K. S. Latourette

VENTURE OF FAITH

ROBERT G. TORBET

VENTURE OF FAITH

The Story of the
American Baptist Foreign Mission Society
and the
Woman's American Baptist Foreign Mission Society
1814–1954

With a Foreword by JESSE R. WILSON

THE JUDSON PRESS
PHILADELPHIA

FIRST EDITION

Library of Congress Catalogue Card Number: 55-10800

Printed in the U.S.A.
for The Judson Press, by the
American Book–Stratford Press, Inc., New York

To My Mother,

whose example of selfless Christian devotion very early kindled within my life a love for the Savior and a zeal for the spread of the gospel into all the world.

Foreword

VENTURE OF FAITH tells the story of fourteen decades of American Baptist foreign missions. Fourteen decades do not occupy a large place in the total span of Christian history. Yet they comprise a very substantial segment of the modern missionary movement.

That movement began in the latter half of the eighteenth century. At the beginning of the nineteenth century, its greatness lay primarily in its possibilities. Not many mission agencies and not many missionaries were involved in it. The Good News of God's everlasting mercy in Jesus Christ had not yet reached many people outside of Western Europe and America. At that time, the great new fact of our day, the existence of the church in almost all lands, was only a dream in the minds of intrepid men of faith like William Carey.

When, therefore, in 1814, the Baptists of the United States formed the Triennial Convention (called after 1845 the American Baptist Missionary Union) to take over the support of Adoniram and Ann Judson and to send out other missionaries, they launched out upon what was truly a "venture of faith."

To be able to go back to those formative years, to discover and sift source material, to select the highlights of the story as it unfolded across fourteen decades (1814–1954), to encompass the story as a whole, and to tell it in a vivid and engaging style—to be able to do all of this calls for great gifts. Fortunately, Dr. Robert G. Torbet, the author of this volume, possesses such gifts. These he has used in carrying through the important assignment given to him in 1950 by the American Baptist Foreign Mission Society and the Woman's American Baptist Foreign Mission Society.

The results of his labors, set forth in the following pages, speak for themselves. Here one finds the antecedents of American Baptist foreign missions and the modest initial efforts of the first Baptists on this side of the Atlantic to take their Lord's command seriously. Here, as in Great Britain and on the Continent, foreign missions was only a minority movement. Hardly within the church, and yet growing out of the church, it was a society or "union," as the Baptist organization was called, sponsored by concerned people with a world vision. It had a membership basis of its own, not at all identical with that of the churches. Although without funds, without past experience, without knowledge of the problems to be encountered, it was never without the sublime faith that God's bidding would be undergirded with God's enabling. So it was that those early mission-minded people went forward "through peril, toil, and pain" until now. . . .

But the story of that venture is Dr. Torbet's, not mine. I only had the privilege of working with him, of reading what he wrote, of getting others to read it, of giving counsel and encouragement—all in the name of the two American Baptist Foreign Mission Societies, which had sought his help.

Readers deserve to know that this monumental work has been done by Dr. Torbet as a labor of love. During all the years of his research and writing, he has carried a full portfolio of work for the American Baptist Publication Society. From that Society he has received his daily bread. Writing this history, therefore, has been labor beyond the call of duty. The only reward to the laborer has been that of having the satisfaction of a worthy task well done. Baptists should be deeply thankful for men like Dr. Torbet.

Whatever else may come to those who read this story, our hope is that all may leave it with a burning realization that it is an unfinished story. That which was most nobly begun in 1814 and which has been extended and enlarged across the years must be continued. It may no longer be a venture in the sense of an undertaking which is uncertain as to outcome, for this venture has proved its wisdom and worth in a thousand ways. But it is nevertheless still a venture in which uncharted ways must be followed—ways which can be followed only by men and women of faith.

It remains, therefore, for us the living to rededicate ourselves to this great unfinished task to which hundreds of men and women have already given, in Abraham Lincoln's noble phrase, "the last full measure of devotion."

JESSE R. WILSON

INTERNATIONAL MISSIONARY COUNCIL

New York, N. Y.
March, 1955

Preface

MANY HISTORIES of American Baptist foreign missions have been written since the movement began in 1814. Each has made its contribution to the treasured story of the inspiring venture of faith in which countless Baptists have been engaged for more than 140 years. This fresh telling of the work of the American Baptist Foreign Mission Society and of the Woman's American Baptist Foreign Mission Society comes at a significant period in their history. Both Societies have engaged recently in plans to integrate their functions for greater efficiency. On the fields, momentous changes have taken place in recent years as leadership has been increasingly transferred from the missionaries to the Christians in those lands where American Baptists have been at work. Therefore, a recounting of the long history of the work of American Baptists through these Societies enables us today to gain a new perspective in the mission task in which we are engaged. Through this new perspective, it is hoped that there may emerge fresh insights for the future as American Baptists at home work together with Baptists beyond the seas as partners in the spread of the gospel of Jesus Christ.

In the preparation of this history, the author has sought to write with an appreciative spirit and an appraising mind. He has made a sincere effort to select from the mass of materials those events which would most accurately present the ever vital and changing enterprise which we know as American Baptist foreign missions. He has sought to interpret these materials in the larger context of the ongoing stream of Christianity at home and abroad, and in the light of world events as they have made their impact upon the church.

As the bibliography indicates, the materials have been drawn from manuscript and printed sources—from records of the Societies and, where available, of the various missions on the fields; from correspondence and journals of missionaries; from biographies and memoirs; from periodicals published at home and on the mission fields; from histories of various aspects of the mission work; and from numerous secondary sources which have been helpful in providing a background for an understanding and interpretation of the available data.

In the task of research, the author is indebted to many people. For assistance in the compilation of material, he wishes to commend the excellent work of three graduate students, Donald Smith, Frederick J. Boehlke, and Bioren Pfaff. For counsel and helpful co-operation in providing access to materials, special gratitude should be expressed to the library staffs of the Samuel Colgate Collection at Rochester, N. Y., of the American Baptist Historical Society at Chester, Pa. (now removed to Rochester, N. Y.), and of The Eastern Baptist Theological Seminary, Philadelphia, Pa. Appreciation is also due to Dr. Richard D. Pierce, curator of the Backus Historical Society Collection at Newton Centre, Mass., for his wise and friendly counsel. For their gracious and tireless assistance in so many ways to the author in his use of the records of the American Baptist Foreign Mission Society and the Woman's American Baptist Foreign Mission Society, deep gratitude is due Mrs. Katherine L. Read, Miss Jessie K. Bates, and Miss Ada P. Stearns. For the wise counsel and kindly encouragement of Dr. Jesse R. Wilson, Dr. Irene A. Jones, and the foreign secretaries of the two Societies the author is most grateful. To Dr. Kenneth Scott Latourette and Dr. William B. Lipphard, he is deeply in debt for the helpful criticisms of the manuscript. And to my colleagues, Dr. Miles W. Smith, book editor, and Dr. Benjamin P. Browne, editor-in-chief, my heartfelt thanks for their encouragement and sympathetic help.

This word of appreciation cannot be closed without calling attention to the helpfulness of many representatives of the field, some on furlough and others at their station. Indeed, to all of the missionaries, past and present, the author owes an expression of eternal gratitude for the inspiration which their deeds and achievements have brought to him in the course of the preparation of this history.

ROBERT G. TORBET

Contents

VENTURE OF FAITH

PART 1 THE FORMATIVE YEARS (TO 1845)

CHAPTER I

Beginning of a Venture

ON OCTOBER 2, 1792, in the home of the widow of a Baptist deacon at Kettering, England, a group of fifteen Baptist ministers met to discuss the formation of a foreign mission society. The gathering was in response to a vote taken by the Northampton Association on the preceding thirtieth of May. Among the fifteen present was William Carey. With characteristic vigor, he challenged his fellow ministers with the words: "See what Moravians are daring, and some of them British like ourselves, and many only artisans and poor! Can't we Baptists at least attempt *something* in fealty to the same Lord?" [1]

The setting was not pretentious; the speaker was a young man of thirty-one who had earned a humble living during his early years making shoes. At the age of seventeen he had become a Christian. But with a lost world weighing upon his heart and a conviction that world missions should be the concern of every Christian, he was to become the pioneer of the English-speaking Protestant foreign mission movement. His program was simple and straightforward: pray, plan, pay. He was so convincing that his challenge was accepted. A resolution was passed which was the beginning of a venture of faith:

> Humbly desirous of making an effort for the propagation of the Gospel amongst the Heathen, according to the recommen-

[1] S. Pearce Carey, *William Carey* (Philadelphia, 1923), p. 90.

> dations of Carey's *Enquiry,* we unanimously resolve to act in Society together for this purpose; and, as in the divided state of Christendom each denomination, by exerting itself separately, seems likeliest to accomplish the great end, we name this the Particular Baptist Society for the Propagation of the Gospel amongst the Heathen.[2]

The fledgling movement thus undertaken was a daring enterprise. A small band of humble men had made a decision which was to acquire a significance for a rapidly changing world all out of proportion to the meagre resources pledged that day. With no financial backing, the fifteen ministers present contributed from their own pockets the sum of thirteen pounds, two shillings, six pence, plus one pound proceeds which had come in that day from the sale of Carey's *Enquiry*. For want of a better depository, the money was placed in a snuffbox. Among those present were John Ryland, pastor of the College Lane Baptist church at Northampton, John Sutcliff, minister of the Olney Church which had sent Carey into the ministry, Andrew Fuller, pastor at Kettering, and Samuel Pearce, minister of the Cannon Street church, Birmingham. At a later meeting, Fuller was elected secretary, and Reynold Hogg of Thrapstone, who had been absent from the initial meeting, was made treasurer.

Three months later, on January 9, 1793, the first missionaries were appointed. Carey had hoped to be the first; but when John Thomas, a British surgeon who had served in Bengal, offered to return as a representative of the society, the young pastor stepped aside in favor of the experienced doctor. It soon became evident, however, from Thomas' reports that a missionary might support himself to a large extent. With hopes renewed, Carey volunteered at once to go with Thomas on that basis. The meeting closed on a note of deep joy as the two men, filled with emotion, embraced and dedicated themselves to work together in the cause of foreign missions.

As an enterprise dependent upon voluntary support of the churches, its promotion fell to Pearce and Fuller, who traveled widely throughout England, preaching and collecting funds. The new project did much to arouse spiritual enthusiasm and to develop a denominational consciousness. As Baptists were awakened to their

---

[2] *Ibid.*, p. 91. Carey's pamphlet referred to was *The Enquiry into the Obligations of Christians to Use Means for the Conversion of the Heathens,* published in 1792.

missionary responsibility, evangelism at home was intensified and membership in some churches tripled within five years.[3]

Antecedents of the Carey Movement

The organization of the Baptist Missionary Society, so briefly sketched here, was the product of a developing concern which was inherent within evangelical Christianity. It is not correct to claim that it was the fountain-head of the modern Protestant foreign mission movement. For more than two centuries prior to Carey's time, Protestants had conducted missions among non-Christians. Chief among these Protestants were the Moravian Brethren, or *Unitas Fratrum,* who traced their spiritual descent from John Huss and possibly from Peter Waldo. With Herrnhut, a village built on the estates of Count Zinzendorf in the present Saxony, as a center, the entire community devoted itself to missions. This was a new phenomenon in Christianity—a voluntary movement of laymen and laywomen impelled by a holy zeal to share the Good News of salvation with those who had never had opportunity to hear of it. Before the end of the eighteenth century, they had begun missions in Russia, India, the Nicobar Islands, Ceylon, in the English colonies in North America, in the West Indies, in Surinam, in Central America, on the Gold Coast of East Africa, in South Africa, and in Greenland and Labrador. Their influence bore fruit in the Wesleyan revival and in the growth of world-wide Methodism.[4]

As early as 1699 (or 1698 in old style dating), the Anglican "Society for Promoting Christian Knowledge" came into existence under the impetus of Thomas Bray, the commissary in Maryland for the Bishop of London. He also assisted in 1701 in the organization of the "Society for the Propagation of the Gospel in Foreign Parts." The aim of both societies was to conduct work among white settlers and Indians in the New World. In 1709 the Scotch began to subsidize a similar work among American Indians.

By the middle of the eighteenth century, John and Charles Wesley

---

[3] Joseph Ivimey, *History of English Baptists, 1760–1820,* 4 volumes (London, 1811–30). Vol. 4, pp. 68-75; David Douglas, *History of the Baptist Churches in the North of England* (London, 1846), p. 241.

[4] Kenneth Scott Latourette, *Three Centuries of Advance, 1500–1800,* Vol. III in *A History of the Expansion of Christianity,* 7 volumes, (New York, 1939), pp. 46-50.

and George Whitefield had led in the rise of the Evangelical Movement in the British Isles, and the Great Awakening had aroused the Thirteen Colonies to a white heat of spiritual fervor. These revivals resulted in an evangelistic concern among Christians which stimulated the development of missions to American Indians and Negroes in the New World, and later to other non-Christian peoples in other areas of the world.

In spite of the hampering effects of the Enlightenment Era, with its over-emphasis upon reason in religion, and of the delaying effects of the American Revolution, the French Revolution, and the Napoleonic Wars, Protestant missionary activities were accelerated in the closing years of the eighteenth century and the opening years of the nineteenth. Within ten years of the organization of the Baptist Missionary Society in 1792, there arose in the British Isles the London Missionary Society, the Religious Tract Society, the Church Missionary Society, the British and Foreign Bible Society, the Glasgow Missionary Society, and the Scottish Missionary Society—all forerunners of the numerous Protestant agencies which were to emerge in the nineteenth and twentieth centuries.[5]

In this outburst of quickened activity among Protestants may be seen the fruition of the basic emphasis of evangelical Christianity, namely, that vital religion is the product of a personal experience of redemption on the part of each individual who has been confronted with the gospel. The corollary to this teaching, which is as old as the New Testament—"and how shall they hear without a preacher?"—became the motivating idea for a missionary effort which has become the marvel of modern church history.[6] Although this concern was inherent within the nature and teachings of the great Protestant reformers, it became most effective among those groups of Christians who were freest from the limitations of medieval Christianity, once they had caught the vision of a world need.

During the early years of the Protestant Reformation, it was the Anabaptists who evangelized with greatest fervor. Having rejected the medieval doctrine of the church which identifies the ecclesiastical with the civil aspects of society, they became a witnessing movement of consecrated laymen and laywomen. Believing that the church is

---

[5] *Ibid.*, p. 50.

[6] The Scripture quotation is from Romans 10:14 (American Revised Version).

a fellowship of those who have been redeemed and gathered out of the world by a personal and voluntary faith in Jesus Christ, they sought to win converts wherever they went. It was their willingness to administer "believer's" baptism to all who entered into this new life which caused them to be nicknamed "anabaptists" or rebaptizers. And because they challenged the established status of Christianity, the Roman Catholics, Lutherans, and Calvinists alike sought to silence their testimony by stern persecution.

Although the movement had won thousands of followers, it was driven underground in Europe during the sixteenth century. Yet it was not destroyed. Through the Mennonites, followers of a converted priest by the name of Menno Simons, the Anabaptist witness was preserved, particularly in Holland and West Friesland. The concept of the church as a fellowship of the regenerated only was not without influence on other Christians.

This basic teaching, as set forth by Mennonite merchants and artisans, influenced John Smyth and his refugee English congregation in Amsterdam, Holland, to reject in 1609 the "covenant" idea of the church in favor of the view of the church as a fellowship of converts gathered out of the world by a voluntary act of personal faith. From this event we may date the beginnings of English Baptists.

Later, a Pietist Movement developed within Lutheranism which stressed the "little church within the church," that is, the truly redeemed among the nominal members. The Moravian missionary movement was a direct result of this teaching. The same concept was inherent within Calvinist doctrine. For in spite of their continuation of the "covenant" idea of the church with the practice of infant baptism, the Calvinists insisted that the true church is composed only of those who have experienced regeneration upon a personal confession of faith in Jesus Christ.

This emphasis upon pesonal decision and conscious acceptance of the gospel by sinners softened the influence of the doctrine of predestination in Calvinism. The Wesleyan revivals in England and the Great Awakening which followed in America contributed much to the emergence of a modified Calvinism which enabled its adherents to become eager to participate in evangelistic efforts to win converts to the church. By the close of the eighteenth century, Baptists of Arminian and moderate Calvinistic views in England and America were aroused to a concern for the salvation of the non-Christian peoples of the world. In this connection, William Carey was "the first Anglo-Saxon Protestant either in America or in Great Britain to propose that Christians take concrete steps to bring their Gospel to all the human race." [7]

A New Era Emerges

The modern era of foreign missions was thus the product of a series of religious awakenings which broke out spontaneously in many quarters and which moved out along several different currents within the sixteenth, seventeenth, and eighteenth centuries. During this period, the greatest impulse to foreign missions came from those Christians whose churches had no connection with the state. Their missions were undertaken by leaders from the humble classes, whereas Roman Catholic missions were led by aristocrats and usually supported by government patronage. Their emphasis was upon the priesthood of believers, whereas the Roman Catholics retained the hierarchy as mediators between God and man.[8] The Protestant missions which were to spread most successfully in the nineteenth century were of this more democratic pattern. In the judgment of a great church historian, Protestantism had broken the old wineskins while Roman Catholicism, with all of its creditable execution of missions, had but stretched them.[9]

Contributing also to the emergence of a sturdy Protestant foreign mission enterprise was the gradual process by which Christian Europe was freed from a provincialism with its vision of need limited to the borders of that continent. This was the by-product of a great era of exploration and colonization. By the sixteenth century Protestants were entering upon their first contacts with non-Christians of other lands through commerce, conquests, and colonizing. These associations stimulated missionary activity on a small scale.

The very first Protestant settlement in the New World was accompanied by a missionary impulse. In 1555–1556 a French clergyman unsuccessfully attempted to win converts while his comrades, under Nicholas Durand (Villegagnon), sought to establish a colony in Brazil near the present site of Rio de Janeiro. Gustavus Vasa, the first Protestant King of Sweden, sent out missionaries to work among

---

[7] Latourette, *Three Centuries of Advance,* p. 68.

[8] *Ibid.,* pp. 16-17.

[9] *Ibid.,* p. 16.

the Lapps in the northern area of his realm. Adrianus Savaria, a Dutch Protestant pastor, advocated foreign missions five years before the first Dutch commercial venture set sail for the East Indies in 1595. To prepare for such a project, a missionary seminary was established at Leyden in 1622. During the following ten years, it sent out twelve young men as missionaries.[10]

English colonization from the first was at least nominally associated with the missionary motive. This was reflected in Richard Hakluyt's *Discourse on Western Planting,* which was written in 1584 at the request of Sir Walter Raleigh to convince Queen Elizabeth of the wisdom of English colonization in America. In his list of reasons for settling the New World, Hakluyt stressed America's need of the gospel, particularly as represented by the Protestant faith.[11] King James I, by charter requirement, placed upon the Virginia Company a responsibility to spread the Christian religion to people who live in ignorance of the true gospel. One of the few Puritans to show a serious concern for American Indians was John Eliot of New England. In the seventeenth century the Society of Friends also undertook work among the Indians.

During the early period of the settling of the Thirteen Colonies, when a remarkable number of Protestant immigrants made their way from Europe, literature urging foreign missions was being circulated in the British Isles and on the Continent. One of the most powerful voices was that of the Austrian, Baron Justinian von Weltz (1621–70), who advocated a "brotherhood of Christ" for foreign missions. He published several treatises proposing organization of societies and outlining plans for the conversion of "unbelieving nations." At Halle, the center of German pietism, August Hermann Francke published in 1705–6 the reports of the Danish-Halle Mission under the title, *A History of Evangelical Missions in the East for the Conversion of the Heathen.* Sermons and addresses by the Wesleys, Whitefield, and later, Thomas Coke, Zinzendorf, and others were circulated widely. The Pietists of the continent and the Methodists of England and America spread the idea of missions by their hymns.[12]

---

[10] *Ibid.,* pp. 42-45.

[11] William Warren Sweet, *Religion in Colonial America* (New York, 1942), pp. 3-8.

[12] William O. Carver, *The Course of Christian Missions.* Revised edition. (New York, 1939), p. 130.

In such a setting an evangelistic concern developed which expressed itself in revivals at home and missions abroad. Like their British cousins, Baptists in America very early entered upon mission work. The Philadelphia Baptist Association, the first to be organized in the country (1707), sent out evangelists or missionaries. Between 1743 and 1762 they established at least four churches along the Atlantic Coast as far south as Charleston, South Carolina. Similar evangelistic activities were carried on by Baptists in New England and Virginia.[13] In 1802 Baptists in Boston founded the Massachusetts Baptist Missionary Society for the evangelizing of new settlements on the frontier. Five years later this society co-operated with the New York Baptist Missionary Society in support of a missionary among the Tuscarora Indians in northwestern New York.[14] Baptists were also active in reaching the Negroes, who were welcomed as members in their churches. By 1795 there were 17,664 Negro Baptists south and east of Maryland.[15] These are typical instances of a growing work among Indians, Negroes, and white settlers along the frontier which reflected the quickening of spiritual fervor following the Great Awakening.

An additional factor to encourage the development of the new missionary spirit was the rise of a humane attitude that began to show itself after 1775 in the dealings of European powers, especially of Great Britain, with Asiatic peoples. Undoubtedly a product of the spiritual awakening of the Wesleyan Movement, it reflected an interest in extending to these peoples the benefits of European civilization, which to their minds were identified with Christianity. There was a new enthusiasm for charity, philanthropy, and reform. In a very real sense, "the new missionary movement was but a phase of that awakening to the rights and dignity and destiny of mankind which in all European countries and America had vast effect in preparing the way for the progress of democracy in the nineteenth century." [16]

---

[13] Robert G. Torbet, *A Social History of the Philadelphia Baptist Association, 1707–1940* (Philadelphia, 1944), p. 19.

[14] Kenneth Scott Latourette, *The Great Century in Europe and the United States of America, 1800–1914,* Vol. IV of *A History of the Expansion of Christianity* (New York, 1941) p. 313, citing *The Massachusetts Baptist Missionary Magazine,* Vol. 2, p. 314.

[15] *Religion on the American Frontier: the Baptists, 1783–1830* (Chicago, 1931), p. 78, citing Asplund, *Universal Annual Register, 1796,* p. 82.

[16] Edward Caldwell Moore, *The Spread of Christianity in the Modern World* (Chicago, 1925), p. 43.

The sense of the value of human life and the enthusiasm for the welfare of mankind which marked the closing years of the eighteenth century were a by-product of the Christian teaching that moral and spiritual needs lie at the roots of human ills. Moreover, Christianity and Western civilization had become "inextricably intermingled in the life of the homelands" because the unity of civilization had been fostered by Christian influence.[17] This explains the reason for the spread of Christianity hand in hand with Western culture during this period. In the minds of missionary enthusiasts, therefore, the superlative value of the gospel was identified closely with the cultural benefits which they believed were the product of Christian stewardship of life and talents.

It is, indeed, significant that the very genius of the vigorous Protestant foreign mission movement which began in the late eighteenth century lay in large measure in this remarkable combination of evangelistic concern for the inner life with the desire to work for social, economic, and cultural betterment in the outward life as well. The democratic character of Protestant missions conducted by Baptists, Congregationalists, and Methodists—sects that were freed from the old pattern of state patronage—found a readier acceptance with the masses to be won to Christianity than the autocratic Roman Catholic missions achieved. Within that democratic teaching was the germ which was to develop among many non-Christian peoples, particularly in Asia and Africa, a fervent desire for self-determination. Once a spirit of nationalism took hold of these people, as it did after 1900, they began to resent the close identification of the gospel with Western culture.

The Protestant missionary movement of the nineteenth and twentieth centuries enjoyed an increasing interest on the part of its followers, whereas Roman Catholic missions which had such a brilliant rise in the preceding period experienced a declining interest, except for a fresh rejuvenation here and there in recent years. Moreover, Protestants manifested a more widespread vitality and eagerness to propagate their religion than Roman Catholics. This may be due in part, at least, to the distinctive instruments for missionary activity developed by Protestants, known as societies. These provided for a large measure of co-operation between laity and clergy. Money was

[17] John Baillie, "The World Mission of the Church: the Contemporary Scene," *International Review of Missions,* Vol. 41, No. 162 (April, 1952), p. 164.

raised by large numbers of the rank and file of church members. Roman Catholics, on the other hand, used very largely monastic orders for missionary work, and retained control of the enterprise in clerical hands. The Protestants' emphasis upon conversion of individuals and their distrust of mass movements into the church also distinguished their methods from the medieval manner by which Europeans had become Christians.[18] In fact, the Protestant focus of attention upon the individual has been a significant factor in the successful appeal of evangelical missions to the masses of non-Christian peoples.

Highlights of Carey's Career

William Carey undoubtedly exerted a formative influence in shaping the pattern of the Protestant missionary movement just described. Because of this fact, it is well to trace briefly here his remarkable career. As we have seen, he belonged to a communion that was unhampered by state church connections and ecclesiastical patterns. He advocated a society which should be autonomous and composed only of those people who actually contributed to the support of the enterprise. Any person would be recognized as a member who would subscribe ten pounds at once, or ten shillings and six pence annually. This became the pattern for other societies in England and America.

Carey and his family arrived in India in 1793, accompanied by John Thomas, his associate who turned out to be financially irresponsible. Within a few weeks of their landing at Calcutta, Thomas had spent a year's allowance. To Carey, he was to be a severe handicap in the years that followed. To support his family and his mission, Carey labored for six years as superintendent of an indigo factory. With amazing versatility, he learned Bengali and Sanskrit and he studied Indian plant life assiduously.

When the English East India Company refused to allow new additions to the mission to settle in the city, the new missionaries found refuge in Serampore, on the Hooghly River about ten miles from Calcutta. The Danish Government, which maintained factories in Serampore, resisted the hostile pressures of the British against the missionaries. Soon Carey joined the newcomers, and Serampore became the center of his mission. Prominent among his colleagues

[18] The foregoing analysis of the early Protestant missionary movement is suggested in part by Latourette, *Three Centuries of Advance*, pp. 50-51.

were William Ward, a printer and editor, and Joshua Marshman, a schoolmaster of wide reading. The Serampore Trio, as Carey, Ward, and Marshman came to be called, set up a press. By 1832 portions or all of the Christian Scriptures had been translated and published in forty-four languages and dialects. In this task, Carey reflected the Baptist position that every person should have the privilege of reading the Bible in his own language.

For this reason and because Carey was committed to the principle of developing an indigenous church life in India, he opened a college to train his converts to reach their people with the Christian message. He also admitted non-Christians, and taught the philosophies and religions of India as well as the Bible and Christian theology. His own proficiency as a teacher and linguist and his respectful attitude towards India's rich culture won respect and influenced many students to become Christians.

Further evidence of his far-sighted statesmanship may be seen in his proposal that missionaries of all denominations should meet every ten years to co-ordinate plans for spreading the gospel to the whole world. Over a century later this idea came to fruition in the International Missionary Council.

Carey's personal interest in plant life and his recognition of India's great need for food prompted him to initiate organization of an agri-horticultural society to improve utilization of the soil.

The young mission was harrassed by many difficulties and obstacles, which included the hostility of the English East India Company, dissensions among the missionaries which seemed to result from friction between younger reinforcements and the Trio, and differences in point of view between the Trio and the society at home. The latter difficulty arose with the passing of the original leadership at home after 1815. With the deaths of Sutcliff and Fuller, changes began to occur in policy making and in attitude towards the missionaries. In place of friendly letters that manifested complete confidence and understanding, formal directives arrived in Serampore from the society at home. These aroused resentment among the Trio, for the missionaries had been sent out to India with an understanding that they should become independent of the society as soon as possible. Actually, they had received little financial support. Instead, they had supported themselves. With their own earnings they had built a mission which included a college and other property. Carey had accepted the post of professor of Indian Languages in the college of Calcutta; Marshman and his wife operated a boarding school for European children; and Ward made profits from the Mission Press. By living together and sharing expenses they were able to put most of their earnings into the mission, a sum which is estimated to have totalled one hundred thousand pounds.[19]

To the newcomers on the committee at home, it appeared that the Trio had been amassing a fortune in property. The Trio, in turn, refused to relinquish control of their own earnings. Finally a division occurred between the home society and the survivors of the Trio. The property was divided so that the college was left in control of Carey and Marshman. The society undertook direction of the remainder of the property.[20]

The influence of the center at Serampore continued, however, to stimulate Baptist missionary activity in Bengal. The work which had been begun through the Baptist Missionary Society under Carey's wise counselling continued to prosper. The controversy which lasted for some ten years had been unfortunate, but the mission enterprise did not die. Moreover, valuable lessons about mission administration had been learned. Serampore's influence upon the Protestant missionary enterprise continued to be felt.

Space does not permit an outline of the work of the Baptist Missionary Society; suffice it to say that its activities had been extended, upon Carey's advice, to Ceylon in 1812. Another mission, also upon Carey's counsel, was developed in 1821 in Orissa, southwest of Bengal, by the New Connexion General Baptists. During the course of the century, British Baptists extended their missionary efforts to North India, African Congo, and China.[21]

During this initial period in Baptist foreign missions, there was considerable correspondence between leaders in England and America. The Philadelphia Baptist Association, for example, received frequent reports concerning Carey's work in India and encouraged

---

[19] A. C. Underwood, *A History of the English Baptists* (London, 1947), pp. 196-98.

[20] Kenneth Scott Latourette, *The Great Century in Northern Africa and Asia, 1800–1914,* Vol. VI of *A History of the Expansion of Christianity* (New York, 1944), pp. 107-8.

[21] For details, see F. Townley Lord, *Achievement: A Short History of the Baptist Missionary Society, 1792–1942* (London, 1942).

the churches to contribute financial assistance.[22] Typical of this affiliation between American and British Baptists is the work of Dr. William Staughton. He was an Englishman by birth and education. In 1792 he had been present at Kettering on the occasion of the organization of the English Particular Baptist Missionary Society, and manifested an intense interest in the enterprise. This interest he brought with him to America three years later. As the pastor of the First Baptist Church in Philadelphia, he found a congenial company of like-minded Calvinistic Baptists. He advocated their support of the East India Missionary Enterprises. In order to raise funds for the support of the British missionaries, he wrote a book entitled *The Baptist Mission in India.* Through an extensive correspondence with Baptists in England and those who were missionaries in India, he was able to be an effective promotional agent in America.[23]

Other associations in the country also manifested a lively interest in Carey's work at Serampore by observing special seasons of prayer and by making generous contributions to its support. In 1806 Baptists along the Atlantic seaboard from Boston to Charleston and in the outlying regions gave $2,500 to that Mission. During the next eight years, they shared in contributing more than $18,000. When the American Board of Commissioners for Foreign Missions was established in 1812 by the Congregationalists, the Baptists collected $3,000 to assist in sending Luther Rice and Adoniram and Ann Judson to India. In the twenty-year period prior to the organization of their own national society in 1814, American Baptists gave between seven and eight thousand dollars through the channels mentioned.[24]

---

[22] *Philadelphia Association Minutes: 1707–1807,* pp. 360, 412, 423, 430.

[23] S. W. Lynd, editor, *Memoir of the Rev. William Staughton, D.D.* (Boston, 1834), chaps. 1-6.

[24] Albert L. Vail, *The Morning Hour of American Baptist Missions* (Philadelphia, 1907), pp. 241, 244, 250-51.

CHAPTER II

Launching a Movement

ON A SEPTEMBER EVENING in 1808, a slim, straight lad, just past his twentieth birthday, stopped at a country inn in western Massachusetts for supper and the night. His genial manner and handsome appearance, with high forehead, keen eyes, and dark hair, prompted a favorable appraisal from the shrewd landlord. Following the evening meal, he was shown to his room. With considerable ado and in an apologetic tone, the host explained that the only available room was next to one in which lay a very ill young man. The traveler brushed aside the explanation with an assurance that this fact would not disturb his rest. So it was that Adoniram Judson, a short time out of Brown University, was left alone with his thoughts.

Uneasy in mind about his future and eager to see something of the world, Judson had set out in August for a tour of the country west and south of his native Massachusetts. For a brief time he had attached himself to a theatrical troupe in New York. But soon tiring of this life, he had returned to the home of his uncle, the Congregational minister in Sheffield, Massachusetts. There, he had met a visiting clergyman who had engaged him in conversation about spiritual matters. Not being a Christian, although the son of a Congregational minister, young Judson had been impressed. But he had refrained from acting upon any inclination that he may have felt in response to the conversation.

As a matter of fact, Adoniram Judson at the time prided himself on being a sceptic—a stand which was considered sophisticated among college youth. It appears that he had been influenced in his thinking about religion by a close friend at Brown, to whom he referred in his writing only as E————. Largely through the example of this young man's agnostic views, Adoniram had adopted a rather hostile attitude towards Christianity. Always honest, he had shared his opinions with his father, who promptly showed his displeasure. His mother, by her tears, proved to be even more disconcerting.

As Judson lay sleepless in his bed, kept awake by the groans of the sick youth in the adjoining room, he kept wondering if the young man were ready to die. Then, remembering his own recent experiences, he began to ask himself whether he, in a similar position, would be ready.

In the morning, when Adoniram inquired of the landlord concerning the young man's health, he was shocked to learn that he had died during the night. When he asked the lad's name, he discovered to his amazement that he had been none other than E————, his college friend who had influenced him to become a sceptic. As the full import of the tragic end of E———— sank into his mind, he became deeply concerned about his own spiritual destiny.

With typical resoluteness, Adoniram Judson abandoned his trip and returned home to Plymouth to settle his spiritual problem. Fortunately, upon his arrival Professors Stuart and Griffin, representing the new seminary at Andover, happened to be in Plymouth. When he sought their counsel, they suggested that he enter the seminary as a special student, on the strength that from the classroom experiences there he would gain help in resolving his doubts. While yet undecided to take this advice, Judson came upon a book by Thomas Boston, entitled *The Fourfold State*. This brought him to a decision, and so, on October 12, he entered Andover.

Adoniram Judson entered the seminary, as he did everything else, with a passion for excellence and an enthusiasm for life. Gradually, his doubts were resolved, and he became certain of the historical basis of the Christian faith. Two months later he had accepted Jesus Christ as his Savior, and had pledged himself to Christian service. When he returned home for the vacation period, he united with his father's church at Plymouth.

This young man of such great promise had become a Christian through a combination of influences. Earliest in effect, certainly, was that of a Christian home. Most dramatic was the death of his friend E————. Andover Seminary undoubtedly was the most immediately effective influence to resolve his doubts. But behind them all was the fact that God was preparing him for a mighty work.[1]

A Mission Band Presents a Challenge

One day in September, 1809, Adoniram Judson read a sermon by Claudius Buchanan, a chaplain for the British East India Company. It was instrumental in setting the direction of his whole life. The sermon appeared in *The Massachusetts Baptist Missionary Magazine*. It had been preached at St. James Parish Church, Bristol, England, for the benefit of a "Society for Missions to Africa and the East." Entitled "The Star in the East," the sermon presented a new and compelling idea to Judson. Its appeal for missions in India gripped his imagination as nothing had ever done before. For five months he did not come to a decision. Then, one cold day in February, 1810, he was walking alone in the woods behind the seminary building, when suddenly the Great Commission came into his mind. Now it held a personal meaning for his own life. That was the decisive moment. Kneeling in the snow, he resolved to become a missionary to peoples beyond the sea.[2]

As in the case of his conversion, there were several factors which influenced Judson's decision to become a foreign missionary. The immediate one seems to have been Buchanan's sermon. Certainly, this was reinforced by other reading in *The Massachusetts Baptist Missionary Magazine,* which regularly carried reports of the English Baptists' work at Serampore. In addition, he had read Syme's story of his *Embassy to Ava*. Still another factor was the interest in international affairs which prevailed in New England at the time. Not only did ships transport cargo to and from distant lands, but they carried English missionaries to India by way of Boston or New York. The impact of the Bible itself exerted a persuasive influence upon Judson, as he contemplated the significance of the Great Commission.

---

[1] Stacy R. Warburton, *Eastward: the Story of Adoniram Judson* (New York, 1937), p. 18. The author is indebted to this excellent biography for the foregoing account.

[2] For Buchanan's sermon, see *The Massachusetts Baptist Missionary Magazine* (Boston), Vol. 2, No. 7 (September, 1809), pp. 202-06. For the letter in which Judson explains what led him to decide for foreign missions (dated December 18, 1837, from Maulmein, to Dr. Chapin, president of Columbian College), see Francis Wayland, *A Memoir of the Life and Labors of the Rev. Adoniram Judson, D.D.* (Boston, 1853), Vol. 1, pp. 51-53. This title will be referred to hereafter as *Memoir of Judson.*

And finally, a prayerful consideration of his own qualifications and his natural response to a challenging task played an important part in his decision.[3]

Adoniram Judson was not alone in his dedication to missions. At Williams College there was already a missionary fellowship of young men who "were accustomed to meet at night beneath a haystack near the college grounds." [4] Of this group, Samuel J. Mills, Luther Rice, and James Richards came to Andover Seminary late in the spring of 1810. Samuel Newell, from Harvard, and Samuel Nott, Jr., from Union, were classmates with Judson at Andover. Rice was a middler. Mills, Richard, and a third seminarian, Edward Warren, who was also interested in missions, were juniors. These young men were attracted to each other at Andover by a common dedication to the cause of missions.

From the first, Judson was determined to devote his life to foreign missions. The Williams men were drawn in part, at least, to work among the American Indians. It was largely the vision of Judson that directed others of the group to a concern for peoples in lands beyond the sea. He was the man of action who took decisive steps to develop an organization which might send him and his colleagues to the mission field.

Their first step was to consult their professors. In this they were fortunate to gain the sympathetic understanding of Professors Griffin and Stuart. Griffin wrote to the London Missionary Society to see if that agency would send out the volunteers. Impatient to secure an early appointment for himself, Judson wrote also to the Society, volunteering his services. Then, on Monday, June 25, 1810, a memorable meeting with the young men was held at the home of Professor Stuart. Those present, in addition to the host, were Professor Griffin, Dr. Samuel Spring of Newburyport, and the Reverend Samuel Worcester, pastor of the Tabernacle Church at Salem, a few other pastors, and one layman, Jeremiah Evarts. It was decided to present the proposal to a missionary movement to the General Asso-

---

[3] Warburton, *Eastward,* pp. 21-22; for the influence of the news of English Baptist missions upon Americans, see *The Massachusetts Baptist Missionary Magazine,* Vol. 1 (1803–08), Vol. 2 (1808–10), and Vol. 3 (1811–13).

[4] Edward Judson, *The Life of Adoniram Judson* (New York, 1883), p. 17. This is an interesting version of the source of the term "haystack" meeting, the other being that the group made their decision to be missionaries in the shelter of a haystack during a rainstorm.

ciation of Massachusetts Proper, which was to meet at Bradford the next week.

Worcester invited Spring to ride from Andover to Bradford in his carriage. On the way, a distance of ten miles, they worked out a plan for a Board of Commissioners for Foreign Missions. According to Worcester's own report later, "the form, the number of members, and name were proposed" by the time they arrived at their destination.[5] On Friday, June 29, the Association adopted unanimously a recommendation to form such a board.

The first meeting of the American Board of Commissioners was held in September. All that was accomplished was preparation of a message to the churches and appointment of a Prudential Committee to explore ways and means of equipping and sending forth missionaries. On December 25, Judson, Newell, Nott, and Hall were examined and approved for appointment, if and when the way should open. Judson was instructed to go to London to ascertain whether or not he and his associates might be supported for a time by the London Missionary Society, without their being wholly under the direction of that agency.

During the voyage, the ship on which Judson was traveling was taken into custody by a French vessel. The crew and passengers were taken to Bayonne, France. Judson was released through the efforts of a friendly American. After six adventuresome weeks in France, he arrived in London. Either forgetting his instructions or ignoring them, the young man gained appointment of himself and his colleagues as missionaries of the London Society. The promise was also given that they would be located together in India. There is no indication that the question of joint support was discussed.

Judson returned home in August, 1811. The next month, he and Nott went to Worcester to give his report to the annual meeting of the board. In his eagerness, he presented the members with the alternative of sending him and his associates as their missionaries, or they would take advantage of their appointment by the London Missionary Society. It seems that he was rebuked mildly by the chairman for his aggressive manner.[6] But he had won his point, for he, Nott, Newell, and Hall received definite appointments as mis-

---

[5] From a letter dated March 23, 1821, included in Wayland, *Memoir of Judson,* Vol. 1, p. 49.

[6] Wayland, *Memoir of Judson,* pp. 78-79, 81-92.

sionaries to work in Burma, or in Surat, or in Penang. The salaries were fixed at $666.66 if married or $445.45 if unmarried, with outfit money equal to a year's salary. A sum of $300 was appropriated, in addition, for books for the missionaries. The vote was taken on the strength of a promised bequest of $30,000 from the widow of John Norris, who had given $10,000 to help establish Andover. The bequest was designated for recruitment of missionaries.

By 1812, there were three more young people to be sent—Nancy Hasseltine (also known as Ann, and hereafter referred to as such), the deacon's daughter in Bradford with whom Adoniram had fallen in love, Harriet Atwood, who was to marry Newell, and Roxana Peck, betrothed to Nott. Luther Rice was added to the list, but on condition that he raise his own expenses. This he did, to the surprise of the members of the board.

On Thursday evening, February 6, 1812, before a congregation of between 1500 and 2000 people who filled to overflowing the Tabernacle Church in Salem, the five young men were ordained. In spite of the bitter cold weather, many people had come from nearby towns. When it was announced that Mrs. Norris' legacy had not yet come in, and that the Board lacked $3,800 of the $5,000 needed, those present were so stirred that they contributed $220. After that, the money poured in, so that in less than two weeks, the Board had $6,000. From the Philadelphia churches alone, contributions amounted to $800.[7]

Soon after the ordination of the men, Ann and Adoniram Judson and Harriet and Samuel Newell were married. On Wednesday, February 18, they sailed on the *Caravan* from Salem. They were bound for Calcutta. On February 24, Samuel and Roxana Nott, Gordon Hall, Luther Rice, and three couples of English Baptist missionaries sailed from Newcastle, Delaware, on the *Harmony*. They, too, were on their way to India.

The American venture in foreign missions had begun. From all practical considerations, the time was not auspicious. For in 1812, Europe was engaged in a life and death struggle with Napoleon. The young American Republic was, itself, on the verge of war with England. Asia was just opening up to western trade under the prodding

---

[7] Warburton, *Eastward,* pp. 41-43; *The Massachusetts Baptist Missionary Magazine,* Vol. 3 (March, 1812), pp. 129-130, 159.

of the British, Dutch, and Danish East India Companies. The economic situation in the United States was precarious.

Yet there were some factors which promised good for the missionary enterprise. In 1807 the maiden voyage of the *Clermont,* on the Hudson, under steam power, had already forecast the ultimate replacement of the graceful sailing vessels that plied between American seaports and the Far East. But more important was the rising missionary zeal that had been awakened in American churches by Carey's mission in India. Equally significant for the future of missionary extension was the church expansion westward toward the Mississiippi that followed in the wake of soul-stirring revivals, strengthening immeasurably the possibilities of financial support.

Far-reaching Decisions

From the time the *Caravan* left the port of Salem, a series of events led to decisions that were far-reaching in their effect upon the Protestant missionary movement. These events began to take place when Adoniram Judson undertook a serious study of the question, "Who should be baptized?"

It was not the first time that the young missionary had been confronted with this subject. As a student in Andover Seminary, Judson's interest in the word *baptizo* had been aroused, while engaged in a private translation of the New Testament from the Greek. In his search for the exact meaning of the Greek word, he found to his consternation that it was at variance with his understanding of it. Although troubled by his discovery, he did not foresee, at that time, its widespread consequences for his ministry. Moreover, other activities diverted his attention and delayed further thought about the matter.

But now that he was on his way to India, with instructions from the American Board to baptize "credible believers with their households," the problem took on a more urgent importance. He began to wonder how he ought to treat the unconverted children and servants of the converted when he reached his destination. He also realized that he would be obliged to defend his position before the English Baptists in Calcutta.

In April, when the voyage was half over, he resumed a serious study of the problem. He continued it until he reached Calcutta in

June. Being troubled by the disconcerting possibility of arriving at a conclusion which would be at variance with the policy of the board, Adoniram consulted his wife. From the first, Ann urged him to drop the matter. She was frightened by the prospects of their losing prestige and friends through a break with the board. But her husband was a determined man. From a boy, he had never allowed a puzzling problem to go unsolved. It is not surprising, therefore, that he threw himself the more earnestly into a thorough examination of the Scriptures.

Upon arrival in India, the Judsons were so occupied for a time with efforts to secure permission to stay in India that there was no opportunity for further reflection on the matter. They soon learned that the British East India Company was unwilling to extend hospitality to American missionaries, whose country was by that time at war with Great Britain. With great reluctance the government finally granted them permission to proceed to the Isle of France.

The next problem was to secure passage to their new destination. When a vessel, *L'Enterprise,* was found to be planning to sail the very week of the government's decision, the hopes of the missionaries were brightened considerably. However, the captain could take only two passengers. Because Harriet Newell was an expectant mother, it was decided that she and her husband should take advantage of the opportunity. The Judsons were to follow as soon as possible.

While awaiting passage, Adoniram and Ann were invited to live in Calcutta, in the home of Mr. Rolt, an Englishman who had married the widow of Brandson, one of the English Baptist missionaries. Once again, they had leisure to resume the study of baptism. Ann continued to hold out against becoming a Baptist. Her husband's reply was steadfast: "But it is my duty to examine the subject; and even if I have to pay dearly for it, I hope I shall not be afraid to embrace the truth." [8]

When the *Harmony* arrived on August 8, with Rice, Hall, and Samuel and Roxana Nott, Judson shared his burden almost at once. Within three hours of their arrival, Adoniram took Nott aside to tell him of his studies. Several days later, the Judson's came to an agree-

---

[8] Warburton, *Eastward,* p. 50; Wayland, *Memoir of Judson,* I, 108.

ment, each on the basis of their independent study, that "the immersion of a professing believer is the only Christian baptism." [9]

Without further delay, Judson characteristically acted upon his decision. On August 27, he wrote to William Carey and his colleagues at Serampore, asking for believer's baptism. A day or two later, he set himself to one of the most difficult tasks of his life —the writing of a letter to Dr. Worcester, chairman of the American Board of Commissioners. Enclosing a copy of his letter to Carey, he offered his resignation, saying that he supposed the board would not want to support a Baptist missionary. At the same time, he wrote to Dr. Thomas Baldwin, pastor of the Second Baptist Church in Boston, transmitting copies of these letters and saying, "Should there be formed a Baptist society for the support of a missionary in these parts, I shall be ready to consider myself their missionary." [10] He likewise corresponded with Dr. Lucius Bolles of Salem.

Dr. Marshman, of the Serampore Trio, upon learning of the request of Ann and Adoniram Judson for baptism, relayed the news at once to Dr. Baldwin in America. He was careful to explain that this decision had not been influenced by consultation with the English Baptist missionaries.

That Judson's decision had been reached privately and independently is evident from a lengthy letter which he wrote to the Third Church in Plymouth, Massachusetts, where he held his membership. In setting forth his reasons for becoming a Baptist, he explained:

> I could not find a single intimation in the New Testament that the children and domestics of believers were members of the church, or entitled to any church ordinance, in consequence of the profession of the head of their family. Everything discountenanced this idea. When baptism was spoken of, it was always in connection with believing. None but believers were commanded to be baptized; and it did not appear to my mind that any others were baptized.[11]

---

[9] These words were expressed in the letter written by Judson to Carey, Marshman, and Ward fom Calcutta on August 27, 1812. See Wayland, *op. cit.,* I, 109.

[10] Wayland, *op. cit.,* Vol. 1, p. 110. For the full correspondence between Judson and Baldwin, Worcester, and Bolles, and the Trio at Serampore, and for the correspondence between Marshman and Baldwin, see *The Baptist Missionary Magazine,* Vol. 3 (March, 1813), pp. 266-70.

[11] Wayland, *Memoir of Judson,* Vol. 1, p. 99.

He went on to point out how inconsistent the Congregationalists were, in that their polity did not admit those who had been baptized to full membership in the church. This he regarded as a violation of the Abrahamic covenant concept of the church to which they appealed in support of their baptism of infants.

On Sunday, September 6, 1812, Adoniram Judson and his wife were baptized by the Reverend William Ward in the Lal Bazaar Chapel at Calcutta. Three weeks later, Judson preached from its pulpit a sermon on "Christian Baptism," which subsequently was circulated in America.[12]

It appears that Judson at first had not felt that his change of denominational affiliation would necessitate the establishing of separate missions or fields on the part of the little band of American missionaries. Not until Hall and Nott had discussed with him the matter of his impending baptism had the step appeared inevitable. Both men and perhaps Rice (for he was not yet a Baptist) felt that the decision of the Judsons had made it unwise to carry out their plan of working together. Their point of view undoubtedly had influenced Judson to present his resignation to the American Board. There is indication of this fact in Judson's words to Dr. Worcester, to whom he offered his resignation:

> My change of sentiments on the subject of baptism is considered by my missionary brethren as incompatible with my continuing their fellow laborer in the mission which they contemplate on the island of Madagascar.[13]

Judson's biographer has suggested that "the sharp divisions in missions along denominational lines might not have arisen," if all four men had insisted upon "a united mission, or intimate co-operation in the same field." [14] In other words, the decision of those first American Protestant missionaries to separate was a formative influence in the shaping of American missions along denominational lines. In support of this viewpoint, it may be pointed out that there was a favorable disposition at home for a united mission. The American Board of Commissioners for Foreign Missions looked for leader-

[12] *The American Baptist Magazine and Missionary Intelligencer,* Vol. 1 (January, 1817), pp. 21-28.

[13] Wayland, *Memoir of Judson,* Vol. 1, p. 110, cited in Warburton, *Eastward,* pp. 52-53, in support of the interpretation set forth.

[14] Warburton, *loc. cit.*

ship to the London Missionary Society, which was organized on a wide interdenominational basis. The American Board, itself, was supported at the outset by contributions from several denominations. The inclination of Christians to co-operate was further evident in the rise of other interdenominational enterprises, such as the British and Foreign Bible Society. Thus it appears that for a brief time at the dawn of the Protestant foreign mission movement, there was the possibility of the development of a pattern of united effort which might well have advanced the cause of co-operative Christianity by a century.

When the Baptists of America learned that Adoniram and Ann Judson had become Baptists, enthusiasm ran high. The fervor with which many had been organizing local mission societies to support Carey's work in India quite naturally found fresh vitality in the possibility of an American field of service. On January 25, 1813, six days after Dr. Baldwin had received Judson's letter, offering his services to the Baptists, the Baptists of Boston began prayer-meetings for missions. On February 8, the "Baptist Society for Propagating the Gospel in India and Other Foreign Parts" was organized in Baldwin's home. It was intended that this society, which was to serve for Massachusetts, should join with other like organizations when they should be formed.

Of course, these developments were unknown to the Judsons, who faced an uncertain future in Calcutta. But they were not alone, for Luther Rice had been baptized on November 1, 1812, having become convinced by his own study of the Scriptures of the validity of Judson's position. Unable to secure transportation to the Isle of France, the three missionaries had considered Ceylon, where Chater of the English Baptist Mission was at work. They also had weighed the possibilities for service in Japan, Amboyna in the Spice Islands, and Brazil. Felix Carey, son of William Carey, on a visit to Calcutta in the fall of 1812 had urged the Judsons to settle in Burma, where he had been working. By October, the Judsons and Rice agreed that Java would offer the most suitable opportunities. But once again, no transportation was available.

About the middle of November, to make bad matters worse, the officials of the East India Company issued strict orders for the deportation of Rice and the Judsons to England. Unless they could find a boat that would take them to a likely mission field, their long voyage to India would prove to have been in vain. To their surprise, they discovered that a ship, the *Creole,* was bound for the Isle of France, their original destination. By now, however, they were without papers, for the authorities had revoked earlier decisions in favor of their immediate departure for England. After acquainting the captain of the *Creole* with their plight, they found that he was not averse to their boarding his vessel secretly. So at midnight, they made their way stealthily through the deserted streets to the waiting ship.

But they were not to reach the Isle of France, for two days down the river they were overtaken by a dispatch boat of the government. The *Creole* was forbidden to proceed with the passengers on board. The captain, however, allowed them opportunity to make another attempt to secure a pass. To this end, Rice hurried to Calcutta while Adoniram went in the opposite direction to Fultah. Alone and frightened, Ann was obliged to wait in a public inn. Both men returned without success, but Adoniram had learned of a ship, the *Commerce,* anchored near Fultah and ready to sail for Ceylon. It was the vessel on which Hall and Nott already were seeking flight from India.

Through some kind act of Providence, Rice turned up with a pass, permitting them to sail on the *Creole,* which had left their point of disembarkation three days before. Undaunted, the three young people hired a small boat which enabled them to overtake the ship at Saugur, at the mouth of the river. Seven weeks later they reached the Isle of France, hopeful of being reunited with the Newells. But Samuel was alone; Harriet had died with her new-born child. It was a keen disappointment and grief to Ann, who felt so alone in a strange land, as she, too, faced motherhood.

In February, 1813, Newell sailed for Ceylon, and thence to Bombay to joint the Notts and Hall. Rice and the Judsons realized in the meantime that the Isle of France offered no missionary possibilities. Knowing that Madagascar was closed to them, and that Burma was hostile territory for missionaries, they decided on Penang, in the Straits of Malacca.

After long discussion, it was determined that Luther Rice should return to America. A severe liver ailment had caused him such intense suffering in Calcutta and on the Isle of France that he felt that he must seek medical help if he were to live. But even more important was the necessity of developing missionary support among American Baptists, if they were to establish a mission. On March 15,

1813, Rice sailed for America, leaving Adoniram and Ann alone with only their faith in God.[15]

American Baptists Organize

As Luther Rice made his way to the United States by way of Brazil, he penned a plea from Bahia on June fifth to a Baptist minister in Boston, entreating American Baptists to form a national missionary society.[16] The tall, impressive young man was a statesman with prophetic insight. He realized that seventy thousand Baptists, scattered along the Atlantic seaboard from Maine to Georgia, needed to be united if the infant missionary enterprise launched in Asia were to be securely established.

Even before his arrival home, the most enthusiastic supporters of foreign missions had been doubtful that they could support Rice and the Judsons without assistance. Daniel Sharp, of Boston, corresponding secretary of the newly organized society for the support of foreign missions (mentioned earlier), had addressed a letter, under date of May 6, 1813, to Andrew Fuller, secretary of the Baptist Missionary Society in England. He suggested a co-operative venture in behalf of Judson. The reply was a kindly refusal on the grounds that it was wiser for the Baptists in America to form their own organization and establish missions for themselves. Indeed, there was no other course open. The British authorities would not allow the American missionaries to stay in Serampore or Calcutta. After Rice's departure, Judson and his wife had been obliged to cast in their lot at Rangoon, a dirty town of some ten thousand inhabitants who lived under Burmese rule. They had landed in the city on June 13, before an answer to Sharp's letter could have been received from England.[17] In fact, American Baptists were confronted with the establishment of an American mission in Burma before Rice's arrival in the United States on September 7, 1813.

Rice lost no time in arousing the churches to the need of the hour. Tirelessly, on horseback and by carriage, he traveled up and down the coast, visiting associations and churches. His eloquence and earnestness engendered an eager enthusiasm wherever he went. Associa-

[15] The foregoing incidents are told thrillingly in Warburton, *Eastward,* pp. 56-60.

[16] *The Massachusetts Baptist Missionary Magazine,* Vol. 3 (September, 1813), pp. 331-33.

[17] Wayland, *Memoir of Judson,* Vol. 1, pp. 124-25.

tions began to organize foreign mission societies after the pattern of the one at Boston. Among these were the Philadelphia Society, which came into existence in the fall of 1813, and the Savannah Society, organized in December of the same year to include Baptists of South Carolina and Georgia. Always, Rice kept before the churches the need for a general convention to organize a national agency. He went so far as to propose that it be held in Philadelphia in June, 1814.[18] To be sure, other men, like Morgan Edwards of Philadelphia (1722–95), had urged unsuccessfully the organization of the Baptists in America into a national body. But it was Luther Rice who supplied the needed missionary incentive to achieve unity.

Under great difficulties of travel, thirty-three delegates from eleven states and Washington, D.C., made their way to Philadelphia for a week of meetings that opened on Wednesday, May 18, 1814. Twenty of the thirty-three came from New York, New Jersey, and Pennsylvania. New England sent three. The southern states, from Virginia to Georgia, sent six. Less than one-third of those present were laymen. All who came were leaders in their areas of the country.[19]

Richard Furman, of Charleston, South Carolina, was appointed president of the Convention. He was fifty-nine years of age, an able minister and a recognized leader in his state, where he had served in its constitutional convention. The secretary was Thomas Baldwin, whose long ministry had been devoted to New England, chiefly to the Second Baptist Church in Boston. He was sixty-one years of age, even-tempered and generous in spirit.

After a preliminary discussion of the purpose of the meeting, a committee of fifteen was appointed to prepare a constitution for a plan of union. Dr. Baldwin served as chairman. A draft presented the next day proved to be unsatisfactory. So a smaller committee composed of Furman, Baldwin, Stephen Gano, and William White was instructed to prepare another. Gano was a New Yorker. He had served as a surgeon in the Continental Army and at the time of this meeting was pastor of the First Baptist Church in Providence, Rhode Island. He was a commanding figure with a powerful voice and an

---

[18] *The Massachusetts Baptist Missionary Magazine,* Vol. 3 (December, 1813), p. 354.

[19] For biographical sketches of the delegates, see *The Missionary Jubilee: An Account of the American Baptist Missionary Union. . . .* Revised edition (New York, 1869), pp. 108-38. For Proceedings of the Convention, see *The Massachusetts Baptist Missionary Magazine,* Vol. 3, Appendix.

easy and natural manner. William White, pastor of the Second Baptist Church in Philadelphia, was a self-educated man who had become an attractive and popular preacher in the city.

On Friday, the new constitution was reported. After some slight amending it was adopted unanimously on Saturday afternoon. Its preamble read:

> We, the delegates from Missionary Societies, and other religious bodies of the Baptist Denomination, in various parts of the United States, met in convention in the city of Philadelphia for the purpose of carrying into effect the benevolent intentions of our constituents, by organizing a plan for eliciting, combining, and directing the energies of the whole Denomination in one sacred effort for sending the glad tidings of Salvation to the Heathen, and to nations destitute of pure Gospel light, DO AGREE to the following Rules or fundamental Principles.

The new organization was called "The General Missionary Convention of the Baptist Denomination in the United States of America, for Foreign Missions." Because it was to meet every three years, it soon came to be known simply as the Triennial Convention. Membership was open to Baptist delegates (not exceeding two in number) from missionary societies and other religious bodies. The right to send delegates "was restricted to bodies contributing to the treasury annually a sum not less than one hundred dollars." Individuals, however generous in their donations, could not make themselves members. The provision that no association be allowed more than two delegates was modified in 1820, so that an additional delegate was permitted for every two hundred dollars contributed beyond the first hundred.

A board of twenty-one commissioners, to act for the Convention for a term of three years, was invested with power to appoint a president, two vice-presidents, a treasurer, a corresponding secretary, and a recording secretary. It was to be called "The Baptist Board of Foreign Missions in the United States."

Although amendments were made at nearly every subsequent meeting, this constitution continued to serve American Baptists for thirty-two years. The pattern which it set was significant for the future. For the first time, the word "convention" was used as a title for an organization of American Baptists.

> It is not the general convention of the societies and other organizations, but of the denomination. . . . The name stands for breadth, universality. It proposes to solicit every Baptist, cuts all the local and partisan limitations, covers the whole denomination. If it had been called the General Society it would have smacked of the limitations of the local societies meeting in it; but it is the Convention, the convening, the coming together, not of societies or churches or other organizations, but of Baptists.[19]

The constituency of the new body was also a departure. It was wholly comprised of organizations, not of individuals. Moreover, it was to be distinctly Baptist, whereas previous organizations for missions, except in the case of the English Baptist Missionary Society, had been interdenominational. This indicates a development in denominational consciousness. Moreover, it became the pattern for most of the foreign mission work conducted by American Protestants.

In this new organization had been focussed the missionary concern of a people whose zeal had been awakened first by Carey's thrilling work in India, and then by Judson's courageous venture in Burma. A scattered and feeble folk, who in 1812 lacked solidarity, had in 1814 become united in purpose and spirit.

For two more days, after adoption of the Constitution, the Convention continued in session. Each night public meetings had been held in the churches and homes throughout the city for preaching and prayer. The final act of the Convention was to vote that a message (prepared by Furman, Baldwin, and Staughton) be circulated among the churches to acquaint them with the purpose and nature of the new organization.

Upon adjournment of the Convention on May 24, the Board met and organized. Dr. Baldwin was elected its president. First vice-president was Dr. Henry Holcombe, of South Carolina, at the time pastor of the First Baptist Church in Philadelphia. Second vice-president was Dr. William Rogers, a New Englander, professor of English and Oratory at the University of Pennsylvania. A layman, John Cauldwell, was made treasurer. Dr. William Staughton was elected corresponding secretary. He had long been a friend of missions, having promoted its cause ever since his arrival in Philadelphia in 1806. He was the first of a series of able administrators of the

---

[19] Albert L. Vail, *The Morning Hour of American Baptist Missions* (Philadelphia, 1907), pp. 394-95.

affairs of the board. William White was appointed recording secretary.

The selection of missionaries was to be governed by Article V of the constitution of the Convention, which provided that missionary appointees were to be persons of genuine piety, talents, and zeal, in good standing in some regular church. Earlier societies had left this point untouched. The principle thus adopted was in keeping with the decision of the founders to establish a *Baptist* missionary convention.

Luther Rice's appointment as a missionary was made on May 25, following a report of his labors in the South. He was to serve temporarily as a promotional agent, interpreting the missionary cause, and organizing societies and institutions for its support. In a letter to Judson, he expressed the hope that this work could be accomplished in five or six months, after which he should be free to join him in Burma.[20]

The next action of the Board was to appoint Adoniram Judson as its missionary, assuming the pledge of support given earlier by the Baptists of Massachusetts, and requesting him to pursue his work in such places as in his judgment might appear most promising.[21] It was voted that the sum of one thousand dollars should be sent to him "by the first safe opportunity." Actually, the news of his appointment did not reach Judson until September 5, 1815, more than fifteen months later. On that date, he wrote in his journal concerning the Convention:

> It unites with all the Bible Societies in Europe and America, during the last twenty years, in furnishing abundant reason to hope, that the dreadful darkness which has so long enveloped the earth, is about to flee away before the rising Sun.[22]

With statesmanlike insight, Adoniram Judson saw the organization of the Triennial Convention as a part of a great Christian movement to evangelize the world.

---

[20] *The Missionary Jubilee*, p. 100.

[21] *The Massachusetts Baptist Missionary Magazine*, Vol. 3, Appendix, p. 13.

[22] Ann H. Judson, *A Particular Relation of the American Baptist Mission to the Burman Empire* (Washington, 1823), p. 53.

CHAPTER III

Gaining a Foothold in the Orient

ON THE GEORGIANA—what Ann Judson called "a crazy old vessel"—Adoniram and his wife embarked on June 22, 1813, at Madras for Rangoon. It was for the young couple the last lap of a long and wearisome voyage, and in many ways the most urgent part of the journey. The trip itself was trying in the extreme. Seasickness and despair all but overcame the young wife. The wretched-looking town of Rangoon, which sprawled uninvitingly at the mouth of the Irawaddy River, was therefore a welcome sight to the Judsons. Tuesday, July 13, was a day long remembered in their lives.

Fortunately, they were able to make a home of sorts in the deserted mission house that had been built by the English Baptist Mission Society when, in 1807, William Carey had sent two missionaries, Chater and Mardon, to Rangoon. Later in the year, Mardon was replaced by Felix Carey, son of the renowned missionary pioneer. Four years later, Chater retired to Ceylon. When Felix Carey entered the employ of the government, the mission was abandoned. Efforts of the London Missionary Society to establish a mission were equally unsuccessful. Only the Roman Catholic missionaries remained, and they were restricted by the government to limit their efforts to the scattered Portuguese population and those of mixed blood.

The Judsons, therefore, were the only Protestant missionaries to the great Burmese Empire, which extended about 1,200 miles to the north between India proper and the Chinese Empire, and was nearly 900 miles wide. Its 19,000,000 people were the subjects of an absolute monarch who ruled at Ava. To the north were mountains; to the south were plains and fertile valleys.

A Beachhead in Rangoon

Settling down in unfinished and comfortless quarters was a severe test of courage for the young couple. There were no English families in the city, and no white woman to share understanding and companionship with Ann. The only compensation for the lack of conveniences was a garden full of flowers and fruit trees. Providentially also, there was one woman left of the old mission, a Burmese.

The first task was language study. In less than a year, Adoniram and Ann were able to read, write, and converse with ease in Burmese. But this accomplishment did not satisfy Judson. He determined so to master the language that he would win the respect and understanding of the best educated Burmese. To this end, he acquainted himself with the literature of the country. Since there were no printed books, he was obliged to read manuscripts engraved on dried palm leaves with an iron stylus or pen, without ink. During the first six months he transcribed a Pali dictionary so as to recognize and understand words brought over from India by Buddhist monks. Then he went to work on a Burmese-English dictionary.

In the meantime, by her charm and friendly spirit, Mrs. Judson paved the way for friendly relations with government officials. It was not long, however, before the menace of bandits forced the Judsons to move from the mission home that was outside the town and off the road to a location within the walls of the town. To add to their loneliness, they received no mail from home for two and a half years after sailing from Salem. In spite of their isolation from friends and familiar places, they never once regretted having come to Burma.

There were times when the severe headaches and eyestrain, which Judson suffered from long hours of study in the hot climate, made him feel that his work was to be short-lived. But he persevered during the long months of severe pain in the preparation of the Burmese grammar. He felt that this must be completed even if it were to be all that he should accomplish. He regarded his work as a pioneer task, to supplement the noble beginning wrought by the English Baptists at Serampore.[1]

---

[1] From a letter to Dr. William Staughton, August 3, 1816, cited in Judson, Ann H., *A Particular Relation of the American Baptist Mission to the Burman Empire* (Washington, 1823), p. 76.

In February, 1815, Ann Judson left Rangoon for Madras for an absence of three months to regain her health. Four months after her return, Roger Williams Judson was born, on September 11. The young parents were not destined long to enjoy their first-born. In eight months the little life was gone, and the first grave was dug in a grove of mango trees in the garden of the mission house.

Experiences like these made a deep impression upon Judson as he reflected upon the type of men who were needed for work in Burma. In a letter to Luther Rice, written on August 3, 1816, he cautioned:

> In encouraging young men to come out as missionaries, do use the greatest caution. One wrong-headed, conscientiously obstinate man, would ruin us. Humble, quiet, persevering men; men of sound, sterling talents, of decent accomplishments, and some natural aptitude to acquire a language; men of amiable, yielding temper, willing to take the lowest place, to be the least of all, and the servant of all; men who enjoy much closet religion, who live near to God, and are willing to suffer all things for Christ's sake, without being proud of it;—these are the men we need.[2]

Without his knowing it at the time, recruits were already on the way in the persons of George H. Hough and his family, the first additions for the mission. Hough was a printer, and therefore especially welcome. The Serampore mission gave a press and Burmese type. Judson had two tracts waiting to be printed. One was entitled "A View of the Christian Religion," which he had written to explain Christianity to the Burmese. The other consisted of a few chapters of the Gospel of Matthew in the Burman language. Also awaiting publication was a small catechism prepared by Mrs. Judson. Within six months, the tracts and first sheets of Matthew were in print.

Taking advantage of the high degree of literacy among Burman men, Judson opened his ministry not by preaching, but by circulation of the printed page. From his first acquaintance with the Burmans, he had been impressed with the great value which they attached to books, particularly in the realm of religion. During the first three months of 1817 he had distributed 1,000 copies of his tract on "A View of the Christian Religion," and 3,000 copies of the catechism. In March the first Buddhist inquirer who was in earnest appeared. By the end of the year, Judson was ready to open his

[2] *Ibid.*, p. 78.

preaching ministry, if he could find a Burman associate among his English Baptist friends.

On Christmas Day, Judson left Rangoon for what he thought would be an absence of three months, while he visited Chittagong, where English Baptists had carried on a brief mission. Owing to sailing difficulties, he did not reach his destination. Instead, he was obliged to leave the ship at Madras and make the return trip overland. As his absence lengthened into several months, his wife's anxieties were increased by the arrest of Hough by the authorities for questioning. Understanding the propensities of Burmese officials for extorting money from frightened prisoners, Ann besought the aid of the viceroy in obtaining Hough's release from prison. The experience had been sufficiently unnerving to prompt Hough to remove his family and the printing press to Calcutta. Even Ann had entertained thoughts of leaving for Bengal, not knowing what had happened to her husband. But a presentiment that he would return shortly changed her mind after booking passage. And well that it did, for Judson arrived home on August 2, 1818, seven months after his departure for Chittagong.

Once more Adoniram and Ann were alone, but this time, not for long. On September 19, 1818, James Colman and Edward Wheelock arrived with their wives. Colman was twenty-three; Wheelock was twenty. The two young men had been ordained and commissioned in Boston on September 10, 1817, a month before sailing for Calcutta. Colman had been discouraged by his friends from his purpose, for they felt that his gifts and temperament gave promise of great use at home. But the foreign mission field was his determined choice.

Early in 1820, Judson and Colman made personal application to the emperor at Ava for permission to preach. It was denied. Fearing that even greater hostility to their mission might develop, Judson sent Colman to Chittagong in the province of Arracan, which was under the protection of the East India Company. Colman was to establish a mission station to which Judson might retreat if the opposition became too intense in Rangoon. He arrived on June 5, 1821. In order to minister to the Arracanese, who lived on the border of the Burmese Empire, he left Chittagong for Cox's Bazar, a town of 30,000, whose people spoke a language similar to that of the Burmese. At first a Buddhist priest from Ceylon incited an attack upon him, but with government protection, he was able to open a school for children. His promising career as a missionary was cut off suddenly, however, by an attack of jungle fever, which took his life on July 4, 1822. His place was occupied temporarily by a member of the Serampore mission.

Meanwhile, back in Rangoon, Judson had adopted a method of religious propagation used by the Burmese. He built in April, 1819, a *zayat,* from which he might preach in the Burmese tongue. A *zayat* is a wayside shelter, usually made of bamboo, which is found in almost every Burman village. Here men gather to talk or rest. Frequently a Buddhist monk or teacher may use the place to instruct his followers or lead them in worship. Judson's Christian *zayat* was a building 18 feet wide by 27 feet long. It stood out in front of the mission house, and consisted of three rooms—a large veranda open to public view, where Judson would sit and read or answer questions; a larger room enclosed for worship and instruction; and a small room at the rear where Ann held her women's classes.

On Sunday, April 4, 1819, this first Protestant Christian gathering-place in Burma was opened. Calling together some neighbors, Judson conducted his first public preaching service, after six years in the country. In attendance were fifteen adults and a number of children. The crowd was disorderly and inattentive, not being accustomed to this type of service. By the next week, however, the order had improved. Within one month, Judson had his first convert, Maung Nau, a man about thirty-five years of age, of moderate ability, with no family, a poor employee of a timber merchant. Day after day he had come to the *zayat* to listen to Judson. Finally, he wrote a letter to the missionaries, confessing his faith and asking for baptism. On June 27, after the usual Sunday service at the *zayat,* the little company of seven retired to a large pond nearby, "and there among the lotus and the water lilies, with a great image of the Buddha silently looking down from the bank, the first Burman convert confessed his Saviour in baptism. It was the beginning of the Protestant church in Burma. The next Sunday, July 4, Burman and American Christians sat down together at the Lord's Supper. The hope of years was fulfilled." [3]

The second convert was Maung Tha Hla, a rather superior and well-read man. Another was Maung Bya, a man of middle age who

---

[3] Stacy R. Warburton, *Eastward: The Story of Adoniram Judson,* p. 77. Copyright, 1937, Round Table Press, New York. Used by permission.

had learned to read in the evening school at the *zayat*. At first, out of fear of persecution, they requested secret baptism. To test their sincerity, Judson advised them to wait for a time. A short time later, they asked for semiprivate baptism, about sunset time, away from public observance. This was granted out of deference to the great price which these new Christians were paying for their faith. So on November 7, the second baptismal service took place. On July 18, 1820, Judson baptized his teacher, Moung Shwa-gnong, and Mah Men-la, a woman fifty-one years old who, like Moung Shwa-gnong, assumed able leadership of the tiny church at Rangoon. By August 21, 1821, he had baptized the eighteenth convert, with two more remaining—Moung Myat-lah and Mah Ing, one deterred by fear of the government, the other by fear of her husband's disapproval.

In the midst of his success, it became apparent that Ann must return to America for medical attention, owing to an ailment of the liver. On August 21, 1821, she sailed for Calcutta and home, leaving a very lonely husband in Rangoon. In the following December, Jonathan D. Price, a physician, arrived to serve in the Burma mission. When appointed by the Board, he had received careful instructions to employ his medical skills for the comfort of his associates, and for the relief of "afflicted heathen." He was warned, however, to regard such service "as subordinate and subservient to your office as a preacher of the doctrine of Christ." [4] Indeed, he had been ordained to the work of an evangelist in the Sansom Street Baptist Church of Philadelphia. In such a devious manner was the medical ministry introduced into missions.

His medical skill soon aroused the interest of the emperor, who invited him to visit the Court at Ava. Judson accompanied him as interpreter, hoping that he might find opportunity to intercede once again in behalf of religious toleration for Burmese Christians and for permission to preach freely in the country. Price was received with much favor and granted quarters in a house near the royal palace. Judson also was invited to remain in the city in order to keep the doctor from becoming lonely. Promising that he would bring his wife to settle in Ava, Judson returned to Rangoon, reaching home on February 2, 1823.

In the meantime, Dr. Price had lost his wife by death just five

---

[4] *The American Baptist Magazine and Missionary Intelligencer,* Vol. 3, No. 5 (Sept. 1821), p. 187.

months after his arrival in Burma. Some time later, he married a Burmese girl, Mah Noo, Judson performing the ceremony. The marriage had come about as the result of an exaggerated sense of obligation on the part of Price, who had been unsuccessful in a cataract operation on the girl which had left her blind.[5]

Mrs. Judson arrived in Rangoon on December 5, 1823. Her return was a double joy to Adoniram, for it reunited him with the one whom he considered the light of his life, and it brought to Burma two newly appointed missionaries, Jonathan and Deborah Wade. During Mrs. Judson's visit to America, the young couple had been influenced greatly by her message and spirit. Their commissioning had occurred in the month that Mrs. Judson was to sail for Calcutta. Accordingly, they had returned with her. Their coming at this time was fortunate for the mission. Judson had just completed his translation of the New Testament into Burmese. Hough was at Rangoon, having returned some time before from Calcutta with the printing press. The Judsons were free to move to Ava to take advantage of the emperor's invitation to make their home there. The Wades, having already studied the language on the way to Burma, were in a position to take leadership of the little church at Rangoon.

The Tragedy of Ava

When Adoniram and Ann arrived in Ava, conditions had changed. An aloofness had replaced the earlier welcome spirit that had persuaded Judson to return with his wife to establish their home in the city. The reason was not far to seek. War was imminent with the English, and the emperor was in no mood to befriend a missionary. Even Dr. Price was out of favor, for all foreigners who spoke English were suspected of being spies for the East India Company. Nevertheless, the Judsons took their courage in both hands and built a small house. Ann opened a school for girls, teaching them to read and sew. The nucleus of the little company consisted of the two daughters of Shwe Ba, a convert. Ann, following a practice of providing native children with Christian names, called them Mary and Abby Hasseltine, after her sisters. On Sundays, Judson preached at the home of Dr. Price. A frequent visitor was Henry Gouger, a

[5] Report by Rev. J. N. Cushing, D.D., of Rangoon, published in the *National Baptist*, Sept. 15, 1887, cited in Walter N. Wyeth, *A Galaxy in the Burman Sky* (Philadelphia, 1892), pp. 37-38.

young Englishman of twenty-five years of age, who was engaged in trade in the city. Through him, the missionaries secured money from the agent of the board in Calcutta, a fact which was later to bring them under suspicion of the Burmese government.

Then, on Sunday, May 23, 1824, at the close of the worship service, news came that war had begun. Rangoon had been bombarded and captured by the British. The attack probably saved the lives of Hough and Wade, who had been imprisoned by the Burman government on May tenth. For Sir Archibald Campbell ordered their release and took them under his protection, threatening to lay the entire country in ruins if the blood of white men was shed. Frightened and feeling that there was little wisdom in remaining in Rangoon, both missionaries left for Calcutta, where they stayed for the duration of the war. Hough printed Judson's translation of the Gospel of Matthew in Burmese, while Wade supervised publication of Judson's Burmese Dictionary.

Worse treatment was in store for their colleagues in Ava. On June 8, while Judson was at dinner, a dozen men rushed into the house and dragged him off. Ann was placed under house arrest for the night. The incident was the result of a discovery by the government that Gouger's accounts showed that he had given money to Judson and Price. This convinced the Burmese authorities that the missionaries were spies. In company with Price and five other foreigners who had also been arrested, Judson was thrown into a wooden building about thirty by forty feet in size. Each prisoner was weighted down by three pairs of fetters on his ankles. Without windows, the building admitted light and air only through a closely woven bamboo door and holes in the walls. Some forty or fifty men and women were lying about, some fastened in the stocks, others bound with chains on their legs—all suffering from heat that was nearly one hundred degrees.

Through persistent intervention with the governor, Ann gained permission to visit the prison with food for her husband. Adoniram and Ann conceived a plan of exchanging notes hidden in the long nose of the tea pot. The unhappy prisoners sought to keep their sanity by passing the long hours playing chess with a rudely constructed set of men carved out of bamboo.

Because their home had been searched ruthlessly by the authorities, Ann had endeavored to save the precious New Testament manuscript in the Burmese language by sewing it in a pillow which she made especially hard, to discourage the jailer from appropriating it. This she brought to Adoniram in the prison.

On January 26, 1825, the brave woman gave birth to a daughter, Maria Elizabeth. By March Ann had gained permission for her husband to move into a bamboo shed in the prison yard, while his companions remained in their overcrowded quarters. Each had a mat and pillow. But the respite was not long, for due to public pressure for their execution, the governor was obliged to return them to the prison to keep them out of sight. Once again the heat and crowded conditions had to be endured. Then suddenly in May, the prisoners were all removed from Ava, and forced to march in the tropic heat to Amarapura. When they could walk no farther, they were taken in carts, more dead than alive, to Aungbinle, a few miles beyond. It was a dilapidated prison, a wooden building standing alone on the plain.

Distraught with anxiety for his safety, Ann followed her husband to his destination. A kindly jailer took pity on her and allowed her the use of two rooms in his house. The first day after her arrival, Mary Hasseltine, the Burmese child under her care, came down with smallpox. Little Maria soon caught the disease from her. To add to Ann's anxiety for the children, who eventually recovered, she never knew for a period of six months at what hour her husband might be put to death. Her fears were not diminished when Adoniram was sent to the Burmese camp to serve as translator and interpreter in the negotiations with the English. He was forced to work in a small windowless hut that stood on the hot sand between the camp and the river. He avoided most cautiously taking any part in political affairs, so that the Burmese might not be able to associate him with British interests.

While Judson was so engaged, Maung Ing, his faithful servant, brought him news that Ann had contracted spotted fever (what is known today as spinal meningitis). Providentially, Dr. Price was freed from prison on the very day that she reached a crisis. Through his care and that of the loyal Moochil, Ann was restored to health.

At last, twenty-one months after his arrest, Adoniram's long imprisonment came to an end on February 21, 1826, following English negotations for release of white prisoners. On March 21, Adoniram and Ann, with little Maria, reached Rangoon by a British gunboat.

The war was over. It had begun in a controversy over Chittagong, the strip of low land lying along the sea and flanking Burma on the west, which was under British rule and provided a refuge for those who were fleeing from Burmese despotism. It ended with the cession of four provinces to the East India Company—Arracan, Ya, Tavoy, and Mergui in the south. The proud emperor was defeated but unbroken in spirit. This was only the beginning of Anglo-Burmese hostilities.

The Judsons' return to Rangoon was brightened by prospects of establishing a stronger work under British protection at Amherst, a new city founded by the civil commissioner on a peninsula at the mouth of the Salween River. Amherst was to be the new capital of Tenasserim, the long and narrow strip of territory in the east that stretched south from the Salween, and which was now in British hands. There, Judson anticipated a freedom to work which he could not have in Rangoon under Burmese rule. On June 29, he moved his family from the city where they had begun their labors. In Amherst, he and Ann selected a pleasant site for a home that looked out to the sea.

Two days after reaching Amherst, Adoniram, still acting as interpreter for the British, was on his way to Ava with Crawford, the civil commissioner, who had urged his help in working out a commercial treaty with the Burmese. Crawford had promised to help Judson in his struggle for religious liberty in Burma by insisting upon a clause for its guarantee in the agreement. With a tender farewell, bright with the anticipation of happier days to come, Ann and Adoniram parted—but never to meet again on this earth. For in October, a violent fever seized Ann. She died on the 24th in spite of the care of the army surgeon and a European nurse. Her body was buried beneath the "hopia" tree that stood between the house and the wind-swept sea. To those who knew her, the tree became a symbol of her courageous life. For Ann had withstood the storms of loneliness and persecution and disease with head uplifted to the heavens and feet planted firmly on the soil of Burma.

A month later, the Wades returned from Calcutta and assumed the care of Maria, seeking also to make a home for the bereaved Judson. On April 24, 1827, just a week after the joyous arrival of George Dana Boardman and his wife, Sarah, little Maria died. It became Boardman's sad duty to make the little coffin, and endeavor to give Judson what comfort he could. After the burial, Boardman did not stay long at Amherst, but removed to Moulmein, about twenty-five miles above the town, on the same side of the Martaban River. Moulmein was the new site chosen by General Campbell as his military headquarters, a fact which quickly caused it to replace Amherst as the chief city of the province. In August, Judson paid the Boardmans a visit, liked the city, and decided to locate the mission there in October. In November, the Wades joined him; and Moulmein became the new center of the mission.

The transition marked a new phase of the work in Burma. Hough and Price had retired from the mission, Hough to be interpreter and teacher and Price to be in the medical service of the Burman ruler at Ava. Judson remained the sole link with the beginnings of the work that had gained ground so slowly in Rangoon, only to be uprooted by the ravages of war.

Lines Lengthen in Behalf of Burma's Karens

In Moulmein, a town of twenty thousand, Boardman and his wife built their home. The presence of the military cantonments, a mile north of Boardman's home, offered them an opportunity to carry on missionary work with both the soldiers and the varied populace. The strategy of the mission at first had been to maintain two stations: one at Amherst under Wade; the other, at Moulmein under Boardman, with Judson free to serve each as duty required. But the rapid decline of Amherst, once the military moved out, prompted the change of plans which had brought Wade to Moulmein.

George Dana Boardman and his wife were exceptionally suited to their task. A native of Maine, George had been trained at a Baptist literary and theological institution at Waterville. Upon his conversion at the age of nineteen, he united with the Baptist church at Waterville. When his alma mater became a college in that same year (1820), the young Boardman became one of its first students. It was there that he first began to consider the claims of foreign missions upon his life. Still unsettled in mind upon his graduation in 1822, he accepted an offer to continue as a tutor. Finally, in April, 1823, he volunteered his services to the Baptist Board of Foreign Missions. His decision had been largely in response to a sense of obligation to fill the place of James Colman, who had died at Cox's Bazar in Arracan on July 4, 1822.

After a period of study at Andover Theological Seminary, Boardman was married in 1825 to Sarah B. Hall, of Salem, Massachusetts. He first had learned of Sarah through an elegy which she had written upon hearing of Colman's untimely death. Deeply impressed by one whose aspirations were so like his own, he had sought her out. Theirs was a fortunate match, for their natures were in complete accord through all of the hardships which they were to face together.

Arriving in Calcutta on December 2, 1825, the Boardmans had found it necessary to await the close of the Anglo-Burmese War before leaving the city. The experience gained through language study, observation of the English missionaries, and study of the schools maintained by the missionaries, stood them in good stead when they opened their own station at Moulmein. Prior to the arrival of the Wades and Judson, the Boardmans gave instruction to all who visited their home. They witnessed in the bazaars and on the highway, and distributed tracts. All the while they continued their study of the Burmese language.

Early in 1828, upon advice of the Board in America that the missionaries spread out from Moulmein in order to encompass more territory, it was decided by the missionaries that Tavoy was the most inviting field for new work.

While the work of Boardman was making progress during that first year, the mission at Amherst was waning as the populace diminished. Accordingly, on October 14, 1827, Mr. and Mrs. Wade and Judson left Amherst to locate in Moulmein. The girls' school which Mrs. Wade had conducted at Amherst was re-established at Moulmein, where it was carried on by Mrs. Boardman and Mrs. Wade. In time it became a significant center of Christian training for girls in Burma. Boardman had opened a boys' school, which was the forerunner of the high schools and higher education which the mission at Moulmein was to introduce to Burma.[6]

Boardman was a young man of a deeply pietistic nature. In theology he was a Calvinist. Never satisfied with his present level of spiritual attainment, he always sought to reach a higher peak. Like Judson, who underwent a similar period of deep soul-searching following the death of Ann, Boardman passed through several months of spiritual struggle during the year 1827. Undoubtedly, the loneli-

---

[6] For the life of Boardman, see Joseph C. Robbins, *Boardman of Burma* (Philadelphia, 1940) and Alonzo King, *A Good Fight; Or, George Dana Boardman and the Burman Mission* (Boston, 1874, improved edition).

ness which he and his wife endured during those months may have had much to do with his state of mind. Their isolation is reflected in an item from Boardman's journal for July 22, 1827. He describes how on each Lord's day morning, he and Sarah read a sermon and engaged in prayer; but on this day, they shared the Lord's Supper.[7]

Early in 1828, upon urging from the Board in America that the missionaries spread out from Moulmein in order to encompass more territory, plans were made to establish a new station at Tavoy about one hundred and fifty miles to the south. A smaller city than Moulmein, Tavoy lay on a low plain, flanked on three sides by mountains. Of its nine thousand inhabitants, six thousand were Burmese. More prosperous than Moulmein, the city was a stronghold of Buddhism, with more than a hundred monasteries and a thousand pagodas.[8] The new site was chosen because Tavoy, like Arracan, had been ceded to the English by the late treaty of peace.

Although they were reluctant to leave Moulmein, which had become very dear to their hearts within less than a year, the Boardmans nevertheless responded to the decision of their colleagues that they should open the new station at Tavoy. They left Moulmein on March 29, 1828, taking with them four boys from the school, a Siamese Christian, and Ko Tha Byu, a Karen convert. The decision to take Ko Tha Byu had been at the urging of Judson. In reality, Boardman had been sceptical of this notorious criminal, who had been guilty of some thirty murders and whose reputation for evil had been so great that Boardman had urged a delay in his baptism so that there might be a longer testing period. But God in his wisdom had directed events. For the presence of Ko Tha Byu was to open the door to undreamed-of results for the Baptist Mission in Burma.

Ko Tha Byu had been born in 1778 in a jungle village near Bassein. He left home at the age of fifteen and entered upon a career of crime. The close of the Burmese War found him in Rangoon, where debt overcame him. He was about to be sold into slavery for this reason when a Burman Christian, Ko Shway-bay, paid his debt. By Burmese law, he became the servant of Ko Shway-bay. But the ungovernable temper of the Karen so discouraged his new master that Judson took him into his employ. Under the influence of Judson's godly life, Ko Tha Byu, the former robber and murderer, was con-

---

[7] King, *A Good Fight,* p. 131.

[8] Robbins, *Boardman of Burma,* p. 98.

verted. The little Burmese church was sceptical of the change in his life; the congregation also looked with some reluctance upon receiving into membership a man from the despised Karen people of the jungle. But in time, they were obliged to admit that his conversion was genuine. The change in the plans of the Mission delayed his baptism until he reached Tavoy.

It was on May 16, 1828, that Boardman baptized Ko Tha Byu, a little more than two months after their arrival in the city. Three Karens who witnessed the baptism urged Ko Tha Byu to accompany them to their own people. This he did. It was to be the beginning of twelve years of most ardent missionary preaching on the part of this remarkable evangelist. By the time of his death at the age of sixty-two, he had broken the ground for the great ingathering of Karens which Boardman, Abbott, and Vinton were to witness during their service in Burma.

Not long after his arrival in Tavoy, Boardman opened a boys' day school in which was taught the Burmese and English languages as well as useful sciences. It was part of a plan which he presented to the Board in America for establishing schools throughout the entire district of Tavoy. The day school at Tavoy, which was under the auspices of the local government with some financial assistance, was to be the central school, under the superintendence of a missionary. Here young men were to be prepared for teaching in the village schools. Each village school, which he estimated would not cost more than ten to fifteen rupees a month, was to select promising young men to send to the central school at Tavoy for training. At the meeting of the Baptist General Convention in Philadelphia, on April 29, 1829, the plan was given approval. In the meantime, Mrs. Boardman was trying to establish a similar plan of schools for girls. At first she found it difficult to secure a teacher. Finally, she had twenty-one pupils taught by a Tavoy woman, who received four rupees a month for teaching each girl to read.

By 1830, Boardman had come to the conclusion that the boarding school, which he had begun alongside of the day school, produced better results. The former afforded an opportunity to influence the religious thinking and the character of the pupils, whereas the day school seldom influenced the pupils in matters of religion.[9] Board-

---

[9] *The American Baptist Magazine,* Vol. 9, No. 11 (Nov. 1829), p. 386; Vol. 10, No. 1 (Jan. 1830), pp. 21-22; Vol. 10, No. 5 (May, 1830), p. 147.

man's strong emphasis upon education was wise in view of the strong Buddhist influence, with its numerous monasteries to teach religion. It was welcomed by the English government as a means of providing general education. Moreover, it exerted a most salutary effect upon the Christian work begun at Tavoy among the Karens, for it provided the basis for the policy that was to develop an indigenous church in Burma. The pattern and method was not new with Boardman. Wade had used it, having observed its effective use by the English missionaries at Calcutta. But Boardman saw its possibilities for the development of a ministry in Burma and brought a well-formulated plan before the Board in America.

Boardman's work fell into three types: daily witnessing in the *zayat* which he did not regard as very successful; preaching to the twenty thousand Burmans and Tavoyans around the city and to the three thousand Karens in the nearby jungle villages; native schools which included the boys' boarding school that was supported by gifts from America, and the day school that was maintained by a monthly allowance from the government. In the day school were Burmans, Tavoyans, Moocoolmans, Portuguese, Indo-Chinese, a Talaing, a Karen, and a Yooan-Shan. They were taught to read, to speak, and to write English and Burmese, arithmetic, geography, and astronomy, and religion. In time ill health compelled Mrs. Boardman to give up her boarding school. At the end of 1829, the little church consisted of three members, one of whom was Kee Keang, a young Chinese who had been baptized on August 3, 1828. By 1830, the church had grown to ten members.[10]

Through the influence of the preaching tours conducted by Ko Tha Byu, Boardman's work expanded to include the Karens. As early as September, 1828, a delegation from the jungle visited his home to show him the sacred book which they had received twelve years before from a white man and which they had worshipped. Not being able to read, they wanted to know whether it was good or evil. When Boardman discovered that it was *The Book of Common Prayer with the Psalms,* published in Oxford, England, he told the Karens that its contents were good. He warned, however, that they should not worship the book, but the God about whom the book told them. This visit was followed by another in the following January, this time by two Karens who had traveled several days' journey to urge the mis-

[10] King, *A Good Fight,* pp. 185-86, 251-57.

sionary to tell the Karens of Tavoy, Mergui, and Tenasserim about his message. Boardman could not resist this appeal. Like David Brainerd, whose example he cherished, he went, on February 5, 1829, with Ko Tha Byu and two of his schoolboys to preach to a people whom he regarded as being like the Indians he had known in America. This was the first of many long and arduous trips through the rice fields, and up the steep mountainside, to lonely Karen villages nestled on the side of the mountain or back in the jungle. Often he was cold and wet upon reaching his destination, but always his heart was warmed by the welcome which awaited him.

The Karens were animists, although Boardman mistook their lack of idols for evidence that they were atheists. Actually, they worshiped the spirits that they believed inhabited nature all about them. Ridden with fears, these people, who had been mistreated and despised by the Burmese, received the message of Christianity gladly. Unlike the Burmese, they had no well-developed form of religion. This explains why there were converts almost from the first.

The year 1829 was one of hardships and heartaches for the Boardmans. Their first-born child, Sarah Ann, died in July. Soon after, Dr. Price died, leaving his two sons to the care of the Boardmans. The climax came with the Tavoy rebellion which broke out in August, during the absence of Major Burney, commander of the troops at the garrison. The Boardmans barely escaped with their lives. Practically all of their possessions were destroyed during the fighting which swept the city for nearly a week. Toward the end of the year, a second son, Judson Wade, was born. Shortly thereafter, Sarah became seriously ill. The burdens placed upon Boardman were too much for him. With broken resistance, he developed a cough which was a warning of his own serious state of health. Yet he drove himself harder than ever, often devoting half of his time to village preaching. Meanwhile, he and Sarah declined steadily in health. In March, 1830, Sarah was obliged to go to Moulmein to recover. About this time, the Wades left Moulmein to rebuild the work at Rangoon, which was under the sole care of Ko Thah-a, the first ordained Burmese pastor. Thus it was that Sarah's coming was welcomed, for she was needed to supervise the work for women and children. But her departure left Boardman to carry on at Tavoy alone.

In the meantime, Judson decided to return to Rangoon. Following the death of his wife, he had spent the year and a half in seclusion at

Moulmein, translating the Old Testament into Burmese. The arrival of Cephas and Stella Bennett at Moulmein on January 14 gave him his opportunity to leave the work in charge of the newcomers. Within a few months, he and the Wades undertook the pressing work at Rangoon. It was not long, however, before Judson left Wade in charge at Rangoon and set out for Prome, which was situated up the Irrawaddy River. It was the chief city between Rangoon and Ava. His plan was to reach the millions beyond these urban centers by establishing a central station in that vicinity. But persecution soon developed, which necessitated his return to Rangoon. Upon his arrival, he found that the Wades had returned to Moulmein, driven out by a renewal of opposition. Judson's presence gave fresh courage to the people, who soon became eager again for his Christian tracts. This was the chief means of spreading the gospel at this time. Because of persecution, public preaching and the conduct of worship services were avoided.

At Moulmein, the Bennetts were hard at work. Cephas Bennett was a printer who had left a thriving publishing business in Utica, New York, because he could not rest until he became a missionary. He took charge of the small English church of twelve members and of the Burmese church of forty members. Mrs. Bennett conducted prayer meetings with the Burmese women. By November, 1830, Bennett was able to report that more than 70,000 tracts had been printed under his direction.[11]

By April, it seemed wise to Judson and Wade, the senior missionaries, that Boardman should come to Moulmein to take over the work there while they devoted themselves to Rangoon. On April 27 Boardman left Tavoy with a sad heart, fearing that his removal might be permanent. During his ministry of two years in Tavoy, in spite of severe trials, he had built a church of twenty members, of whom fifteen were Karens. To console the Karens whom he was leaving, he promised to return after the rains if they would meet him halfway at a place where they might build a *zayat* in which to hold services. Thereupon, he was accompanied to Moulmein by Ko Tha Byu and several other workers.

Although the Boardmans were ill much of the time at Moulmein,

---

[11] Ruth W. Ranney, *A Sketch of the Lives and Missionary Work of Rev. Cephas Bennett and His Wife, Stella Kneeland Bennett, 1829–1891* (New York, 1892), pp. 17-25.

they fulfilled a heavy schedule of work. George preached or taught every day and conducted three services on Sundays. He corrected proof sheets for the press, prepared lessons for the boys' school, and superintended the erection of a new house to replace the old mission home which had fallen into disrepair. Sarah conducted the boys' boarding school, with the assistance of Mrs. Bennett.

Then in September, the Boardmans lost their infant son, Judson Wade, who had been weak and ailing since birth. He was buried at Moulmein. By the time Wade returned to Moulmein in November, it was evident that the Bennetts were sufficiently experienced in mission work to absorb the duties of the Boardmans so that they might return to their beloved Tavoy. The Boardmans arrived home early in December, accompanied by Ko Tha Byu. They found a growing church; not one Christian had fallen away during their absence.

Late in November, 1830, reinforcements arrived at Moulmein in the persons of Eugenio Kincaid and Francis Mason and their wives. The Masons had been assigned by the Board to Tavoy. When they landed there on January 23, 1831, they found Boardman in such a weakened condition that he had to be carried to the jetty in a chair in order to welcome them.

Although Boardman realized that he did not have long to live because of the tuberculosis that was sapping his strength, he determined to make one more trip to the villages of the Karens. They had promised to carry him all the way, if he would but come to them with the gospel. Against the judgment of his wife, he planned to set out with Mason. Sarah insisted upon accompanying them, taking with her little George. For three days, Boardman was carried on a cot over the rocky, mountainous paths. More than one hundred Karens were awaiting him. Their love and eagerness for the gospel cheered him. But in spite of his joy at seeing them, his health became dangerously worse. By February 10, it was apparent that he must return to Tavoy at once. This he agreed to do if the examination and baptism of the new converts might be accomplished that day. That evening, as the sun was about to set, Boardman witnessed the baptism of thirty-four persons by Mason, as he looked on from his cot by the side of the stream. Overcome with emotion, he felt that his life-work was completed.

The next day was a nightmare for Sarah. The trip home was one long anxiety for the welfare of her husband. Although his cot was drenched by rain, Sarah's plea for shelter in the house of a Tavoyan was refused because she and her husband taught a foreign religion. The next morning, February 11, the Karen Christians carried Boardman to the boat that was to take him the rest of the way to Tavoy. But before they could get under way, his flickering strength ebbed away. On learning the news of Boardman's death, Judson said: "One of the brightest luminaries of Burma is extinguished." [12]

For three years following Boardman's death, Sarah continued her husband's work. Encouraged by the sympathetic understanding of Judson, who promised to assume responsibility for the care and education of her son, George, in the event of her death, she determined to stay with the Karens for whom her husband had given his life. With a fine command of the Burmese language and some knowledge of the Karen, she was well prepared. So well did she re-establish the village and station schools that the Commissioner looked to them as a model for other schools to be opened in the province. She continued to tour among the Karen villages, preaching in Burmese with the aid of an interpreter.

The Masons labored with her in Tavoy, devoting their time to the study of the Karen language and assisting her in the schools. During this period, Judson kept in touch with the work in Tavoy. Before long, his admiration for Mrs. Boardman led him to ask her to become his wife. On April 10, 1834, they were married. Her only regret was leaving her schools. But she found Moulmein equally challenging.

The work at Moulmein had undergone considerable change and growth since her previous visit. The arrival of the Kincaids and Masons from America in 1830 had freed Wade for evangelistic tours in the outlying villages. Turning the responsibility for tract distribution over to the native disciples, he and Bennett, the printer, went a hundred miles up the Salween River. At the first village, they found it necessary to convince the people that they were not government agents come to oppress them. Once confidence had been established, the Karens asked for the "Karen books." Nonplussed, Wade asked what they meant. He was told that they had once had books, which were now lost; that their ancestors had told them that the white foreigners had God's word, and would come one day to give it to them. Deeply impressed, Wade then and there determined to reduce

[12] Robbins, *Boardman of Burma,* p. 148.

their language to writing in order that they might have the word of God in their own tongue. This became the great achievement of his life. In two years he had prepared a spelling book, translated a tract, and begun to establish schools. He used the Burmese alphabet, which was possible because of similarities in the dialects of the two peoples.[13]

In February, 1831, John Taylor Jones arrived at Moulmein from America. He was placed in charge of the native preachers at Rangoon, where he and Judson alternated in service. This made it possible for Wade and Kincaid to make a second tour about two hundred miles from the city. They were accompanied by three native catechists. As a result of the tours, a Karen church of fourteen members was established at Wadesville, named in honor of the missionary who first preached the gospel there. The missionaries at the time adopted the plan of encouraging the new converts to establish their own villages, as a means of remaining true to their new kind of life.

At Moulmein there were three flourishing churches—one Burmese, with about one hundred members, and two Karen churches, with nearly the same number when combined. There was also an English church, composed of soldiers from the English army. From Kincaid's arrival in November, 1830, until he took up his work at Ava in 1833, he served as its pastor. Eighty-nine were added in 1831, bringing the total up to 113. The city was also the seat of the second printing establishment of the Baptists in Burma. In 1832 Bennett was reinforced by the coming of two additional printers, Oliver T. Cutter and Royal B. Hancock. The number of presses had increased to four. Since Bennett's arrival, 200,000 tracts had been printed, together with the entire New Testament and 20 other works—all for circulation in Burma.[14]

In 1831 a new work was opened at Kyouk Phyoo, a town on the island of Ramree in the Province of Arracan. It was discovered quite by accident. The Wades had been on their way to Calcutta for the health of Mrs. Wade, when a storm prevented their reaching their destination. Instead, they stopped off at this little town, where they found the people speaking the Burmese language. In three months they were back in Moulmein, but left almost immediately for Mergui, again on account of Mrs. Wade's health. They stayed at Mergui for

[13] Wyeth, *The Wades,* pp. 82-84.
[14] *The American Baptist Magazine,* Vol. 13, No. 1 (Jan., 1833), pp. 9, 13.

more than five months, establishing a small church there. When they departed, they left Moung Ing as pastor.[15] In the autumn of 1832, the Wades were obliged to return to America for a rest. They were the first missionaries to return since the visit of Ann Judson ten years before.

Nineteen years had passed since the Judsons set foot in Burma. Since that time, thirty-three missionaries and their wives had been sent out by the Board. Of those, nine had sailed in 1832—more than one-fourth of the total. Since the first three baptisms in 1819, about four hundred had been received into the churches at Rangoon, Tavoy, Moulmein, and the outlying stations. This represented about two-thirds of the total number of accessions on all fields in Burma. Two printing establishments had been set up, one at Rangoon, the other at Moulmein. There were now four presses and three printers. In addition, there were about 170 schools for Karens—boarding schools, day schools, and village schools for study during the rainy season. Village preaching, which had been introduced by Boardman around Tavoy, was continued by Mason. Judson also adopted this method of evangelism in the vicinity of Moulmein and between Rangoon and Prome. It proved to be an effective way to make use of nationals in tract distribution and witnessing in the villages where interest had been aroused.[16] The support for the work came from America. Judson, the senior missionary in Burma, on one occasion explained that he did not ask the Burmese for contributions "because Buddhist doctrine of merit was so ingrained in them that they might think their gifts were gaining merit with God, instead of being used by His free grace." [17] In time, however, the Karen Christians were to undertake support of the work by their own contributions.

Expansion Beyond Burma

The years from 1833 to 1837 have been called "a notable period in the history of American Baptist missions." [18] The reason is that the swelling enthusiasm for the extension of the gospel to lands beyond the sea had overflowed the barriers of Burma, and entered into new

[15] Wyeth, *The Wades,* p. 93.

[16] *The American Baptist Magazine,* Vol. 13, No. 1 (Jan. 1833), pp. 11-13, 20-21.

[17] Warburton, *Eastward,* p. 133 (footnote 14).

[18] Edmund F. Merriam, *A History of American Baptist Missions* (Philadelphia, 1900), p. 41.

areas hitherto unreached by the preaching of the Christian message. Excitement was heightened by the return to the United States of the Wades in 1833. They arrived in May, just after the annual meeting of the Board of Foreign Missions. Six weeks later, they were engaged in an experiment of the Board to train new missionary candidates in language study prior to their sailing. For this purpose, Mr. and Mrs. Wade spent nine months at Hamilton, together with Moung Shway Moung, a Burman, and Ko Chet-thing, a Karen, whom they had brought with them. There they gave instruction to eight students in both Karen and Burmese.

In November, the Wades were invited to attend a Convention of Western Baptists at Cincinnati, Ohio, where antimission feeling had caused some unfavorable reaction. The presence of the missionaries proved, however, to be more than convincing. In fact, Mrs. Wade was so persuasive in her appeal that ladies cast their jewelry as well as money into the mission treasury. During the spring of the following year, the Wades went with Dr. Lucius Bolles, the corresponding secretary of the Board, into the South, creating a stronger missionary fervor wherever they went. When they sailed from Boston on July 2, 1834, they were accompanied by the largest number of missionaries hitherto sent out at any one time by American Baptists. The group included Hosea Howard, Justus H. Vinton, Grover S. Comstock, William Dean, and Sewall M. Osgood with their wives, and Miss Ann P. Gardner. The entire party arrived in Burma on December 6.[19]

The year 1833 was significant also for the important decision to open a new mission field in the Orient. It was Siam, a country which lay to the southeast of Burma and which represented to the missionaries in that country a door to China. Accordingly, the staff at Moulmein selected John Taylor Jones of their own number to establish a mission among the Siamese across the border in Bangkok. He and his wife left Moulmein and arrived at their destination in March, 1833.

Jones found a city in which more than one-half of the population were Chinese immigrants, many of whom occupied important positions in the economic life of Siam. Although his work was among the Siamese, he saw the wisdom of beginning a mission to the Chinese. Accordingly, he urged the Board at home to send him a colleague

[19] Wyeth, *The Wades,* pp. 97-103.

for this purpose. Meanwhile his ministry was varied, including preaching, translating the Scriptures into Siamese, and engaging in an elementary kind of medical practice. Each Sunday in his home he conducted worship for interested Chinese, who were more responsive to his message than the Siamese.

In 1834 the Board in America responded to Jones' request and appointed William Dean to minister to the Chinese at Bangkok. Dean and his wife arrived in Singapore in January, 1835. On March 5, Mrs. Dean died shortly after the birth of a baby girl. Although bereaved by his loss, Dean joined with Jones at Bangkok to undertake work among the Chinese. This left Mr. and Mrs. Jones free to continue their medical ministry and translation efforts. In December, 1835, Dean baptized three Chinese converts and organized "the first Protestant church in all Asia composed of Chinese members." [20] With Dean as pastor, this church ministered to the large transient population of Chinese. It was the first organized Baptist work among these people.

In 1836 the mission at Bangkok was strengthened by the arrival of R. D. Davenport, Alanson Reed, and J. Lewis Shuck with their wives. They brought with them a press and materials for printing. The work was by now well-established, but as yet there were no converts among the Siamese. The main results were still among the Chinese.

Meanwhile, at home, the missionary enthusiasm of American Baptists had reached a new peak in 1835 at the eighth triennial meeting of the General Missionary Convention in Richmond, Virginia. With a surplus of funds in the treasury and missionary interest mounting, it was resolved to raise at least $100,000 to send reinforcements to the hard-pressed missionaries on the field, and "to establish new missions in every unoccupied place where there may be a reasonable prospect of success." [21]

The immediate spearhead of advance was to be a mission among the Telinga, or Telugu, people of South India. The opportunity had been presented to the Convention at Richmond by the Rev. Amos Sutton of the English Baptist Mission in Orissa, India. He had married, it may be recalled, the widow of the Rev. James Colman, one of the early victims of disease in the American Baptist Mission in Arracan. Mrs. Sutton was at the time of the Convention in the

---

[20] Francis Wayland Goddard, *Called to Cathay* (New York, 1948), p. 23.
[21] Merriam, *op. cit.*, p. 43.

United States visiting her relatives. Through this seemingly providential combination of circumstances, Baptists were confronted with a new challenge which was to become as famous in achievements as the Burma Mission.

As a result of this remarkable Convention, the Rev. Howard Malcom was appointed to visit the mission fields in Asia. He sailed in September, 1835, with a large group of missionaries, including the Rev. Elisha L. Abbott and the Rev. Samuel S. Day, who were appointed for the new Telugu field. Upon their arrival in Calcutta, it was decided, in consultation with the missionaries at Moulmein, to assign Day and his wife to open the new field in South India, while Abbott was to proceed to the Karen mission in Burma. Before leaving for his post, Abbott was married to Miss Ann P. Gardner, who had come out to Rangoon with the Wades on their return from furlough.

Abbott divided his attention among the Karens around Moulmein, Rangoon, and a cluster of villages about forty miles north of Rangoon called Maubin. His success with these people brought opposition from the Burmese authorities, forcing Abbott early in 1840 to move with Kincaid to Araccan, which was under English control.

Day and his wife landed first at Vizagapatam in India, but after a time they removed to Madras. In 1840 they established themselves at Nellore, which became for twenty-six years the only station in the Telugu mission, hence referred to as the "Lone Star." The Telugu territory stretched along the coast southwesterly from Orissa for six hundred miles, nearly to Madras, and about four hundred miles into the interior. It offered several advantages for mission work. The climate was comparatively cool. The territory was under the protection of the East India Company. The New Testament had been translated already into the Telugu language by Serampore missionaries, and it was in printed form. Tracts, hymns, a catechism, and a translation of Bunyan's *Pilgrim's Progress* had been published in Telugu by the Madras Auxiliary Bible Society and the Religious Tract Society of Madras.[22]

A third area of advance in this inspiring period was Assam. An invitation to open a mission in that country had been issued by Captain F. Jenkins, the governor-general's agent and commissioner in Assam. Jenkins, who was resident at Gauhati, had written to Mr.

[22] *The American Baptist Magazine,* Vol. 16, No. 6 (June, 1836), pp. 149-50.

Trevelyan, of the Civil Service in Calcutta, suggesting that the missionaries among the Burmans and Siamese might be interested in extending their work to people called Shans, in the hills of northeastern Burma. This tribe or family of tribes extended over into Assam, where they were called Khamtis. He explained, quite mistakenly, that there was very little difference in dialects among the Khamtis in Assam and the Sing-phos (now known as Jing-paws, or Kachins) in northeastern Burma. Moreover, he offered the missionaries British protection. Mr. Trevelyan was sufficiently interested to promise a subscription of one thousand rupees if a family would establish a mission at Sadiya, a town northeast of the Kachin Hills and at the northeastern extremity of the Assam Valley.

The proposal of Jenkins was transmitted in 1835 to the Board in America by the Rev. William H. Pearce of the English Baptist Mission at Calcutta. When the missionaries at Moulmein were consulted by the Board, Nathan Brown replied that Jones at Bangkok could ascend the Siam River about two-thirds of the way to Sadiya. Hence, the new field represented a plausible approach to China. He also reported that a Roman Catholic missionary priest had gone up the Irrawaddy River during the previous year, seeking entrance into China, but had been stopped at Ava and sent back. The ever fertile mind of Brown advanced still another argument in favor of the new move. He saw the possibility of another line of communication between Sadiya and Ava by way of the Katheh (Cassay) country, the capital of which was Manipur, some two hundred miles from both Sadiya and Ava respectively, but in line with each. Manipur district was reportedly a fine country and independent of the Burman Government. It becomes apparent that two considerations were uppermost in the minds of the missionaries at Moulmein: the importance of finding a fresh entrance to China and the necessity of reaching into the heart of Burma from the north as well as from the south.

Accordingly, the Board designated Brown for Sadiya. With Oliver T. Cutter and a printing press, Brown arrived from Calcutta on March 23, 1836, after a tedious journey of four months. He found the town beautifully situated in the center of a plain, surrounded by mountains. The climate was temperate and healthful; the soil was fertile; but the population was sparse, owing to wars that had depopulated the country. Nearby, at Suikhwa, he noted the beginning of tea plantations, to which thousands of tea plants had been sent from China. Because the missionaries identified the Khamtis with the hill people whom they called Shans in northeastern Burma, the new mission was opened under the name "mission to the Shans." [23]

From this brief review of more than two decades of pioneer mission work, it becomes apparent that a foothold had been gained in the Orient, but with great difficulty. The cost in human life has been revealed only partially by the scattered references to the sacrifices made by individual missionaries during the period under consideration. It was an initial and very necessary phase of the great missionary expansion that was to follow. The advances gained had to be held if the work were to acquire permanence and stability. We turn now to that story.

---

[23] *Ibid.*, Vol. 16, No. 1 (Jan. 1836), pp. 19-22; Vol. 17, No. 5 (May, 1837), pp. 116-19.

CHAPTER IV

Holding the Line Under Trial

THE FOOTHOLD had been won in the Orient over a period of twenty or more years at great sacrifice of lives and money. American Baptists, who in 1835 numbered not more than 452,000, were not a wealthy people. But they were rich in evangelistic fervor and in young people whose all-consuming passion in life was to take the gospel to peoples who had never heard its glad tidings. The result was the establishing of missions, not only in Burma, but in Siam, South India, Assam, and, as we shall see in the next chapter, in West Africa and Europe.

After the first waves of enthusiasm had reached their crest in 1835, the stark realities of maintaining these missions under the most discouraging circumstances remained to be faced. At home, the task of sustaining, year by year, adequate support of an expanding program was in itself a mounting problem that became the more urgent in the midst of a national financial depression and internal dissension over the slavery issue. This story we shall trace in Chapter VI. On the mission fields, extremes of climate, disease, hostile governments, wars, and the lack of sufficient missionary personnel combined to test severely the capacity for endurance of the pioneers in the foreign mission enterprise.

The trends in the mission fields in the Orient during the dozen years just prior to 1845, when the schism occurred in the General Convention at home, had important consequences for Baptists then and now: then, because so much depended upon beginnings; now, because valuable lessons may be learned from the experiences of the past.

Developments at Moulmein

It will be recalled that Adoniram Judson took his wife, Sarah Boardman, to Moulmein in April, 1834. They worked together for eleven years. She brought to his ministry a gentle and cheerful disposition, and a deep devotion to Christ. Their home was very simple, made of bamboo mats with a roof of thatch. There were three rooms along the front with two smaller rooms behind, a detached kitchen, and a wide veranda that ran the full length of the house. It was situated on a principal street, easily accessible to visitors. The printing house was not far away. Close by was the school for Burmese and Karen children. The chapel and residences for the other missionaries completed the group of buildings on the mission compound. In another part of the town were a chapel for the English-speaking congregation and Bennett's English school.

During these years Judson completed the Burmese Bible (1834), worked on the Burmese dictionary, preached regularly in the chapel, directed the daily work of the Burmese evangelists, and gave counsel to the younger missionaries. He and Sarah had eight children—one daughter, Abigail Ann, and six sons, Adoniram Brown, Elnathan, Henry, Henry Hall, Charles, and Edward. Another child was stillborn, to whom was given the name, Luther.

At her husband's suggestion, Sarah undertook a study of the language of the Peguans, or Talaings, a people who comprised a large part of the Moulmein population. In time she translated tracts and the New Testament into their language. In addition, she became an expert in Burmese, translating Bunyan's *Pilgrim's Progress* into that tongue and adding twenty hymns to the hymnbook.

Toward the close of 1838, as Judson passed his fiftieth birthday, he began to suffer from a cough and inflammation of the throat and lungs. It was the beginning of the pulmonary disease which eventually cost him the use of his voice above a whisper, and which ultimately took his life. Because he loved preaching, it was a severe blow to him. Yet, it forced him to settle down to the translation work and the dictionary, both of which were so important for the future of the mission.

During these years Judson seems to have crystallized his views of missionary work. He placed preaching in the foreground, considering it more important than translating and distributing Christian literature and the Scriptures. He longed to be free of the dictionary, the preparation of which was pressed upon him by the Board of Managers in America. Whenever possible, he took time for evangelistic tours among the Karens. His preaching was practical and down to earth, never vague and abstract. His remarkable linguistic gifts enabled him to communicate the gospel with warmth and accuracy. For many years, he was the only missionary able to preach in Burmese.

He subordinated mission schools for children to the preaching of the gospel to adults. He rebelled against becoming a school-teacher or maker of textbooks. In keeping with what he believed was the method of the apostles, he made his appeal to the parents, for they were the ones who should have to face persecution involved in accepting a new faith. To be sure, he conducted schools, but not for the purpose of teaching the culture of western civilization. He seems to have had little patience with those who sought to prepare the Burmese mind to accept Christianity by means of astronomical and geological concepts which broke down the cosmology of the Buddhist religion.

Judson trained his national workers informally, by taking them on evangelistic tours, and by sending them in pairs into distant villages to witness. He had the gift of inspiring promising youth to become teachers and preachers. In letters written in 1835 to Dr. Lucius Bolles, corresponding secretary of the Board, he advised that each missionary train a few boys and young men for a year or two, and then send from each station at least two or three of the most promising to Moulmein or Tavoy for further training. In this way, a seminary might be developed. He had little patience with a theological curriculum that was not Bible-centered. Metaphysics and related subjects were to him a waste of time. The essential purpose of a seminary training was to prepare ministers to communicate their message intelligibly and persuasively by the spoken and written word.[1]

Sarah Judson, never strong and often ill even during the early years at Tavoy, began to suffer again from dysentery. By the close of 1844, her health had declined to such an extent that her return to America seemed imperative. It was decided that she should take the

---

[1] For an excellent discussion of Judson's views on missionary work, see Warburton, *Eastward,* pp. 82-88, 381-82.

older children with her. Adoniram accompanied her, intending to see her to St. Helena; it is well that he did, for on September 1, 1845, just off the island, she died. The bereaved husband and father continued on to America with the children. By October 15 he was in Boston, his first visit home in thirty-two years.[2]

The educational work at Moulmein was quite extensive. The Moulmein Free School, established by Cephas Bennett in 1834, was intended to exert a Christian influence upon the children so that even if they should not be converted, they would see the folly of idolatry. In 1836 there were 122 enrolled, of whom 54 were Burmese, 20 Chinese, 18 East Indian, 13 Portuguese, and the remaining 17 of eight different nationalities.[3]

The theological seminary, which had been opened by Wade at Tavoy in 1835 and closed two years later because of his illness, was reopened in Moulmein by Edward A. Stevens in March, 1839, with fourteen pupils in attendance. By 1841 it became necessary to close the school for lack of funds. The Moulmein High School in charge of Hosea Howard, was kept open by a gift of four hundred rupees from the Moulmein Missionary Society, which was composed chiefly of missionaries and European citizens, with some assistance from Christian Burmese. This organization supported ten assistants in mission work, one of whom was a Peguan, two were Burmese, and seven were Karens.[4]

It was about this time that the Karen Christians at Moulmein were beginning to contribute to the support of evangelistic work. In 1838, for example, they gave seventy rupees, not a large sum, but a significant start. At the same time, the missionaries were beginning to sell the Karens bound books at one-half of their real value. Justus Vinton wrote to friends in America that "If the gospel ever spreads extensively in this country, the native Christians must take hold of the work; and the sooner they are trained to it, the better." [5] His policy was justified by the developments in later years.

---

[2] The foregoing account is based largely upon Warburton, *Eastward,* chap. 9, and Wyeth, *Sarah B. Judson* (Philadelphia, 1889).

[3] Based on Bennett's Journal, *The American Baptist Magazine,* Vol. 16 (1836), pp. 104-08, 246-49.

[4] *The Baptist Missionary Magazine,* Vol. 20, No. 4 (April, 1840), pp. 78-80; Vol. 22, No. 6 (June, 1842), p. 168; Vol. 23, No. 6 (June, 1843), pp. 150-51; Vol. 24, No. 5 (May, 1844), pp. 115-16.

[5] *Ibid.,* Vol. 19, No. 9 (Sept., 1839), pp. 218-19.

Opposition at Rangoon and Ava

The mission at Rangoon, where Judson had opened his work in 1813, enjoyed no such successes as occurred at Moulmein. From the first, the shadow of Ava fell upon the struggling efforts of the missionaries to gather a church there. There were times, to be sure, when government officials close to the emperor manifested towards the mission a degree of friendliness that surprised Judson and his colleagues. But for the most part, persecution was the studied policy of the authorities. Under these circumstances and because Rangoon and Ava were keys to the opening of the entire country and of China to Christianity, the missionaries never slackened their efforts to win the favor of the government at Ava.

As we have seen, the chief success of the mission in Burma was among the Karens, a people oppressed and despised by the Burmese and therefore especially vulnerable to persecution by a government that was hostile to Christianity.

Early in the spring of 1832, Eugenio Kincaid removed from Moulmein to Rangoon with a view to encouraging the secret converts there who were afraid to come out in the open because of the attitude of the government. Although he did not know the language, he helped in the schools already established. At the close of that year, he went to Madras to marry Miss Barbara McBain, daughter of a military officer in the service of the East India Company. During his absence from Rangoon, his assistants who were in charge of the schools came under the persecution of the authorities, and the work was disrupted. Upon his return, however, he began again, undismayed.

Realizing that the basic problem lay with the government at Ava, Kincaid obtained permission from the viceroy to sail up the Irrawaddy River on April 6, 1833, for Ava. He was accompanied by his wife and her sister, and Ko Shoon and Ko Sanlone, two native preachers. They covered the seven hundred miles in fifty-four days, preaching in villages and cities along the way and distributing tracts.

It was Kincaid's plan to establish himself in Ava for a year or two in the hopes that he might win the Burmese ruler to a policy of toleration. But he found no welcome upon his arrival. Delay after delay met his efforts to secure a permanent place to live—all because the government did not wish to have "peddlers of a foreign religion."

Yet a flood of visitors came to him for counsel. On several occasions he was invited to the Palace to talk with Prince Lekara, who desired to study the Bible. By the end of Kincaid's first year in Ava, a church had been planted. For the remaining three years of his stay, many heard the gospel, and there were some secret disciples.

Ever alert to discover ways of spreading his message beyond Burma, Kincaid learned through travelers to Ava of a people known as Shyans (the Shans mentioned in the previous chapter), who occupied the provinces on the northern frontiers of the empire. When he planned to visit them, he was forbidden by the Burmese government to distribute his religious books to the north. Finally, however, through the intervention of the British Resident at Ava, he received permission and on January 27, 1837, he embarked on the Irrawaddy River.

On the way he met a party of about thirty Shans, dressed in dark blue cotton and smoking pipes with stems about three feet long. They spoke Burmese, and explained that they were on a pilgrimage from their home some 250 miles to the northeast to find peace through the gods of Burma at Amarapura, Ava, and Pagan. When Kincaid presented to them the message concerning the true and living God, they heard him with great interest.

After twenty-two days of travel, Kincaid reached Mogaung, the most northern city of Burma; it lay beneath the shadow of the Himalaya Mountains. He had hoped to go on to Sadiya, but was compelled to turn back for want of men and provisions. On his return to Ava, he was twice attacked by robbers and barely escaped death at their hands.

He arrived in Ava on March 11, to find the populace in turmoil. Prince Thur-ra-wadi had overthrown his brother, the king. The mission families were obliged to accept the invitation of Colonel Burney, the British Resident, to take temporary refuge under his roof. When the prince, who had been friendly to foreigners, became king, he adopted the same attitude of intolerance toward Kincaid as had his predecessor, forbidding him to distribute his books. As the king, he felt an obligation to protect the traditional religion of his country. Realizing the hopelessness of the situation, Kincaid left Ava on June 17, 1837, reaching Rangoon on July 6.[6]

---

[6] The foregoing account is based largely on A. S. Patton, *The Hero Missionary: Eugenio Kincaid* (New York, 1858); *The Baptist Missionary Magazine,* Vol. 18, No. 3 (March, 1838), pp. 69-71.

He found that because of the revolution, most of the missionaries had gone on to Moulmein. He learned that the native pastor, Ko Sanlone, had been arrested earlier while preaching, and had escaped execution only because he was a native of Moulmein and therefore under British protection. He was not released from prison, however, until his wife had bribed the officials with a sum of money and he had promised that he would discontinue preaching in the territory.

From this time on, the people were afraid even to visit the missionaries. Fortunately, within a few months the alarm had subsided, and tracts were once more accepted. Native preachers from Moulmein were able to preach unmolested, but no Rangoon Christians dared do it. It was virtually impossible to gather a church in the city. On June 17, at Ava, the mission was closed.[7]

It is not surprising, therefore, that even the intrepid Kincaid proceeded in August, 1837, to Moulmein, and thence to Tavoy, and then to Mergui in the British-protected province of Tenasserim. There he worked until the autumn of 1838, when he returned to Moulmein. Through a disciple, he learned that it was unsafe to return to Ava, whereupon he set his face towards Arracan in the company of Elisha Abbott.

When the Vintons visited Rangoon in November, 1842, they found the Karen Christians facing severe trials. Although none had apostasized, some who had requested baptism had turned back, saying that the teachers had forsaken them. To Burmese persecution was added the test of Roman Catholic proselyting. First, native assistants were offered by the Catholics three or four times the money paid them by the Baptists. When this failed to dissuade them, their Protestant faith and even their personal character were attacked.[8] It was a trying time for the Karens, many of whom were hopeful that the impending struggle between the Burmese government and East India Company would end in a British victory.[9]

Progress Among Karens

After the death of Boardman in 1831, Francis Mason had carried on at Tavoy, assisted only by Mrs. Boardman until her marriage to

---

[7] Based on report of Howard Malcom in Journal kept during his visit to Burma in 1836. *The Baptist Missionary Magazine,* Vol. 17, No. 5 (May, 1837), pp. 100-01; Vol. 18, No. 6 (June, 1838), pp. 148-52.

[8] *Ibid.,* Vol. 24, No. 5 (May, 1844), p. 106.

[9] *Ibid.,* Vol. 22, No. 5 (May, 1842), p. 133.

Adoniram Judson. The return of Jonathan and Deborah Wade from America in 1834 was, therefore, a welcome relief to Mason. For the Wades went at once to Tavoy to lend what assistance they could. There in an area that extended several hundred miles along the eastern shore of the Bay of Bengal, were the Sgaw and Pwo Karens to whom the Wades devoted the rest of their lives. Their station was established at Matah, which lay over the mountains from Tavoy. With Mason, they had made the journey on foot; Mrs. Wade having to be carried in a chair most of the way. There she remained as teacher and leader, while her husband and Mason went down the Tenasserim River to preach in all of the Karen villages between Matah and Mergui. At Matah, Mrs. Wade supervised the distribution of tracts and the visitation evangelism carried on by the Karen Christians. She conducted services in the *zayat* which was set up near her dwelling. Within a month of her arrival, she witnessed a transformation among the people. Housekeeping habits were revolutionized and temperance sentiment became universal.

Upon the return of Mason and Wade, the examination of new converts began. The conditions imposed upon the newcomers to the church were severe. Each person had to give evidence of a new life in Christ. The decision of his being received for baptism lay with the Karen church itself. Their vote had to be unanimous. Each new Christian was obliged to know how to read; he had to renounce liquor and pledge himself to total abstinence, a measure which was taken to test the sincerity of the convert inasmuch as drunkenness was a prevailing vice among non-Christian Karens. In addition, each new believer was expected to promise to observe the morality set forth in the Bible.[10] In this way the door to the church was closed to those who were insincere and unworthy.

During the rainy season, the missionaries returned to Tavoy to work. This was usually the time when instruction might be given to those who were preparing for leadership in the church. During this period many of the Karens from Matah came to town for the purpose of learning to read. For this privilege, many of them traveled forty miles over swollen streams, and through jungles infested with wild beasts.

---

[10] The foregoing account and what follows is based upon Wyeth, *The Wades,* pp. 112-32, and *The Baptist Missionary Magazine,* Vol. 17, No. 2 (Feb., 1837), pp. 30-35.

In November, 1835, the Wades, in the company of Burmese and Karen assistants, made another evangelistic tour along the Tavoy River southward, distributing tracts and preaching from their boat at each village along the way. When the rains were over in December, they visited Matah again. By the end of the year, there had been sixty baptisms at Tavoy. A Karen boarding school had been in existence for five months with sixty pupils under the care of Mrs. Wade. At Matah, the number of members in the church reached a total of 230 by March, 1836. A year later, the church at Tavoy numbered three hundred.

Such rapid growth placed heavy responsibilities upon the missionaries, who were looked to for the development of a wholesome Christian community. Because the climate was unsuited for healthful living, the Wades led the Christian Karens to establish a new town at a site a few miles above Tavoy which was dry and approachable all the year around. Because the people had few possessions, the move was not so difficult as might be thought. Yet, the full responsibility for assisting the families in the actual moving, the transporting of building materials, the planting of their rice paddies, the purchase of farming utensils and cattle, all fell to the missionary. In fact he provided for these essentials out of his own allowance. The new town was named Newburg, apparently at the suggestion of Wade.

This project was in line with the practice of the missionaries generally. For Judson had founded two Christian communities, to which converts came and made their permanent homes. One was called Newville, established in 1832; the other was Chummerah, on the bank of the Salween River sixty miles north of Moulmein. Mason, as we have seen, also established such a community in the province of Tavoy. He called it Matah (City of Love). As has been already indicated, it became the seat of a flourishing church and schools.

Such a course was possible among the Karens because they were in the transition from a migratory kind of life to one more settled. It was not difficult to persuade them to settle down to a life of agriculture and trade. Christians, who soon developed habits of cleanliness, welcomed a superior kind of environment from that to which they had been accustomed before coming in contact with the gospel.

In a very real sense these Christian communities provide an example of the way in which the missionaries sought to minister to the whole man. This service was especially effective among the Karens because they were a people who had little of this world's goods and less resistance to that which offered them a measure of security and happiness which their animism had never provided.

The success of the Baptist work among the Karens is indicated by the fact that by 1843 within the limits of Moulmein, Tavoy, and the Rangoon missions, there were nearly 30 churches with more than 1,500 members. There were also between two and three thousand Karen converts not associated in churches and tens of thousands waiting and eager to receive the gospel. With only five missionaries available for work among these people, the practice of placing increasing confidence in Karen assistants grew. Abbott, who was in charge of the Rangoon Mission in the early 1840's, used them where there was no missionary residing among the Karens of Burma proper. It was a policy which did much to develop an indigenous church in Burma.

In 1835 the province of Arracan, which was in British hands, attracted the attention of the Baptists. It was "a long, narrow strip of sandy coast, with several good seaports, but a sickly climate, extending from about latitude 15° N. to the southern boundary of Chittagong, and separated from Burma by the lofty range of the Western Yoma Mountains." [11] It had been ceded to the British East India Company after the First Anglo-Burmese War of 1824–26. Thus it had the advantage of a friendly government, and it afforded an opportunity to minister to the Karens, who were scattered along the eastern edge of the territory.

The first missionaries to come were Grover and Sarah Comstock. They had applied to the Board in 1832. Grover was a convert of the revival that swept Rochester, New York, in 1831. He united with the First Baptist Church, of which his father was pastor. Feeling a call to preach, he spent a year in general theological study at Hamilton, and a half year more for instruction in Burmese under the guidance of the Wades, who were then on furlough. It was there that he met Sarah Davis of Brookline, Massachusetts. They were married on June 24, 1834. Five days later they were commissioned in the Baptist Meeting House at Baldwin Place, Boston, along with William Dean, Justus H. Vinton, Hosea Howard, and Sewall M. Osgood and their wives, and Miss Ann P. Gardner. On July 2, the entire party

---

[11] L. P. Brockett, *The Story of the Karen Mission in Bassein, 1838–1890* (Philadelphia, 1891), p. 24.

sailed on the ship *Cashmere,* which required five months to make the voyage to Amherst.

Following a brief stay there, the Comstocks went on to Moulmein. After some delay, they, together with Rev. Thomas Simons, chartered a small schooner, and made their way up the river to Kyouk Phyoo, an important town and military station of the British. They reached their destination on March 4, 1835. In his first three months there, Comstock made remarkable headway in his evangelistic work. He was aided by the fact that Burmese was spoken by many, and by the availability of Judson's Catechism and other material. Moreover, there was a general hunger of the people for a religion that would provide more comfort in the presence of death than Buddhism. Some Araccanese objected to Christianity on the grounds that they had heard and observed that Christians treated their wives with respect and affection, regarding them as companions rather than servants. Sarah's work consisted primarily of supervising the day schools for children from 9 A.M. until 3 P.M. on week days, and administering medicine to the sick, either at the mission house or in the huts of the people.

The ardor of these young pioneers was tested severely by climatic conditions. Frequent and sudden changes of weather affected their health. Marshes made the place an area subject to malaria, especially after the heavy rains. It became necessary for them to take a boat trip down the river in an effort to regain their health in Moulmein. In the meantime, Levi Hall and his wife, upon their arrival at Calcutta, were diverted from the Telugu Mission to reinforce the Comstocks. But they both died within a few months. This great loss determined the Comstocks to relinquish the mission. So in December, 1837, they went to Calcutta and thence to Moulmein, arriving in April, 1838.

After a year in Moulmein, the Comstocks accompanied by the Rev. Lyman Stilson and his wife, new arrivals from America, returned to Arracan, spent ten days in Kyouk Phyoo, and then went on to Ramree, a town of 10,000 and the center of a large population. There was less opposition there than at Kyouk Phyoo, and more interest was manifested. The entire district of Ramree, including its capital, had a population of 63,000. On May 29, 1839, a church was constituted by the Comstocks and the Stilsons. The membership numbered eight persons, four of whom were nationals. In a short time, it grew to eleven. There were two native assistants. Mrs. Comstock commenced a school for boys and girls at Ramree, and gathered the women about her for instruction. For the children she prepared "The Mother's Book" and a "Scripture Catechism."

Although there were no converts until February 20, when Comstock baptized a Mohammedan, he was convinced that Arracan was a fertile field for mission work, if only enough missionaries could be made available to settle down and live among the people. With this in mind, he called upon the Board to furnish six men for the province. Fortunately, reinforcements became available in 1840 from Burma, where the persecution at Rangoon and Ava had forced Kincaid and Abbott to relinquish their work for the time being.[12]

Since 1836 these two men had been preaching with great success to the Karens around Rangoon, Kemmendine, Maubin, and Moulmein. As a result of their labors several hundred Karens were baptized. In the course of his work, Abbott had entered the Bassein district in December, 1837. This district, which lay between the Rangoon River on the east and the Bassein River on the west, formed the southwestern portion of the province of Pegu. It extended north to the 18th parallel and westward to the foothills of the Western Yoma range that separated it from Arracan. In size it was as large as the State of Massachusetts. The population included Sgaw and Pwo-Karens, Burmans, Talaings, Tamils, Telugus, Chinese, and Shans. At the time, the Burmese, who were merchants and traders, governed the district. They held as virtual serfs the Karens, who were small-scale farmers and laborers. The Karens were forbidden the possession of books or the privilege of learning to read. Severe penalties, which extended to beheading or crucifixion, were dealt to those who violated these restrictions.[13]

To Abbott it was a surprise, therefore, to find a number of believers among the Karens who desired baptism. It seems that two years before an old man among them had purchased two little books in Burmese by Judson: *The Golden Balance* and *The Ship of Grace*. They had been distributed by Thomas Simons in 1835, as he passed through Bassein from Arracan to Rangoon. The old man had trav-

---

[12] The foregoing is based on A. M. Edmond, *Memoir of Mrs. Sarah D. Comstock, Missionary to Arracan* (Philadelphia, 1854) and Wyeth, *A Galaxy in the Burman Sky*, Chap. 4.

[13] Brockett, *op. cit.*, pp. 25-27. This excellent account is drawn upon for the narrative that follows.

eled nearly a hundred miles, through a thick jungle infested with wild beasts and robbers, to Maubin for further instruction. Others followed his example in their eagerness to obtain the Christian message. Abbott was able, on his brief tour, to baptize forty-nine persons who had been converted by means of these tracts. None of the converts, however, were natives of Bassein proper.

In June, 1838, a young chief, Shway Weing, a man of superior gifts who had been converted during Abbott's visit in 1837, arrived at Maubin with nine other young men of much promise whom he desired to leave with the missionary for instruction. Shway Weing had been baptized by Abbott on June 22. He was the first convert from the Bassein district proper. Six weeks later, he was arrested in Rangoon, and tortured and beaten for possessing books of the white men. When, after three weeks, he was released, he begged the missionary for more books to take back to Bassein. When warned that he would lose his life if caught again, he merely replied: "I should so much sooner get to heaven."

Through the courageous labors of Shway Weing, more than two thousand Karens were ready in 1839 to live for Christ, although they knew that it meant severe persecution. For a brief period at the close of this year, the viceroy at Rangoon was friendly to Kincaid and Abbott and did not molest their work among the Bassein Karens. But his fall from power brought renewed hostilities. The door to the Bassein Karens was closed, except for a base of operations to the northwest of the Bassein district, in Arracan. It was known that Karens, for some years, had crossed the Yoma Mountains and settled in Arracan in order to escape Burmese oppression. There they found freedom, if not a healthful climate and the fertile soil they were accustomed to in Bassein.

So it was that Abbott and Kincaid set out from Moulmein on February 11, 1840, to occupy stations in Arracan. Abbott and his wife, with Ko Tha Byu, the aged Karen apostle, and two other assistants, established a station at Sandoway, a small Burmese town, fifty miles south of Ramree, situated up a small river about fifteen miles as the river runs (five otherwise) from the sea.

Mr. and Mrs. Kincaid proceeded farther up the coast to Akyab. With characteristic vigor, Abbott made a tour from December, 1840, to January, 1841, among the Karens on the eastern frontier of the province. From Sandoway he distributed more than six thousand books and tracts during the year, in spite of a cholera epidemic which swept away one-eighth of the population, and also in spite of the Burmese persecution of Karens who were found with Christian books. In Bassein to the south of Arracan, Karens were forced to conduct worship services in small companies of two or three families in order to avoid discovery by the government. Abbott sent his two assistants to Bassein and Rangoon to invite young Christian Karens to come to Sandoway for instruction. Within a month, eighty arrived from Bassein, and he baptized twenty-seven of them. During the rainy season, he had thirty Karen students preparing for the ministry. This number grew to nearly sixty within a short time. Within five years of his arrival in Arracan, Abbott and the pastors under his charge baptized upwards of three thousand converts.[14]

In an effort to relieve the Karen Christians from the intense sufferings which they were obliged to endure at the hands of the Burmese, Abbott appealed to Arthur P. Phayre, the Assistant Commissioner of the British Government in Arracan. Phayre at once responded by offering sites for Karen Christian villages and a loan of timber and rice and seed for the first year. Nearly five hundred families removed in 1842 to three new village sites: Ong Khyaung, Magezzin, and Baumee. Additional villages were established also at four other locations farther down the Arracan coast.

The next year was one of severe trial, as disease and poor crops almost wiped out the Karen villages. Those who survived returned home in terror. But in Bassein, matters were still worse, as cholera swept away five hundred Christians. The tide was turned, however, the following year when deserted villages were restored and many new ones started.

Facing an almost impossible task of providing pastoral leadership for these people, Abbott decided to ordain two of his most capable and devout assistants, Myat Kyau and Tway Po, for service in Bassein. He intended that they should establish churches and strengthen the suffering converts. Accordingly, on January 8, 1843, he called a council to examine the young men for ordination by the Magezzin church. His faith in them was more than vindicated, for Myat Kyau baptized 1,550 Karens that year, as the result of a four months'

---

[14] Wyeth, *op. cit.*, chaps. 6-12; William Gammell, *A History of American Baptist Missions* (Boston, 1849), p. 158.

tour in the Bassein district. In 1844 he nearly equalled this record, and Tway Po was almost as successful.[15]

Abbott's action in ordaining these assistants and placing upon their shoulders full responsibility of leadership was an innovation in the policy of the mission. His policy was not approved by the Board at home or by some of the older missionaries.[16] In a very real sense, Abbott was a pioneer in developing a self-governing and self-supporting leadership.

Until this time, it had been customary for native pastors to be supported by missionary funds. Abbott, however, felt that the strength of the church would depend upon an early development of responsibility upon the part of its members. He developed two types of leaders. The first were called assistants. They were requested and approved by the people of their own respective villages. They were really pastors of their own congregations and served as evangelists. Abbott argued that they should be ordained, since God had called them and since they were doing the work of the ministry. The second type of leaders were like the "class leaders" among the Methodists. They received no pay from the mission and did not itinerate and preach. They simply led the religious services in their own villages.[17]

Abbott's championing of the principle of self-support was far in advance of his times. It was not until the twentieth century that it came to be generally recognized among Christian groups. Much credit is due, therefore, to this pioneer missionary and his successors in the Karen mission in Burma for developing "the earliest mission station in the world to demonstrate on any large scale how superior to the older system of missionary subventions is the policy of throwing the burden of supporting their own pastors on the native Christians." [18]

With Comstock at Ramree and Abbott at Sandoway, a third center of work in Arracan was established in 1840 in the city of Akyab

---

15 Brockett, *The Story of the Karen Mission in Bassein, 1838–1890,* pp. 43-45.

16 *Ibid.,* p. 45.

17 *The Baptist Missionary Magazine,* Vol. 24, No. 1 (Jan. 1844), pp. 4-5; Vol. 24, No. 12 (Dec. 1844), p. 352.

18 Helen Barrett Montgomery, *Following the Sunrise: A Century of Baptist Missions, 1813–1913* (Philadelphia, 1913), p. 43; see also C. H. Carpenter, *Self-Support, Illustrated in the History of the Bassein Karen Mission from 1840 to 1880* (Boston, 1883).

by Kincaid. In spite of temperatures that rarely fell below ninety degrees, Kincaid preached three times on Sundays in his own house and four times during the week in three different places in town. Anywhere from twenty to a hundred persons attended his meetings. He was assisted by two native preachers.

About this time, Kincaid learned of the great revivals which had been bringing thousands of Karens to Christ in the Bassein province since 1837. Even Moung Shway Moung, the governor under the Burmese emperor, was reported to be a Christian.

In May, 1841, a "mountain chief" by the name of Chet-za came to Akyab to invite Kincaid to establish a school in his area. He had brought with him a list of the names of 273 boys and girls whom he wished to place in the school, if the missionary would come. So on December 29, 1841, Kincaid and Stilson (from Ramree) set out to the Kemmee country of the chief. From the Akyab harbor it was about 75 miles up the Ko-la-dan River. The missionaries found the Kemmees to be a very neat people. Although they had no religious services, they believed in a Supreme Being. They considered murder, adultery, stealing, and falsehood to be great crimes. Moreover, they had a tradition concerning the Book which one day should be brought to them by the white man.

In response to the appeal of these people, the missionaries established a station about 150 miles north of Akyab. Stilson remained with them to study the language and reduce it to writing, a task which made possible eventually the supplying of the Kemmees with the Christian message in writing. Kincaid made several subsequent visits among them. At a still later period, Ingalls paid them a visit. His labors resulted in many conversions. Among the converts was Paiting, son of the "mountain chief." It became his constant prayer that a teacher be sent to his people from America.[19]

In 1843, after twelve years of service in Burma, the Kincaids returned to America. They brought with them the two oldest children of the Comstocks to be educated in the homeland. The parting had been difficult for the parents. Yet, Comstock's parting word to Kincaid was, "Remember, brother Kincaid, six men for Arracan!"

Such faith was tested severely when Mrs. Comstock died on April 28, 1843, even before the children arrived in the United States. She

---

[19] Patton, *The Hero Missionary: Kincaid,* pp. 175-76.

was but thirty years of age. Within a few weeks, the two younger children died, leaving Comstock alone in Ramree, for Stilson had gone to Akyab and the Abbotts were in Sandoway. Then his two assistants became ill and died. On April 25, 1844, at the age of thirty-five, he, himself, succumbed from fever at Akyab, where he had gone to finish a textbook for publication. His legacy to the missionary enterprise was the memory of remarkable conscientiousness and decision of character combined with a passion for Arracan. He was the founder of the Arracan field. He left able leadership in Kincaid, Abbot, and Stilson. Although it had taken seven years to win the first convert, the ingathering thereafter was rewarding, for up to Comstock's death there had been 489 baptisms.[20]

The severity of climate continued to take its toll of life and health. In October, 1844, Abbott reported to the Board that he suffered from pulmonary consumption which prevented him from continuing to preach. His anxiety for the three thousand Christians and their two ordained pastors and thirty native preachers was touching, as he requested that a missionary be sent to the Karens at Sandoway. In the same letter he told of the death of his fifteen-month-old son two months before. On January 27, 1845, his wife died of a heart attack, after a trip south in the jungle to care for her husband during one of his evangelistic tours.[21]

The cost in human life had been great, but Arracan had demonstrated its importance as a mission field. With the exception of Kyouk Phyoo, the climate was not prohibitive for work; the proximity of the province to Burma on the east had enabled the missionaries to continue their contacts with the Karens within the areas where opposion from the government was most severe. The withdrawal of the English Baptists from this field in favor of the American Baptists had left them with an open field. But the major need was for reinforcements. For by 1845, the Stilsons alone remained in Arracan, Abbott having returned to America in 1844. This comparatively new field in Burma was dear to the hearts of the missionaries. It is not surprising, therefore, that while in America they should make a strong plea for its continued support.[22]

---

[20] Wyeth, *A Galaxy in the Burman Sky,* p. 63.
[21] *The Baptist Missionary Magazine,* Vol. 24 (1845), pp. 91, 139-40.
[22] See Chapter VI.

Difficulties in Assam

Tragedy played its grim role in the early days of the Assam Mission. The scene was within a few miles of Sadiya, the first station occupied in that country. In 1837 reinforcements were sent out by the Board in America to give needed assistance to Cutter and Brown, who had begun the work there in 1836. The Rev. Jacob Thomas and his wife had made the long journey from America to Calcutta in safety. Then they had proceeded by land and river across Bengal and up the length of the Brahmaputra River without mishap until they came almost within sight of their destination. On July 7, as they were securing their canoes along the bank of the river for encamping for the night, a tree on the bank which had been undermined by flood waters fell upon the boat in which Thomas sat. He was crushed to death almost without warning. Following the burial the next day, the bereaved party of Mrs. Thomas and Mr. and Mrs. Bronson continued on their way. On July 17 the party arrived at Sadiya.[23]

The next few years were most trying for the mission. An attack on Sadiya in March, 1839, and the subsequent commotion due to plundering, coupled with the inability of the British garrison to handle the situation, forced the removal of the mission to Jaipur. The new location was a thriving town to the southwest which was expected to become the headquarters for tea operations. It had the additional advantage of being only five-days distance from Jorhat, the great center of the Assamese population.

Through tours in the Nam Sang Noga Mountains lying southeast of Jaipur, Bronson not only found an exhilaratingly cool climate but also a people known as the Nagas, who appeared to be more receptive to the gospel than the Hinduized Assamese who resisted the message of the missionaries. The Nagas were animists, and hence free from the practice of idolatry. They had a strong attachment to their own language. By 1840, Bronson had established a school for some twenty pupils in the Naga Hills, and in April removed from Jaipur to his new station. He was assisted by new missionaries. Cyrus Barker and his wife, and Miss Rhoda Bronson, Bronson's sister. Through Captain Jenkins, who had long been interested in opening mission work in Assam, the Commissioner of Upper Assam contributed 1,200 rupees for the school in the first year.

[23] *The Baptist Missionary Magazine,* Vol. 18, No. 3 (Mar. 1838), pp. 68-69.

In October, 1840, Miss Bronson died. The Barkers were assigned to work among the Assamese at Sibsagor to the southwest of Sadiya in 1841. It was a favorable spot, having some 700,000 population in the area, and enjoying means of communication by water to Jorhat. Since it was the headquarters for the British Army, it had a resident physician and reasonable protection for the mission. A government school was established in which English and Bengali were taught.

In the same year, Bronson opened a new station at Nowgong, which lay southwest of Jorhat and northeast of Gauhati on the Brahmaputra River. He had made this move on the advice of Captain Jenkins. In 1843 a third center was established at Gauhati, which was still nearer Bengal. These stations continued to be the bases of missionary work in Assam for thirty-three years, with the exception of Goalpara, directly west of Gauhati, which was opened in 1867 for work among the Garos, a hill tribe.

During these initial years of the mission, Brown's principal employment was the translation of the New Testament into Assamese. Cutter conducted six village schools at Sibsagar. In spite of poor health, Barker established schools in the vicinity of Gauhati. Plans were under way in 1845 for the building of a chapel and schoolhouse at Gauhati by private subscription. Bronson founded the Nowgong Orphan Institution in 1842. It became the training school for practically all of the Assamese leadership of the churches during the 19th century. Although much patient labor was expended, in these early years, in behalf of the winning of the Hinduized Assamese, the results were slight because of their resistance to Christianity. The major success in Assam was to be among the animists of the hill tribes, the Garos and the Nagas whose culture was less developed and hence less resistant to the gospel.[24]

Discouragements in South India

Between 1836 when the Days arrived in India and 1840 when a permanent station was developed at Nellore, the Baptist work was carried on briefly at Vizagapatam and Chicacole. It was then moved to Madras on advice of Dr. Howard Malcom while on his deputa-

---

[24] Merriam, *A History of American Baptist Missions,* pp. 122-24; *The Baptist Missionary Magazine,* Vol. 19 (1839), pp. 279, 281-87; Vol. 20 (1840), pp. 29-30; Vol. 21 (1841), pp. 113-17, 192, 341; Vol. 22 (1842), pp. 64-67, 69-70; Vol. 25 (1845), pp. 184-85.

tion trip to Southeast Asia. During this period, Day, accompanied by Gordon, a missionary of the London Missionary Society, conducted evangelistic tours in all of the district around Madras, and as far north as Ongole. On August 4, 1838 a Baptist church, with fifteen members, was constituted at Madras. The membership increased to eighteen by the following year.

In the fall of 1840, Day was joined at Nellore, the new station, by the Van Husens, a new missionary couple from America. On September 27, Day baptized the first Telugu convert connected with this mission. He had been a believer for three years. He was a man about forty years of age, and engaged in civil service for the government. His baptism attracted a vast throng of spectators.

Nellore was regarded by Day and Van Husen as fortunately situated on the south side of the Pennar River, fifteen miles from the Bay of Bengal and 110 miles from Madras. It had suburbs and three adjacent villages, with a combined population of about 20,000 inhabitants. Being a civil and military station of the British East India Company, it afforded protection for the missionaries and medical care as well. Since it was a center of trade with communications to Madras, Calcutta, Hyderabad, Nagpur, and other places, tourists and traders might be relied upon to carry the gospel into the interior of the country. A further advantage was that the male population among the Telugus could read.

The usual methods of missionary endeavor, preaching, distribution of tracts, the founding of a school on the mission compound, and personal conversation were all used, but with little success. Here, as at Rangoon and Ava, the gospel met greater resistance than it had from peoples of a less developed religious life and culture. Hinduism, like Buddhism, was a more formidable barrier to Christianity than animism. During the annual festival at Janavadu in May, 1844, the preaching of Day and his assistants almost resulted in their death. They were assailed violently by some Brahmans, and forced to retreat through a narrow street, walking backwards to ward off the blows and to avoid being thrown down and trampled to death. Because of British protection, several arrests were made and the affair was investigated. But the opposition was indicative of an open hostility to a foreign religion. By October, however, it was possible to organize a church of eight members, which included the missionaries.

But Van Husen was in poor health.[25] The picture did not look bright; and it was not to improve greatly for the next several years.

Problems in Siam and Expansion into China

The Baptist Mission at Bangkok in Siam was the training ground for missionary work in China. From its founding in 1833, the efforts of the missionaries were divided between the Siamese and the Chinese laborers who worked in the city. Between the two, the greatest success was had with the Chinese. Under the direction of William Dean, the first Chinese Baptist church grew by 1845 to twenty-four members. The little band supported two preaching stations in outlying districts.

At the end of August, Alanson Reed, who had arrived in Bangkok in 1836 with J. L. Shuck to reinforce the Chinese mission, died from dysentery. Shuck soon left for the Portuguese colony on the island of Macao. There, on January 31, 1837, he baptized the first convert in China, Ahea A. Loo, who had come under the influence of Christian books a few years before Shuck's arrival. The baptism took place in a river, within a few rods of a large Portuguese fort, with its mounted ramparts. Mrs. Shuck was the only witness. Because the new convert could read and write his own language, he was taken into the service of the missionary. In the company of A. Loo, Shuck visited Hainan in February. An attack by pirates compelled him to return to Macao. It was at this time that Shuck was able to commence preaching in Chinese.

Meantime in Bangkok, on December 16, 1840, reinforcements arrived in the persons of Rev. Josiah Goddard and his wife. Five years later he was authorized by the Board in America to remove to Hong Kong, to which city Shuck had moved in 1842 in order to help in the revision of the Chinese version of the Scriptures which was then in progress. From there he eventually went to Ningpo, where he pioneered in the evangelistic work of the East China Baptist Mission.

Just as Shuck opened the mission in South China which was to come under the Southern Baptist Convention after 1845, just so Dr.

---

[25] The foregoing account is based upon reports in *The Baptist Missionary Magazine*, Vol. 18 (1838), pp. 158-59; Vol. 19 (1839), pp. 172-78, 209-15; Vol. 20 (1840), pp. 145-46; Vol. 21 (1841), pp. 122-23; Vol. 23 (1843), pp. 97-100; Vol. 24 (1844), p. 351; Vol. 25 (1845), p. 185.

D. J. Macgowan, a physician, opened the East China field. In 1843, Dr. Macgowan opened a hospital. It closed for a time, but was re-opened in April, 1845. During the first year, he ministered to two thousand patients and conducted preaching services. But the real beginnings of evangelistic work may be dated from Goddard's arrival in March, 1848, which is a story that will be told later.

Shuck's work in Hong Kong made singular progress. Nine years after he had sailed from America, there was an organized church, with Dean as pastor, and a Baptist mission schoolhouse, a building of two stories, which was fifty-five feet in length and twenty-five wide. Upon the arrival of Dr. and Mrs. Devan on October 22, 1844, a Chinese temple was procured for a dispensary at Kowloon, one of the out-stations on the mainland. In April, 1845, the missionaries entrusted the chapels at Hong Kong to the supervision of Chinese assistants and the missionaries of other societies, and left for Canton for the purpose of constituting a Baptist church there. Shuck was chosen to be its pastor.[26]

The long-awaited entrance into China had come to pass. Siam had been the port of entrance. Along the way, the New Testament had been published in the Siamese language, and some converts had been won. But the principal achievement was the establishing of a Chinese work there which provided a base for entering China with the gospel.

---

[26] *The Baptist Missionary Magazine,* Vol. 18 (1838), pp. 55-61, 95; Vol. 19, pp. 220-22; Vol. 20, pp. 143-44; Vol. 22, pp. 54, 261, 341-42; Vol. 23, pp. 156-58, 246, 315-16; Vol. 24, p. 45; Vol. 25, pp. 91, 105-06, 179-80, 184, 272-73.

CHAPTER V

Beachheads Outside of Asia

ALTHOUGH THE LAND of Burma claimed the major portion of foreign mission interest among American Baptists prior to 1845, there were other concerns outside of Asia that occupied their attention. The earliest of these, which really antedated the organization of the Triennial Convention in 1814, was the winning of the Indian Americans to Christ. Second in point of chronological development was the extension of concern for the American Negroes who had been deported to Liberia in Northwest Africa. The third was the establishing of missionary activities in various European countries. These early endeavors may be grouped together for convenience under the heading of "beachheads outside of Asia." For in a sense, they were but the beginnings of a more intensive work which was to be developed in the latter half of the nineteenth century. Their importance in this early period lies in the fact that they represented a breadth of missionary concern within the vision and faith that characterized Baptist leadership prior to 1845.

The Mission to American Indians

As we have seen in a previous chapter, early efforts to evangelize Indian tribes within the United States were initiated and supported by local societies. But with the establishment of a national convention, the lines began to lengthen into the Middle West territory of Indiana, Michigan, and Illinois. In 1817 the Board of the Convention appointed the Reverend Isaac McCoy to minister to several tribes of Indians in Indiana and to the Ottawas in Michigan.[1] By

[1] See Chapter II.

1821 he had established a church at Fort Wayne, Indiana. His genuine concern for the welfare of the Indians took him many times to Washington on their behalf. He continued as a missionary until 1842, when he became the corresponding secretary of the American Indian Association.

The General Convention continued to send missionaries to various tribes in different parts of the country. In co-operation with the United States Government, schools were established. The missionaries, in some cases, sought to reduce tribal languages to writing in order to make the Bible available to the people in their own tongue. Efforts were also made to provide industrial training. Indian men were given instruction in blacksmithing, carpentry, and weaving; women were taught household skills.[2]

It is only possible, in the brief space allowed, to summarize the work of American Baptists among the various tribes of American Indians. It was supervised by the same Board that conducted missions in foreign lands. By 1845, missionaries of the General Convention were laboring among the Cherokees in North Carolina and in the Indian Territory, to which they were removed after 1838; among the Creeks in Georgia and Alabama, until their removal to the Indian Territory about 1840; among several tribes in New York; among the Ottawas and Ojibwas in Michigan; among the Choctaws in the Southwest from 1826 to 1844, after their removal to the Indian Territory; and among several tribes along the Mississippi.

It is to their credit that the missionaries supported the Indians against the injustices which were dealt them when they were removed by the United States Government from their homes and forced to establish themselves in new and frequently undesirable territories allotted to them in the West. In many instances, the work was broken by this removal of tribes, but it continued among several tribes, especially the Cherokee and Shawanos, under the auspices of the American Baptist Missionary Union, as the General Convention was called after 1845.

Up to the outbreak of the Civil War, a total of sixty missionaries had been commissioned by the Board to serve among the Indians. Through their efforts, there had been two thousand baptisms among the Indian converts by that time.[3]

---

[2] Charles L. White, *A Century of Faith* (Philadelphia, 1932), pp. 81-83.
[3] *Ibid.*, p. 83.

The Mission in Liberia

The initial interest in Africa was manifested by Lott Cary, a Negro Baptist of Richmond, Virginia. Converted in 1807, he united with the First Baptist Church (white) of that city. There were then no organized colored churches in the South. From his accustomed seat in the gallery of that church, he caught a vision of the needs of his people for the gospel. Determined to preach, he learned to read the New Testament with the help of a young white man, and was licensed to preach. By 1813 he had saved the sum of $850 with which he purchased his freedom and that of his children. His wife had already died. In 1815 he was a leading spirit in the founding of the African Missionary Society of Richmond, one of the first established in America for the purpose of sending missionaries to Africa.[4]

At first funds came in slowly, for Negro Baptists were poor. But by 1818 they had gathered the sum of $700. In the meantime, white Baptists had become interested through the organization of the American Colonization Society in 1816 for Negro deportation to Liberia. They saw in this plan not only a possible means of solving the country's freed-Negro problem, but a new field of missionary endeavor. Inspired by the sacrificial efforts of the Negro Baptists, the General Convention, meeting in Baltimore, Maryland, appointed on April 28, 1820, Lott Cary and Coelin Teague, another Negro preacher, as missionaries to the new colony in Liberia.

The new appointees sailed from Norfolk in January, 1821, and settled first near Free Town, Sierra Leone. The colony sent out by the American Colonization Society, with which Cary and Teague were connected, was later located at a place called Montserado, the name of which was soon changed to Monrovia.

The country, itself, came to be called Liberia. It is situated along the western coast of Africa. Several rivers flow from the hinterland to the sea. Along these were established villages and trading posts. Monrovia, the largest town, was the capital of the country. The inhabitants were known as Bassas.

Teague left the mission in 1823. Cary was joined early in 1824 by Reverend Colston M. Waring, also from Virginia. By 1824, a Baptist church was organized, a school was opened, and nine converts

---

[4] B. F. Riley, *A History of the Baptists in the Southern States East of the Mississippi* (Philadelphia, 1898), pp. 315-17.

were baptized. In the midst of this evident progress, the little colony was threatened with invasions by the savage tribes that surrounded them. Many of the colonists, fearing extermination, proposed to return to Sierra Leone. But Cary persuaded them to stay and face the enemy. During a period of two months, when native tribes were attacking the colony, Cary gave courageous leadership, co-operating with Governor Ashmun, in defense of the people. At one point during an attack, Cary actually rallied the broken forces of the colony to drive the enemy out of the territory.

Cary's services extended also to include the role of mediator between the Negro colonists and the governor. Although he stood for law and order, he expressed sympathy with the claims of the settlers for reforms in the government. Possibly due to his loyalty to the governor, on the one hand, and to his intercession on behalf of the people, on the other, the reforms were granted in 1824.[5] He died on November 10, 1828.

In 1826 Calvin Holton, a graduate of Waterville College in Maine, joined the mission in Monrovia. He was the first white man to be sent to Africa by American Baptists. His appointment reflects their deepening interest in the Christianizing of Africa. But it was the beginning of a tragic chapter in the history of this mission. Until 1845, most of the missionaries and their wives who were sent out either died or were obliged to return home to regain their health. The climate of Liberia was too severe for white people. Accordingly, it became the practice to send out only Negroes.

The heroic story of the noble efforts of the missionaries who went to Liberia is highlighted by an almost incredible persistence and courage in the face of heartbreak and death. For example, Reverend William G. Crocker and Reverend and Mrs. William Mylne arrived in Monrovia in August, 1835. Before the end of September, Mrs. Mylne had died of fever. The next year Mylne, himself, nearly died of disease. Yet, the two men persevered in the study of the Bassa language, with a view to preparing the Scriptures in the native tongue of the people. Finally, illness forced Mylne's return to America in 1838. Miss R. Warren, a new arrival in September, 1839, and Crocker were married in 1840. They were working at Edina, a new

---

[5] G. Hervey, *The Story of Baptist Missions in Foreign Lands* (St. Louis, 1886), pp. 203-04.

station when she died in August of the same year. Crocker was obliged to return to the United States the next year for a furlough. Reverend Joseph Fielding and his wife, new missionaries who had arrived in December, 1841, both died a month later of fever.

The only missionaries of the Board left in Liberia were Ivory Clarke and his wife, who had arrived at Edina in 1837, and John Day, at Bexley about seven miles away, who was assisted by Kong Koba, a native convert, and Mr. J. C. Minor, a printer who began work at Edina in 1842. Clarke had charge of two schools, one for boys and the other for girls, which were attended by a total of seventy pupils. In addition, he saw through the press the publication of two books in the Bassa language, *Easy Lessons* and *The Bassa Reader*. Crocker returned to Monrovia from America on February 23, 1844. He preached on Sunday and died of a hemorrhage the next day. Such is a glimpse of the cost in human life of the Liberian Mission.[6]

Direct operation of the Board in Liberia ceased in 1856. Difficulties in making satisfactory business arrangements for the mission and the grave problem of the loss of missionary lives due to climatic conditions combined to bring about this decision. The mission continued, however, on a basis of self-support, with some assistance from Negro Baptists of the South. Interest of American Baptists in Africa did not end, however, as an examination of almost yearly resolutions to reopen the work will testify.[7]

The Liberian Mission is of particular interest because it marked the first joint effort of peoples of two races to carry on a foreign mission enterprise. Moreover, its origin was stimulated, not only by an evangelistic motive, but by a social concern to solve the freed-Negro problem in America. Perhaps even more important to the development of our story is the fact that this mission provides a vivid illustration of the intense spirit of self-sacrifice that moved young men and women to lay down their lives that people in Africa might hear the gospel. Devotion of this kind is one of the finest evidences

---

[6] *The American Baptist Magazine,* Vol. 16 (1836), pp. 22-23, 69-70; *The Baptist Missionary Magazine* (same periodical under a new title), Vol. 18 (1838), pp. 145, 214; Vol. 19 (1839), pp. 195-201; Vol. 20 (1840), pp. 135-36; Vol. 21 (1841), 347-48; Vol. 23 (1843), pp. 52, 148; Vol. 24 (1844), p. 142.

[7] Merriam, *A History of American Baptist Missions* (Philadelphia, 1900), pp. 41, 182-83.

of the purity of missionary purpose which has marked Baptist foreign mission work.

Beginnings in Europe and Haiti

The religious life of Europe, the ancestral home of so many American Baptists, was predominantly Roman Catholic, Eastern Orthodox, Lutheran, or Reformed. Few Christians bore witness to the Anabaptist tradition of the sixteenth century. Because it had been ruthlessly suppressed by Roman Catholic and Protestant state churches alike, the voice in behalf of religious liberty and a free church was little heard. Yet, here and there small groups or single individuals gave some allegiance to the concept of a gathered fellowship of regenerate believers, separate from the state and free of ecclesiasticism.

In some measure, the emergence of a Baptist witness in Europe at this time was "parallel to and, in some respects, a product of the Pietistic movement of the late eighteenth and early nineteenth centuries—a movement largely of laymen who were deeply troubled by the sterility and aridity of the state religion which had produced alarming infidelity, secularization, numberless empty churches, religious indifference and widespread intemperance among the clergy." [8]

Among these were a small company of people in French Flanders, in the village of Noumain. Through a study of the Bible, a copy of which a farmer had uncovered in a corner of his old house, they had been aroused to fellowship together. A young man by the name of Henri Pyt, who had been converted under the preaching of Robert Haldane, the Scotch evangelist, became their spiritual guide in 1820. He taught them Baptist principles during his eighteen-month stay with them. After his departure, his followers shared with others what they had learned.

About this time, assistance came from an unexpected quarter. An American Baptist minister, the Reverend Howard Malcom, secretary of the Triennial Convention, was traveling in France in 1831 for his health. Being impressed with the evangelistic opportunities there, he urged American Baptists to establish a mission in that country. In response to his appeal, Ira Chase, professor at Newton Theological Institution, was appointed general director of the new venture.

---

[8] From an address by Dr. W. E. Garrison at Faith and Order Conference, Lund, Sweden, August, 1952. Cited in Dorothy A. Stevens, editor, *Baptists Under the Cross* (Philadelphia, 1953), p. 19.

John Casimir Rostan, a brilliant young native of Marseilles, who had become a Baptist pastor in America, was appointed the first missionary. Together, in October, 1832, they sailed for France.

Professor Chase reported that there were a number of congregations throughout France which shared Baptist views, in part or in whole. In some cases the polity and principles were indistinct, but in every situation there was a striving for a New Testament kind of Christianity in opposition to the sacramentalism and ecclesiasticism of the Roman Catholic Church. Because the constitution of the French Government, adopted in 1830, provided a measure of religious freedom to all, the times seemed to be favorable for missionary work.[9]

Meanwhile, Rostan had established himself at Paris, where he was offered the use of a Methodist chapel. He sought to gain support among prominent men in the city for establishing an *evangelical society* among French Catholics. His mature learning qualified him to lecture for Pyt, who was professor of Christianity at the Society of Civilization, while Pyt spent the summer of 1833 in England. The pre-eminently useful career of this remarkable young man was brought to an untimely end on December 5, 1833, when he was stricken fatally with cholera.[10]

Rostan was replaced the next year by the Reverend Isaac Wilmarth, who had been converted in Paris some years before. When about to sail from New York on April 30, 1834, Professor Chase reminded him that he was going forth "as an ambassador of God, not a political emissary." He urged the young man to remain aloof from "the strife of party politics." [11] It was a timely warning, for the early efforts of Baptists in France were hindered by persecution from the state in spite of previous guarantees of toleration.

During Wilmarth's five-year ministry in France, he organized the First Baptist Church in Paris on May 10, 1835, and made contact with the Baptist followers of Pyt in northeastern France. When failing health forced his return to America, D. Newton Sheldon and Erastus Willard, two missionaries who had arrived in Paris in 1835, continued the mission. Upon the departure of Sheldon from Paris in 1837, that station remained vacant, but Willard continued with a

---

[9] *The American Baptist Magazine,* Vol. 13 (1833), pp. 325-36.
[10] *Ibid.,* pp. 282-84; Vol. 14 (1834), pp. 163-65.
[11] *Ibid.,* Vol. 14 (1834), p. 363.

school at Douai. He was the only American Baptist missionary in the country. Under French leadership the work grew until in 1845 there were seven churches.

The Board's interest in Germany had been aroused as early as 1833, as the result of correspondence from Professor Barnas Sears of Hamilton College in New York, written on September 21 from Halle while on a trip to Europe. He told of meeting, in Hamburg, Johann Gerhard Oncken, an impressive man about thirty years of age, who had requested baptism of him.

Oncken was a native of Varel, in Oldenburg. As a lad of thirteen, he was taken to Scotland by a Scottish merchant who had become interested in him on one of his visits to Varel. For nine years, Oncken worked for the merchant, traveling extensively in Scotland, England, France, and Germany. During this time his Lutheran up-bringing underwent change as Presbyterian and Congregational influences were brought to bear through his life in Scotland and England. In the home of an Independent (or Congregational) family in London, he was converted. Immediately, he determined to devote his life to evangelism.

In 1823 he accepted appointment by the Continental Society as a missionary to Germany. He settled down in Hamburg as a member of the English Reformed Church. When his preaching opened him to persecution, he opened a bookshop and became a citizen of the town. From this vantage point he distributed Bibles, circulated tracts, helped to establish Sunday schools, and continued his preaching ministry.

A reading of the Scriptures led him, in 1829, to make inquiry of British Baptists concerning baptism. The presence of Professor Sears in Germany in 1833–34 gave him his opportunity to receive believer's baptism. On April 22, 1834, a little band of seven persons, including Oncken and his wife, rowed in a small boat at midnight to a point several miles from the city. There in the river Elbe under the cover of darkness for fear of incurring persecution they were baptized.[12]

Oncken's identification of himself with the Baptists, a despised group in Germany, brought him under more severe persecution than

---

[12] For Professor Sear's correspondence, see *The American Baptist Magazine*, Vol. 14 (1834), pp. 290-93.

he had endured as an Independent. He was disowned by the Edinburgh Bible Society under which he had been serving prior to his baptism. In 1835, upon the recommendation of Professor Sears, he was engaged by the Triennial Convention in America as its agent.

Under Oncken's vigorous leadership, the church at Hamburg began to grow in spite of hostile efforts instigated by the Lutheran clergy. For a time a friendly member of the Hamburg Senate protected the little Baptist church from destruction. In the meantime, a church of six members had been organized at Berlin in May, 1837, and still another at Oldenburg in September of the same year. In October, 1838, Oncken organized a church of twenty-three members at Stuttgart. Thus were his constant travels through Germany bearing fruit as he distributed tracts and Bibles, preached, and baptized.

By the fall of 1839, Oncken and his associate, Reverend Julius Köbner, of Denmark, were able to organize a church in Copenhagen, after baptizing six or seven converts. This event thoroughly aroused the Lutherans, who began to warn everyone against the Baptist heretics. Undaunted, an engraver by the name of Peter Mönster, a man forty-four years of age, became pastor of the little congregation.

By May, 1840, Oncken's friends in Hamburg could protect him no longer. The Senate sentenced him to four weeks of imprisonment and payment of the expenses of his trial. His crime had been preaching, baptizing, and administering the Lord's Supper outside of the Lutheran state church. It was the first open infliction of punishment since the formation of the Baptist church in Hamburg six years before. By this time the congregation numbered nearly one hundred persons, and the authorities were determined to uproot the heresy. In Denmark the story was the same. Shortly after Oncken's release from prison, Köbner was arrested and imprisoned for fourteen days.

During the next several months, Oncken was obliged to conduct religious services for small groups of the congregation, meeting in various homes throughout the city on Sundays and during the week. But still the work grew as new churches were organized in the following year in Germany and in Denmark.

In May, 1842, the congregation in Hamburg was delivered unexpectedly from persecution when a great fire left a third of the city's inhabitants homeless. The sacrificial service of Oncken and his congregation in behalf of the suffering citizens won the gratitude of the

Senate and prevented further acts of hostility. By 1845 there were 380 Baptists in the city.[13]

The Danish Baptists were not so fortunate. The pastor of the church and his brother had been imprisoned twice and released only upon payment of a heavy fine for which all their goods had to be sold. Baptists in America were so disturbed by such treatment of their Danish brethren that the Triennial Convention in 1842 sent Professor Horatio B. Hackett of Newton Theological Institution to Copenhagen. The American and Foreign Bible Society, a Baptist organization, took similar action by sending Professor Thomas J. Conant of Hamilton College to join with Hackett in interceding with the Danish Government. Their mission did not secure immediate results, for Pastor Mönster was imprisoned a third time in December, 1842. Yet the church had grown in three years from eleven members to more than two hundred in spite of the constant threat of fines and imprisonment for those who refused to have their infants baptized and who persisted in attending Baptist meetings.[14]

The first American Baptist missionaries to be sent to Greece were the Reverend Horace T. Love and Cephas Pascoe, who arrived at Patras on December 9, 1836. They obtained permission to preach and distribute the Scriptures. They also established a mission school with sixteen pupils. In 1839 or 1840 the mission was changed to Corfu, with Love and the Reverend R. F. Buell engaged in the work, assisted by Mrs. H. E. Dickson, a former teacher of the government-supported Boarding School for Girls. The first convert was received in 1840.

In 1841 rioting broke out against Buell in resentment against his distribution of tracts at the temple of St. Spyridion on a festival day. He and his wife were obliged to remove to Athens, leaving Love and Mrs. Dickson to continue the work. Later the Buells opened a work on the Island of Malta. In 1842 Love returned to America to regain his health.

Early in 1844 reinforcements arrived in the persons of the Reverend Albert N. Arnold and wife, of Providence, Rhode Island, and Miss S. Emily Waldo, of Charleston, Massachusetts, who were to

---

[13] The foregoing account is based on reports in *The Baptist Missionary Magazine*, Vol. 17 (1837), p. 207; Vol. 18 (1838), pp. 145-46, 227-32; Vol. 19 (1839), pp. 190-95, 268; Vol. 20 (1840), pp. 103-07, 257-60; Vol. 21 (1841), pp. 180-81.

[14] *Ibid.*, Vol. 22 (1842), pp. 308-14; Vol. 23 (1843), pp. 10-11, 73-76, 192.

work with Mrs. Dickson at Corfu. It was the beginning of a missionary enterprise which did not make a sufficient impact upon the people to persuade them to leave their state church in any great numbers. Although the mission was continued, it never thrived.[15]

An unsuccessful attempt to begin a mission in Haiti occurred in 1835, when the Board of the General Convention appointed William C. Monroe, an educated Negro, to work at Port-au-Prince. He held services in his own house, and gathered twenty-one converts during his first year of service. He was unable to find a suitable site on which to build a church. Even more of a problem was the lack of funds. Early in 1837 he visited the United States to make known the needs of the mission. He met with very little encouragement, possibly because a reaction had set in due to the Board's overexpansion. Upon his return to Port-au-Prince, he was ill for a time. Finally, finding the little church languishing, he withdrew from the services of the Board.[16] It was not until 1919 that American Baptists resumed work in Haiti under the auspices of The American Baptist Home Mission Society.

No one of the three efforts presented in this chapter met with outstanding success. The missions to the Indians in the United States and the abortive attempt in Haiti were not given the same intensity of interest and concern that the fields in Southeast Asia received. The Liberian Mission in West Africa was the victim of circumstances beyond the control of the missionaries or the Board, namely a climate to which white people were unsuited. The European Missions, which showed varying degrees of success, met with the resistance with which an old and highly developed culture reacts to a new message that challenges the institutionalized religious life of the people. Yet, by 1845 there were in France, Germany, Denmark, and Greece a total of 28 churches with an over-all membership of 900 members.[17]

---

[15] See Merriam, *A History of American Baptist Missions,* pp. 199-200; and *The Baptist Missionary Magazine,* Vol. 18 (1838), pp. 146-47; Vol. 22 (1842), pp. 31-34, 108-11, 166; Vol. 23 (1843), pp. 146-47, 221; Vol. 24 (1844), p. 44.

[16] Gammell, *History of American Baptist Missions,* pp. 263-64.

[17] *The Baptist Missionary Magazine,* Vol. 25, No. 7 (July 1845), p. 186.

CHAPTER VI

Supporting the Venture at Home

WHILE A FOOTHOLD was being won in faraway Burma, Assam, Siam, South India, Liberia, and on the continent of Europe, Baptists in the homeland were being faced with surmounting problems as they met year by year the responsibility for maintaining and expanding a mission program. This included not only the sending out of missionaries, but also the development of a denomination at home financially strong enough to support the venture abroad.

Although the fledgling mission in Burma had been the motivating force for uniting the Baptists of America in the General Baptist Convention in 1814, there soon emerged other interests and concerns which vied with foreign missions for encouragement and support. It is at this point that we may begin the story of what was happening at home prior to 1845.

An Expanding Program (1817–1826)

The second session of the General or Triennial Convention which opened on May 7, 1817, in the Sansom Street Baptist Church, Philadelphia, symbolized the expansion which characterized the next decade. Four major decisions were made which enlarged the purpose for which the organization had come into existence. *The American Baptist Magazine and Missionary Intelligencer,* formerly *The Massachusetts Baptist Missionary Magazine,* was adopted as the Convention's official organ. The constitution was amended to enlarge the membership of the Board of Managers to thirty-one, to double the number of vice presidents, and extend the powers of the Convention "so as to embrace home missions and plans for the encouragement of education." Accordingly, John Mason Peck and James E. Welch were commissioned for service among the white settlers and Indians in the Western Mission in the vicinity of St. Louis, Missouri. Plans were set in motion to organize a seminary for the training of ministers, which resulted in the founding of Columbian College in Washington, D.C. In addition, the churches were called upon to observe the first Monday in every month as a day of prayer for missions.[1]

The decision to include education within the responsibility of the Convention met with some misgivings on the part of delegates who feared that the action might weaken support of foreign missions, for which the Convention had been organized. But because the move had the powerful backing of the president, Richard Furman, of Charleston, South Carolina, of William Staughton, of Philadelphia, Luther Rice, the agent of the Convention, and others, it was not formally opposed.[2]

The administrative activities of the Board also had come under criticism. For this reason, a committee of seven with the Reverend Jesse Mercer of Georgia as chairman was appointed by the Convention at the request of the Board for an investigation of their conduct. The report commended the Board and expressed disapproval of individuals who were seeking to undermine public confidence in its work.[3]

During the next three years, the Board turned its attention, some thought excessively, to new phases of the work, for which provision had been made in the amended constitution. The only missionaries sent to foreign lands were Jonathan M. Price, M.D., to Burma, and Collin Teague and Lott Cary to West Africa. Several home missionary appointments were made, including that of the Reverend Isaac McCoy to labor among "the aborigines on the Wabash," and the Reverend Humphrey Posey, among the Cherokees in North Carolina and Georgia. Although plans for the new school, to be at Washing-

---

[1] *The American Baptist Magazine and Missionary Intelligencer,* Vol. 1 (1817), pp. 133-35; *The Missionary Jubilee: An Account of the Fiftieth Anniversary of the American Baptist Missionary Union* (New York, 1869), pp. 101-02.

[2] *The Missionary Jubilee,* p. 101.

[3] *Ibid.,* p. 102.

ton, D.C., were well received in the Middle and Southern States, many thought that foreign missions were being sacrificed for its support. It is altogether likely that Baptists of New England, in particular, may have felt that Rhode Island College was sufficient to train young men for the ministry.

Pursuant to the enlarged functions of the Convention, its name was changed at the triennial session in 1820 to "The General Convention of the Baptist Denomination in the United States for Foreign Missions, and other important objects relating to the Redeemer's Kingdom." Further amendments were made to the constitution. One was to allow societies and churches to send an additional delegate for every two hundred dollars contributed beyond the first hundred. A second was to transfer the power to appoint executive officers from the Board to the Convention. A third was to assure the constituents that funds given for distinct purposes would be kept inviolate. A fourth provided for the management of "an institution for educational purposes." These changes were sanctioned by the Legislature of Pennsylvania when the Convention became incorporated in 1823.

When a committee presented the plan for the establishment of a school at Washington, D.C., several of the delegates opposed it on the grounds that money thus used would hinder the mission cause. It soon became apparent, however, that the Convention was being asked to approve what had already been done. For land had been purchased and a building was under construction. After a somewhat stormy session, peacemakers stepped into the breach to effect an understanding.[4]

The 1820 Convention also dealt with matters pertaining to its missionary work at home and abroad. When it became evident that the United States Congress was to appropriate the annual sum of ten thousand dollars for the welfare of American Indians, the Board sent a representative to Washington to solicit some portion of the amount. Thus began a practice of receiving annual subsidies from the government, a practice which continued throughout the course of its Indian mission work.

Because the Board expressed disfavor over the decision of George Hough to remove himself and his family from Rangoon to Seram-

---

[4] For a brief account of this Convention session, see *The Missionary Jubilee*, pp. 103-105.

pore, in 1818, without permission, the Convention enacted "rules for the general government of the conduct of missionaries and their associates." In substance, missionaries were obliged to occupy a station until removed by consent of the Board. This action proved to be most objectionable to the missionaries, who did not hesitate to express their disapproval of it.[5]

During the next three years, the Board sent no missionary to Burma, and only one, a Negro from Virginia, was sent to West Africa. The seat of the Board's operations was transferred from Philadelphia to Washington. The move was in keeping with the plan of Luther Rice and others to establish a denominational center in the national capital. It was also to enable Dr. Staughton, the newly elected president of Columbian College, to serve as corresponding secretary of the Board.

At the same time, there were evidences of a difference of viewpoint within the Board itself. The difference became acute in the Board's dealings with Luther Rice, its agent, and in its handling of the financial problems associated with Columbian College. In 1821 the Board's report reflected a disappointment that Rice's preoccupation with the educational program at Washington had prevented his giving the degree of attention to missionary promotion which had marked the preceding years. As a practical expedient, a temporary loan of ten thousand dollars was made to the college. In taking this action, the Board made it clear that the loan had been made from monies designated for missions, and was therefore only "a temporary convenience" to the educational department of the Convention's work.[6]

The triennial session of the General Convention, which opened on April 30, 1823, in the First Baptist Church, Washington, D.C., was illustrative of the ever-widening responsibilities and problems confronting American Baptists.[7]

First to be considered was the issue of representation. The Convention was composed of but fifty-three delegates from ten states

[5] *Ibid.*, p. 104; *The American Baptist Magazine and Missionary Intelligencer*, Vol. II (1820), p. 399.

[6] *The American Baptist Magazine and Missionary Intelligencer,* Vol. III (1821), p. 182.

[7] The following account is based on *The American Baptist Magazine and Missionary Intelligencer,* Vol. IV (1823), pp. 137-43.

and the District of Columbia. Of that number, thirteen were residents of Washington, D.C., ten were from Virginia, and seven were from Massachusetts. Pennsylvania and New York were represented by six each. It is obvious that travel conditions and costs were prohibitive to a larger attendance. Under the circumstances, it is not surprising that some contended that a delegate should be permitted to cast as many votes as the number of societies which had chosen him to attend. But Professor Ira Chase, although he represented two societies, argued that he was rightly entitled to but one vote. He warned that any other view was dangerous to a democratic basis of operations. In this position he was upheld by Dr. Baldwin and Dr. Staughton, and the constitutional provision for each delegate to have one vote was left unchanged.

The underlying criticism of Luther Rice's devotion to Columbian College was reflected in his letter sent to the Convention during his absence. It expressed his strong conviction that the educational institution would aid rather than deter the cause of missions.

Interest in the Burma and Arracan Missions was enlivened by the presence of Ann Judson in the city and by the volunteering for service by Jonathan Wade of Edinburgh, New York, and George Dana Boardman, a teacher at Waterville College in Maine. The Committee on the African Mission reported favorably concerning the work of Lott Cary and Collin Teague in Liberia, and emphasized the supplemental social influence of the mission to aid in suppression of the slave trade on the coast of Africa.

At this same Convention, it was decided to approve the state conventions, which had been in process of organization in various states since 1802, when the Massachusetts Domestic Missionary Society came into existence. Being convinced that the state agencies could not interfere with the rights of the churches, the Convention leaders recognized their value for bringing together "the wisdom, piety, and talent of the denomination."

An incident occurred on a rainy and chilly Sunday evening, October 26, 1823, which was to have far-reaching effects upon the cause of foreign missions. A young man, Francis Wayland, who was only twenty-seven years of age, preached to a small congregation in the First Baptist Church of Boston on the subject, "The Moral Dignity of the Missionary Enterprise." The occasion was the anniversary of the Boston Baptist Foreign Mission Society. His hearers represented three churches which had united to hear the annual sermon. His text was "The field is the world." Throughout the service, the speaker was obliged to wear his overcoat to keep warm.

The next morning, he visited a friend's home to share his disappointment over the meeting. Throwing himself on a sofa, he complained in a depressed mood: "It was a complete failure. It fell perfectly dead." A week later, however, he preached the same sermon before the Bible Translation Society at Salem. The message made a profound impression upon Deacon Loring and his son, who were engaged in the printing business. They insisted that the discourse must be published.

When the first edition came from the press in December, it was exhausted almost at once. A second was issued in February. Then a third and cheaper edition appeared. It was adopted by the American Tract Society as one of their permanent series. The sermon was thereafter given wide circulation both in the United States and England. Little did those who heard the message preached realize that it was "to mark an era in the history of the missionary enterprise."[8] Yet, such was its influence in the years which followed that Wayland became a tower of strength of the missionary movement, first as associate with Dr. Thomas Baldwin in editing *The American Baptist Magazine* from 1823, and then as chief editor on Baldwin's death in 1825.

During the intervening years before the next session of the General Convention in 1826, several important decisions were made which comprise a part of the emerging policies of the Convention's Board of Managers, of which Dr. Baldwin was chairman.

For example, in 1824 the sum of two thousand dollars, appropriated for the Burma Mission, was sent to the Reverend John Lawson, a British Baptist missionary in Calcutta, who was to serve as a treasurer for the missionaries. At the same time, the missionaries at Ava and Rangoon were authorized to spend up to a thousand dollars for the construction or purchase of new buildings at Ava, which were to become the property of the General Convention.

In September of the same year the Board at Washington, D.C., requested a committee in the Boston area to give general direction and superintendence of the Baptist Foreign Mission. This action was

---

[8] Francis and H. L. Wayland, *A Memoir of the Life and Labors of Francis Wayland,* Two Volumes (New York, 1867), I, p. 165.

taken to remedy what was felt to be a declining interest in foreign missions owing to the divided attention of Luther Rice between Columbian College and the missionary enterprise. The responsibility was accepted on October 14 in the home of Dr. Baldwin. The plan worked out to advantage because of the large degree of missionary enthusiasm in New England at the time and also because commerce with India was then being conducted through northern seaports.[9]

In spite of the opening of the Anglo-Burmese War in 1824 and the ensuing arrest of Adoniram Judson and Jonathan Price, the Board was optimistic about sending out Boardman on July 16, 1825. They believed that the war would be of brief duration, and that it would end in a British victory which, in turn, would strengthen the position of the Burma Mission. It was planned that Boardman should join Wade at Calcutta for language study until conditions permitted his entrance to Burma.

The year, 1825, proved to be a difficult one for American Baptists. The treasury was depleted after expenditures had been made for outfit and support of foreign missions and the Western Indian Mission. Then, on August 29, Dr. Thomas Baldwin, the president of the Board of Managers and a trustee of Columbian College, died while on a speaking trip to Waterville, Maine. He had been a minister for forty-two years, and editor of the *Massachusetts Baptist Missionary Magazine* fourteen years and senior editor of its successor, *The American Baptist Magazine,* for eight years. His death was not only a loss to the cause of missions but to the concept of denominational connectionalism and strength which he championed.[10]

Foreign Missions Become Sole Concern

The year 1826 marks a watershed in the history of the General Convention. The triennial session opened on April 26 in the Oliver Street Baptist Church, New York City. It lasted twelve days. Momentous decisions were reached which changed the direction of denominational activity for nearly a century.

The constitution was revised so as to limit the Convention's opera-

---

[9] The foregoing paragraphs are based on *The American Baptist Magazine and Missionary Intelligencer* (name was shortened to *The American Baptist Magazine* in 1825), Vol. IV (1824), pp. 422, 456; Vol. V (1825), pp. 215-17.

[10] *Ibid.,* Vol. V, pp. 252, 318-19. For memoir of Baldwin, see Vol. VI (1826), No. 1, pp. 2-17, and No. 2, pp. 6-49.

tions to foreign missionary concerns, which were to include Indian Missions within the United States. All connections were dissolved with Columbian College, except a slight one which involved no responsibility. The office of General Agent was abolished. The seat of operations was transferred to Boston, with executive responsibilities being entrusted to an Acting Board, resident in New England. The latter move was made in response to an offer of New England Baptists to underwrite the maintenance of the missions during this period when the treasury was financially depleted.

With the exception of Dr. William Staughton, of Washington, D.C., who was elected president, the other officers were of New England: Dr. Lucius Bolles of Boston who was made corresponding secretary, Francis Wayland, of Providence, Rhode Island, who became recording secretary, and the Honorable Heman Lincoln, of Boston, who was elected treasurer. It was reported that "the session was a peculiarly laborious and trying one." On some subjects of great importance there was considerable conflict of opinion and feeling. But it is believed that toward the close much harmony both of feeling and judgment prevailed.[11]

The reasons which were given at the time for the action of the Convention in restricting its operations "exclusively to Missionary business" were five in number: (1) a disavowal of any necessary connection between the missionary and educational concerns of the denomination; (2) a lack of provision in the constitution for dispersal of funds for both missionary and educational purposes; (3) a divided sentiment between missionary and educational interests which weakened promotional endeavor; (4) a flagging of missionary zeal and diminution of receipts ever since the two interests were united in the Convention; (5) the failure of the Convention to have control over the funds invested in education owing to the fact that trustees of Columbian College, although originally nominated by the Convention, had the power to replace their number. When the College went into debt, the seriousness of the situation brought matters to a head, and forced the abandonment of a project which threatened the entire missionary enterprise.[12]

Thus circumstances had combined to bring about the triumph of

---

[11] *The American Baptist Magazine,* Vol. VI (1826), p. 181.
[12] *Ibid.,* Vol. VI, pp. 208-10.

what may be termed the society method of denominational co-operative activity as over against a denominational connectionalism. The latter plan, which had long been advocated by men like Luther Rice and President Francis Wayland of Brown University, sought the strength of united action in a convention which would assume leadership in all phases of denominational life and activities. In fact, as late as April, 1826, there were proposals for the revision of the constitution of the General Convention so that all members might be appointed by state conventions, which could bear the traveling expense of delegates and thus bring to triennial sessions representatives from frontier states. It was argued that such a plan would represent more equitably the churches than one by which nearly one-third of the delegates resided in Washington, D.C., and by which some delegates represented a society of twenty-five or thirty persons, instead of a state. The proposed scheme was intended to develop a strong connection between all parts of the country. Thus, it was proposed that the General Convention should represent state conventions as they, in turn, represented associations, which were composed of representatives of the churches.[13]

It is significant that President Wayland, in the face of the financial situation of 1826, reversed his position and did more than any other man at the Convention in New York "to secure the separation of the college from the Convention." Thereafter he rejected the concept of a denominational organization based upon the churches in favor of the society method in which those were members who actually contributed to the work of the societies. In this respect, he was supporting the view of those who had founded the General Convention in 1814.[14]

From this time on, the meetings of the General Convention were in the interest of foreign missions. The work of Christian education and publications was the special concern of the American Baptist Publication Society, which had been organized in 1824 as a General Tract Society and enlarged in function later. Responsibility for home missions was invested in The American Baptist Home Mission Society, which came into existence in 1832. Three national agencies,

---

[13] *Ibid.*, Vol. VI, pp. 114-19.

[14] Wayland, *A Memoir of the Life and Labors of Francis Wayland,* p. 180. See also Robert A. Baker, *Relations between Northern and Southern Baptists* (Fort Worth, Texas, 1948), pp. 15-17.

then, instead of a single convention, became the channels through which Baptists operated co-operatively at home and abroad.

Under the plan of reorganization, the General Convention engaged the services of Ira M. Allen to raise funds for foreign missions. Unlike Luther Rice, he was not an administrative officer of the Convention. But like Rice, he traveled extensively, combining local mission societies into more effective units. In the larger communities he established 137 primary societies and 11 auxiliary societies. Typical of the local societies was the Female Missionary Society of the First Baptist Church in Philadelphia. In 1827 it had 100 members, each of whom contributed no less than one dollar a year. State conventions frequently commended the Burma Mission to their churches for special consideration. In 1827 Adoniram Judson presented more than $4,000 to the mission funds, which comprised the accumulated gifts made to him by individuals and payment for services that he had rendered to the Bengal Government. Yet, for lack of funds, the Board was unable to strengthen appreciably the Burma Mission. It urged every church to establish what were called "male and female mission societies." By April, 1828, the receipts for a twelve-month period amounted to $14,603.38. The number of Baptists at the time was estimated at 283,381 in 4,056 churches.[15]

The administration of the foreign mission enterprise fell to Dr. Lucius Bolles, the corresponding secretary. As executive officer of the Board of Managers, he was responsible for superintending the operations of missionaries, for attending to their wants, directing their movements, and corresponding with them. He was also to study world conditions and to ascertain the best fields for missionary labors. The task of recruiting new missionaries, of visiting the Indian Missions at home, and of raising funds also fell to him. For this herculean service he was paid one thousand dollars, half of which he received in compensation as editor of *The American Baptist Magazine*. As yet, the treasurer of the Board was not paid for services rendered.[16]

When the triennial session of the General Convention was held in Philadelphia at the close of April, 1829, several important decisions were made.[17] Application was made to change the name of the body

---

[15] *The American Baptist Magazine,* Vol. VII (1827), pp. 29, 139-40; Vol. VIII (1828), pp. 174-75, 182, 249; Vol. IX (1829), pp. 322-23.

[16] *Ibid.,* Vol. VII (1827), pp. 173-74.

[17] The following account is drawn from the Convention proceedings in *The American Baptist Magazine,* Vol. IX (1829), pp. 185-216.

to "The Baptist General Convention," whose aim "shall be to promote Foreign Missions, and other important objects relating to the Redeemer's kingdom." The committee on the Burma Mission approved the use of "native assistants" by the missionaries. The advantage of this innovation was strategic, from the point of view of the missionaries and the Board, for such leaders could be obtained for one-eighth the cost to maintain an American or European teacher on the field. Moreover, it was felt that national leadership would exert "a more direct and powerful influence" in the evangelizing of Burma. It cost about one hundred dollars a year to support a national preacher in that country.

In view of the exclusive concern of the Convention for foreign missions, plans were formulated for the re-enforcement of the Burmese and Karen stations and to replace Lott Cary, whose death in Liberia was reported early in the sessions. Some talked of reaching China by means of work in Tavoy, where the Boardmans had gone in 1828. Greece was regarded as a field to develop. South America presented a challenge, although no way seemed open at the moment for actual operations.

Underlying all of the ambitious plans for expansion was the basic problem of financial support at home. The retarding factor, which was recognized at the time, was the lack of "mutual knowledge and co-operation" within the denomination. The churches were not united to the point where concerted action could be achieved most effectively.[18] Nevertheless, progress went on apace on the foreign fields. Reports from Burma were encouraging, as the missionaries looked to the success of their schools "for the spiritual emancipation" of the country. At least four missionaries and their wives sailed in 1830 for service in Africa and Burma.

From 1831 there appears to have been a rising tide of missionary zeal. Receipts made a steady advance, after the slump of the previous years, which indicated that the foreign mission task had taken root in the denomination. The triennial meetings of 1832, held in the Oliver Street Baptist Church, New York City, were attended by 122 delegates, exceeding by 50 persons the attendance at any previous convention. The host church had indicated its enthusiasm by sending a printing press with Oliver T. Cutter, who had sailed on October 12,

---

[18] *Ibid.*, Vol. IX, p. 241.

1831, to assist Cephas Bennett at Moulmein. There were fourteen missionaries in Burma, five new missionaries ready to sail, and another five in school awaiting appointment.

The Convention of 1832 was notable for several reasons. A new national agency was organized on April 27, during a recess of the general sessions, with the full blessing of the delegates. It was The American Baptist Home Mission Society, established "to aid in the spreading of the kingdom of Christ in North America." The Convention adopted a resolution to consider the feasibility of undertaking mission stations in France, Germany, and Greece. The principle of designating the purpose and object of gifts was introduced, when the Convention voted to amend the bylaws so that any person who paid four hundred dollars a year to maintain a missionary on the field might select the one he wished to support. Individuals were encouraged to contribute one hundred dollars a year for the maintenance of a "native preacher." All such contributors were to be entitled to membership on the Board of Managers. As a further incentive to more generous financial support, the Convention voted to increase the number of delegates by allowing each association, society, or church to send an additional representative for each additional hundred dollars contributed annually.[19]

In November, 1832, Alfred Bennett, a minister long active in mission interests in New York State, became an agent of the General Convention. He was the father of Cephas Bennett, printer-missionary at Moulmein. His service to the denomination and the foreign mission enterprise was notable. Until his death in 1851, he traveled throughout the country, tirelessly devoted to the cause to which Luther Rice had awakened him early in his ministry. During his long tours, he endured many hardships. For example, on his way from Erie, Pennsylvania, to Cleveland, Ohio, on one occasion, the stagecoach in which he was traveling had a drunken driver. Twice in the night it overturned. During the winter months, Bennett often suffered colds and hoarseness, which finally induced a lung infection. Always conciliatory in spirit, his stabilizing influence was felt wherever antimission controversies raged, and later, where the abolition issue was

---

[19] The foregoing paragraphs are based on *Ibid.*, Vol. XII (1832), pp. 169-85; William J. Longley, *The First Thirty-five Years: A Short Account of Foreign Mission Beginnings in the United States* (A manuscript history of 66 pages), chaps. 4 and 5.

threatening division and diminished funds for the missionary enterprise. He represented the dedication which was aflame in many human hearts at home, without which the light of the gospel could not have been kept burning on foreign fields.[20]

The raising of missionary funds was perhaps the most serious obstacle to progress at a time when enthusiasm was relatively high. By 1833 there were nearly 5,000 Baptist churches in the United States, of which it was estimated that only one-half were financially strong enough to contribute to missions. Of that number, only 200 were strong enough to raise $300 to $500 a year for foreign missions. Three hundred were able to raise $200 annually, while 2,000 churches could only contribute $50 yearly. Yet, it was computed that were these 2,500 churches to do their full share, an annual amount of $290,000 would have been raised to provide the cost of maintaining 1,500 missionaries on the field (at the standard figure of $400 each) with the sum of $50,000 left to cover contingent expenses. The actual contribution of American Baptists fell far short of these figures, amounting to only $47,496.29. At the same time, English Baptists, who numbered only about 65,000 members (less than 17 per cent of the total membership of American Baptists), contributed not less than $60,000 annually for missions, in spite of taxation and the obligation to pay church tithes for the support of the Established Church.[21]

Yet there was a mounting optimism among missionary-minded Baptists. For in the same year, the Mission Board opened a new field in Siam, as a possible threshold to China. At the same time, they talked of establishing "a well-conducted Protestant mission in Mexico . . . as a barrier between the Romanism of South America and the Great Western Valley" in the United States.[22]

In the midst of plans for expansion, there arose in 1833 a debate concerning the proper length of a missionary's term of service. Opinion was divided between two points of view: that a term of ten years was the maximum if the health of the individual were to be safe-

---

[20] For an account of his work, see H. Harvey, *Memoir of Alfred Bennett* (New York, 1852).

[21] Based upon calculations reported in *The American Baptist Magazine*, Vol. XIII (1833), pp. 117-18; 230-31, and *The American Baptist Register* for 1832, p. 407.

[22] *The American Baptist Magazine*, Vol. XIII, p. 208.

guarded, and the view that a missionary should serve for life. Advocates of the limited term argued that this course would attract more volunteers and even men of mature years. Returned missionaries would be available to teach new recruits the language; and money spent for widows and orphans of missionaries who died on the field, owing to long years of service, would be saved. The supposition was that the Board was entirely absolved from such responsibility if the missionary died after his return home. Adoniram Judson spoke for the missionaries on the field when he wrote with considerable feeling: *"I hope that none will come, unless they come for life.* I am afraid it will become fashionable to come out *for a limited term of years.* Do inveigh everywhere against this pernicious system. I regard it as a regular scheme of the devil to sap the foundation of missions." [23]

The year 1834 witnessed gathering momentum in the rising missionary enthusiasm. The Reverend Isaac Wilmarth was sent to the new mission in France which had been approved the year before. Professor Barnas Sears, of Hamilton College in New York, baptized Johann Gerhard Oncken and six others in the Elbe River, near Hamburg, Germany, thus inaugurating what was to become the great German Baptist Mission which ministered eventually to Scandinavian countries and Russia. In the same year, a mission was opened in Haiti. Although short-lived, as we have seen in an earlier chapter, it reflected a growing sense of responsibility for peoples everywhere. The receipts for the year reached over $63,000, exceeding those for 1833 by more than $16,000. Of this sum, $7,500 came from the American Bible Society and $4,000 from the American Tract Society for translation work. The year closed with a total of 21 stations in Burma, Siam, Liberia, France, and the Indian fields in the United States. There had been 1,500 converts since 1813 when the first station was opened in Rangoon. In 1834, there were 16 mission churches and 109 missionaries and their assistants.[24]

It is little wonder that missionary fervor at the triennial meeting of the General Convention at Richmond, Virginia, in 1835, reached a higher peak than ever before attained. With a surplus in the treasury and with encouraging reports from the fields, the delegates instructed the Board "to establish new missions in every unoccupied

---

[23] *Ibid.*, pp. 137, 199-200.

[24] *Ibid.*, Vol. XIV (1834), p. 236; Vol. XV (1835), pp. 31-36.

place where there may be a reasonable prospect of success." In addition, a resolution was passed that the Convention should endeavor to raise at least $100,000 during the coming year for foreign missions.

Owing to the enlarged work of the Board, provision was made for two corresponding secretaries instead of one. Baron Stow, of Boston, was selected to complement the work of Lucius Bolles, who had been serving the Board since 1824. The treasurer, whose services had been gratuitous up to this time, was to receive annual compensation. The Reverend Jesse Mercer, of Georgia, was elected president of the Board of Managers. Under the spell of an address presented by the Reverend Amos Sutton of the English Baptist Mission in Orissa, India, the Convention voted to establish a mission at once among the Telinga, or Telugu, people of India. The Burman Bible was reported as having been completed on January 31, 1834, although the last revision was not to be accomplished until October 24, 1840. In every respect, the Convention was marked by a high degree of optimism.[25]

Actions taken at the Convention of 1835 had far-reaching results. Foremost among these was the appointment of the Reverend Howard Malcom, a member of the Board and former pastor of the Federal Street Baptist Church, Boston, to make the first deputation tour of the mission stations in the history of American Baptists. Sailing from Boston on September 22, 1835, for Calcutta, his first appointment was to arrange for favorable commencement of the Telugu mission. Traveling with him was a large company of missionaries, among whom were Elisha L. Abbott and Samuel S. Day, who were to establish the new work in South India.

At the close of March, 1836, he attended a Missionary Conference at which were present a dozen missionaries from Burma, including Adoniram Judson. In his journal, Malcom describes the veteran missionary who was then forty-seven years of age, as a vigorous person of moderate size, his auburn hair growing grey. He was pastor of a congregation that numbered over a hundred persons. It was his practice to walk a mile or two almost every evening, to which he attributed his health.

The importance of the Conference, which set the pattern for future planning sessions, may be indicated by Malcom's list of the topics discussed: (1) establishment of a seminary to train pastors—its

[25] *The American Baptist Magazine,* Vol. XV, pp. 205-63.

location, teacher, course of study, and bylaws; (2) new fields of labor; (3) "native" schools; (4) polygamy and its relation to the baptism of converts; (5) the problem of reducing the number of characters in the Burmese language; (6) the practice of giving English names to "native" children in place of their pagan names; (7) boarding schools; (8) the best mode of endowment; (9) assignments for new missionaries.

The good which Malcom's visit did for the missionaries may be measured not only in counsel, but also in spiritual fellowship. When Malcom preached on the first Sunday in April, it was the first sermon in English which Judson had heard in fourteen years.

Malcom's tour of the missions took him to Siam and South India. He visited thirty-one mission stations, including some of other denominations. By the time of his return to the United States, he had been absent two and a half years and had traveled 53,000 miles.[26]

Attributable also to the enthusiasm of the Convention of 1835 was the opening of new missions within the next year in South India, in Greece, and in Assam. Because this story has been told in a previous chapter, the facts are merely repeated here to show their relationship to the scene at home.

Growing Problems (1835–1845)

As if to chasten the spirit of optimism that possessed Baptists in this period, a number of problems combined to test the very endurance of the missionary movement. In August, 1835, because of dissension over policy, the first problem arose. American Baptists sought a financial appropriation from the American Bible Society to assist in the printing of a Bengali version of the Scriptures, prepared by William Yates, a Baptist missionary in Calcutta. Yates, in his version had followed Judson's lead in Burmese by translating the word *baptizo* by the word meaning "to immerse." After months of discussion, the Bible Society Board voted on March 17, 1836, to grant $5,000 to the Baptist Board of Foreign Missions subject to the restrictions adopted in a resolution on March 25, 1836, that only such versions should be encouraged "as conform in the principles of their

---

[26] *Ibid.*, Vol. XVI (1836), p. 153; selections from Malcom's journal are to be found in Vols. XVI, No. 10 through Vol. XVIII, No. 6. His observations were published in two volumes entitled, *Travels in South Eastern Asia, Etc.* (Boston, 1837).

translation to the common English version, at least so far as that all the religious denominations represented in the society can consistently use and circulate said versions in their several schools and communities."

When informed of the conditions set forth, the Baptist Board declined the funds, on the grounds that its own policy of Bible translation, adopted in April, 1833, would be violated. For according to a resolution passed at its meeting in Salem, the Board had instructed missionary translators to ascertain the precise meaning of the original text and "to transfer no words which are capable of being literally translated." Faced with the consequent loss of important revenues, the Board proceeded to adopt resolutions calling on the churches, associations, and missionary societies of Baptists to undertake measures to augment their own funds for the continuance of translation work.[27]

The churches responded with enthusiasm to the call of the Board. A convention of 390 delegates from 23 states met in Philadelphia in April, 1837, to organize their own agency for printing and distributing the Scriptures. It was called the American and Foreign Bible Society. Dr. Spencer H. Cone, a New York minister, was elected president; Dr. Charles G. Sommers, also of New York, was the first corresponding secretary; and William Colgate, a prominent manufacturer, was the first treasurer. Soon it became evident that some wished not only to publish "literal" translations of the Bible on mission fields, but also a "literal" English version at home. Others regarded the printing of a Baptist version in English as unnecessary and costly. When the Society decided in May, 1850, to circulate only the standard version in English, a rival society was organized, known as The American Bible Union. Thereafter, neither society fared well financially.

Earnest efforts to win Adoniram Judson's support for a Baptist version in English were frustrated by his death, just as the new project was getting under way. His son was of the opinion, however, that Judson's name could not be claimed on the side of such a version. This was based on a letter written by Judson's widow within three years of his death, in which she explained that:

---

[27] *The American Baptist Magazine,* Vol. XIII (1833), pp. 209-10; Vol. XVI (1836), pp. 122-23.

> The circular of the new society reached Maulmein a month too late; but previous to that he had spoken to me in terms of strong reprobation of the movements of the New Versionists. He was a strong, thorough Baptist; he admired the Baptist principle and policy, well carried out; despised all imitations of other denominations, and thought the Baptists ought to be willing to stand for what they really are—the only true representatives of religious freedom in the world. But the abandonment of a word in common use for centuries, and so slightly equivocal in its meaning, he would have regarded as the very extreme of childishness.[28]

This unfortunate controversy was finally settled when a Bible Convention was held in Saratoga Springs, New York, in May, 1883. There it was decided that Bible work at home was to be carried on by the American Baptist Publication Society, while that for foreign distribution was to be the responsibility of the foreign mission officers. Thus the agency for distributing versions in foreign dialects was separated from that which handled the English versions for home use, leaving each free to carry out its own policy.

A second factor to complicate the situation at home was the decline in receipts during the year, 1836. The Board reported that expenditures exceeded income by $20,000. This was, of course, due in part, at least, to an overexpansion of missions and to a lack of understanding of needs in some parts of the United States. At the same time, the number of missionary volunteers had fallen off. Yet there were reports of evident progress from the mission fields. At home, the flow of workers and materials continued. Three couples sailed for Burma, with six printing presses and a huge supply of paper.

Illustrative of the momentum on the fields is the over-all picture in 1838. By that year, the number of mission stations had increased to 69, the number of missionaries to 98, and the number of native workers to 70; there were 38 native churches, of which 20 had been constituted since the Convention of 1835. Fifty schools and five printing establishments had been set up, while books had been prepared in 15 foreign languages. During the three year period, 53 missionaries had been sent out, and there had been 1,100 baptisms. In the fiscal year ending April 15, 1838, the Board had spent over $107,000, which was in excess of receipts by more than $44,000.

[28] Edward Judson, *Life of Adoniram Judson* (New York, 1883), pp. 408-09.

Reinforcements were needed for the Siamese, the Chinese, the Telugus in India, and the Indian tribes in the United States. Several missionary candidates were awaiting sailing instructions, but the funds were depleted.[29]

At this critical juncture, Howard Malcom, who had but recently returned from his tour of the mission fields, was appointed to the newly created post of financial secretary of the Board of Foreign Missions. His task was to co-ordinate the efforts of district agents and superintend the collecting of funds. In a circular address to the churches he pointed out the dilemma in which the Board found itself, having been authorized to enlarge its operations on the strength of a promised subsidy of $100,000 a year. The average annual contribution to missions by American Baptists was but seven cents per member. In only six states was this figure higher. In three states and the District of Columbia there were no contributions at all.[30] Appeals to the churches were intensified during the years that followed. It was the ultimate goal of the Board that each pastor should serve as its promotional agent. The perennial task of fund raising called for a measure of planning and organization which the Baptists of that day had not yet achieved. Moreover, the denomination was being threatened by schism, owing to unresolved differences over the slavery issue.

In spite of these difficulties, however, missionary interest did not diminish, although some of it was undoubtedly dissipated in controversy. Nevertheless, in the three year period between 1838 and 1841, the Board employed 31 additional missionaries, while in 1840 the mission presses printed 13,000,000 pages of Scripture and tracts. All this was achieved in the face of a general cut-back on expenditures, which went into effect on April 1, 1840. The income for the three years did not meet the expenditures, being only $238,000 as over against an outlay of $261,000. To help meet this amount, the American and Foreign Bible Society contributed $50,000 in the three year period.[31]

---

[29] *The Baptist Missionary Magazine,* Vol. XVIII (1838), pp. 125-26.

[30] *Ibid.,* p. 262. States giving more than seven cents per member were South Carolina (10¢), Georgia and Pennsylvania (11¢), Rhode Island (12½¢), Maryland (15¢), and Massachusetts (25¢). Missouri, Delaware, and Arkansas gave nothing.

[31] *The Baptist Missionary Magazine,* Vol. 21 (1841), pp. 137-212.

The triennial meeting of the General Convention in 1841 in Baltimore reflected the variant currents of uneasiness and distrust which the troubled times within and without were setting in motion. The financial straits faced by the Board raised again the issue of the basis of representation and organizational efficiency. The decision to curtail operations on all mission fields raised the issue of missionary-board relationships. Accordingly, it was decided that "the Board recognizes entire equality of rights between themselves and their missionaries; the right of ultimate decision respecting the amount of appropriation to the missionaries, belonging to the Board,—and the right of determining whether on a reduction of appropriation they will continue in the service, belonging to the missionaries." [32]

The tensions and controversial atmosphere of the times undoubtedly gave rise to plentiful criticism of the Board's policies. This is reflected in the detailed reports provided for the 1841 Convention concerning the relations of the Board to other institutions and agencies, and to the Convention, itself. It was explained that the Board's powers were plenary between sessions of the Convention only with reference to missions, and not to "the right of inquisition" which belonged to the Convention alone. The allusion was to charges by some that the Board intended to select as missionary candidates only those who did not own slaves, and to the plea from others that the Board should not select slave-holders for missionary service. Conscious of sectional tension, the Board explained that its "Acting Board" of fifteen members at Boston carried responsibility only between quarterly meetings of the entire group. Having also come under criticism for overexpansion and extravagant expenditures, the Board offered rebuttal, and pled for unity and generous support of the missionary enterprise, regardless of differences over slavery and other issues.

Appeals and temporizing were to no avail, however, for the slavery issue lay deep within the moral consciousness of altogether too many people, especially in the North. The controversy had broken out into the open among Baptists as early as April, 1840, when the American Baptist Anti-Slavery Convention met in New York City. It gave expression to the radical opposition to slavery among some northern

---

[32] *Ibid.*, p. 158.
[33] *Ibid.*, Vol. XXII (1842), pp. 105-08.

Baptists, and among certain Baptist missionaries in Burma who had severed their connection with the General Convention to form a Foreign Provisional Missionary Committee under whose direction they might work without association with slave-holders.

In November, a threat on the part of the Alabama Baptist Convention to withhold funds from the Board of Foreign Missions was met by assurances of the Board's policy of official neutrality, regardless of the private opinions of its members. The Baltimore Convention in 1841 likewise avoided an open break by "disclaiming participation in the doings of the abolition Baptists. . . . The understanding was that slavery was a subject with which the Convention had no right to interefere." [34]

In the same year, the American Baptist Home Mission Society issued a similar declaration of neutrality.

When the Provisional Foreign Mission Committee of the American Baptist Anti-Slavery Convention sent a circular letter to one or more of the missionaries of the Board of Foreign Missions, presumably inviting them to receive their support, Solomon Peck, the secretary of the Board wrote a strong reply on November 15, 1842. He insisted that the Board members had not "yielded their *personal* neutrality," as they were accused, but that they refused to be subservient to either the South or the North. He admitted, however, that they were no apologists for slavery.[35]

As abolitionist sentiment grew stronger among the common people, many church members wished to send their missionary funds through a channel that was openly opposed to slavery. Consequently, the American and Foreign Free Baptist Board of Foreign Missions was formed in Boston in 1843, but the Baptist Board of Foreign Missions, which exclusively administered the missionary funds of the Convention, ruled against the existence of such an organization.

When in 1844 the General Convention met in Philadelphia, there were 460 delegates present, 80 of whom were from states below the Mason and Dixon line. The proportion of Southerners and Midwesterners was small because of distance. With delegates of other societies of the denomination who were holding annual meetings at

---

[34] Mary B. Putnam, *The Baptists and Slavery, 1840–1845* (Ann Arbor, Mich., 1913), pp. 27, 29-30.

[35] *The Baptist Missionary Magazine,* Vol. XXIII (1843), pp. 169-70.

the same time, the number of visiting Baptists was swelled to almost 700. It was not an unreasonably poor representation of the 700,000 Baptists in the United States at the time. Massachusetts sent the largest delegation, having 103 representatives of the state's 31,843 Baptists, whereas, Virginia with 82,732 Baptists had only 43 delegates present. Pennsylvania had 46 delegates to represent the 28,044 Baptists in the state.[36] This percentage of representation was not large for the state in which the Convention was being held.

Dr. W. B. Johnson, the retiring president of the Convention and a Southerner, declined re-election for reasons of health and in order to allow the office to go to someone out of the South, since it had been held by Southerners for twenty-one out of thirty years. Dr. Francis Wayland, president of Brown University in Rhode Island, and a moderate on the abolition question, was chosen as president. A Virginian, Dr. J. B. Taylor, became secretary.

On Thursday evening, April 25, Dr. Richard Fuller, a Baptist minister of South Carolina and a slave owner, presented a resolution calling upon the Convention to restrict itself solely to its missionary enterprise. Dr. Spencer H. Cone, a prominent minister of New York City, supported his effort. It was opposed, however by Dr. Nathaniel Colver, pastor of Tremont Temple, Boston, who regarded the move as an avoidance of the issue at hand. After much debate, a second effort to maintain unity by a noncommittal policy on slavery was made by Dr. George B. Ide, who was then pastor of the First Baptist Church in Philadelphia. He urged that the Convention continue to co-operate in the work of foreign missions, disclaiming "all sanction either expressed or implied, whether of slavery or of anti-slavery," but as individuals, being free to express and promote whatever views they held. The resolution was adopted unanimously on Friday morning. Thus the whole matter was again laid on the table.[37]

The stark realities of an indebtedness of $27,000 added to the problems of the delegates. On Saturday morning, Eugenio Kincaid, on furlough from Burma, addressed the Convention, after which 16 persons subscribed $400 each to support that number of missionaries on the field. William Colgate, chairman of the Committee on Finance,

---

[36] *The Baptist Missionary Magazine,* Vol. XXIV (1844), pp. 145-51; Putnam, *op. cit.,* pp. 35-36. The membership of Baptists per state is based on figures in *The Baptist Register* for 1845.

[37] *The Baptist Missionary Magazine,* Vol. XXIV, pp. 155, 157-58.

appealed to people of wealth to make generous gifts, and pled with pastors to assume responsibility for raising funds in their churches.

Although the receipts had climbed from $45,883 in 1843 to $62,-062 in 1844, the indebtedness had mounted from $3,000 in 1842 to $40,000 in 1845, as expenditures for an expanded program of operations exceeded $94,000. Accordingly the Board was obliged to retrench further by voting to discontinue the French and Greek Missions as soon as expedient.[38]

Meanwhile, tension mounted in the slavery controversy. When the Georgia Baptist Convention presented a test case to the American Baptist Home Mission Society by offering James E. Reeves of Georgia, a slave-holder, for appointment as a missionary to the Cherokee Indians, the Board voted seven to five against appointing him. This response led the Alabama Convention in November, 1844, to confront the Board of Foreign Missions with a set of resolutions, calling upon the national agency to grant the same privileges to slave-holders and non-slave-holders. In December, the Acting Board at Boston gave a reply which in reality was a departure from the principle of neutrality laid down by the Convention at its annual meeting. Their decision was as follows: "If any one should offer himself as a missionary, having slaves, and should insist on retaining them as his property, we could not appoint him. One thing is certain, we can never be a party to any arrangement which would imply approbation of slavery." [39]

This decision of the Foreign Mission Board set off a vigorous debate. Southerners did not attempt to defend the evils in the slavery system, but described the institution as an inherited disease to be cured slowly. There were many who justified its continuance on biblical grounds, some claiming that the Negroes' contacts with white masters brought them in touch with the gospel. Northern abolitionists were unconciliatory, insisting that the nefarious practice violated the inherent dignity and worth of the individual in the sight of God. At the same time, there were those who sought to conciliate the two groups.[40]

---

[38] *Ibid.*, Vol. XXV (1845), pp. 146, 152, 157.

[39] *Ibid.*, p. 222.

[40] For summaries of debates between Dr. Francis Wayland and Dr. Richard Fuller of the North and South respectively, see James O. Murray, *Francis Wayland* (New York, 1891), pp. 263-64; also *The Baptist Record* (Philadelphia weekly), Nov. 20, 1844.

Despite all efforts to maintain a semblance of unity, the deeply seated tensions within the denomination finally precipitated the long-threatened schism. It was initiated, however, not by the General Convention, but by The American Baptist Home Mission Society, which decided at a meeting in April, 1845, that it would be more expedient for its members to conduct their work in separate organizations in the North and in the South. This was the signal for the Virginia Foreign Mission Society to issue a call for a convention to be held in May. Meeting in Augusta, Georgia, 328 delegates from the churches of the South on May 8, 1845, organized the Southern Baptist Convention. It was a new type of Baptist organization, being a firmly centralized denominational body functioning through various boards. Thus it was unlike the General Convention, which in reality had been principally a foreign mission society, and which it continued to be even after the division when it changed its name to the American Baptist Missionary Union. The newly constituted Convention was of a type of organization that "had the denominational emphasis of the Associational method which had been rejected by the Northern leaders after 1820." [41]

On September 24, 1845, the Board of Foreign Missions of the General Convention met in special session in the rooms of the American Baptist Publication Society in Philadelphia. Committees were established to facilitate the transfer of certain missions and to handle any claims resulting from the separation. It was commonly agreed by both parties of the division that the property should remain with the General Convention. A call was issued for an extra session of the Convention to be held in November at the Baptist Tabernacle in New York.

When the meeting opened on November 19, Adoniram Judson was in attendance. He had arrived in Boston on October 15, bereft of his wife, Sarah, who had died six weeks before while en route home. It had been more than thirty-three years since his departure for India. Eugenio Kincaid and Elisha Abbott, his Burma colleagues were also present. In many ways, the presence of these three men had much to do with the success of the meeting.

---

[41] Robert A. Baker, *Relations between Northern and Southern Baptists,* footnote 4 on p. 280. See also Torbet, *A History of the Baptists,* pp. 309-10. The actual change in the nature of the General Convention came in 1826.

On November 20, the Convention drew up a new constitution and made arrangements to secure from the Legislature of Pennsylvania permission to change its name to "The American Baptist Missionary Union," and also to obtain incorporation in the State of Massachusetts under the same title. Dr. Edward Bright was elected the corresponding secretary, a position which he retained until 1855, serving with distinction.

Not being allowed to speak in public owing to his throat ailment, Judson was unable to address the delegates. But when economies were suggested on the third day of the Convention, and the proposal was made to abandon the Arracan Mission, the veteran missionary arose to his feet and burst out, disregarding the warning of doctors: "I must say a few words. I must protest against the abandonment of the Arracan mission!" Then his voice sank back to a whisper as Dr. Spencer H. Cone, former president of the Convention, repeated his words to the delegates: "If the Convention thinks my services can be dispensed with in finishing my dictionary, I will go immediately to Arracan; or if God should spare my life to finish my dictionary, I will go afterward and labor and die, and be buried there." [42]

Dr. Cone broke down with emotion in the midst of repeating this touching appeal. The audience was likewise moved deeply. Kincaid then made a stirring appeal. Immediately it was voted not to abandon Arracan, but to reinforce and strengthen the mission. The inspiration had been provided. The debt of $40,000 was repaid, with an additional $5,000 to reinforce the mission work.

Judson's spirit was conciliatory when he visited the South during the winter of 1846. At Richmond, Virginia, he congratulated the churches on the formation of the Southern Baptist Convention, suggesting that the size of the country called for two organizations.[43] On June 2, he was in Hamilton, New York, being united in marriage to Emily Chubbuck, a writer of considerable renown whose readers knew her as "Fanny Forester." They sailed together from Boston on July 11 for Burma, arriving in Amherst on November 27. There was something symbolic in the presence of the great Judson in the United States at the crucial hour of separation within the Convention. His spirit of conciliation, his undaunted courage and undy-

---

[42] Warburton, *Eastward,* p. 192.

[43] Edward Judson, *Life of Adoniram Judson,* pp. 475-76.

ing faith, and his determination to give pre-eminence to the missionary task of the church gave much needed inspiration to Baptists as they were about to enter upon the second phase in their venture of faith.

PART 2 THE ERA OF EXPANSION (1845–1914)

CHAPTER VII

An Era of Expansion

OUR STORY thus far has covered that period during which the venture of faith was in its first flush of enthusiasm. It had begun with the dramatic challenge of two young people, Ann and Adoniram Judson, in Rangoon very much in need of support from the Baptists of America. It had gathered momentum as a number of other young men and women gave themselves selflessly to the great missionary enterprise. The newness of the cause not only aroused the imagination of Baptists north and south, but it drew them together into a national organization which did much to strengthen the Baptist witness in America and to enlarge the vision of Baptists for a world mission.

To be sure, there were problems, tensions, and discouragements which confronted those early pioneers. They arose from the inevitable frictions which accompany the administration of a complex enterprise that takes place in several parts of the world at one time. They arose also from the fact that, at best, only a minority of Baptists were committed to support the cause which had brought the Triennial Convention into existence. These perplexing problems and tensions arose, too, out of the almost insurmountable obstacles which were present on the mission fields—perils to health and personal safety, hostile governments, language barriers, cultural differences, and the very great distances from the homeland.

Sources of tension within the home scene also contributed to difficulties abroad. In many localities there was an antimission sentiment which withstood every effort to raise funds to support the extension of the gospel through organized means. It stemmed in part from a theological preoccupation with the doctrine of divine election, and in part from an antipathy to organizations which raised funds and appeared to some to infringe upon the prerogatives of the local congregation. The fear of centralization among Baptists was a disturbing factor many times during the formative period of their organizational life. Indeed, this fear is still present. Sectionalism, which was influential in American political and social life, reflected itself in church affairs as well. In a country of such size as the United States, it was a phenomenon not to be wondered at, for great distances and limited means of travel and communication made provincialism inevitable, east and west as well as north and south. Involved in this diversification of outlook in American life was the very divisive issue of slavery.

It was the slavery question, as we have seen, which became the occasion for a split in the Baptist forces. That issue was aggravated by a growing dissatisfaction of Baptists in the South with the administration of home mission work in the lower tier of states. Thus, by 1845, the long threatened schism occurred, and the Triennial Convention reorganized itself as the American Baptist Missionary Union, while Southerners brought into existence the Southern Baptist Convention.

Because the next period in the history of the American Baptist Missionary Union extends for nearly seventy years, it seems best to pause here to point out the general characteristics of this segment of time and to call attention to the trends which were present on most of the mission fields of American Baptists.

Within the United States, from which the impetus came for the ever enlarging missionary enterprise abroad, changes were emerging with startling rapidity. The American frontier was being pushed farther and farther west, aided by new means of transportation and communication. The economy of the nation was being shifted from agriculture to industry, a trend which was accelerated by the Civil War. The resultant expansion of manufacturing and commerce brought a series of alterations in the way of life for most Americans. For some there was increased wealth; for others increased poverty. The factory system changed the face of cities, particularly in the

East. Towns developed into metropolises. Labor became a commodity over which bloody conflicts were waged in the struggle to gain wealth. The family tended to disintegrate as individuals were taken for long hours out of the home into factories and shops. Machines not only made for cheaper and more plentiful commodities for nearly everyone, but they augmented the destructiveness of war. The world began to shrink in time and space.

As society sought to reorganize itself for the spread and preservation of the new prosperity, a *laissez-faire* economy emerged to undergird capitalism and the political democracy of the nineteenth century. Only here and there were there radical voices calling for some form of socialism by which the wealth might be shared more equitably. For the most part, it was an era of comparative freedom from heavy taxes and of unusual opportunities for building financial fortunes. And with it all, the Christian impulse inspired generous philanthropy which came to the support of worthy causes including missions.

In this period of rapidly increasing wealth and creative inventiveness, Americans developed an abounding optimism which combined with new intellectual currents to produce a climate of opinion that was suited to the furtherance of the missionary enterprise. It must be admitted, however, that missionary zeal was mingled at times with a degree of national pride which confused the spread of the gospel with the sharing of western civilization with other parts of the world.

On the international scene, trends were in motion which strengthened, at least indirectly and often directly, the progress of missions. The imperialistic expansion of Western and Northern European peoples, which had begun three centuries earlier, reached its climax in the period under consideration. By 1914 most of the world's land surface was politically subject to European peoples or at least touched by their commerce and culture. This included Africa, Burma, India, Ceylon, China, Japan, the Pacific Isles, Australia, New Zealand, Siberia, and the Americas. Because the English-speaking peoples were outstanding in this period, Protestant missions received favorable reception and even encouragement in many lands where the West exerted political and military influence.

A further trend that aided the progress of Christian missions was the disintegration of non-European cultures under the impact of the Western advance with its scientific "know-how." The cultures of primitive tribes succumbed quickly; the higher civilizations of the Near East, India, Ceylon, Burma, Siam, Indo-China, China, and Japan yielded less rapidly and less completely. There emerged a synthetic world culture which was more an extension of European civilization than a true synthesis. Underneath the deep-felt and smoldering resentment of Western patronage and exploitation was always present, ready to burst forth from time to time in antiforeign riots in China and elsewhere. Throughout the entire period, Baptist missions were aided by the protective presence of British rule, wherever it existed, and to some extent by a kindly attitude on the part of Eastern peoples to American democracy.[1]

These trends made their impact felt within the churches. Moreover, older religious patterns were giving way to changing ideas and methods. In American Protestantism, in particular, the principle of voluntary support achieved a measure of initiative in Christian work which would have amazed Europeans. The freedom of the churches from political support and influence led to a more purely religious expression of Christianity than had been true before. In fact, the great missionary movement of the nineteenth century was not motivated by political considerations as had been true in earlier centuries of missionary expansion.

The perennial revivals that characterized a large segment of Protestantism in the United States during the nineteenth century provided a vigor that expressed itself in the Sunday school movement, the Y.M.C.A.'s and the Y.W.C.A.'s, significant student Christian movements such as the Student Volunteer Movement, and the World Student Christian Federation, Christian publishing ventures, and widespread philanthropic support of Christian causes.

The rich and varied intellectual endeavors of Christian scholars in Great Britain and Europe exerted a strong influence during the latter years of the period under consideration. Their attention to biblical criticism and to an intensive study of the records of the life of Jesus and to the nature of his message and purpose weakened for some the traditional sanctions for missionary endeavor that were associated with the concept of Christianity as the only true faith without which men would die in their sins. Some who had supported

---

[1] For a fuller discussion of these trends, see Kenneth Scott Latourette, *The Great Century in Europe and the U. S. A., 1800–1914* (Vol. IV of *A History of the Expansion of Christianity*), ch. 2.

missions on that premise shifted their motivation to a new basis of sharing truth by a process of education and humanitarian social uplift in the name of Jesus. The number who took this position was not large, and American Baptist missionaries were not among those who did; but undoubtedly this changed point of view affected to some extent the support of Baptist missions, which appealed to the traditional sanctions.

Fortunately, the fresh outburst of vigor within Christianity in this period which gave rise to widespread translation of the Bible into many languages and dialects, to the building of hospitals, and to the erecting of educational systems met with favorable response in many lands. This was especially true near the close of the nineteenth century in China and Japan. In these countries the influence of Western peoples with their technical skills had weakened resistance to Christianity. Indeed, missionaries enjoyed the prestige of being associated with the highly successful Western Civilization.[2]

During the latter years of this period, the missionary movement itself gave rise to efforts within Protestantism for church union. These efforts resulted at home in some mergers of similar denominations and in various federations for co-operative work; abroad, they resulted in the emergence of national Christian councils by which work on the fields was carried on through joint planning and consultation wherever feasible. In this, American Baptists participated from the start.

On American Baptist mission fields, these trends reflected themselves in varying degree. The successful spread of British rule and protection to missionaries was hailed as a boon in Burma, South India, Assam, and Bengal-Orissa. The first entrance into China came about under the protection of foreign powers through diplomatic arrangements at the so-called "treaty ports." The co-operative spirit in Protestant missions was evident, as has been mentioned, among American Baptists who usually participated in joint efforts of work whenever to do so avoided unnecessary duplication and promised to advance the cause of Christ.

The strong individualism of American Protestantism was clearly evident in the spirit of the missionaries who represented the American Baptist Missionary Union on the fields abroad. This in time gave rise to strong differences of opinion with the Board at home regard-

[2] *Ibid.*, pp. 45-46.

ing administrative policies, even threatening the existence of the Burma Mission in the middle of the nineteenth century. When the Board sought to develop centralized field supervision early in the twentieth century, strong opposition again was aroused among some of the missionaries. But that same spirit which resented any hint of the employer-employee relationship in connection with the missionary calling carried the great enterprise through times that tried the very souls of men and would have defeated men and women of lesser spirit.

Between 1845 and 1914, we note a changing emphasis in the processes by which the gospel was spread by missionaries of the American Baptist Missionary Union. There was a gradual decline of tract distribution, without abandoning the method entirely. More emphasis was placed upon schools as a means of making an impact upon the national culture and of developing Christian leaders. On this point there was strong difference of opinion, especially in Burma. New methods of missionary service and influence were developed, such as medical work, industrial schools, and agricultural missions. Women became increasingly prominent as full-fledged missionaries. The work of translation and publishing Christian literature was enlarged.

There was always tension within the Board at home and among the missionaries on the fields over the relative merits of two diverse methods of missionary work. One was the winning of converts one by one, which was the natural expression of evangelicalism's emphasis upon the individual soul's direct access to God. The other was the supplementing and strengthening of the evangelistic effort by the aid of schools of higher education whereby the national leadership might be influenced by Christian teaching and example, even though not every student of these schools might become a professing believer. While Baptists were unanimous in emphasizing evangelism and in giving it primacy in missions, not all were agreed on the wisdom of this more intensive impact upon society and its culture through educational means. Near the close of the period under consideration, this problem merged with the financial need of retrenchment to initiate the so-called "intensive policy" as over against the purely "extensive policy" of spreading the gospel. The new policy was not accepted without opposition as we shall see in Part Three of this story.

American Baptist missionaries were for the most part agreed on the need of developing self-supporting and indigenous churches. At times, however, there was disagreement as to the methods by which this might be achieved to best advantage, and as to the speed with which it should be effected. This was particularly true in Burma between missionaries who worked among the Karens and those who labored with the Burmese; it was also true in South India and in China.

Throughout the entire period there was a general faithfulness to Baptist principles on the fields. Converts were won, instructed carefully, admitted to believer's baptism, and organized into churches which had a democratic polity. To be sure, the extent of democratic procedure varied with different missionaries and with the readiness of converts to assume leadership responsibility. Converts were encouraged to express their Christian faith in their own words. Christianity for Baptist missionaries was non-creedal, the Bible being the only guide to faith and practice.

The lot of the missionary's life had lightened in some respects by the close of the period. Travel conditions had improved in most countries, and furloughs were more frequent and less arduous to make by sea-voyage. Medical care for missionaries and their families had become somewhat improved in older mission stations, although the frontier missions were still destitute of the commonest comforts of home. The number of missionaries had increased greatly by 1914, and likewise the number of supporters at home. From a small beginning, with only one missionary and his wife a century earlier, the number of missionaries had increased to 700. During those 100 years, American Baptists contributed $31,000,000 to their foreign mission agency. Within the century a total of 315,983 converts had been won on ten mission fields around the world, and organized into more than 1,500 churches.[3]

We turn now to the story of this remarkable venture of faith as it unfolded at home and on mission fields in Asia, Africa, and Europe from 1845 to the opening of the First World War in 1914.

---

[3] Howard B. Grose and Fred P. Haggard, *The Judson Centennial, 1814–1914* (Philadelphia, 1914), p. 205; P. H. J. Lerrigo and Doris M. Amidon, *All Kindreds and Tongues* (New York, 1940), pp. 8-9.

CHAPTER VIII

Developments at Home: A Period of Trial and Error, 1846–1866

AMERICAN BAPTISTS entered upon the second phase of their venture of faith in the year 1846. For those in the South, it meant the launching of a southwide convention through which a degree of denominational connectionalism was to be achieved which was new to Baptists up to that time. For those in the North, it meant the reorganization of the old Triennial Convention under the new name, "The American Baptist Missionary Union." The record of these significant changes has been set down in Chapter VI. It remains for us here only to point out that Baptists in the North were faced with depleted membership, a burden of debt, and a continuing responsibility for the work overseas at a time when the nation itself was engulfed in controversy and the ever increasing threat of civil war.

During the twenty-year period from 1846 until 1866, there were three corresponding secretaries: Dr. Solomon Peck of Massachusetts, who administered the foreign affairs of the Union's work from 1838 to 1856; Dr. Edward Bright, of New York, who wrestled with the problems of home support of the missions overseas from 1846 to 1855; and Dr. Jonah G. Warren, successor to Dr. Bright, in the period from 1856 to 1873. Upon the shoulders of these administrative officers fell the chief burden for the effective operation of an enterprise which in 1846 enrolled 99 missionaries and assistants, 155 native workers, and supported and supervised 82 churches. The total membership of native converts was 5,300. For the purpose of Christian instruction there were 50 schools which enrolled 2,000 pupils. Mission stations were located in Burma, Siam, China, Assam, India, Africa, France, Germany, Denmark, and Greece. In addition, the Union bore responsibility for mission stations among several tribes of Indians in the United States.[1]

It was not without a touch of the prophetic that the Union adopted in 1847 the seal which it has retained to the present time. It portrayed an ox standing between a plow and an altar, and inscribed on the seal were the words, "Ready for Either." The idea had been borrowed from a medieval inscription belonging to an Augustinian monk of the sixteenth century who was connected with the Vatican Library. It expressed in Latin the thought: "Ready for Either, Ready for service or sacrifice, as the Lord may call." [2] Certainly, the sense of dedication in the face of such alternatives characterized the work of The American Baptist Missionary Union throughout its history. Not always were the results completely satisfactory or entirely free from the errors of judgment to which human leadership is susceptible. The men and women who carried responsibility for the great enterprise of foreign missions at home and abroad were earthen vessels subject to the limitations of their kind. But the willingness to be "ready for either"—for service or sacrifice—was used by God for the spread of the gospel in a remarkable way.

In those early years in particular, following upon the schism of 1845, the Union passed through a period of trial and error as its members faced numerous problems growing out of support and administration and also out of expansion as the work grew.

Securing Financial Support

First among these problems was that of developing sufficient financial backing to carry on alone the work once undertaken by Southerners as well. Dr. Bright was largely responsible for the successful eliciting of needed funds for the Union. He set about to systematize the giving of local churches and state missionary conventions. This was done with the assistance of a few promotional agents, some full-time and some part-time. Interest was stimulated by the story of the actual work on the field as told by returned missionaries and through letters and journals from those still on the field as published in *The*

---

1 American Baptist Missionary Union, *Annual Reports* for 1846, p. 48.

2 *The Baptist Missionary Magazine,* Vol. 77, No. 11 (Nov. 1897), p. 579.

Missionary Magazine, a monthly publication of the Union. As a result of these efforts, the funds increased from over $82,000 in 1845 to more than $100,000 in 1846. Thereafter, they continued to average approximately $15,000 in excess of the last few years of united giving by both North and South until the figure of $120,826 was reached in 1851. In the years that followed, the receipts never fell below $100,000, except in 1858, immediately following the financial panic of 1857 and during the first two years of the Civil War. Yet, notwithstanding such progress, there were only five years in the period between 1846 and 1866 when the work was operated without a deficit. The largest deficit was experienced in 1855, when expenditures exceeded receipts by $61,333.[3]

This resulted in a policy of retrenchment which caused keen disappointment on the field. Missionaries lamented the fact that this action had been taken by the Executive Committee without consultation with them. What had happened was that the Executive Committee had decided to send to the field only the money which came into the treasury instead of the previous practice of borrowing a sufficient amount to cover the appropriations requested by the missionaries. Accordingly, missionaries found it virtually impossible to pay their assistants and to meet the expenses involved in carrying on their schools. In many cases, they were obliged to use their own limited income in order to carry on the work. It was a trying period as the officials at home wrestled with a growing burden of debt, and the missionaries on the field struggled valiantly in the face of shrinking resources.[4]

The main financial support came from Massachusetts, New York, and Pennsylvania. All of the missions contributed something to the reduction of the debt. For example, in 1860, Burma gave $679, while the Baptists of France presented nearly $100. The Executive Committee of the Union recommended that the expenditures for 1861 should not exceed $110,000. As a further measure, the Executive Committee had spent over $9,000 to employ agents to raise funds during the year. Although the outlay shocked their sense of economy, they were obliged to admit that the results had justified their action, for they emerged out of debt for the first time in many

[3] *Ibid.,* Vol. 55, No. 5 (May, 1875), p. 159.

[4] *Ibid.,* Vol. 36, No. 8 (Aug. 1856), pp. 340-41; Vol. 37, No. 3 (March, 1857), pp. 77-79; Vol. 37, No. 11 (Nov. 1857), pp. 405-14.

years. Their caution in this uncharted course of fund-raising is evident, however, from their report to the Union that they did not expect to spend so much for that purpose in the future.[5]

The problem of obtaining sufficient financial support for the expanding mission work of the Union was accentuated in those years by several factors. One was the ever-present difficulty of arousing in the churches of the denomination a sense of responsibility to the missionary enterprise. Baptist polity, being local in its applications, had not developed in Baptists generally a corporate sense of responsibility. All too many were quite willing to regard the problem of support as belonging rightly to the Union, not to the churches. A second factor was the failure of the officers of the Union to win the full co-operation of the pastors in fund-raising. The annual visit of the Union's financial representative or of a missionary home on furlough was not adequate to meet the need. Every year, the annual meeting of the Union gave expression to this complaint. A third factor was the procedure of planning expenditures for the coming year, not upon previous receipts but upon the needs expressed by missionaries on the field. Undoubtedly, a fourth factor was the modest economic circumstances in which most Baptists found themselves. But having made that concession, it is still necessary to admit that missionary enthusiam had not pervaded the rank and file of Baptist churches across the country. Only a relatively small percentage of church members actually bore the burden of financial support for the missionary enterprise. The wonder of it all is that so much was accomplished with the meager support.

Administering the Mission Fields

A second major problem faced by the Union in this period of trial and error was that of administering work on fields thousands of miles away. The chief means of contact with the missionaries was by letters which were months in arriving at their destination. The only alternative was to await the return to America of missionaries for furlough. When it is recalled that the administrative officers in the homeland were dependent upon such limited means of contact for the information upon which they based their allocation of funds, it is not surprising that the Executive Committee voted in September, 1852, to send a deputation to Asia in 1853. The purpose of this all-

[5] *Ibid.,* Vol. 40, No. 7 (July 1860), pp. 221-23.

important decision, which was to have such far-reaching effects, is found in the minutes of the Committee:

> In view of changes now occurring in the civil relations of the Burman Empire demanding increased vigor and wisdom in the effort for its evangelization; in view of questions which are consequently arising among our missionaries as to changes of location, etc.; and in accordance with desires expressed by some of the missionaries,
>
> *Resolved,* That a deputation from this Committee to the Convention of Missionaries proposed to be held at Maulmain [*sic.*] in the Spring of 1853 is eminently desirable.
>
> *Resolved,* That the Rev. S. Peck, D. D., the Foreign Secretary, and Rev. Wm. R. Williams, D. D., be appointed to this service and requested to undertake it.[6]

Subsequently, the Executive Committee appointed Reverend J. N. Granger, of Providence, Rhode Island, in place of Williams, who had declined the invitation to go.

The convention of missionaries met at Moulmein from April 4 until May 17, 1853. Those in attendance included all of the workers from the Burmese and Karen Missions, except Beecher of the Sandoway station, Moore of the Arracan Mission, and Francis Mason of the Tavoy Mission. William Dean had come from Hongkong by invitation, as had Nathan Brown from the Assam Mission. Dr. Solomon Peck, the foreign secretary, and the Reverend J. N. Granger represented the Executive Committee.

The convention was opened with a sermon by the foreign secretary. Dr. Jonathan Wade, the honored and long-time missionary to the Karens, was chosen president, while Reverend Cephas Bennett and Dr. J. Dawson were selected as secretaries. After the preliminaries of presenting the formal call for the convention by the Executive Committee, the business under consideration was referred to sixteen different committees. Each committee included three missionaries. Dean and Brown served on these committees, although not missionaries in Burma; but the members of the deputation from the United States did not. All topics were discussed thoroughly with an

---

[6] American Baptist Missionary Union, Records of Executive Committee, Vol. B, pp. 169-70. This source, *The Missionary Magazine* for 1853 and 1854, and biographies of leading missionaries involved provide the chief sources of information for this complicated story.

encouraging degree of harmony. The parties concerned understood that the decisions reached were not final, but awaited consideration of the Executive Committee. The last day of the meeting was spent in prayer for the Missionary Union, which was then about to assemble for its annual sessions at Albany, New York.[7]

The topics covered by the committees included the relative importance of different methods of evangelism, the future of the Arracan Mission, different methods of preaching, the standard of missionary character and qualifications, the care of native churches, the advisability of preaching in English, the distribution of the Burmese Bible, the location of the Press and the advisable number of printing establishments, the general system of schools, the principles which should govern missionaries in entering upon or relinquishing stations or duties assigned to them, the expediency of having Karen missionaries laboring with the Burmese during the rainy seasons when jungle work was impractical, the work of native assistants, the future work among the Burmese in Tavoy and Mergui, the role of Moulmein in the work of the Burma Mission, the problem of occupying Burma proper which was not under British protection, the use of money given directly to missionaries, the theological training of native preachers, the expediency of holding triennial conferences for missionaries, and the missionary's dependence upon the Holy Spirit.

The conclusions reached by these committees are worthy of close attention because they reflect the thinking and experience of the missionaries at the time. Moreover, an understanding of them will lead to a fairer evaluation of the grave differences of opinion regarding missionary policy that resulted from the deputation's visit to Moulmein.

The missionaries agreed that oral preaching was the divinely ordained method of evangelism and the most effective, although tracts and the distribution of books and of the Scriptures should not be neglected. There was a disposition, however, to place less emphasis upon the free distribution of the printed page than had been done in the earlier years of the Mission. The special committee recommended a more extensive use of medical practice as a missionary method in Burma, for it would effectively bring non-Christians under the in-

---

[7] *The Missionary Magazine,* Vol. 33, No. 10 (Oct. 1853), pp. 436-39; No. 11 (Nov. 1853), pp. 441-57; No. 12 (Dec. 1853), pp. 473-85; Vol. 34, No. 1 (Jan. 1854), pp. 5-19.

fluence of the gospel. They urged the establishment of a dispensary at every station not otherwise supplied with medical assistance.

It was made clear that no one plan of preaching should be adopted to the exclusion of all others. There was agreement that all preaching should be concerned with Jesus Christ as the way of life. House-to-house preaching was commended as a supplement to the regular chapel services at each station. Missionaries were discouraged from becoming side-tracked into work which required only the use of English, unless they first obtained permission from the Executive Committee for such a course. Behind this conclusion was the feeling that a missionary's primary duty was to preach the gospel to men in their own language.

The missionaries agreed that candidates for such services abroad should possess a genuine and practical Christian experience; a sturdy physical constitution; personal qualities of caution, courage, and mental capacity; and the finest possible education. Missionaries on the field should avoid engaging in personal business apart from missionary work in order to augment income. It was conceded that every missionary should teach by example as well as by precept, and that he should cultivate the closest sympathy with the people of the area in which he worked and study their language and thought patterns and ways of life.

The committee on pastorates for native churches urged that the care of such churches be placed in the hands of nationals as soon as possible, and that native preachers be ordained for these churches as soon as they could qualify.

The committee concerned with the future of the printing business of the Mission recommended that Moulmein be continued as the locale of the Press, and that there be only one Press for all Burma, the Karen Mission Press at Tavoy being merged with that at Moulmein. The purpose of this move was to economize and to facilitate a greater degree of uniformity in the spelling of names and the use of scientific terms.

The committee responsible for a consideration of the general system of schools recommended that the strictest economy of time and money should be observed in the establishing and administering of schools. Where there was a demand from non-Christians for schools in the villages, it was urged that they should be established sparingly and only where the missionary could supervise them, and then only for the purpose of Christian education rather than secular education. It was agreed that no missionary should give time to such schools for any other purpose than for general superintendence and providing religious instruction. In the case of schools for Christians, it was agreed that normal schools were valuable for training teachers and preachers for an indigenous Christian community. But boarding schools were frowned upon as unnecessary since the missionaries could reach the people in Burma readily without gathering non-Christian children, even though orphans, into such schools, as was being done in some stations. This latter conclusion was to arouse much opposition among missionaries already engaged in this type of work. The committee strongly emphasized that each mission should decide these issues between itself and the Executive Committee.

Another point on which there was to be great difference of opinion was the recommendation that a missionary should adhere to the field and duties assigned to him by the Executive Committee unless, for some reason, the missionary and the Committee should agree on a change. In the case of an emergency, a missionary might leave his post to supply a vacancy or occupy a new field without delay, but only when it was done on the recommendation of the misssion to which he was attached, pending a reference of the matter to the Executive Committee. It was also underscored that a missionary had no right to suspend or alter orders which he had received from the Executive Committee, unless he was convinced that the Executive Committee was laboring under a misapprehension or unless the execution of such an order would be injurious to the work. In such case, a mission to which the missionary was attached could defer action on such orders until they could obtain further instructions from the Executive Committee. If a missionary and the Executive Committee could not agree, the only alternative was a dissolution of his connection with the Missionary Union.

It was this report that aroused much feeling on the part of those missionaries who contended that their relationship to the Union was not that of employees to employers, but rather that of equal partners in a Christian enterprise. They insisted that there were times when only the missionary on the field, and not always even his own associates at the Mission Station Headquarters, knew best what decision he must make in his work.

A related question concerned disposition of money placed in the hands of a missionary to be used at his discretion or for a specific object. The committee considering the matter realized that there might be times when the individual missionary would be right and the group of missionaries in his mission might be wrong, but, in general, it would be safer to trust the opinion of the majority. In other words, such moneys should be spent only with the consent of the mission, unless there were some precedent to go by in the expenditure for that particular object. It was generally agreed that the greatest economy was needed in the use of mission funds, and that the nationals' support of their own work should be encouraged as much as possible.

Other recommendations included a proposal for a single theological seminary for the Karens at Moulmein, for strengthening of the work in the Arracan among the Karens and the Kemmees, and for reaching the Burmese in Tavoy and Mergui. It was agreed also that missionaries to the Burmese and Karens would benefit from a triennial conference for spiritual refreshment and for better co-ordination of their work. The conference was planned for October, 1855.

Upon the return of the deputation to America, the Missionary Union adopted its report which followed in general the recommendations of the missionary convention at Moulmein. It was decided to establish permanent stations at once at Rangoon, Bassein, Henzada, Prome, Toungoo, and Shwegyin. But Kyouk Phyoo, Mergui, and Sandoway—stations in Arracan and Tenasserim—were to be abandoned and the missionaries shifted to new locations. (On this decision the missionaries were not agreed.) Preaching was to be the chief work of missions. Each missionary was to engage in oral preaching throughout the dry season and at other times to the extent of his ability. His connection with auxiliary agencies such as schools was to be adjusted to this plan. Karen preachers were to be ordained more speedily than heretofore. The English church at Moulmein was to be disbanded and the members, all Eurasians, were urged to join the Burmese church there and thus save the missionary's time. The printing department was to be consolidated at Moulmein and placed under the direction of a publication committee and an auditing committee which should work under the policies of the Executive Committee of the Union. Schools were to be a "means of Christian instruction," not of "imparting a secular education." Only three types of schools were fully approved by the deputation—primary schools for children of converts in the villages, which were to be taught by native Christians and to be self-supporting; normal schools to train teachers and ministerial candidates; and theological schools, of which there was to be one for all the Karens and another for the Burmans. Boarding schools, which had been established by missionaries to attract non-Christians, and the teaching of English (which was associated with higher secular education) were to be discouraged.[8]

The momentous decisions arising from this conference met with approval from the majority of the missionaries. Many regarded them as being on the whole beneficial and speeding up developments which otherwise would have come slowly. Yet, the regulations adopted concerning the conduct of mission schools and the personal relationships of some missionaries with the Executive Committee aroused a storm of protest and resulted eventually in several resignations. On the field it prompted the separation of the Rangoon Sgaw Karen Mission from the Union for seventeen years, and of the Bassein Sgaw Karen Mission for thirteen years.

Here it is only possible to summarize the conflicting relationship between the missionaries and the Executive Committee, which began in 1852 when Elisha Abbott was accused of immorality, a charge of which he was cleared, and Justus Vinton made certain decisions during the tumultuous days of the Second Anglo-Burmese War that were at variance with the policy of the officials at home. The coming of the deputation to Burma in 1853 accentuated the differences. When the decisions of the Union with respect to the deputation's report became known, letters of protest were received from individual missionaries and articles, critical of the Union's action, appeared in religious periodicals in the United States. As a result, the Board of Managers met for seven days in March, 1855. Although there were differences in point of view among those present as to the degree of authority vested in the Executive Committee, the general conclusion was in favor of the action taken by the Union.[9]

An analysis of the primary causes that led to the alienation of several missionaries from the Union at this time has been preserved

---

[8] *The Missionary Magazine,* Vol. 34, No. 7 (July, 1854), pp. 227-40; Edmund F. Merriam, *The American Baptist Missionary Union and Its Missions* (Boston, 1897), pp. 48-49.

[9] *The Missionary Magazine,* Vol. 35, No. 5 (May, 1855), pp. 129-64.

in the autobiography of Dr. Joseph P. Binney, who devoted twenty-six years chiefly to educational work in Burma. They were: (1) The mission policy of the Executive Committee in appropriating funds to the mission station rather than to each individual missionary. This practice, which developed as the number of missionaries increased, caused difficulties because a majority vote of one could prevent allocation of funds for repair of a roof on a missionary's house. Because the missionaries to the Karens were in the minority in the Burma-Karen Mission, they felt that their interests were often disregarded and outvoted. To meet this objection, Binney recommended a separation of the Karen and Burmese work so that each department might receive its own appropriations. Eventually this was done, but not until disaffection had become a serious reality. (2) The feeling of some missionaries that the relationship between them and the officers of the Union was not "fraternal," but rather that of "employees and employers." This sentiment was expressed in a joint letter prepared in February, 1856, by several missionaries in Burma. They gave as their reason for dissatisfaction that they felt they were unduly subject to the power of the Executive Commitee. They took exception to the right of that Committee to "appoint, instruct, and direct" the missionaries, "to fix their compensation," and to have the authority to remove them "for sufficient cause, and to appoint others in their stead." (3) A third cause for alienation was misunderstanding which arose over actions of the Executive Committee that seemed to the missionaries on the field to be made arbitrarily without sufficient information concerning the actual situations involved.

An illustration of this kind of misunderstanding is provided by Binney's own record of how he had been authorized by the Executive Committee to help straighten out the business accounts of the late Dr. Justus Vinton. These accounts had become confused as he had developed the mission station at Kemmendine upon the annexation of Pegu by the British in 1852, and later as he had fed starving Karens during the postwar period. Many at once became suspicious of Binney that he might hurt the interests of Mrs. Vinton and the Karens. Wisely, he allayed these fears by recommending to the Executive Committee that the issue be closed and that the Karens or their advisers be allowed to take over the entire property at Kemmendine. To this the Executive Committee agreed, and the matter closed without incident.[10]

The conciliatory attitude of the officials in America was all the more welcomed in Burma because Vinton, prior to his death, had joined with Elisha Abbott in opposition to the policies laid down by the deputation and backed by the Executive Committee. Abbott was not returned to the field. He died in Fulton, New York, on December 3, 1854, just ten months after having been informed of the Committee's action.

The relations with Vinton were more drawn out. In May, 1855, the Committee voted to remove him from Rangoon, center of the Karen Mission, because he had persisted in teaching English in the mission schools contrary to the new policy of the Union. The following February the issue over the title deed of the property at Kemmendine came up for review. It was Vinton's contention that it was rightfully in his name and really belonged to the Rangoon Karen Home Mission Society for whom and with whose help he had acquired the land and erected a school building. The Executive Committee claimed that the title belonged to the Union. It gave therefore power of attorney to Lovell Ingalls, treasurer of the Burma Mission, to pay Vinton for the purchase price of the land and the buildings and to take steps to force him to transfer the title, if he refused to do so. Vinton's purchase of the property had been, from the point of view of the Executive Committee, an unauthorized debt. The issue had been joined when he said that he would "transfer the property, if he continued in connection with the Union," which implied that he had the right to keep title to the property, if he did not maintain his connection.[11]

Unquestionably Vinton's concern was not selfish, but was for the welfare of the Karen Christians. Beneath the surface seems to have been a conflict of policy between Vinton, who believed in developing a self-supporting work among the Karens, and the Executive Committee, which was not ready to accept the implications of this course, especially with respect to property-holding. But it is also apparent that he resented the supervisory function of the Executive Com-

---

[10] J. P. Binney, *Twenty-Six Years in Burmah,* pp. 285-88; *The Missionary Magazine,* Vol. 36, No. 8 (Aug. 1856), p. 332.

[11] American Baptist Missionary Union, Records of the Executive Committee, Vol. C, pp. 74-82.

mittee. In this he was typical of several missionaries—all able and devoted men, but strong individualists who had become accustomed to a free hand in the affairs of the Mission in earlier years when the Union had been obliged by great distances and perhaps by inexperience to leave a larger degree of decision about policy-making in the hands of its missionaries than it now felt to be wise.

In November, 1856, Vinton's resignation was accepted by the Executive Committee. In the same month, the Reverend J. S. Beecher, who was at the time in Philadelphia, was dismissed as a missionary because he had insisted that if he were to be returned to the field, he must be assured of a free hand in the management of the gross appropriation and also of the conduct of his mission work on the field.[12]

On February 28, 1857, the Reverend Eugenio Kincaid appeared before the Executive Committee soon after his return to the United States. He explained the grounds for the dissatisfaction of the missionaries in Burma with the Union. It appears that a chief cause of unrest lay in a lack of confidence in Dr. Solomon Peck, the foreign secretary. For on April 21, 1857, the Executive Committee gave considerable attention to a lengthy letter from Dr. Peck, defending his administration in the face of criticisms of Dr. Kincaid and others that his decisions had been high-handed or dictatorial. He insisted that he and the Executive Committee had been functioning in accord with the Constitution. He further explained that while on the field in Burma he had foreseen that his holding of councils would eventuate in some dissension and even loss of capable missionaries.

Although the Executive Committee expressed a note of confidence in the integrity and efficiency of the foreign secretary, the tide had begun to turn in favor of the missionaries' viewpoint. On May 7, Peck presented new regulations concerning relations with the missionaries of the Union to replace those of 1827. These were based on proposals made by the missionaries in Burma. Moreover, they were adopted with the understanding that they should be acceptable to the missionaries, and that the "words 'mutual' and 'mutually' be so construed that, in case of disagreement between any missionary and the Executive Committee after fraternal and deliberate consultation, the right of ultimate decision shall belong to the Executive Com-

[12] *Ibid.*, Vol. C, pp. 170-74.

mittee, and the right of determining whether in view of such decision he will continue in the service shall belong to the missionary."

The provisions included: (1) the right of a missionary to determine the field of service where he will labor; (2) the decision that each mission shall have a chairman, a secretary, and a treasurer selected from the ranks of the missionaries; (3) the agreement that missionary wives and children shall be included in the Union's financial care of the missionaries; (4) the regulation that no missionary shall engage in secular employment; (5) the policy that any missionary accused of misconduct shall have benefit of investigation by his own colleagues; and (6) the rule that no missionary shall undertake new work or expense without the approval of his mission and the concurrence of the Executive Committee.[13]

Under the prodding influence of the Missionary Union, whose members were deeply regretful of the loss by resignation of at least six missionaries since the conflict had begun, the Executive Committee dealt on January 19, 1858, with a resolution of the Union that some way be found to restore all of the missionaries to the organization of the Union. Members of the Committee expressed doubt that such a course was possible, but they promised to make efforts toward conciliation. In line with this agreement, upon the death of Justus H. Vinton in the following June, the Executive Committee paid a high tribute to his work.

Further indication of the conciliatory policy was the adoption by the Executive Committee, on March 15, 1859, of "A Plan for Reconstruction of Missionary Policy." It included several new features: (1) All missionaries henceforth were to be on the same basis as ministers of the gospel in the United States. (2) All matters of difference between the missionaries and the Union were to be adjusted to individual cases instead of on the basis of general rules arbitrarily laid down. (3) Wives of missionaries were no longer to be regarded as assistants and hence were not to be held responsible for missionary service. (4) Missionaries were to be free to form their own associations for mutual consultation and encouragement on the field. (5) Organized missions in respective countries were dispensed with, and each missionary was placed under the immediate direction of the

[13] For the foregoing actions, see *Ibid.*, Vol. C, pp. 211-20, 223-25. For correspondence involved in the resignations of missionaries, see *Free Mission Record. Letters of Resignation from Messrs. Vinton and Brayton, etc.* (New York, 1857).

Executive Committee. This was a concession to the individuality of the missionaries in their respective stations. (6) Missionaries were not to be required to account for salaries paid to them, but they were obliged to give account for other funds. (7) Each mission field was to have a treasurer through whom remittances shall be made to each missionary. (8) Separate mission presses were to be dispensed with, and each missionary was to have an appropriation for printing needs. (9) Missionaries were to avoid demands, as far as practicable, on the treasury of the Union for support of schools. School expenses were to come from the field where the school was located.

It will be observed that the new policy of 1859 preserved the best features of the conclusions of the deputation of 1853 while introducing important concessions to the initiative and individual needs of the missionaries on the field. In a very real sense, it was the product of a period of trial and error in solving the difficult problems involved in field administration by a co-operative relationship between officials at home, who were responsible to the American constituency, and missionaries on the field, who were responsible to those officials on the one hand and to the nationals whom they served on the other. The action of 1859 produced desirable results, for by October, 1861, upon their request, three missionaries, Brayton, Harris, and Rose, were reappointed as missionaries. This was viewed widely as a good omen that the unhappy differences which had arisen since 1853 were being healed.[14]

Although the executive officers of the Union, Dr. J. G. Warren and later his associate, Dr. J. N. Murdock, worked faithfully for reconciliation, the achievement of their goal was complicated by the fact that the dissenting missionaries had associated themselves with The American Baptist Free Mission Society, which had come into existence in 1843 in protest against the failure of the Triennial Convention to take a strong stand in favor of abolition of slavery. Later, this Free Society added another principle to its platform, that "Christian missionaries are the servants of Christ and not of man." By this, they meant that no board should stand between the missionary and the churches or individuals who supported them.

---

[14] Records of the Executive Committee, Vol. C, pp. 277-79, 309-10, 376-83; Vol. D, p. 109. The missionaries who had resigned, either on their own initiative or by request, as a result of differences with the Executive Committee included D. L. Brayton, J. S. Beecher, J. H. Vinton, Harris, Rose, and Nathan Brown.

With the settling of the slavery issue by the Civil War and the removal of leading personalities, like Vinton and Beecher, by death and the return of some missionaries, including Nathan Brown, who resigned from the Free Mission Society to enter upon translation work in Japan under The American Baptist Missionary Union, the way was paved by 1868 for reunion. Dr. Binney of Rangoon and Mr. Douglass of Bassein were instrumental in facilitating the disposal of the Free Society's property in both places. Thus came to a close one of the saddest chapters in the history of the Union.

We have dwelt at length on the story here because it represented a significant milestone in the development of missionary administration. Indeed, its formative influence has been felt to the present time as new procedures have grown out of the lessons learned in those trying years.

Perhaps the conflict was inevitable in the very nature of the situation. For years, the Executive Committee in whom was vested policy-making authority had allowed a large degree of freedom to the missionaries on the field. Then, in the 1850's when the growing complexity of the Union's work demanded closer supervision, co-ordination, and realignment, the Executive Committee took a more active part in the direct administration of the missions. When the new policies challenged the basic concept of mission work as held by some missionaries of strong personality who had been accustomed to a free hand, they naturally felt that they were being restricted unfairly. On the other hand, the majority point of view was expressed by Dr. Jonathan Wade, who felt that the Executive Committee had saved the missions from an extremely dangerous trend toward a preoccupation with education at the expense of preaching. There is every reason to believe that the point of view of the Executive Committee was shared by the majority of Baptists at home. Nevertheless, it is also clear that the administrative officers of the Union had not been entirely wise in their handling of the personnel problems nor in the formulation of policy. Yet, the complexity of the over-all situation is evident in the fact that the same kind of differences with respect to missionary policies have arisen from time to time to the present.

This period of twenty years (1846–1866) which we have been surveying was tumultuous in many ways. Not only did the Missionary Union find it necessary to wrestle with the problems that accompany growth in a major enterprise of world-wide scope, but it was buffeted by the stirring events of a nation at war. During the first half of 1863, the financial agent for the Middle States south of New York reported that "the people have been burdened as never before, in taxation, in providing for sick and disabled soldiers, in helping the families of the noble defenders of our government, in paying high prices for the necessities of life." Yet he could conclude with the cheering news that more money had been contributed and more churches and individuals had participated than in any former year of his service.[15]

As a measure of economy, Dr. J. G. Warren served as the sole corresponding secretary of the Union, bearing administrative responsibility for the home and foreign departments. It was not until 1866 that he obtained an assistant in the person of Dr. John N. Murdock.

The jubilee year of the Union's history was celebrated in 1864 with much optimism in spite of the war. Plans were laid for raising $100,000 as a special fund with which to reinforce the missions in Burma, Assam, and South India. The receipts in 1864–65 exceeded $197,000, allowing a surplus of more than $21,000—a rare occurrence in the experience of the Union. Accordingly, interest was revived in re-establishing support of the mission in Africa, which had been cut off since 1856. The interest persisted in spite of the refusal of the Executive Committee to reopen its work in the Liberian Mission where many missionaries had succumbed to the climate and disease. Actually a permanent work was not achieved in Africa until 1884, when the Belgian Congo was accepted by the Union as a new field of operation. (See Chapter XVII.)

Decisions Concerning Retrenchment

The story of these two decades cannot be closed without mention of another major problem faced by the Missionary Union in this formative period. It concerned the ever-pressing question of whether to maintain missions of slight success in favor of those which gave more evidence of growth. A dramatic example occurred at the Convention in 1853 when the Union actually considered closing the Nellore station in South India. The delegates were dissuaded by Dr. Edward Bright, the home secretary, who pointed to a large map which hung

[15] *The Missionary Magazine,* Vol. 43, No. 7 (July, 1863), p. 225.

above the platform, declaring "that he would never write the letter calling for the blotting out of the 'Lone-Star' on the map of India." That night, Reverend S. F. Smith, author of the anthem, "America," went to his room to pen the memorable poem, "The Lone Star." When it was read the next morning, the assembled delegates were moved by deep emotion, a fact which saved Nellore from abandonment.

Again in 1862 the Union considered closing the field, but were dissuaded this time by the passionate pleading of Dr. Lyman Jewett, who had just returned from Nellore, where he had served since 1848. Though in declining years and poor health, Jewett vowed that he would return to his beloved station. Once again the mission was saved, and the Union voted to send a young man with him—"to give him Christian burial" as someone facetiously remarked.[16] The wisdom of that decision is known to all who know the story of the Pentecostal revival which occurred in the years that followed, during the ministry of that young man, John E. Clough.

Another example of the problem is to be found in the disposition of the Union's work among the Indians in the United States. It will be recalled from a previous chapter that missions to various Indian tribes had been an integral part of the responsibility of the Triennial Convention virtually from its beginning. After the schism, the Missionary Union was still carrying on a ministry to the Ojibwas and Ottawas in Michigan, to the Tonawandas and Tuscaroras in New York, and to the Shawanos, Cherokees, and Delawares in the Indian Territory in the vicinity of Oklahoma and Arkansas. The mission to the Tuscaroras was transferred wholly to the New York Baptist State Convention in 1850.

There were many difficulties which prevented the Indian missions from gaining appreciably in strength. One was the frequent removal of tribes by government treaty. Another was the ever-present evil of intoxicating liquors and their debilitating effect upon the Indians. A third was the slavery issue which became divisive among the Cherokee Nation by 1860. Border-state newspapers exerted every effort to stir up opposition to the missionaries. John B. Jones, of the mission, was expelled from his post by a hostile Indian agent from Georgia. He took refuge in Illinois. Another missionary, Mr. Upham,

---

[16] Howard B. Grose and Fred P. Haggard, ed., *The Judson Centennial, 1814–1914* (Philadelphia, 1914), pp. 200-01.

eventually resigned his post because of opposition to his school and the constant personal danger connected with his work. Reverend Evan Jones, the father of the mission, was the last to leave, going to Kansas in 1861 until the time was more favorable to continue his work with the Cherokees.

It is significant that the Christian Cherokees were loyal to the United States. In fact, Baptist churches in the Cherokee Nation were regarded as centers of antislavery principles. When the Federal Army reached Cherokee country during the course of the war, the missionaries were able to resume their work, and reported a willingness of the Indians to hear the gospel.[17]

By the close of the war, the affairs of the Indian missions were so distracted, with buildings destroyed and personnel scattered, that the Missionary Union viewed with pessimism their future success. Moreover, a fourth factor was involved, namely the preoccupation of the Union with overseas work, which left to the Indian missions only a marginal concern.

It is not surprising, therefore, that the Executive Committee terminated its connection with American Indian Missions in 1866, and released to The American Baptist Home Mission Society all title to real and personal property in the states of Michigan and Kansas and in the Cherokee Nation. This action was the conclusion of at least twelve years of exploratory planning, for the first proposal had been made in May, 1854, to the Board of Managers of the Union by the Committee on Indian Missions. At the time of the transfer, only two active missions remained. These were among the Cherokees and the Shawanos and Delawares in the Indian Territory. For the Indian missions the transfer was fortunate. Under the auspices of the Home Mission Society, the work was given a place of importance which it had never enjoyed as a part of the foreign mission enterprise.

Broadening the Base of Representation

During the formative years after the schism in 1845, pressures were exerted from several sources in behalf of a change of the basis of representation for membership. Representation in 1814 had been based upon individual contributions of members from missionary

---

[17] *The Missionary Magazine,* Vol. 40, No. 7, (July, 1860), pp. 271-73; Vol. 41, No. 7 (July, 1861), pp. 272-73; Vol. 42, No. 7 (July, 1862), pp. 304-05; Vol. 43, No. 7 (July, 1863), pp. 288-90.

societies and other Baptist religious bodies. The amount to be contributed was to be not less than one hundred dollars annually. There were several reasons for this policy. According to the severe Calvinistic conception of the church as an ecclesiastical institution, the church had no function to engage in missionary operations to the heathen. It was also believed that a Baptist church had no right to delegate its powers to an outside organization of any sort. Thus, the only way by which missionary-minded people could circumvent this impasse was "to organize outside the church little missionary societies." It was from these individualistic and spontaneously organized societies in states along the seaboard that the Triennial Convention was formed. In the words of a later home secretary for the Union:

> This was the only form of representation that then was practicable, and yet would preserve the moral aims of the movement. It was a case in which the spirit, latent in a remnant of our churches, far transcended the letter of their formal constitution as viewed by the great mass of Baptist churches of the time. It was the expression of the church within the church.[18]

In 1820 the second stage occurred when an amendment was adopted which allowed constituent bodies the right to send an additional delegate for every two hundred dollars contributed beyond the first hundred. This was to extend the privileges of membership to a greater number of people. Moreover, it made possible a widening of missionary sentiment, which resulted in the opening of individual churches and associational gatherings to appeals and collections for the cause that had been hitherto closed.

The third stage came in 1845, following the schism, when the American Baptist Missionary Union was formed under a new constitution. A new policy, adopted at that time, confined membership to life members only. Accordingly, former members of the old Triennial Convention who were present at the first meeting of the Missionary Union became constituent members. Other persons could become life members by paying the sum of one hundred dollars at one time. The new pattern did not meet with complete approval,

---

[18] Henry C. Mabie, *The Basis of Representation in the Missionary Union: A Historical Survey*. 12 pages. The author is indebted to Dr. Mabie's fine analysis for much of the material in this section.

as is indicated by the fact that the very next year, the Reverend Alfred Bennett, of New York State, introduced a resolution which aroused much debate for the following three years. It raised the issue whether a church could become a member of the Union by making a contribution of one hundred dollars. Bennett's proposal was to introduce the "representative principle," by which churches would be represented in proportion to their membership.

Bennett's move was resisted by those who feared the legislative authority that would go along with representation. Some argued that the principle would violate the New Testament concept of the autonomy of the local church. In reality, they feared that the representative principle would bring into visible and organic form a Baptist congress with legislative powers for all phases of church life. The Union, they insisted, was only intended to be an agency for mission work. If the Union were to be composed of "representatives" of the churches, they foresaw a possible sabotage of the missionary cause inasmuch as the task was not popular with many church members. In 1849 it was finally decided by a narrow margin of vote to allow the constitution to stand unchanged. The reason was that the majority of members of the Union were fearful of broadening the base of representation to allow voting privileges to persons or groups who were not actual contributors to the missionary task.[19]

The fourth stage was an historic compromise when, in 1854, those who had supported the traditional basis of membership agreed that each church which contributed to the Union might send one annual delegate to the Union. With slight variations, this remained the policy of the Union for the rest of the century. Thus there were four classes of membership possible: that of missionaries in service with the Union, Life Membership, Honorary Life Membership, and Annual Membership. It should be noted that when the privilege of representation of churches was granted, it was conceded only to those churches which demonstrated their rapport with the purposes of the Union by their contributions to its work.[20] The action of 1854 was a compromise in that the individualistic principle on which the Union

---

[19] *Ibid.*, pp. 6-7; *The Baptist Missionary Magazine,* Vol. 27, No. 7 (July, 1847), p. 209; Vol. 28, No. 7 (July, 1848), pp. 196-97; Vol. 28, No. 9 (Sept., 1848), pp. 367-84; Vol. 29, No. 7 (July, 1849), pp. 204-06.

[20] Mabie, *op. cit.*, p. 8; *The Baptist Missionary Magazine,* Vol. 34, No. 7 (July, 1854), p. 217.

had been organized had not been set aside, while a limited number of representatives of the churches were admitted to membership in the organization. Once again the Missionary Union had solved a problem involved in its growth in this period of trial and error.

CHAPTER IX

Developments at Home: A Period of Progress, 1866–1893

THE YEAR 1866 provides a suitable dividing point between the first two decades of the American Baptist Missionary Union's separate existence that followed the secession of Southern Baptists in 1845 and the half century that was to round out one hundred years of missionary endeavor. It marked the beginning of a Reconstruction Era in American politics. The Civil War was over, and a wounded nation had set about to recover by peaceful means the unity for which the conflict had been waged. On the international scene, the Western World entered upon a period of comparative peace, although warfare was at no time completely absent as nations maneuvered for advantage in the continuing struggle for the balance of power. It was a time of industrial expansion and growing prosperity in English-speaking countries. The extension of British rule in particular and of western imperialism in general opened new doors of opportunity for mission boards. A boundless optimism took hold of Christian leaders which was compounded of faith in the eternal destiny of the church to be victorious over evil and of a reliance upon the ingenuity of western civilization to find new means by which to extend the blessings of Christianity to all parts of the world.

Within the American Baptist Missionary Union, the year 1866 brought to leadership a man whose missionary statesmanship combined with favorable world conditions to usher in an era of progress hitherto unknown in Baptist missionary history. He was Dr. John

Nelson Murdock, a native of New York State. As a young man he had engaged in the practice of law. His religious training had been received among the Methodists by whom he eventually had been licensed to preach. It was not until 1843, at the age of twenty-three, that he became a Baptist and was ordained to the Baptist ministry at Waterville, New York. Pastoral changes took him in 1858 to the Bowdoin Square Baptist Church in Boston. His services on the Executive Committee of the Missionary Union were enlisted almost at once. It is not surprising, therefore, that he was called eventually from his Boston pastorate to become assistant secretary of the Union in 1863 and then secretary three years later. Although he resigned in 1891 and was made Honorary Secretary, he continued to carry responsibility for the Union's leadership for another two years. He remained Honorary Secretary until his death in 1897. In the nearly thirty years of active leadership as an executive officer of the Union, the extent of Dr. Murdock's influence justifies our reference to the period as the "Murdock era."

Postwar Trends

Changes which had been occurring in American life for many years were accelerated by the Civil War. In 1867, for example, the *Colorado,* first of a new line of steamships to China by way of California, completed her maiden voyage as quickly as did ships of the old English line. Dr. William Dean, veteran missionary to Siam, wrote in the same year that the passage from the United States to Bangkok could be made in half the time that it had required thirty years earlier. He marvelled that communications could be received from Boston in less than three months whereas it had once required three years. Telegraphic messages of news events in the United States were read in Bangkok a month after they had occurred.[1] This acceleration of the means of travel and communication was destined to facilitate a closer supervision of the work on mission fields. Certainly it was to lighten the sense of isolation which bore so heavily upon missionaries.

Under the energetic direction of Dr. Murdock, new stations were opened, old stations were strengthened, and schools were reinforced. In 1868 alone, the Executive Committee spent about $225,000. The rapidly enlarging program resulted in a mounting indebtedness. Yet, the mood of optimism prevailed. It was typified by Dr. M. B. Ander-

[1] *The Missionary Magazine,* Vol. 47, No. 11 (Nov., 1867), pp. 427-31.

son, president of the Missionary Union, whose annual address in Chicago in May, 1871, stressed his confidence that missions were in a favorable state of transition. He pointed out that opposition to the gospel was disappearing in non-Christian lands. He saw an opportunity to give to the nations of the East the Christian civilization which had been developed in America. To this end, colleges and seminaries were needed on mission fields. The Board responded to the president's challenge by approving a plan for the Rangoon Baptist College, which was established the next year for youth of all races in Burma.[2]

This attitude was noticeably different from that which so clearly had prevailed in the 1850's. Then, only a minority of the missionaries foresaw the need for providing higher education for qualified converts. It is likely that the change in missionary outlook was the product of a number of factors. The growing number of Christians on the foreign fields undoubtedly forced the problem into plainer view for the supporters of the cause at home. Then, too, there was the growing desire of nationals for education which would equip them for government service and for professional leadership in their country. Episcopalian and Roman Catholic schools openly made provision for meeting this need, thereby creating serious competition for Baptist missionaries who were anxious not to lose their converts. It is also possible that American Baptists to a larger extent were themselves becoming more appreciative of higher education.

In a very real sense, the Union's missions were in a transitional stage. Statistics for 1874 indicate that 22 of the 132 missionaries at work in the several Asiatic missions were unmarried women. This was a departure from earlier policy which had refused full missionary status to single women. Connected with these Asiatic missions were more than 500 native preachers and assistants who served 400 churches which had a combined membership of about 25,000. Obviously, a national leadership was being developed with considerable success. The effectiveness of the work being done is reflected in the fact that there were 2,311 baptisms during the year.[3]

The coming of Dr. Murdock to the Union was followed soon after by the passing of three notable leaders—Nehemiah Boynton, the Honorable Heman Lincoln, and Dr. Baron Stow. In a way they were

[2] *Ibid.,* Vol. 51, No. 7 (July, 1871), pp. 194-95, 198-200
[3] *Ibid.,* Vol. 54, No. 10 (Oct., 1874), pp. 345-46.

typical of the devoted leadership of laymen and ministers respectively who served on the Board of Managers.

Boynton was a New Englander, born in Gloucester, Massachusetts, in 1804. The early years of his mature life were spent in business in Maine. In 1845 he moved to Boston, where he remained for the rest of his life. Between 1859 and 1865 he held public offices in the State Senate and as a member of the Governor's Executive Council for Suffolk County. It is not surprising that a man of his gifts was made chairman of the Finance Committee for the Missionary Union in 1853, and treasurer two years later. For nine years he carried the heavy burden of debt that rested upon the Union, and did not retire until the indebtedness was paid off and the Union had achieved a firmer financial basis. He died in Boston on November 22, 1868.

Heman Lincoln sustained a continuous official connection with the Missionary Union of almost forty-five years. Indeed, he had been one of the earliest friends and supporters of Baptist missions. Elected treasurer of the Union in 1824, he held the office for nearly twenty-two years without monetary compensation. Upon his retirement from the treasurer's office, he was chosen a member of the Executive Committee, a position that he held for twenty-three consecutive years. He was always a generous donor to the Union's work. He died in Boston on August 11, 1869, in his ninety-first year.

Just four months later, Lincoln's pastor and close friend, Dr. Baron Stow, died in the same city at sixty-nine years of age. For about forty-four years he had been related intimately to the cause of foreign missions, and for the last thirty-seven years he had served as a member of the Acting Board of the Executive Committee. He combined in his leadership elements which were at once conservative and progressive. He was invaluable as reconciler of conflicting ideas in the committee room. Indeed, he was largely influential in shaping the organic structure and practical relations of the Missionary Union. When Heman Lincoln's failing health forced him to retire from the chairmanship of the Executive Commitee, it was Dr. Stow who was selected in his place. He served in that capacity until his death.[4]

A further development in this period was the organization of Baptist women into two auxiliary agencies for the support of foreign missions. The story is so important that it will be told in detail in

---

[4] For the foregoing biographical sketches, see *ibid.,* Vol. 49, No. 1 (Jan., 1869), pp. 29-31; Vol. 50, No. 7 (July, 1870), pp. 208-10.

the next chapter. Suffice it to say here that in 1871 the women of the East met at Newton Centre, Massachusetts, to establish the Woman's Baptist Foreign Missionary Society; and just a short time later, the women of the West met in Chicago to organize the Woman's Baptist Foreign Missionary Society of the West. It was the beginning of a significant united effort of women in behalf of the work of the Union. By 1914, they had raised more than $4,000,000. On mission fields, they were represented by a corps of single women who gave devoted and able leadership in education, evangelism, and medical missions. At home, they were instrumental in developing a program of missionary education for children and youth which has paid rich dividends in continuing support of missionary work to the present time.

The contribution of women to missions antedated their period of national organization. However, the war years from 1860 to 1865 had afforded a large opportunity for women to take leadership through the work of the Sanitary Commission and the work of the Christian Commission which nobly served the war effort. The impetus thus provided gathered momentum in the years following the war, and the growing insistence of Baptist women that they have a more direct part in the missionary program of the denomination reflects the trend toward the wider participation of women in all affairs of life.

The year 1872 holds more than passing interest for several reasons. It marks the opening of a new field of responsibility for the Missionary Union. The Board of Managers accepted on May 21 the Japan Mission of the American Baptist Free Mission Society. It was another step toward reconciliation between those missionaries who had left the Union in earlier years over the slavery issue and differences regarding field administration. Dr. Nathan Brown, who had been serving with the Free Mission Society in Japan, was welcomed back to co-operation with the Union. At the same meeting, it was voted to transfer the Chinese Mission in Siam to China proper, although missionaries continued to work in Siam until 1909. While not related to this expansion program, another matter of importance came before the meeting. It was a proposal to alter the Union's constitution so as to place the Union fully upon a plan of church representation. This was a revival of earlier efforts to effect the same change. The next year, the Union rejected the proposal, but did agree to hold mass meetings in all states from which delegates to the Union were sent, so that the churches might receive firsthand reports from members of the Union.[5]

Closely associated with the trend toward expansion of the Union's work on the mission fields was the ever-present problem of debt. By 1875, the annual expenditures had mounted to nearly $242,000. The accumulated indebtedness totalled close to $53,000. Measures of economy were taken, such as cutting the budget for 1876 by $30,000. The Board of Managers adopted a resolution urging the Executive Committee to dispense with collecting agencies, undoubtedly to cut down on overhead expense. It was hoped that the churches and pastors would respond sufficiently to their responsibility of raising funds. The actual fact, however, was that the rank and file of Baptist church members were not supporting missions. A comparison of statistics for 1875 indicates that Baptists were by far the smallest contributors to the work of foreign missions of the four oldest and largest societies in the country in proportion to their total church membership. Fortunately, the operations of the collecting agents were not abandoned, but only cut about twenty per cent. But unfortunately for the efficient management of the Union, in 1876 the offices of foreign secretary and home secretary were for a time combined.[6]

When delegates arrived for the annual meeting on May 22, 1877, in the historic First Baptist Church, Providence, Rhode Island, the financial picture was not bright. By careful economizing, the debt had been reduced to $47,000. But the needs remained most pressing. Dr. Murdock presented the matter squarely before the delegates. He placed the responsibility for retrenchment or advance upon the ministers and churches. He urged seminaries to train students to be missionary-minded, and churches to include this quality among others when calling a pastor. It was difficult to see why 8,000 Baptist churches in the North, with approximately 660,000 members, should not be able to raise the funds necessary for so great a cause.

The next morning, a remarkable enthusiasm took hold of the delegates. By subscriptions and gifts of watches, diamond rings, and even

[5] *The Baptist Missionary Magazine,* Vol. 52, No. 7 (July, 1872), pp. iii, viii of Annual Report; Vol. 53, No. 7 (July, 1873), pp. 198, 203-04, 218-19.

[6] *Ibid.,* Vol. 55, No. 7 (July, 1875), pp. 206, 210, 293; Vol. 56, No. 4 (April, 1876), pp. 102-03; Vol. 56, No. 7 (July, 1876), pp. 207, 215.

a fifty-cent piece from a poor woman, the sum of $30,000 was raised before adjournment for the noon meal. In the afternoon the scene was reproduced, until all but $11,000 of the deficit had been pledged. Of that amount, one individual promised to contribute $5,000 if the whole debt were cancelled.[7] The debt was soon liquidated, and the Union was free once again to enter upon a program of expansion, which in turn led characteristically to further indebtedness. There were few years, indeed, when the Union was free from the burden of debt.

Problems of Missionary Policy

The policy of strengthening the educational phase of the missions abroad, which had been commended in 1871, had resulted in increased expenditures for boarding schools for girls in Burma, for two colleges (at Rangoon, Burma, and at Ongole, India), and for a theological school at Ramapatnam, India. In 1878 a special committee reported to the Executive Committee that the principles on which the missions were operated should be reviewed in the light of these developments. This report indicated a fresh recurrence of the fear that schools might usurp the primacy of evangelism in the work of the Union. While the committee admitted that higher education should be provided to train Christian leaders, it regarded the establishment of the Baptist colleges at Rangoon and Ongole as premature, and warned that there was the danger of founding too many boarding schools "where girls are accustomed to a better style of living than is common with people." [8]

During the same year, Dr. M. B. Anderson, former president of the Missionary Union, presented a resolution urging the Executive Committee to send to the Orient "intelligent Christian laymen, practically trained in commerce, farming, and the mechanic arts, who shall be charged with the duty of instructing native Christians in various branches of industry, with a view of making them better able to support their pastors and schools, and generally in becoming more efficient agents in economic production." [9] His far-sighted recommendation was adopted. It revealed the dual concern that was present during those years in the leadership of the Union: to retain the

---

[7] *The Baptist Missionary Magazine,* Vol. 57, No. 7 (July, 1877), pp. 163-77.

[8] American Baptist Missionary Union, Records of the Executive Committee, Vol. H, pp. 157-62.

[9] *The Baptist Missionary Magazine,* Vol. 58, No. 7 (July, 1878), p. 198.

primacy of evangelism while at the same time educating the new Christians to become self-supporting and constructive leaders in their own communities. There does not seem to have been strong disposition to choose between the two concerns; instead, there was an urgent desire to maintain the proper relationship between the two.

Indicative of the trend to give more consideration to what might be called the auxiliary or subordinate phases of missionary work is the fact that in November, 1878, the first medical missionary was appointed by the Woman's Foreign Missionary Society of the West. She was Dr. Caroline H. Daniels, of Kalamazoo, Michigan. Her appointment was to China in response to a call from Swatow. Because the American Baptist Missionary Union was not yet ready to endorse this specialized type of missionary, she was obliged to "consider herself as appointed by the Union for evangelistic work as others had been, but that there would be no objection to her using in her work any medical knowledge which she might possess." By an appeal to Michigan Baptists, she initiated a "hospital fund," which made possible the erection of two buildings at Swatow in 1882. In 1884 illness forced her to return to America. For five years the hospital was closed, until it was reopened by Dr. Anna K. Scott, who had served for twelve years in Assam with her husband and then, following his death, had taken up the study of medicine in order to be of further service. Once again, the Baptist women were taking the lead in medical missions.

By the close of the century, the position of medical missions in the work of the Union had become sufficiently advanced so that 29 physicians were laboring under its direction, with 12 hospitals and many dispensaries. The only mission field in which American Baptists had no medical work was Japan, where the progressive program of the government seemed to make medical work by outsiders unnecessary. Yet, it was only a step in the right direction, for in 1902, out of a total of 480 missionaries of the Union (including those appointed by the Women's Societies), only 27 were doctors (18 men and 9 women). Even more revealing of the Union's slow progress in changing its basic point of view was the fact that these physicians were obliged to go out first and foremost as preachers and secondarily as medical personnel.[10]

---

[10] *Ibid.*, Vol. 78, No. 5 (May, 1898), pp. 164-75; Vol. 82, No. 3 (March, 1902), p. 94.

Industrial work in missions had been gaining popularity throughout the nineteenth century. Many of the schools provided opportunity for boys and girls to learn trades which would enable them to earn a living. By the end of the 1890's there was a more inclusive conception of the importance of this phase of mission work. In South India, the need was particularly great, for wages were only one-third what they were in Burma. Nearly all of the converts to Christianity in the Telugu Mission were from the poorest classes, farm laborers or coolies who were barely able to earn a subsistence. Dr. John E. Clough had this in mind when he sought to establish at Ongole an industrial mission school where young Christians could be trained to be shoemakers, carpenters, tailors, blacksmiths, brickmakers, masons, or goldsmiths. At Kurnool, girls were taught needlework. At Allur, boys were trained in agriculture. Because Africa presented the same need as South India, industrial mission work was the rule for all schools. In China and Japan, however, where people were well trained in industrial pursuits, the same need was not felt. It was important, though, to teach converts to earn their own way in society. The industrial phase of mission work was justified as a means of helping Christians to make a living. It was never intended as a means of making people Christians.[11]

Dawn of a New Missionary Epoch

Events were conspiring to make for great optimism in the Missionary Union by 1879. In Burma there were eleven Baptist mission stations, seven of which had been opened since the Missionary Convention of 1853 at Moulmein. There were great advances in the development of indigenous churches, especially among the Karen Christians. In Assam, where progress had been slow, Baptists were on the threshold of success among the animistic peoples of the Garo Hills and among the immigrants who had entered the country to work in the tea gardens. The most dramatic occurrence of mass conversions had taken place in 1878 at Ongole, India, where 2,222 persons were baptized in a single day. By 1879 the total number of converts had reached 10,500.[12]

Dr. Murdock saw a "new missionary epoch" dawning. Before the

[11] *Ibid.*, Vol. 79, No. 8 (Aug., 1899), pp. 424-32.

[12] American Baptist Missionary Union, *Annual Reports* for 1879, pp. vii, xv-xvi.

annual meeting of the Union in Saratoga, New York, in 1879, he outlined the great changes which were taking place in world affairs that were opening the "heathen world" to the Christian faith—first Japan, then Siam, China, Burma, the islands of the sea, and at last Africa. Then he went on to say: "The great centre of Mohammedanism in Asia has just passed under the protectorate of England." In Europe he saw the revolutions in Austria and Italy as omens of good for Protestant missions at a time when political power was being wrested from the Roman Catholic Church. His mood reflected the optimism that was prevalent in all of the reports of the various field committees.[13]

At the next annual meeting, this great secretary outlined the "signs of promise" in American Baptist missions: (1) the great ingathering in South India; (2) the rapid strides towards self-support especially in Burma; (3) the great potential of the native ministry which missionaries need to develop more freely; (4) the large annual additions to the mission churches and the increasing efficiency of the educational institutions; (5) the expansion of the Japan Mission; and (6) the hopeful outlook of the work in Spain, and the great revivals in Sweden where 3,200 accessions by baptisms were received in 1879 alone.[14]

The progress enjoyed by Baptists was matched by other Protestant missions. In 1881 it was pointed out that there were more than 70 Protestant missionary societies enrolling nearly 2,500 ordained missionaries, not including thousands of native teachers, preachers, and helpers. This was in sharp contrast to the situation 80 years before, when there were only seven societies with a total of 170 missionaries. In the same period of time, the number of converts to Christianity on foreign fields increased from approximately 50,000 to 1,650,000. The amount of money contributed to foreign missions did not exceed $250,000 in 1800; by 1880 the sum for the year was $6,250,000. Of this grand total $1,700,000 came from American churches. In 1800 the schools of the missionary societies numbered only 70; in 1880 there were 12,000 schools giving instruction to nearly a half million pupils. Against the 50 translations of the Bible in 1800, the Scriptures, in whole or in part, were published 80 years later in

---

[13] *The Baptist Missionary Magazine,* Vol. 59, No. 7 (July, 1879), pp. 169-73, 176-87.

[14] *Ibid.,* Vol. 60, No. 7 (July, 1880), pp. 170-76.

226 languages and dialects.[15] Truly it was a century of Christian missions, and the momentum gained in the early years from pioneers like William Carey, Adoniram and Ann Judson, Robert Morrison, and James Moffatt, to mention only a few, was carried on by a host of equally devoted men and women at home and abroad.

Problems of Administration

Quite naturally, the expanding responsibilities borne by the American Baptist Missionary Union raised new problems of administration. In 1882 the Board of Managers voted to meet a full day prior to the annual meetings of the Union in order to receive reports and recommendations from the Executive Committee. This action was designed to recover for the Board members, who were scattered across the country, a closer supervision of policy making. Some of their prerogatives had been lost by a constitutional revision of 1859 which made the Executive Committee directly responsible to the Union.[16]

The office of treasurer was one of increasing responsibility in this period. Fortunately for the Union, there had been a succession of dedicated business men who occupied this position for long periods of time. Since the retirement of Nehemiah Boynton in 1864, Freeman A. Smith, who had been his assistant, served as treasurer of the Union until failing health forced his resignation on November 1, 1882.

Smith's retirement was darkened for a brief time by charges and insinuations that the Board of Managers had dealt unfairly with missionaries in financial matters and that he in particular had benefitted personally. The specific objection was that the savings made by the Union through the benefit of favorable rates of international currency exchange when salaries in Burma were paid in the currency of that country were not passed on to the missionaries. It was alleged that $50,000 had been "pocketed" in this way between 1874 and 1879. As usually happens in such cases, unwarranted statements were issued to the press and complaints were made anonymously which resulted in unfavorable publicity. To make bad matters worse, the man who was supposed to have made the initial complaint was the Reverend A. T. Rose, one of the missionaries who had severed connections with the society during the controversy that followed the

---

15 *Ibid.*, Vol. 61, No. 7 (July, 1881), p. 181.

16 *The Baptist Missionary Magazine,* Vol. 62, No. 7 (July, 1882), pp. 193-96.

missionary conference of 1853 at Moulmein. Later, as it will be recalled, he returned to the service of the Union. Rose vigorously denied the charge. An audit of the treasurer's books cleared Freeman Smith of the unpleasant charges made against his management of the finances of the Union. The Board of Managers hastened to explain that savings in payment of salaries that resulted from a favorable rate of exchange were accumulated for distribution to the missionaries during periods when the rate was unfavorable to American currency.

While the rumors were proved to be false, there were serious expressions of dissatisfaction made by some of the missionaries concerning their relationship to the Union. To allay such unrest and possibly to avoid the recurrence of resignations, the Union adopted a resolution in 1884 which was intended to assure its missionaries that they were "trusted fellow-workers" and "equal partners" whose counsel on missionary policy was welcomed. As further evidence of good faith, the members of the Union voted to admit to full membership in the society all missionaries during their term of office on the field or while on furlough.[17]

In the same year, the Missionary Union took a major step of faith, when they accepted the Livingstone Inland Mission in the Belgian Congo from H. Grattan Guiness, a wealthy English benefactor of foreign missions. It was a courageous act because the Union was burdened by an indebtedness of nearly $50,000. Undaunted but realistic about the situation, the Union adopted a series of resolutions at the annual meeting in 1885 which directed the Executive Committee to take several courses of action: (1) The officers of the Union were authorized to enter into joint action with the American Baptist Home Mission Society and the American Baptist Publication Society in an effort to raise together their combined indebtedness. (2) The Executive Committee was urged to limit new appropriations to the amount which it felt might reasonably be raised. (3) Retrenchment was to be made in the area of educational work on the fields rather than in the evangelistic program.

It is indicative of the caution with which the Union viewed any tampering with the women's societies that a fourth resolution was

---

[17] *Ibid.*, Vol. 62, No. 12 (Dec., 1882), p. 410; Vol. 63, No. 7 (July, 1883), p. 194; Vol. 63, No. 10 (Oct., 1883), pp. 363-70; Vol. 64, No. 7 (July, 1884), pp. 172-73, 193-94.

not adopted. It called upon the Woman's Foreign Mission Societies to give more of their funds to evangelistic work than to the educational projects which they were currently supporting. This plea was reinforced by the Committee on Burma, whose report explained that most of the $294,600 which had been expended on education over the past ten years had been so designated by the Woman's Societies.[18]

It was a trying time for the Union, but once again the debt was liquidated, as in 1877, with the same outpouring of sacrifice and devotion to a great cause. Dr. Murdock called it "the healthy process of the unforced action of the churches." Several devices had been used. Dr. Edward Judson, president of the Union and son of the renowned pioneer of American Baptist missions, had made a successful appeal to the Sunday schools across the country. Dr. M. H. Bixby, home on furlough, aroused great enthusiasm for carrying the gospel into Upper Burma, which had just come under British rule. Appropriations had been cut by nearly $59,000. These factors, together with a growing interest in the Congo Mission, combined to sweep away the financial obstacles. Within a week the debt of nearly $50,000 was raised and a balance of $3,000 was in hand. Again the way was open for the advance demanded by the pressing new needs of a changing world.[19]

As the era of Dr. Murdock's leadership drew to a close, the Missionary Union was better organized and functioned more smoothly than ever before. It was composed of three distinct bodies: the Union itself, the Board of Managers which included seventy-five members selected from all areas of the country plus the general officers of the Union and the presidents of the Woman's Societies (*ex officio*) and three members of the Executive Committee, and the administrative nucleus known as the Executive Committee. The Union met annually in the May meetings at the same time and in the same place as the other national agencies held their sessions. The Executive Committee met regularly throughout the year. Its membership had been increased from nine to fifteen in 1895. Headquarters of the Union had been located for many years in the Tremont Temple, Boston, until the fire in March, 1893, when they were removed temporarily to 2A Beacon Street. In 1896 they returned to the new and fireproof Tremont Temple.

---

[18] *Ibid.,* Vol. 65, No. 7 (July, 1885), pp. 177-80, 187.
[19] *Ibid.,* Vol. 66, No. 7 (July, 1886), pp. 177, 191.

Contact with the churches was maintained by various means. Ten district secretaries worked under the direction of the home secretary, visiting the churches frequently to bring information and pleas for support to the people. They arranged for occasional mass meetings at which time missionaries home on furlough would be heard. The Woman's Societies had their own rather elaborate plan of organization in the churches whereby children and youth as well as women were reached with the missionary message.

The chief printed channel of missionary information was *The Baptist Missionary Magazine,* which had been established in 1803 under the title, *Massachusetts Baptist Missionary Magazine.* In 1817 it became *The American Baptist Magazine and Missionary Intelligencer.* The title was shortened in 1824 to *The Baptist Missionary Magazine.* Until 1835 it was the organ of both home and foreign missions, but in 1836 it became strictly a publication for foreign missions. For most of its history, the magazine was edited by the corresponding secretaries of the society, including Dr. Lucius Bolles, Dr. Edward Bright, and Dr. John Murdock. In 1893 the office of editorial secretary was created and occupied with great efficiency by Dr. Edmund F. Merriam and later by Dr. Fred P. Haggard. In 1897 the magazine was enlarged and became the first missionary periodical in America to employ the make-up and liberal use of photographs characteristic of secular periodicals. After 1910 the magazine was to be known as *Missions.*

There were other publications which carried missionary information into Baptist homes. One was *The Macedonian and Record,* which was supported in the 1870's jointly by the Missionary Union, the American Baptist Publication Society, and the American Baptist Home Mission Society. It carried a variety of articles drawn from the work of the three societies. In 1877, *The Macedonian and Helping Hand,* as it was then called, was transferred to the Woman's Societies for publication. They gave it the simplified title of *The Helping Hand.* In the 1890's a little illustrated four-page paper called *The Kingdom* was also published by the Union.[20]

---

[20] For an historical sketch of *The Baptist Missionary Magazine* from 1803 to 1903, see Vol. 83, No. 12 (Dec., 1903), pp. 747-49. See also Vol. 51, No. 7 (July, 1871), pp. 211-12 and Vol. 57, No. 7 (July, 1877), p. 182. For description of the organization of the Union, see Edmund F. Merriam, *The American Baptist Missionary Union and Its Missions* (Boston, 1897), pp. 22-26.

As the Union grew, the provisions of previous acts of incorporation no longer covered current necessities of property holding. Therefore, in 1894, a full act of incorporation was obtained from the Legislature of New York. In the same year the Massachusetts Legislature passed an act permitting the Union to receive by gift, purchase, or devise, and to hold in fee simple, real estate not exceeding the value of $1,000,000, and personal property to an amount not exceeding $2,000,000.

In the 1890's the Missionary Union was also taking note of the wide expanse of its home territory. In 1888 the annual meetings were held in Minneapolis, Minnesota. It was the first time that the Union had met away from the Eastern seaboard. The increasing awareness of the importance of the constituency in the West was manifested in a resolution adopted by the Board of Managers in May, 1890, which urged that no pains be spared "to maintain a sympathetic connection between the churches of our denomination in the West and the Missionary Rooms in Boston." In 1893 the annual meetings were held in Denver, Colorado, with a large delegation of Baptists from the Western states and from the Pacific coast.[21]

Missionary salaries came under review in 1890 for the first time since 1859. The cash pay for the first three years of service was to be reduced from $1,000 annually to $800 for married men and $600 for single men. But in addition, all expenses of the missionaries and their families were to be paid by the Union except house rent. Expenses had not been cared for adequately by previous policy. The reason for reducing the cash pay in the first three years was due to the fact that many missionaries dropped out during this crucial period. The initial investment of funds for a missionary's equipment and for travel to his station became almost a total loss if the missionary decided to return home. During the next seven years of service, married men were to receive $1,000 and single men $800 annually. During the next period of ten years, married men were to receive $1,500 and single men $1,200. The salary of "female assistants" was to include medical attendance and travel, and was to be $500. Certainly no one could accuse missionaries of choosing their vocation for monetary reasons!

---

[21] *The Baptist Missionary Magazine,* Vol. 69, No. 7 (July, 1889), p. 212; Vol. 70, No. 7 (July, 1890), p. 215; Vol. 73, No. 8 (Aug., 1893), p. 383.

Widening Horizons

The effect of change was felt on the field as well as at home. Far-sighted missionaries were reshaping their approach to the task of evangelizing non-Christian peoples. Dr. William Ashmore, of the South China Mission, who served briefly as a secretary of the Union in the late 1880's, pointed out in 1887 that there were missionary methods which had to give way to a more effective approach. He noted the earlier practice of missionaries to give American names to the children of nationals, the purpose being chiefly to flatter contributors who were led to sponsor the youngsters. He also called attention to the former policy of relying almost entirely on the press to do the work of the preacher. Now, he observed, most missionaries rely more upon preaching and make a small charge for New Testaments which they distribute. He lamented the custom of sending converts to America to be educated for the ministry. In his quaint way, he pointed out that the results were disappointing because the lad became too broad for his "old fashioned stool." His keen insight was reflected in the statement that: "It is better and more enduring workmanship to draw theological ideas fresh and first-hand from the Scriptures, and to let a theological system grow up with the growth of the young church." His basic caution was against proclaiming a combination of Christianity and Western civilization.[22]

Indicative also of the enlarging conception of the world mission of the church was the London Missionary Conference of June, 1888. It was a forerunner of the ecumenical movement which has been associated so intimately with missions. Dr. Murdock represented the Missionary Union. He was impressed by the variety of topics which came under serious consideration by the fifteen hundred delegates present. They included the relationship of schools to evangelizing agencies, the place and value of medical missions, conditions and degrees of training for the "native" ministry, methods of dealing with the various ethnic religions, the treatment which should be accorded new converts who are confused by conflicting practices in their own culture, such as the practice of polygamy, methods of developing indigenous churches, and the work of the press in the distribution of the Scriptures and tracts. Dr. Murdock's impressions were not all

---

[22] *Ibid.*, Vol. 67, No. 12 (Dec., 1887), pp. 453-56; Vol. 68, No. 1 (Jan., 1888), p. 12.

favorable. He resented the absence of a fair proportion of Americans on the program.[23]

Closely related to the enthusiasm which surrounded great missionary conferences such as the one in London was the Student Volunteer Movement, which was organized in 1886. The infectious missionary spirit which was aroused on college campuses throughout the country, was felt in every denomination. The American Baptist Missionary Union was no longer faced with a problem of securing missionary recruits. Young men and women were knocking at the doors, ready and eager to be sent forth. It is to the credit of the Union that it responded to their challenge. In 1890 the Union appointed and sent abroad forty-two new missionaries with eighteen older missionaries who were returning to their fields. This was done in spite of a decline in the value of American exchange in Asia, owing to passage of the Silver Bill in the United States and its effect on India. This changed situation added nearly $120,000 to the expenditures of the Union. In 1892 the Union sent out eighty-one missionaries, the largest number ever before sent abroad in a single year. Of this number, fifty-two were going out for the first time. The majority were destined for stations in Burma, India, and the Congo. Others were assigned to Assam, China, and Japan.

It was a glorious climax to the era of Dr. Murdock's leadership. He was obliged to resign in 1891 because of failing health. For the next two years he was urged to continue service in the absence of a successor. Then, in May, 1892, Dr. Henry C. Mabie, who had been elected home secretary in 1890, received two new associates in the appointment of Dr. S. W. Duncan as foreign secretary for Burma, Assam, Siam, China, Japan, and Europe, and Dr. Edmund F. Merriam as foreign secretary for India and Africa, with additional responsibilities for legacies and the editorship of *The Baptist Missionary Magazine.*

During the term of Dr. Murdock's official duties as corresponding secretary, the number of missionaries had been increased from 84 in 1863 to 378 in 1891; the income had increased from $92,606.66 to $472,174.21 in addition to permanent funds which amounted to nearly $27,000. The Telugu mission had become a huge success; Sweden had become a new field in 1865, with remarkable ingather-

---

[23] *Ibid.*, Vol. 68, No. 9 (Sept., 1888), pp. 356-58.

ings of converts; Japan and the Belgian Congo had been added to the Union's responsibilities in 1872 and 1884 respectively. In a burst of gratitude for his outstanding services, the Union elected Dr. Murdock honorary secretary for life in 1891.[24]

The year 1892 marked the centenary of the Carey movement which had launched the great Protestant foreign mission enterprise of the nineteenth century. For Baptists it was a notable year. Under the direction of Dr. Henry C. Mabie, the Union raised over a million dollars in a special memorial fund. The number of converts on all fields totalled for the year 18,549. The largest number (8,000) was in South India and the next largest (3,600) was in Sweden.[25] It was a fitting culmination to a significant period in the history of the American Baptist Missionary Union.

---

[24] *The Baptist Missionary Magazine,* Vol. 70, No. 11 (Nov., 1890), pp. 426-27; Vol. 72, No. 11 (Nov., 1892), p. 447; Vol. 71, No. 7 (July, 1891), pp. 210-11.

[25] *Ibid.,* Vol. 73, No. 7 (July, 1893), pp. 189-94; Vol. 72, No. 7 (July, 1892), pp. 208-09.

CHAPTER X

Developments at Home: An Era of Transition, 1893–1913

ALTHOUGH PROGRESS continued in American Baptist missions, it is not amiss to gather the events that occurred in the twenty years from 1893 under the caption, "an era of transition." For it was a time in which developments at home and abroad were undergoing major changes in response to forces which were at work that called for new procedures, new organizational patterns, and a fresh approach to the missionary task.

To summarize briefly, we may enumerate on the home scene the growing influence of women's work, the rise of the laymen's movement, the influence of an emerging ecumenical movement, the organization of the Northern Baptist Convention and the merger of American Free Baptists with that body, and the revision of the administrative structure of the American Baptist Missionary Union by which it was renamed in 1910 The American Baptist Foreign Mission Society.

On the international scene, events were unfolding which had a marked effect upon world missions. The Spanish-American War in 1898 resulted in the acquisition by the United States of Cuba and the Philippine Islands. Mission boards of major denominations lost no time in establishing work in the newly opened territories. The Missionary Union entered the Philippines almost at once. The revolution in China in 1911–1912, which overthrew the imperial power in favor of a republic, was hailed in English-speaking countries as a great victory for democracy and as a providential opportunity for Christian missions. The era of Western imperialism had brought material benefits to peoples of the East, but it also had aroused a restlessness which broke forth in many places in anti-Western riots. An emerging national consciousness in Eastern countries found expression among Christians in a growing desire for leadership in their church life. This trend hastened the movement towards a new relationship between organized missions and the so-called "younger churches."

The missionary movement in the United States reached its peak in the years from 1890 to 1921. During this time there was in the country a very strong enthusiasm both for evangelizing peoples of other lands and for social uplift and humanitarian reform at home. It was the era of Rooseveltian Progressivism. It was also a time when the Student Volunteer Movement had as its goal the "evangelization of the world in this generation." At the same time, hosts of women's missionary societies and the Laymen's Missionary Movement that arose in 1907 marshaled the support of church members across Protestantism in behalf of foreign missions.

The deepest religious motivation in these years stemmed from the spirit of Moody revivalism, which imbued converts with the conviction that they were vessels of the Holy Spirit to bring salvation and blessing to all mankind. This expressed itself in the missionary movement by a determined purpose to save the heathen from damnation. By 1900, however, this traditional sanction for missions was undergoing change. The contemporary currents of humanitarianism and democratic thought that exalted the dignity of man also led to a decline in the former emphasis upon man's sinfulness. In this connection it is revealing that the report of the World Missionary Conference, held at Edinburgh in 1910, made no mention of the fact that the heathen would suffer the torments of hell if unconverted. In all fairness, it should be said that this silence was probably due more to a deference to the growing public repugnance to the traditional concept than to a basic change of notion as to the ultimate destiny of the heathen. Nevertheless, the changing attitude of the public mind was a formative influence in the shaping of a new philosophy of missions.

The increasing concern in the United States with foreign markets, particularly in Asia, contributed to the growing favor with which many people viewed the missionary enterprise. In other words, many saw that missions might pave the way for more prosperous commercial relations, and so gave the cause their blessing.

The strong humanitarian feeling that was current in the latter years of the nineteenth century reflected itself in missions, especially with the publication in 1897 of James S. Dennis' two-volume work, *Christian Missions and Social Progress: A Sociological Study of Foreign Missions.* The author's assumption was that Christianity had been the supreme force in the social regeneration of the Western world, and could render the same service for the Eastern world. He wrote out of a missionary's experience in Syria, and his outlook was most optimistic. To be sure, he saw that the goal of social regeneration was to be reached, not by an all-out social reform program, such as the Social Gospel Movement called for at home, but by the conversion of individuals to Christianity. In 1912 the Reverend H. K. Wright, a missionary to China, began to espouse a completely social-reform type of program. It is notable that this changing viewpoint was linked especially to the missionary work in China. As Christians became increasingly enthusiastic about the transforming influence of the gospel in Chinese society, they developed quite naturally a strong interest in the future of China as a nation. When they saw the apparent triumph of democracy in the Revolution of 1911–1912, they became even more convinced of the concomitant benefits of Christianity and Western civilization.[1]

With this brief background, we may turn more specifically to the story of the American Baptist Missionary Union in this period of transition. Because the threads of major developments were interwoven during these years, it seems wise to separate them as far as is possible by topics, while maintaining the inner chronological order of events. We shall be concerned with the changing emphasis on educational missions, the trend towards more direct supervision of the fields, the emergence of denominational support of missions through organization of the Northern Baptist Convention, changes in organizational procedures and mission policy, and the centennial year of 1914.

---

[1] The foregoing interpretation of the shifting motivations for missions after 1890 is based largely upon the excellent analysis provided by Paul A. Varg, "Motives in Protestant Missions, 1890–1917," *Church History,* Vol. 23, No. 1 (March, 1954).

Changing Emphasis on Educational Missions

At the annual meeting in July, 1894, President Alvah Hovey of Newton Theological Institution in Massachusetts presented to the Board of Managers a significant report concerning higher education on mission fields. His figures revealed that there were more than 1,246 schools under the care of the Union. Of the 1,470 teachers responsible for them, only 105 were missionaries, while 1,350 were nationals. The total number of pupils was 18,000. The over-all cost of the educational work of the Union for the year 1893, including ocean-passage of missionary teachers, salaries, and buildings was more than $140,000, although the nationals bore a large portion of the expense involved in the support of elementary and boarding schools. Of the 57 station schools maintained at strategic points in fields occupied by the Union, not fewer than 50 were boarding schools in such places as Nellore, Ongole, Bassein, Rangoon, Moulmein, Toungoo, Swatow, Yokohama, and Tokyo. The majority of them were in charge of women supported by the Woman's Societies. Besides these station schools, there were nine boarding schools for girls—two in India, two in Burma, one in China, and four in Japan; and also three schools for training Bible women—one in Burma, one in China, and one in Japan; and a school for Eurasian girls in Moulmein. The Union had but two colleges, one at Rangoon, which had been in eixstence twenty years, and the other at Ongole, which had just been opened.

The details have been provided in order to give a background for the issues which were raised in the report. The question still lingered in the minds of many about the need of boarding schools as an aid to evangelization. The committee's reply was indicative of a changing attitude towards these schools which were staunchly supported by the Woman's Societies. It was pointed out that many young people who were candidates for the ministry had their only chance to obtain a good grammar school education through this means. To the objections expressed by some missionaries in South India concerning the need for the college at Ongole, the committee offered a strong conviction that the Mission should provide collegiate education for Christian youth.

A further issue which had become important by this time was the question whether missionaries should continue to receive "grants-in-aid" from the British Government in India, Assam, and Burma in return for the educational services rendered the people and the government in those communities where mission schools provided the main source of secular training as well as that which was religious. The amounts were not great, totalling less than one-eleventh of the whole expense involved in maintaining the schools. But to many Baptists, the principle of the separation of church and state was involved, and they interpreted the acceptance of such aid as a violation of that doctrine. So strongly did the Union feel on this issue that it was voted that the reception of state aid for mission school work should be discontinued.

The recommendations of Dr. Hovey's committee, which were adopted, crystallized the policy of the Union in the troublesome problem of maintaining a balance between evangelism and education in the administration of the funds provided for missions. In summary, they included instructions that: (1) the present methods of school work should be continued, with such changes as will promote efficiency in evangelizing; (2) the native Christians should be impressed with their duty to provide for the education of their children; (3) only Christians should be employed as teachers in mission schools; (4) the primary purpose of all teachers should be the imparting of Christian truth; (5) high schools and colleges should not be founded until assurance of a following and support is obtained; (6) boarding school girls who receive free education should be obliged to perform some manual service; (7) single women missionaries should be used in educational work as far as possible to avoid arousing prejudice against women leaders in Oriental countries.[2] It is obvious that the Union had adopted a milder attitude on the school question than in previous years. It was prophetic of a more radical change of policy that was yet to come.

Closely related to the concern of the Union to maintain some schools for higher education was the basic aim of developing self-governing and self-supporting churches. In this connection the records of the Board of Managers indicate that there was an increasing disposition of the Union to relate self-direction and self-support in such a way as to encourage the emergence of an indigenous Chris-

---

[2] *The Baptist Missionary Magazine,* Vol. 74, No. 7 (July, 1894), pp. 190-201.

tianity. This was intended to help avoid transplanting of American religious forms and institutions upon other cultures.

The largest degree of self-support was to be found in Burma, where 441 of the 640 churches were maintaining themselves in 1898 without assistance from American funds. Of the 532 mission schools in that country, 327 were entirely self-supporting. The over-all picture was not so bright as far as schools were concerned. Only 383 of the total number of 1,235 mission schools received no help from America. However, 524 of the total number of 853 churches were self-sustaining. In Europe the work was largely independent financially, receiving only small sums from America to supplement the pitifully small salaries of pastors of smaller churches.

The degree of self-support varied with each mission field. In South India, for example, the great poverty of the people ministered to by American Baptists and the reticence of the missionaries to place too great emphasis on sacrificial stewardship were significant factors. In China, the cultural background of the people did not encourage individual self-reliance. The same quality may have been a factor to a lesser degree in Japan. In the Belgian Congo Mission, on the other hand, the people were peculiarly well-adapted to the development of self-support and a democratic type of life.[3]

Dr. S. W. Duncan, foreign secretary of the Union, in 1898 outlined the position of the society clearly when he said that self-support should be the cardinal point in the missionary policy of the future. He also urged that decisive steps be taken to introduce industrial pursuits among the native Christians so that they might become economically self-sufficient. The principle that had been advanced and argued by Elisha L. Abbott of the Sandoway Sgaw Karen Mission and by C. H. Carpenter at Bassein in the 1850's had finally come to general acceptance.

An important factor in influencing a rethinking of policy with respect to better support of the mission schools was the enthusiastic response of the Chinese to education. By 1904, the Foreign Department of the Executive Committee was going on record as convinced that schools were not only an auxiliary to evangelism, but perhaps a direct route to the hearts of the people. Indicative of the changing policy was the taking over of a high school for boys at Nellore from

---

[3] *Ibid.*, Vol. 75, No. 7 (July, 1895), pp. 202-04, 423; Vol. 78, No. 3 (March, 1898), pp. 87-91.

the Free Church Missionary Society of Scotland, the establishing of an academy in the East China Mission at Hangchow, plans for a strong central school at Swatow in the South China Mission, the initiation of school work at Suifu in western China, and preliminary planning for higher development of Duncan Academy in Tokyo and for the beginning of school work at Jaro in the Philippine Islands.[4]

In order to strengthen further the educational work, the Board, in 1904, made its first great effort to raise endowments for the higher schools abroad. It was justified on the grounds that an effective school system was vital to the development of indigenous churches. But the trend produced a tension because many still felt that an excessive emphasis was being placed on education to the weakening of evangelization. Although this factor and the accumulation of a deficit prevented the successful achievement of the endowment fund, the new attitude toward education prevailed and became an important phase of the new mission policy of the early twentieth century.

Trend Towards Greater Field Supervision

In 1895 the Board of Managers took steps to consider the propriety of constituting advisory committees on the mission fields in order to relieve the Executive Committee of many of the details of managing the work abroad. That there was need for such a plan is indicated in an article written in 1899 by Dr. David Downie, who had been mission treasurer at Nellore, India, for twenty-five years. He called attention to the deplorable lack of organization on the field, which made it possible for an individual missionary to draw up his recommendations for appropriations and send them directly to the Executive Committee without sharing them with any of his associates. He also pointed to the lack of audits of accounts as an indication of inefficiency which should be corrected.[5]

Upon the basis of a pattern worked out by the missionaries in Japan and South India, the Executive Committee adopted in 1899 a plan of administering the fields through Missionary Conferences set up in each major mission. It called for an annual meeting of the missionaries of all stations on a particular field, at which time a

---

[4] *Ibid.*, Vol. 84, No. 7 (July, 1904), pp. 295-96.

[5] *The Baptist Missionary Magazine*, Vol. 75, No. 7 (July, 1895), p. 214; *The Baptist Missionary Review* (a monthly of the South India Mission), Vol. 5, No. 11 (Nov., 1899), pp. 407-11.

secretary was to be appointed to conduct the official correspondence with the Home Board. The Conference also was to appoint annually a Committee of Reference, an Examining Committee (to administer language examinations of new missionaries), a Property Committee, and a Statistician. Although all missionaries were still to have the right to correspond freely with the foreign secretary of the Board, it was understood that all requests were to be presented first to the Committee of Reference and then to the Missionary Conference for consideration in the light of the total needs of the mission. All requests which were thus approved were forwarded to the Executive Committee in the United States as recommendations of the Conference. It was recognized that any missionary had the right to appeal from the decision of any committee to the Conference, and from the Conference to the Executive Committee. The new plan was to give expression to the Executive Committee's respect for the experience and judgment of the missionaries, and to develop a more efficient and harmonious administration of the fields.[6]

By 1901 the plan was in operation throughout the missions of the Union. By that time also, the Executive Committee voted to divide itself into five groups for more specialized attention to the increasingly complex tasks coming before it. Accordingly, there were set up the Committee on Burma, the Committee on Assam and South India, the Committee on China and Siam, the Committee on Japan and the Philippines, and the Committee on Europe and Africa.

Reactions from missionaries to the new procedures were on the whole favorable. Editorial comment in the monthly publication of the South India Mission is typical:

> The advantages of such a committee are so numerous that one wonders now how we ever got on without it, or why it should have taken so long for us to come to understand the matter aright. The fear of centralization—of putting too much power in the hands of a few—is being proved to have been largely imaginary by the fact that no one has been discovered who had any such inclination; while the provision which changes the personnel of the committee entirely every four years prevents the possibility of any one man acquiring dictatorial power, even if, by chance, such a person should be found on the committee.[7]

---

[6] American Baptist Missionary Union, Records of the Executive Committee for Nov. 20, 1899, pp. 414-19.

[7] *The Baptist Missionary Review,* Vol. 10, No. 2 (Feb., 1904), p. 59.

From 1906 on and after 1910 when the administration was revised, the actions of the Executive Committee and of the Board of Managers were usually introduced by such words as: "in accordance with recommendation by the South India Conference Committee."

In 1908 a second step in the development of new procedures for field administration was adopted. It was a plan for the appointment of two "general missionaries" who should serve as counsellors to the missionaries of the respective mission fields. The Executive Committee carefully explained that they were not to be "overseers," but "fellow helpers." Dr. W. L. Ferguson and Dr. J. L. Dearing were selected, but there was so much opposition to the idea, especially in Burma, Assam, and South India, that they resigned. The real objection was that the plan contained the seeds of episcopacy. So much tension was aroused by the matter that the Northern Baptist Convention, at Portland, Oregon, in 1909, voted to appoint a committee to consider the issue. The committee recommended that the plan be carried out in the China, Japan, and Philippine fields for the proposed period of two years, but held in abeyance elsewhere until the foreign secretary should have opportunity to make a visit for conference with the missionary bodies.[8]

In 1910 additional authority was granted to the missionaries on the field when the procedure was adopted by the Board of assigning a gross allotment of funds to each field to be distributed through the Missionary Conference. This relieved the officials in the home offices of having to approve the apportionment of funds to each missionary. Moreover, it enabled those on the field to meet emergencies without undue delay. It was also a concession to the wisdom of relying to a greater degree upon the first-hand experience of the missionaries for decisions which were difficult to make fairly by a committee in the United States far removed from the situations that demanded attention.

Emergence of Denominational Support of Missions

The financial receipts of the Union in 1893 amounted to nearly $767,000. The expenditures for that year and the next were arranged not on the basis of the large receipts of the Carey Centennial in

[8] *Ibid.*, Vol. 14, No. 11 (Nov., 1908), pp. 425-43. American Baptist Missionary Union, *Annual Reports* for 1908, p. 60; American Baptist Foreign Mission Society, *Annual Reports* for 1910, pp. 30-33.

1892, but upon reasonable expectations based on the increases of the immediately preceding years. But to the dismay of the Board, the receipts of 1894 fell below those of 1891, the amount being just under $466,000. Although the donations for 1895 increased by about $12,000, the hoped-for gains were not forthcoming. The debt in 1894 stood at $203,595. Accordingly, only 12 men and 7 women were appointed for the fields during the year in contrast to 25 men and 13 women in 1893. In 1895 the number dropped to 9 men and 14 women, while the appropriations were reduced by $109,000. In spite of valiant efforts to stem the decline in donations, they dropped steadily in the next two years. By 1897 the debt was at an all-time high; it totalled $292,721.32. The Home Mission Society was faced with a deficit of $181,761.59, bringing the combined indebtedness for missions up to $474,482.91.

The situation obviously called for joint planning, for all of the denominational agencies were faced with budgetary problems. Moreover, there had been a persistent appeal from many quarters for some plan of unified appeal to the churches to avoid the scattered approaches and the inefficiencies of traditional procedures. Accordingly, the three national agencies, foreign, home, and publication societies, appointed three representatives each to constitute a Commission on Systematic Christian Beneficence. It was to plan for the total giving of the denomination. Actually, the agencies represented were more than three, for the Baptist Young People's Union of America and the Woman's Societies, both Home and Foreign, also sent representatives. The Missionary Union sent two of its secretaries, Dr. Henry C. Mabie and Dr. Thomas T. S. Barbour, and also Stephen Greene, a lawyer from Newton Centre, Massachusetts. Barbour was elected chairman and Greene, secretary of the Commission. The Commission recommended to State Conventions that state commissions, associational commissions, and local church commissions be formed. Through suitable literature and inspirational leadership, Baptist people were to be trained to systematic and proportionate giving. The plan was in essence the forerunner of the kind of missionary promotion program that developed later in the Northern Baptist Convention.

In June, 1897, the foreign and home mission societies joined in a determined effort to raise, through a co-ordinated plan of approach to the churches, the sum of $700,000 to wipe out the combined debts. Through the rallying of Baptist laymen across the country, the campaign was successful. It was helped greatly by a large contribution from John D. Rockefeller, the oil magnate and generous Baptist layman.[9]

The experiment of co-operation between the various societies in raising the indebtedness paved the way for further conversations in behalf of their working together. To this end, a Commission on Co-ordination of the National Agencies met in New York on October 17-18, 1900. The meeting resulted in two recommendations: (1) that steps be taken to secure for each society a uniform basis of membership, so that delegates of the three major societies might be, as far as possible, identical; (2) that a mid-year conference of the executive boards of the national societies be held to deliberate on problems related to the collection of funds. The first of the mid-year meetings was held in the Madison Avenue Baptist Church, New York City, December 3-4, 1901.

At the May meetings of the societies in St. Paul, Minnesota, in 1902, resolutions were adopted by the Missionary Union which authorized appointment of three members to participate in a Committee of Fifteen (seven ministers, five laymen, and three laywomen, none of whom were to be paid officers of the societies). The purpose of the Committee of Fifteen was to determine "whether there be any lack of proper adjustment and proper co-operation between the three great societies, including their associate societies, as to fields of labor." When the Committee made its report the next year, it became obvious that union of the three societies was inadvisable. However, it was agreed that systematic co-operation was necessary, and that a Committee of Reference of nine persons be appointed from among the several societies to work out differences among them. It was also agreed that the societies should organize and unify their financial appeals and collecting procedures.[10]

The Missionary Union also was confronted with the persistent desire of many people to "designate" their missionary funds for specific missionaries, hoping thereby to receive letters or information from

---

[9] *The Baptist Missionary Magazine,* Vol. 76, No. 2 (Feb., 1896), pp. 33-34; Vol. 76, No. 7 (July, 1896), p. 197; Vol. 76, No. 8 (Aug., 1896), pp. 431-32; Vol. 76, No. 10 (Oct., 1896), pp. 503-06; Vol. 77, No. 8 (Aug., 1897), pp. 461-64; Vol. 77, No. 9 (Sept., 1897), p. 532.

[10] *Ibid.,* Vol. 81, No. 7 (July, 1901), p. 271; Vol. 82, No. 1 (Jan., 1902), pp. 10-12, 258-64; Vol. 83, No. 7 (July, 1903), pp. 245-46.

those whom they were supporting. This, of course, placed an undue burden upon already overworked servants of the Union. For this reason, the "station plan" was devised by the Executive Committee in 1901, whereby churches might interest themselves in contributing towards a specific station. This would not create the problems involved in designations to a specific missionary or to a native preacher or teacher.[11]

In 1905 the Union felt that it was necessary to change the name of the society from The American Baptist Missionary Union to The American Baptist Foreign Mission Society. The move was dictated by confusion which had arisen over the interpretation which many people gave to the word "Union." For many it designated home and foreign missions, whereas the founders had only intended to indicate the union of the "Home" and "Foreign" Departments. Final approval for the change was not forthcoming until 1910.[12]

After some delay in efforts to co-ordinate the activities of the various agencies of Northern Baptists, a call was issued in 1906 for a general meeting of all the societies to be held in connection with the May meeting in 1907 at Washington, D.C. Accordingly, in the Nation's capital, the three general societies previously named, together with the auxiliary women's societies, met on May 16-17 at the Calvary Baptist Church. Dr. W. C. Bitting of St. Louis, Missouri, who was to serve as corresponding secretary of the new national organization for a period of twenty years, proposed that a committee of fifteen draft a plan of organization which would preserve the independence of the local church and yet provide co-ordination of denominational work. The product was not to be a legislative body.[13] The committee was appointed and undertook a task which was completed three years later.

The move thus begun was of momentous significance to the future of American Baptist missions. It was hailed by many as a great forward step in obtaining general denominational support of the primary purpose for which all Baptist agencies existed—the world mission of evangelization. Dr. Clifton D. Gray of Dorchester, Massachusetts, expressed the general point of view when he said: "We used to say

---

[11] *Ibid.*, Vol. 81, No. 7 (July, 1901), pp. 288-89.

[12] *Ibid.*, Vol. 87, No. 1 (Jan., 1907), p. 8.

[13] W. C. Bitting, *A Manual of the Northern Baptist Convention, 1908–1918* (Philadelphia, 1918), p. 9.

that the societies belonged to us. We now say that we belong to the societies. We want them to feel that we are behind them." [14]

The organization of the Northern Baptist Convention had the wholehearted backing of Baptists in the Laymen's Missionary Movement, which had come into existence during the previous year. It was an interdenominational effort of laymen to arouse an interest in missions within their respective denominations by preparing material, offering suggestions, and otherwise assisting the individual denominations. One of the first suggestions was that a body of at least fifty men should plan to visit all the mission fields of the world for the purpose of making a first-hand study of missions. This resulted twenty-five years later in 1932 in the Laymen's Inquiry which brought forth varied reactions among Baptists as we shall see. Baptists were interested in the movement from the first, hoping to turn the general tide of enthusiasm into a strong movement on behalf of their own joint budget needs for missions. But because of lack of organizational planning at the outset, the Baptist Laymen's Missionary Movement was slow to get under way. It is significent, however, that the executive secretary of the interdenominational organization was a Baptist of tremendous promotional energies, the Reverend H. A. La Flamme.

The need was truly great, for the Union was struggling in 1907 with an accumulated debt of over $43,000. In fact, it had been free of indebtedness only nine years since 1850. The laymen's enthusiasm was badly needed, for the difficulty lay in arousing the rank and file of church members to increase their support of missions. Out of receipts that nearly reached $1,000,000 in the year ending April 30, 1907, only $441,225.61 represented "donations" by churches, Sunday schools, young people's societies, and individuals. To meet the demand for more specific response from the churches, the Apportionment Plan was inaugurated. It involved an "assessment" of a loose sort upon the churches, as a portion of the budget was assigned for voluntary acceptance by each congregation. Although it aroused some objections, it proved very successful.[15]

When the Northern Baptist Convention met in Oklahoma City in May, 1908, the White Temple was filled to overflowing, and a spirit

---

[14] *The Baptist Missionary Magazine,* Vol. 87, No. 7 (July, 1907), p. 262.

[15] American Baptist Missionary Union, *Reports* for 1907, p. 14; for 1910, p. 21; *Missions,* Vol. 1, No. 1 (Jan., 1910), p. 33 ff.

of intense enthusiasm prevailed. At this gathering, plans were completed for co-operation through the new organization. The Woman's Societies, both home and foreign, voted to unite with the Convention. The Missionary Union agreed to modify its structure so as to enter into co-operative relations with the Convention. This meant regulating its expenditures in accordance with the annual budget approved by the Convention. It meant also that there would be no solicitation of funds or incurring of indebtedness without approval of the Convention in its annual session, or in an emergency between sessions, of the Convention's Finance Committee of nine members. The co-ordinated budget of the Convention was to be prepared by the Finance Committee on the basis of budget recommendations from the various co-operating agencies. The Convention approved a budget for the fiscal year, April 1, 1908 to March 31, 1909, which totalled one and a half million dollars. Of this amount $284,000 was for reduction of the indebtedness of the three national societies. Of these amounts, the Missionary Union was allotted $547,000 for its current operations and $158,000 for reduction of its deficit.

Reactions to this initial effort in denominational co-operation were varied. The 956 delegates present at Oklahoma from 33 states and territories were enthusiastic and surprised that so much committee work and free discussion could result in the unanimity that characterized decisions of the Convention. Laymen regarded the new procedures as a step forward that was in keeping with the practice of large business enterprises. To be sure there was not complete approval across the country. There were those who had misgivings that the new organization would deprive Baptist churches of their democratic polity. But on the whole, the constituencies of the national societies showed a marked degree of enthusiasm and patience in working out the numerous details involved in the process of working together.

The Convention of 1909 met in Portland, Oregon. A "Million Dollar Budget" was adopted for the fiscal year, 1909–1910. The various societies voted to publish jointly a new missionary magazine to be called *Missions*. The board records of the co-operating agencies were hereafter to be published with those of the Northern Baptist Convention in a single Yearbook. The Woman's American Baptist Home Mission Society was admitted into equal membership in the Convention as a co-operating society.

At Chicago, in 1910, the Northern Baptist Convention was incorporated legally under the Laws of the State of New York. The purpose of the organization, as stated in its Act of Incorporation was to provide a means of giving "expression to the opinions of its constituency upon moral, religious, and denominational matters, and to promote denominational unity and efficiency in efforts for the evangelization of the world." Delegates were to be appointed by the churches and co-operating organizations—not, as heretofore, on the basis of money contributions, but of membership representation—with the voting privilege extended by each Society to all delegates seated in the Convention. The Executive Committee was to be composed of officers, former presidents, and thirty others, fifteen of whom were to be laymen. The term of office was to be a maximum of six years. This Committee was to act for the Convention between sessions. The legal independence of each co-operating organization was guaranteed, and the relationship between a Society and the Convention could end on one year's notice from either party.[16]

Following the Chicago Convention, the national organization of the Baptist Laymen's Missionary Movement was effected. The Reverend W. T. Stackhouse, who had given significant leadership to a similar movement in Canada, was elected general secretary of the organization. In 1911 it was the goal of the laymen to persuade each Baptist to contribute ten cents a day to missions. Until his health broke in 1913, Stackhouse gave vigorous and inspiring leadership to this movement.

Through the generous donation of $50,000 by "the Man from Pennsylvania," as Mr. M. C. Treat of Washington, Pennsylvania, was called, an incentive was given to the Convention to raise $200,000 for a fund for retired ministers and missionaries. The offer was made in 1911 when the Convention was meeting in Philadelphia. Dr. Henry C. Morehouse, executive secretary of the American Baptist Home Mission Society, gave devoted service to the successful completion of the campaign to raise the sum required. Just before Christmas in that same year, Dr. Morehouse inspired several wealthy laymen to contribute the last $100,000 by offering his own life sav-

[16] For a fuller account of the Northern Baptist Convention, see Robert G. Torbet, *A History of the Baptists* (Philadelphia, 1950; revised edition, 1952), pp. 453-57. See also *The Baptist Missionary Magazine*, Vol. 88, No. 7 (July, 1908), pp. 268-80; *Missions*, Vol. 1, No. 6 (June, 1910), pp. 271-80, 387-99.

ings of $10,000. Through such valiant beginnings the Ministers and Missionaries Benefit Board began the work which has continued successfully with blessing to many servants of Christ in the later years of life.

When the Northern Baptist Convention met at Des Moines, Iowa, in May, 1912, a budget of nearly $2,500,000 was adopted, and a campaign was launched to raise $3,000,000 in order to liquidate the combined deficits of the co-operating societies amounting to $208,-616. At the same time, the American Baptist Foreign Mission Society (as the Union was now called) requested the Convention to appoint a committee to investigate the internal expenses for operations in order to stop the persistent criticisms of too much overhead and waste. Officers of the Society explained that they had cut the operating expenses of the organization to $130,000. The committee's only suggestion was that some savings might be effected through limiting the output of missionary literature. The Convention expressed full confidence in the management of the Society and granted $200,-000 for its expenses.

Under the chairmanship of Dr. Shailer Mathews of the Divinity School of the University of Chicago and president of the Federal Council of Churches of Christ in America, the Three Million Dollar Campaign was successfully launched. John D. Rockefeller offered $100,000 if the Baptists would raise $250,000 more than in the previous year. The response was varied. Giving per capita east of the Rockies was one dollar for all three general societies, whereas it was $2.31 west of the mountains. On the whole, the Campaign was good for the denomination.

By the time the Convention met in Detroit, Michigan, in May, 1913, a new spirit of unity and zeal had taken hold of the denomination. The enthusiasm was enhanced by the merger of the Woman's American Baptist Foreign Mission Societies and their inclusion within the Convention that year. The editor of *Missions* observed that it was the first time since the organization of the Convention that the old time enthusiasm of the anniversaries had been combined effectively with the best methods of conducting denominational business. In a burst of optimism, the 1,600 delegates voted to discontinue their Campaign and join with the United Missionary Campaign, which was a great forward movement of home and foreign mission societies in the United States and Canada to culminate in a great every member canvass of church members in the two countries.[17]

Changes in the Society's Procedures and Policy

Two events necessitated changes in 1912 within the organization of the American Baptist Foreign Mission Society. One was the organization of the Northern Baptist Convention in 1907 which we have just explained in some detail. The other was the merger in 1911 of the Free Baptists with the Convention. The actual transfer of Free Baptist funds and properties involved in turning the Bengal-Orissa Mission over to the American Baptist Foreign Mission Society was concluded at formal ceremonies in Kingsley Hall of the Ford Building in Boston, on October 5, 1911. To facilitate this friendly amalgamation, the Foreign Mission Board united with the Boards of the Home Mission Society and the Publication Society in asking Dr. A. W. Anthony, general secretary and treasurer of the General Conference of Free Baptists until the merger, to become joint secretary of Free Baptist affairs for the three bodies until the transition could be completed. This he did with great tact and wisdom.

In 1911, the Foreign Mission Society began operating under a new Board of Managers which had replaced the old Executive Committee in accordance with the new bylaws adopted in Chicago in 1910. The majority of members were within easy reach of Boston, so as to be able to attend semimonthly meetings. Quarterly meetings were held in various cities across the country.

In 1912 Dr. Thomas S. Barbour, the foreign secretary, resigned because of impaired health. He was succeeded by Dr. James H. Franklin of Colorado Springs, Colorado. Dr. Franklin had held several pastorates in the North, and had served for two years as district secretary of the Home Mission Society. For four years he had been a member of the Board of Managers of the Foreign Mission Society, and had served on the Africa Commission appointed to investigate conditions in the Belgian Congo and in Nigeria. He also had been recording secretary of the Executive Committee of the Northern Baptist Convention, and was in close touch with the work of the denomination.

---

[17] *Missions,* Vol. 2, No. 8 (Aug., 1911), pp. 518-20; Vol. 3, No. 2 (Feb., 1912), pp. 90-91; Vol. 3, No. 7 (July, 1912), pp. 505-06, 515-23; Vol. 4, No. 1 (Jan., 1913), p. 29; Vol. 4, No. 3 (Mar., 1913), p. 183; Vol. 4, No. 7 (July, 1913), pp. 522-45.

About the same time, Mr. Ernest S. Butler was appointed to succeed Mr. Charles W. Perkins as treasurer of the Society. For some eighteen years Butler had been a businessman in Boston, and was prominent interdenominationally as well as among Baptists. He was typical of the important contribution of laymen to missions.

At the quarterly meeting of the Board of Managers in Chicago in March, 1912, it was voted to have a general secretary to co-ordinate the activities of the foreign, home, and treasury departments of the Society. The general secretary was to be the chief officer of the executive force of the Society. He was to be the general representative of the Society on both the home and foreign fields. President Emory W. Hunt of Denison University in Granville, Ohio, and former president of the Society, was elected to the new office. Although in poor health, he accepted the position. In the home office, in addition to his general duties, he assumed special responsibility for obtaining candidates for the mission fields.

On November 12, 1913, the Board adopted a revised plan of administration which called for: (1) An Officer's Council, to consist of the executive officers of the Society, with the chairman of the Board of Managers *ex officio;* its function was to unify and harmonize the work of the several departments and to serve as an advisory body to the Board. (2) The General Secretary. (3) The Home Department. (4) The Foreign Department. (5) The Treasury Department. The work of the Foreign Department was divided eventually into two groups: Burma, Assam, South India, and Bengal-Orissa under the direction of Foreign Secretary Arthur C. Baldwin; and China, Japan, the Philippine Islands, the Belgian Congo, and Europe under Foreign Secretary James H. Franklin.[18]

The task of missionary education which formerly had been carried on directly by the Society was now entrusted to what was called the Baptist Forward Movement for Missionary Education. In its report for 1912, the Foreign Mission Society indicated that the new effort, which was largely the product of the Woman's Societies, was accomplishing far more at less cost than the Society had ever been able to

[18] The foregoing account is based on the following sources: *Missions,* Vol. 2, No. 7 (July, 1911), pp. 461, 469; American Baptist Foreign Mission Society *Reports* for 1911, pp. 15-16, for 1912, pp. 18-20; Records of the Board of Managers of A.B.F.M.S. for July 1, 1912, p. 1, for March 20, 1912, pp. 136-39, for Nov. 12, 1913, pp. 8-11, for Feb. 11, 1914, p. 135.

do. The Movement gave special consideration to missionary education in Sunday schools.[19]

In 1912 the Foreign Mission Society was confronted with the necessity of another major decision, which this time concerned mission policy. The Convention that met that year at Des Moines was challenged by reports of an increasing number of converts in the Kengtung area of northern Burma and in South India and the Belgian Congo. The growing burdens being placed by the ingatherings upon the limited staff of workers in the respective fields obliged the Society to consider a strategy for the future in the light of the difficult financial situation at home. Accordingly, a conference was held at Newton Theological Institution in Massachusetts following the Convention. Officers, board members, and missionaries home on furlough were present. On September 12, 1912, as a consequence of the deliberations, what eventually came to be known as the "intensive" policy was adopted.

The Intensive Policy in essence was a directive that the Society, for the present, should undertake more intensive work on currently operated fields, rather than open new fields. Such a policy was not to be construed as retrenchment, but a progressive step in the direction of establishing self-supporting and self-perpetuating churches on Baptist fields. It was the judgment of the Board that entrance upon new fields would sacrifice those on which work was then being conducted under the handicaps of insufficient workers and inadequate equipment. In the interest of penetrating most effectively the countries involved with strong Christian churches, the strategy was to establish strong Christian centers at pivotal points from which further evangelization by national leaders could be carried out more successfully. To implement this program of self-sustaining church life, the educational facilities of such stations were to be given primary consideration. Contrary to earlier views with which we have become familiar, the Board now was convinced that the Christian education of youth was the only means of a lasting penetration of the life and culture of the nation. It was also determined wise to co-operate, to the utmost practical extent, with other Christian bodies working in the same fields. This co-operation was regarded as particularly important in the department of higher education, where the number

[19] A.B.F.M.S. *Reports* for 1912, p. 26.

of students was relatively small and the expense proportionately great.[20]

In the execution of such a policy, there were several consequences which aroused the opposition of many who placed primary emphasis upon aggressive evangelism in untouched areas. The Central China Mission was closed in 1913 in order to give more support to the other American Baptist Missions in China. The relatively new work in Japan and the Philippines was narrowed to certain areas where a concentrated effort could be effected. However great the need appeared to be, no new stations were to be opened. An increasing proportion of mission funds were to be applied to educational work. This was regarded by many Baptists as a betrayal of the Christian's primary responsibility to evangelize. Although arguments were set forth to support the Society's position that education was regarded as a means of evangelizing, opposition continued. Following the First World War, this opposition burst forth into open hostility, as will be reported later.

Indicative of the growing concern of the Board for the educational phase of its work on the fields, was the vote of February 12, 1913, that representatives of the Convention's Executive Committee and of the Board of Education confer with its own Educational Committee. The purpose of the joint conference was to consider establishing an educational department of the Foreign Mission Society with a view to strengthening and extending the educational work of the Society in the Orient. The conference was held on March 11. The next day the Board of Managers approved a recommendation from the conference to create an advisory committee on educational work to counsel with the Society. The Society approved the plan in June.[21]

Although there had been consistent interest shown by officers of the Society in such ecumenical developments as the great Edinburgh Missionary Conference of 1910, the Student Volunteer Movement, and the Laymen's Missionary Movement, the most notable developments in interdenominational co-operation took place in educational work on the mission fields in the Far East. For example, in 1914, the Baptists were co-operating in Japan with the Presbyterians in

---

[20] Records of Board of Managers of A.B.F.M.S. for Sept. 12, 1912, p. 94; for full statement of the Intensive Policy, see A.B.F.M.S. *Reports* for 1914, pp. 223-42.

[21] Records of Board of Managers of A.B.F.M.S. for Feb. 12, 1913, p. 234; for March 12, 1913, p. 174; for June 18-19, 1913, p. 363.

the lower grades of college work. In China the Board had been able to enter into a plan of interdenominational support of the graduate schools of Nanking University. This freed Baptists to give more attention to the Shanghai Baptist College, which was the joint responsibility of Northern and Southern Baptists. Proposals were under consideration for union in medical colleges at Chengtu in West China and at Canton in South China. In South China there was a strong movement toward co-operation in educational work between the South China Mission and the English Presbyterians.[22]

Field administration was improved in 1914 by adoption of two plans. The first was a plan offered to the missionaries by the Board of Managers in the autumn of 1912 whereby they should receive the annual appropriations for their work in gross amounts, to be distributed among the several stations and missionaries by the Mission Conference or the Reference Committee. This was accepted by the East China, Japan, South China, and Philippine Missions. The alternate plan, which was less radical than the first, placed an enlarged emergency fund at the disposal of the mission at the beginning of the year to be used for unforeseen needs that arose after the original schedule of appropriations had been made by the Board. This plan was accepted by the West China, South India, Bengal-Orissa, and Congo Missions. On the request of the Assam and East China Missions, the Board approved a plan for a conference or mission secretary, who would not only act as correspondent for the mission, but would visit the stations and confer and advise with the missionaries. Accordingly, Dr. A. J. Tuttle of Gauhati was appointed for Assam, and Dr. J. T. Proctor of Shanghai for East China.[23]

From this brief survey we may gather that the Foreign Mission Society had achieved a more harmonious relationship with its missionaries than ever before. We may conclude also that the Society had come under a new leadership, progressive in outlook and eagerly desirous of achieving the goal of an indigenous Christianity on the mission fields in which much money had been invested and for which many lives had been spent during the one hundred years since American Baptists had begun their work.

---

[22] A.B.F.M.S., *Annual Reports* for 1914, p. 61.

[23] *Missions,* Vol. 5, No. 7 (July, 1914), pp. 563-64.

The Centennial Year, 1914

Preparations had been in the making for almost five years prior to the actual celebrations which took place at Rangoon, Moulmein, Mandalay, and Bassein in Burma. They began at Rangoon on December 10, 1913, and terminated at Bassein on January 4, 1914. To attract Baptists from the United States a tour of the mission fields was arranged, which brought them to Burma in time for the centenary of the establishment of Baptist missions in that country. The Christians and missionaries together contributed Rs. 66,000 ($22,000) as a thank-offering. It was fitting that the anniversary pilgrimage was concluded at Bassein, in the Sgaw Karen Mission. For there was to be found "more nearly the completed product of missionary activity, self-support, and self-propagation, along evangelistic, educational, and industrial lines than in any other American Baptist foreign mission." Bassein was symbolic of the great success in developing an indigenous Christianity in Burma, where there were over a thousand organized churches, seventy-six per cent of which were self-supporting.[24]

On June 24-25, 1914, the Judson Centennial Program was observed jointly by the Northern Baptist Convention and the Foreign Mission Society. It was particularly suitable that the place of meeting should have been Tremont Temple in Boston, where for so many years the Board of Managers had conducted its faithful work and from which a host of missionaries had followed Adoniram Judson to the East. During those two days, a number of events occurred that reflected the deep hold which missions had upon Northern Baptists. The deficit of $276,000 which was being carried by the Foreign Society, the Home Society, and the Woman's Foreign Society was eliminated almost completely by pledges and gifts. Of this amount, $100,000 was given by John D. Rockefeller. Dr. Edward Judson was made honorary president of the Foreign Mission Society as a tribute to the son of the great pioneer missionary of American Baptists. Twenty-six missionaries were commissioned, which brought to 1,474 the total sent out since 1865.

The centennial provided a study in contrasts. In 1814 there had been but four missionaries on the roll of the Society. One hundred

[24] Howard B. Grose and Fred P. Haggard, editors, *The Judson Centennial, 1814–1914* (Philadelphia, 1914), pp. 291-99.

years later there were 701, reinforced by 6,106 native workers. During that century the missionaries of the Society had been engaged in an enterprise through which 308,605 persons in non-Christian lands had become Christians. When that figure is added to the number in Europe, the total is 585,351—more than half a million. These Christians had been organized into 1,575 churches, of which 908, or 57 per cent, were self-supporting in 1914. From responsibility for a single field in Burma in 1814, American Baptists had responsibility for ten fields by 1914 scattered around the world—Burma, Assam, Bengal-Orissa, South India, East China, South China, West China, Japan, the Philippines, and the Belgian Congo—besides giving assistance to European Baptists. It was a tremendous undertaking into which approximately $31,000,000 had been poured, in addition to the lives of brave men and women who gave their all for Christ and his kingdom.[25]

---

[25] *Ibid.*, pp. 25-142, 205, 300-02.

CHAPTER XI

Baptist Women Marshal Their Forces

WOMEN HAVE BEEN in the forerank of the Protestant missionary movement from the beginning. Indeed, they have been almost as numerous as men, inasmuch as missionaries with few exceptions were accompanied by their wives. Although the women were given for many years only the rank of assistant missionary, they took their full share of responsibility and bore with unflinching courage the same burdens which fell upon their husbands. In the public mind, the stirring adventures of great women like Ann Hasseltine Judson, Harriet Newell, and Roxana Nott, who had sailed with their husbands for India in 1812, inspired as great interest as the experiences of their men. For Baptists, Ann Judson was the "heroine of Ava." To them, she was as truly a missionary as her illustrious husband.

It was a different situation, however, in the case of unmarried women. They were obliged, if they got in at all, "to slip quietly into the mission without attracting much notice." Boards were under the impression that "unmarried females" were helpless creatures, subject to every imagined evil and peril. This prejudice, which was an overtone of the prevailing concept of the world as man's domain, was very difficult to overcome. It was responsible for many of the limitations which were placed upon the leadership of women at home in the missionary endeavor of the nineteenth century.[1]

[1] For an excellent treatment of this subject, see R. Pierce Beaver, "Pioneer Single Women Missionaries," Missionary Research Library Bulletin, Vol. IV, No. 12 (Sept. 30, 1953).

Because women overcame these obstacles and gave sacrificial service to Baptist missions at home and abroad, their story is deserving of special attention. In this chapter the entire record cannot, of course, be narrated. In such brief space only the main outlines of the development of women's organized work can be traced. But the reader will be impressed by the ever-recurring allusion to the influence of women missionaries and their supporting societies as the story of the respective mission fields unfolds.

Women's Work Prior to 1871

In the first half of the nineteenth century, women organized many local missionary societies. The first of these was the Boston Female Society for Missionary Purposes, established in 1800 and supported by Baptists and Congregationalists. At first, it planned work among Indians in the United States, then became interested in William Carey's mission to India. The first secretary and treasurer of the society was Miss Mary Webb, a helpless cripple whose only means of locomotion was a hand carriage. Other local societies followed—the Female Mite Society and the Boston Baptist Female Education Society organized in 1815, a growing number of Female Primary Societies, and a Woman's Monthly Concert of Prayer for Missions. Their purpose was to assist the established mission work by their gifts and prayer. There was at that time no organized effort undertaken "by women for women." That was to come later in response to the desire of single young women to enter foreign mission service, when the boards were unwilling to send them out unprotected.

The earliest illustration of the reluctance among all mission boards to approve appointment of single women was provided by Baptists in 1815. Shortly after the organization of the Triennial Convention in 1814, the Board appointed a printer, George H. Hough, with his wife and two children, to reinforce the Judsons in Burma. When this news was made public, a widow by the name of Mrs. Charlotte H. White addressed a letter to the Board, requesting that she be granted permission to accompany the Hough family to Burma, where she desired to be of service to the children and women of that country. To reinforce her proposal, she offered her property to the Society, which amounted to about fifteen hundred dollars. This raised the question as to what the Board meant by the term "missionary." A special committee was appointed to consider Mrs. White's proposal.

On July 11, the majority voted to allow her "to attach herself to the family of brother Hough, to accompany them to India, and to render service to the mission." A minority of the committee insisted that only preachers were to be appointed as missionaries, and that it was never intended that women should be employed by the Society in any way. The incident caused much discussion and difference of opinion, even the resignation of some members of the Board. Later, the issue was resolved when Mrs. White married an English missionary, Joshua Rowe, a few months after her arrival at Serampore, where the American party had stopped for a time with the English Baptists. The Board at home reported to its constituents that it had incurred no expense in sending out Mrs. Rowe, and decided that the remainder of the money she had contributed to the fund should be returned to her.[2]

The first stimulus to organization of women's missionary societies in American Protestantism came from an appeal of the Reverend David Abeel, an American missionary, who addressed some women in London in 1834 while returning to China from his furlough in America. He urged them to send to the mission fields in the Orient educated and consecrated women who should visit the homes of non-Christians and win the mothers and gather the girls into mission schools. As a result, a group of women of varying denominations formed a missionary society for promoting female education in the East. It became the first woman's foreign mission society.

Upon reaching America, Abeel made the same appeal in New York City. The response of the women was the same, but the denominational boards vigorously opposed it. Accordingly, the work of women in the Orient was delayed for twenty-seven years. Nevertheless, events were conspiring to overcome the obstacles placed in the way of women's work abroad.

Freewill Baptist women took matters into their own hands in 1847 and organized the New Hampshire Yearly Meeting Benevolent Association for the purpose of raising funds for home and foreign missions. They followed this up by founding in Sutton, Vermont, later in the same year, the Freewill Baptist Female Missionary Society. Men could not attend their meetings without paying an extra fee for

---

[2] *Ibid.*, pp. 3-4; Board Reports of the General Missionary Convention of the Baptist Denomination in the United States, Vol. 1 (May 18, 1814–April 19, 1820), p. 33.

missions. Funds were sent directly to the treasurer of the home and foreign mission societies of the Freewill Baptist denomination. The Society made itself responsible for spreading missionary information, urging pastors to preach on missionary themes once in three months, raising funds, and securing information about missionaries for the Freewill Baptist publication, *Morning Star*. Mrs. M. M. Hutchins was the first corresponding secretary. In 1863 its name was changed to Freewill Baptist Ladies' Systematic Beneficence Society.

Miss Sarah P. Merrill, of Stratham, New Hampshire, was the first single woman missionary among Baptists. She was sent out by the Freewill Baptist Missionary Society in 1846. Within a year she married O. R. Bacheler, pioneer missionary to Bengal-Orissa. Miss Lavinia Crawford, of Arkwright, New York, went to the same field as the first single woman missionary sent out by Freewill Baptist women after the organization of their own society in 1847.[3]

In the spring of 1860 a second event occurred to change the course of missionary history. The wife of Dr. Francis Mason of Burma arrived in Boston on furlough. She went at once to the home of Mrs. John D. Richardson in South Boston, a friend with whom she had been sharing correspondence. Her appeal was for the needs of women in Burma which only women missionaries could meet. With characteristic energy, Mrs. Mason held numerous conferences with officials of the American Baptist Missionary Union and with other boards, urging them to appoint single women as teachers and Bible readers. Her efforts met with failure. Whereupon she and other women of like concern set about to organize an interdenominational society patterned after the English organization of 1834.

From small groups of women in Boston, New York, Brooklyn, and Philadelphia, there was incorporated in February, 1861, the Woman's Union Missionary Society of America for Heathen Lands. Its specific purpose was to employ unmarried women to labor in the Orient. In recognition of the inspiration provided by Mrs. Mason, her own station, Toungoo, Burma, was selected for its first appointees, Miss S. H. Marston, Miss S. J. Higby, and Miss S. S. LeFevre. In addition, the Society supported during that first year, four native Bible women in Burma, India, and China.

---

[3] Mrs. Henry G. Safford, *The Golden Jubilee* (New York, 1921), pp. 1-2; Mary A. Davis, *History of the Free Baptist Woman's Missionary Society* (Boston, 1900), pp. 15-19; *The Free Baptist Woman's Missionary Society, 1873–1921* (Providence, 1922), pp. 39-40.

The Woman's Union Missionary Society had a significant influence upon the development of women's work. Its success disarmed prejudice and opposition on the mission fields and at home. Well-trained young women became a source of strength to over-worked missionary wives. They were able to give assistance in educational, evangelistic, and medical work. As the demands increased, it became obvious that the one interdenominational society was insufficient. Between 1868 and 1870 the Congregational women, the Methodists, and the Presbyterians organized their own Woman's Boards.[4]

The impact of these developments did not go unnoticed by the American Baptist Missionary Union. On January 30, 1866, the Executive Committee gave extended attention to the question of engaging unmarried women missionaries. Although subscribing to a continuance of their general policy of engaging single women only in subordinate departments of the work and only when under the protection of a missionary family, the Committee showed signs of weakening. They recommended that "large discretion should be given to the Corresponding Secretary in discouraging or encouraging applications from unmarried women." By June, 1867, the Committee polled their missionaries in Asia to determine "how far the interests of the Missions may be subserved by the more liberal appointment of female helpers." Two years later, the Executive Committee was taking note that men were hard to find for missionary service, whereas there were scores of Christian women, well qualified to be teachers and missionary assistants, who were anxious to go to the mission fields. Then, showing a remarkable change of attitude, the Committee admitted that they had no right to shut the door in the face of competent women who were willing to enter foreign missionary service. It was generally agreed that they should be assigned to educational work, where they could serve best without arousing the prejudice of Orientals against women in public life.[5]

The organization of an independent society of women in Canada about this time was due to the faith and courage of a young woman, Miss Hannah M. Norris. Because Canadian Baptists were contributing to foreign missions through the American Baptist Missionary Union, she applied in 1869 to be sent to Burma. Because of lack of

[4] Safford, *op. cit.*, pp. 3-5.

[5] American Baptist Missionary Union, Records of Executive Committee for 1866–1867, pp. 8-9, 173-74; *The Baptist Missionary Magazine*, Vol. 49, No. 2 (Feb., 1869), pp. 38-43.

funds the Board could not send her. She was determined, however, to go to the field even if it meant raising the funds herself. The Reverend E. M. Saunders, pastor of the First Baptist Church in Halifax, Nova Scotia, urged her to appeal to the women of the churches for support. At once she set about to form Woman's Mission Circles in the churches. The first was organized on June 18, 1870. In two months thirty-two had been formed. In September she was able to sail for Burma with her first year's support assured. It was out of this beginning that the United Baptist Woman's Missionary Union of the Maritime Provinces emerged in 1884.[6]

By 1870 the stage was set across Protestantism for the development of women's missionary work on a national scale. The unceasing and devoted service of women during the Civil War had been a major factor in their success. For through their display of executive ability and their sacrifical shouldering of responsibility, they won recognition and respect. But they also became conscious of their power, and of their rights in public service. Thus they were especially well qualified for the period of national organization into which they entered in the 1870's. Added to this was the success of young unmarried women on mission fields which had done much to break down prejudice on the part of mission boards. Finally, the money-raising power of women proved to be a persuasive influence upon denominational leaders in giving them a measure of initiative in organizational leadership.

Beginning of Organized Societies (1871–1881)

In 1870 Mrs. C. H. Carpenter, wife of the famed missionary to the Karens at Bassein in Burma, wrote frequently of the needs of her field to her sister, Mrs. Alvah Hovey, wife of the president of Newton Theological Institution at Newton Centre, Massachusetts. She outlined the way in which women teachers could minister to Burmese and Karen women and children. Then in January, 1871, she proposed that her sister undertake "the forming of women's societies, auxiliary to the Missionary Union" for the purpose of sending out and supporting such teachers. Mrs. Hovey, being a woman of determination, lost no time in setting the plan in motion.[7]

---

[6] George E. Levy, *The Baptists of the Maritime Provinces, 1753–1946* (Saint John, New Brunswick, 1946), pp. 191-95.

[7] Safford, *op. cit.*, p. 6.

At a preliminary meeting of interested women in the Baptist Church at Newton Centre, a committee was appointed to circularize all Baptist ministers in Boston. Nearly everyone approved of the idea. At the same time, the Executive Committee of the Missionary Union was approached. On March 13, it gave approval to the proposed society on the condition that the officers of the Union be entrusted with the direction of its work. More specifically, this involved direct appointment and distribution of all missionaries, the fixing of their salaries, the appropriation of funds for their support, and the direction of their work on foreign fields. Every effort was to be made to avoid "needless increase of machinery and expense." The Union's officials welcomed the prospects of increased funds through the work of the Baptist women in the churches.[8]

With the blessing of the Missionary Union in hand, about two hundred Baptist women met in the vestry of the Clarendon Street Baptist Church in Boston on April 3, 1871, to form a society to be known as the "Woman's Baptist Foreign Mission Society." A constitution was adopted, and officers were elected. Mrs. Gardner Colby, of Newton Centre, was chosen president. There were six vice-presidents, a secretary, a treasurer, and an executive board of eleven members. In its constitution, the purpose of the Society and its auxiliary relationship to the Missionary Union were made clear:

> The leading object of this Society shall be the Christianization of women in foreign lands. This object it shall seek to accomplish, as far as possible, by furnishing support through the American Baptist Missionary Union to Christian women employed by said Union as missionaries, native teachers or Bible readers—together with the facilities needed for their work—such laborers being recommended by this Society.[9]

On May 3, an invitation was sent to the Baptist women of the West to join the new Society. But by the time the contact was made, it was too late. On May 9 the Woman's Baptist Missionary Society of the West had been organized in the lecture room of the First Baptist Church of Chicago. The inspiration for this move had come from Mrs. Cyrus F. Tolman, daughter of Dr. Miles Bronson and a mis-

---

[8] A.B.M.U., Records of the Executive Committee for March 13, 1871, p. 61.

[9] Woman's Baptist Foreign Missionary Society (East), Records of Executive Board, Vol. 1, p. 3.

sionary for several years with her husband in Assam. On her return to America for rest, she had stirred up the women to action. Mrs. Robert Harris, of Chicago, was elected president. Mrs Tolman was the first corresponding secretary.

At a meeting of representatives of the two societies in New York in 1872 the matter of uniting was discussed, but without agreement. It appears that the idea had been initiated by the women of the East. The western women were not so minded. Accordingly, the Eastern Society embraced New England, the Middle Atlantic States, and Washington, D.C.; the territory of the Western Society included Ohio and Michigan on the East and as far as the Pacific Coast on the West. The two societies worked intimately together from their respective headquarters in Boston and Chicago. They freely exchanged missionaries and fields of labor, and united in many publications.

In October, 1874, the women of California organized a third society, and were joined the next year by those of Oregon, Washington Territory, and Nevada. The new organization was called the Woman's Baptist Foreign Missionary Society of the Pacific Coast. Mrs. Bunyan Spencer was elected president and Mrs. M. E. Bridges, corresponding secretary. The Board was located in San Francisco. It maintained a separate existence until 1893, when it became auxiliary to the Woman's Baptist Missionary Society of the West.

Closely associated with this Society was the Oregon Woman's Society, composed of Baptist women of the northwestern states who had separated sometime after 1875 from the Pacific Coast Society because of great distances. The latter then came to be known as the California Society. Officers of the Oregon Society included Mrs. M. L. Briggs, president, and Mrs. E. S. Latourette, corresponding secretary.

For the sake of economy and unity in the missionary enterprise, all of these societies were auxiliary to the American Baptist Missionary Union. The Woman's Boards were to seek out suitable young women and recommend them to the Executive Committee of the Union for appointment. They were also to provide for their support. All contacts with the field were to be through the Executive Committee. The membership in the Woman's Societies was kept at one dollar a year so that every woman who desired could afford to belong. Payment of twenty-five dollars constituted life membership.[10]

The main contribution of the young women sent out by the Woman's Societies was made in behalf of women and girls in the Orient. They gave themselves in particular to mission schools for girls, to medical treatment of women and children, and to direct instruction of women in the truths of Christianity. The most urgent calls for educational work came from Burma.

Four unmarried women assistants who had been sent to Burma by the Missionary Union before 1871 were transferred to the list of the Woman's Boards. They were Miss Susan E. Haswell, who was with her parents at Moulmein; Miss A. R. Gage, who was stationed at Rangoon with her sister, Mrs. Bixby, and later with the Bennetts, who were in charge of the printing press there; Miss Rosa Adams at Henzada; and Miss Isabella Watson at Bassein. On December 16, 1871, the first new recruits sailed from New York—Miss Alvira L. Stevens (West) and Miss Katherine F. Evans (East). The three centers of women's work in Burma were at Rangoon, Moulmein, and Tavoy.

The Woman's Society of the West led in the work for women and girls in Assam. It adopted from the Union Miss Maria Bronson at Nowgong and Mrs. Anna K. Scott, M.D., at Gauhati, and added Miss Mary D. Rankin as an additional worker at Gauhati. In time the Board erected schoolhouses at both stations.

For South India, the Woman's Boards gave missionaries to Nellore, Ongole, and Ramapatnam. Miss Lavinia Peabody (later Mrs. Pearce), the second missionary sent out by the Western Society, was assigned to Ramapatnam in 1872, where she devoted herself for six years to the educating of women and girls. In 1874 Miss Mary A. Wood (later Mrs. Newhall) went from the West to take charge of the girls' boarding school at Ongole which had been founded by Mrs. John E. Clough.

East and West co-operated in establishing work at Swatow in South China. The Society for the West inaugurated medical work in 1878 by the appointment of Miss C. H. Daniels, M.D., as a medical missionary to Swatow. She was allowed only $250 for medical equip-

---

[10] The foregoing account is based on W.B.F.M.S. (East), Records of Executive Board for 1871, pp. 5, 35-36; Safford, *op. cit.*, pp. 1-10; *A Century of Service by Baptist Women* (New York, 1933), p. 6.

ment. Upon her resignation or death, all books and medicines purchased by her were to become the property of the mission. For medicine and appliances she was allowed to use $150 a year from the fees earned for her services as a doctor. All remaining fees were to go into the treasury of the Society. Such was the status of a medical missionary in those days.[11]

When the first decade of work in the Orient closed for both Societies, 2,387 local women's mission circles and children's bands in the East and West had contributed to the support of 56 missionaries, 98 schools with 2,839 pupils, and 98 native Bible women. Total receipts in 1881 for the Society of the East exceeded $50,000, and for the Society of the West amounted to $21,534. In both cases substantial increases had been made over preceding years. The combined contributions for 1881 were over ten times the amount ten years earlier.[12]

Two Decades of Progress (1881–1901)

The initial problems of organization of the Woman's Societies had been met with a larger measure of success than had been anticipated. The entrance of women into the sphere of national leadership was modest but effective. It gave expression to the enthusiasm for the cause of missions which had been long held in check. Relationships between the Societies and the Missionary Union were cordial, although the officials of the Union were careful to maintain the subordinate position of the women's agencies as auxiliaries.

During the decade, 1881–1891, the Woman's Societies extended their work in several directions. Salaries were provided for women Bible readers for France and Sweden. When the Missionary Union gave up the Liberian Mission in Africa, the Western Board assumed support of Mrs. C. M. Hill in response to her earnest plea to be allowed to carry on the schools which gave much promise of success. Likewise, Mrs. Jacob Vonbrunn's station and three village schools were taken over by the Eastern Board.

When the Reverend Henry Richards of the Congo called for single women workers to give assistance in training the new converts of the

---

[11] For more details concerning the work of these societies, see Safford, *The Golden Jubilee,* chap. 1; see also W.B.F.M.S. for the West, Records of Meetings and of the Executive Board for 1878, pp. 98-99.

[12] Safford, *op. cit.,* p. 36; *Baptist Missionary Magazine,* Vol. 72, No. 6 (June, 1872), p. 228; Vol. 61, No. 8 (Aug., 1881), pp. 283-84.

great revival that began in 1878, both Societies responded by sending Miss L. Faulkner and Miss L. Hamilton to Lukunga and Miss Louise Fleming to Palabala. In 1885, the women were called upon to give aid to the pioneer work begun in Upper Burma after it had been opened by the British.

The Swatow Woman's Bible School, which had been established by Miss A. M. Fielde in 1871, became a major factor during the 1880's in the success of the South China Mission. In 1886 women's work was begun in the fledgling Baptist Mission in Japan through the services of Miss Harriet M. Browne and Miss Nellie E. Fife sent out by the Society of the West.

Both East and West added new boarding and day schools to their schedules for South India. Special prominence was given to direct evangelistic work among women of caste as well as among those of the poorer classes. Several caste girls' schools were opened in Ongole and Madras. One began with 47 pupils and increased to 162 within four years. These schools did much to modify the attitude of caste people toward the Mission.

Medical work was begun almost simultaneously in Burma and China by the Societies of East and West. For some years the policy had been to allocate some funds for the care of sick children at boarding schools. Miss Susan Haswell, seeing the great need of this kind of service, organized a hospital in 1883 in a building on the compound of the Morton Lane School. She employed a nurse and used older pupils of the school to assist in caring for the patients. The work was financed locally. This hospital represented the beginning of Baptist medical work in Burma.

The first medical personnel to be sent out by Northern Baptist women were Dr. Ellen E. Mitchell, a woman fifty years of age, and Miss A. M. Barkley, a trained nurse. The two women reached Moulmein in January, 1880. Both women were supported by the Society of the East. At the same time, the women of the West sent Dr. C. H. Daniels, of Michigan, to Swatow, where a hospital later was built with funds raised by the Baptists of her state. In 1887 Dr. M. C. Douglas, a medical missionary of the Society of the East since 1872, was invited by Lady Dufferin, wife of the Viceroy of India, to take charge of the Government Hospital and Nurses' Training School in Rangoon. In 1888, Dr. Marie M. Coté was assigned to the Carpenter Memorial Hospital in Bassein by the Board at Chicago. Dr. Emma

J. Cummings, of the East, was the first physician to respond to the call from South India. She reached Bapatla in December, 1886, but took up permanent work a few months later at Ramapatnam, where the climate was less trying.

By 1891 a total of sixty-five new missionaries had been sent to the field during the second decade of organized work—thirty-five by the Eastern women and thirty by the Western. More than sixty thousand dollars had been invested in new buildings and extensive additions to older equipment. In 1890 the Woman's Baptist Foreign Missionary Society (East) had secured the excellent leadership as home secretary of Mrs. N. M. Waterbury, a missionary's wife for five years in India. For the next seventeen years, her influence gave new impetus to the work at home and abroad.[13]

During the third decade of organized work, 1891–1901, Northern Baptist women gave to the foreign mission enterprise an insight into the need for schools and for Christian influence on family life. They also instilled on the field the temperance ideals which women were upholding so valiantly at home through the Women's Christian Temperance Union.

In the United States, attention was given early in the 1890's to the preparation of missionary candidates. To this end the Eastern Board established "Hasseltine House" for missionary candidates at Newton Centre, where the girls were invited to spend a year before sailing. The home was in charge of Mrs. O. L. George, who had spent seventeen years in Burma. The candidates were received cordially by the faculty of Newton Theological Institution. In October, 1892, the Baptist Training School for Christian Workers was opened in Philadelphia. For a time it was under the direction of the Woman's Foreign Mission Society of Pennsylvania. The leading spirit in its founding had been Mrs. J. N. Cushing, a gifted missionary from Burma. Another institution that provided Bible training for girls as well as men was the Boston Bible and Missionary Training School, which had been established by Dr. A. J. Gordon in 1889, five years after the Belgian Congo Mission had been taken over by the American Baptist Missionary Union.

Bible schools also were organized in the Orient to train Christian workers. Among these was the Burman School at Rangoon, founded in May, 1893, and later removed to Insein. For six years it was fi-

[13] Safford, *The Golden Jubilee,* p. 68.

nanced by the Board of the East. Since 1899 it has been supported by nationals. A second was the Karen Woman's Bible School, which was the outgrowth of a training class that had been carried on for three years by Miss Lawrence in Thatone. It was opened in Rangoon in May, 1897, with twenty-two students, under the direction of Mrs. M. M. Rose, daughter of D. L. Brayton, the veteran missionary to the Pwo Karens. A third institution was the Bible School at Swatow which became the responsibility of the Western Society.

During this decade there was a marked advance in medical work. Up to this time only three physicians had been sent to the Orient—Dr. Daniels to China, Dr. Mitchell to Burma, and Dr. Cummings to India. From 1891 to 1901 fourteen new physicians were sent out, eight from the East and six from the West. Because of ill health four of these were obliged to return to America within a short time. The others made history in medical missions. Among these was Dr. Anna K. Scott at Swatow, China; Dr. Josephine Bixby at Kityang, also in South China; Dr. Caroline Coates at Nellore in South India; and Dr. Catharine L. Mabie, usually identified with Kimpese, but stationed in the early years at Banza Manteke in the Belgian Congo.

For the entire ten-year period the Woman's Societies had added 77 missionaries, bringing its illustrious staff to 113. They supported 284 Bible women, maintained 454 schools with 16,500 pupils, and operated 13 hospitals. The two Societies appropriated approximately $70,000 for new buildings and repairs. At home, they owned three homes for the children of missionaries—at Newton Centre, Massachusetts; Chicago, Illinois; and Burton, Washington. In addition they maintained the home for missionary candidates at Newton Centre. The combined receipts from these Societies annually amounted to $150,000.[14]

Within the brief span of thirty years since its organization in 1871, women's work had become a permanent part of denominational life. Baptist women were successfully promoting missionary giving through local church circles and associational and district meetings. In addition they were preparing literature and educating children and youth concerning missions. Besides maintaining their own projects on mission fields and at home, the Woman's Societies were making financial contributions for distinctively Missionary Union work, over

---

[14] *Ibid.*, p. 109; *The Baptist Missionary Magazine,* Vol. 75, No. 7 (July, 1895), p. 194.

which they had no control. For example, during the fiscal year, 1893–1894, they gave more than thirty thousand dollars to the Union for this purpose. But even more important, the women were providing a corps of able and self-sacrificing missionaries.

The New Century and Merger

The fourth decade of organized women's work that opened in 1901 was marked by a growing appreciation of their contribution to missions on the part of the denomination generally. It was a period that presented increasingly complex problems in the face of new demands and changing circumstances abroad and at home. Responsibilities for administration of the fields became more involved in the face of antiforeign tensions in China, rapid ingatherings of new converts in South India, and the emergence of the new field policy set up by the American Baptist Missionary Union which we have traced in the last chapter. Moreover, the Woman's Societies were entering into co-operative relationships with other denominations in the support of schools and hospitals in areas where joint work was more economical and effective. This trend reflected the influence of the growing ecumenical spirit that characterized the new century. A further problem concerned relationships to the Missionary Union and also to the Northern Baptist Convention following its organization in 1907.[15]

The work on the mission fields continued along the lines outlined in the previous chapter. In 1903 the Societies began to send single women to the Philippines. In 1906 a great revival swept over India that affected the South India Mission. It began in the Kassia Hills and spread rapidly. Impetus had come chiefly from the work of that remarkable Indian Christian woman, Pandita Ramabai, whose self-sacrificing work in behalf of the girls of low caste at Mukti was accompanied by a highly emotional revival that had begun in 1901. In the Telugu field, its influence was felt especially in the boarding schools. Under the wise leadership of the missionaries, the spiritual awakening accomplished much good. With the merger of Baptist and Free Baptist work in 1911, the Bengal-Orissa Mission of India, southwest of Calcutta on the Bay of Bengal, brought additional responsibilities to the Woman's Societies. They contributed

[15] For a discussion of these problems, see Helen Barrett Montgomery, *Western Women in Eastern Lands* (New York, 1911), chap. 6.

leadership to educational, industrial, evangelistic, and medical work conducted on the five stations of that field.

Perhaps the most dramatic development in women's work in the period under consideration was the merger of the Societies, and their affiliation with the Northern Baptist Convention. The initial steps were taken by the western women in 1902. At that time, a Co-ordination Committee, which had been set up by the Board of the Society for the West to effect closer relations with the Missionary Union, expressed a readiness to consider the wisdom of uniting all woman's foreign missionary societies. The committee expressed an unwillingness, however, to merge with the Missionary Union, as some had suggested. They were convinced that women were needed on the foreign field and that their educational influence was needed at home —tasks which could be accomplished best by separate women's organizations. At the same time, they pressed for representation on the Reference Committees which had been established on the mission fields to make recommendations to the Executive Committee of the Union (see Chapter X).[16]

Although the Missionary Union's officials admitted the need for the kind of educational work for women and children that the Woman's Societies were doing, they stressed the subordinate position of those organizations to the Union in a communication of 1902. In view of later developments, the contents are of sufficient importance to quote here:

> We consider that there is already one treasury for the foreign work; we regard the women's societies in the light of helpful and efficient auxiliaries, whose several treasuries are really places of deposit for funds to be used in the foreign mission work; which funds are duly sent to the treasury of the Missionary Union, and are finally administered by the Executive Committee of the Union. The title to all property in foreign countries acquired by the payment of money collected by the women's societies is held by the Missionary Union; all women candidates are appointed and their fields designated by the Executive Committee, and their salaries are paid by order of the Executive Committee through the treasury of the Missionary Union; every appropriation for the foreign work of the women's societies is submitted to the Executive Committee,

[16] Records of the Meetings of the Woman's Baptist Foreign Missionary Society for the West and of the Executive Board, Vol. 7 (1901–03), pp. 108-10, 114, 124-28.

and can only become operative with their approval. The women's societies also appropriate large sums for educational, medical, and evangelistic work at the request of the Executive Committee to support work where the women's societies have no representative.[17]

The first definite step towards merger came in March, 1903, when the Woman's Societies of California and Oregon voted to unite organically with the Society of the West. The next major move came five years later, when the Societies of the East and the West approved a Proposed Movement for Co-operation in Missionary Education that already had been accepted by the Missionary Union, the Home Mission Society, and the Publication Society in February, 1908. It was especially aimed for young people. The plan was to develop in them a sense of stewardship with respect to missions.

In May, 1908, the Western Board agreed to participate in the Committee of Twenty-One set up by the major national agencies and the Northern Baptist Convention "for the preparation of budgets of the societies mentioned therein and the apportionment of the same among the states, associations, and churches . . . beginning with the fiscal year 1909–1910." In December, 1909, the Board agreed to present its budget with that of the Missionary Union to the Northern Baptist Convention. These were important steps in the direction of affiliation with the Convention.[18]

At the annual meetings of the Woman's Societies in April, 1909, the two Boards adopted a resolution to unite in closer co-operation on the field and at home. The territory of the Convention was to be divided into four districts for promotional purposes: Eastern States, Central States, Mountain States, and Pacific States. For each district there was to be a secretary. A certain percentage of funds collected was to constitute a common fund for the prosecution of this united promotion work. A general council was to be appointed, composed of three members from each Board, and a chairman who was not a member of either Board was to be chosen by the two Boards.

In the course of discussion later in the year concerning affiliation with the Northern Baptist Convention, the question of the relationship of the Woman's Societies to the Missionary Union emerged

---

[17] Cited in the Records of the Meetings of the Woman's Baptist Missionary Society (East), Vol. 3 (1898–1907), pp. 131-32.

[18] Records of the Meetings of the W.B.M.S. for the West and of the Executive Board, Vol. 10 (1907–09), pp. 152-53; Vol. 11 (1909–12), p. 69.

once more. At the meeting of the Executive Board for the West on December 7, 1909, it was brought out in discussion that:

> . . . 'legally' according to the charters of the two Woman's Foreign Missionary Societies, the two societies are separate organizations apart from the American Baptist Missionary Union, and that the term of 'auxiliary' is one of permission and convenience rather than an actual fact legally, and is based upon the by-laws of the societies and reaffirmed in reports made from time to time since the organization of the two Woman's Societies.[19]

It is apparent that the charters of the Societies provided much more independence than the women had claimed through the years.

On July 8 and again on September 6, 1912, representatives of the general society and the two Woman's Societies met in the Baptist Headquarters in Boston to confer on the proposed merger. The women insisted upon preserving their identity within the Convention. They also made plans for a projected union with Free Baptist women. The Society of the West was agreeable to union with the women of the East, provided that the headquarters were not in Boston. These meetings paved the way for a general conference of a joint council of seven persons, representing the general society, the two women's societies, the Executive Committee of the Northern Baptist Convention, and the General Conference of Free Baptists. The meeting was held in Boston on December 17, 1912.

After an enlargement of the joint council to sixteen members, a two-day meeting was held in Rochester, New York, January 16-18, 1913, to outline a plan for formation of one Woman's Baptist Foreign Mission Society. It was agreed that the administration of foreign work should be conducted from Boston, while home administration should be centered in Chicago.

The actual organization meeting for the merger was held in Detroit, Michigan, May 17-19, 1913. There sixty delegates from each Society met in the Woodward Avenue Baptist Church. Mrs. Andrew MacLeish, president of the Society for the West, called the meeting to order. Mrs. M. Grant Edmands, president of the Society in the East, joined her in leading a devotional service. Mrs. H. E. Goodman, of Chicago, was elected chairman of the meeting, and Mrs. M. J. Twomey, of Portland, Maine, was chosen secretary. The rec-

---

[19] *Ibid.*, Vol. 11, p. 69

ommendations for unification which had been adopted by both Societies at their annual meetings were read. Then, in a solemn ceremony, Mrs. Edmands presented Mrs. Goodman with a gavel made from the wood of the "hopia" tree which grew out of the grave of Ann Hasseltine Judson in Burma. On motion of Mrs. Edmands, the delegates voted to proceed with the organization of the Woman's American Baptist Foreign Mission Society. A constitution was prepared, and the following officers were elected: Mrs. Helen B. Montgomery, president; Mrs. M. Grant Edmands, vice-president for the Foreign Department; Mrs. Andrew MacLeish, vice-president for the Home Administration Department; Mrs. R. E. Ramsay, recording secretary. A temporary Board of Managers was chosen to serve until the Districts were organized and could elect their own representatives. It was decided that business should be conducted by the officers of the Woman's Baptist Foreign Missionary Society (East) until a charter had been secured for the new organization. Meantime, the new officers would be perfecting the Districts. On the last day of the session, Mrs. Edmands relinquished her position as vice-president for the Foreign Department, and Mrs. Henry W. Peabody was elected in her place. The new constitution and bylaws were to go into effect on May 15, 1914, following a formal vote of the two Societies to merge their organizations.[20]

The closing meetings of the two Societies in the spring of 1914 were memorable occasions. The Woman's Baptist Foreign Missionary Society (East) met in the Newton Centre Baptist Church on April 28-30; it was the site on which 11 women, all members of that church, had issued the call on February 28, 1871, which had resulted in organization of the Society. During the 43 years of its history, the Society had supported 219 missionaries. To the churches had been added 1,430 young people, chiefly from the schools which it maintained. In 1913–14, the Society had 96 missionaries on the field, with nine under appointment. In addition, 67 married missionaries were receiving appropriations for work among women and children. A total of 523 schools that served 21,189 pupils came under the responsibility of the Society. Likewise, the Society supported 165 Bible women and hundreds of native teachers.[21]

---

[20] *A Century of Service,* pp. 10-11.

[21] *Annual Report of the Woman's Baptist Foreign Missionary Society (East),* Vol. 8 (1912–14), p. 97.

The Woman's Baptist Foreign Missionary Society for the West held its closing business session in the First Baptist Church of Chicago on May 6-7, 1914. Although it was not the same building in which the first meeting had been conducted in 1871, the church was the same. A total of 169 missionaries had served the Society on the field in the 43 years of its history. In the current year, there were 65 on the field; 5 others were under appointment. The Society maintained 529 schools ministering to 17,001 pupils, two hospitals and four dispensaries, four Bible-training schools and three kindergartens. Of the missionary staff, three were doctors and three nurses. The number of Bible women engaged by the Society was 182.[22]

The result of the merger was the gathering into one great organization all of the resources which hitherto had been working co-operatively, to be sure, but separately. It was a step forward which was hailed by Baptists across the country, particularly when the new Society became a co-operating agency of the Northern Baptist Convention.

---

[22] *Annual Reports of Woman's Baptist Foreign Missionary Society for the West,* Vol. 7 (1911–14), pp. 72, 164-73.

CHAPTER XII

Success in Burma

AGAINST THE BACKGROUND of the developments at home, through which we have caught glimpses of the work abroad, we shall sketch now the thrilling story of the actual unfolding of the great work being done on the respective fields. As we shall see, there was great success in some cases and discouragement in others. The determining factors were often beyond the control of either the missionaries or the Board. There were the vagaries of cultural differences which frequently presented serious obstacles to effective evangelizing of the peoples involved. There were also the geographic problems of communication and of climatic conditions. At times, internecine strife between various tribes and hostilities between Eastern peoples and Western imperialists complicated the relation between missionaries and nationals. In some instances, however, the lack of effective achievement was due to the insufficient support from home or from the unwise choice of station sites or of mission policy. Where there was great success, the credit must be shared by the dauntless missionaries, the faithful and zealous pastors and teachers from the national churches, the tireless energy of board members and secretaries at home, and the host of Baptist people, few of whom were wealthy but without whose financial support the enterprise would have failed completely.

The first field to claim our attention quite naturally is Burma, where in 1813 American Baptists first began mission work overseas. In previous chapters we have traced the story of those early developments to the schism at home in 1845. For the purpose of recall at this point, it may be well to describe briefly the nature of the country. The Burma which Baptist missionaries were entering in increasing numbers throughout the second half of the nineteenth century was almost equal in size to the State of Texas. At the two extremes it was 1,000 miles long and 600 miles wide. Its population in 1914, numbering nearly 13,000,000, was equal to that of New England and the Middle Atlantic States combined. The country was divided into Upper Burma, which was hilly to mountainous and rich in mineral resources, and Lower Burma, which was a fertile plain devoted to the rather profitable raising of rice and other crops.

Approximately three-fourths of the population of Burma was engaged in agriculture. The average landowner held six and a half acres of arable soil, while 2,750,000 people had no land at all. Nearly one-eighth of the land under cultivation was in the hands of large landowners. The populace represented 40 different racial strains, with as many languages and dialects.

When the Baptist mission began in Burma, the country was ruled by a despotic king and his council of landowners. Through two wars between the British and the government of Burma, in 1824–26 and again in 1852, portions of Lower Burma fell under the rule of the British Viceroy of India. In 1886 the domains of King Theebaw, which constituted Upper Burma, were annexed to India. In 1897 Burma was made once more a separate province with its own lieutenant-governor. This acquisition of Burma by the British government in India was a major factor in enabling the Baptists to establish strong missions in the country.

Religiously, the people of Burma were a mixture. The great majority, nearly 10,000,000 by the first quarter of the twentieth century, were Buddhists. The rest were chiefly animists, whose fear of evil spirits was relieved only by the Christian message. Because Buddhism was the accepted religion of the Burmese and also of the Shans, both groups were more difficult to win to Christianity. The animistic hill tribes were more easily won because their culture, being less developed than that of either the Burmese or the Shans, offered little resistance to the Christian gospel.

There had been outstanding missionaries in the pioneer period of the Burma Mission. Among them, of course, were Adoniram and Ann Judson, who planted the initial station at Rangoon, and George Dana Boardman and his wife, Sarah, who established the Karen mission. Jonathan Wade and Elisha Abbott were formative influences in the Karen churches. Intertwined in the history of the Karen work is the name of Justus Vinton, who landed with his wife at Moulmein in December, 1834. For the next fourteen years, the Vintons evangelized village after village in the district around Moulmein. Then there was Eugenio Kincaid, the great evangelist to the Burmese. These are but a few of the long list of devoted men and women prior to 1845 who helped to establish the work in Lower Burma.

Because of the variety of racial groups with whom Baptist missionaries worked in the period to 1914, it is difficult to trace the story of the various missions in Burma without creating some confusion. Therefore, it will be the plan of this chapter to trace first the main developments of the work generally from 1846 to 1914. The chapter will conclude with a summary of special phases of mission work, such as education, medical work, and publications. This will be followed in the next chapter by a survey of the slow progress made among the Burmese and the Shans, then of the dramatic successes among the Karens, and finally of the later efforts to reach the hill peoples of Upper Burma.

Developments to the Organization of the Burma Convention (1846–1865)

The year 1846 was freighted with problems both at home and on the field. The Missionary Union had emerged from the schism with a measure of success, but the financial future was as yet uncertain. Accordingly, attention was given to the possibility of retrenchment. Meanwhile, the situation in Burma was precarious owing to numerous cases of sickness and death among the missionaries. Lovele Ingalls, at Moulmein, wrote a strong appeal to the Board on January 7 for reinforcements. He pointed out that there was not a single missionary whose time was devoted to preaching to the Burmese. The few who understood and spoke Burmese well were engaged in the Karen work. In Moulmein, those who were ministering to the Burmese were occupied with teaching rather than direct evangelistic preaching.[1] Obviously, Ingalls' analysis of the situation implied a criticism of the use of schools as a method of reaching the Burmese. It foreboded the coming conflict over mission policy that was to be precipitated by the visit of the Deputation a few years later.

[1] *The Baptist Missionary Magazine,* Vol. 26, No. 6 (June, 1846), pp. 145-47; No. 7 (July, 1846), pp. 207-10.

On December 5, 1846, Judson arrived at Moulmein, accompanied by Harris and Beecher and their wives. It was his last term of service. His visit to America had been spent in seeking to arouse further support for the mission. Almost at once he went to Rangoon to revive the work there. The Burmese church had barely more than eleven members surviving. Services had to be conducted in secrecy to avoid persecution from the hostile government. Lack of funds added to his discouragement, and in September, 1847, he felt obliged to abandon Rangoon for the time being. Accordingly, he returned to Moulmein to complete the Burmese-English Dictionary and to preach at least one sermon each Sunday.

In the latter part of the year, Justus Vinton and his wife left Moulmein for their first visit to America since their arrival fourteen years before. Vinton spent his entire furlough traveling across the country, seeking to arouse the lagging enthusiasm of the churches. His efforts were not in vain, for in 1850 the Missionary Union was able to send out one of the largest groups of missionaries in its history—a total of thirteen men and women, including Dr. Dawson, a physician.

Before the middle of 1850 the great Judson was gone. Following a cold contracted in the fall of 1849, he declined rapidly in strength. Although reluctant to leave Moulmein, he had yielded to the advice of his physician to take a sea voyage, and it was while aboard the ship *Aristide Marie* that he died quietly on April 12, 1850, his breath growing shorter and shorter until it ceased altogether. He was buried in the Indian Ocean, while the sad news of his passing was taken to his wife at Moulmein.

The English-Burmese Dictionary had been completed by Judson, himself, at the close of 1848, and soon afterwards was sent to the press. The Burmese-English Dictionary, which was left incomplete upon his death, was entrusted to Edward A. Stevens, at Moulmein, in whose ability Judson had placed great confidence. Stevens was not to finish the Dictionary until 1852.

Less than a year after Judson's death, Eugenio Kincaid and Dr. Dawson visited the governor at Rangoon to gain entrance once again to that city and eventually to secure permission to establish a mission in Ava, capital of Burma proper. In the face of great hostility from the authorities, the two men wrested permission to stay in the city and conduct religious services in a rented house. Dr. Dawson established a regular dispensary on the first floor, while the second floor furnished accommodations for a chapel and living quarters.

From his vantage point in Rangoon, Kincaid saw the plight of Karen Christians, many of whom were being persecuted by the Burmese. Their villages were being burned, and many were put to death. Within seven miles of Rangoon were five thousand Karen refugees, Christians and non-Christians alike. Seeing their desperate need, Kincaid sent for Vinton, who knew their language and worked among Karens at Moulmein. Without waiting for permission from the Board in Boston to relocate (a cause for its censure of him later), Vinton went at once to Rangoon in April, 1851. He was welcomed by Karens from all quarters. To care for the spread of smallpox amongst the Karens, he set up a hospital. Mrs. Vinton established a school which soon attracted some two hundred pupils. A remarkable ingathering of converts followed, beginning in July.

Meanwhile, Kincaid was having some success among the Burmese. By November, he was able to report the baptism of several persons in the city. Encouraged by these favorable results, Kincaid, Dawson, and Vinton prepared strong recommendations to the Missionary Union to maintain a permanent station at Rangoon. They explained that without a strong church there and the assistance of missionaries, the Burmese Christians would be unable to cope with the inevitable persecution which would follow any successful inroads of the gospel upon Buddhism.[2]

Fortunately for the future of the Rangoon mission, events transpired about this time that led to the fall of the Province of Pegu to British rule. It began on November 23, 1851, when a steamer and three British warships appeared off the mouth of the Rangoon River, to the consternation of the Burmese governor. They were there to redress alleged wrongs done to British subjects by the Burmese government. So dangerous did the situation become for foreigners in the city that Kincaid and Dawson had to seek refuge on one of the vessels. After a siege of more than a month, a report came from Ava that the king desired friendly relations with the British. However, open fighting broke out when the Burmese fired from the stockades of the city on the vessel bearing a flag of truce and seeking a com-

---

[2] *Ibid.*, Vol. 31, No. 11 (Nov., 1851), pp. 409-16; Vol. 32, No. 2 (Feb., 1852), pp. 33-37; No. 4 (Apr., 1852), pp. 97-108; Vol. 38, No. 9 (Sept., 1858), pp. 342-43.

munication with the governor. The British openly declared war, and sent an army into the country. Martaban was taken on April 5, and Rangoon on April 14. The city was left a shambles by fires set by the Burmese and by the shelling from the English ships. Kincaid and Dawson returned at once to recover their possessions, but obtained only a few books. Under British protection they reopened their work in a Buddhist monastery within the boundaries of the stockade.

Soon afterward, Bassein also fell to the English. Elisha Abbott, who had fled for safety to Moulmein, was able, with British protection, to return with H. L. Van Meter. He took up residence there in a Buddhist monastery on July 12, 1852. A few months later, ill health forced him, however, to return to America.

As a result of the British victories, the Province of Pegu was incorporated into British India. By the close of 1852, it was divided into four districts, Rangoon, Prome, Pegu, and Bassein. Bassein district was to include Sandoway, which had been formerly under the Commissioner of Arracan. Martaban district was to be subject to the civil jurisdiction of the Commissioner at Moulmein.

The war had significant effect upon the Baptist work in Burma. It demoralized the missions greatly. The Karen Christians suffered extreme oppression, and nearly all of their chapels were destroyed. Even after the end of Burmese rule, they were subjected to famine, disorganization, and the terrorism of roaming groups of Burmese bandits. But recovery was rapid especially at Kemmendine, a site two miles from the stockade at Rangoon, to which Vinton moved the Karen mission. Buildings were erected there for his home and a school. Vinton bought a shipload of rice in order to feed the starving Karens. In the years that followed, thousands were baptized, churches were organized, and schoolhouses were built.

The war had assured the safety of Baptist missionaries in Lower Burma. From 1852 on, persecution of Christian Burmese and Karens was made illegal. It is little wonder that the missionaries regarded the British victory as a providential act of God, an attitude which the Burmese were to resent in later years. Moreover, new areas were open to missionary advance, a fact which figured largely in the decision of the Missionary Union to send a Deputation to Burma in 1853.[3]

---

[3] The account of the Second Anglo-Burman War and its effects upon Baptist missions has been drawn from biographies of Vinton, Kincaid, and Abbott,

The work of the Deputation and its effects upon the missions have been described in detail in Chapter VIII. Here it is only necessary, therefore, to call attention to its importance to the Burma Mission, with which it was chiefly concerned. By bringing about the resignation of several able missionaries, it weakened the staff. By its insistence upon a change of policy with respect to schools, it placed a serious check upon the educational work which had been developed among the Burmese and the Karens. By its stress, however, upon the importance of an ordained native ministry, the Deputation provided a wholesome corrective to a reluctance on the part of some missionaries to share responsibility with national leadership. The decision of the Deputation to recommend an expansion of the work of the Burma Mission was a step in the right direction. Rangoon, Bassein, Pegu, and Prome were to have two missionaries each.

One of the most rewarding actions in 1853 was the founding of a new station at Toungoo, about 175 miles north of Rangoon and situated on the Sitang River. There were four distinct tribes of Karens in the area: the Sgaws in the mountains to the west; the Bghais in the mountains to the northeast, extending far beyond the British territories; the Pakus to the east of Toungoo; and the Maunie-pghas to the southeast. In the absence of Dr. Francis Mason in America, the new mission was entrusted to a remarkable Christian Karen, Sau Quala. After Mason returned to Burma in October, 1854, he was occupied with completing his translation of the Scriptures into Pwo Karen. Thus he was able to give only indirect supervision to Toungoo. He had instructed Quala to throw into the work every promising young man whom he could train, without waiting for them to take a regular course of instruction. The results were beyond all expectancy. The young preachers comprised a body of assistants unequalled in the history of the Burma Mission up to that time.

Mason and his wife established residence at Toungoo in January, 1857. With keen appreciation of the initiative and ability already manifested by the native leadership, he left the care of the churches completely in the hands of the pastors. Even the village schools were given an importance that was not overshadowed by the school he taught in Toungoo. For the training of teachers, Mason planned a

---

and from the detailed accounts provided by missionaries in *The Baptist Missionary Magazine* in Volumes 32 and 33 that includes issues for May, 1852 through April, 1853.

normal school in Toungoo with a native instructor and supported by the Karens themselves. Mrs. Mason opened a girls' school on the same principle.

At the same time Mason began preparation of books in Bghai Karen. He urged the early appointment of a missionary to work among the Burmese in the area, and with the Shans on the northern borders of the empire who were more numerous and less devoted to Buddhism than the Burmese.

From the start, the Toungoo mission was a phenomenal success, and it deserves a prominent place in the history of the work among the Burmese and the Karens. It is an outstanding example of the accomplishment of the faithful and effective Karen preacher, Sau Quala, who had been in full charge of the work until May, 1855, when Daniel Whitaker came to help him. It is a thrilling illustration of the transforming influence of the gospel upon community life. Whereas there had been deep-seated fear and enmity between Bghai Karen villages so that a man's life might be forfeited if he were found outside of his own district, Christianity had developed a free and happy intercourse among villages. An intemperate people had given up the use of intoxicants. Literacy replaced ignorance, and liberality became an outstanding quality of the new churches.[4]

The year 1859 was memorable for several reasons. In the first place, the seat of the Burmese government was removed from Ava to Mandalay. Within eight months the new capital had 300,000 people. The king remained friendly to the missionaries, and offered to build a mission house when asked for a plot of ground upon which to establish a compound.

A second event of note was the entrance of the first Protestant non-Baptist mission into Burma. The Society for the Propagation of the Gospel in Foreign Parts established a center at Rangoon for the circulation of Christian literature and the promotion of Christian education. The coming of the Church of England into Burma proved to be a source of irritation to some of the missionaries who regarded Burma as exclusively a Baptist field. The Executive Committee of the Missionary Union fortunately did not share this view.[5]

---

[4] *The Baptist Missionary Magazine,* Vol. 35, No. 7 (July, 1855), pp. 290-92; Vol. 36, No. 7 (July, 1856), pp. 262-66; Vol. 38, No. 7 (July, 1858), pp. 241-44.

[5] *Ibid.,* Vol. 39, No. 11 (Nov., 1859), pp. 395-96; Vol. 45, No. 2 (Feb., 1865), pp. 33-35.

A third development in 1859 was the change of policy initiated by the Executive Committee, whereby organized local missions were to be replaced by larger units based on racial groupings. Henceforth, therefore, the mission stations were to be identified respectively with the Burmese department or the Karen department. It was a step in the direction of greater co-ordination on the field.

Within the next few years, both departments showed evidence of marked progress. In 1860 there were forty Burmese baptisms, thirty-seven of which had resulted wholly from preaching in Burmese. Two of the converts were Mohammedans, one of whom was a man of prominence and well known in Ava, who had devoted six years to a careful comparison of the Bible with the Koran before asking for baptism. In 1860 the "Rangoon Burman Missionary Society" was formed by missionaries and English residents for the sole purpose of spreading the gospel among the Burmese. In the same year a Burmese Association of Baptist churches was formed at Thonze (then called Thongzai), in the territory of the Rangoon mission. It was the first strictly Burmese association. At Bassein, the work among the Pwo Karens had developed to the point where there were thirteen churches and a total membership of over five hundred Christians. In February, 1863, they were organized in a Pwo Association, thus giving them an opportunity to develop separately from the much larger body of Sgaw Karens.[6]

Consolidation and Organizational Development (1865–1885)

In October, 1865, a Burma Baptist Missionary Convention was organized with the approval of the Executive Committee of the Union. It was intended to develop among the missionaries a unity of purpose and harmony of viewpoint on major issues. It was also an important step in the direction of transferring the work of evangelization to the national leadership of the churches in Burma. The conference that brought the new organization into being was composed of all the missionaries of the Union; it also enrolled Beecher, Vinton, and M. Luther, who were no longer connected with the Union, together with seventy native preachers and leading laymen. Membership in the Convention was to be comprised of all missionaries, ordained minis-

[6] *Ibid.*, Vol. 41, No. 7 (July, 1861), pp. 229-31; Vol. 44, No. 7 (July, 1864), pp. 238-40.

ters, and authorized preachers of the gospel who were in the fellowship of the denomination and in agreement with the constitution. In addition, there were to be one lay delegate from each church and an additional layman for each fifty members in the church. The officers included a president, four vice-presidents, a recording secretary, a corresponding secretary, a treasurer, and twelve additional members. These composed a Committee of Management to conduct the affairs of the Convention between annual meetings.

The Reverend Cephas Bennett was elected president. The four vice-presidents were J. S. Beecher, Syah Ko En, Sau Quala, and Thrah Po Kway. The Conference adopted a resolution affirming the general principle that the Convention would regard education in the vernacular for the great body of people as of first importance. But it also expressed the belief that before the Christians of Burma could be made even comparatively independent of the guidance of the missionaries, their leaders must receive, either in Burma or abroad, an education which would approach in breadth and thoroughness that of the foreign teachers. The Conference then pointed to the Anglo-Vernacular Normal and Industrial Institute of Bassein as the ideally indigenous school for this purpose.[7]

It is noteworthy that the school so designated had been started by Beecher in defiance of the rules set down by the American Baptist Missionary Union in the 1850's and after he had left the Union's service for that reason. In a sense, therefore, the attitude expressed by the Conference was a triumph for Beecher's policy over that of the Deputation of 1853. It is also significant that this Conference went on record in favor of an indigenous church in Burma, which again represented the victory of the point of view of Elisha Abbott and C. H. Carpenter as well as of Beecher in the Bassein mission.

True to its purpose, the Burma Baptist Missionary Convention sent out Karen preachers to the Chins (at first called Kyens), a tribe in the Prome field that was allegedly more numerous in that area than the Karens. In 1867 an exploring tour was authorized to go up the Irrawaddy River to Mandalay and thence to the Shan regions north and east of that city. The journey was committed to Rose, who was associated with the mission to the Burmese, and to Cushing, of the mission to the Shans. At the end of November, these men carried

---

7 *The Baptist Missionary Magazine,* Vol. 46, No. 7 (July, 1866), pp. 220-26.

out their survey as far into the Shan States as the unsettled conditions of the country permitted.[8]

Another new development in the Burma Mission about this time was a change of policy among the missionaries to the Karens concerning the priority of schools. In 1867 the Missionary Union's Executive Committee took note that the Karen missionaries, almost to a man, were urging the establishment of boarding schools among the Burmese. On May 29, the Committee approved the proposal. The decision reflected a great change from that expressed twenty years before by prominent leaders on the field and at home who doubted the value of spending as much money as was then being used to educate the people of Burma. A factor largely responsible for the new viewpoint was the competition in many areas from the Church of England and Roman Catholic schools. Baptist missionaries saw that they soon would lose their converts if they did not offer equal opportunities for education. Accordingly, they were urging the Executive Committee to send missionaries to supervise schools, and unmarried women to teach in the normal schools. Fortunately, it was at a time when many young women of the churches in America, in the East and West, were interested in this kind of missionary service. Within the next few years the Baptist women of the country were organizing their own national societies for this purpose.[9]

In 1868 the newly laid Atlantic Cable was used for the first time by the Executive Committee to contact its missionaries. The dispatch, which concerned arrangements to fill a vacancy made in the Bassein mission by the death of Benjamin C. Thomas, read cryptically, "Carpenter transferred to Bassein, and Smith to Rangoon." It required three days for the message to reach Burma from the headquarters in Boston. The event marked a milestone in the history of the administration of the mission.[10]

In 1871 the Rangoon Baptist College was established by the Union in response to an urgent plea from all the Karen missionaries in Burma. It was to provide a good higher education for the children of the twenty thousand Karen Christians who otherwise might be

[8] *Ibid.,* Vol. 46, No. 7 (July, 1866), pp. 264-66; Vol. 48, No. 7 (July, 1868), pp. 223-25.

[9] *The Baptist Missionary Magazine,* Vol. 47, No. 8 (Aug., 1867), pp. 325-28.

[10] *Ibid.,* Vol. 49, No. 3 (March, 1869), pp. 75-76; No. 7 (July, 1869), pp. 239-40.

tempted to obtain it in Roman Catholic or Church of England schools. There is no doubt that Baptist missionaries were seriously concerned over the superior educational advantages and higher salaries which the other communions were offering. This attitude was reflected by the Committee of Management of the Burma Baptist Convention when it ventured the opinion that any one who had joined the Baptists for worldly gain was welcome to go where he could better himself, but there should be at least one general institution where the people could obtain for themselves and their children a sound higher education.

The compound of Cephas Bennett, with the buildings on it, was purchased for the college. Its beginnings were not encouraging. Dr. J. P. Binney, who had been head of the Karen Theological Seminary, was elected president. He was succeeded in about a year by the Reverend C. H. Carpenter of Bassein, who resigned in two years when his plans to remove the school to Bassein did not win favor. In March, 1875, Dr. J. Packer assumed the presidency. When an accident necessitated his return to the United States in 1879, the college was closed until 1881.

Near the close of Packer's second term of service, the school was affiliated with Calcutta University with the status of a high school whose pupils were eligible for the Matriculation Examination that permitted entrance to the University. For a time, Dr. B. P. Cross was associated with President Packer, but in 1887, he was transferred to the Karen Theological Seminary. When ill health compelled the Packers to return to the United States, the school came under the direction of Dr. J. N. Cushing for a few months, until the arrival of Professor E. B. Roach and his wife from America in October, 1887. In 1890 the Reverend D. C. Gilmore and Miss Gertrude Clinton joined them as co-workers.

When Roach became superintendent of the Mission Press in May, 1892, Cushing took temporary charge. On February 11, 1895, he was chosen president. The school prospered under his leadership. For example, in 1893, a Normal Department had been opened, with a generous government grant. The new department supplied certificated teachers for the mission schools. In 1894 the institution was raised to a first arts or second grade college, and affiliated with Calcutta University. In the same year reinforcement arrived in the field of science in the person of a college professor, L. E. Hicks, Ph.D.

During the next two years, seven additional missionaries were added to the teaching staff. The enrollment arose from 122 in 1892 to 438 in 1896. The Christians of the country began to take a financial interest. By 1896, the old seminary compound in Rangoon provided a new campus for the college, on which had been erected two dormitories, a laboratory, and a hospital. Almost all of the students in the high school and college were Christians, and the percentage of non-Christians in the lower departments was comparatively small.[11]

During the period of the early development of Rangoon Baptist College, educational work had received a marked impetus from the Woman's Societies, which it will be recalled had been organized in 1871. On mission fields across Protestantism, there was a demand for increased educational facilities. This was equally true among Baptists, not only in Burma, but in Japan, China, and South India. The shifting emphasis in missionary methods was viewed at home by the Missionary Union with some alarm, although there was no disposition, as formerly, to restrict the educational work. Instead, it was urged that the station schools be left, so far as possible, to the care of women, while the men carry on an aggressive itinerant ministry of preaching. The warning was sounded repeatedly that schools must not become the main means of evangelization.[12]

Meanwhile, on the field, the educational policy of the Union was meeting with criticism from another angle. It came from Dr. C. H. Carpenter, head of the Sgaw Karen Normal and Industrial Institute at Bassein, which was regarded by the British as the model school of Burma. His contention was that the Union was spending three times what the Roman Catholics and the Church of England were investing in education in Burma, without achieving the same level of work. The explanation, he insisted, was that the Baptists lacked co-ordination and continuity. They maintained, for example, in Toungoo two schools for Karens alone, teaching them in the same dialect. In Rangoon, they had four schools for the Karens with considerable duplication of effort. In Rangoon and Bassein separate schools and teaching staffs were maintained for the Pwos at great cost, which were inferior to those established for and supported largely by the Sgaws. Carpenter advocated a consolidation of schools wherever

---

[11] *Ibid.,* Vol. 51, No. 7 (July, 1871), pp. 241-42; Vol. 52, No. 7 (July, 1872), pp. 236-38; Vol. 77, No. 11 (Nov., 1897), pp. 598-601.

[12] *The Baptist Missionary Magazine,* Vol. 56, No. 7 (July, 1876), pp. 223-25.

possibile, and the establishment of Bassein as the Karen educational center. He argued that Rangoon was not a proper site for the college because it was removed from the population center of the Karens, who were more numerous than the Burmese Christians. Other missionaries contended that Rangoon was the strategic educational center for a college which would serve Burmese as well as Karens. Always there was in their minds the concern to reach the Burmese if at all possible.[13]

By 1880 Baptist missionaries were scattered throughout the southern part of Burma proper. This had been made possible by the extension of British rule in 1853. Prior to that time, the stations were confined to the Tenasserim Provinces, with Moulmein and Tavoy as centers. Now, there were important stations at Rangoon, Bassein, Henzada, Shwegyin, Prome, and Toungoo. The results had been impressive. Within ten years, 126 churches had been formed at Toungoo, with a total of 6,000 members. In Henzada, within a very few years, there were 56 churches, with 2,000 members. In Bassein there were nearly 6,000 members in 51 churches. In all Burma, the Baptists maintained 400 churches, with over 20,000 members. In gross financial contributions to the Missionary Union for the year ending April, 1879, the Christians of Burma were led only by Massachusetts and New York.[14]

Expansion and Steady Growth (1886–1914)

With the annexation of Upper Burma by the Viceroy of India in 1886, the Executive Committee of the Union took immediate steps to establish missions there. J. A. Freiday and W. H. Roberts were already in the territory, as Shan and Kachin interpreters for the British Army. Rose was authorized to proceed to Mandalay to begin work in the capital itself. Others were to be transferred from older stations as soon as the country became settled and safe for residence.[15]

---

[13] *Ibid.,* Vol. 60, No. 1 (Jan., 1880), pp. 6-12; No. 6 (June, 1880), pp. 146-50.

[14] *Ibid.,* Vol. 60, No. 7 (July, 1880), pp. 183-86; No. 8 (Aug., 1880), p. 294. Massachusetts contributed $41,312.72; New York, $39,469.46; and Burma, $31,616.14, of which amount $30,478.78 was raised by the Karen churches in the Bassein district to pay for the erection of the Normal and Industrial Institute buildings. The Karens then sought to raise an additional $25,000 for endowment of the schools.

[15] *The Baptist Missionary Magazine,* Vol. 66, No. 3 (March, 1886), p. 59.

By 1889 there were fifteen associations of churches in Burma, an increase of four in twenty-five years. Three were Burmese and Talaing (or Mon), five were Sgaw Karen, two were Pwo Karen, two were mixed Sgaw and Pwo, two were Bghai Karen, and one was Chin. The Burma Baptist Missionary Convention was achieving gradually a gratifying measure of co-ordination. Every station had its central school to which were sent the more advanced pupils from the villages. Some of the town mission schools had attained the academic rank of middle grade according to British standards. Four editions of the Burmese New Testament had followed one another over a quarter of a century. Two or three editions of the New Testament in Sgaw and Pwo Karen respectively had been produced during the same period. Cushing had made the New Testament available in the Shan language, and the Old Testament in Shan was going through the press by 1889. In spite of a rigid discipline required of all converts, there were 30,000 Baptist communicants in Burma. Fine buildings had been erected entirely with native funds, such as the brick chapel at Prome, the Ko Tha Byu Memorial Hall at Bassein, and the Thomas Memorial at Henzada.[16] They stood as evidence of a vigorous and self-sacrificing Christian community.

The decade from 1890 to 1900 was characterized by similar evidence of steady growth. The number of mission schools increased from 468 to 518, and the pupils from 11,477 to 15,021. The Christians of Burma had raised $211,575 for schools over the ten-year period. Rangoon Baptist College had experienced an increase in enrollment from 113 to 567 students of all grades. By 1900 the theological seminary at Insein was the largest in the Orient. During the decade there were 22,231 baptisms in Burma. Contributions from the churches amounted to $491,612. A gain in membership of over 200 per cent had been achieved in the Burmese work at Bassein and Henzada, in the Chin and Burmese work at Sandoway, and at Bhamo among the Kachins. At Manadalay and at Thayetmyo the gain was 400 per cent in stations serving the Burmese and Chins respectively. Two small stations which had shown still greater gains were Shwegyin (366 per cent for the Burmese work) and Thaton (600 per cent). These notable successes contributed to Baptists' achieving third place in the list of Christian denominations in Burma, Assam, and India—

---

[16] *Ibid.,* Vol. 69, No. 11 (Nov., 1889), pp. 427-29.

Roman Catholics and the Church of England occupying first and second place respectively.[17]

During this period of expansion it was understandable that the missionaries, scattered as they were throughout Burma, should seek an annual meeting together prior to the Convention sessions for inspiration and fellowship. Although the idea was broached several times in the 1880's or earlier, it was set aside out of concern lest such a meeting should appear to the nationals as having a political significance. By 1887, however, the missionaries decided to hold a devotional meeting; such gatherings were repeated until 1898, when a Burma Baptist Missionary Conference was organized with officers, a few committees, and a constitution. Two years later, a Committee of Reference was set up according to the pattern adopted first in South India and approved by officers of the Missionary Union.[18]

With the reorganization of the Foreign Society at home under strong executives, following its affiliation in 1907 with the Northern Baptist Convention, new policies on the field were inevitable, as we have seen in an earlier chapter. Dr. Thomas S. Barbour, the foreign secretary, and Dr. Fred P. Haggard, the home secretary, guided this reorganization. The Missionary Conference became the seat of final authority on the field. It worked through various subcommittees, chief of which was the Committee of Reference that acted for the Conference between annual meetings. In 1904 women missionaries were given representation on this committee. After 1910 the Committee of Reference assumed initiative and executive powers, dealing with many business matters concerning work on the field that were formerly handled by the executive officers in the United States. All personal matters concerning the missionaries were still handled directly by the Board.[19]

---

[17] *Ibid.*, Vol. 80, No. 7 (July, 1900), pp. 246-50; No. 10 (Oct., 1900), p. 586; Vol. 84, No. 6 (June, 1904), p. 193. Statistics for the various denominations showed 1,202,039 Roman Catholics; 435,612 Church of England; 220,863 Baptists; 155,455 Lutherans; 76,869 Methodists; 53,829 Presbyterians; 37,876 Congregationalists—a total of 2,182,543. Baptist figures include adult believers only.

[18] See description of the Burma Baptist Missionary Conference as it was from 1900 to 1925 in Lizbeth B. Hughes, ed., *The Evangel in Burma* (Rangoon, 1926), pp. 13-26. For background concerning the Committee of Reference, see Chapter X.

[19] For Rules of Procedure of the Committee of Reference, see *The News from the American Baptist Missions in Burma and Assam,* Vol. 13, No. 6 (Dec., 1900), pp. 1-2; see also Vol. 16, No. 5 (Nov., 1903), p. 1.

As a direct result of the interest aroused in co-operative Christianity by the World Missionary Conference of 1910, held in Edinburgh, Dr. John R. Mott met at Rangoon, on January 14-16, 1913, with representatives of the various missions in Burma. To the surprise of nearly everyone, including the Baptists, the meeting resulted in definite action on comity and co-operation in Burma. A doctrinal basis of unity was established in the common belief of all denominations "in the divinity of our Lord Jesus Christ, as expressed in the Apostles' and Nicene creeds, and in the conviction that Holy Scripture doth contain all things necessary to man's salvation." A Council of Christian Missions in Burma was set up to represent all missionary societies and church organizations working in the country which desired to participate. Its functions were to be purely advisory. The Council was to consider such questions as were referred to it by the different missions, and to organize subcommittees for different aspects of the work. In particular, it was to set up an interdenominational committee on education. Once in every ten years, the Council was to make a united survey of the whole field, "to see how fully it is occupied, and what the further needs are." The new plan of comity and co-operation was hailed by a Baptist missionary spokesman as a step in the direction of "greater efficiency and more rapid progress of the work of missions in Burma." [20]

By the celebration of the Centennial of the Burma Mission in December, 1913, there were 185 missionaries on the field, working in 30 mission stations among Karens, Burmese, Shans, Chins, Kachins, and more recently among the Lahus. The total membership of 65,000 Christians was only 20,000 less than the total number of Baptists in the United States when Judson began his work in Burma. Of the 916 churches, 717 or 78 per cent were self-supporting. More than 2,100 nationals were serving as pastors, teachers, and evangelists. There were 708 schools serving 26,235 pupils. While the American Baptists at home appropriated nearly $250,000 in 1914 for the work in Burma, contributions from the churches of Burma totalled almost $94,000.[21]

From this survey of the Burma Mission in general, it is evident that a century of missionary effort had been crowned with success.

---

[20] *Missions,* Vol. 4, No. 4 (April, 1913), p. 273.

[21] *Ibid.,* Vol. 4, No. 10 (Oct., 1913), p. 760; Howard B. Grose and Fred P. Haggard, *The Judson Centennial, 1814–1914* (Philadelphia, 1914), p. 17.

To be sure, the enterprise had been costly, but the rewards were gratifying. Changed lives and transformed communities gave testimony of the power of the gospel from Lower Burma to the hill country of the north. As always, Baptists were making their strongest appeal to the plain people, especially to the disinherited of society. Yet, they also were making headway amongst the more literate Burmese and Shans. Their schools had won the respect of nationals and of the British government alike. Through education, medical work, and a program of agricultural and industrial guidance, the Baptist Mission in Burma was making a significant contribution to the social uplift of the depressed classes in particular and to the ability of the churches to become self-supporting. For the future of Christianity in the country, the missionaries were making their most important achievement in the gradual development of a trained leadership to direct the churches and perpetuate the evangelization of their own people.

Special Phases of Mission Work

From the survey just concluded it is evident that education played an important part in the Burma Mission. Naturally, the largest and most prominent schools were developed in the main centers of the work. The earliest Anglo-Vernacular and English Middle Schools for Karens and Burmese (corresponding to junior high schools in America) were developed between 1845 and 1865 in Moulmein, Rangoon, Shwegyin, Tavoy, Bassein, and Toungoo, in that order. Two were for girls, the Karen School at Rangoon founded by Mrs. J. H. Vinton, and the Karen School at Shwegyin established by Mrs. Vinton Harris. The number of schools increased appreciably with the organization of the Woman's Societies in America in 1871. Between that date and 1914, there came into existence thirty-nine Anglo-Vernacular and English Middle Schools. In addition, seven high schools were opened between 1893 and 1914. Among these were the Ko Tha Byu High School at Bassein, with 800 pupils by 1914; the Morton Lane Girls' School at Moulmein, with a strong normal department; the Kemmendine Girls' School at Rangoon, with nearly 400 girls enrolled; the English Girls' High School at Moulmein, which was performing a valuable service to the English-speaking and Eurasian population; and the Mandalay High School, which was the only Baptist school of its grade for boys in Upper Burma.

Six normal schools also were founded between 1883 and 1914 to serve Burmese, Karens, Shans, Chins, Eurasians, and other smaller groups.

In addition to these secondary schools, there were, of course, the primary village schools, the Bible schools for women, two theological seminaries for Burmese and Karens respectively, and the college at Rangoon. Most Burmese and Shan parents demanded separate schools for their daughters, but co-education came to be accepted eventually among the Karens.

The role which the mission schools played in Burma has been notable. They brought to illiterate peoples their first taste of education; and especially to girls and women, they brought the first opportunity to emerge from a subordinate position in society. The schools not only developed leadership for Christian communities, but also provided trained personnel for government service and the professions. Throughout their history, these schools were evangelizing agencies, for most of the non-Christian students were led to a commitment to Christ or at least to a sympathetic understanding of Christianity and the purpose of the mission.[22]

To Susan Haswell must go the credit for the beginning of institutional medical work in Burma. To be sure, nearly every missionary had been obliged to render assistance to the sick in connection with his many other duties. But it was the appeal of Miss Haswell that brought to Burma the first woman physician, Dr. Ellen Mitchell, in 1879. For twenty-two years Dr. Mitchell used a house on a hillside in Moulmein for a hospital in which to care for the health needs of women and children. She also inaugurated the Moulmein Leper Asylum, which was eventually organized in a formal manner in 1898 as a branch of the English society known as the Mission to Lepers in India and the East.[23] It later was named for Susan Haswell.

The Reverend Arthur Darrow came to Moulmein in 1902, the year after Dr. Mitchell's death. He worked among the Talaings, causing the church to make genuine progress within a few years. As a thank offering, this church gave ten thousand rupees to purchase a site for a hospital. This gift was presented to the Foreign Mission

[22] For a complete list of American Baptist secondary and normal schools, see the *Burma News,* Vol. 40, No. 10 (Oct., 1927), pp. 75-76. For a summary of women's work in education and medicine, see Randolph L. Howard, *Baptists in Burma* (Philadelphia, 1931), chap. 7.

[23] *The Baptist Missionary Magazine,* Vol. 84, No. 5 (May, 1904), p. 169.

Societies at the celebration of the Judson Centennial in 1913. The hospital and nurses' home were not completed, however, until 1918. The Ellen Mitchell Memorial Hospital, as it was called, became in time the center of the Leper Asylum which was then carried on jointly by the American Mission to Lepers and the city of Moulmein.

A second hospital was established in Burma prior to 1914, under the direction of Dr. W. C. Griggs. It was the Bessie Richards Memorial Hospital in Bhamo, dedicated in 1896 in honor of a Baptist woman of Philadelphia, Pennsylvania, who had organized in the Nicetown Baptist Church a mission circle to support two nurses for the Karens. Just before her death she had urged the women not to let the work cease. In her memory, therefore, they raised funds for a building, forty-four feet long, which provided two wards and a combination dispensary and operating room. The Second Baptist Church in Germantown, Philadelphia, furnished a microscope.[24] This is illustrative of the manner in which the meager supplies for medical work were provided when medical missions were in their infancy.

Perhaps no single agency of the Burma Mission accomplished more for the spread of the gospel in that country than the American Baptist Mission Press. From previous chapters, it will be recalled that the first printer, George H. Hough, was sent to Burma to assist Judson in 1816. He set up in Rangoon a press which was a gift of the English Baptist Mission at Serampore. During the First Anglo-Burmese War, the press was moved to Calcutta, and then located in Moulmein after hostilities had ceased. In 1830 Cephas Bennett, also a printer, arrived in Moulmein with the first press to be sent from the United States. Between 1832 and 1843, the Missionary Union employed a number of printers, stereotypers, and engravers to labor at Moulmein. These years constituted a great period of printing in Burma. There was a heavy demand for the Scriptures in various languages, and missionaries and the supporters at home were interested in getting the Bible into the hands of the people. Bennett even opened a second press at Tavoy in 1837 to serve the Karens. By 1841, however, with Burma proper closed to missionaries, there was an oversupply and the presses were standing still. By 1851, therefore, all the printers at Moulmein had been transferred to other

[24] *Ibid.*, Vol. 76, No. 10 (Oct., 1896), pp. 512-13.

missions or had returned to America except Cephas Bennett and T. S. Ranney.

Four years later, as a result of the visit of the Deputation to Burma in 1853, the press at Tavoy was merged with that at Moulmein. In 1862, the entire printing establishment was removed to Rangoon, which by then was the chief social and commercial city in Burma.

Publications of the presses had included Bibles, books for the schools, hymnals, and two monthly papers, the *Morning Star* in Karen, which had been established at Tavoy in September, 1842, and the *Religious Herald* in Burmese, which had been started at Moulmein in January, 1843.

In February, 1865, the Executive Committee of the Union evolved a new plan for conducting the mission press in Burma, replacing the policy adopted by the Deputation in 1853. They abolished the Publication Committee, which had not really functioned for some years, and placed the management of the press wholly in the hands of Bennett, the superintendent, and the Executive Committee. It was hoped that eventually the supervision of the press would be taken over entirely by the missionaries, or by a combination of missionaries and nationals. Lucrative job work was to be subordinate to the printing work for the mission.[25]

The progress of the Mission Press at Rangoon was steady, as the work in the country was enlarged, and as sales increased. Upon the retirement of Bennett in 1881, after fifty years of service as superintendent of the Press, he was succeeded by Frank D. Phinney, who served until 1892 when Professor E. B. Roach, of Rangoon Baptist College, took over the responsibility. On September 13, 1903, the cornerstone was laid for a new building, which was completed by December 15, 1904. A fine salesroom on the street level increased sales fifty per cent within the first two weeks of occupancy of the new quarters. In addition to other materials, Sunday school lesson papers were being produced in Burmese, Sgaw Karen and Pwo Karen. In the year 1913–14, the Mission Press did a gross business of more than $158,000.[26]

---

[25] The foregoing account is based on *The Baptist Missionary Magazine,* Vol. 44, No. 7 (July, 1864), pp. 230-38; Vol. 45, No. 7 (July, 1865), pp. 213-20.

[26] *Ibid.,* Vol. 85, No. 6 (June, 1805), p. 227; *The News from the American Baptist Missions in Burma and Assam,* Vol. 20, No. 10 (Oct., 1907), p. 1; *Missions,* Vol. 5, No. 7 (July, 1914), p. 565.

By the time of the Judson Centennial, the Bible had been translated and printed in six of the languages of Burma, and portions of the Scriptures had been produced in other dialects. The six major versions were Judson's Burmese, Durlin Brayton's Pwo Karen, Josiah Cushing's Shan, Francis Mason's Sgaw Karen, Ola Hanson's Kachin, and the Mon or Talaing version produced by James Haswell and Robert Halliday.

CHAPTER XIII

Success in Burma (Continued)

WE TURN NOW to a brief summary of the work accomplished among the various racial groups in Burma. In order to avoid repetition of the story just unfolded, the emphasis will be upon the main characteristics of the approach to these people and of their response to the gospel.

Slow Progress Among the Burmese

As we have seen, the earliest efforts of Judson and his associates were devoted to winning the Burmese to Christianity. From the first, except in occasional instances, the resistance of the Burmese to the gospel was determined and unrelenting. Their devotion to Buddhism and its educational system was not easily shaken by preaching. They found it hard to believe that there was any truth to be discovered outside of their own monasteries. Parents who could be persuaded to send their children to the primary schools would send them, as soon as they were able to read a little, to Buddhist schools where they would be taught in their religious books and in the Pali language, which was used by better educated Burmese. Many parents were afraid not to send their sons to a monastery school lest they lose merit. Moreover, they could be persuaded to send their daughters to the Christian schools only with the greatest difficulty because such parents believed that girls who learned to read "would go to the lowest hell" in the life hereafter.

The missionaries from the first sought to avoid any political alliance with the British; yet the Burmese resented the protection to Christians given by British officials wherever they were in control. During the Second Anglo-Burmese War in 1852, Kincaid was blamed by the Burmese governor at Rangoon for the coming of the British warships to the city. Later, when the missionaries openly manifested satisfaction that Lower Burma had come under British rule, the resentment of the Burmese was deepened. Although it was not given open expression until recent years, it remained as a source of Burmese resistance to Christianity.

Until the opening of Lower Burma in 1852, Baptist work among the Burmese was restricted to Tennaserim Province, which was under British protection, and to Rangoon. In Tennaserim, the stations were Moulmein and Tavoy. In both places the approach to the Karens met with greater response than among the Burmese, although it was possible to establish some organized work among the latter. At Rangoon, as we have seen, circumstances were so discouraging that Judson was obliged to abandon the city in 1847 and retire to Moulmein where he worked until his death three years later. Although Kincaid and Dr. Dawson sought to resume work in Rangoon against great odds in 1851, it was not until after the British victory in 1852 that any permanent work could be established.

With Lower Burma thus opened to missionaries, new stations were occupied for reaching the Burmese people. For example, Lovell Ingalls, who had served in Arracan for several years, was transferred in 1853 to Rangoon, where he labored with marked success until his death in 1856. His wife continued on, giving able leadership to the educational work.

In November, 1854, Reverend J. L. Douglass opened a Burmese Department of the Bassein Mission. It was the first Burmese work within the radius of a hundred miles, yet there were sixteen thousand Burmese within an hour's walk from the town. Earlier in the year, Thomas Simons had joined Kincaid in Prome, where religious services were conducted among the Burmese with the assistance of three Burmese Christians. Similar work was being carried on in Shwegyin, Toungoo, and Henzada.

On March 26, 1856, Ko Thah-a, the venerable pastor of the Burmese Baptist Church at Rangoon, died. He was succeeded by Ko En, formerly of Moulmein. Ko En had been baptized by Judson in 1828. He later was associated, as an assistant, with Wade at Rangoon, then with Judson on a visit to Prome, then successively with Bennett, Kincaid, and others. During his pastorate at Rangoon, which was to last until his death in 1868, he baptized 143 persons.

He was unusually familiar with the Scriptures, having assisted Judson in his earlier years with the preparation of the Burmese translation for the press. Ko En was typical of the pastoral leadership that was being encouraged by the missionaries in Burma.[1]

For many years missionaries had been endeavoring to establish a permanent work at Ava, the capital of Burma proper. Only sporadic success had brightened their discouragement. In 1856 Kincaid and Dr. Dawson paid a second visit to the city. They were well received by the king and his councillors and encouraged to establish permanent residence. Ko Shway Nee, one of the oldest and most influential members of the remnant church in the city, was ordained to take charge of the eight members that remained. Dr. Dawson rendered medical aid to several notable people, and once more there was hope of a successful work in Ava. But soon the capital was removed to Mandalay.

On August 20, 1859, at Bassein the first Burmese convert was baptized by Douglass, after several years of patient labor. He was an old man who endured bitter reviling and persecution from his neighbors and his family because of his stand. His example led to other baptisms until, by the close of the year, there was a small Burmese church of eight members.

The Burmese department of the mission at Rangoon continued to enjoy favorable results. It had been aided appreciably by the support of the Rangoon Burman Missionary Society, which had been organized in 1860 by missionaries and English residents. By 1863, the close of the first decade of this mission's existence, a total of 237 Burmese had been baptized. Of these a good number lived in villages more or less remote from the city and the pastoral supervision of the mission staff. Most of them remained faithful and were instrumental in leading others to Christ. The establishment of the Burmese Baptist Association in 1860 at Thonze (then called Thongzai), with sessions in the Burmese language, was a source of strength to the churches. When the annual meeting was held in Rangoon in 1863, more than two hundred Burmese Christians were present.[2]

When the Burmese Association met in Bassein in January, 1864, there were twenty-one members in the church there. The total membership of the Burmese churches at Rangoon, Thonze, Letpadau,

---

[1] *The Baptist Missionary Magazine,* Vol. 48, No. 10 (Oct., 1868), pp. 385-86.
[2] *Ibid.,* Vol. 43, No. 7 (July, 1863), pp. 241 ff.

Henzada, and Bassein was 341. The Burmese delegates were invited to the Sgaw Karen Association, a day's journey from Bassein, at a village called Pauah-thang. For the first time, the Karen and Burmese Christians were united in a single fellowship.[3] It was a glowing testimony to the transforming power of the gospel which had been able to bring these two peoples together on an equal basis of Christian love.

Douglass' strategy at Bassein is illustrative of the difficulties encountered by the missionaries and native pastors in winning the Burmese to Christianity. At first he had planned to build up a church at Bassein which would be a center for missionary outreach into the whole area. But results were slow. Many Christians found it difficult to resist the numerous temptations of a commercial center. Hence, Douglass developed the strategy of itinerating as far and wide as possible into the villages, establishing little churches wherever he found enough converts. Each church then became a center of further evangelization under the leadership of a native evangelist. The Executive Committee of the Missionary Union was so pleased with Douglass' method that they commended it to all of the Baptist missions.[4]

The organization of the Burma Baptist Missionary Convention in 1865 was undoubtedly a source of inspiration and encouragement to the Burmese churches, for it brought them into close association with the strong Karen congregations. The leading centers of work for the Burmese were six in number. At Tavoy, Dr. Wade, now over 70 years of age, was still in charge of the station. The church was pitifully small, with only five members, but he looked for better days if he could secure the help of a native preacher. At Moulmein, where Dr. and Mrs. Haswell had labored a long time, Norris directed the boys' school, Miss Susan Haswell had charge of a boarding school for girls which she had established in 1867, and the English church continued to function. At Rangoon, Mrs. Ingalls carried on the work begun by her husband, assisted by Miss Rosa H. Adams. The Reverend A. T. Rose carried on the itinerating work in the villages. Slowly but steadily the Burmese church was growing. Arthur A. Crawley brought his ministry to a close at Henzada in 1867, being transferred to Bassein for the health of his wife. Douglass, in turn, moved from

[3] *Ibid.*, Vol. 44, No. 7 (July, 1864), pp. 238 ff.
[4] *Ibid.*, Vol. 45, No. 7 (July, 1865), pp. 231 ff.

Bassein to take his place. In addition to a healthy church at Henzada, there were in the district seven Burmese preachers, a school teacher, and a woman Bible reader. At Prome, the Burmese work was but a segment of a varied ministry on the part of Thomas Simons and Edward A. Stevens and his son, Edward O. Stevens, who served Karens, Chins, Shans, Chinese, Eurasians, and British soldiers. Upon the annexation of Upper Burma by the Viceroy of India in 1868, the missionaries at Prome hoped to establish a mission station in the capital. Accordingly, Stevens and his son visited Mandalay to preach and distribute tracts, but few responded out of fear of the hostility of the Burmese government to Christianity. At Bassein, the work which was described earlier, continued with a measure of success.[5]

In 1894 to 1897 the Missionary Union became involved in most unpleasant relations with the English-speaking Baptist church at Rangoon. The story is told here even though it was not strictly a part of the Burmese work because it illustrates problems of administration on the field. To understand the situation, some background is needed. From 1860 to 1890 the church had been served by missionaries, chiefly in connection with their other duties. But from 1882 to 1887, the Reverend L. J. Denchfield was assigned to be pastor. In October, 1890, the Reverend F. T. Whitman was sent out by the Missionary Union to serve in the same capacity. He, however, claimed to have been appointed as a special representative of the Union in Burma, and therefore in charge of all other missionaries.

Needless to say, Whitman's pretension of authority was opposed by the missionaries, many of whom had been in Burma before he was born. In the face of their resistance and without the knowledge of the church, Whitman wrote to Dr. Duncan, the foreign secretary of the Union, on August 17, 1894, demanding the removal of two missionaries from Rangoon, and the placing of certain school and church property in his control, or he would resign. When Dr. Duncan accepted his resignation, he gave his congregation to understand that the Union had "peremptorily recalled him."

Thoroughly aroused by what they regarded as unjust treatment of their pastor, the church voted in November, after his departure, to

---

[5] This brief survey is based on the report in *The Baptist Missionary Magazine,* Vol. 48, No. 7 (July, 1868), pp. 226-32, and Vol. 51, No. 7 (July, 1871), pp. 229-31.

sever its connection with the Union. In spite of kindly entreaties on the part of Dr. Duncan, the congregation claimed complete independence and ownership of the property. Because many of the missionaries in the church disapproved of the high-handed methods of its members, they withdrew and on July 14, 1896 organized the Immanuel Baptist Church of Rangoon. The following month, the Union filed an ejectment suit against the old congregation. On December 21, after a court trial, the decree was given in favor of the Union. Accordingly, the recalcitrant congregation was obliged to relinquish the property, which was occupied shortly thereafter by the Immanuel Church that had remained loyal to the Union.[6]

By the turn of the century, Rangoon had become the main center of Burmese Christian strength. In 1904 fully 75 per cent or 3,000 of the more than 4,000 Christians at the Burmese Baptist Association were from Rangoon churches. A major factor in the progress among the Burmese, although slow, was the unfailing faith of generation after generation of missionaries who never gave up hope that the Burmese could be won to Christ. Through schools, through the translation of the Scriptures, through books and tracts, and through patient preaching and tireless debates, an impression had been made and by 1913 a nucleus of Burmese churches had been formed, one hundred years after Judson's first contacts in Rangoon.

The Mission to the Shans

The Shans were a hill people who occupied the northeast provinces of Burma. Indeed, their territory extended into China on the one hand and into Assam on the other. The Shan States, as their district was called, was about 900 miles long and 400 broad. All told, they numbered about 7,000,000 people. They were Buddhists, and in some respects similar to the Burmese; in other respects, they were like the Siamese. Although more literate than the animistic hill tribes in their area, they were not so highly developed culturally as the Burmese. Shy and retiring by nature, the Shans were not easy to reach, for they were suspicious of the motives of the missionaries who sought to lead them to Christ.

The first Baptist missionary among them was the Reverend Moses

---

[6] *The News from the American Baptist Missions in Burma and Assam,* Vol. 9, No. 2 (Aug. 1896), p. 1; *The Baptist Missionary Review,* Vol. 4, No. 1. (March, 1898), pp. 92-95.

H. Bixby. He was appointed in 1860, at a time when the Shans were moving down into the vicinity of Toungoo to escape warlike disturbances in their native region. Bixby had gained valuable experience as a missionary for a few years in Moulmein. He arrived at Toungoo in March, 1861, to discover that there were ten thousand Shans in the vicinity of the town. During the first year he preached in Burmese to the Shans and the Burmese. Meanwhile, he began to prepare a vocabulary of the Shan language and wrote two Shan tracts. He built a chapel on the site of a ruined pagoda which had been donated by the English Deputy Commissioner. At the end of the year a church was organized and there was a school of thirty pupils. In 1863 he built a house. That year, the little congregation gave, besides the ordinary church expenses, forty rupees towards the printing of Shan tracts.

In December, he and his wife and three native preachers set out into the mountains beyond Toungoo for a tour of the Shan States. He was obliged to turn back en route when he learned that three of his coolie bearers had made a plot to murder him and Mrs. Bixby, thinking they had a large sum of money with them. But he did not give up, for he believed that the mountain area around Toungoo would open up a way for the gospel to the Shan States and on into western China. Ill health, however, forced his return to America in 1868, where he became a pastor in Providence, Rhode Island. He continued his interest in missions as a member of the Board of Managers of the Union. On the field he left three churches, over a hundred members, ten chapels, ten native workers, a training school for pastors, and a successor in the person of the Reverend Josiah Nelson Cushing, who with his wife had joined the mission in 1867.[7]

In 1871 a young graduate of Newton Theological Institution, Edwin Delmont Kelley, was appointed to the Shan Mission. He arrived at Toungoo in February, 1872. With remarkable aptitude for the language, he preached in Shan for the first time late in September. His death by drowning in an effort to retrieve a waterfowl which he had shot, brought to a premature end a promising missionary career.[8] His going was a severe loss to Cushing and to the mission

[7] Henry C. Vedder, *A Short History of Baptist Missions* (Philadelphia, 1927), chap. 5; see also Jennie Bixby Johnson, *The Life and Work of Moses Homan Bixby* (New York, 1904).

[8] Jennie B. Kelley, *A Consecrated Life: Portraiture of Rev. Edwin Delmont Kelley, Missionary in Burmah* (Boston, 1879).

Cushing's contribution to the Shans was very significant. He was chiefly responsible for the translation of the Bible into the Shan language. This he accomplished by 1891. He also produced a Shan grammar and a dictionary. In 1876, Cushing and his wife sought entrance into Upper Burma by way of Bhamo. About that time, the China Inland Mission offered to relinquish to the Baptists prior rights to occupy the city, if they could send a man at once. Not willing to let the opportunity pass, Mrs. Cushing agreed to carry on the work in Toungoo while her husband established a station at Bhamo. They lived and worked 600 miles apart, for nearly a year, until reinforcements arrived.

In February, 1878, Albert J. Lyon and J. A. Freiday reached Bhamo. It was a terrible blow to Cushing, however, when Lyon died of consumption a month later. Cushing carried on, nevertheless, revising his Shan Dictionary and reducing the Kachin language to writing. By 1879, he returned to Toungoo, leaving Freiday and his wife in charge of the Shan work of the Bhamo mission, and the Reverend W. H. Roberts and his wife in charge of the work for the Kachins. The Kachins were pressing southward and eastward from their mountain habitat to extend their domain, and were displacing the Shans and the Burmese. It was thought that they might become a link between the Burma Mission and the Assam Mission.[9]

In 1885, the work at Bhamo was disrupted seriously by the war between the British and the Burmese which led to the annexation of Upper Burma by British India in 1886.

By 1890 the north country was safe enough for the opening by M. B. Kirkpatrick of the first station in the Shan country at Thibaw. Two years later a new station was started at Moné. Medical work was to occupy an important place in both stations. In 1893 Dr. Cushing left the Shans at Toungoo to assume charge of the Rangoon Baptist College. At Namkham, the center of a large Shan population, W. W. Cochrane opened another new station. By 1895, the Shans were being ministered to by twelve missionaries and nine native preachers. There were also many Shans in Burmese churches in Toungoo, Thaton, and elsewhere.[10]

---

[9] *The Baptist Missionary Magazine,* Vol. 60, No. 8 (Aug., 1880), pp. 296-98.

[10] *Ibid.,* Vol. 71, No. 7 (July, 1891), p. 234; Edmund F. Merriam, *The American Baptist Missionary Union and Its Missions* (Boston, 1897), pp. 84-87.

About 1901 another pioneer outpost for the Shans was opened by the Reverend William M. Young in Kengtung State on the far eastern border of Burma. He had come from a Shan station at Hsipaw in the Northern Shan States. As he preached in the market place in Kengtung towns, he experienced a much greater response from certain hill tribes than from the Shans themselves. However, he gathered a nucleus of Shan converts and established a church.

Schools and medical work developed slowly in the years that followed. Shans were not easy to win to Christianity, but work among them continued. This was true not only because of the persistency of the missionaries from America, but also because the mission was fortified effectively by the ministry of Karen missionaries who had been sent out by the Karen Home Mission Society of Lower Burma.

Dramatic Successes Among the Karens

We turn now to a summary of the more rewarding work among the Karens. In previous chapters we have traced the thrilling beginnings of this mission under the Boardmans, Francis Mason and his wife, the Wades, and Elisha Abbott. The main centers of activity were Moulmein, Tavoy, Amherst, and Mergui in Tennaserim Province, Sandoway along the west coast of Arracan Province, and Bassein in Bassein District. Some Karens had been won in the vicinity of Rangoon. Missionary fatalities had been high in Sandoway because of the difficult climate. No missionary had been able to enter Bassein prior to 1852 because it was under Burmese rule. Yet, Abbott could report in 1845 that there were nearly 3,500 baptized believers, 32 preachers, and 2 ordained pastors in the Arracan and Bassein missions. By 1846 there were 32 churches, 34 preachers unordained and 2 ordained, and over 4,000 members, besides nearly 1,500 who were requesting baptism.[11]

It is significant that Abbott had built a wonderful foundation for the work among the Sgaw Karens in Bassein during the period from 1837 to 1847, without ever having been permitted to enter Bassein itself. Most of his leadership had been given from the Arracan, under British protection, and from more than a hundred miles away and in spite of the barriers of mountains and jungles. He had been able

---

[11] L. P. Brockett, *The Story of the Karen Mission in Bassein, 1838–1890* (Philadelphia, 1891), p. 47. This history is a helpful supplement to the records of this great mission.

to gather over four thousand Karens into churches pastored by their own leaders. The secret in part had been the careful training of pastors in his home at Sandoway. Beyond this he counselled with the leaders of the churches once a year in a three or four week conference at each of the associational meetings on the frontier of Arracan.

In 1847 the Board sent out the Reverend John S. Beecher and his wife to be Abbott's associate at Sandoway. Two years later, the Reverend H. L. Van Meter arrived to be a missionary to the Pwo Karens in the same field. At that time there were already two or three Pwo Karen churches.

Abbott's policy during these years was to develop Karen churches which would be self-supporting and self-governing so far as possible. He found it necessary, however, to convince many of his fellow missionaries of the wisdom of his plan. But he remained firm in spite of criticism even from the Board at home, which was accustomed to granting financial support to native pastors who worked under the direction of missionaries. In support of his point of view, Abbott reported that some of the pastors who did not rely upon their congregations for support became "as lazy as Buddhist priests."

Under the inspiration of his leadership, the Karens organized a Home Mission Society in 1851, which contributed to sending out its own missionaries to other parts of Burma and Siam. The Society also subsidized in part the salaries of pastors of needy churches. Although the Karens emerged from the ravages of the Second Anglo-Burman War of 1852 greatly impoverished, they determined to continue their home mission work.

The British victory in the war opened Bassein to the missionaries. Hence, Abbott and Van Meter transferred the headquarters of the Karen mission from Sandoway to Bassein in July, 1852, in order to be closer to the main body of Karen churches. Ill health, however, forced Abbott to return to America in December. He died at Fulton, New York, on December 3, 1854, at forty-five years of age, after eighteen years of arduous missionary service had exacted its toll.

During this period further developments of importance were occurring at other stations where Karens were being reached by the gospel. At Moulmein, in May, 1845, the Karen Theological Seminary was opened for the training of pastoral leadership for the churches. Dr. J. P. Binney was its founder and head. At first it was difficult to develop in the students a discipline and humility in their studies. But by 1847 the first four graduates were ordained to the Karen ministry by a council of missionaries and Karen Christians who were members of five churches in the area. This policy of encouraging an ordained ministry among the Karens had been initiated by Abbott. It represented an earlier disposition to give leadership to nationals than was manifested by some of the missionaries in the other stations in Burma.

Mrs. Binney was responsible for establishing the Karen Normal School in April, 1846. It opened with only nine children. Within four years the number had increased to forty boys and girls who were taught to read in English and Karen, and to acquire some skill in manual labor. The purpose of the school was to encourage the wives of theological students to remain in town during the dry season while their husbands were in school. It was also hoped that the training of the children would improve some of the habits of the Karens in the direction of greater industry and cleanliness. The ultimate objective of the school was to prepare youngsters who might enter the seminary, to train teachers for village schools, and to educate a few to give a Christian literature to their nation.

Important support was given to the Karen Normal School and to mission stations and schools maintained for Karens and Burmese alike by the Moulmein Missionary Society, which had been organized in 1837 as an auxiliary to the Board of the Triennial Convention in the United States. Its members included missionaries and interested Britishers and Europeans who made monthly contributions to its work.

Another singular achievement for Karen work was Francis Mason's completion, on January 10, 1851, of the translation of the entire Bible into Sgaw Karen. Writing from Moulmein on that date, the great missionary who had prepared the Sgaw New Testament at Tavoy in 1843, recorded the completion of the Old Testament on which he had been at work at Moulmein since 1847. He had labored there rather than at his own station, Tavoy, because he felt the need of consultation with his fellow missionaries, especially Dr. Binney. Meticulous in his scholarship, Mason prepared a study of the animals, insects, plants, and birds of Burma so that he might more accurately translate the names of various forms of life found in the Bible. Thus a by-product of his Bible translation was the 900 page book, *Burmah, Its People and Natural Productions,* which was first printed in 1852 at Moulmein and was reprinted in a second edition at Rangoon in 1860.

Like William Carey, Francis Mason had been a shoemaker by trade in England. He had been converted after his arrival in America. Again like Carey, he became a great missionary and linguist. His version of the Bible in the Sgaw language, which was printed at Moulmein in 1853, is still used by Karen Christians "almost exactly as Mason printed it a century ago." Later, he translated parts of the Bible into Pwo Karen and Bwe Karen, and at seventy-four years of age, he "sat in the market-place at Bhamo noting down the spoken words of Kachin people who came to trade." [12]

At Rangoon during the Anglo-Burmese War of 1852 there developed, as we have noted previously in this chapter, a great awakening among Karens who had sought refuge outside the city from persecution by their Burmese over-lords. The effects of this revival were felt as well in the Burmese work at Rangoon, and its influence extended also to Sandoway and Bassein.

It will be recalled that the Deputation from the Board of the Missionary Union arrived in Burma in 1853, holding its famous conference at Moulmein. The Karen work was affected by the unhappy results of this event. Beecher, who had left Sandoway for Bassein in 1846, was dismissed by the Board for having left his station without permission. Accordingly, he returned to Bassein under the auspices of the American Baptist Free Mission Society, where he erected the Karen Mission House in 1858 and opened the Bassein Sgaw Karen Normal and Industrial Institute in 1860. Between 1854 and 1855, Justus Vinton, who had developed a growing Karen mission at Kemmendine just outside of Rangoon in 1853, Durlin L. Brayton just recently transferred from Mergui to Kemmendine, A. Taylor Rose at Akyab in Arracan Province, Norman Harris of the Shwegyin station, and Nathan Brown of the Assam mission also resigned from the Union in protest to the Deputation's decisions. They accepted a nominal connection with the Free Mission Society in order to continue their labors in Burma.

---

[12] *The Baptist Missionary Magazine,* Vol. 31, No. 6 (June, 1851), p. 167; quotations are from a photostatic copy of an address by the Rev. H. C. Williams of the Burma Bible Society delivered at Tavoy on November 21, 1953, in recognition of the Sgaw Karen Bible Centenary.

In spite of these disruptions to mission harmony, remarkable advances were made during the next several years. At Bassein the churches grew in strength and self-reliance. By 1870, not one of the fifty-eight preachers received support from any foreign source.[13] Beecher's Normal and Industrial Institute was providing a vernacular education for Sgaw Karens which enabled them to make an adequate living and take their place in community life. An English department was added in 1860, at the solicitation of the Karens, to provide special training for leaders. It was the first Christian school in Burma established on the basis of indigenous support.

When the Burma Baptist Missionary Convention was organized in 1865, the Sgaw Karens at Bassein remained aloof from it. Their attitude undoubtedly had been influenced by the controversy which the Deputation's visit to Burma had aroused between their missionary leaders and the Board. The failure of the Free Mission Society to provide funds for the Bassein Mission led the Karen pastors, with Beecher's knowledge, to appeal in 1866 for help from the Missionary Union. Too ill to continue his work, Beecher left the same year for England, where he died. This combination of circumstances opened the way in 1868 for a reunion of the Karen missionaries with the Union. Through the services of Binney of Rangoon and Douglass of Bassein, the Free Society's property in the two areas was disposed of, and the unhappy schism caused by the Deputation of 1853 was healed at last. Under the new leadership of C. H. Carpenter, who had been transferred from Rangoon by the Union in November, 1868, new buildings were erected with Karen funds for the Normal and Industrial Institute. Moreover, by 1870, the Bassein Sgaw Karens joined the Burma Convention.

Typical of the advance made in this period was the establishment of the Toungoo mission in the closing months of 1853. To reach the numerous tribes of Karens and the Shans in this area, the town of Toungoo was chosen. It was an excellent center from which to advance up into the hills that bordered on Siam. Because we have alluded to this station previously in this chapter, suffice it here to summarize the work being done among the Karens and the peculiar problems faced.

Three main dialects were spoken in the area—Sgaw, Pwo, and

---

[13] *The Baptist Missionary Magazine,* Vol. 50, No. 11 (Nov., 1870), pp. 412-13.

Bghai Karen. The pioneer missionary at Toungoo, Dr. Francis Mason, was equal to the task of learning all three. Moreover, there were able native leaders who carried the work forward during Mason's absence in America in 1854, and for several years thereafter. Chief among these was Sau Quala, whom we have mentioned earlier. He was a convert of the famed Ko Tha Byu, first Christian among the Karens. Sau Quala was typical of the younger generation of pastors who had the advantage of education and the status of ordination. After fifteen years of service at Tavoy with Mason, he gave twelve years of able leadership to the growing mission at Toungoo, baptizing hundreds of converts, training pastors, helping to organize churches, and preaching with effectiveness in both the Sgaw and Pwo dialects. His great ministry and usefulness came to an end when he, for a brief time, was guilty of immorality. Repenting bitterly, he retired from the work, but lived an exemplary life thereafter. His experience is a reminder of the severe temptations to which Christians, so soon out of paganism, are subjected. It is also a reminder of the frailty of the human vessels which God uses to convey his grace.[14]

Mrs. Mason, the first white woman to enter Toungoo, established in 1857 the Karen Female School, which was supported by the tribal chiefs and their people from the start. For this purpose an educational society of 60 chiefs was organized. Later it increased to 260 from six clans, with a Board of Managers composed of one from each of the tribes. Mrs. Mason was convinced that the hope of the children of Burma lay in the freeing of the minds of women from ignorance, superstition, and fear.[15]

It is regrettable that the able work begun by Mrs. Mason was marred by certain aberrations in her thinking which became so disruptive to the harmony of the station that in 1864 the Executive Committee was obliged to withdraw support from her. Even more unfortunate was the fact that the Union found it necessary to take similar action against Dr. Mason in 1865, when he steadfastly supported and shielded his wife in her erroneous teaching. The action of the officers of the Union had been taken only after Sau Quala

[14] The story of Sau Quala is told serially in *The Baptist Missionary Magazine,* Vol. 36 (1856); see also Hervey, *The Story of Baptist Missions,* p. 455.

[15] *The Baptist Missionary Magazine,* Vol. 40, No. 2 (Feb., 1860), pp. 45-48. See also Mrs. Francis Mason, *Civilizing Mountain Men, or Sketches of Mission Work Among the Karens* (London, 1864).

and other Karen preachers had broken with the Masons over the teachings of Mrs. Mason and also because of the autocratic control which Dr. Mason exercised over the Association of churches.

Mrs. Mason's strange teachings, which were first expressed in 1862, came to be known as the "God language." She announced that she had found the language in which God spoke to Adam "in the embroideries of the Karen women's dresses, in the pagodas, and other appendages of Buddhist worship." She taught that all nations have this "God language," the key to which she claimed to have received from God himself.[16] Moreover, she sought to introduce Anglican ritualism to the Karens.

For the Toungoo station, the effects of her leadership were extremely serious. The Association of churches in Pegu, where Dr. Cross worked, was divided—one group following the Masons, the other following Cross. The Bghai Association also split into two groups. In 1871 Mrs. Mason brought in a representative of the Society for the Propagation of the Gospel to instruct her followers in the Anglican liturgy. However, when he sensed the situation in the mission, he wisely withdrew. In the meantime, Dr. Mason, himself, had at last openly opposed his wife's teaching. Accordingly, he was reinstated by the Union in July, 1871, with the status of a single missionary. Mason's stand resulted in a reunion of the two Bghai Associations in 1872. Even the Pegu churches which had followed Mrs. Mason gave signs of cordiality towards those who sought to win them back to the fold.[17]

About the same time that the Karen work was opened in Toungoo, the Reverend Norman Harris was appointed by the American Baptist Missionary Union to begin a new station at Shwegyin. He came with the experience of seven years of work among the Karens at Moulmein, and he remained at Shwegyin for thirty years. During this time he was virtually the only missionary there.

He and Mrs. Harris had arrived in August, 1853, after a journey of three weeks in a small Burmese boat, with their four small children and a few Christian Karens from Moulmein. Their coming brought forth no welcome. But undaunted, they held a service on

---

[16] *The Baptist Missionary Magazine,* Vol. 54, No. 6 (June, 1874), p. 163.

[17] The story of the Mason difficulties at Toungoo is given in *The Baptist Missionary Magazine,* Vol. 45, No. 7 (July, 1865), pp. 221-27; No. 9 (Sept., 1865), pp. 347, 408-11; Vol. 52, No. 7 (July, 1872), pp. 252-54; Vol. 54, No. 6 (June, 1874), p. 163; No. 7 (July, 1874), p. 233.

the following Sunday, and were observed by a passing pagan Karen who saw in the missionary the long-awaited white man who should bring the Sacred Book of salvation. Within seven weeks, on November 13, this man, Sau Tah-ree, and six others were baptized along with one Shan on November 13. On the evening of the same day, a church was organized and the Lord's Supper was celebrated. Later that night, as if to heighten the price for such a victory, Mrs. Harris took ill with a disease contracted on the way from Moulmein. Ten days later, just after sharing with her loved ones a vision of Karens dressed in white bearing palms of victory in their hands, she died with a smile on her face.

The bereaved husband took the four children to Rangoon to be taken to America by the daughter of Justus Vinton, Miss Miranda Vinton, who had been a companion of the family at Moulmein. Sau Tah-ree and his family moved to the mission compound to look after Harris' needs. Soon the Karen Christian learned to read, and he, for the next fifteen years, became a co-laborer with the missionary.

One year from the start of the mission, there were 577 converts in six churches. On January 10, 1854 they were organized into an association. Evangelistic and eager for education, the new Christians helped to support a school at Shwegyin. Early in 1856 Harris married Miss Vinton of Rangoon. The couple made the trip to Shwegyin on an elephant. But within five months, the bride died of jungle fever, and Harris was once more left alone. This sad event shook the faith of many of the new converts, who turned away from the gospel. Harris, himself, was obliged to return for a time to America to overcome the effects of recurring attacks of fever. While at home, he married a third time, taking as his wife the widowed sister of the first Mrs. Harris. She with Julia, her five-year-old daughter, returned with him to Burma.

During Harris' absence from Shwegyin, the mission was under the care of Sau Tah-ree and Sau Doo-moo. The Karens built a house for the missionary family three days' journey from Shwegyin in Sau Doo-moo's village, where the people wanted a school. One was established and eighty pupils were enrolled.

Illness and death stalked the path of the courageous missionaries. Within three weeks, little Julia was dead. At the end of the year, Harris' health and unfavorable news concerning his children in America forced a second visit to the homeland. This time, he took two Karen lads with him to be educated—Kah-chur, age fifteen, and Pah-kau-too, the eleven-year-old son of Sau Tah-ree. These boys were graduated with honors from Madison University in New York State. While the Harrises were in America, the Karens sent 200 rupees to the Missionary Union to pay toward their missionary's passage back to Burma. On March 7, 1865, Harris returned to Shwegyin alone. In 1868 Mrs. Harris, although her sight was failing, rejoined him and entered into the work. But in 1871, attacks of fever drove her back to America.

In 1873 reinforcements arrived in the persons of Kah-chur, from his studies in America, and of the Reverend and Mrs. B. P. Cross. Cross was the son of the pioneer missionary who had labored with Mason at Toungoo. In 1874 a new chapel, a large dormitory, and a dining hall were erected for the school. The next year, Pah-kau-too returned from America, but took up work in Rangoon. Illness forced Harris to give up his work near the close of 1875. By that time, the Reverend and Mrs. H. W. Hale had arrived, and they were left in charge, assisted by Kah-chur.

The next several years saw a coming and going of missionaries. Harris returned in 1877, but in 1882, because of illness, he was obliged to leave the mission for good. He died in America two years later. His place was taken for brief periods by W. I. Price, David Smith, and E. J. Miller. Permanent leadership was not attained until 1893, when Harris' youngest son, the Reverend E. N. Harris, reached the field with his wife, the daughter of Thomas Allen, an early missionary to the Burmese. A number of single women were sent out during the next few years by the Woman's Societies to assist in the school work at Shwegyin and the neighboring town of Nyaunglebin.

Until 1899 the progress of the Shwegyin mission was slow. The town had ceased to be headquarters of the district in 1885, when the railroad was completed from Rangoon to Toungoo, deflecting travel from Shwegyin. In view of the changing circumstances, Harris urged the Shwegyin Karens to open a mission field to the east at Papun in the Salween District, where his father had visited years before. Accordingly, in 1900, the Association sent Thrah Kah-nah, pastor of one of the strongest churches, to be evangelist in that area. About the same time, the Association opened two out-stations at Kyaukkyi, a small town thirty-five miles to the north, and at Nyaunglebin, a thriving community twelve miles west on the railroad. This was the beginning of great growth. Schools were developed at the new stations and contributions and membership increased generally. The Papun station organized an association with about one hundred members in 1903, and took over from the larger Rangoon Karen Association responsibility for missionary operations in the Mainlungyi District of Northern Siam. Thus missions outside of Burma were being supported by the young churches which had been established by American missionaries.[18]

The period from 1870 to 1914 was one of great advances in Karen work generally. This was especially true in educational development. At Bassein, for instance, under the able direction of C. H. Carpenter, several new buildings had been erected with Karen funds at the Normal and Industrial Institute. These included the principal building, "Ko Thah Byu Memorial Hall," which was dedicated on May 16, 1878, the fiftieth anniversary of the baptism of the first Karen convert by Boardman in Tavoy. In ten years, the Sgaw Karen Christians of Bassein had contributed $36,564 for permanent buildings and an endowment of over $15,000 for the school.[19]

Elsewhere, the cause of Christian education likewise was being advanced. The Rangoon Baptist College had been established in 1872 for Karen and Burmese youth. The Karen Theological Seminary was removed in 1890 from Rangoon to Insein, where it was thought the climate would be more favorable to the health of the students. At other mission stations, boarding and normal schools were being maintained with a large degree of Karen support and with personnel supplied by the Karens and also by the Woman's Missionary Societies in America.

The advance in self-support and self-direction of the Karen churches and schools was truly remarkable. Carpenter, like Abbott and Beecher, his predecessors, pointed out the contrast between the Bassein Mission, which had supported practically all of its work since 1854, and the other missions in Burma. He cited the fact that twenty-eight per cent of all the mission funds from America in 1880–81 was being used for the support of native pupils and teachers in the schools. He argued that this money could have been used for

[18] This account has been based largely upon a *History of the Shwegyin Karen Mission* by Mrs. J. E. Harris and revised by her son, Rev. E. N. Harris (Chicago, 1907).

[19] C. H. Carpenter, *Self-Support Illustrated in the History of the Bassein Karen Mission from 1840 to 1880* (Boston, 1883), p. 378.

establishing new missions if all of the missionaries in Burma had been willing to adopt the principle of self-support.[20]

The degree to which the Karen Christians had engaged in missionary efforts beyond their own borders was equally impressive. For example, the Bghai Karen Mission in Toungoo supported from 1867 to 1899, without aid from America, native missionaries among the Karennis or Red-Karens (so called because of the copper color of their skin). These people lived in what was known as the Karenni Plateau, about 900 to 1,000 square miles in size. Because of the good work done, the Karenni chiefs in the fall of 1899 expressed a desire for missionaries and medical help. In response, the Missionary Union sent Dr. Truman Johnson, a medical man, and Dr. Bunker, from Toungoo, to establish a permanent station at Loikaw, about seventy-five miles northeast of Toungoo.

In spite of opposition at first, a small church was gathered at Daushe-ee, thirteen miles south of Loikaw. In less than five months, a mission house was built for the medical work of Dr. Johnson. During his second year at Loikaw, the doctor was left in charge. He built a fine schoolhouse and thus ensured the permanency of the work. By 1903 the Reverend and Mrs. Samuel E. Samuelson and Miss Johanna Anderson joined the station. Few missions have had such success in so short a time. There were 19 churches and out-stations, with 3,468 Red Karens under instruction from 22 preachers and teachers. The total number of church members was 112, with double that many enrolled in the schools.[21]

By 1910 the strength of Karen Christians had grown to nearly seven per cent of the number of Karens in Burma. There were 50,000 church members in 774 churches, all but 91 of which were self-supporting. In addition, the Karens were maintaining responsibility for the building of their chapels and for sustaining their schools and other institutions.[22] Moreover, the transformation in the life of these people was an important factor in winning Burmese respect for Christianity, and in part accounts for the relative progress in gaining Burmese converts in the later years of the nineteenth century.

---

[20] *Ibid.*, footnote on p. 397.
[21] *The Baptist Missionary Magazine,* Vol. 84, No. 5 (May, 1904), pp. 170-71.
[22] *Missions,* Vol. 1, No. 3 (March, 1910), pp. 154-55.

Reaching the Hill Peoples

Almost from the beginning of the Burma Mission, the eager eyes of the Baptist missionaries were turned towards the hills that bordered on China and Siam. For in those heights lived numerous and varied tribes, some of whom found their way to trading centers to the South and thereby became known to the missionaries, both American and Karen. Not only were these hill peoples an object of their evangelistic concern, but they were regarded as a possible contact with China, the coveted empire to be won for Christ.

Among the hill tribes were the Kachins, a wild and savage people. They were regarded by Dr. J. N. Cushing, missionary at Toungoo, as the most numerous people occupying the mountainous regions stretching from Upper Assam across Northern Burma beyond the Chinese boundary into Yunnan Province. From 65,000 to 100,000 of them were in Burma, and many more in China. They put constant pressure upon the Shans, forcing them southward. So far as contacts with the missionaries were concerned, the Kachins were shy and not easily won. Since about 1840, they had interested missionaries, both Protestant and Roman Catholic, on the Assam side and also on the Burma side. Because of similarities in language, Baptist missionaries thought that they might become the connecting link between the missions in Burma and Assam. Religiously, they were animists and therefore not as resistant to the gospel as the Buddhists, once their confidence was won.[23]

The first white man to meet the Kachins was Dr. Eugenio Kincaid, co-worker of Judson, who went into Upper Burma for a brief visit in 1837. He called them "Ka Khyens." But actual work among them was not begun by Baptists until 1876, when Thra S'Peh, a Karen teacher, was sent to the Kachins from Bassein. The next year, Dr. Cushing visited the mountains east of Bhamo, with a young Sgaw Karen Christian, Bogalay by name, who had been commissioned by the Bassein Home Mission Society to work among the Kachins. Thus a station was opened at Bhamo. Although Dr. Cushing's main responsibility was for the Shans to the south at Toungoo, he began to prepare a Kachin grammar and dictionary, using the Burmese alphabet. Certain manuscripts which had been prepared by Dr. Mason

---

[23] Vedder, *A Short History of Baptist Missions,* pp. 127-28; *The Baptist Missionary Magazine,* Vol. 60, No. 8 (Aug., 1880), pp. 296-98.

and which had been turned over to Cushing when he entered the hill country formed a sound basis for his work.

Other missionaries to the Kachins were Dr. Miles Bronson, of Assam, Dr. A. Taylor Rose, of Rangoon, and W. H. Roberts, who replaced A. J. Lyon, the Shan missionary at Bhamo, upon his death. Roberts worked among the Kachins for thirty-four years. Using a permit that had been granted to Lyon by the Burman king, Roberts gained entrance to Bhamo. There he was welcomed by Bogalay, S'Peh, and three other Karen preachers. By 1880, Roberts had baptized the first seven Kachin converts, who had been won by the Karen missionaries.

In need of more room for his growing school at Bhamo, Roberts appealed to the king at Mandalay for land in Bhamo. He received three acres outside of the city. There the missionaries erected a dwelling, a school-building, dormitories, houses for the Karen teachers, and a chapel. Twenty-five pupils were enrolled in the school. On December 7, 1884, the Kachin mission was destroyed by a band of Chinese and Kachins who were in rebellion against the Burmese. Even the Shan mission of Freiday was damaged. Roberts was blamed by the Burman authorities for aiding and abetting the rebellion, and so was ordered out of Bhamo. He went to British Burma, but was soon enabled to return when the British defeated King Theebaw and annexed Upper Burma in 1886.

Through funds provided by the Kachins, the British in Burma, and friends in America, a two story brick building was erected for the school and a chapel. It was known as the Lyon Memorial Hall. The Kachin church had seventy members, and the Woman's American Baptist Foreign Missionary Society sent Miss Eva C. Stark and Miss Fannie D. Manning to take charge of the school. They were followed in 1891 by the Reverend Ola Hanson and his wife. With youthful enthusiasm and ability, Hanson, a capable linguist, undertook a study of the Kachin language. He developed Kachin writing in Roman letters, compiled a dictionary, prepared school textbooks, a catechism, a number of religious works, and a large part of the Kachin hymnal. In addition, during his forty years with the Kachins, he wrote a standard work on Kachin anthropology. But his greatest achievement was the translation of the entire Bible into the Kachin language, which he completed on August 11, 1926. For his outstanding services Colgate University at Hamilton, New York, conferred upon him in 1909 the honorary degree of Doctor of Letters, and the British government in 1922 presented to him the Kaisar-i-Hind gold medal and a gift of money.

In the vicinity of Bhamo, there were ten schoolhouses by 1904, which had been built by the Hansons. Three of them were self-supporting. The Bhamo church had well over 100 members. In the meantime another church of 70 members had been developed in 1894 by the Reverend George E. Geis and his wife at Myitkyina, more than 100 miles north of Bhamo. In 1908–10 still another station was opened at Namkham, where a hospital was eventually established.[24]

A second hill people among whom American Baptists commenced work about 1880 were the Chins, who lived in the mountainous regions between lower Bengal and Upper Burma. They numbered less than 200,000, and, like the Kachins, were animists and of a primitive culture. The first Chin convert was baptized by Francis Mason, at Tavoy, in 1837. In 1854 a number of them were baptized by Kincaid at Prome. In 1868 E. O. Stevens wrote from Prome concerning them. He called them "Khyens," and described their home as being in the Western Yoma Mountains, which stretched north from Arracan to the Naga hills in Assam. The more southern Chins were divided into four tribes, distinguished from each other by dialectical peculiarities. When the Chins lived near the Burmese, the men more readily adopted the Burmese dress than did the women, whose tattoed faces indicated at once their origin. In the jungle villages the men did not tattoo themselves, and wore very little clothing.

Stevens had gained his first information concerning the Chins from a Karen preacher of Henzada, who could speak the Chin language a little, and so was persuaded to visit Prome around 1865. Stevens had discovered that the Pwo Karen alphabet, with slight modifications, could express most of the Chin sounds. Thus he was able to reduce the Chin language to writing and prepare a version of the catechism, a few hymns, and the Gospel of John from the Burmese and Sgaw

---

[24] *The Baptist Missionary Magazine,* Vol. 84, No. 5 (May, 1904), pp. 172-73; John E. Skoglund, *The Spirit Tree* (Philadelphia, 1951), pp. 32-42; Randolph L. Howard, *Baptists in Burma* (Philadelphia, 1931), pp. 80 ff. See also Gustaf A. Sword, *Light in the Jungle: Life Story of Ola Hanson of Burma* (Chicago, 1954).

Karen. Although not free from defects, these materials were understood by several Chins whom the Karen preacher taught to read.[25]

In 1884 the Reverend W. F. Thomas traveled extensively through the Chin country on both sides of the Yoma Mountains. He baptized 29 Chins at Gyatedau, in Arracan, where the first Chin Association was formed. In 1888 he made Sandoway the center of work among the Chins in Arracan. By 1890 there were nearly 300 Chin Christians in the vicinity. Meanwhile, the Reverend A. E. Carson made a tour of the Chin country, and opened a station at Thayetmyo, on the eastern side of the Arracan Yoma Mountains. In 1892 the Reverend Ernest Grigg replaced Thomas at Sandoway, when he was transferred to Rangoon. By 1895 there were 17 Chin churches with 547 members, and 16 schools with 235 pupils. Eight missionaries and 25 native preachers were serving the Chins at Sandoway and Thayetmyo.[26]

At Henzada, Mrs. B. C. Thomas in the meantime had opened a school which did much to evangelize and civilize the Chins. In 1899 a new station was started at Haka, in the Chin hills north of Arracan. The Carsons were assigned to this mission, but Mrs. Carson was obliged to carry on alone after the early death of her husband. For twenty-one years she was to serve at Haka in the midst of great privation and danger.

In 1907 preachers and laymen gathered at Haka from four towns within a radius of a hundred miles or more to establish the Chin Hills Baptist Association. Five dialects were spoken at the week-long sessions. The event gave new impetus to the work, and by 1913 a thousand Chins were Christians. That year, the Reverend J. Herbert Cope, who came to Haka in 1908, reported that four schools had been established on his field to meet the hunger for education. The Chin teacher's day began at 5 A.M. and closed at 9 P.M. He preached during the day and taught school in the evening.[27]

A third hill tribe ministered to by Baptists were the Lahus, or Muhsos as the Shans called them. There were about 150,000 of them in a territory that included Kengtung State in Burma, Yunnan Province in China, Siam, and Indo-China. They were animists. Along with their belief in evil spirits, they believed in a creator God; they

---

[25] *The Baptist Missionary Magazine,* Vol. 48, No. 10 (Oct., 1868), pp. 407-08.

[26] Merriam, *American Baptist Missionary Union and Its Missions,* pp. 88-89.

[27] *Ibid.,* Vol. 87, No. 8 (Aug., 1907), pp. 330-31.

abhorred intoxicants; and were in search of teachers who would tell them of the will of God.

Work among the Lahus began in 1901, when the Reverend William M. Young came in contact with them among the Shans with whom he was laboring in Kengtung Town. As the Lahus began to respond to his preaching, he endeavored to push up into China. He actually got nine miles over the border to a Lahu village called Bana, a hundred miles north of Kengtung. There he and his two sons built a very large mission house, where he lived and from which he conducted a very simple primary school. His purpose was to teach his converts to read enough so that they could go into the villages to preach. Many of these workers were ordained so that they could baptize the new converts more readily.

From 1905 onward, Young began to reap the harvest of his sowing. In that one year, 1,800 converts were baptized. Thereafter, mass movements brought ten thousand into the churches in five years, and one hundred villages became Christian. In 1913, reinforcements arrived in the person of Adoniram Judson's grandson, the Reverend A. C. Hanna.[28]

Young encouraged a hasty acceptance of baptism in his zeal and high-pitched enthusiasm, expecting to give his converts training later. This he was not always able to accomplish because there were not enough able teachers. The men he had to help him were Karens and a few Lahus who were very inadequately prepared to understand the meaning of the Christian life. Many of the Karens were legalists in their approach to Christianity, emphasizing negatives as the requirement of a devoted life. Nevertheless, the great ingatherings among the Lahus, which extended into the period beyond 1914, made a deep impression upon the Baptists in America. Moreover, their influence was felt among other hill tribes, like the Akhas and the Was, among whom mission stations were established in later years.

Baptist missionaries labored also among small groups who were not hill tribes. Among these were the Talaings (or Mons), who once were the dominant people in Southern Burma where Pegu was their capital. They were subjugated, however, by the Burmese in 1753. Mission work among the Talaings centered in Moulmein, where there

---

[28] Vedder, *op. cit.*, p. 128

were developed schools, a few churches with a total membership of less than five hundred, and a hospital and leper asylum. Baptists also maintained four centers for work among Eurasians scattered throughout Burma—Moulmein, Rangoon, Mandalay, and Maymyo. These people were the product of intermarriage between Asians and Europeans. The Reverend C. L. Davenport at Manadalay was known as the "apostle to the Eurasians." In addition, the Burma Mission developed missions for the Tamils and Telugus, who had migrated from peninsular India. Ahlone, Rangoon, and Moulmein were the main centers for their schools and churches. One entire church was composed almost entirely of converts from Islam.[29]

True to the genius of Baptists for making a successful appeal to the plain people of society, the Burma Mission had reached across the plains of Lower Burma and into the hills and mountains of Upper Burma, to the very borders of China, until the principal peoples of the country had been touched. The Karens and hill tribes had made the largest response and had furnished significant and growing Christian communities. The Burmese and Shans were gathered more slowly, yet an effective nucleus had been won. Within a single century, the dream of Judson had been realized to a remarkable degree.

---

[29] Robbins, *Following the Pioneers,* p. 78; Montgomery, *Following the Sunrise,* pp. 56-57.

CHAPTER XIV

Baptist Missions in South India

On the west coast of the Bay of Bengal, just opposite Lower Burma, is the country of the Telugus, among whom American Baptists began a mission in 1836. In a previous chapter, we traced the trying and often disappointing developments of those early years, first in Vizagapatam, then in Madras, and finally in 1840 at Nellore. Samuel Day and his wife had been the pioneer missionaries to the Telugus, and it was their dauntless faith in the Telugus' ultimate receptivity to the gospel that kept the mission open. On October 12, 1844, with the assistance of the Reverend S. Van Husen and his wife, the Days established a church of eight members at Nellore. It was a small beginning of the station that was to become, within less than thirty-five years, the center of one of the most widespread mass movements to Christianity in the history of Protestant missions.

The Telugu country included the Madras Presidency, that was governed by the British, and the northwest portion, which was under the rule of the Nizam of Hyderabad. Allegedly to protect the Nizam from a foreign invasion, the British maintained a military force at Secunderabad, supported at the Nizam's expense. Actually, the British strategy was to protect British India from the Nizam. The presence of the English in India did put a stop to the bloody invasions of warring peoples of Central Asia and Afghanistan, and it did give the country peace. But even more important to the missionary enterprise, British rule was regarded as providing a welcome protection for the spread of the Christian message.

The Telugus, as we have seen earlier, were a Scythian people of a proud ancestry. Their status in society had been overshadowed by the Aryans who had spread over Southern India. The Aryan Brahmans and Kshetryas retained for themselves the first and second places, or castes, in a rigidly stratified social structure. A fair portion of the Scythians were admitted into the third or Vysia caste, but the majority were left in the fourth or Sudra caste. The Sudras claimed to be the only true Telugus. Outside of the Telugu country, there were settlements of these people in Madras, Mysore, and in Burma, chiefly at Rangoon and Moulmein.

By the nineteenth century the Sudras, who once were the menial servants of the Brahmans, had become owners of the land. Although generally illiterate, they were rising in the intellectual and social scale and occupied the important position of being the chief cultivators of the soil in the country. Their pride of caste made it exceedingly difficult for them to accept Christianity. Indeed, no stronger proof could be given "of a man's conversion than his willingness to break his caste." [1]

Early Discouragements (1845–1866)

In April, 1845, the Van Husens were obliged to leave Nellore because of failing health. The following year, Day's physical condition necessitated a return to America. In his absence, the mission was left in the care of two Eurasians, who proved faithless. They caused the church to be scattered, and held drunken revels in the mission bungalow. It was well that these facts were not known in America when the Executive Committee was considering in 1848 the abandonment of the Telugu mission. The Committee was dissuaded only by the eloquent pleas of Day, whose timely arrival in the country saved the mission. He was backed by the Reverend William R. Williams, chairman of the Telugu committee. That year, which has been called the darkest in the history of the Telugu work, was the one in which Lyman Jewett gave himself to work among the Telugus.

Jewett and his wife sailed with Day from Boston on October 10, 1848. It was a sad sight which confronted them upon their arrival in Nellore. But heartened by the companionship of the new mis-

---

[1] David Downie, *The Lone Star: the History of the Telugu Mission of the American Baptist Missionary Union* (Philadelphia, 1893), p. 24. This book is an excellent source of information concerning the South India Mission.

sionaries, Day set the station in order and resumed chapel services on March 26, 1849. Jewett, who was a gifted linguist, acquired the language easily. By constant touring among the villages, the Jewetts saw results. Mrs. Jewett organized a girls' boarding school, although it numbered only two or three for a time. Day, himself, opened several day schools in which English as well as Telugu was taught.

Some 270 pupils were receiving instruction in these schools when the Executive Committee of the Missionary Union ordered them to be closed, and cut off appropriations for them as of October 1, 1850. The decision reflected the strong sentiment at home against the use of schools as a missionary agency. The teaching of English was opposed in particular as an encouragement to secular pursuits. The order was a source of deep disappointment to Day.

In 1853 four events occurred that were of great significance for the future of the mission. The first was the visit of the Deputation, whose decisions had brought such disruption to the Burma Mission. Unable to see large and tangible evidences of progress at Nellore, the Board representatives made an unfavorable report upon their return to America. In consequence, a second event occurred which threatened to bring the station to an untimely end. At the annual meeting of the Missionary Union in Albany, the fate of the mission was pending again, as in 1848. This time, as was indicated in an earlier chapter, it was the home secretary, Dr. Edward Bright, who arose to intercede for what he dramatically called, "the Lone Star Mission." The emotion aroused in the heart of the hymn-writer, Dr. Samuel Francis Smith, issued the next morning in a poem, "Shine On, Lone Star," the sentiments of which turned the tide. And once again, the mission was saved.

A third event was the conversion of a young man, Tupili Rangiah, and his baptism by Jewett in 1853. In consequence of his action, Rangiah was ostracized by his family. Alone and deserted, he began a ministry of witnessing in the villages around Nellore. That single convert was destined to become the outstanding pioneer evangelist and father of the first "foreign" missionary to the Telugu people in South Africa.[2]

A fourth event of importance to the mission was the prayer meet-

---

[2] *Natal Indian Baptist Association News,* Vol. I, No. 4 (Apr.-June 1953), pp. 7 ff.

ing at Ongole, during the visit of the Jewetts to the city at the close of the year. Before dawn on New Year's Day in 1854, the missionaries and three Telugu Christian women, Nursu, Julia, and Ruth, ascended the hill which overlooked the city. On the great road leading north to Calcutta and northwest to Hyderabad, it was but seventy-seven miles from Nellore and only six or eight miles from the sea. As they looked down upon the town with its Hindu temples and Mohammedan mosques, and counted some fifty outlying villages, their hearts were strangely stirred. Kneeling down, each in turn prayed that God would send a missionary to Ongole. Then Jewett pointed out a piece of ground nearby and prophesied that the day would come when a mission bungalow should stand on that site. Downie, in referring to this occurrence later, marked it as the turning point of the mission's history.[3]

For many years, it did not seem as if the prophecy or the prayer would be fulfilled. In 1855 the Reverend F. A. Douglass and his wife arrived to replace Day, who had been forced home because of illness. One of his earliest converts was Konakiah, who became the first ordained pastor and who later married Julia of Nellore. Another was Lydia, a caste woman, who became known as "Anna, the Prophetess" because of her witnessing. Confident of ultimate success, Jewett urged the Missionary Union to establish a new station at Ongole, and to place one missionary there and two at Nellore.

Then came the Sepoy Mutiny of 1857 with its threat to all foreigners in India. The rebellion of the Indian troops had been caused by several circumstances. The British annexation of the province of Oudh, resentment over the government measures to outlaw infanticide, burning of widows, and other inhumane practices, and the introduction of greased cartridges for use in the Enfield rifles which violated a religious taboo—these all combined to create the outburst of antiforeign feeling.[4] Although the Mutiny did not directly threaten the Nellore mission, the missionaries sought safety in Madras until January, 1858, when order had been restored. During their absence the Telugu assistants kept the schools in operation.

For the next few years the mission barely held its own, being confined to an area within fifteen miles of Nellore, with little possibility

---

[3] *The "Lone Star" Jubilee* (Madras, 1886), p. 29.

[4] Based on a report from Jewett in *The Baptist Missionary Magazine,* Vol. 37, No. 10 (Oct., 1857), pp. 369-70.

of expansion due to the scarcity of workers. It is little wonder that in 1862, while Jewett was on his way home to America, broken in health, the Union debated for a third time whether to abandon the mission. The story of Jewett's self-sacrificing appeal to maintain the mission and his own determination to return has been told elsewhere.[5] The decision of the Board to send him back with a new missionary, John E. Clough, of Iowa, began a new chapter in the history of the Telugu mission.

The choice of Clough was almost miraculous. Because he was a strong individualist, trained for engineering rather than theology, and not prepossessing, the Board was somewhat uncertain about his qualifications. When convinced that he was determined to go to India even if turned down, the Board capitulated and appointed him. At the time, they were not aware that the young Clough was to prove to be "a missionary genius" who saw that "the Western forms of civilization are not necessarily adapted to an Eastern community," and so was freer than many of his contemporaries to develop new patterns of missionary work that made his work "unique in the annals of Christian missions." [6]

The arrival of Jewett and the Cloughs in Nellore in 1865 was simultaneous with the adoption of a new plan of missionary work. The Telugu assistants were sent out on itinerant journeys by themselves, rather than in the company of missionaries, as heretofore. It was a step in the development of a self-directing leadership among the Telugus.[7] The reinforcements at Nellore freed the Douglasses for a return to America later in the year to regain their health. The year closed with several baptisms and high hopes for the future.

A New Era (1866–1876)

It is generally recognized that "the great achievement of the Telugu Mission followed the establishment of the Ongole station in 1866." [8] Twelve years after the prayer meeting of Jewett's little band on a hill overlooking the town, the prayer for a missionary was answered. For John E. Clough began a work there in September in response to an invitation from Yerranguntla Periah, an Indian teacher who desired

---

[5] See Chapter VIII.

[6] Henry C. Vedder, *A Short History of Baptist Missions* (Philadelphia, 1927), pp. 69-70.

[7] *The Baptist Missionary Magazine,* Vol. 45, No. 7 (July, 1865), pp. 243-44.

[8] Vedder, *A Short History of Baptist Missions,* p. 69.

to know more about Christianity. Clough was accompanied from Nellore by Rangiah, Ezra, and Lutchmiah with their families. Periah and his wife were the first to be baptized.

With the help of Periah, Clough undertook his preaching ministry. On January 1, 1867, a church was organized. Shortly thereafter, twenty-eight persons were baptized as the result of meetings held in a neighboring village. Most of these were Madigas, or workers in leather, who were outcastes. Their enthusiasm for the gospel at once presented a problem to the missionary, for the church at Ongole was composed of caste people. At first, Clough was able to pacify the church by reminding them that the Madiga converts were some distance from Ongole, and would do their status no harm. But as the outcastes continued to respond to his preaching, he was forced to decide whether to allow them in and lose the caste peoples, or to shut them out. As he and Mrs. Clough separately sought guidance from the Bible, they each found the answer in 1 Corinthians 1:26-27—that God has called the weak and ignorant rather than the mighty and the wise.

From that time, the die was cast. Clough was insulted by the caste people with the words, *Madiga Dhora,* which means "Mr. Madiga," or "Outcaste White Man." For a time, attempts were even made upon his life, but he persisted in his course. On October 13, 1868, he dedicated a chapel for the Madigas, and baptized 42 of them on August 1, 1869. The door was opened, and they who had come by the tens began to come by hundreds. At the end of five years' work in Ongole, the church had 1,500 members.[9]

Of his new converts, Clough expected three evidences of a changed life—the abandonment of idol worship, of eating carrion (Hindus were forbidden to kill cattle for food), and of working on Sunday. In each instance his requirements were intended to assure a clean break with paganism. On other matters of cultural significance, which were of secondary importance, he was lenient. He carefully avoided any semblance of imposing Western patterns of life upon the people. He allowed his preachers to stay as close as possible to the model of the Hindu Guru, or spiritual teacher. He built up a rudimentary sort of church government on the basis of the primitive system of self-rule that prevailed in the villages. Where there was

---

[9] Herbert Waldo Hines, *Clough: Kingdom-Builder in South India* (Philadelphia, 1929), pp. 59-102.

evident lack of freedom, he was careful to suppress his American indignation.

Clough made every effort to meet men in their own environment, "not as detached units away from home." He planted centers of Christian activity at the very heart of Indian village life. The older missionary objective had been to convert individuals and disengage them from their former life, one by one, and organize them into churches. Although he did not discard this aim, he recognized the importance of the social group, and left men in it, seeking to Christianize the group. Always he reckoned sympathetically with the family unit and tribal characteristics. He possessed a natural gift for handling successfully the gregarious instincts that dominated Eastern tribes. The most successful feature of his plan was to make the village elder a Baptist deacon, thus uniting community leadership with the church and assuring a Christianizing of the former.

Clough's acceptance of large numbers of converts, his failure to organize local churches after the Western fashion, and his reticence to put the work on a more self-supporting basis opened him to criticism. Ongole was the nucleus of his hundreds of converts, scattered as they were in outlying villages. He justified his procedure on the ground that the lack of a theological seminary to train adequate leaders prevented the organization of new converts into manageable churches.[10]

Faced with such a need, Clough, Jewett, A. V. Timpany, and John McLaurin petitioned the Executive Committee of the Missionary Union for funds to be used in the building of a seminary at Ramapatnam, a sea-coast town halfway between Ongole and Nellore. The missionaries decided that Clough should return to America to help raise these funds, to enlist new missionary candidates, and to regain his failing health. When he arrived home in 1872, the Board tried to dissuade him from his plan to raise $50,000 for the seminary. But it capitulated when Iowa Baptists endorsed the project with a gift of $5,000. By the time the financial panic of 1873 set in during September of that year, Clough's objective had been met. On January 31, 1874, he sailed for Ongole.

---

[10] Clough's missionary methods and point of view are discussed fully in John E. Clough, *Social Christianity in the Orient* (New York, 1914). See the preface by his widow, Emma Rauschenbusch Clough, and his own statements throughout the book.

During Clough's absence, McLaurin had done well, but now he went on to work in Cocanada, where Baptist missionaries from Canada were at work. Meanwhile, the Reverend David Downie and his wife had arrived in 1873 to relieve the Jewetts, who returned to America. Downie was plunged at once into the task of mission treasurer.

In 1876 came the dreadful India famine, one of many that periodically destroyed the lives of thousands of men and women in a land dependent upon favorable monsoon winds to bring rain that meant the difference between crops and starvation. Hunger-driven people dragged themselves into the mission compound at Ongole, crying for help. Some were so weakened that they died at the gate. Others, too hungry to wait to be served, ate half-boiled grain out of the cauldron in which it was cooking. Then they lay down and died. Even caste people came begging Clough to buy their jewelry so that they might procure food. Native dealers would not give them a fair price, and they had come to trust the missionary.

Clough wrote for aid to friends in America and England, and appealed to the Baptist missions in Burma and Assam. Karen Christians of Burma sent at once several thousand rupees. Aid came also from the West. The Madras Government imported 30,000 tons of rice and distributed it over the affected districts at a rate within the people's reach. Baptist missionaries at Nellore, Ongole, Ramapatnam, and Kurnool were appointed government agents for distributing relief in their respective areas. In addition, the government set up the Buckingham canal and unfinished railways as relief work-projects.

At Nellore, a "relief camp" was established on a small scale at the Baptist mission. Mrs. Downie superintended funds provided by the civil officials, feeding a hundred children daily. Clough, at Ongole, took a contract with the government to excavate some four miles of the Buckingham canal as a relief work for the Madiga Christians, who were loath to work under foreign overseers. With the help of his preachers, Clough supervised construction work at Razupallem—a task for which his earlier engineering training well fitted him. During rest periods, meetings were held for Bible study and prayer. Clough described the project in the following words:

> It was Christianity applied in practice on our portion of the canal. The weakest were cared for most. There were children who had survived their parents, and were given protection. There were

women without husband or brother, who were yet safe in our camp. Those who were too weak to work were given food just the same. All were treated well—yet they were Madigas. They would have hesitated to go to any other camp.[11]

After several months of struggle with cholera and with the gigantic task of supervising the work of many hundreds of persons seeking help, Clough returned to Ongole. The famine lasted into the third year. During this period of great stress, the missionary's hair turned white. But he won the undying affection and acclaim of all peoples, caste and outcaste alike. Although not yet forty-five years of age, he became known to the Telugus as *Tahta,* a term of great respect which means "grandfather."

During the course of the famine, mission work was suspended. Since March, 1877, there had been no baptisms, chiefly because Clough did not want to allow any suggestion to enter the minds of the people that there was an association between relief and becoming Christians. Then, on June 16, 1878, when the worst of the famine was over and the people could be held back no longer, the decision to receive the new converts was announced. On July 2, in the Gundlacumma River, at a place called Velumpilly, on the Northern Trunk Road, about 10 miles north of Ongole, 614 were baptized. The next day, six ordained pastors took turns, in pairs, baptizing from sunrise to sunset. A total of 2,222 received the ordinance of baptism. The third day the baptizing was resumed, until the total number of converts received into the church at the great Pentecost at Velumpilly was 3,536. By the close of the year, 9,606 converts had been baptized in a period of six months, bringing the membership of the Ongole church up to 12,004.[12]

In the missionary conferences for South India and Ceylon, Clough was criticized severely by his fellow missionaries of various denominations because he took so many into the church. Among American Baptists, however, the news was electrifying. The Executive Committee of the Missionary Union called for a day of thanksgiving in the churches.[13]

Meanwhile, the ingathering continued and responsibilities rested

---

[11] Clough, *op. cit.,* p. 249. For relief work at Nellore, see Downie, *The History of the Telugu Mission,* Chap. 9.

[12] Downie, *op. cit.,* pp. 111 ff. See also Hine, *Clough: Kingdom-Builder in South India,* p. 146.

[13] Hines, *op. cit.,* p. 149.

heavily upon an overburdened staff. Mrs. Clough returned to America in 1879 because of failing health, accompanied part way by her husband. The Reverend W. B. Boggs, a new missionary, was left in charge. Although Mrs. Clough lived fifteen years longer, she was never able to return to India. Sometime later, Clough married Miss Emma Rauschenbusch, sister of Dr. Walter Rauschenbusch, famed advocate of the "social gospel." She was a missionary of the Woman's Society of the West, serving at Ongole.

In January, 1880 Clough toured his field with rewarding results. The number of baptisms reached 3,000 during the year. By 1882, the Ongole church had more than 20,000 members, which made it the largest Baptist church in the world. Although the vast congregation was divided nominally into twenty-seven different congregations, practically they were under the management of the missionaries at Ongole. Under the pressure of circumstances and of counsel from his fellow missionaries, Clough finally consented to a plan of reorganization in 1883. The field was divided into five areas, of about thirty square miles each. A single area had its central station, its missionary in charge, its churches, and its own native helpers. The new stations under this plan were developed at Cumbum, Vinukonda, Narasaravupet, and Bapatla. Yet, the Ongole church, after the division, still had over 14,000 members.

By the close of the year, 1884, there were in the Telugu mission, 12 stations, 204 out-stations, 40 missionaries, 154 native preachers, 38 Bible women, 323 other native helpers, and 42 churches with 26,396 members. The total number of baptisms in that single year had been 15,556. There were also about 300 schools with 341 teachers and 4,898 pupils. These included village schools, the Ongole High School, which had been opened in 1880, and the theological seminary at Ramapatnam. A mission press at Bezwada was conducted by the Telugu Baptist Publication Society, which had been formed in 1868. Scriptures were distributed widely by colporters and Bible women.[14]

The remarkable growth on the field was not matched by proportionate support at home. Instead, the supply of funds was reduced seriously in 1885. Moreover, there were repeated urgings from many who did not understand the problems of the South India field that

[14] *The Baptist Missionary Magazine,* Vol. 66, No. 2 (Feb., 1886), p. 51; Vedder, *A Short History of Baptist Missions,* pp. 77-78.

the Telugu churches should be made self-supporting. The example of the Karen Christians in Burma was constantly a source of comparison. Under the strain of overwork and heavy responsibility, Clough's health again began to be impaired, but he did not slacken his pace.

The Jubilee, or fiftieth anniversary of the Telugu mission was held February 5-10, 1886. Dr. and Mrs. Jewett, to whose work so much of the success of those years had been due, were on their way to America. In their absence, their chairs were decorated with flowers and remained unoccupied in their honor. It was a fitting tribute to these early missionaries whose devoted faith had overcome all obstacles and had prevailed repeatedly against efforts to close the mission prematurely.

Continued Advance (1887–1914)

As growth continued, the American Baptist Missionary Union was confronted with a problem of comity relations. It occurred in connection with a protest from the Evangelical Lutheran Association which was at work among the Telugus. When the Baptists had reorganized the Ongole church in 1883, they established a station at Guntur in the Kistna District, north of Bapatla. Although the Baptists had been at work among the Telugus twenty-one years earlier than the Lutherans, the latter complained that their territory was being invaded, when some six thousand villagers sought baptism from Baptist missionaries. The two societies in the United States agreed to maintain their present stations in that area, although neither would enter a new station in which the other was at work, or use undue influence to withdraw members away from the other. The Lutherans on the field were unsympathetic with the agreement, and purchased property a year later at nearby Narsaranapetta, where Baptists had a station. When confronted with their violation of the agreement, the Lutheran representatives announced that they had withdrawn their consent to it.[15] The incident is worthy of mention only because it illustrates a kind of problem which ultimately gave rise to serious efforts towards co-operative planning on the part of mission boards working in the same areas.

Medical work was begun on the Telugu field in 1890 at Secun-

---

[15] *The Baptist Missionary Magazine,* Vol. 68, No. 9 (Sept., 1888), pp. 358-60.

derabad by Dr. Ida Faye (afterward Mrs. F. H. Levering). A most notable work was established at Udayagiri, a jungle district fifty miles from a railway, when a hospital was set up in a mud hut in 1892 by Dr. M. Grant Stait, wife of the Reverend T. W. Stait. People came for a hundred miles around to receive care. Its influence was responsible for raising the living standards of the entire community. Within the next thirty years, the one-room hospital was to grow into the Etta Waterbury Memorial Hospital. Dr. J. S. Timpany, son of A. V. Timpany, early associate of Clough in South India, went out in 1896, and shortly thereafter began medical work at Hanumakonda, which developed in time into the Victoria Memorial Hospital. In 1897 the Baptist Mission Hospital for Women and Children—the first institution of its kind—was dedicated at Nellore.

On January 1, 1900, Dr. Ida Scudder, daughter of a veteran missionary, returned to India to assist her father. But he died five months after her arrival. That first summer, single-handed, she faced the dread bubonic plague. In 1902 the Women's Hospital at Vellore was completed, and was for a time her chief care. In 1906 she began the weekly use of an ambulance along the roadside to minister to outpatients. The next year, the Nursing School at Vellore was opened. Such were the beginnings of the Vellore Medical School and Hospital which were later developed with the support of American Baptists and many other church groups. Dr. Scudder gave notable service to the women of India, especially in gynaecology and obstetrics.[16]

From this brief survey of early medical missions in South India, it becomes evident that it was largely the work of women sent out by the Woman's Societies. In this, as in education, they made their greatest contribution to the women and children of that land.

As the Telugu mission grew in size, organization and support became problems of increasing importance. In 1885, Dr. David Downie, of Nellore, urged the Missionary Conference, meeting at Madras, to divide the mission into three associations: the Southern for all south of Ongole, the Northern for all north of Ongole, and the Western for the Deccan. The scheme was adopted and became the beginning of an adequate plan for organization. In 1887 Downie established the little paper, *The Lone Star,* which published mission news. Within a few years, it gave place to the *Baptist Missionary Review,* of which

---

[16] Mary Pauline Jeffery, *Dr. Ida: India—The Life Story of Ida S. Scudder* (New York, 1938).

he became the first business manager and subsequently editor-in-chief.

A remarkable revival occurred in 1890–91 which brought 8,000 additional converts into the churches within a six-month period. To meet the expanding needs, the missionaries urged the Executive Committee of the Missionary Union to send 25 new men and raise $50,000. By September, 1891, six missionaries had been appointed and $15,000 had been raised. Upon the heels of this request came a petition from the leading officials of Ongole, asking the Union to convert the High School into a college of the second grade. This was granted, and enlargement of the mission together with an endowment fund for the college were provided by a sum of $100,000 which had been raised by Clough and Downie while home on furlough.

By 1893 the number of churches had increased to 77, with 48,815 members. Besides the missionaries, there were 245 native preachers and 107 Bible women. In the entire field there were more than 12,000 pupils in over 800 Sunday schools.[17] Such expansion made necessary further reorganization, and the Nellore field alone was divided in 1894 into four areas.

In spite of the great progress on the Telugu field, there was great need for missionary leadership, for only a few converts were out of paganism for as many as 20 years. Self-direction and self-support were to come slowly. Although in 1897 the Telugu churches exceeded by 20,000 the membership in Burma, only 34 of the 108 churches in South India were self-supporting, whereas 441 out of the 640 churches in Burma were supporting their own ministry. Yet the first Telugu Baptist Convention met at Ramapatnam in August, 1897. On the Kundakur field, the Reverend Wheeler Boggess had introduced the policy of complete self-support. Most missionaries believed that it should be brought about more gradually among a people of great poverty and unaccustomed to bear responsibility. Nevertheless, the Executive Committee of the Union urged in 1899 that Boggess' plan have the fullest and fairest trial possible throughout the entire mission.[18]

The senior missionary most aware of the need for more effective

---

[17] *The Baptist Missionary Magazine,* Vol. 73, No. 7 (July, 1893), p. 201.

[18] *Ibid.,* Vol. 77, No. 12 (Dec., 1897), pp. 619-28; Records of the Executive Committee of A.B.M.U. for Nov. 13 and Nov. 20, 1899, Vol. 15, pp. 408-10, 420-21.

administration of the Telugu mission was Downie. While on furlough in America in 1900, he recommended that an advisory board be established on the field to oversee the general interests of the mission. The plan was approved by Dr. Murdock, the foreign secretary. In 1901 the name of the "Advisory Board" was changed to the "Committee of Reference." In an earlier chapter we have noted that this eventually became a generally accepted procedure in other missions as well.

Perhaps the most dramatic evidence of the organizational changes which growth was making inevitable was on the Ongole field. It occurred when the Reverend James M. Baker took over the big church which Dr. Clough personally had led for so long. Baker had come to South India in 1895 to teach and serve as principal of the Ongole Baptist College. When Clough was obliged to return to America following a hip injury which he incurred in a fall in February, 1901, he commended Baker to the people in his absence. With considerable reluctance to take over the great man's work, the younger missionary faced several problems. First, he had to raise the standard for mission workers. This he sought to do by subjecting them to a study course and examination on the portions of the Bible studied. Second, he had to face the problem of reducing the number of children to be admitted to the Ongole Orphanages which Clough had been developing after the famine of 1898–99. With a subsidy of 4,000 rupees a month supplied by *The Christian Herald* magazine in America, Clough had cared for over 300 boys and about 240 girls. The girls attended the Ongole Girls' School, managed by Miss Sarah Kelly. The boys were organized by Dr. Gerrit J. Huizinga into the Ongole Industrial School, where leather and aluminum work were taught. Baker realized that Americans would not likely sustain the same amount of contributions. He also saw that drawing the children away from the villages actually weakened the hamlet schools. He therefore accepted for the orphanages only such children as could not be cared for by their relatives.

A third task was to reduce the size of the Ongole church membership from 25,000 to about 19,000. From the original Ongole pastorate, Baker also set apart two more stations, assigning the Reverend John A. Curtiss and the Reverend W. T. Elmore to Donakonda and Podili respectively. This move reduced the Ongole church by 8,000 additional members, the schools by 132, the number of pupils by

2,767, and the area of the Ongole station by 1,220 square miles. A fourth problem involved the settlement of several court cases over differences between the caste people and Christian outcastes for the use of water. Baker also helped to organize a Leather Workers' Union to prevent some of the Madigas from undercutting the price on their fellow workers.

Dr. Clough returned at the end of twenty-three months, unable to walk without aid. He carried on after a fashion until Baker's return from a furlough in America. On September 11, 1905, the Board of the Missionary Union accepted Clough's resignation and appointed Baker in his place. The veteran missionary wanted to stay at Ongole, which Baker resisted unsuccessfully, the Board giving permission as did also the Reference Committee in India. Ill health, however, forced Clough's departure to America, where he died in November, 1910, in New York State.[19]

In a certain sense the passing of the great pioneer missionary marked the end of an era. During his latter days changes occurred which gained momentum following his death. The problem of self-support was given increased attention. Baker, unlike Clough who had been rather indulgent with the Christians at Ongole, preferred not to give money outright. Instead, he sought to train Christians to earn a livelihood. To stimulate giving, he established an annual Harvest Festival. The offering received was used to assist scores of villages to build substantial chapel-schoolhouses.

The Telugu Baptist Home Mission Society, which had been organized in 1897, was in many ways the greatest stimulus to Baptist church life in India. Its work included both home and foreign missions. It conducted work among pagan tribes in India and sent the Reverend John Rangiah and his wife in 1903 to minister to Telugu immigrants in Natal in South Africa. A third missionary, the Reverend V. C. Jacob, an able professor in the seminary at Ramapatnam, was sent in 1910.

A problem closely related to self-support was that of industrial betterment. Because the caste system deprived many of the right to make an adequate living, missionaries found very early that attention must be given to the economic welfare of outcastes and caste people who had been ostracised for becoming Christians. In 1904, for ex-

[19] The foregoing account is based largely on James M. Baker, *Contending the Grade in India* (Ashville, N.C., 1947).

ample, at Hanumakonda, the general Missionary Conference appointed a committee to study the whole question of industrial education, especially of establishing a normal agricultural training school. An industrial experiment station was set up at Ongole later, and the Reverend S. D. Bawden was sent out as the first industrial missionary. There, pumps were used to irrigate the soil, and efforts were made to introduce looms so that Christian weavers might compete more successfully against the Sudras and local merchants.

At Bapatla, the Reverend G. N. Thomssen developed the Co-operative Association, Ltd., in 1909. Caste people, Moslems, and Christians became members, each cultivating land that belonged to the Association. During 1910 the dumping ground at Bapatla was abolished, refuse and sweepings were converted into fertilizer, a swamp was drained, and the town protected against floods. This was the first land association ever formed in India.

At Donakonda, schoolboys were used to plant the compound with 5,000 trees. It was a long-range plan for a source of income from the sale of lumber when the soil was too poor for farming. At this station, Mrs. J. A. Curtiss developed dairy farming. At Ongole, gardening was taught to the boys by Miss Amelia E. Dessa, and to the girls by Miss Bertha M. Evans.

Caste, with its rigid grip upon the life of India, was weakening somewhat by 1913, although it was still a major problem. Even in the Christian communities, the stratification of caste left its influence. Because the great ingatherings under Clough's ministry had occurred almost entirely among the Madigas (or tanners), caste peoples were alienated. This was due to the fact that the Madigas were at the very bottom of the social scale. When a few Malas (or weavers) were converted and baptized in Nellore, some antipathy arose between them and the Madiga Christians, who were very strong in the area around Ongole. This feeling reflected the ingrained sense of superiority of the Malas over the more numerous Madigas, although both groups were outside of the pale of caste-privileges.

The health needs of the people of South India constituted a fourth major problem. In 1910 patients came from 529 villages to the single American Baptist hospital, which was at Hanumakonda. They were Hindus, Moslems, Parsees, Europeans, and Eurasians. We have noted already the gains made by medical missionaries in the early years of the twentieth century, particularly for women and children.

A fifth concern of the missionaries was education. By the close of the period under consideration in this chapter, the Telugu Mission had a Normal School at Bapatla, Boys' and Girls' High Schools at Nellore, Ongole, and Kurnool, scores of station boarding schools, and six hundred elementary village schools.[20]

In February, 1911, the seventy-fifth anniversary of the Lone Star Mission was held at Nellore. Dr. Downie reported that the membership of the Telugu Mission had increased from 27,500 to 56,500 within the past 25 years. The number of churches had jumped from 52 to 140. There were 640 schools with 16,000 pupils.

The Missionary Conference, which met at Nellore in connection with the celebration, made administrative changes for the entire field. A Property Committee was set up to be responsible, with the builder, for mission equipment and expenditure of building funds. A plan was formulated for closer relations with the Burma and Assam Missionary Conferences. A committee of three missionaries and two Indian Christians were appointed to adjust questions connected with the churches and their members. A decision was made to open a new station at Janumpet, and to send annual delegates to the Free Baptist Mission Conference in Orissa. Industrial matters and the support of students in mission schools were discussed.[21]

It was evident that the spirit of co-operation was growing in the Telugu Mission. Moreover, the sharing of leadership with national Christians was increasing slowly. By 1914 the South India Conference had participated in the organization of the Telugu Christian Convention, to represent all Christian bodies in the Telugu area.[22]

The American Baptist Mission in South India had enjoyed a dramatic success among the Telugus since the beginning of the great ingathering in 1877. By 1914 it had achieved a reputation that was far different from its earlier status when there was serious doubt about its survival. The accomplishments of the Mission were far-reaching in effect. There was in South India a Christian community of more than 56,000 Baptists. The Christian standards upheld by these converts was a constant witness to the transforming power of Christ in human life. Under its influence an impression was being

---

[20] For a fuller development of these problems, see Montgomery, *Following the Sunrise,* pp. 115-31.

[21] *American Baptist Foreign Mission Society Reports* for 1911, p. 69.

[22] Records of the Board of Managers of A.B.F.M.S. for March 11, 1914, p. 167.

made on caste and other social evils. The churches were growing in their national leadership. Illiteracy was being lifted gradually by the work of mission schools. Medical assistance and sanitation reforms brought needed benefits to thousands. The introduction of relief measures in the face of famines and the program of agricultural and industrial guidance made an impact upon the economic life of the country. The lot of women and children was lifted appreciably by the work of missionaries.

In a sense, the Christian message in India was a significant factor in the social and political awakening of that great country. To be sure, the full impact of the Christian concept of the worth of the individual in the sight of God and hence of his fellow men was felt only by degrees. It did not culminate in full fruition for the outcastes until later decades. But the seeds had been sown in the process of Christian evangelization prior to 1914.

CHAPTER XV

Baptist Missions in Bengal-Orissa and Assam

As we continue our story, we proceed north in a clockwise rotation about the Bay of Bengal. First, we reach Bengal-Orissa, which is northeast of the South India field and closest to American Baptist work in that area. Although not so old as the Assam Mission farther to the east, the Bengal-Orissa field dates back to 1836 as a project of Free Will Baptists. Because Bengal-Orissa is associated closely with India proper, we shall consider this field first. Then we shall turn to Assam, the story of which we began in an earlier chapter.

Baptists in Bengal-Orissa

The earliest Christian missions in Bengal-Orissa were begun by Nestorian Christians who arrived in the eighth century. Roman Catholic efforts began in 1542 under the intrepid missionary-priest, Francis Xavier. The first Protestant mission was opened around 1700 by Zieganbalg at Tranquebar, a Danish possession. William Carey established Baptist work at Calcutta, and later at Serampore, from 1793 on.

It was for American Baptists to enter Bengal-Orissa proper, upon the urging of the Reverend Amos Sutton, an English General Baptist missionary in Orissa, which was a province of India. He was at the time a resident of Puri, where Hinduism was all but universal. Badly in need of help, he was persuaded by his American wife, the former Mrs. Coleman, to address a letter to Baptists in America through *The Morning Star,* publication of the Free Will Baptists of New England. The letter was written but not mailed because she could not recall the address. But miraculously, a package arrived from England, wrapped in an old copy of the periodical, which gave the necessary information. As a consequence, the letter reached its destination and was published in the April, 1832, issue. Sutton's plea gave rise to the organization of a Free Will Baptist Foreign Mission Society in the autumn of 1832 at North Parsonfield, Maine, in the meeting house of the Reverend John Buzzell, who became the first president. The new society was incorporated under charter from the Maine Legislature on January 29, 1833. Soon afterward, Sutton visited the United States, and served for a year as corresponding secretary. He also induced American Baptists to undertake work among the Telugus, as we have seen earlier.

The first American appointees were the Reverend and Mrs. Eli Noyes, assigned to Cuttack, and the Reverend and Mrs. Jeremiah Phillips, designated for Balasore. They were to serve as colleagues of the British missionaries who had been in Orissa for fourteen years. But it soon became evident that the Americans would do better on their own. So they selected Sambalpur, about 250 miles northwest of Cuttack and 200 miles directly west of Balasore. On December 12, 1836, they set out by boat for their destination. The town was the seat of a raja, or petty ruler. The only foreigner in a population of 15,000 was Babington, an English merchant. His generosity kept the missionaries in funds for several months. The raja himself became friendly after a visit from the newcomers and their presentation of a Bible.

Those first efforts met with deep discouragement. The missionaries made their home in a pagan temple, where they were allowed to cook, eat, and sleep. From Cuttack, tracts were sent which were written in the Oriya language, one of the five spoken in Bengal-Orissa. A native preacher, Daitari, assisted in evangelistic work. Then came famine and illness. The infant daughter of the Noyes' family died, while both parents were ill. The Phillips' baby likewise succumbed to disease, then the mother. When Phillips, himself, contracted fever, he and six children whom he had adopted to save from starvation were sent in January, 1838, to friends at Cuttack. Sambalpur did not again become a mission field until sixty years later.

The English missionaries then offered the Americans a station on the coast at Balasore, the chief city of Northern Orissa, where the

English General Baptists were conducting a small mission, but were glad to give way to others. Although a difficult situation, the city had the advantage of being on the road used by pilgrims to the Ganges and Puri. There were no other Protestant missionaries in the district, yet there were nearly 4,000,000 people in an area of 12,000 square miles. In February, 1838, Balasore was occupied. Phillips became the station missionary and Noyes the evangelist to the villages. A year later, Phillips married Miss Mary Ann Grimsditch, an English lady of Serampore. The first convert was Chakradhar, father of two of the six children whom Phillips had adopted at Sambalpur. In March, 1839, Mr. Woodstock, the English magistrate, and his wife were baptized by Noyes. In February, 1840, the first preacher was licensed. He was a lawyer who had come to Balasore in the previous summer and had been converted. By April, 1840, a chapel was dedicated.

Several institutions were developed at Balasore. Noyes had thirty-five orphan boys during his last year, 1840–41. His successor, Dr. Otis R. Bacheler, an ordained minister and medical doctor, built at his own expense two houses for these boys. In 1849, the government rescued sixteen Khono boys from being made human sacrifices by the people in their ceremonial rites. They were taken into the orphanage. The next year, thirty-four more were received. Of the boys who remained there, some became good workers in the mission; others were settled in Christian communities at Santipore and Metrapore.

A girls' orphanage was organized at Balasore, under the care of Mrs. Bacheler. In 1851 Miss Lavinia Crawford took this work over, and later removed the institution to Jellasore. Through the donation of the Reverend J. L. Sinclair of New Hampshire, a building was purchased in 1886. It was named the Sinclair Girls' Orphanage. By 1870 there were 110 boys and girls in the Christian school at Balasore. In 1879 a mission girls' school was started by Mrs. Marshall. A normal department was added in 1881, to train women teachers. In 1886 it was united with the Sinclair Girls' Orphanage as a middle grade school (comparable to American junior high schools).

The zenana work (in the homes of high caste women) was begun in 1869. Women missionaries reached into scores of homes, teaching girls and older women the Christian message. The influence of the missionaries upon the life of women is indicated by the fact that in

1888, 200 were being taught, and 381 were enrolled in girls' schools and zenanas.

The Balasore station had excellent native teachers. Among these was Rama, the first preacher ordained in the mission at Jellasore on November 9, 1847. He helped Bacheler, Cooley, and Smith until his death in 1859. There was also Kamal Nayak, who served more than thirty years as a preacher at Balasore. His son, Solomon, was pastor of the Balasore church from 1880 until his death at the close of 1884.

The Boys' Industrial School was the outgrowth of the orphanage work in Balasore. The missionaries felt that handwork was needed to train boys to support themselves and to develop their spiritual nature. Tailoring, carpentry work, blacksmithing, machine work, bookbinding, and the like were taught. The school became in time the largest and best equipped of its kind in all India. In fact the school was able to maintain itself by the sale of its products.

Not only was education of primary interest in the development of the mission, but medical work proved to be most successful in winning a hearing for the gospel. In this connection, Dr. Bacheler was a pioneer. He established a dispensary at Balasore in 1840. He then formed a medical class of native students. In 1850, six of them had completed a two years' course, and four of the six were prepared to practice. When Dr. Bacheler left Balasore in 1851, the dispensary was continued by native physicians. During the eighteen years before this dispensary was closed in 1863, an average of 2,200 patients were treated annually, a large number of which were surgical cases. Dr. Bacheler performed the first operation in that district with the use of chloroform. He published a medical work in Oriya and a large volume later in Bengali. His revision of the latter was adopted as a textbook in the medical schools of India. In 1863, he established a dispensary at Midnapore.

Dr. Bacheler was assisted at Belasore by Dr. James L. Phillips. In 1881 Dr. Nellie M. Phillips went to the field to engage in medical work at Dantoon and Santipore. In 1888, she established a new dispensary at Balasore. In 1886, Dr. H. M. Bacheler went to the field to work with his father at Midnapore until the close of 1888, when he was stationed at Jellasore. On November 26, 1890, he died very suddenly at Balasore. That same year, Dr. Mary W. Bacheler, a daughter of the pioneer doctor, returned to Bengal-Orissa, supported by the Woman's Society.[1]

In the Midnapore District of Bengal Province, the Free Will Baptists maintained five principal stations for about 1,000,000 population, working among three races, the Bengalis, Oriyas, and Santals. Midnapore was first occupied in 1844, although not permanently until about 1869. In 1866 zenana work was begun at Midnapore by Mrs. J. L. Phillips and Miss Julia E. Phillips (later Mrs. Burkholder). In 1879, a Bible School was established in the town for training preachers. The first principal was Dr. James L. Phillips. There were sixteen preachers enrolled that first year. Classes were held in an old building formerly used as Sepoy quarters. Phillips served for seven years as its head, then returned to America. The school was named the Phillips Bible School in honor of Jeremiah Phillips, who laid the foundations for Baptist work in Bengal-Orissa. A building was erected for the institution in 1890.

Another station was opened in 1865 at Santipore. It had been an out-station since 1852, seven miles north of Jellasore. Bhimpore, which was twenty miles northwest of Midnapore, was started in 1873 by Dr. and Mrs. James L. Phillips. From 1874 to 1878, Dr. O. R. Bacheler had charge of the stations, assisted by the Reverend R. D. Frost. In 1880 the Reverend T. W. Burkholder and his wife occupied it. On January 1, 1874, a church for the Santals, a hardy and animistic aboriginal people, was organized, with 42 members. Dr. James L. Phillips, who had returned from America in 1865, devoted himself to a study of the Santali language. He was the first exclusively Santali missionary to the Orissa Mission. In time, Bhimpore became the center for Baptist work among 200,000 Santals.

Stations were established also at Dantoon in 1877, thirty-five miles south of Midnapore, and at Chandbali in 1886, a seaport town fifty miles south of Balasore. Contai, close to eighty miles south of Calcutta, was opened about 1902, under the leadership of Howard R. Murphy. Here in 1904–06 a pentecostal type of revival broke out which did much to bring Santals and caste Christians together. Sensing deeply the need for a doctor, Murphy returned to America, after

---

[1] A Manuscript History of the Free Will Baptist Work in Bengal-Orissa has been of help in this survey. The work was prepared under the chairmanship of William C. Osgood. Hence we shall refer to it as the Osgood MS. It is an uneven work, having been contributed to by several persons.

nine and a half years of service, to prepare to be an accredited physician and surgeon. In addition to his medical work, Murphy was in charge of 100 village schools scattered over an area about the size of four counties, all in the jungle vicinity of the foothills of the Neilgere Mountains. During the First World War, he was to supervise the education of the Santals.[2]

Within the next few years following the establishment of the station at Contai, an additional center was developed at Khargpur, a railroad junction in Bengal. By 1914 nine stations had been occupied more or less permanently by missionaries—Bhimpore, Midnapore, Khargpur, and Contai in Bengal; and Jellasore, Santipore, Balasore, Bhadrak, and Chandbali in Orissa. The work in Contai and Chandbali was carried on by nationals, and that in Jellasore and Bhadrak was superintended by missionaries in Balasore.

The Bengal-Orissa Mission had developed through the years five departments of work. First was the medical work. Although all missionaries found it necessary to give some medical care, qualified doctors were a part of the staff. Dr. A. L. Kennan was at Sterling Memorial Hospital in Bhimpore, and Dr. Murphy at his Dispensary at Midnapore.

Educational work was second. There were schools in all stations and even in small communities. The more important were at Bhimpore, the center of the Santal work. There were about sixty schools scattered through the jungles. Many of the teachers were trained in the Santal Normal Training School at Bhimpore. The Phillips Bible School at Midnapore strengthened the quality of the ministry for the entire territory. Zenana work was carried on in Midnapore, Santipore, Jellasore, and Balasore. Hindu girls' schools were carried on by national Christian workers. There were also boys' schools in the towns and districts under supervision of the Mission. They were supported partially by the Mission and partly by the government. Most of them were taught by Hindu teachers, but when a Christian teacher was available, Sunday school was provided also. When the school was taught by a Hindu, the missionary tried to send a worker to give Christian instruction. The Boys' High School at Balasore, organized in 1890, was maintained as the only distinctly Christian secondary school in the two provinces.

---

[2] Howard R. Murphy, From Lone Prairies to Teeming Jungles. An unpublished manuscript loaned to the writer.

A third department of the Bengal-Orissa Mission was the industrial. At Bhimpore a workshop provided training in a means of livelihood for boys of the orphanage and the Christian villages. At Santipore, there was a weaving plant. The industrial department at Balasore was the best organized and most extensive, teaching a variety of trades. A fourth phase of the work was to provide a refuge for orphans. At Bhimpore in Bengal and Balasore in Orissa, orphanages cared for about 200 boys and girls.

The fifth department was for evangelism. There were about twelve out-stations where there were churches and small Christian communities. Street preaching was carried on in these stations. Colporters did their work there also. Bible women visited women in the homes. The evangelistic element was prominent throughout all phases of the Mission's work. There have been no mass movements on this field. Converts have been gathered individually. To be sure, however, the Santals, like the Karens in Burma, have responded in great numbers. The transformation that has come about in their villages is indicative of a vital personal faith. Moreover, a good proportion of the converts have been from caste people. This is in marked contrast to other fields which we have surveyed thus far. This fact alone has made for a larger influence of the Christian community in Bengal-Orissa. Moreover, the prominence given to education in this Mission has made for a good supply of strong Christian leadership, some of whom have been capable of directing the work of a whole station. In 1914 there were 23 churches and 1,621 members.[3]

The decision of the Free Baptists to merge with the Northern Baptist Convention in 1911 brought under the oversight of the American Baptist Foreign Mission Society and the Woman's Societies a strong and wholesome field of labor. Although it is not one of the larger and more spectacularly successful fields, the Bengal-Orissa Mission is one worthy of study. For it demonstrates the wisdom of the balance between evangelism and education in the development of indigenous Christianity.

---

[3] *Missions,* Vol. 5, No. 6 (June, 1914), pp. 482-86; Helen Barrett Montgomery, *Following the Sunrise: A Century of Baptist Missions, 1813–1913* (Philadelphia, 1913), pp. 131-35; *Annual Report of A.B.F.M.S.* for 1914, p. 115.

The Assam Mission (1845–1867)

Assam, which was a province of British India after 1838, very early came to the attention of American Baptist missionaries who were at work in Burma. It is located in the northeast corner of India, lying between East Pakistan and Burma, north of the Bay of Bengal. The province consists of the fertile valley of the Brahmaputra River that flows into the Bay of Bengal, and of the hill country to the east and southward. The climate is very hot and the rainfall is heavy. The tea industry is the main source of revenue, with nearly a half million acres under cultivation. Cotton is also a staple crop. Minerals and forests add further wealth to the country.

In a population of some six million people, eighty languages are spoken. One-fourth of the inhabitants are Assamese, who live in the valley. Religiously, they embrace a degraded form of Hinduism. The Bengali immigrants from the west are both Hindu and Moslem in religious faith. The Laos and Shan peoples, who have come to work in the tea-gardens and rice plantations, have been influenced by Buddhism. The hill tribes—the Garos, Nagas, Mikirs, and others—are chiefly animists. When the missionaries first came in contact with them, they were a savage and bloodthirsty people.

Because the beginnings of the Assam Mission have been traced in a previous chapter, it will be sufficient here merely to summarize the progress of the work to 1845. It will be recalled that American Baptists were invited into the region in 1839 by Major Jenkins, the British Commissioner at Gauhati. Nathan Brown and Oliver T. Cutter, a printer, opened work at Sadiya, far to the northeast. There a press was set up, textbooks were printed in Assamese, and the translation of the New Testament into Assamese was begun. Schools were established in nearby villages, and plans were laid for developing an experimental farm. Reinforcements were provided with the coming of the Bronsons and the Thomases. But unfortunately for the future of the work, an insurrection of the Khamtis in 1839 forced the abandonment of the mission. It was not to be reopened until 1906.

The next station and the second phase of the work was undertaken at Jaipur in 1839 or 1840. The Bronsons gave their entire attention to the Nagas; Cutter cared for the press which had been removed to Jaipur; and Brown looked to preaching and literary activities. At the urgent request of Bronson, the Reverend Cyrus Barker and his wife and Miss Rhoda Bronson were appointed to labor with the Nagas. But the plan did not materialize, for Miss Bronson died soon after her arrival, and the Barkers went on to work in the plains among the Assamese. Then, because the first convert, after six years of labor in Assam, was an Assamese (Nidhi Levi), the missionaries turned their attention from the hill tribes to the plains people. By 1843, Sibsagar became the new center of activities. The Cutters brought the printing press from Jaipur. Brown preached and continued his translation work. While Barker studied the language, Mrs. Barker established a school for girls. Meanwhile, Bronson opened a new station at Nowgong, where he initiated a new method of evangelization—education of the youth. To this end, he also established an orphanage. In time a revival broke out in the school which justified his confidence in the experiment.

Thus by 1845, Sibsagar, Nowgong, and Gauhati were the three central stations in Assam, and remained so for the next twenty years. In 1845 the first three churches were organized at these towns, with the main congregation at Gauhati. Sadiya and Jaipur had been abandoned. At Sibsagar alone there were six hundred pupils by 1846, and the mission press had issued four million pages of school books, hymnals, catechisms, tracts, and Gospels. Yet the progress among the Assamese was very slow. The trying climate, the poverty and ignorance of the people, the faulty location of early mission stations, such as Sadiya and Jaipur, had combined to hinder the work.

In 1848 further reinforcements arrived in the persons of the Reverend A. H. Danforth and his wife, who were assigned to Gauhati, and the Reverend Ira J. Stoddard, who with his wife was placed in charge of the Nowgong Orphan Institution. The total number of church members at the three stations was over fifty, with the largest portion at Gauhati. Mission schools were maintained at each station, and several village schools in outlying areas. The missionaries continued to send word to the Board at home concerning the work to be done among the hill tribes, particularly the Nagas and the Miris, whom they regarded as much like the Karens of Burma.[4]

In October, 1851, delegates of the three branch churches dissolved their relationships so that each might become a local church. On

---

[4] *The Baptist Missionary Magazine,* Vol. 28, No. 7 (July, 1848), pp. 268-69.

October 30, 1851, these three congregations (Nowgong, Sibsagar, and Gauhati) formed the Assam Baptist Association. Plans were made for assistant preachers and colporters, and for the extension of work to Golaghat and Mongoldai. The organization of the Association was of great importance to the mission because "it gave the isolated missionary a basis upon which to formulate a working plan." [5] Moreover, it was a significant step in the development of an indigenous Christian community.

A crisis came in the affairs of the mission, however, when the Deputation from America, led by Solomon Peck, discouraged the educational efforts of Bronson at Nowgong in favor of emphasizing direct preaching as the proper means of evangelism. Dr. Peck felt that secular education should be taken care of by the government. Therefore, he regarded the orphan school and the boarding school for girls as a dissipation of missionary effort. As a compromise arrangement, the Nowgong Orphan Institution was to be changed to a central normal school for the preparatory training of native teachers and preachers, with primary and normal departments. The effect of this change was that the institution died. It was a deep disappointment to Bronson in particular, for he had hoped that the school would become a means of developing a Christian community through the instruction of the youth of the country. The Assam missionaries were united in seeing in the school a proper means of evangelizing non-Christians and of training converts to be missionaries to their own people.[6]

Another calamity that befell the mission at this time was the resignation of Nathan Brown, after twenty-two years of service. Poor health and discouragement over the turn of events contributed to his decision to leave Sibsagar in February, 1855. The work was weakened further by the effects of the Sepoy Mutiny in 1857, which together with disease cut the staff of missionaries down to one each in Sibsagar and Gauhati and to a single native assistant at Nowgong. Danforth at Gauhati was obliged to render daily military service for a period during the summer of 1857, and the Whitings at Sibsagar were ready to retire from the station if violence broke out. Fortu-

[5] Victor H. Sword, *Baptists in Assam: A Century of Missionary Service, 1836–1936* (Chicago, 1935), p. 82.

[6] *Ibid.*, pp. 85-86; *The Baptist Missionary Magazine*, Vol. 35, No. 2 (Feb., 1855), pp. 33-37; No. 7 (July, 1855), pp. 306-11.

nately for the mission, they were eventually able to resume their work in safety.[7]

When the Danforths returned to America in 1859 for reasons of health, the Reverend Cyrus F. Tolman and his wife were sent out to reinforce the Nowgong station. Meanwhile, Whiting at Sibsagar was giving general supervision of all the stations during the absence of the Bronsons in America.

While the condition of the Assamese churches was discouraging because of the lethargy among the people, the hill tribes were making continual advances to the missionaries for instruction. This was particularly true of the Mikirs who pled with Tolman to come to the mountains to preach to them. Beginning in December, 1859, with the approval of the Executive Committee of the Missionary Union, the Tolmans made a tour of the Mikir mountains. They visited 150 villages, where they were moved by the deplorable condition of the people, many of whom were enslaved by opium and all of whom were terrified by fear of evil spirits. By 1862 the Tolmans had produced a primary reading book in the Mikir language, and were teaching several of the tribe to read. But the toll of travel and disease contracted during exposure in the hills brought Tolman's work to a premature close. Upon Bronson's return to Assam, he found the valiant missionary in a precarious state of health, which forced his return to America. It was a severe blow to the mission at Nowgong and a great loss to the Mikirs to whom Tolman had been so devoted.

To add further to the discouragement of the Assam missionaries, discontent was rising rapidly at this time among the masses over a greatly increased rate of taxation which they interpreted to be foreign exploitation. Rumors were abroad that the government intended to force Christianity upon the people. At home, the Civil War was depleting sources of support for the mission, and causing division among the missionaries. During these years, there seldom were more than two missionaries in charge in Assam; each station was left under the direction of a single lady or with none. The work among the Mikirs was followed up by the Reverend Edward Payson Scott and his wife, who arrived from America in 1862. In spite of ill health, the Scotts sought to carry on their work with what help Bronson

---

[7] *The Baptist Missionary Magazine,* Vol. 37, No. 11 (Nov., 1857), pp. 389-91; No. 12 (Dec., 1857), pp. 438-39; Vol. 38, No. 7 (July, 1858), pp. 249-50.

could give at Nowgong. But it was an uphill struggle. Increasingly, the missionaries realized that they must locate their stations in the hills among these people who were so desirous of the gospel, if they were to serve them effectively. A decision was inevitable between the slow and discouraging work in the plains and the more promising possibilities of the hills.[8]

Shifting Emphasis to Hill Tribes in Assam

The year 1867 marked a new epoch in the Baptist Mission in Assam; for at that time a reversal of policy turned attention from the plains to the hill peoples. Prompting such action had been the numerous visits of the Mikirs to Nowgong. They had given every appearance of being interested in Christianity, and, as we have seen, had responded to such efforts as were exerted in their behalf. The Cacharis had appealed to Danforth at Gauhati for instruction as early as 1857. The Garos also had asked for missionaries, and had requested schools of the government. Major Jenkins, the British Commissioner, was particularly interested. Accordingly, the government established a school at Goalpara for Garo boys. Seven of the first ten lads soon became Christians. Not long afterwards, some of the Garos sought help from Dr. Bronson. Consequently, he visited them in 1867 in the Garo Hills, and baptized thirty-seven converts. With the help of Omed and Ramhke, two of the earliest Garo converts, Bronson organized them into a church of forty members, and ordained Omed to be its pastor.

That same year, the Reverend I. J. Stoddard and the Reverend M. B. Comfort arrived in Assam to serve as the first missionaries to the Garos. Bronson settled in Goalpara, which became the center of activities among these hill people. In 1870 the government invited the missionaries to establish a new station at Tura. This they did not do at once, partly because of a lack of workers and partly because Stoddard felt that the Garo Christians would resent the mission being used to aid in pacifying the hill tribes. But with the coming of Marcus C. Mason and Elnathan G. Phillips to Goalpara in 1874, the wisdom of the move became more apparent. In 1877 Phillips settled at Tura, and organized a church of seven members the follow-

---

[8] Almost every issue of *The Baptist Missionary Magazine* in the years from 1855 includes information concerning the hill tribes and their appeals for missionaries.

ing year. He was joined in 1878 by Mason. The most important work of these two men, aside from their evangelistic labors, was the translation of the Bible into the Garo language. This task was especially difficult because a written language had to be devised, and also because of the inadequacy of the Garos' religious experience to provide words that would convey Christian thought. In their laborious translation, Mason and Phillips had the able assistance of Miss E. C. Bond.

Tura soon became the center of Christian work among the Garos. An important school for the training of girls was developed there under the guidance of the Woman's American Baptist Foreign Mission Societies. A Bible school for the training of ministers also was established. In 1899, Dr. G. G. Crozier, a medical missionary, was appointed for this field. Under his direction a hospital was started, which became a base for ministering to a large area by means of touring clinics and dispensaries.[9]

Mason, the veteran missionary, recommended a program of industrial education for the Garos. He saw that only in this way could they become strong Christian communities with economic independence. Moreover, he realized that these simple people, almost destitute of industrial skills, yet living in country rich in timber, arable soil, and water supply, would be exploited by outsiders. He frankly urged that the Garo people be taught to improve their opportunities and to make money for God. "Without this instruction," he said, "they will soon become perpetual slaves to incoming capitalists. With instruction they will rise and keep in advance of progress, and be themselves the capitalists, farmers, mechanics, manufacturers, and merchants, examples and instructors to others, especially to the future Christians of adjoining tribes." [10]

The progress of missionary efforts in the hills was phenomenal as compared with the work in the plains. By 1886 there were 1,473 baptized Garos, with 766 pupils in 44 schools. The village schools were strong evangelizing agencies because they were entirely under the supervision of the mission by an arrangement with the government. With the help of the government and of various Christian publication agencies, the Baptists were able to get into print a grammar,

---

[9] John E. Skoglund, *The Spirit Tree: The Story of Baptist Work Among Primitive Peoples* (Philadelphia, 1951), p. 59.

[10] *The Baptist Missionary Magazine*, Vol. 63, No. 6 (June, 1883), p. 146.

an arithmetic, and other textbooks for the Garos. From 1902 the Garo literature was printed in Roman characters, and the Garos themselves maintained a press for the publication of books in their own language. By 1905 the church membership had grown to 4,340, and a total of 7,326 people had been baptized. There were 109 village schools ministering to 2,221 pupils. Thus did education go hand-in-hand with evangelism.[11]

Perhaps among few other peoples did the gospel produce more dramatic change than among the Garos. A primitive and cruel people were transformed into literate and kindly Christians. Dense jungles were replaced by churches, schools, and bungalows. Industrial and agricultural training developed within communities a sense of economic well-being and confidence. Moreover, the Garo churches had been founded on a basis of self-support. By 1900 they were sending their own missionaries to neighboring tribes.

Equally impressive was the work carried on in this period among the peoples of the Naga Hills between the Brahmaputra Valley and Burma. The Nagas were known by a variety of tribal names—the Angami, the Ao, the Lhota, the Sema, the Rengma, the Tangkuhl, the Kabui, the Nzemi, the Khairao, and the Konyak Nagas. Bronson had been the first missionary to visit the Naga Hills, making his initial tour as early as 1838. In 1839 he had built a house at Mansang and spent eight months among them. In 1851, the Reverend S. W. Whiting, then the missionary in charge of the Sibsagar station, baptized a Naga from Morangkong village of the Ao tribe. The new convert lived at Sibsagar and became associated with the church there. But after a few years he returned to the hills, where he died.

Not until 1869, thirty years after the first contacts with these wild head-hunting people, did Edward Payson Scott go up into the hills with his Bible and a violin. He occasionally had seen at Nowgong on market days these strange looking Naga men, short in stature and sturdy in build—with only a loin cloth and colored feathers and wads of cotton in holes in their ears, and carrying sharp spears decorated

[11] Sword, *Baptists in Assam,* pp. 97-99; Henry C. Vedder, *A Short History of Baptist Missions* (Philadelphia, 1927), p. 124.

with black (human) and red (goat) hair. They were very dirty and unkempt in appearance. He was warned by a British officer not to go among them since they were head-hunters. Every young Naga had to take human skulls before he was considered brave enough to defend a wife. But Scott was not intimidated.

As he approached the first Naga village, he was met by twelve naked warriors with spears poised to strike him. Quickly he began to play his violin and to sing the hymn, "Am I a Soldier of the Cross?" Entranced, the men dropped their spears and shouted for more. He had won his way with music. Several young men went back to the plains with him to enter school at Nowgong. But that year, Scott died of cholera.

Fortunately for the Nagas, the Reverend E. W. Clark, who arrived in Assam in 1871, became interested in them. With the help of Godhula, an Assamese Christian, Clark acquired a knowledge of the vernacular of the Ao Nagas living in the vicinity of Sibsagar. From the spring of 1872 he, himself, made frequent trips into the hills to minister to them. In March, 1876, when he could leave responsibility for the printing press and translation work to the Reverend A. K. Gurney, he settled in the hills, establishing churches and schools, with Molung as a center. In 1885 he was reinforced by the coming of Dr. S. W. Rivenburg, a medical missionary, and his wife. Two years later, the Rivenburgs replaced C. D. King at Kohima, who had been working among the Angami Nagas since 1878. In 1889 the Ao Naga territory was annexed to the British Crown and head-hunting was stopped. Meanwhile, the church at Molung had grown strong enough to have its own ordained pastor.

Then a more central location for the mission was established at Impur, ten miles from Mokokchung, the government center. There a training school for pastors and lay workers was established by the Reverend S. A. Perrine in 1898, and a church was organized. Clark translated the Scriptures into Ao Naga and prepared a dictionary of the language. In the years that followed, mission stations were established at fifteen places for as many Naga tribes, a separate literature being prepared for each. Among these was Ukrul in Manipur State, a station which was opened by the Reverend William Pettigrew for the Tangkuhl Nagas in 1896. The work at Ukrul and Kohima, both of which towns were near Burma, became a point of contact with the Burma Mission.[12] Although head-hunting still flourished within a day's journey of Impur, Christian communities were growing rapidly.

In the meantime, work continued among the Assamese on the plains at Sibsagar, Nowgong, and Gauhati. But growth was slow. Most of the converts were from the immigrants who worked in the tea gardens. Among the missionaries there was difference of opinion with respect to a wise mission strategy. O. L. Swanson, John Firth, and later Joseph Paul felt that less stress should be placed on the Mundaris, or working peoples, and more on the Assamese. In time, however, they came to agree with Clark and Petrick that the emphasis should be placed upon the laboring class in the tea gardens. Swanson accordingly settled down at Golaghat in 1898 to do that work. These different points of view illustrate the weakness in the Assam Mission from the lack of co-ordinated planning. Each missionary did that which was wise in his own eyes.

The first evidence of an over-all strategy in the Mission was the establishment of an educational center at Jorhat in 1905 by the Reverend S. A. D. Boggs. This was the first effort in fifty years of work in Assam to unify the Mission, except in the Nowgong Orphanage that had come to an untimely end. Jorhat became the location of a Bible School to train pastors. In 1909 agricultural instruction was begun by Charles Tilden, in addition to industrial and manual arts training. The significance of the Jorhat Schools for the effectiveness of the Assam Mission was to increase in future years.

In 1903 the Assamese Bible was completed. It had been begun by Nathan Brown soon after his arrival in the country, more than half a century before. The project was continued by Nedhi Levi Farwell, Whiting, and Ward, and finally completed by Gurney. The long delay had been caused by the inability of the missionaries to devote their whole time to the work.[13]

In 1906 Sadiya was reopened after a long absence of missionaries from that northern center. Dr. and Mrs. H. W. Kirby went there to minister to the Abors and Miris, and to open a medical center with a grant provided by the Arthington Fund, a legacy obtained by the

[12] The foregoing survey is based upon Sword, *Baptists in Assam,* chap. 13, Skoglund, *The Spirit Tree,* chap. 5, and entries in *The Baptist Missionary Magazine*.

[13] *The Baptist Missionary Magazine,* Vol. 84, No. 9 (Sept., 1904), p. 617; Vol. 87, No. 6 (June, 1907), pp. 219-20.

Missionary Union. In 1901 they moved to Jorhat. Other centers of medical work opened prior to 1914 were at Kohima, Manipur, and Impur.

According to a report in 1908, the membership of the churches in Assam had grown in 20 years from 842 to upwards of 9,000. The major number were drawn from the hill tribes. Because so little was being done by the government in Assam for the hill peoples, the Mission devoted much attention to providing schools for their general instruction and for the training of national leaders. Training schools for workers were developed at Tura for the Garos; at Impur, Kohima, and Ukrul for the Nagas; and at Jorhat for the immigrant peoples and others in Upper Assam. The "Assam Valley Preachers' Training School" at Jorhat was reconstituted in 1914 as "The Jorhat Christian Schools." It was intended to provide a central Christian institution of higher education for all Assam, where young people might receive training in theory and in industrial skills. There was a middle English and high school, a Bible school, and an industrial school. In this program, the students combined a schedule of work and study.

In January, 1914, an "All Assam Baptist Convention" was organized at Golaghat, on the occasion of the celebration of the Judson Centennial. About 1,000 persons were in attendance, representing more than 20 different languages and tribes. At that time there were in the Assam Mission 13,000 converts.[14] The advance in the Mission since the entrance of Baptist missionaries in 1839 had not been phenomenal. Indeed, discouragements had marked the early years of work in the plains. It was not until stations were developed among the hill peoples that signs of genuine progress could be seen. Yet, in the plains as well as in the hills, a Christian witness had been planted against great odds by the persistent labors of a corps of missionaries and national leaders. By a combination of evangelism, education, and medical aid, a firm basis had been established by 1914 upon which more rapid success was to be achieved in later years.

---

[14] *Reports of American Baptist Missionary Union* for 1908, pp. 93-94; for 1911, p. 63; for 1914, pp. 50, 90; *Missions,* Vol. 5, No. 10 (Oct., 1914), pp. 772-75.

CHAPTER XVI

Meeting China's Challenge

CHINA IS ONE of the truly great countries of the world. Its history lies in the remote past. Its population includes nearly one-fourth of the people of the world. Yet, contrary to popular opinion, it is not over-populated. Within its 22 provinces that cover more than 1,500,000 square miles, its citizens are found crowded into but one-third of the vast area. This unbalanced distribution, especially in the North, is due to the lack of transportation facilities. The country is rich in resources. Anthracite coal, iron fields, oil territory, mineral wealth, great rivers, undeveloped areas for growing wheat, are all part of the potential wealth of China.

The civilization of the Chinese people dates back to 3000 B.C. For some reason, there came a setback in China's culture soon after the opening of the Christian Era. From that time, her people began to live in the past. This static quality of life continued until 1912 when the country entered upon a revolution, the effects of which have been felt in all areas of life ever since. The future of China is veiled in as much mystery as her beginnings. Yet, the virility of the people, their tenacious qualities, their courage, and their frugality, give hope for a more stable and progressive country than they have achieved to the present.

A Preview of the China Missions

Because the New China is in many respects the product of Christian missions and of the impact of Western culture, it is not amiss to relate the story of Baptist missions in China against the backdrop of the stirring events that have caught up the nation within the past century. As we have seen in an earlier chapter, China presented to the early American Baptist missionaries an enigma and a challenge.

How to gain entrance into the fabulous land was the problem in the first years of the nineteenth century. That the establishment of missions there would be desirable was an accepted conclusion among Baptists at home and in Burma. We have noted how William Dean and his wife founded a mission in Bangkok, the capital of Siam, in 1834. There they found great numbers of Chinese workmen, many of whom heard the gospel gladly and became Christians. Within eight years there were five churches with a total of five hundred members.

This initial work among the Chinese was followed in 1837 by the winning of the first convert on the mainland of China by J. L. Shuck. Then, following the Opium War with Great Britain and the treaty of 1842, fresh opportunities presented themselves. Hong Kong was ceded to the British, and five port cities in China were opened under treaty agreements for commerce and rights of foreign residence. They were Amoy, Canton, Foochow, Ningpo, and Shanghai. Almost at once, three Baptist missionaries, William Dean, J. L. Shuck, and J. L. Roberts moved to Hong Kong to establish the long-coveted mission station on Chinese soil. They were soon joined by Dr. D. J. Macgowan, the first Baptist medical missionary to the country. In November, 1843, he went to Ningpo, where he founded the East China Baptist Mission.

After the second Opium War (1857), the port of Swatow in South China was opened to foreign trade and residence. In 1860 the mission at Hong Kong was transferred to Swatow, which became the first station of what is now the South China Baptist Mission. William Ashmore and his son gave a total of ninety years to this mission. They purchased the Kakchieh mission compound, on the island across the bay from Swatow, and developed a theological seminary there for the training of a national leadership.

For a time the Tai-ping Rebellion (1845–1865) against the Manchu Dynasty subjected the country to turmoil and great suffering. There were many who felt that the readiness of its leaders to destroy the idols and to uproot the ancient patterns of the country presented at the time a golden opportunity to Christian missions for great advance, had they been ready to take advantage of it. On the other hand, there were those who regarded the rebellion as only superficially related to principles congenial to Christianity, although some of its leaders were nominal Christians. At least it may be admitted that another opportunity for change and progress did not come to China for several years. For the rebellion ultimately was suppressed by the forces of reaction.

After two decades of peace, another period of upheaval followed in 1884, when a war with France aroused antiforeignism. This in turn was followed by a time of Baptist expansion, when the East China field was enlarged by the planting of new stations in Shaohing, Kinhwa, Huchow, and Hangchow. About the same period, the West China field was opened in 1889 in the province of Szechuan, far into the interior of the country, by W. M. Upcraft and George Warner. In Chengtu, the outpost of Baptist missions in China, there was stiff opposition; in 1895 there were antiforeign riots which hindered but did not defeat the new effort.

The next few years saw great expansion in all three fields, and a fourth was opened in Central China in 1893 at Hankow. As converts increased, new churches were organized; additional schools were established; and hospitals and dispensaries were built. By 1900 there were 15 churches and 699 members in East China, two churches and 68 members in West China, 12 churches and 2,500 members in South China—a total of 29 churches and 3,267 members for three of the four fields. The Central China field was too new to offer any tangible results. For all China, the missionary personnel totalled 65, including wives and single women missionaries.

Then came the terrifying Boxer Rebellion in 1900. In some respects, it was the last stand of the old China, as the dowager Empress Tsi-an virtually deposed the young ruler, Kwah-Su, whose attempts at reform were regarded as dangerous and in the direction of Western influence. Combined with the internal dissension was a bitter resentment of foreign occupation and privilege in the country. Only incidentally was the uprising an anti-Christian movement, and that only because the spread of the Christian message had been through the efforts of peoples from the Western World. The worst effects of it were felt in Shantung and Shansi Provinces in North China. In southern and central China, missionaries fared better. In all, 135 missionaries' lives were lost, representing several denominations, and much mission property was destroyed.

There followed another period of quiet and constructive effort in the Baptist missions. The chief advances were in educational and medical work and in the development of administrative policies which prepared the way ultimately for a transfer of leadership from foreigners to Chinese Christians. In 1906 the West China Union University was established at Chengtu, an interdenominational project in which American Baptists participated. In 1908 the Shanghai Baptist College was established, with joint support from Northern and Southern Baptists. A new station was established at Ninyuenfu in West China, while Hopo and Sunwuhsien were opened in South China.

Then came the Revolution of 1911 by which the ancient dynasty of the empire was overthrown, the traditional educational system was abolished, and the Chinese Republic was proclaimed on February 12, 1912. The rapid succession of events gave Christianity a great opportunity, for the democratic background of Protestant missions in particular placed them in something of a favored position in the new climate of opinion that came with the revolution.[1]

Up to 1912, the greater progress in evangelistic work was in the South China Mission. The number of churches increased from about 50 to 106 between 1900 and 1912, and the membership grew from 2,073 to 3,583. In the East China Mission, the increases were from 13 to 24 churches, and from 683 to 1,311 members. In both Missions there had been retrogression in the number of churches that were independent of foreign aid. Although self-support was slow to develop on all the fields, it made more progress in the South because it was stressed more there.

Education received more emphasis in East China than in South China. While South China gave no thought to a college, East China got one firmly established at Shanghai. In medical work both Missions aimed at expansion, with hospitals in their main stations as a goal. Administratively, missionaries in South China were less anxious for centralized oversight of the work than in East China because of their previous experience with the autocratic control of a few leading missionaries. This fact made the South China missionaries jealous of their individual rights and district autonomy. Accordingly, East China developed during the early years of the twentieth century more centralization of administration, more concentration and efficiency, and a larger degree of autonomy on the field in their relationships to

---

[1] For supplemental surveys, see William B. Lipphard, *Out of the Storm in China* (Philadelphia, 1932); Helen Barrett Montgomery, *Following the Sunrise: A Century of Baptist Missions, 1813–1913* (Philadelphia, 1913), chap. 5; Henry C. Vedder, *A Short History of Baptist Missions* (Philadelphia, 1927), chap. 6.

the Boards at home. One writer has summarized trends in these words:

> Both missions were envisaging the day of complete devolution, when the native church would assume full responsibility for conducting the work. Both had taken first steps in that direction, but the East China Mission was really farther advanced along that line since it had a more efficient native organization to which authority could be committed.[2]

On these two fields, climate, natural resources, and the inhabitants all presented a similar picture. There was, however, a degree of urbanization in the lower Yangtze Valley of East China that did not exist in South China. Except for Swatow, the cities of the South, had commercial but not cultural importance. Outside contacts were not with Hongkong and Canton, but with distant Singapore and Siam. Whereas in East China, around Ningpo, the most prominent and wealthy business leaders of Shanghai exerted their influence. The growth of cities which had cultural as well as economic importance in East China, and their relative absence in South China influenced greatly the lines of development of the two Missions.

Although the territory of the East China Mission was larger than that of South China, a network of canals and rivers aided traffic. In South China, however, there was no such canal system to facilitate travel. The South China Mission worked among peoples of two distinct languages, so that two separate church conventions had to be maintained (one among the Tie Chiu peoples and the other among the Hakkas). In East China, although there was a difference of dialects, the Mission had only one convention that embraced all of the churches.

Growth was more rapid in the South China Mission because the people had a more venturesome spirit and a more open-minded attitude. Those of northeastern Chekiang, in East China, were more bound by the glories of traditional and ancient China.

---

[2] This comparison of the two major fields of American Baptists in China is drawn from an admirable study by Kenneth G. Hobart, A Comparative History of the East China and South China Missions of the American Baptist Foreign Mission Society, 1833–1935: A Study of the Intensive vs. the Extensive Policy in Mission Work. A typed doctoral dissertation at Yale University, 1937, pp. 429-40.

Methods of work generally were the same in the two Missions—evangelistic preaching, tract distribution, personal evangelism, faithful instruction of sincere inquirers and converts individually and in groups, and educational work through small schools for boys and girls. The one difference was that the Ningpo Mission (the earliest center in the East China field) introduced medical work at the outset, and kept it up all through the years. It proved to be a potent factor in overcoming opposition and winning the confidence of the Chinese. At Hong Kong in South China, on the other hand, there was no medical service. However, it did have one factor which was absent in Ningpo, the protection of the British flag.

Net results remained about the same. While there were slightly more baptisms at Hong Kong than at Ningpo, the loss, due to the instability of the Tie Chiu people, was greater in South China. On the other hand, South China had about four times as many churches and nearly three times as many members as East China by 1900. Evangelistic expansion was stressed more evidently in South China, whereas an intensive policy of educational and institutional development was emphasized in the East China Mission. The latter sought to train an indigenous leadership and Christian community by educational work. By further contrast, however, it may be noted that the concentration of most of the missionaries in South China, at Kakchieh, actually strengthened the educational set-up there. South China had a more thorough and successful training plan for volunteer lay helpers through the "quarterly meeting" and a week of guided study prior to administration of the ordinance of the Lord's Supper. Laymen were also welcomed into the theological class, and local preachers were urged to conduct classes for their members. The better trained rank-and-file membership in South China was indicated by the greater willingness and ability there to share the financial burden.[3]

Although the change of government in China in 1912 freed the missionaries from restrictions and brought recognition to graduates of mission schools for positions of leadership in the country, the American Baptists were not prepared to take full advantage of the growing opportunities which the new developments were making possible. Unable to expand and strengthen existing work simulta-

---

[3] *Ibid.*, pp. viii, ix, 39-41, 114-15, 268-71.

neously, the leading missionaries of the China Missions met with the new and enterprising foreign secretary, Dr. James H. Franklin, on October 9, 1912 to prepare a clear statement concerning the work in China. They explained that a development of the intensive policy, which they saw as the solution to the dilemma, meant a greater emphasis upon education to train Christian leaders among the Chinese. This plan seemed to be favored by the "fever of intellectual acquisitiveness that (was) sweeping over China" at the time. As the backbone of China's ancient educational system had been swept away, the people were looking to the missionaries to provide education for them. At the same time, from the Chinese point of view, medical work was continuing to be the most popular type of Christian ministry. Accordingly there was increasing need for special missionaries for technical service.

The intensive policy was also in answer to a manifestly growing desire among Chinese Christians for a voice in church control. Small beginnings had been made in the development of Chinese home mission work whereby evangelists were sent out to open out-stations through Chinese direction and financial support. Plans were being formulated to allow these societies to control, at first, a share and ultimately all of the money appropriated by the Foreign Mission Societies in America for evangelization and church aid in China. In fact, the Boards were eager to apply the intensive policy first in China because the facilities for training Christian leaders there were inadequate.

As a further measure taken to implement the new policy, the Board voted in 1913 to withdraw from Central China. Because the resources were not adequate to send additional missionaries and equipment to strengthen that field, it was thought best to turn it over to other Societies in the area. This move was opposed vigorously by the South China Mission which favored an extensive policy. On the other hand, it was received with warm approval by the East China Mission, where the intensive policy was acceptable. At home opposition was led by Dr. Frank M. Goodchild, who had visited Central China following the Judson Centennial Tour of 1914.

By 1914, the American Baptists were supporting in China a total of 72 missionaries in 21 stations on three fields. They were spending over $250,000 annually for this work. Moreover, they were faced with the prospects of increasing that expenditure by 75 per cent if the enterprise were to be maintained without curtailment.[4]

Although American Baptists did not enter into organic union with other denominations in China, their missionaries did co-operate in union projects in educational and medical missions. They also participated in a conference on comity which was held at Shanghai in 1913 by Dr. John R. Mott in keeping with proposals previously made at the World Missionary Conference in Edinburgh in 1910.[5] They stood on the threshold of significant changes, chiefly in the direction of a greater emphasis upon education and the development of a trained leadership among nationals. In this respect, they lagged behind the Presbyterians, Methodists, and Congregationalists, who also were at work in the country. For most of their history in the nineteenth century, Baptists had laid their chief stress upon evangelism. Such schools as they had were small and poorly equipped. In the judgment of one historian:

> The fruit of this policy was failure to develop strong leaders among the Chinese and limitation of the growth of the mission to the numbers who could be influenced by the direct evangelistic labors of the missionaries with such helpers as they could train.[6]

The story of the main developments on the major fields of service in China will be traced here briefly against the general background just provided. The chief accomplishments of the intensive policy, as it was worked out after 1913, will be summarized in a later chapter.

The South China Mission

As we have seen, the beginnings of Baptist work in China took place in Hongkong, where the Tie Chiu church was organized on May 28, 1843, with three members under the pastorate of William Dean. Intimately associated with this pioneer effort were the Shucks. Mrs. Henrietta Shuck was the first American woman missionary in China. Not long after the Southern Baptist Convention had been formed in 1845, the Shucks separated themselves from the American Baptist Missionary Union for service with the Southern Board. It was a natural move, for the Canton station and the work for the Can-

---

[4] *Missions,* Vol. 4, No. 7 (July, 1913), pp. 547, 561; No. 11 (Nov., 1913), pp. 873-75; Vol. 5, No. 7 (July, 1914), pp. 561-63.

[5] *Ibid.,* Vol. 4, No. 9 (Sept., 1913), pp. 671-75.

[6] Montgomery, *Following the Sunrise,* pp. 160-61.

tonese peoples had been turned over to the Southern Baptists in 1845. From that time the work of American Baptists was confined in South China to the vicinity of Hong Kong, until Swatow was opened in 1863. Although Dean argued for a permanent station at Hong Kong, the workers early began to feel that it was only a stepping-stone to a more stable community of Chinese. For in Hong Kong, the missionaries were dealing with a somewhat floating population of Tie Chiu people.

On the mainland, Swatow was in 1860 "little more than a small dirty village, located on the mud flats formed by the delta of the Han River." [7] But its natural harbor gave it promise of later becoming the ninth among the ports of China. By June of that year, the Reverend John W. Johnson and three of his assistants had completed the transfer of the Mission from Hong Kong to Swatow. After thirty years of work among the Chinese people, first in Siam, then in Hong Kong, the work was at last centered in the homeland. Although Swatow was designated as a station from the beginning, the headquarters of the Mission were maintained for some years at Masu, where anti-foreign feeling did not make itself felt.

In March, 1863, William Ashmore and his wife sailed for China, arriving in July. The following year he purchased for Mex. $800 the nucleus of the present Baptist Mission Compound at Kakchieh, a site across the bay from the city proper. It consisted of some rocky treeless hills and the upper end of a gully or two. For the purpose of foreign residence, the situation surpassed Swatow, but as a mission center, it was too isolated. As a consequence, the hospital which was erected there in later years did not grow as it would have done in Swatow. By contrast, the English Presbyterian Mission in Swatow enjoyed a greater growth than the Baptist Mission. This was due in part to location. It is the opinion of some that Ashmore would have done better to have waited until he had sufficient funds to buy property within the city.[8]

The early years of the Swatow mission were notably successful. Chinese assistants gave devoted service. Although not able preachers, they were well acquainted with the Scriptures and they lived among the people, doing much personal work. The Mission was associated

---

[7] Hobart, A Comparative History of the East China and South China Missions, p. 116.

[8] *Ibid.*, pp. 123-24.

inseparably with William Ashmore, under whose direction early converts were trained in self-reliance and self-support. But the policy of developing independent churches was premature. The result was that the Mission went over to the other extreme. "Thereafter, for nearly thirty years there was only one church in the Mission—the central church at Kakchieh. All baptized disciples were regarded as members of it, and to it they repaired once a quarter to celebrate the communion." [9]

When Ashmore returned from a furlough in America early in the 1870's, he took over the task of biblical instruction of ministerial students. He had twelve, all of whom were over thirty years of age. In 1873 a building for these students was erected. From the beginning, theological training was a combination of class-room and field work. Up to 1898, the theological school produced nine ordained and forty-two unordained preachers. Although Ashmore bore the responsibility for this work through the years, he had the assistance of the other missionaries. Indeed, the availability of the missionaries under the plan of a central headquarters at Swatow made such instruction easier than it would have been if the Mission had been more decentralized.

Chinese women were trained to be Bible teachers by Miss Adele M. Fielde, the first single woman missionary to China. In 1873 she opened what came to be known as the Swatow Woman's Bible Training School. Her plan was simple but effective. After a brief period of instruction, she would send the women out, two by two, to teach the Bible in the homes. Then they returned for further training, after which they would go forth again. By such a blending of theory and practice, Miss Fielde developed able leadership for the women's work in South China. In the first 21 years of the school's history, 212 women received instruction. Miss Fielde distinguished herself also by publication of a *Dictionary of the Swatow Dialect* in 1883, which was given wide acclaim by Chinese scholars.[10] She also aided William Ashmore's son in the preparation of a colloquial version of the Scriptures.

Ashmore's program of developing an indigenous church was farsighted and required the co-operation of the Board at home. In 1872,

[9] *Ibid.*, p. 133.

[10] Hobart, A Comparative History of the East China and South China Missions, p. 165; *The Baptist Missionary Magazine*, Vol. 63, No. 10 (Oct., 1883), p. 361.

for example, he requested the Union to permit the Chinese congregation "to use under their own direction all the funds collected on the field." [11] At the same time, he encouraged the Kakchieh church to undertake the support of two evangelists at a salary of eight dollars per man for a period of two months. He further insisted that the thousands of villages in the Tie Chiu area (the northeastern part of Kwantung Province) should be evangelized by the Chinese church members as far as possible. Although the missionaries engaged in a tremendous amount of itinerating, they at times left out-stations vacant in the hope that the Chinese Christians would assume responsibility for their Sunday services. In some cases the plan worked. By July, 1897, the Mission notified the chapels that beginning the next year, they would be expected to support their own preachers so far as possible.

The Mission also sought self-support with respect to local schools. Because every local chapel wanted its own elementary school, the treasury would have been emptied if this policy had not been encouraged. In 1880 the Chinese Christians were made responsible for the educating of their own children. Through the years that followed, even small grants to chapel schools were diminished gradually.

Medical work began in the South China Mission with the arrival in 1878 of Miss C. H. Daniels, M.D., at Kakchieh. By 1880 she had a dispensary there, where she treated about 400 patients during the latter part of the year. In 1884, after having opened a hospital, she had to leave because of ill-health. Late in 1889, Mrs. Anna K. Scott, M.D., arrived to reopen the hospital at Kakchieh. She had been formerly a missionary's wife in Assam. Upon the death of her husband, she had returned to America to prepare herself to be a doctor. In 1890 she reported over 4,000 treatments. Before the close of that year, she opened a dispensary at Kityang, and still another at Chaoyang in 1891. She was known throughout the countryside for her ability to cure people of the dread opium habit. In 1893, Dr. Scott erected a small hospital building at Kityang. About the same time, she took in some Chinese Christian men as medical students. In 1894 six were enrolled for a three-year course. The following year she turned this hospital at Kityang over to Dr. Josephine M. Bixby, who had arrived in China the previous year. Dr. Bixby was the first missionary to make Kityang a permanent residence. She was joined

[11] Hobart, *op. cit.*, p. 168.

shortly by the Reverend and Mrs. Jacob Speicher, and from 1896 Kityang was regarded as a regular mission station. Such were the beginnings of medical missions in South China. They had been achieved by representatives of the Woman's Societies in America. To them must go the credit for the pioneer development of two hospitals which by 1900, were to develop, during succeeding years, into well equipped medical institutions.[12]

Further evidence of the virility of the South China Mission during these years of evangelistic expansion was the opening of a new work among the Hakkas in the 1880's. It had begun when the Reverend W. K. McKibben and his wife, of the Swatow staff, undertook in 1881 to labor exclusively among this highland people of a different dialect. Their headquarters were at Kaying. During later years they were joined by the Reverend George Campbell and his sister, and still later by the Reverend and Mrs. George E. Whitman, Miss M. L. Ostrom, and a medical missionary, Dr. Edward Bailey, and his wife. By the close of the century, McKibben was able to resume his labors at Swatow, leaving Campbell and Whitman to carry on at the Hakka Mission. The Hakka people were found to be among the most intelligent in China. In time, something like a mass movement was to develop as inquirers increased from among the upper classes.

Translation work progressed slowly in view of the heavy burdens that fell upon the Mission staff. It was not until the end of 1895 that the New Testament in the Tie Chiu vernacular was completed. The bulk of the work had been done by Dr. William Ashmore, Jr., with some help from other missionaries. He was not to complete the translation of the Old Testament until 1922. Unlike his father, who was essentially an evangelist and planter of churches, the son, who had begun his missionary service in 1879, was by gifts and temperament a scholar. Although he bore responsibility for the general work of a missionary, his great accomplishments were to translate the Scriptures and to share with his father in the development of the Ashmore Theological Seminary. He also was one of the founders of the China Baptist Publication Society, which was organized in Canton in 1899.[13]

The Publication Society was formed as an independent organiza-

---

[12] Hobart, *op. cit.*, pp. 146, 175-78.

[13] George H. Water, "Missionary Statesmen: The William Ashmores—Father and Son," *The Chronicle*, Vol. 14, No. 1 (Jan., 1951), pp. 40-45.

tion, but its property virtually was owned jointly by the Foreign Mission Board of the Southern Baptist Convention and the American Baptist Foreign Mission Society. The press was conducted under the management of a Board of Directors representing the missionaries of the two societies and the Chinese Christians. The first general secretaries were Dr. R. E. Chambers and the Reverend Jacob Speicher. Support of the enterprise came from Northern and Southern Baptists and also from the English and Swedish Baptists who likewise had work in China.

By the end of the nineteenth century, the territory of the South China Mission was fairly well marked out. There were 90 out-stations and preaching places reported, with 2,073 baptized church members served by 44 ordained pastors and preachers. During the year 1899, a total of $3,632 was contributed by the Chinese for general purposes. The results had been achieved by continuous evangelistic efforts, in which evangelists of the Chinese people and Bible women had borne a heroic part.[14]

The administration of the South China Mission during this period of expansion had been without a formal plan of over-all organization. Since 1859, it will be recalled, the Board of the Missionary Union had done away with organized missions as such, and had made each missionary responsible to the Executive Committee, although allowing the missionaries to form such associations of their own for free conference as they might desire. This meant that each missionary made his own requests for appropriations and administered his work independently of the other missionaries in the Mission. Undoubtedly, there was consultation and informal planning, but there was no corporate planning required.

For forty years the South China Mission operated under this policy. The encouragement which it afforded for individual initiative in a period of intensive evangelism and expansion was in its favor. But the frictions which arose between missionaries who did not see eye-to-eye on plans and methods issued in serious trouble by the close of the century. This was accentuated by the fact that a one-man domination had developed on the field. The long experience and seniority of Dr. William Ashmore, Sr., coupled with his dynamic personality made him something of an autocrat in the Mission. The missionaries who came in the 1890's found the lack of representative

---

[14] Hobart, *op. cit.,* p. 150

control irksome. By the close of the decade, bitter feelings had broken out into open revolt. Eleven missionaries appended their signatures, on September 22, 1899, to a letter to Dr. T. S. Barbour, the foreign secretary. In it they brought charges against Dr. Ashmore of duplicity and intentional effort to alienate missionary workers one from another. A visit of the foreign secretary was required to straighten out the misunderstandings and restore harmonious relations. It was obvious that the friction had arisen over a misapprehension of Ashmore's aggressive oversight of the various stations and over differences of mission policy between Ashmore and some of the newer missionaries. The settlement of the conflict gave opportunity to establish independent churches and so decentralize the Mission.[15]

The tensions over Ashmore's leadership were not alone responsible for changes in the administration of the Mission. Indeed, the thinking of Board members and secretaries concerning mission programs, methods, and policies was being modified by a combination of circumstances which we have noted in an earlier chapter. The Finance Committee raised the question as early as 1898 as to whether the wisest use was being made of resources. "It suggested the possibility of an undue emphasis on evangelism to the neglect of Christian nurture, and urged that efforts and expenditures be strategically massed." [16] Along the line of this thought, Dr. S. W. Duncan, Dr. Barbour's predecessor as foreign secretary, recommended to the Union in 1898 that a larger emphasis be placed on educational work in China in order to train leaders for the churches. At the same time, the Executive Committee was seeking a plan of administration of the fields whereby it might be relieved of the ever growing burden of detail. Accordingly, in 1899, a proposal was submitted to all the missions of the Union that called for advisory action by "reference committees" on the fields, which would at once free the Board of numerous details and assure the missionaries of greater initiative in planning their work together. The plan was adopted ultimately on all the fields of the Missionary Union.

Between 1900 and 1912 there were many developments which

---

[15] Hobart, A Comparative History of the East China and South China Missions, pp. 179-84; Records of the Executive Committee of the American Baptist Missionary Union for July 28, 1899, p. 315; for December 4, 1899, pp. 426-27; and for March 11, 1901, pp. 108-10.

[16] Hobart, *op. cit.*, p. 282.

we can only summarize here. The Boxer Rebellion of 1900 actually enhanced the prestige of the foreigner and his religion in China, hence there was a readier acceptance of evangelistic efforts in the years that followed. A home mission society was organized in October, 1905, and nearly enough money was raised to support three evangelists in 1906. The Hakka Mission suffered from a constantly changing missionary personnel, yet there was progress. By 1912 three stations had been occupied and work was well established in two of them.

In keeping with the new concern for Christian nurture, educational work was given an impetus. A Bible Institute was established in 1903 to meet an urgent need for trained leadership. In 1905 Dr. Ashmore, Sr., made a gift to the Union of $10,000 in land and money to erect seminary quarters at Kakchieh. The presentation was made in Boston on his eightieth birthday. The new building for the Ashmore Theological Seminary, opened in 1907, was situated on a commanding site overlooking the Bay of Swatow. Its president was Dr. William Ashmore, Jr. In 1908 the Mission began to develop Sunday schools. Within three years, there were about one hundred organized schools, attended mostly by adults. The great desire for popular education stimulated the development of chapel schools. In 1909, for example, twenty-five such schools were opened in the Kityang field, with over five hundred pupils. Although not all of them survived, they represented a trend that was growing. By 1912, the Mission had ten boarding schools for boys and girls with 433 students, and 56 primary schools that served 1,100 pupils.[17]

During this twelve-year period, two new hospital plants were established at Kityang and Kakchieh. At Hopo a hospital was being requested by the citizens with a promise of financial aid, but no staff was available. There were two instances of co-operation with other denominations in medical work. One was at Canton, where the Mission designated Dr. Henry Newman to the staff of the medical school that was being organized interdenominationally. The other was with the English Presbyterian Mission at Swatow for medical work and theological training.

Although there had been during this period a continued emphasis upon trained leadership and self-support, there had been no transfer of administrative control from the Mission to the churches. Associa-

[17] *Ibid.*, p. 325

tions provided inspiration, instruction, and an opportunity to make requests of the missionaries. Home mission societies, supported by the Chinese Christians, conducted evangelistic work, but it was only a beginning of participation in the administrative responsibility of the work.[18] The process of devolution by which the Chinese assumed full responsibility and control of the churches, schools, and hospitals was to come in the period after 1914.

The East China Mission

The East China field was the second developed by American Baptists in China. All of the stations except Nanking and Shanghai (which are in Kiangsu Province) were located in Chekiang, the smallest and most eastern province of China. Its population of 11,000,000 people was crowded into a territory no larger than Ohio. Yet, it was a wealthy section of the country, dotted by large cities of 200,000 to 1,000,000 population.

It will be recalled that the first station established was Ningpo, to which Dr. D. J. Macgowan went in 1843. There he founded a hospital which won him favor with the people. By 1845, the American Presbyterians, the Church Missionary Society of England, and the English General Baptists had commenced operations in the same city. On October 31, 1847, just a few months after the arrival of the Reverend E. C. Lord and his wife to reinforce the station, the First Baptist Church was organized on the site of the West Gate Chapel that was to be completed in 1852. On November 21, the first convert was baptized. He was Tsiu Tsu-lin, teacher of Dr. Macgowan. Subsequently he became a preacher of the gospel.

On April 8, 1849, the Reverend Josiah Goddard and his wife and four children arrived. He had labored eight years among the Chinese in Bangkok, but in 1848 pulmonary tuberculosis forced him out of the hot and humid climate. At Ningpo, he sought recovery of health. Unable to preach to any great extent because of his condition, he gave himself almost exclusively to completing a translation of the New Testament which he had begun in Siam. In 1853 the first copy came from the press. Its fine classical style was applauded by Chinese scholars. While working on the Old Testament, Goddard's worn body gave way, and he died at the age of forty, on September 4, 1854. His missionary career was a link between the Siam Mission

---

[18] *Ibid.*, pp. 352, 364

and the East China field, for he labored devotedly in both countries. Moreover, he was a close friend and kinsman of William Dean, the pioneer missionary to the Chinese people. His son, Josiah Ripley Goddard was to return to China in 1867, to devote forty-six years to the East China Mission.

The vacancy left by Goddard was filled by the Reverend Miles J. Knowlton, who had arrived in 1853. While Dr. Macgowan managed the hospital and Mrs. Macgowan got a day school for girls under way, Lord supervised a boys' school at the West Gate Chapel, and Knowlton established a new station on the Island of Chusan. In 1855 eight of the thirteen baptisms in Ningpo were of persons living on Chusan. Although funds were cut in 1857, two Chinese preachers were sent to begin a third station in Kinhwa. By the close of the first ten years of the West Gate Chapel (1857), there had been twenty-five baptisms, four deaths, and two exclusions, leaving nineteen Chinese Christians.[19]

In December, 1858, Dr. Macgowan closed the dispensary and left Ningpo for the United States. The support he had been receiving from the Medical Missionary Society of China was cut off, and his health was precarious. Five years later, he resigned his connection with the Missionary Union. After the American Civil War, he returned to Shanghai to a private medical practice, and later entered service on the staff of the Imperial Customs at Wenchow. He died in Shanghai on July 21, 1893.

In 1860 the Reverend Horace Jenkins and his wife arrived to strengthen the Ningpo station. It was help gladly received, for Mrs. Lord had died only a few months before of pulmonary tuberculosis. The same year, the city was disturbed by fighting of the Tai-ping rebels. The missionaries were faced with the care of hundreds of refugees who flocked into the mission compounds which had been declared by the government out-of-bounds for the fighting. When the rebels were driven out of Ningpo in May, 1862, by French, English, and Chinese troops, Knowlton saw a weakening of Chinese confidence in their idols and a greater receptivity to the Christian message. The next year there were 41 baptisms in Ningpo, and a church of 13 members was organized at Kinhwa. Knowlton himself

---

[19] J. R. Goddard, *The East China Baptist Mission, Historical Notes* (Ningpo, 1911), pp. 7-8; *The Baptist Missionary Magazine,* Vol. 45, No. 1 (Jan., 1865), p. 2.

had baptized 159 persons between his arrival in 1854 and 1864. In the latter year, there were in the East China Mission four churches with 126 members in contrast to one church of eight members ten years before. In addition there were seven out-stations and nine assistant preachers.[20]

The year 1867 was significant for a number of reasons. In the first place, it was a time of unusual expansion of the Mission. Four members of the Ningpo church formed themselves into a Baptist church at near-by Hangchow, where they lived. By the close of the year, the Ningpo church had 74 members; the Jih-z-kong church had 39; the Chusan church, 38; the Kinhwa church, 21; and the Hangchow church, 8; bringing the total to 180 in 13 meeting places. Because of this expansion of the field, the Board abandoned the name "Ningpo Mission" in favor of "East China Mission."[21] In the same year Josiah R. Goddard and his wife received their appointment to China.

On June 1, 1868, the young Goddards arrived in Ningpo. Within a month and without warning, Goddard was given the heavy task of being mission treasurer, a position which he held for the next forty-three years. His boyhood knowledge of the language served him in good stead, and soon he was deeply involved in the work. But tragedy was not far away. In September, he lost both his wife and their newly born child. This was his second wife to die shortly after their marriage.

Fortunately, the demands of the Mission eased his sorrow to a degree. He made a trip to Shaohing to study possibilities of opening a new station there. As a consequence, the Jenkins family took up residence there in the spring of 1869. When Knowlton left for furlough in March, 1870, Goddard assumed the sole responsibility for the work in Ningpo. He served as pastor of the city church, as instructor of a class of young theological students, and gave general administrative oversight to the station. The following fall, he received a visit from William Dean and his daughter, Fanny. The meeting with Fanny was a solace to the lonely man, and shortly thereafter they were married. Mrs. Goddard was eminently successful

---

[20] Hobart, A Comparative History of the East China and South China Missions, pp. 187-89.

[21] Goddard, *op. cit.*, p. 14.

in teaching Chinese women to read. Together, husband and wife launched a literacy campaign for adults.

In spite of every effort to win the people, the number of conversions were few and scattered. As Goddard sought the reason for such slow progress, it occurred to him that the little struggling churches were too weak and widely scattered to make a strong impact upon non-Christians. Accordingly, he organized on December 22, 1873, the Chekiang Baptist Association. There were six churches represented by two missionaries, 18 preachers, and five laymen. The total membership reported was 205, and about $100 Chinese currency was in the treasury. Dr. Knowlton was elected chairman, while Goddard and one of the Chinese preachers were chosen clerks. In 1879 the churches of the Southern Baptist Mission in Kiangsu Province were admitted to membership, and the name was changed to the "Chekiang and Kiangsu Baptist Association." In 1895, when the Kiangsu churches had grown large enough to separate into their own association, the name reverted to the "Chekiang Baptist Association." It was this organization of churches which provided the core of strength for the Chinese Christians in later years when they were to pass through severe trial in the absence of foreign leadership.[22]

By 1875, Knowlton was gone, having died the previous year. Badly in need of help, Goddard persuaded E. C. Lord, who had been with the mission twelve years before and had then resigned to become U. S. Consul, to resume his relations with the Mission. This he did without salary, since he retained his diplomatic position. His return brought to the Mission his son-in-law, Dr. S. P. Barchet, a medical man who had been engaged with him in an independent work in the city. "They brought with them the North Gate Church and the chapels and work at the South Gate, at Nying-kong-gyiao, and at Kong-keo, and also the girls' boarding school, which had been established and carried on by aid of gifts from friends in England."[23] Thus the Mission was strengthened and the medical work which had been discontinued upon Dr. Macgowan's departure in 1858 was reopened. Barchet was a skilled surgeon, and even without a hospital, he gained a reputation for successful cataract operations. Yet, he was at heart an evangelist and combined a preaching ministry with the

[22] *Ibid.*, pp. 17-18; Francis W. Goddard, *Called to Cathay* (New York, 1948), pp. 72-73.

[23] Goddard, *The East China Baptist Mission*, p. 18.

practice of medicine. In consequence of the large addition which Dr. Lord brought, the East China churches numbered nine in 1877, with 23 chapels in the city and out-stations, 21 preachers, and 307 members.[24]

Recruits for the Mission began to come faster now—five in 1888, two in 1889, and eleven between 1890 and 1893. They were distributed among all the stations except Hangchow. Unfortunately, self-support did not keep pace with these evidences of growth. The Mission was not successful in persuading parents to pay toward the expenses of their children in the schools. At Kinhwa the idea of supporting their own church ministry did not take hold of the congregation. The Ningpo West Gate Church did assume one-half of the support of its pastor in 1884, and achieved complete support about 1898. But this was the exception rather than the rule. The idea of self-support was alien to the Chinese mind. The small temple up-keep, in the days before they became Christians, had been met by fees paid there for fortune-telling, purchase of incense, and the like. In appraising the situation, Dr. Hobart, himself a missionary of long experience in China, wrote:

> These facts would seem to indicate that either the Chekiang Chinese were far poorer than those of South China, or that the Mission had not rightly assessed the financial ability of its constituency and so had failed to apply sufficient pressure to secure larger native support of the schools. The latter alternative seems the more probable.[25]

In 1896 two forward steps occurred at the meeting of the Chekiang Baptist Association in Shaohing. One was the projection of a plan for a Chinese Home Mission Society, which was perfected in 1897 at Huchow. The other was the organization of the "Chekiang Baptist Missionary Conference." An "advisory" committee, consisting of one member from each station and two of the Woman's Society, was created; and other committees related to special phases of the work were set up. This advisory committee was to ascertain the judgment of the entire mission on important Board proposals. In these two actions we see far-sighted policies being developed. The first was in terms of self-direction on the part of the Chinese Christians. The

---

[24] *Ibid.*, p. 20.

[25] Hobart, A Comparative History of the East China and South China Missions, pp. 225-26.

second was in terms of a responsible administrative machinery through which the missionaries might function on the field in behalf of the Board. This step preceded by four or five years the Board's proposal for organized missions and the "reference committee." The Chekiang Baptist Missionary Conference later developed into the East China Baptist Mission Conference.[26]

During the forty-seven years of the Mission's history, from 1843 to 1900, educational and medical work had been a supplement to the great amount of evangelistic work done. By the close of the century, there were three boarding schools with seventy-five pupils, and five other schools with a total of eighty-six students. The schools were staffed by Chinese teachers and supervised by missionaries. Yet, only the foundations had been laid for a sound system of education under mission supervision.

The medical work likewise was given a secondary place, and only the basic structure for later institutions could be developed. As we have seen, Dr. Barchet resumed in 1875 the medical work begun by Dr. Macgowan in Ningpo. Then from 1881–83, Barchet was on furlough, during which time the hospital was kept open by his Chinese assistants, with the oversight of Goddard. Upon Barchet's return in 1883, the medical work was resumed. In 1889 Dr. and Mrs. J. S. Grant arrived to relieve Barchet. Grant had the same evangelistic zeal as Barchet, and was well suited to carry on his ministry. In 1894 when the Barchets returned from furlough, they were transferred to Kinhwa to open medical work there. In May, 1895, he succeeded in establishing a hospital in the town. Although the Ningpo Hospital was closed temporarily for lack of funds in 1899, the medical work had a footing in two of the Mission stations, at Ningpo and Kinhwa. With cramped facilities and a staff never larger than one foreign doctor and two or three poorly trained assistants, a beginning had been made and the way was outlined for the future development of medical missions in the East China field.

Literary work was given more place in this Mission than in the South China field. In 1860 Dr. Lord prepared expository notes in Chinese on books of the Bible. Dr. Jenkins published also in Chinese a Reference New Testament in 1873, and completed by 1898 commentaries on most of the books of the New Testament. Lord revised

---

[26] *Ibid.*, p. 223.

Josiah Goddard's version of the Wenli New Testament and translated all of it, with a large part of the Old Testament, into Ningpo romanized colloquial. His task was completed later by Dr. J. R. Goddard, who finished the Old Testament in March, 1901, after six years of labor. The printing establishment, begun in 1877 by the Reverend W. W. Sweet at Shaohing, and later removed to Hangchow, greatly stimulated literary production. This was known as the Wayland Press. It was housed at the Wayland Academy for boys in Hangchow, a school which Sweet had founded in 1899. The Press furnished employment for worthy students, and supplied Sunday school helps and devotional literature for the churches.

In 1899 there were in the entire East China Mission 13 organized churches, only two of them self-supporting. There were also 22 outstations and 683 members in the combined church enrollment. Serving these churches were 9 ordained and 19 unordained preachers, and 6 Bible women. Numerically, the results were not impressive. But when measured against the developments of later years, they represented a worthy investment of life and money, for there was being shaped a small but effective Christian community that was to stand the test of trial and persecution.[27]

During the Boxer Rebellion of 1900, the churches faced severe testing. Kinhwa suffered worse than any other station in the East China Mission. A mob stormed the mission compound, forcing the Bousfields to flee for their lives. They escaped over a rear wall to the city magistrate's office, where they received passage by boat to Shanghai. Although the uprising disrupted the work on all of the stations, forcing the missionaries to the coast, no one of the staff or of the Chinese Christians lost their lives. Only at Kinhwa was damage done to the property.

The gathering of the missionaries at Shanghai during the uprising made them first aware of the responsibility which they had for that great city. They found a considerable group of Baptists from Chekiang Province, most of whom had come from Ningpo and Chusan to work. These they gathered into a church which was formally organized on April 5, 1903. Dr. J. R. Goddard preached the sermon for the occasion. The first missionaries to reside permanently in

---

[27] The foregoing summary is based upon Hobart, *op. cit.,* pp. 224, 230-37, 250-51, 265; and Frank A. Ufford, The East China Baptist Mission: 1843–1943 (a paper presented in Ningpo in 1948), p. 18.

Shanghai were the Reverend and Mrs. Frank J. White, who joined the staff of the Shanghai Baptist Seminary in 1906.

The period from 1900 to 1914 was characterized by marked extension of the work, but mainly within the limits already set. The exception was the occupation of the Shanghai area just described. The largest tangible results were not in the field of evangelism and church planting, as in the South China Mission, but in founding and developing educational and medical institutions.[28]

Many new schools were opened in this period, and the standards of efficiency were raised. For example, the boys' day school at Kinhwa was transformed into a boarding school; and a boarding school was established at Huchow. Wayland Academy was opened at Hangchow in 1900. After six years of joint effort to establish a college and seminary at Shanghai, Northern and Southern Baptists crystallized plans for both institutions in 1906. The seminary was opened in that year. A campus of twenty-seven acres was purchased along the harbor of the city. Dr. R. T. Bryan, a Southerner, was selected president of the seminary, and Dr. Frank J. White represented Northern Baptists. Dr. J. T. Proctor of the East China Mission was made president of the college. Construction work was begun in May, 1907. The seminary was moved to the campus later that year, and the college was opened in 1909, with forty-five students enrolled. The faculty was made up of two Americans and six Chinese. By 1911 the two divisions were united as the University of Shanghai under the presidency of Dr. White.

By 1912 the total appropriations for the East China Mission totalled $76,615, which represented an increase of more than 100 per cent over the $30,000 provided in 1905. Much of this amount went to educational work, especially for Shanghai University and Seminary.[29]

During these years there was a general trend of co-operation with other denominations in educational and hospital work, as well as in evangelistic and church activities. In 1911 Baptists entered into plans for a Union Educational Commission to include five missions (Southern Methodist, Northern and Southern Presbyterian, Northern and Southern Baptist). It became the East China Educational Union for

---

[28] Hobart, A Comparative History of the East China and South China Missions, p. 364.

[29] *Ibid.*, pp. 408-09.

the entire lower Yangtze Valley, giving needed co-ordination to the program of higher education. Baptists were full partners in Ginling College in Nanking, which was founded shortly after the revolution in 1911. The East China Missionary Conference of 1912 approved a Baptist share with two Presbyterian Missions in a Union Institutional Evangelistic Centre at Hangchow. Co-operation with the China Inland Mission was approved in evangelistic and educational work in the Kinhwa region.

Similar progress in medical work was noticeable at this time. In 1904 Dr. Grant built a new hospital at Ningpo. About the same time a medical program was being developed at Huchow by Dr. M. D. Eubank. In 1908 Dr. C. H. Barlow was added to the staff. Two years later gifts were provided from friends in America and the Woman's Society to erect a hospital there. In 1910 a large hospital building was dedicated at Shaohing, where Dr. Francis W. Goddard, son of J. R. Goddard, was at work. The same year, Dr. MacKenzie was building a hospital at Kinhwa, which was made possible by gifts from America.

The East China Missionary Conference stressed self-support of medical work, and endorsed in 1910 co-operation in the proposed Union Medical College at Nanking to train doctors. By 1915, Baptists and Southern Methodists had entered upon a union medical work at Huchow.[30]

The administration of the East China Mission was strengthened greatly by the efficient functioning of the Chekiang Baptist Missionary Conference, which had come into existence in 1896. By 1911 the number of regular committees through which it worked had increased to eight. In addition there were four special committees and four boards of managers for the direction of specific institutions under the care of the Mission. Instead of doing its business in two days before the annual association meeting, twelve days were required.

Among the problems faced by the Missionary Conference was that of supervising language examinations for new missionaries. In the early days, the acquiring of the language was left to each newcomer. Because some delayed in achieving facility in this respect, regulations were developed and an examining committee was set up to conduct examination of all new missionaries engaged in language study. By

[30] *Ibid.*, pp. 410-11, 419-21. See also notes on individual stations in Goddard, *The East China Baptist Mission.*

1906 a curriculum was adopted, and in time the Mission entered into co-operation with the Union Language School in Nanking.

A second concern of the Missionary Conference was the guidance of the Board at home in policy making relative to the advance of the Mission. In 1904 the Mission opened seven new stations including Shanghai, Chusan, Songkian, Dongai, Donglu, Siaoshan, and T'ang-p'u. To carry out this expanded program, request was made for 47 new missionaries and $151,500. By 1910, however, the thinking of the missionaries on the field had changed to the point where the Conference, after consulting with the West China Mission, urged the Board to consolidate the two Missions. They had come to see that "the demands upon the funds of the Foreign Society call for intensive development rather than expansion in missionary work." [31] Thus the year 1911 marked the end of the expansionist movement.

Thereafter, the American Baptist Foreign Mission Society chose to concentrate on fewer units in China, and so inaugurated what we have come to know as the Intensive Policy. Accordingly, increased emphasis was placed on education. Trained nationals were to be employed with foreign support only until they were capable of self-support. Chinese leaders were to be given a larger place in administration. Illustrative of good faith in this respect was the vote by the Missionary Conference in 1911 to admit the Chinese to representation on the Board of Shanghai Baptist College. It also was intended that the Mission should co-operate closely with Chinese home mission organizations as they assumed increasing responsibility for certain areas and forms of work. Ultimately, the goal was to be the transfer of all administrative and financial responsibility to the Chinese.

A further step in administrative change in the East China Mission was the appointment in 1913 of Dr. J. T. Proctor as the first full-time mission secretary. His early experience in the Huchow evangelistic field, and his later term as president of Shanghai Baptist College provided an excellent background for his new duties. He became the executive for the Mission, and as such sat on all committees, but without the right to vote on any. Although there was some opposition to the creation of the office, he maintained it with dignity and exerted great influence as advisor to the Mission and the Chinese churches. He also helped greatly in guiding the growth of Shanghai Baptist College and Theological Seminary. In union projects his counsel was

[31] Ufford, The East China Baptist Mission: 1843–1943, p. 25.

in demand. The most notable achievements of his office came in the period after 1914.[32]

An important phase of the working out of the Intensive Policy was what came to be known as the "devolution process," whereby an easy but steady transition was to be made in the control of the Mission from foreigners to Chinese. The Mission put into operation the first steps in this process by changing its constitution in 1912 "to eliminate the exclusively foreign educational and evangelistic committees and substitute for them joint committees consisting of Chinese and missionaries" in equal number.[33] Since these were departmental committees with no final jurisdiction, this action did not involve turning over executive authority to nationals, but it was aimed toward that eventual end.

The West China Mission

The first station of the West China Mission was opened in 1889 at Suifu by William Upcraft and George Warner, forty years after the start of Baptist work in China. It was located far inland on the western edge of the Empire, in Szechuan Province. Szechuan was the largest and most populous of the provinces of China. Its 68,000,000 people lived in an area greater in size than California. The country was mountainous, although the Chengtu Plain, 90 by 40 miles, provided a level spot for raising rice which was exported to other parts of China. Szechuan produced in addition tea, tobacco, and medicines. Copper and brass ware were manufactured, and salt was produced. Because of wretched roads and poor means of communication, the farmers were always poor and very provincial, never having been far away from their villages.[34]

Although the Nestorians introduced Christianity into China as early as the seventh century after Christ, it was not until the end of the seventeenth century that Roman Catholic missionaries made their way into Szechuan Province. Protestants did not arrive until the latter half of the nineteenth century.

When Upcraft and Warner, the first American Baptist missionaries

---

[32] *Ibid.*, pp. 27-28.

[33] Hobart, A Comparative History of the East China and South China Missions, p. 561.

[34] Much of the material in this section on the West China Mission is drawn from a mimeographed manuscript of considerable value by Joseph Taylor, West of the Yangtze Gorges (Los Angeles, 1936).

to the area, came up the Yangtze River in 1889, they adopted Chinese dress to avoid being conspicuous in the face of extreme hostility. Baptist work began in a house on Water Well Street in Suifu. The first converts were baptized in the pool in the garden, and the first church was organized in that house. Reinforcements came in 1892 when Dr. and Mrs. Finch arrived from Ningpo and Miss Forbes and Miss Inveen came from the United States. Still others were needed, and so Upcraft returned home to make his plea. He arrived at a favorable time, for American Baptists were celebrating the centenary of Baptist foreign missions (1892). The Board responded with enthusiasm and assigned to West China eleven of the one hundred missionaries being sent abroad. Those who actually reached the field were Openshaw, Salquist, Bradshaw, Beaman, and Miss Bliss who later became Mrs. Beaman. New stations were opened at Yachow and Kiating in 1894.

The period, 1895 to 1900, was a difficult time, for following anti-foreign riots in 1895, several missionaries were transferred to other parts of China. But the Finches, Mrs. Wellwood, and Salquist returned to Suifu. The Beamans went to Kiating, to be joined later by Bradshaw, after Upcraft and Openshaw had returned to Yachow from a trip to Burma. The first educational enterprise of West China was opened in 1895 in the chapel at Suifu, a small school for boys and girls. By the end of the period, in spite of frequent riots, the Baptists managed to have three churches with sixty-eight members and about two hundred registered inquirers.

When the first interdenominational West China Mission Conference was held in Chunking in January, 1899, Baptists participated. Areas of work and responsibilities were mutually agreed upon. The West China Religious Tract Society was organized to facilitate more economical publication work. A third achievement of the Conference was the initiation of *The West China Missionary News,* a monthly magazine printed in English for the benefit of the missionaries at work in the three provinces of West China. This experiment in co-operation was basically successful, and continued with general conferences being held every ten years.

The Boxer uprising once again drove the missionaries out of West China. Upon their return, the Mission entered upon a time of great evangelism. During this period inquirers came by the hundreds and even thousands. Two hospitals were built, one at Suifu and the other at Yachow. A new station was opened at Ningyuan in 1905.

In the interest of standardizing the work of the schools, the workers of all denominations in West China organized the West China Educational Union in Chengtu in 1906. The need for higher institutions of learning led to union efforts such as the Union Middle School at Chengtu in 1909, the Union Normal School for Young Women, and the West China Union University, also at Chengtu. Distinctly Baptist schools for women and girls were opened also under workers sent out by the Woman's Society in 1904. These included the Girl's School at Suifu and the first kindergarten in the province.

Szechuan Province again became an area for fighting when an outbreak occurred over the railroad from Hankow to Chengtu in 1911. It became the signal for a general uprising and the *coup d'etat* in Central China which overthrew the Manchu Dynasty and ushered in the Republic on January 1, 1912, under President Sun Yat Sen. Thrilled by the prospects of expansion in the New China, American Baptists sent out new recruits to West China in 1912–13. From this time on, there was steady progress in the Mission. An increasingly large number of trained Chinese co-workers participated in the work. Moreover, the abandonment of the Central China Mission in 1913 brought several additional workers to West China. It also made possible the development of work for women and children in the hospital at Suifu, which was sponsored by the Woman's Board.[35]

The West China Mission is an excellent illustration of the effective results of co-operation between missions of various denominations at work within the same area. Without sacrificing its distinctiveness, the Baptist Mission entered into several union projects, as we have seen, with notable success. Perhaps because the field was developed later than the others, lessons had been learned about the importance of co-operative planning which were put to good use by most of the denominations in the area.

The Central China Mission

The Central China Mission was the fourth and last of the fields developed in China by American Baptists. It was established at the in-

---

[35] A basic source of information relied upon in this survey has been West China Baptist Mission Records, 1889–1944, a typescript prepared by Mrs. Salquist.

dustrial heart of the country in the Province of Hupeh. Ocean steamers were able to come six hundred miles up the Yangtze River to Hanyang, Hankow, and Wuchang, the three centers of China's new industrial civilization. In this area were iron and steel works, arsenals, gun-works, brick-kilns, and docks.

In 1893 the Reverend Joseph S. Adams removed from the East China Mission to Hanyang. There he conferred with missionaries of other denominations at work in the area, and was assigned to a territory 150 miles long and 100 miles wide, with a population of 5,000,000. It lay directly west of the East China field. The first station to be opened was Hankow in 1893. Situated at the head of ocean navigation on the Yangtze, it linked the stations on the coast with the missionaries in West China and served the provinces of Hupeh and Hunan. Adams and his wife, who had labored for many years at Kinhwa, and the Reverend W. F. Gray and his wife were stationed there. The permanent station of the Mission, however, was established later at Hanyang, a city on the north bank of the Yangtze, and more accessible to people of the interior.

In the process of over-all planning, the Board decided in 1913 to discontinue the Central China Mission because it required more reinforcements than could be provided to make it a success. The decision was a part of the application of the Intensive Policy adopted by the Board for all of its fields. There was much criticism for abandoning the Central China field. The South China missionaries in particular opposed the move as needless retrenchment. The East China staff, on the other hand, viewed it as a necessary move if the more settled stations were to be strengthened. After hearings from interested persons, the Board, on April 22-23, 1914, reaffirmed its decision to close the Mission.[36]

In this survey of American Baptist work in China, several facts are notable. First, it is obvious that the challenge of China, which had gripped the imagination of Judson himself, exerted an increasing claim upon the attention of both missionaries and the churches at

[36] Records of the Board of Managers of The American Baptist Foreign Mission Society for Sept. 10-11, 1913, pp. 459-64; for March 11, 1914, p. 175; for April 22-23, 1914, p. 204.

home. The story is therefore a thrilling one of persistence and achievement, often in the face of the gravest dangers. Second, one observes the close relationship between the fluctuating fortunes of the Chinese people and the reception accorded Baptist missionaries at work in China. The intimate association between Christianity and the Westerner is most marked in its effect upon the Chinese attitude toward the Christian message. Third, nowhere else do we find a better illustration of the two tendencies which always provide tension on every mission field—expansion through evangelism, and the intensive strengthening of the work through education. A study of the East China and South China Missions is particularly valuable at this point. Fourth, one may study the results of the application of the Intensive Policy most readily in the China Missions, from the extreme of discontinuing the Central China field to the virtual institutionalizing of the East China Mission. The latter trend was to be more prevalent in the period after 1914.

CHAPTER XVII

Maintaining the Light in Africa

THE LIGHT of the gospel has been kept burning in Africa at a dreadful cost of human life. Or to put it in another way, "The African frontier has advanced on the stepping-stones of missionary graves." [1] Certainly, this was true of the Baptist efforts in Liberia which began in 1821 and continued only under extreme personal sacrifice. And so it was also the case in Belgian Congo, where English and American Baptists undertook work following Henry Stanley's dramatic trek across Central Africa to the mouth of the Congo River at Boma in 1877.

Many have been the obstacles to the spread of the Christian message in the great continent of Africa. One is Africa's vastness, which may be comprehended by the fact that the entire United States, all of Europe, together with India and China could be set within its boundaries. A second deterrent is the more than five hundred distinct languages and over three hundred dialects. A third is the expanding influence of Mohammedanism which has come to dominate almost the entire northern portion of the continent, where Christianity once had taken root. A fourth obstacle in many parts of Africa is the climate. Where Baptists have been at work, the climate has been particularly difficult. In Liberia and in the Congo in the early years, heat, humidity, and disease combined to defeat almost every effort of white men to establish themselves. Fortunately, modern medicine

[1] A statement made by W. T. Stead, cited in Helen Barrett Montgomery, *Following the Sunrise: A Century of Baptist Missions, 1813–1913* (Philadelphia, 1913), p. 217.

and sanitation have reduced the hazard appreciably in recent times, but not until after many courageous missionaries had laid down their lives in a sacrifice without which the story that follows could not be told.

The Mission in Liberia after 1845

The story of the brave attempts to establish a lasting work in the strip of land along the western coast of Africa known as Liberia has been traced in an earlier chapter. The ever-present enemies were the almost unbearable climate and disease. The principal station of the Mission was removed in 1845 from Edina to Bexley, in the hope of finding a more healthful center of activity. By means of a combination of preaching and teaching, native workers sought to win converts from among the Bassas, the prevailing tribe, and also to minister to the needs of colonists. The missionary in charge was the Reverend Ivory Clarke, who devoted himself principally to translation work and the publication of a dictionary and spelling book in the Bassa language. But unable to withstand the recurring onslaughts of fever, he died at sea on April 24, 1848, while en route to the United States. His wife continued home to gain strength enough for a return to the work to which she was devoted. Meanwhile, the Mission was carried on by native assistants, principally Jacob Vonbrunn and L. Kong Crocker. Vonbrunn had been taken as a child from his native Bassa country to Sierra Leone and educated by the Church Missionary Society of England. Later, he had left the work of that organization to labor among his own Bassa people, as an assistant to Clarke. To his faithfulness much credit is due for the continuance of the Mission in those trying days.[2]

In 1853, reinforcements arrived in the persons of the Goodmans and Shermers who accompanied Mrs. Crocker to Liberia, following her furlough. They found the mission premises and press in good order. The boarding school had twenty pupils, and the Sunday school had forty. Vonbrunn had been preaching regularly to a church membership of sixteen at Bexley. At once the newcomers took up the work which Clarke had been forced to relinquish. But death was not ever far away, and by September of that year, Mrs. Shermer had died of African dysentery. Because of a heart ailment, Shermer himself was obliged to leave the tropical climate, but before he could secure

---

[2] The Baptist Missionary Magazine, Vol. 27, No. 5 (May, 1847), pp. 151-52.

passage, Mrs. Crocker succumbed to an attack of fever. Yet, in spite of the death of missionaries, the work among the Bassas continued, although ineffectively, under the supervision of the native pastors.

At home, however, the news of missionary losses was regarded with the greatest gravity. After careful survey of the prospects for the Mission, the Executive Committee of the Union urged the Board to discontinue the work. This was done in 1856, and the Mission was transferred to the Foreign Mission Board of the Southern Baptist Convention. Within but a few short years, however, involvement in the Civil War prevented Southern Baptists from continuing support of the Liberian Mission. Once again the Bassa leaders were left to their own resources.[3]

The year after the cessation of hostilities, the American Baptist Missionary Union considered the possibilities of re-opening the Liberian Mission, especially if any large number of freed Negroes should emigrate to the country. At the annual meeting in 1868, plans were laid for the re-establishment of the Mission. The following year four missionaries were appointed, including Vonbrunn, for labor among the Bassas. The results were so encouraging that the Executive Committee proposed in 1870 to extend their work in Africa and to open a training school for preachers. Meanwhile, the Baptist churches in Liberia had organized the Liberian Baptist Missionary Union, which was to be the counterpart of the Missionary Union in America. It is notable that English was the language used in all of the schools because of the great variety of dialects. Moreover, there was no effort to translate or print in the dialects. The hope was expressed to the Union in America in 1875 that there might be developed in Liberia "an English and Christian civilization." [4]

During this revival of interest in the Liberian Mission, the Southern Board had sent two missionaries to that field. It seems that white Baptists, both north and south, hoped that the Negro Baptists of the United States might assume responsibility for this Mission. In time, this proved to be true, for in later years the Lott Cary Baptist Foreign Mission Society and the Foreign Mission Board of the National Baptist Convention, both organized by Negroes in the United

---

[3] *Ibid.,* Vol. 36, No. 7 (July, 1856), pp. 213, 242, 298.

[4] *The Baptist Missionary Magazine,* Vol. 46, No. 2 (Feb., 1866), pp. 41-44; Vol. 48, No. 7 (July, 1868), pp. 200-01, 206; Vol. 49, No. 7 (July, 1869), pp. 211, 289-90; Vol. 50, No. 7 (July, 1870), pp. 291-96; Vol. 51, No. 7 (July, 1871), pp. 287-90.

States, carried chief responsibility for the American support of the churches in Liberia.

Faced with the realization that white men were unsuited to the climate of Liberia, the Missionary Union began to consider other parts of Africa in which it might take up work. A possibility presented itself in an offer made by Robert Arthington, a Baptist of Leeds, England, to give the Missionary Union seven thousand pounds to establish a mission in the Sudan and to place a steamer on Lake Chad. The proposal was declined as impracticable in view of the conditions which accompanied the offer.[5] Shortly thereafter a second offer came from England, this time from H. Grattan Guiness, a wealthy Christian layman who had developed in 1878–79 the Livingstone Inland Mission along the Congo River, and had found that it was expanding beyond the possibility of private control and support. This offer the Union accepted.

The New Mission in Belgian Congo

The Livingstone Inland Mission was largely the creation of H. Grattan Guiness, who had undertaken work in the Congo about the same time as the Baptist Missionary Society of England was beginning its work there. The Mission was named after the great missionary-explorer, David Livingstone. Supported by a few friends in England, the enterprise increased from year to year until there were seven stations extending up the Congo for more than seven hundred miles. Up to 1883, the Mission had sent out fifty missionaries and had launched the steamboat *Henry Reed* in the upper Congo for their use. The Ki-Kongo language, used on the Lower River, had been reduced to writing and a grammar and dictionary had been published. In the five years of its existence, about $150,000 had been invested in the Mission.

Guiness' connection with American Baptists came through two points of contact: his long-time friendship with Dr. J. N. Murdock, the corresponding secretary of the Missionary Union, and correspondence conducted by Dr. Edmund F. Merriam, also a secretary of the Union, with the Reverend George Pearse of England, who had opened a mission in Algeria which he was desirous of transferring to the Missionary Union. Because Pearse was in Algeria at the time when Merriam's letter arrived, it was forwarded to Guiness, who was

[5] *Ibid.,* Vol. 62, No. 3 (March, 1882), p. 57.

acting in an advisory capacity for Pearse's Mission. Taking advantage of American Baptist interest in Africa, Guiness wrote at once to Dr. Murdock in May, 1883, offering him the Livingstone Inland Mission on the Congo.[6]

After several months of careful investigation, the American Baptist Missionary Union accepted the offer in May, 1884 and effected the transfer in September. The seven stations which were turned over to the Union were Mukimvika, located at the mouth of the Congo on the south side; Palabala, 112 miles from the sea and 12 miles south of the river; Banza Manteke, 40 miles beyond Palabala; Mukimbungu and Lukunga, which were 69 miles beyond Banza Manteke; Leopoldville at the head of Livingstone Falls on Stanley Pool; and Equator Station, where the Congo crosses the equator. The station at Mukimbungu was turned over at once to a new Swedish Mission. The steamboat *Henry Reed* was chartered to the Congo Free State on the condition of a guarantee of free passage for missionaries and cargo. Nine of the twenty-six missionaries of the Livingstone Inland Mission staff came over to the Union and gave loyal support. They were instructed to baptize their converts and organize them into Baptist churches in accordance with the policy of the Missionary Union. Outstanding among the missionaries who remained were Henry Richards, Dr. Aaron Sims, Arthur Billington, Peter Frederickson, Charles Harvey, and Joseph Clark.[7]

At first, some Baptists in America had misgivings about the possibility of success of this new venture. The arrival in the United States of Dr. Sims, a medical missionary with the Mission, and his visits to the churches aroused confidence in the enterprise. But even more convincing was the ringing editorial published by Dr. Edward Bright in 1886 in the *Examiner,* of which he was editor. In a manner reminiscent of his famous plea to keep alive the "Lone Star Mission" of South India, Bright set forth the advantages of the Congo Mission. Opposition melted, and when the Union held its annual meeting at Asbury Park that year, it was voted to reinforce the Mission with funds and additional missionaries.

Bright's faith was vindicated by the remarkable revival that com-

---

[6] Edmund F. Merriam, *A History of American Baptist Missions* (Philadelphia, 1900), pp. 183-85.

[7] For an account of these decisions of the Executive Committee concerning reorganization of the Mission, see *The Baptist Missionary Magazine,* Vol. 66, No. 7 (July, 1886), pp. 295-97.

menced at Banza Manteke in August, 1886. After six years of discouraging efforts there to win converts, Henry Richards had begun a fresh study of the missionary emphasis of the first apostles. Convinced that their message was the good news of grace, he undertook a simple translation of Luke's Gospel for the people, twelve verses each day with a brief explanation. When he came to the thirtieth verse of the sixth chapter, he hesitated because he knew how readily the people would take advantage of him, requiring him literally to give them all that he possessed. And that is what happened—but only for the night. By the next morning, many who had come under conviction of sin returned the things which they had taken from the missionary, and began to believe that he was God's man. The first convert was Lutate, a man whom Richards had to shelter in his own house from enemies who sought to poison him because of his Christian stand. When the chief's son was converted, others began to come. With these first disciples as evidence of the transforming grace of God, Richards went throughout the territory telling of the love of Christ. Within a few weeks, more than a thousand persons placed their idols at the feet of the missionary, professing faith in Jesus Christ as their Savior.

When the news reached America, it electrified the churches. Clarendon St. Church in Boston, of which Dr. A. J. Gordon was then pastor, sent to Banza Manteke a chapel in sections, all ready to be assembled. African Christians transported it sixty miles up the river, carrying the parts on their heads. The task required seven hundred loads. Some were obliged to make the week-long journey five times. Their willingness to be of service now that they were Christians was a marked feature of the Congolese converts. Despite the obstacles of distance and poor communications, this wave of conversions spread to other stations up and down the Congo. It was rightly called the "Pentecost on the Congo." [8]

In many ways the Congo was a different type of mission field from the others begun by American Baptists. There were no highly developed religions in this area. Like the hill tribes of Burma and Assam, the people were animists, attributing to the natural world identification with evil spirits who made their lives one prolonged terror. The majority of people in the Congo basin were known as Bantus, a language term rather than a designation of race. They were broken

[8] Montgomery, *Following the Sunrise,* pp. 226-29.

up into many tribes and clans. Their 160 dialects fell into four distinct language groups—the Ki-Kongo, spoken on the Lower River in Northern Angola, Cabinda, and French Equatorial Africa; the Lingala, spoken in the Middle River and Upper River areas; the Swahili, used in and beyond Stanleyville; and Tshiluba, used in the south. The language problem made it necessary for missionaries to be fluent with more than one dialect at a station, as well as capable of speaking the government medium of communication, which was French. The task was not made easier by the fact that African languages were highly inflected and complicated in grammar.

The Bantus, prior to the days of the European penetration of the Congo, practiced cannibalism, polygamy, witchcraft, and engaged in tribal warfare. Their life was dominated by fear. The witch-doctor, the priest of fetishism, exerted unparalleled power over their social relations and personal well-being. The coming of the Christian missionary to the Congo brought medical missions which did much to discredit the witch-doctor, "the true ruler of all central Africa." Henry Richards saw clearly the power of the witch-doctor and pointed out that the animistic Congolese called themselves "the children of the devil" in contrast to the Christians who were known as "the children of God." [9]

The tribal life of the Congolese people has presented a serious concern to missionaries who have sought to bring the gospel to them without violating the wholesome values in their African culture. Missionaries found that in the Congo, land belonged to the community, to the tribe, not to the individual. The person's use of the soil, therefore, was by virtue of his belonging to the social group. In a very real sense the tribal chief was the father of the villagers. At this point in particular, missionaries had the problem of developing a new kind of community, based upon mutual love in Christ, to replace the tribal loyalties where they conflicted with Christian standards. In this task there were serious problems, some of which arose because the missionaries did not understand sufficiently the cultural patterns which were deeply ingrained in the African mind.

For example, missionaries discovered that the structure of family life in the Congo had been based traditionally upon the matriarchal line, rather than upon the patriarchal as in the West and in certain areas of Asia. The wife's brother, not her husband was responsible

[9] *Developing Africa's Riches in Christ* (New York, 1935), pp. 4-5.

for the upbringing of the children of a marriage. This sometimes gave rise to a conflict in standards if the brother was not a Christian and the parents of the children were. Moreover, marriage practices for the African differed from those acceptable to the Christian. The "bride-price," which was exacted of the groom and arrived at by a "palaver" or period of bargaining, sometimes was not paid in full to his wife's parents for years. In the meantime, cohabitation was permissible and children were born before the marriage arrangements were concluded. According to Congolese custom, a wife who was nursing her child (which she might do for as long as two years) did not engage in marital relations with her husband. He, however, might take a temporary wife, or another permanent one. This practice of polygamy was frowned upon by both the government and the Christian churches. Yet, because a woman had no standing in society except as she was married, the monogamous standard of Christianity placed some Christian girls in a difficult position.

Against such a background, it is easy to see why the discipline exercised by Christian churches resulted in the excommunication of members for reverting to polygamy, witchcraft, and in the disciplining of those who engaged in heathen practices, drunkenness, or unlawful dances (good dances, which were so much a part of African life, were not usually forbidden to Christians). To make certain that new converts understood the transition which they were called upon to make, many inquirers were kept in training for five years before being admitted to baptism. But even then, there were great losses from the Christian ranks.[10]

The penetration of the Congo by Europeans also produced serious problems. The establishment of the Congo Free State by the Berlin Conference of 1885 did not actually benefit the Africans. Under the presidency of King Leopold II of Belgium, the new government allowed a wanton exploitation of the people. The traffic in slave labor and the demoralizing influence of the liquor business gave the Congo Mission great concern. Year by year letters and reports sent home to the Board protested against the infringement of the Africans' rights and the abuse of the people generally. Missionaries wit-

---

[10] In addition to the many fine volumes which discuss the anthropology of African culture, the reader may profit from a Christian discussion of these problems in G. J. M. Pearce, *Congo Background* (London, 1954), chaps. 2 and 3.

nessed with alarm the policy of terrorism and murder systematically resorted to for the purpose of forcing the natives to work for the rubber companies which had been given concessions in the territory. These conditions had a dampening effect upon mission work. By 1896 the revival that had begun ten years before at Banza Manteke had come to an end. The missionaries and Board members alike attributed the fact to the state of affairs in the Congo. Conversions did not cease entirely, but the unusually large ingathering was curtailed by the unfavorable influence of a selfish government which offset the good which the Mission was accomplishing.[11]

Meanwhile the basic and constructive work in the stations continued. By 1900 there were 1,500 church members at Banza Manteke. Within a radius of 30 miles, 56 native preachers and teachers were at work through 25 out-stations. The 953 baptisms for that single year were almost 50 per cent of the previous total church membership of the Mission, which was 1,925. In one year a dispensary at Banza Manteke cared for the physical ills of 16,000 persons. At the Lukunga Station, a successful effort was being made to place the work on a self-supporting basis. There was little success, however, in gaining support for the school because the people had not yet come to value education sufficiently to pay for it.[12]

In the early years of the twentieth century, protests against conditions in the Congo mounted, first in England, then in the United States, Germany, and other countries. The American Baptist Missionary Union co-operated with the Congo Reform Association, which was seeking to awaken Americans to protest the sufferings of the people of the Congo under the Belgian king. In 1907 the Union called upon the United States Government to intervene.[13] These efforts were not in vain, for on October 18, 1908, the Belgian Parliament annexed the Congo State and began the removal of abuses that had accumulated under Leopold's personal rule.

After twenty-five years of work on the Congo, the stations on the Banza Manteke field achieved a degree of maturity and permanence

---

[11] *The Baptist Missionary Magazine,* Vol. 76, No. 7 (July, 1896), p. 377. This is typical of reports to be found regularly in this periodical during these years.

[12] *Ibid.,* Vol. 80, No. 7 (July, 1900), pp. 246, 263; Vol. 76, No. 7 (July, 1896), pp. 379-82.

[13] *American Baptist Missionary Union Report* for 1907, pp. 48-51, 228-29.

which was signalized by the organization of the Lower Congo Training School. It had grown out of Richard's Monday morning class for preachers. In 1908 it was merged into the Congo Evangelical Training Institution at Kimpese, a union school jointly supported by the Baptist Missionary Society of England and the Missionary Union. It opened in 1909, with the Reverend S. E. Moon as the American Baptist representative on the faculty. The principal was Lewis of the English Society. There were thirty-three students in attendance, nineteen men and fourteen women.[14] In 1911, Dr. Catherine L. Mabie, who had been serving valiantly since 1898 as a traveling medical missionary without a hospital and with very little equipment, came to Kimpese to conduct medical work and to offer courses at the school in physiology, sanitation, and hygiene.

In the meantime, the Baptist Mission had been extended up the Congo to include Leopoldville, which was opened in 1883, but was left for many years without a resident missionary. In 1897 Leopoldville was abandoned and Bolengi, a post near the equator, was transferred to the Foreign Christian Missionary Society of America. The Congo Balolo Mission, in charge of H. Grattan Guiness, was at work in the interior and took over some of the American Baptist responsibilities as they sought to restrict their activities to the Upper Congo.

By 1900 the Mission began to extend in another direction, into the Kwango region somewhat to the east of Leopoldville. It is an area drained by a network of great rivers that are tributary to the Congo. About 1900 Dr. W. H. Leslie, a medical missionary at Banza Manteke, decided to penetrate into the area. For several years, he and his wife lived alone in that wilderness, as he sought to establish what is known as the Vanga station almost directly east of Leopoldville. With but two axes, a saw, a hammer, a box of nails, two bales of cloth, and ten sacks of salt to start with, he eventually cleared a plateau above the river. From this beginning, he built a village, with houses for the missionaries, a church, a school, and a dispensary. Vanga became a very influential center for the spread of Christianity. As the result of the visit of a Commission sent to the Congo by the Missionary Union in 1910, plans were made in 1911 to enlarge the

---

[14] *The Baptist Missionary Magazine,* Vol. 89, No. 9 (Sept., 1909), pp. 313, 332.

work in the Kwango District and in neighboring areas. Reinforcements were also to be sent to the older stations.[15]

By 1913 the Congo Mission maintained seven boarding schools —at Banza Manteke, Lukunga, Sona Bata, Ikoko, Tshumbiri, Palabala, and Kimpese. Enrollment in each ranged from nine to forty-four pupils. The equipment in most cases was meager. American Baptists were slow to realize the need for well-equipped schools of this type in which to train future leaders. The English Baptists, on the other hand, had a better developed system of station schools because they gave more attention to education. Their influence was felt at Kimpese, where the Congo Evangelical Training Institution had by 1913 seven double brick-houses for dormitories, built by the students under the direction of the English missionaries. The central building, known as Bentley Memorial, contained lecture rooms. Industrial and agricultural instruction was provided in addition to eight grades of general education. Dr. Mabie was preparing for the school a set of primary text-books, and was beginning a course with the women on home-making and church membership. Throughout the entire Congo Mission, there were 247 village schools, with 7,602 pupils.

In a land where the witch-doctor was priest and medicine man, the missionary found it necessary to be both preacher and doctor. Every missionary, therefore, shared so far as he was able in giving medical aid. In 1912 at Sona Bata, for example, Mrs. Frederickson, with only crude huts for dispensary buildings, treated nearly 6,000 cases, cared for 46 in-patients, and collected 1,344 francs in medical fees. In the same year, at Banza Manteke, Mrs. Bain, during Dr. Mabie's furlough, assumed charge of the medical work, pending the arrival of Dr. Parsons. She reported 1,017 treatments, 18 in-patients, and 100 calls in the villages. At Tshumbiri, Mrs. Billington did splendid medical work. At Ikoko, Rodgers kept up an active dispensary service. The regular medical staff of the Mission included Dr. Sims, for 30 years at Matadi, Dr. F. P. Lynch at Mukimvika, Dr. Nauss at Sona Bata, Dr. H. Ostrom at Ikoko, Dr. W. H. Leslie at Vanga, and Dr. C. L. Mabie at Kimpese. In the early years, all of these doctors were obliged to work without hospitals.[16]

---

[15] Vedder, *A Short History of Baptist Missions,* p. 273; *Missions,* Vol. 2, No. 2 (Feb., 1911), pp. 112-13.

[16] Montgomery, *Following the Sunrise,* pp. 235-42.

In keeping with the general policy followed on older mission fields, the Board approved efforts being made by the Congo Missionary Conference to develop self-support in all of the stations. Beginning in 1912, the missionaries reduced appropriations for evangelistic and district school work ten per cent until the maximum funds provided should not exceed $200 a year. The Board of Managers of the Society also approved a Station Council Plan recommended by the Missionary Conference. It called for a council meeting of the missionaries at each station, upon their return from the annual Conference. At this time the work of the station should be divided so as to care adequately for evangelistic, educational, medical, and general needs. The station councils were also to meet weekly for prayer and consultation relating to the work of the area. This was a step in the direction of a more efficient management of mission affairs.[17]

Another trend developing in the opening years of the twentieth century was interdenominational co-operation. In 1903 a General Conference of Missionaries of the Protestant Societies Working in Congo Land was organized. Represented in the new effort were American Baptists, English Baptists, the Swedish Missionary Society, the Congo Balolo Mission, the American Presbyterian Congo Mission, and the Foreign Christian Missionary Society. At their meetings, they discussed such problems as school work, payment of native teachers, polygamy, intemperance, and mutual co-operation. Always they were conscious of the growing influence of Roman Catholic power exerted through a sympathetic Belgian government and through aggressive Roman Catholic institutions on the field. This General Conference of Protestant Missionaries was the beginning of a significant movement in Protestant co-operation in the Congo.

As early as 1914, annual reports from the field indicated that changes were occurring in the life of the Congo and its people, as the railroads began to pierce the jungles, dividing Africa east and west, and north and south. A general restlessness was beginning to pervade the villages. Frederickson at Sona Bata complained that many of the young Christians were giving up their teaching posts in the mission schools to take more lucrative work with the railway company. English Baptists also felt the pressure of the influence which the railway companies were exerting in drawing the young men away from the

[17] Records of Board of Managers of the American Baptist Foreign Mission Society for Sept. 11-12, 1912, pp. 79-80.

humdrum life of the villages.[18] It was a trend which was to develop into serious proportions after the First World War. Secularism was just beginning to invade the life of Africa, vying with Christianity for the loyalty of her most ambitious young people.

---

[18] *American Baptist Missionary Union Report* for 1914, p. 145.

CHAPTER XVIII

Witness in Japan

THE LAND of the rising sun, as Japan has been called, consisted in the nineteenth century of five principal islands, extending twenty-five hundred miles, a distance approximately equal to that from Maine to Florida. The total area was about the size of New England and the Middle Atlantic States combined. It was not rich in natural resources, yet had a huge population. Consequently, there was always a struggle for existence. About three-fifths of the soil was worked by peasant-proprietors, a people of perseverance, courage, good humor, politeness, and self-confidence. In temperament the Japanese were passionate and esthetic. They possessed the virtues of a feudalistic society—courage, loyalty to a chief, and personal honor. The two pillars of their ethics and life were loyalty and filial piety.

The geographic location of Japan played an important role in the life of its people. A temperate climate, plentiful rainfall, fairly fertile soil, and reasonable proximity to other civilized nations combined to bring the Japanese into the main stream of history. Their insular position contributed to making them the greatest seafaring people of Asia. Yet, until the middle of the nineteenth century, Japan, for the most part, remained culturally and politically aloof from other nations. Isolation made the Japanese a highly self-conscious people, "unaccustomed to dealing with foreigners individually or as a nation." [1]

The principal religious influences in Japanese life were Shintoism and Buddhism. The latter religion, which was introduced into Japan about A.D. 552, served as a medium for the influence of Chinese

[1] Edwin O. Reischauer, *Japan, Past and Present* (New York, 1947), p. 8.

culture upon the nation. Consisting chiefly in reverence shown to imperial ancestors, it aroused patriotic feeling. Japanese students who had served on embassies to China sought to introduce change in their country along the Chinese pattern. To this end, they formed a clique at the Yamato court in the year 645, and seized power through a carefully engineered coup. For a time they were successful; then in the ninth century, reaction set in and Japan ceased to send embassies to China or to encourage the spread of Chinese influence.

During the next three or four centuries there developed in Japan a feudalism which weakened the central government in favor of the provincial governors whose political and economic power grew. By the thirteenth centry, Japan's emperor was reduced to a mere puppet in the hands of a private government of feudal lords. Accompanying this era of political transformation was a religious awakening in which a reform sect of Buddhism arose that held special attraction for the feudal lords because it stressed the disciplined life.

When European merchants entered Far Eastern waters in the early part of the sixteenth century, they found that the Japanese were in the ascendancy on the seas. The influence of the rising commercial class was accompanied, however, by the emergence of a powerful figure, Oda Nobunaga. In 1568 he crushed the military power of the landed aristocracy and took over the commercial city of Osaka. By this time, Buddhism had replaced Shintoism as the dominant religion in the country. It was not, however, without a rival in Confucianism, which was slowly becoming the strongest intellectual and ethical force in the country.

Christianity enjoyed a temporary introduction into Japan during a visit of Francis Xavier in the mid-sixteenth century. But it failed to survive the persecution which arose in 1638 when the Japanese rulers sought to wipe it out because they feared the political power of the Pope at Rome.

A period of unprecedented peace in Japanese national life followed under the Tokugawa dynasty. Although the leaders clung to a rural economy and the supremacy of the landed aristocracy, an expanding merchant class was developing in the country. By 1868 the Tokugawa rule came to an end, when the new imperial government, centered in the person of the emperor, replaced feudal influence. The young *samurai* or military class embarked on a course of rapid modernization of the country. Once the doors of Japan were opened to

Western culture, Christianity was regarded more kindly as a diplomatic concession to the West, whose favor the Japanese rulers wished to win. Yet behind the new façade of Western culture, the political and social institutions of the country remained substantially the same.

It was against such a background, so briefly sketched on these pages, that Japan's Christians were recruited in the nineteenth century. Most of them were from the influential circles of society. Many were *samurai,* the backbone of the feudal system on which the Tokugawa rulers had based authority in earlier days. Of the three forms of Christianity which engaged the attention of the Japanese, the Roman Catholic, the Russian Orthodox, and the Protestant, the last was the most important numerically and in influence. Protestant missionaries began to enter Japan after a treaty arrangement had been consummated in 1858 between the United States and Japan which won freedom for foreigners to propagate their religion. This agreement climaxed several years of American effort, led by Commodore M. C. Perry of the United States Navy, to open Japan to Western trade. In 1859 the Protestant Episcopal Church, the Presbyterian Church of the U.S.A., and the Dutch Reformed Church sent representatives. Additional societies entered the country from 1869 on, including the American Board of Commissioners for Foreign Missions, the American Baptist Missionary Union, and the Methodist Episcopal Board.

Christian missions enjoyed remarkable growth in the 1880's as things Western became more popular, and as revivals occurred around 1883. Between 1882 and 1888 the number of churches inceased for all groups from 93 to 249, the number of communicants from 4,987 to 25,514, the number of missionaries from 145 to 451, the number of ordained Japanese ministers from 49 to 142, and the number of seminaries from 7 with 71 pupils to 14 with 287 pupils. The United Church of Christ in Japan, which had been organized in 1877, contained in 1888 more than one-fourth of the Protestant Christians. In the 1890's Japanese Christians became restive under missionary control, and pressed for increasing self-government.

Between 1900 and 1914 there was another period of decided growth. By 1913, Protestants numbered 90,000. The major successes had been with the intellectuals. Mission work was conducted primarily in the cities. Much use was made of the printed page in disseminating the gospel, since the Japanese people were predominately literate. Institutions, particularly schools, were developed by mission agencies. There was a strong disposition to united effort and the minimizing of denominational lines by the Japanese Christians themselves. In spite of the growth, however, the Christians of all communions, Roman Catholics, Protestants, and Russian Orthodox, remained a small minority in 1914, with only 200,000 members, or less than one-half of one percent of the population. Of this number, Protestants constituted more than one-half and were increasing more rapidly than either Roman Catholics or Russian Orthodox. Christianity's gains in Japan were slower than in China in the same period because by 1914 the cultural structure of the nation had not crumbled as it had in China. Yet, in proportion to its numerical strength, the influence of Christianity was very significant in Japanese life, making itself felt in education, in humanitarian movements, in encouraging the development of parliamentary government, and in its impact upon Buddhism.[2]

Baptist Beginnings in Japan

The first Baptist missionary to conduct work in Japan was a sailor aboard one of Commodore Perry's ships in Tokyo Bay. He became interested in missionary opportunities when he was allowed to go ashore in 1853. His name was Jonathan Goble. In returning to America, he brought with him to Hamilton, New York, a Japanese sailor. There the lad was baptized in Goble's home church—in all probability the first convert of modern Protestant missions to the Japanese. In 1860 Goble and his wife returned to Japan under the American Baptist Free Mission Society, an abolitionist group. For ten years he served as a free lance missionary, earning his living making shoes and doing carpentry work. When his wife became ill and unable to walk, he contrived a small two-wheeled vehicle—a cross between an English gig and an American baby carriage—which in time became the pattern for the famed Japanese jinrikisha, which is generally called in Japan a *kuruma*. As a missionary he preached and taught in Yokohama, translating the Gospel of Matthew into

---

[2] Kenneth Scott Latourette, *The Great Century in Northern Africa and Asia, A.D. 1800–A.D. 1914,* Vol. VI of *A History of the Expansion of Christianity* (New York, 1944), chap. 6.

colloquial Japanese. In 1870, the Gobles again returned to America. On the voyage home, they came into contact with an embassy of Japanese leaders, led by Prince Iwakura, who were coming to the United States to seek a revision of treaties between the two countries. Goble impressed the diplomats to the point that they invited him to explain Christianity to them.

Upon his arrival home, Goble presented a favorable report to his own Mission, but it was unable to give him further support. Instead, the officials requested the American Baptist Missionary Union to include Japan in their field of operations. This proposal was received favorably, and Dr. Nathan Brown, veteran missionary to Burma and Assam and an able linguist, was persuaded to become the first missionary to Japan. With him were associated the Gobles as free lances. They were not long back in Japan before they felt the need for more independence and resigned from the Union. They continued to carry on missionary service in their accustomed way of distributing literature, without making any effort to build a church.[3]

With the arrival of Dr. Nathan Brown in Yokohama on February 7, 1873, began the real history of the Baptist Mission in Japan. There was no church, for the Free Baptists, under Goble's leadership, had organized none. Brown found, however, that other leading denominations already had laid the foundation of their work and were in favorable positions. Therefore, the contribution of the Baptists to the Christian work of the city was overshadowed by that of the Presbyterians, the Congregationalists, the Episcopalians, and the Methodists.

Nathan Brown's success in Japan was all the more remarkable because of his age. When he took up his work in Yokohama, he was sixty-six years old and feeble in health. His unusual linguistic abilities and his generous Christian spirit were to enshrine him in the affectionate memory of Japanese Christians. At once, he undertook a study of the language, and began to preach and to gather converts into a church. Then he resolved to translate the New Testament into the vernacular, in the event that he should be spared ten more years of life. With great difficulty, he completed the task while continuing his ministry to the church. His New Testament did not gain a wide

---

[3] William Wynd, *Seventy Years in Japan: A Saga of Northern Baptists* (no date), pp. 2-3. This is a useful account of work conducted by the American Baptist Missionary Union.

circulation, although it was an excellent translation from the Greek text. The plain people for whom he had produced his work had not reached the stage to appreciate its message. Those who were primarily interested in the New Testament were intellectuals who desired a version which would challenge their literary tastes.

Fortunately, a committee of various denominational representatives were at work on such a translation. When it was published, it became the accepted version. The Baptist representative was Dr. C. K. Harrington, one of the teachers in the Baptist Seminary at Yokohama, who was not only learned in Greek and Hebrew but also in Brown's translation. Thus the influence of Brown's work was preserved in the Revised Version of the Bible Societies, which was finished in 1919 and is now in general use in Japan.[4]

One of the early converts of Brown, Tetsuya Kawakatsu, who was baptized on May 14, 1877, became a fine leader and served for eleven years as an associate of the great missionary. When Brown died in 1886, Kawakatsu carried the work on in Yokohama. This Japanese was one of a long series of Christians in the Baptist Mission in Japan upon whom has rested responsibility for the effective continuance of the Christian witness. Brown also had been assisted by two women sent out by the Missionary Union and the Woman's Societies. They were Miss Clara A. Sands and Miss Anna H. Kidder, both of whom arrived in Yokohama in 1875. They became pioneers in Baptist women's work. Miss Sands took advantage of the eagerness of Japanese mothers for the training of their children by opening Sunday schools and day schools in different parts of the city and its suburbs. Churches later developed out of the work of these schools.

In 1879 Dr. and Mrs. Albert A. Bennett arrived to relieve Brown of some of the burdens which he had been carrying in spite of failing health. Bennett took on the evangelistic work in the city, and for a time was pastor of the church. As he observed the feeble efforts of the deacons to preach and assume leadership, he realized their need for instruction. Accordingly, he invited four of these lay preachers to his home once a week for guidance in sermon preparation. They soon expressed a desire to come twice a week, and eventually, to come daily. By October, 1884, Bennett had organized a formal seminary, with five students, and more the following term. In addition, he pub-

[4] *Ibid.*, pp. 8-9.

lished a small monthly paper for the jinrikisha men called the *Jinrikisha.* He also visited the prisons, and was a welcome speaker to the sailors of the Japanese Fleet. When Brown died in 1886, Bennett was obliged to finish the revision of the New Testament and see it through the press. Then he closed up the printing office, so as to have more time for his teaching and the frequent evangelistic tours which he conducted into the country regions. Bennett's only furlough in his thirty years of service in Japan was from 1902–04. On October 12, 1909, he died and was buried in his beloved Yokohama. His ministry came to an end just twenty-five years after the founding of the Baptist Theological Seminary. The imprint of his life was felt on the city, on the students whom he taught, and on the churches which he served.[5]

Baptist work was extended to Tokyo as early as 1874, only a year after the Mission had been opened in Yokohama. The Reverend James Hope Arthur and his wife opened a station there with great promise, but within three brief years, Arthur died of tuberculosis. He left, however, a girls' school, through which an evangelistic influence was exerted. It is significant that Arthur was obliged to obtain a Japanese patron, whose employee he became for all public purposes, in order to avoid the displeasure of those who objected to a "Christian" school. Eventually it became possible to teach Bible to voluntary classes outside of regular school hours. It was to this school that Miss Kidder came in 1875. She remained with it until her death in 1913, working closely with Miss Sotome, a Japanese Christian.

On June 14, 1876, two years after the girls' school, the first Tokyo Baptist church was organized. The relationship between the two was very close, the church holding its earliest meetings in a room of the school building. The first woman to be baptized was Mrs. Hama Uchida, who remained active in Christian work for more than fifty years. By 1877 the membership had increased to eighteen, making this church larger than its parent congregation in Yokohama. After the death of Arthur the work was maintained by Miss Sotome and two evangelists, Seishin Toriyama and Shigei Suzuki.

In 1883 the Reverend and Mrs. C. H. D. Fisher and Miss Marie Antoinette Whitman arrived to take over direction of the work at

[5] For an interesting account of his life, see *A Sketch of the Life and Character of Albert Arnold Bennett* (Providence, Rhode Island, 1913).

Tokyo. They suffered a severe testing because of government opposition. With unusual patience, Fisher turned from one place of service to another as opposition broke out. Eventually outstations were developed in nearby areas. During the years that followed, the girls' school was strengthened by the addition of new teachers. A Sunday school and kindergarten work were also developed.[6]

Meanwhile other stations were being established to the northeast and southwest of Tokyo and Yokohama. From Tohoku, 250 miles north of Tokyo, came a call for workers from the Baptist Mission. The contact had come through the influence of Nathan Brown's books in that section. In response to the request, the Missionary Union appointed T. P. Poate, a professor of English in Tokyo and a British subject. He served until 1892 when an accident to one of his eyes compelled his retirement to America. In the interim, he traveled 900 miles on foot through the Tohoku district and another 900 by jinrikisha and coastal boats, preaching and organizing churches. Although he met opposition from the government in Morioka, where he had a school, he persisted in his work. He was reinforced in 1889 by the coming of the Reverend and Mrs. R. L. Halsey to Sendai, the principal town of the district. There they established a school. The progress of the gospel in the entire area was slow because of a general hostility which lasted into the early years of the twentieth century. Later missionaries in this northland included E. H. Jones, S. W. Hamblen, Henry Topping, C. Howard Ross, and George E. Haynes and their wives. The main centers of work were Sendai and Morioka.

Nearly three hundred miles southwest of Tokyo lay another district in which Baptists undertook to establish several new centers of activity. In 1882, Dr. and Mrs. H. H. Rhees opened a station in Kobe. Because of a narrowly sectarian background and a training in law, Rhees was quite legalistic about matters and did not engage in the interdenominational activity which was a pleasing feature of the work in Japan. Mrs. Rhees was his opposite, full of love and kindness, modifying happily her husband's sternness. They adopted a Japanese boy and a girl and began a day school in a corner of their garden. In their home was housed the church which they organized that year. Taheita Yoshikawa, of a *samurai* family of Himeji which had broken with tradition and had become Christian, became the

[6] Wynd, *op. cit.*, pp. 19-29.

teacher in the school. In 1884, G. H. Appleton and his wife joined the mission, and for four years worked chiefly at Shimonoseki, an outstation of Kobe. When they returned to America in 1888, Robert A. Thomson and his wife were on the field. He was a Scotsman, whose brother was in charge of the Scottish Bible Society in Yokohama. They worked with the Rheeses until the death of Dr. Rhees in 1899, when they took charge of the field. Mrs. Thomson was particularly interested in kindergarten work, which was an important means of entering into the home life of the people. It was a popular type of ministry among the Japanese, although a source of some irritation to the Board at home because of the expense involved. The Board was of the opinion that the churches were strong enough to support their own kindergartens.[7]

In the meantime, another station was developed at Himeji, a small city forty miles southwest of Kobe. From 1875 to 1885 several missions had tried in vain to gain an entrance to Himeji. Then a change of attitude on the part of the people took place, and G. H. Appleton of the Baptist Mission was granted a permit to live there. It was a first step. Rhees and Thomson in Kobe made occasional visits, and in the end received help from the Woman's Board in the person of Miss Ella R. Church, who was transferred to Himeji from the Yokohama School for Girls. She established a school in 1892 and served as its first principal. In the beginning she met the same opposition, but by 1893 she had gained permission from the central government in Tokyo, in spite of the hostile *samurai* influence at Himeji. Because the school maintained high standards, it attracted favorable attention and won a place in the community.

A fourth major area for Baptist work was far to the north, on the island of Hokkaido. In 1886, Dr. C. H. Carpenter and his wife, after 15 years in the tropical regions of lower Burma, came to Japan to improve their health and carry on missionary work. They rented a house at Nemuro, a town of 12,000 people on the east coast of the island. Although Carpenter lived only four and a half months after their arrival, Mrs. Carpenter carried on the work there with the aid of her husband's elder brother, Lucius D. Carpenter, who had come to Japan with his wife and a niece, Miss Lenore Ayres, to help her. Soon the Lucius Carpenters had to return to America, but Miss Ayres remained for a time. In 1889–90 new missionaries arrived to

[7] Wynd, *Seventy Years in Japan,* pp. 71-72.

assist Mrs. C. H. Carpenter. They were Miss Louisa Cummings and the Reverend W. B. Parshley. Mrs. Carpenter retired from the Mission in 1906.

Because Nemuro was not a progressive town that could hold its young people, another station was opened on the island at Otaru. T. E. Shumaker and his wife took charge of this work in 1902. They were succeeded by F. W. Steadman and his wife in 1907. In 1911 Mr. and Mrs. Takahashi returned from study abroad at Newton Theological Institution in Massachusetts to be their associates.

In 1886 the outstation at Shimonoseki, in Southern Japan, was made a full-fledged mission station. Later this work was removed to Chofu, a suburb, where Miss Harriet M. Browne established the first home for orphans under Baptist auspices in Japan. Two years later Mr. and Mrs. Thomson of Kobe commenced a ministry at Osaka, the second largest city in the country and a center of industry. Mr. Chuhachi, a young Japanese from Sendai, assisted them. He lived in the city in a rented room near the Umeda Station, where he preached regularly. The Thomsons went up from Kobe three times a week to teach young men in the little chapel. This they continued to do until Dr. Rhees went on furlough, leaving them in complete charge at Kobe. A full-time missionary was secured when the Reverend J. W. McCollum and his wife, who were Southern Baptists, volunteered to relieve the Thomsons during the absence of the Rheeses. Accordingly, the McCollums built a home and in 1891 organized a church in Osaka. Six months later, Dr. Rhees' return to Kobe prompted the raising of the question concerning the wisdom of Northern and Southern Baptists working in the same field. As a result, a mutual agreement placed the McCollums on the island of Kyushu, and the new station at Osaka lost an able leader.

Fortunately, the Reverend William Wynd, one of several new appointees to Japan in 1891, was assigned to Osaka, which became from that date a regular station of the Northern Baptist Mission. In 1892 the Reverend J. H. Scott and his wife arrived in Japan and became Wynd's associates. They remained in Osaka for twenty years.

In their strategy these early missionaries in Osaka made two mistakes. They either failed to study the traditional religions of the country so as to be able to find points of contact with the people, or they regarded rival faiths as "worn-out garments" to be discarded. To the Japanese mind, this approach was inadequate. Buddhist priests, on the other hand, studied Christianity diligently, visited Christian churches, and invited Christian teachers into their temples to explain the Bible. As a result Buddhism was modified so that Buddha became to his followers more like the Heavenly Father revealed by Jesus Christ. In the second place, the missionaries overestimated the importance of preaching and underestimated the power of contact with the people in their everyday life. To be sure, the Sunday schools and English schools which missionaries conducted brought them into some contact with the daily life of the people, but it was only a step in the right direction.

Seeing this need, the Woman's Board in 1908 enlarged the scope of its educational work in Osaka. A Bible school was erected in the western part of the city and placed in charge of Miss Lavinia Mead, who had been in Japan for eighteen years and understood the people. The school quickly attracted a select band of women, who were trained to present the gospel message to people who worked in the factories and who, all too frequently, lived in the slums of the city. In 1909 the American Baptist Missionary Union strengthened the work by erecting a church building through joint efforts with the Christians of the West Church in the city. In the years that followed, a number of additional missionaries came and went, indicating that Osaka had gained a place of importance in the planning of the Union.[8]

We have traced briefly the establishing of key stations in scattered sections of Japan from 1873 to 1890. Something of their progress has been noted. In some cases success was hampered by an inadequate understanding of the mind of the Japanese; in other cases progress was made possible by a wise blending of educational work with evangelism. In every instance there was courage and sacrifice on the part of missionaries and national leaders alike in the face of government hostility. The situation, however, improved perceptibly after 1890 when the first signs of democratic procedures began to be introduced into Japanese life. For in that year the first elections were held in the country. In 1891 the newly organized Diet, or legislative body, began to function.

Although education was encouraged by the government as a means of developing a competent citizenry, the schools became increas-

---

[8] *Ibid.*, pp. 80-101.

ingly a medium for teaching people what to think rather than how to think. As the government expanded its influence in other areas of life, including the economic, a strong nationalism developed. The nation, with its problem of over-population, began to cast eager eyes toward China and Korea as areas for imperialistic expansion. It will be recalled that Japan won Formosa as the result of her war with China over Korea. By the close of the century, all of the Western Powers had come to recognize the growing influence of Japan. Indeed, that nation was the first in Asia to free itself of extraterritoriality, a practice of granting special privileges to foreigners living in their own settlements within certain Far Eastern cities. By 1911 Japan had resumed complete control of her own tariffs, and had quietly annexed Korea. Thus, on the eve of the First World War, she was ready to take full advantage of the opportunity which the occasion presented for pressing for recognition as a world power.

In these developments, it is significant to see the role which Christian schools played in spreading democratic ideas in Japan. Moreover, business men, eager to gain representation in government, encouraged an attitude of friendly appreciation of Christianity, which they viewed as helpful to their cause because it was associated intimately with Western democracy and economic progress.[9]

The effect of these new developments upon missionary work was most favorable. For example, when extraterritoriality came to an end in 1899, aliens were permitted to travel and reside in the interior of the country. Missionaries, accordingly, shared in the privilege of freer movement, and some mission societies adopted new methods of spreading the gospel to hitherto unreached peoples. Among them was the introduction of a new type of mission by the American Baptist Missionary Union in 1898—a gospel ship ministry to the peoples of the Inland Sea who lived on numerous islands in Southern Japan. The opportunity to reach this neglected area presented itself when Robert Allan, a shipowner of Glasgow, Scotland, made an offer of a ship for evangelistic use. The missionary-mariner chosen for the unusual task was Captain Luke W. Bickel, a stalwart man of action, thirty-two years of age, six feet tall, a lover of the sea, and a brilliant conversationalist who found contacts with people easy to make. He was the son of a German Baptist emigree to America, Philipp Bickel,

---

[9] Reischauer, *Japan, Past and Present,* pp. 128-47.

who had established the first German Baptist church in Cincinnati and later had become a colporteur of the American Baptist Publication Society to manage the German Baptist publication work in Hamburg, Germany.

When Luke Bickel accepted the appointment of the American Baptist Missionary Union, he was serving the London Baptist Publication Society. After a brief course at Spurgeon's College, he made his way to Japan. During the first year, Bickel visited 62 islands in the chain that stretched for 500 miles from Shimonoseki in the west to Osaka in the east. He held meetings in some 350 towns and villages, reaching approximately 40,000 people. Being a practical and orderly man, he devised a plan of strategy which proved highly successful. He divided the chain of islands into three groups, establishing an evangelist on a central island in each. Bickel took his ship wherever the people gave consent, and where no work was being conducted by other Christian missions. His ministry was to all men of all races. He kept the number of paid workers to a minimum, placing responsibility upon the Christians themselves. His message was orderly and clear, following a definite arrangement of topics as he explained the gospel message—God, man, sin, the Savior. By 1900 Bickel had on his visiting list 400 towns and villages on 60 of the chief islands of the Inland Sea. There were 40 organized Sunday schools, two kindergartens, many mother's meetings, night schools, week-day Bible classes, traveling libraries, and a monthly magazine.

In 1913 a new ship, provided by the same donor but built under Captain Bickel's instructions, was dedicated to replace the Little White Ship that had served so well for thirteen years. It was called "Fukuin Maru," which means "Ship of Good News." The First World War was to curtail temporarily its activities, but not the progress of the work, for centers of Christian influence had been established firmly throughout the islands of the Inland Sea.

The new type of evangelism was especially significant because, up to that time, sixty per cent of all Protestant missionaries had been found in the eight largest cities of the country. Yet three-fourths of the population of Japan were located outside of the cities, in small towns and farm-villages. Indeed, unlike other Baptist mission fields, Japan was unique in that the *samurai* class rather than the plain people had been the first to receive the gospel. Thus, the introduction of the gospel ship was an important step in the direction of reaching the peasant class in the rural areas of the country.[10]

Further evidence of the growing interest in the neglected peoples of the more remote islands may be seen in the concern of the Reverend R. A. Thomson, of Kobe, in the Liuchiu, or Pendant Tassel Islands, lying northeast of Formosa. In 1891, he succeeded in arousing the interest of Mrs. Alexander Allan, a tourist from Scotland, to make a donation for establishing work among these people. Accordingly, a Japanese evangelist was sent to work among them. At the end of the first year, he had baptized 11 converts and organized the first Baptist church at Naha. By 1913 there were 800 members, 225 of whom had been baptized during the preceding year. The Japanese Christian women had been very active on these islands, devoting much voluntary service to the work.[11]

Educational Work and Other Developments

The first major educational institution to be developed by American Baptists in Japan was the Baptist Theological Seminary in Yokohama. The school grew out of a Bible class for preachers which Dr. Albert A. Bennett started in 1880, the year after his arrival. In 1884 the little Mission signified its approval of what Bennett was doing by formally announcing that the class was to become a seminary of which he was to be the principal, assisted by three other missionaries residing in the vicinity. In 1886 Dr. C. K. Harrington was sent out by the Board to become Bennett's associate in the seminary. In 1894 Dr. J. L. Dearing was added to the staff as president, thus relieving Bennett for teaching. For fourteen years Dr. Dearing gave excellent leadership to the school. In 1908 he was succeeded by Dr. W. B. Parshley, who two years later led in uniting the institution with the Southern Baptist Seminary at Fukuoka on Kyushu Island. The new location chosen was Tokyo, and the merged institution was operated by the Japanese Baptist Convention, the American Baptist Missionary Union, and the Southern Baptist Convention. It was named the Union Baptist Seminary.

For a long time the work of Baptists in Japan was crippled be-

---

[10] For additional accounts, see Charles K. Harrington, *Captain Bickel of the Inland Sea* (New York, 1919); Wynd, *op. cit.*, pp. 129 ff.; Helen Barrett Montgomery, *Following the Sunrise: A Century of Baptist Missions, 1813–1913* (Philadelphia, 1913), pp. 197-203.

[11] Montgomery, *op. cit.*, pp. 194-96.

cause they had no academy, while other denominations provided Christian college-preparatory training. The little Mission seems to have been preoccupied with the translation and distribution of the Scriptures. Moreover, many missionaries conducted their own schools or taught in government schools. Through this lack in secondary education, the quality of the students in the theological seminary remained low. The matter was remedied, however, when Professor Ernest W. Clement of Beaver Dam, Wisconsin, was persuaded to come to Japan to teach English in a government high school. He became so convinced of the need for Christian schools in the country that he resigned his post in 1891 and returned to America to arouse concern. In due course, he went back to Japan as a missionary under the American Baptist Missionary Union. An academy was opened in 1895, with eighteen students, nine of whom were candidates for the ministry. It was called the Tokyo Baptist Academy. When Dr. S. W. Duncan, foreign secretary of the Board in America died just on the point of a visit to the new institution, Mrs. Robert Harris made a gift for a dormitory in his memory. In 1900 the English name of the school was changed to the Duncan Academy, although the Japanese continued to speak of it as "Tokyo Gakuin." A new site was purchased and buildings were erected.

During the furlough of the Clements in 1903, Mr. Henry Topping became acting principal. The institution served sixty-five students. Two years later, Duncan Academy was awarded the coveted government recognition, which made the students eligible for privileges and patronage. Clement, who was an advocate of a limited enrollment met with opposition from others who felt that a larger school would attract more attention. In 1911, on his return from furlough, Clement resigned to re-enter government service. Dr. H. B. Benninghoff, his successor in the principalship, encouraged a growing enrollment. By 1912 it reached more than one hundred. Later leaders saw the need for additional space, and by 1917, Duncan Academy was closed at Tokyo, and a new Middle School was established at Yokohama, known as Mabie Memorial College in honor of the home secretary of the Missionary Union from 1890 to 1908. To the Japanese, it was still known as "Kanto Gakuin."

The Woman's Societies made a significant contribution to the Japan Mission through the establishment of schools for girls and women. The Sendai Baptist School ("Shokei Jogakko") was organized as the result of a conference of three women missionaries some time in 1890—Miss Nellie E. Fife, senior missionary who had come out in 1887, Miss L. Adele Phillips and Miss Lavinia Mead, both of whom had arrived in 1890. All three were representatives of the Woman's Baptist Missionary Society of the West. In 1898 Miss Annie S. Buzzell became principal, and led the school for twenty years. On December 18, 1891, "Soshin Jogakko" (which means "Truth-Seeking Girls" School) was dedicated. It was called in English the Mary L. Colby School in honor of the president of the Woman's Board who was also the first donor in behalf of the buildings erected. The institution had grown out of a small class of six girls which had met in a shed at the back of Mrs. Nathan Brown's house years before. She had secured the services of Miss Chiyo Yamada, who in 1890 became the able associate of Miss Clara A. Converse, the first principal appointed by the Woman's Board. They worked together for forty-five years.

By 1913 there were in Japan four boarding schools for girls—at Tokyo, Yokohama, Himeji, and Sendai. In addition, Baptist women supported a Bible Training School at Osaka, which had been opened in 1908 under the leadership of Miss Lavinia Mead and Japanese teachers. Kindergartens, which had been started in Tokyo in 1897, were to be found also in Morioka, Kobe, and Naha in the Liuchiu Islands. The Kindergarten Training School in Tokyo, which was founded in 1911, provided necessary preparation of teachers in this strategic type of educational work which reached into the homes of Japan. Baptist kindergartens were regarded as effective evangelizing agencies because they provided recruits for the Sunday schools and opened many homes to visits from Sunday school missionaries. The small boarding schools, though costly per student, likewise served as effective evangelistic centers.

Another distinctive contribution to educational work in Japan was the Christian dormitory or hostel as an evangelizing and Christianizing influence on university campuses. In 1908, Dr. Benninghoff and his Japanese associates undertook to provide such a service in connection with the Waseda University in Tokyo. The building became headquarters for the Christian activities in the university, and provided a Christian home environment for Christian students attending the institution. The effort was so successful that the University authorities requested Dr. Benninghoff to open a similar dormitory for middle-school boys. Bible classes, prayer meetings, student conferences, social life, and an atmosphere of Christian friendliness constituted the program. A carry-over of the same plan was the Dormitory for Business Men which Dr. Dearing established in Yokohama. It opened with twenty-eight boarders, and developed a fine institutional and club life. In 1909 a Christian hostel was opened for women in Haramachi by the Woman's Board.

An important move for Christian higher education was made by the Board of the American Baptist Foreign Mission Society in 1912, when it approved a proposal from Dr. W. B. Parshley, president of the Union Baptist Seminary, for establishing a Christian University in Japan. The vote included a decision to maintain this concern in all future appropriations of the Board.[12]

The trend in education had been accompanied by one in interdenominational co-operation. Baptists were participating, as early as 1900, with other Protestants in Japan in an evangelistic movement. They were uniting also with the Congregational and Presbyterian churches in the publication of a Union Hymn Book. Moreover, these three denominations, together with the Methodist churches, jointly issued Sunday School Lesson Helps.

At the same time, Baptists were uniting their own ranks. In 1890 the Yearly Japan Baptist Conference of Missionaries was organized under the leadership of Dearing, Taft, and Hamblen. About the same time the Japanese Baptists brought the Japan Baptist Convention into existence along parallel lines. It was composed of pastors, evangelists, Bible women, and lay representatives from the churches. Missionaries were invited as delegates. This body in turn sent delegates to the Missionary Conference. By 1900 the missionaries of the American Baptist Missionary Union and the Southern Baptist Convention were co-operating in a Union Conference, which published a news-letter known as *Gleanings* and a monthly sheet in the vernacular called *The Baptist Recorder*.

In 1912, Dr. James H. Franklin's first visit to Japan as foreign secretary hastened the day of fuller co-operation. The Japanese Baptists proposed a Union Reference Committee to consist of members

---

[12] For an account of educational work in Japan, see Wynd, *Seventy Years in Japan,* chaps. 10-17; Montgomery, *Following the Sunrise,* pp. 186-90, 205-06; *The Baptist Missionary Review* (Madras), Vol. I, No. 6 (June, 1895), pp. 216-18, Records of Board of Managers of A.B.F.M.S. for Sept. 12, 1912, p. 99.

of the Japan Baptist Mission Conference and the Japan Baptist Convention. It was to function with respect to all matters except items which concerned personal affairs of the missionaries. Thus began a closer relationship between Japanese and missionaries in administration of the Mission. Although in 1912 there were not yet any Japanese on the Reference Committee, or on the committee that transacted the Mission's business, or on the property committee, the era of sole missionary supervision had ended. In later years not only were Japanese represented on these committees, but in time they came to hold the majority membership.[13]

As self-direction made progress in Japanese church life, so did self-support. In 1898 a policy of self-support had been called for by the Conference of Missionaries. The Board of the Missionary Union approved a plan to give help from mission funds only to those churches which were maintaining the rent and incidental expenses of their chapel buildings.[14]

Another significant development in the Japan Mission was the creation of the institutional church at Tokyo in 1908. It was largely the work of Dr. and Mrs. William Axling, although the Reverend C. H. D. Fisher had overseen the erection of the building. At what was known as the Tabernacle, the Axlings developed a Japan Baptist Center which became more than a church. It served as a school, as a home for boys' clubs, for girls' guilds, for associations of young women, as a library, and as a clinic for those in need of medical counsel. Baptists had not developed medical work on any significant scale in Japan, chiefly because the government so early developed medical services for the people. But the Tabernacle gave evidence of the fact that the Christian community in Tokyo was conscious of the need for a well-rounded ministry to the whole life of men and women. More than 300 persons were enrolled in the night school classes and 100 in the Bible classes for men and women. Japanese supporters contributed more than a third of all the money needed to maintain the program. When the entire structure was burned to the ground in February, 1912, friends in America set out to raise $30,000 for a new plant. An equal concern was shown by the Japa-

---

[13] Wynd, *op. cit.*, pp. 265-79; *The Baptist Missionary Magazine,* Vol. 81, No. 10 (Oct., 1901), pp. 627-28.

[14] Records of the Executive Committee of A.B.M.U. for July 11, 1898, pp. 98-100.

nese who had come to value the contribution which the Tabernacle made to the community.[15]

By 1913 there were more than 4,000 Baptists in Japan, including about 500 who were under Southern Baptist affiliation. Of the 962 missionaries in the country, there were 81 Baptists, representing nearly one-twelfth of the total force. Japanese Baptist Christians numbered one-twentieth of the Protestant communicants. The increase in Japanese Baptist churches had averaged 10 per cent annually.[16] Although education played a more important part in the total enterprise in Japan than on some other Baptist fields, it was not so vigorous as that carried on by other denominations. For the most part American Baptists responded to the Japanese desire to minimize sectarian differences which were imported from abroad. Accordingly, there was a larger degree of interdenominational participation on the part of Baptists in Japan than elsewhere, except perhaps in West China and East China. The most notable effort of Baptists to reach the peasant classes of society was the gospel-ship evangelism conducted in the Inland Sea. This was the more impressive because Protestant work generally had been directed to the middle and upper classes. This in turn was due to the unusual political conditions in the country during the nineteenth century which made these classes relatively more open to the gospel.

---

[15] Wynd, *op. cit.*, pp. 255-64; Montgomery, *Following the Sunrise*, pp. 204-05.

[16] Montgomery, *op. cit.*, p. 211.

CHAPTER XIX

Outpost in the Pacific

THE PHILIPPINE ISLANDS were discovered in 1521 by Ferdinand Magellan, twenty-nine years after Columbus had reached the New World. Since that time they have been in the orbit of Western civilization, first as the possession of Spain and later as the responsibility of the United States of America. Under Spanish rule, the administration of the province fell almost entirely to the Dominican and Franciscan Orders of Friars to whose missionary endeavors the Filipinos owe their introduction to Christianity. Until 1896, the friars were the virtual rulers of the islands. But with their gain of political and economic control over the life of the people, there came a decline in their missionary zeal. During the eighteenth century the jealous wrangling between the Orders left only the Jesuits to carry on an active missionary work on the frontiers. Then, following 1850, there came a steady disintegration of Roman Catholic influence in the Philippines, as a reaction set in against the abuses of the friars.

Gregorio Aglipay, a native priest ordained in Manila about 1890, became closely associated with the leaders of the revolutions which took place in 1896 and 1898. For his pains he was unfrocked by the Spanish bishop. This did not deter the rebellious Filipinos from making him "vicar general," or chaplain general, of the revolutionary forces under Aguinaldo in 1899, following American occupation of the Islands. He set himself up as archbishop in Manila and head of the dissenters. Actually, he had little popular support from the general public until the Vatican issued a bull in 1902, upholding the friars against the Filipino clergy. From that moment the leading Filipinos allied themselves with Aglipay. While his movement was supported by many out of non-religious motives, it was essentially an effort to throw off the yoke of the papacy and to free the Filipino church from foreign rule. Coming, as it did, at the time when Spain lost control of the Islands to the Americans, the reform movement furnished a favorable background for Protestant missionaries when they entered the country after 1898, in spite of the fact that many in the movement rebelled against American rule.[1]

The startling news of Admiral Dewey's successful attack upon the Spanish ships in Manila Bay on May 1, 1898, brought to the attention of Americans a heterogeneous collection of tribes and races, some quite uncivilized. To American Protestants the challenge to evangelize these peoples was not in the least dampened by the fact that Roman Catholic missionaries had been at work among them for nearly four centuries. On July 13, 1898, in anticipation of prospects of an American victory in the Spanish-American War then in progress, missionary officials of various mission boards met at a conference in the Presbyterian House in New York. Dr. S. W. Duncan, secretary for the American Baptist Missionary Union, served as chairman. The purpose of the conference was to consider how the gospel might enter the West Indies and Pacific Islands, now opened by the hostilities with Spain. A committee was appointed to determine a suitable division of the fields among the denominations participating. The American Baptist Missionary Union was prepared to appoint missionaries and begin work in the Philippines as soon as the way was open.[2]

When the Philippines were ceded by Spain to the United States by the Treaty of Paris signed on April 11, 1899, Protestant mission societies were ready to move at once. On April 21, Dr. J. B. Rogers of the Presbyterian Board arrived, followed by a representative of the Methodist Board in March, 1900. In May of the same year, a Baptist, the Reverend Eric Lund began work on the Island of Panay. The danger of overlapping prompted representatives of the mission boards involved to gather in Manila on April 24-26, 1901, to organize the Evangelical Union of the Philippine Islands. By comity agreements, Presbyterians were assigned the territory in Luzon to the east and south of Manila; the Methodists were given the territory in Luzon between Manila and Lingayen Gulf. Baptists and

[1] For an interesting interpretation of Roman Catholic influence in the Philippines, see Charles W. Briggs, *The Progressing Philippines* (Philadelphia, 1913).

[2] *The Baptist Missionary Magazine,* Vol. 78, No. 9 (Sept., 1898), p. 523.

Presbyterians were to work together in Panay and Negros, two islands of the Visayan group. The rest of the Visayan Islands were to be assigned later. The Congregationalists were to be responsible for the Island of Mindanao. The Disciples and Episcopalians, who were also present, did not agree to the comity arrangement and so did not participate. The Episcopalians planned to confine themselves to work among the Moros and the wild tribes. Thus from the very beginning, Protestant missions in the Philippines, with the two exceptions named, were placed upon a basis of interdenominational co-operation.

Establishment of a Baptist Mission

By the comity arrangement, Baptist work was to be among the Visayans, who numbered more than three million and comprised the largest tribe on the Islands. The Visayans were found on the islands of Panay, Negros, Cebu, Samar, Leyte, and Bohol. Like the less numerous Tagalogs, the Visayans were progressive and civilized, having benefitted from Roman Catholic influence. The Negritos, on the other hand, were uncivilized. The Moros were Mohammedans. In addition there were in the Philippines about fifty thousand Chinese and some Japanese. Baptists became responsible for establishing stations on Panay and Negros. The dominance of the Visayan dialect in this area made a successful literary work possible. Moreover, there was a hearty response from the peasants who had been influenced by the reform efforts of the Filipino clergy.

Among the people there were only two classes, the landowners and the landless. The peasants, who lived in a somewhat feudal type of social unit known as the *barrio* or village, were practically serfs. They had suffered greatly at the hands of the friars whose economic mastery of the country was a source of constant irritation. When American rule was introduced, the rebellion of Aguinaldo was essentially a demonstration against foreign control of any kind. Inherent within the Filipinos was a liberty-loving spirit which found expression in an eager reception of the Christian message as it was proclaimed by the Protestant missionaries. In this respect there was a particular appeal in the democratic character of Baptist church life.

Because the term "Protestant" had negative implications in this Roman Catholic country, all missions agreed to use the word "evangelical" to describe themselves. (They will be so designated in this chapter.) This was a fortunate choice, for many of the Roman Catholic clergy among the Filipinos were eager for reforms that paralleled the Reformation of the sixteenth century in Europe.

In such a favorable atmosphere, the Baptists entered upon their work, being responsible for the greater part of the provinces of Iloilo and Capiz on Panay Island, for the western part of Negros Island, and for Romblon and Masbata, two small islands farther north. The combined population of this area was about a million. Believing that a man with experience in a Spanish-speaking country would be most effective among these people, the American Baptist Missionary Union appointed the Reverend Eric Lund, a Swedish Baptist who had served for ten years in Barcelona, Spain. On March 24, 1900, he sailed for the Philippines, accompanied by Braulio Manikan, a native of the Philippines who had come under his influence in Barcelona. The two men took with them a supply of Christian literature. They were singularly prepared in spirit for the new assignment. For both had dreamed of the day when they might go to the Philippines to preach the evangelical faith instead of leaving the field wholly to Roman Catholic influence. To this end they had begun in Barcelona a translation of the Bible into Panayan Visayan. Manikan was a native of the province of Capiz, and hence familiar with the Visayan dialect. After they had been in the Philippines for some time, they completed the translation (1912).

It was natural that the two missionaries should go first, upon their arrival, to the province of Capiz, the home of Manikan. From there, they proceeded to Iloilo province. Finding that the Presbyterians were established already in Iloilo City, they set up headquarters in Jaro, a nearby town. Shortly thereafter, a delegation of peasants presented Lund with a petition signed by several thousand people, requesting that they be taught the evangelical faith. The major portion of this group were known as the Bolo Battalion because of the sharp knives or bolos which they carried as weapons. They were known to both Spaniards and Americans as "belligerents" because of their resistance to the Spanish rule and later because they engaged in guerilla warfare against the American troops. They had turned to the American missionaries on the advice of Gregorio Lampinio, popularly known as "Papa Gorio." The members of this Bolo Battalion were remarkably receptive to the gospel, and within a year one thousand persons were baptized by Dr. Charles W. Briggs, who had joined Lund and Manikan in the latter part of 1900. From this nucleus there grew eventually the churches which later were organized into the Convention of Philippine Baptist Churches.[3]

Eric Lund, the pioneer Baptist missionary to the Philippines, was described by his colleagues as "tall, portly and dignified, with a short closely cropped black beard." At first he suffered much from the heat and had severe attacks of indigestion, which caused him to return to Sweden where he remained until persuaded by Dr. Briggs to return to continue his translation work. This he agreed to do if a printer and press were made available. His rigidly conservative nature both in temperament and in theology made him quite unyielding. His translation of the Bible might have become the accepted colloquial version had not his insistence upon the use of the word "immerse" for *baptize* prevented its use by other denominations.

Lund's ministry and that of Manikan, his associate, were opposed vigorously by Roman Catholics. Filipinos in some villages who were known to have attended evangelical meetings frequently lost their jobs. Yet the response among the villagers was great. In 1901 there were 113 baptisms in Jaro, while 8,000 in the area announced a desire to become evangelical Christians. To protect themselves against ostracism from hostile neighbors, converts from six towns of the province of Iloilo settled a new town on the mountain side near the market town of Janiway, a few miles north of Jaro. They named it Calvary; it was exclusively a community of evangelicals.[4]

In 1901 the little Baptist Mission was reinforced by the arrival of the Reverend and Mrs. J. C. Robbins, the Reverend and Mrs. A. A. Forshee, and Dr. P. H. J. Lerrigo, a medical missionary, and his wife. In 1902 W. O. Valentine and his wife were transferred from the Mandalay High School in Burma. In 1904 the Reverend and Mrs. H. W. Munger and Dr. R. C. Thomas, a second medical missionary, with his wife, began their work.

Because of the widespread illiteracy of the people and their lack of technical skills, the missionaries faced the task of developing

---

[3] An excellent account of this early work is provided in the Fridell Manuscript, an historical account prepared by Dr. Elmer A. Fridell, foreign secretary for the Orient with the A.B.F.M.S. See also *The Baptist Missionary Magazine,* Vol. 80, No. 5 (May, 1900), p. 164.

[4] R. Fred Chambers, Central Philippine College: An Historical Study in the Light of Philippine Historical and Cultural Background (a doctoral dissertation at the University of Colorado, 1949), pp. 3-5.

schools to train national workers for the churches and also to provide vocational skills whereby the peasants might be equipped to make an adequate livelihood. In addition, the need for medical work was great. The survey of these developments are an important aspect of the story of these early years in the Philippine Baptist Mission and therefore deserve special attention.

Beginnings of Institutional Work

On June 13, 1904, the Baptist missionaries met at Jaro to organize the Philippine Baptist Conference of Missionaries, with Briggs as president and Forshee as secretary. There were three standing committees—one on Reference (which referred requests of missionaries to the Board at home), one on Property, and one on Publication. At this time there were 11 Baptist churches, eight in Iloilo and one in Capiz, all on Panay Island, and two in western Negros. The combined membership totaled 1,606, most of whom were in the province of Iloilo. The conference voted to establish a Bible school and an industrial school, both to be under one management. It was decided also to publish a small quarterly periodical of missionary information for home consumption which should be called, "The Pearl of the Orient."

The Bible School opened in the home of Mr. Valentine in Jaro on June 1, 1905. A few weeks later it was moved to a rented house. Twelve pupils were enrolled and some Bible women attended. The teaching staff was composed of the missionaries who gave such time as they could spare from other responsibilities. On October 1 of the same year the Jaro Industrial School opened. Like the Bible School, it was the product of Valentine's vision of the need of the Filipinos for adequate education. His plan, which had been approved by the Board in Boston the previous year, called for a school in which boys could learn to help themselves. Students were to be taught English and crafts. By a practical plan of combining book study with actual experience in farming and business, pupils could earn their way while they learned. The school was situated on a campus of sixty-five acres. To develop actual experience in democracy, the student body was organized into the "Jaro Industrial School Republic," with a congress composed of three representatives from each class and two senators, and an executive department. It was the oldest form of student government in the Philippines. Because the Industrial School was the only one of its kind on the islands, it attracted the attention of government officials and of Bishop Brent, who was commencing an Episcopal school in Baguio. The farm which was operated in connection with the school won wide acclaim.

The first president was W. O. Valentine. His ideal was to train Filipinos in Christian principles and to appreciate the dignity of work. He sought to make the institution the center of evangelical influence on the islands. In 1911 he was succeeded by Victoriano Diamonon, who was later to receive the degree of doctor of philosophy from the University of Iowa, and return to take leadership in the Department of Justice in Manila, and in other posts of influence. Plans were formulated in 1911 to begin high school work at the institution. In 1913, the Jaro Industrial School was incorporated and the courses were standardized in keeping with the public schools. The move was stimulated by the general lifting of academic standards which accompanied organization in 1908 of the University of the Philippines. It was the beginning of a period of advance which was to culminate in later years in the development of a junior college in 1923 and finally of the full-fledged Central Philippine College. In the course of these changes, the Bible School gradually fell behind. In 1912 it was discontinued, but teaching of the Bible remained a part of the curriculum of Jaro Industrial School. Financial support of the institution came from the United States and from the income earned by the farm. Until 1914 no student paid tuition. Management of the school was entirely in the hands of the missionaries and the American Baptist Foreign Mission Society until 1923.[5]

Other types of educational institutions were developed during these early years. Among these was the Woman's Bible Training School which was organized by Miss Ana V. Johnson in Jaro to prepare Bible women for the Visayan Islands. Another was the Home School or orphanage started in 1906 at Capiz on the northern tip of Panay by Dr. and Mrs. Lerrigo. By 1910 there were seventy-five children under the care of Miss Suman. This Home School was the forerunner of Filamer College, which was founded later at Capiz (now called Roxas City). An Academy for Girls was founded in Iloilo, with Miss Caroline M. Bissinger as principal and Miss Alice M. Stanard as associate. It was the only school in the Philippines for girls of the upper classes. Still another type of educational work and one

[5] *Ibid.*, pp. 7-33.

which was introduced by the Baptists and imitated by other denominations was the student dormitory or hostel. Forshee founded such a dormitory in Bacolod on Negros Island so that the pupils of the public high school might have a Christian atmosphere while away from home.[6]

From this brief survey it becomes clear that Baptists did not seek to develop a complete system of schools as on other mission fields. There was no need for such a plan inasmuch as the government was supporting a public school system. The role of the missionaries was to provide Christian influence and instruction wherever it was needed to supplement and complement the work of the government.

Medical work was introduced almost from the first by evangelical missionaries and was received warmly by the Filipinos. The need was great. Tuberculosis was everywhere and the prevalence of the hookworm caused widespread anemia. In 1900 Dr. J. Andrew Hall, a pioneer medical missionary to the Islands, began the Presbyterian medical mission at Iloilo. In a short time he had established a small bamboo hospital. By 1906 there was a fine two-story building on the main thoroughfare of the town. It provided thirty beds. The next year the Baptists were invited to join in this medical work. The invitation was accepted, and the Union Hospital at Iloilo came into being. The staff was composed of one medical missionary from each denomination, two American trained nurses, and a corps of a dozen Filipino nurses and ten other Filipino helpers. Several thousand patients were treated each year by this institution. The first Baptist medical doctor to serve there was Dr. R. C. Thomas. Later a Training School for Nurses was established.

A hospital and dispensary was started by Dr. Lerrigo at Capiz, supported largely by medical fees. His busy schedule was typical of the heavy responsibilities placed upon medical missionaries in the early years of the Mission. In addition to treating in a single year 8,085 out-patients, 2,165 in-patients, and making 672 visits to patients at home, Dr. Lerrigo supervised a large evangelistic field and had oversight of the boys' dormitory. In later years the hospital came to be known as Emmanuel Hospital, and, as at Iloilo, a Training School for Nurses became an important part of the work.[7]

---

[6] Helen Barrett Montgomery, *Following the Sunrise: A Century of Baptist Missions, 1813–1913* (Philadelphia, 1913), pp. 262-70, 279.

[7] *Ibid.*, pp. 271-72; *The Baptist Missionary Magazine,* Vol. 88, No. 12 (Dec., 1908), p. 451.

It will be recalled that Dr. Lund had seen the need for a printing press while he was engaged in translating the Scriptures into the Visayan language. In 1900 Dr. Briggs brought an upright second hand press with him as a gift from friends in Boston. But a separate building was not seriously considered until 1907, when Mr. E. R. McIntyre was sent out by the Missionary Union to erect a press building and take charge of the publishing business of the Mission. For the building the Executive Committee had appropriated $15,000. Unfortunately, however, McIntyre planned a much larger structure than he had money to finance. Consequently, the funds ran out long before the building was completed. The officials at home therefore refused to give any more money until Dr. Barbour, the foreign secretary, could visit the field in 1908. Sometime later, at the recommendation of Dr. Barbour, the building was completed, the upper story being used for a Bible School. By 1913 the Mission Press at Iloilo provided Testaments, tracts, and a monthly magazine in Visayan, as well as Sunday school helps and general school outlines for the use of the missionaries.[8]

Dr. Barbour's visit to the field in 1908 resulted in a proposal to centralize the administration of the Mission. He introduced to the mission staff the plan advanced by the Board of Managers of the Union to have two "general missionaries": Dr. Dearing assigned for the work in China, Japan, and the Philippines, and Dr. Ferguson, for the work in India, Burma, and Assam. Although it was explained carefully that the new posts did not carry supervisory powers, but only a liaison relationship between the missionaries and the Board, the plan aroused protests from India and Burma in particular, as we have seen in an earlier chapter. Formal approval was given by the missionary conferences in China, Japan, and the Philippines. Nevertheless, the opposition continued and the two general missionaries resigned their special assignment, so that the plan was never carried out.[9]

When Dr. Franklin became foreign secretary, it will be recalled that the Society introduced the intensive policy for all of its fields. As a result, the Bible School at Iloilo was abandoned temporarily, in the anticipation that the Mission might unite with the Presbyterians

[8] H. W. Munger, History of the Philippine Baptist Mission (a typescript, 1925 or 1929), pp. 113-16.

[9] *Ibid.*, pp. 113-14.

in establishing one central Bible Training School. By 1913 the situation on the field was greatly in need of strengthening. The staff of 26 missionaries could rarely muster more than half of its strength at any one time, owing to the heavy drain on health and the consequent necessity of frequent furloughs. Yet the progress in the Mission had been encouraging. The number of Baptist churches had grown from 34 in 1911 to 57 in 1913, a gain of 67 per cent. The number of self-supporting churches were eight in 1911 and 17 in 1913, a gain of over 112 per cent. In 1911 there had been 44 Sunday schools, whereas four years later there were 55. The total membership in the Filipino Baptist churches was 4,337 by 1913. The people from the villages had built and paid for their own chapels. Their spiritual vigor was manifested in the extensive witnessing which they carried on under severe persecution.[10]

In less than fifteen years, the Philippine Mission had become a part of the life of the people, furnishing two hospitals on Panay Island, several schools on Panay and Negros, and a growing church life which was moving in the direction of self-support and self-government. Through the medical work, the missionaries were interpreting the human concern of the evangelical missionary movement. Through the educational program, an effort was being made to develop appreciation for Christian principles and democratic practices. Through the maintainance of the primary purpose of evangelism, the churches were growing steadily. Finally, through a readiness to co-operate with other evangelical denominations at work on the Islands, Baptists were enabled to accomplish more than they might have been able to do alone.

[10] Montgomery, *Following the Sunrise,* pp. 261-62, 274.

CHAPTER XX

Strengthening the Witness in Europe

The progress of modern Baptist missions in continental Europe may be traced by following the succession of midnight baptismal services that in the nineteenth century introduced the witness to country after country. It will be recalled that the first such service was conducted in 1834, in the River Elbe, near Altoona, Germany. On the night of October 30, 1838, the first Danish service was held in the Elsinore River near Copenhagen. At midnight on September 21, 1848, the earliest Swedish converts to Baptist principles were immersed in the Cattegat at Vallersvik. The initial Finnish service was conducted some years later in the Baltic, near Jakobstadt. Soon there were converts to be baptized in Norway, where the Skager-Rak touches Skien. This led in turn to baptisms in Russia in the River Neva, at St. Petersburg.[1] In every case there was dramatized afresh the New Testament principle of believer's baptism as the source from which issues a regenerate church. In spite of stern persecution from many quarters, the witness did not die, but rather was strengthened.

We have traced in chapter five the rise of this modern Baptist witness in France (1832), Germany (1834), Denmark (1838), and Greece (1836), and within those countries the main developments up to 1845. It remains to survey briefly the strengthening of that witness and its spread to other lands during the next seventy years. During this time the American Baptist Missionary Union manifested a keen interest in Europe as a mission field. Until about 1882, mission-

[1] Frank Peterson, *Missions in Europe* (Boston, 1911), p. 5.

aries were sent from America not only by the Union, but also by the American Baptist Publication Society, which carried on colportage work abroad as well as at home. After 1882 the Union abandoned all attempts to evangelize Europe by "outsiders," preferring instead to lend moral and financial assistance to Baptist leaders within the various countries on the continent where a work had been begun. For this service the Union invested in Europe about one-seventh the amount of money that was expended in pagan lands.[2] This indicates in part at least the great importance attached by Baptists in America to their European cousins in spite of the fact that Europeans were nominally Christian.

Slow Progress in France

In 1845 the withdrawal of Southern Baptists from the Triennial Convention left a heavy responsibility upon the body which remained, known as the American Baptist Missionary Union. Consequently, there was some disposition to discontinue the French Mission which had been begun in 1832. A decision was rendered, however, in favor of maintaining the work, and the Reverend Erastus Willard, one of three missionaries previously sent out, was returned to his field of labor at Douay. At the time, he faced the hostility of both Roman Catholics and Protestants of the Reformed Churches. Fortunately for the struggling churches there was a friend at court working on behalf of religious liberty. He was Count A. de Gasparin, who frequently presented to the Chamber of Deputies petitions of the Baptists for religious freedom and counselled French Baptist preachers how to conduct themselves in the face of intolerant local authorities.[3] With the Revolution of 1848, a better day dawned, for the Second Republic which came into being at that time guaranteed religious toleration. Growth of the work thereafter was steady, though not spectacular.

In 1848 Willard was joined by Dr. T. T. Devan, formerly a missionary to China. He undertook preaching in Paris, while his wife established a Sunday school. In time he sought to extend the work to the South of France, and Paris was given up as a suitable center for Baptist effort. In June, 1849, the first Association of French Bap-

---

[2] *The Baptist Missionary Magazine,* Vol. 62, No. 7 (July, 1882). The figures cited are for the fiscal year 1881–82.

[3] *Ibid.,* Vol. 26, No. 9 (Sept., 1846), pp. 284-85.

tists was organized, followed in October by the establishing of a Ministerial Conference. The acknowledged leader of the Mission was Willard. Devan lent his support to southeastern France, while Willard devoted most of his efforts to a training school for preachers at Douay. In 1853 Devan terminated his services, and Willard withdrew three years later. From that time the work was left almost entirely in the hands of the French Baptists, with only financial aid from America.

During the next several years the Mission faced much discouragement. The American Civil War curtailed the amount of assistance from the Mission Union. The Franco-Prussian War in 1871 precipitated a public hatred of the Protestants in France, owing to the fact that the invader was of that persuasion. One pastor was imprisoned as a spy because he inquired if a town in which he was preaching was prepared to defend itself. Most of the male members in several of the Baptist churches were called into the army, thus disrupting church life. The effects of the war increased the poverty of the members, none of whom was prosperous.[4]

Nevertheless the Mission continued to operate, although the progress was slow. With substantial assistance from the Missionary Union, a Baptist chapel was erected in 1873 in Paris at a cost of approximately $60,000. It became an attractive center for Baptist work in the capital city. From 1877 to 1881 the average number of accessions to Baptist churches in the country was 35 per year, which represented an average increase of 7 per year over the previous 20-year period. By 1882, after 50 years of work, there were only 9 churches, with 700 members, and 9 preachers. By contrast the work in Germany and Sweden was flourishing. In Greece and Spain it was even more difficult than in France.[5]

A fresh impetus to French Baptist work came in the 1880's from a remarkable movement begun in Paris by R. W. McAll, a young Englishman, who sought to reach the working people who had drifted from the church. The McAll Mission, as it was called, proved a phenomenal success. In time a French assistant, Reuben Saillens, joined the work. Protestant churches in Paris, including the Baptists, worked in close harmony with the new evangelistic effort. Saillens, who had

---

[4] *The Baptist Missionary Magazine,* Vol. 51, No. 1 (Jan., 1871), pp. 22-26; No. 7 (July, 1871), pp. 261-63.

[5] *Ibid.,* Vol. 62, No. 7 (July, 1882), pp. 187-89.

long had sympathy with Baptist principles, finally associated himself with the Paris Baptist church in Rue de Lille as acting pastor without breaking his connection with the McAll Mission. In 1889 Saillens organized the second Baptist church in Paris, holding services in a hall in Rue St. Denis. Two years later he decided to withdraw from the McAll Mission to devote his full time to Baptist mission work. His leadership was utilized at once, for he was elected general secretary of the French Baptist Missionary Committee. Against such a background a revival developed from 1888, partly the result of the influence of the McAll Mission and partly the effect of the zealous evangelistic efforts of the veteran Baptist preacher, the Reverend J. B. Cretin. Within fifteen months, the two churches in Paris nearly doubled their membership. The Rue de Lille church maintained four mission halls, while the Rue St. Denis church had two, in addition to operating daily meetings in their own places of worship. The combined membership of the two churches by December, 1891, was 978.[6]

The enlargement of the work led to the development of regional organizations known as the Franco-Belgian and the Franco-Swiss Committees. Under the care of the first were the churches in northern France and Belgium where French also was spoken. Under the care of the second were the churches in eastern France and French Switzerland. For want of a theological school, French ministerial students received preparatory training with one of the pastors, followed by a course at Spurgeon's College in England.

By 1900 there were in France 30 Baptist churches with approximately 2,500 members. While the number of churches had decreased to 27 by 1908, 10 had become self-supporting. Through a French Baptist Missionary Committee, the churches were supporting a missionary among the Moslems in Algeria, and were conducting their own work in Belgium and Switzerland. At home Baptist scholars were assisting in the preparation of a new French translation of the Bible which won wide acclaim.[7]

---

[6] Peterson, *Missions in Europe,* pp. 25-27; *The Baptist Missionary Magazine,* Vol. 71, No. 6 (June, 1891), pp. 162-64.

[7] *Proceedings of the first European Baptist Congress,* 1908, p. 162; *Proceedings of the second Baptist World Congress,* 1911, pp. 44, 438. These citations will be referred to hereafter by the initials, E.B.C. and B.W.C.

Enlarging Work in Germany

By 1845, just eleven years after the organization of the first Baptist church in Germany by Gerhard Oncken, there were 380 Baptists in Hamburg. Two years later the first chapel was erected in that city, and the following year another chapel was opened in Berlin under the leadership of G. W. Lehmann, a friend of Oncken. At this time there were Baptist centers at Breslau, Stettin, Bremen, Elbing, Memel, Cassel, Marburg, Bitterfield, and Oldenburg. The chief advance was in East Prussia; the least in Mecklenburg, Saxony, and Bavaria, where religious life was of a more reactionary character. There were three hostile forces that beset Baptist work. The first stemmed from a traditional German antipathy to Anabaptists, who were associated with the hated Münster rebellion of an earlier period. The second was the fear and resentment of the Lutheran clergy to Baptist growth among the plain people. The third was a policy of intolerance on the part of the government, and encouraged by the Lutheran clergy, by which Baptists suffered indignities, imprisonment, and loss of property. With the Revolution of 1848, however, the way was paved for the eventual triumph of official toleration, although in some parts of the country persecution continued for several years.

In view of the more favorable circumstances and continued growth, four Associations of Baptist churches in Prussia, in northwest Germany, in south-central Germany, and in Denmark were united in a "Union of the Associated Churches of Baptized Christians in Germany and Denmark." In pattern and purpose it was modelled after the Triennial Convention which had existed until 1845 in America, even to meeting every three years. Through its facilities, an active missionary program was carried on in neighboring countries. The leading spirit in this work was Oncken. At the time, he was about fifty years of age, a well proportioned man. Rapid and energetic in movement, yet dignified and firm, he was a striking figure when addressing an assembly from the pulpit or on the floor in debate. Few men have been more consumed with the evangelistic passion than Oncken, whose untiring efforts took him into Denmark, Lithuania, and Switzerland to strengthen existing churches and establish new centers of activity. By 1851 there were 41 churches with a combined membership of 3,746 persons, 137 Sunday school teachers, and 1,035 pupils. With the help of funds supplied by the American Baptist Missionary Union in America, Oncken was enabled to engage assistants to aid him in the expanding program.[8]

Between 1850 and 1854 persecution of Baptists was resumed. It was instigated chiefly by the Lutheran clergy, who resented the opposition of Baptist people to infant baptism and to payment of the church tax. In some towns, ministers of Baptist chapels were refused the right to administer the ordinances and to conduct public worship. They were harassed in the performance of their pastoral duties at funerals; public gatherings were disrupted by mobs, while the police tacitly withheld protection; many were imprisoned and treated as common criminals; infants on occasions were forcibly seized to be carried off for baptism by the state church. Through British and American intervention, both on the part of church groups and state authorities, as well as by Baptist constituencies within Europe itself, the attention of King Frederick William the Fourth was called to the plight of German Baptists. Persecution did not cease, however, until that monarch's illness brought Prince Wilhelm to the throne as Regent. The state church even then continued to be unfriendly. In 1858 the Baptist church in Hamburg obtained from the Senate of the city recognition as a religious corporation, thereby making valid their church records of births and marriages. This was the first victory won by Baptists in their struggle in Germany for religious equality.[9]

Although German Baptists were fearful of a trained ministry which they regarded as autocratic and purely professional, Oncken persuaded them to establish a theological seminary at Hamburg in 1880. It was an outgrowth of an effort which he had begun 20 years before to train candidates for the ministry on a less formal basis. By 1910 the new institution had given instruction to 316 students. Many of them became pastors and missionaries in Germany, Hungary, Roumania, Russia, Austria, Switzerland, Holland, Bohemia, India, Africa, and the United States. The business acumen of Dr. Philipp Bickel, chairman of the committee of management, gave stability to the school. Bickel also placed the publishing department of the German Baptist Conference on a secure footing. The publishing house at Hamburg grew out of a small book store which Oncken had

---

[8] *The Baptist Missionary Magazine,* Vol. 29, No. 9 (Sept., 1849), p. 343; Vol. 30, No. 3 (March, 1850), p. 66; J. H. Rushbrooke, *The Baptist Movement in the Continent of Europe* (London, 1915), p. 21.

[9] See regular reports appearing in *The Baptist Missionary Magazine* for the years concerned, especially Vol. 38, No. 9 (Sept., 1858), pp. 330-31.

established as a base of supplies for his colporteurs. In 1871 the government granted a license for printing and publishing. In 1898 the publication headquarters were removed to Cassel, where a four-story building was erected to house its various departments. The publishing house issued three weekly papers, books, tracts, Bibles and smaller portions of the Scriptures for distribution to German-speaking peoples throughout the German Empire, Russia, Switzerland, South Africa, and Australia.[10]

The number of German Baptists increased from 11,275 in 1863 to 45,583 by 1913, and were enrolled in 213 churches. Their property was valued at nearly one million dollars. During the early years of the twentieth century, in addition to supporting missions in neighboring European countries, German Baptists expended approximately $15,000 annually on work in Africa and India.[11] Thus within 80 years there had developed under the leadership of men like Oncken, Julius Köbner, and Lehmann, and with the financial assistance of English and American Baptists, a well-organized fellowship which provided a nucleus for the spread of the Baptist witness far and wide.

The Witness in Scandinavian Countries

Baptist work in Denmark, as we have seen, was an outgrowth of that which had begun in Germany at Hamburg. For many years, therefore, it was identified with the German Mission and enjoyed the able guidance of Julius Köbner, its founder. In 1865 a separate Danish Baptist Conference was organized, and from 1888 appropriations from the American Baptist Missionary Union were separated from those of the German Mission. From that time the work in Denmark was under the direction of a committee of Danish Baptists. The main strength of the Baptist witness in that country was in Copenhagen, the capital, where there were three Baptist churches. By 1910 there were in Denmark 31 churches with a total membership of 4,082, while 40 pastors and missionaries together with 60 lay preachers gave direction to the work. During the years, many of the preachers were sent to America to be trained in the Danish-Norwegian Department of Morgan Park Seminary, now the Divinity School of the

---

[10] Peterson, *Missions in Europe*, pp. 13-15, *The Baptist Missionary Magazine*, Vol. 78, No. 10 (Oct., 1898), p. 567.

[11] *Ibid.*, p. 15; Rushbrooke, *op. cit.*, pp. 28-29.

University of Chicago. Within Denmark there were two schools maintained by Baptists, an academy and a missionary training school. In addition there was a book store and publication department located at Söby in the northern part of Jutland, which prepared a weekly paper and Sunday school materials. The upward advance in membership began to level off by 1914, the total number not exceeding 4,226 in 1915.[12]

The Baptist witness in Scandinavia enjoyed its greatest success in Sweden. In the providence of God, the way was paved for its beginning in that country when two Swedish seamen were converted in America. One was G. W. Schroeder, a sea captain, who joined the Baptist Mariners' Church in New York City in 1843. The other was F. O. Nilson, who did not become a Baptist at once, but who returned to his native land as a missionary to his fellow sailors. In 1845 he came in contact with Schroeder at Gothenburg, and was persuaded to accept Baptist views. Thereupon he went to Hamburg to be baptized by Oncken on August 1, 1847. Upon his return, he was instrumental in establishing the first Baptist church in Sweden, in 1848, near Gothenburg. The next year Nilson was ordained at Hamburg in order to assume responsibility for the Swedish church. His ministry resulted in an increase in the membership of the congregation to fifty-two, but this increase came in spite of the most severe persecution from the authorities, who were determined to protect Lutheranism. After several imprisonments, he was banished in July, 1851, whereupon he went to Copenhagen, to serve as pastor of a Baptist church there until 1853. At that time he accepted the invitation of a band of twenty-four harassed Swedish Baptists to lead them to the United States where they might find religious freedom. Nilson remained in America until 1860, when the King annulled his banishment, making possible his return the following year to become pastor of the newly organized Baptist church in Gothenburg.

A second center of Baptist work in Sweden was Stockholm, where a church had been organized on June 18, 1854, by two furriers, D. Forsell and P. F. Hejdenberg, the latter of whom had been ordained in Hamburg during the previous May. A year later he undertook

[12] Peterson, *op. cit.*, pp. 15-16; *The Baptist Missionary Magazine,* Vol. 46, No. 1 (Jan., 1866), pp. 17-18; Rushbrooke, *The Baptist Movement in the Continent of Europe,* p. 42.

evangelistic work, and Andreas Wiberg, a learned convert from the Lutheran clergy, replaced him as leader of the growing congregation. Following a debate with Oncken and Köbner upon a visit to Hamburg, Wiberg had become convinced of the validity of Baptist teaching. He was baptized by Nilson before sailing for the United States to recover from a period of illness. While in America, Wiberg accepted appointment by the American Baptist Publication Society to superintend its colportage work in Sweden. Upon his return in 1855 he found to his surprise that a small book he had published earlier on the subject of believer's baptism had been instrumental in convincing many people to adopt Baptist views. By the close of the year there were three hundred baptized believers in different parts of the country. That was the beginning of a dramatic ingathering which continued unabated into the next century.

With the support of the American Baptist Publication Society, Wiberg was enabled to engage four evangelists to assist him in establishing new churches, Sunday schools, and eventually a publishing enterprise. The first Conference of Swedish Baptists was held in 1857, with 19 delegates from eight different provinces present. When the second gathering met the following year, there were 100 delegates present. The third Conference, which met in Stockholm in 1861, was able to report that there were 125 Baptist churches in the country with a total of 4,930 members. Seeing the need of a trained ministry, the delegates authorized the Executive Committee of the Conference to establish a seminary. With financial help from England and America, Bethel Seminary was founded in Stockholm in 1866. In that same year the American Baptist Publication Society transferred its work in Sweden to the American Baptist Missionary Union, which gave liberal support until near the end of the century. Wiberg, Knut Oscar Broady, and John Alexis Edgren were appointed missionaries of the Union to direct the publication and educational work to which American support was being given.[13]

By the close of 1874, Wiberg was able to report that there were more than 10,000 Baptists in Sweden, organized into 225 churches, with 67 buildings for worship and 141 pastors. In addition there

---

[13] The foregoing account is based on Peterson, *Missions in Europe,* pp. 16-18; a history of Swedish Baptist work to 1865 by Wiberg in *The Baptist Missionary Magazine,* Vol. 46, No. 2 (Feb., 1866), pp. 35-39; see also Vol. 46, No. 7 (July, 1866), pp. 307-15.

were evidences of the influence of Baptist teaching upon the Lutheran State Church through converts to Baptist views who remained within the established church. By 1914 there were 21 Associations, 635 churches, 54,159 members, 377 ministers, 699 local preachers, 70 students for the ministry, 65,404 Sunday school members, and 623 chapels. The Baptists of Sweden had contributed during the preceding year nearly $300,000, of which approximately $17,000 was spent for foreign missions. Outside of the country, work was conducted on the Aaland Islands in the Baltic, at St. Petersburg in Russia, and in Estonia. Within Sweden, membership was largely recruited from the middle class and the more prosperous members of the laboring classes.[14]

The unusual success of Baptist efforts in Sweden may be attributed in part, at least, to a number of factors. From the first there was sustaining support from the United States, first from the American Baptist Publication Society, and then from the American Baptist Missionary Union. The able leadership within Sweden also gave an advantage to the movement. The early founding of a theological seminary to train ministers was an important factor that contributed to a higher standard of church life. The attractiveness of Baptist teaching to the middle class as well as to the laboring classes undoubtedly contributed a stability to the movement. Although there was some persecution in various localities, the national government did not lend strong encouragement to the practice, hence the greater degree of freedom enjoyed by Swedish Baptists after the 1860's. The early organization of the churches into a Conference after the pattern in Germany was likewise an asset to the ongoing ministry of the Baptists in Sweden.

The introduction of the Baptist witness to Norway came by way of Frederik L. Rymker, a Danish sailor who had been converted and baptized in America. He settled at Prosgrund, near Skien, where a pietistic element in the Lutheran Church was becoming vocal in behalf of the necessity for conversion. Under Rymker's leadership the first Baptist church in Norway was constituted on April 22, 1860, at Tolnaes, a farm near Skien, with seven members present. Another church was founded at Larvik in 1860, although it was destined not

[14] *The Baptist Missionary Magazine,* Vol. 55, No. 11 (Nov., 1875), p. 469; Rushbrooke, *The Baptist Movement in the Continent of Europe,* p. 66; *Proceedings of B.W.C.,* 1905, p. 180.

to survive for long. In 1862 a third church was established at Kragerö. The lack of an educated ministry and of sufficient funds combined with severe persecution by the Lutheran State Church to hinder the progress of Baptist work in the country. Heavy fines, imprisonment, and other indignities were endured by those early Norwegian Baptists. Baptisms were held of necessity at night in some secluded spot to avoid arousing further hostility.

In spite of these handicaps the number of congregations continued to increase until it was possible to organize, at Skien in 1872 a "Southern District Association." Five years later a similar district association for the churches north of the polar circle was established, with Tromsö as a center. In the same year (1877) the Norwegian Baptist Conference was formed at Bergen. It was composed of 14 churches, with 511 members and 12 ministers. In the entire country there were only two Baptist meeting houses—those at Tromsö and Bergen. Without the financial assistance of English Baptists and the American Baptist Missionary Union, the work in Norway might not have survived. After 1900 the course of Baptist advance was more heartening. The membership increased 30 per cent between 1900 and 1910 as over against a mere 7 per cent gain in the population of the country. When the Jubilee Anniversary was observed in Christiana in 1910, the king sent his message of congratulations. The day of persecution clearly was over. During the Jubilee year Norwegian Baptists founded a theological seminary at Christiana with the financial assistance of the Missionary Union. It was a forward step to provide an adequate leadership for the 40 churches then in existence with their nearly 4,000 members.[15]

The Baptist work in Finland was established by the Reverend Eric Jansson, who had been associated first with the Swedish Baptist Mission. The earliest Finns to identify themselves with the Baptists were Franz Victor Heikel and his sister, Anna, whose father was professor in the University of Abo. In June, 1868, they were baptized at Stockholm by Wiberg. Their witness was impressive because of their parentage, and it resulted in further conversions. The first baptisms in Finland took place on July 14, 1868, when two friends of the Heikels received the ordinance in the Baltic Sea near Jakob-

[15] For an excellent account, see Peder Stiansen, *History of the Baptists in Norway* (Chicago, 1933); also Peterson, *Missions in Europe,* pp. 18-19; Rushbrooke, *op. cit.,* pp. 133, 136.

stadt, as other believers watched from the shore. This became the first center of Baptist work in Finland. For several years it was associated with the Swedish Mission, but its growing importance caused it in time to be given a separate place in the reports and appropriations of the Missionary Union. By 1900 a Conference of Swedish-speaking Finns was organized. In 1911 its constituency numbered 29 churches with 1,992 members. There were 21 full-time pastors, and 40 part time. In 1905 a Conference of Finns proper was organized; by 1917 it totaled 25 churches. Although persecution was negligible in Finland, the lack of education and the emotional instability of the people weakened their influence. Financial assistance came in the main from Swedish and British Baptists.[16]

The Witness in the Russian Empire

Although Baptist work began in the Russian-dominated Baltic Countries—Lithuania, Latvia, Estonia, and Poland—before it did in Russia proper, there was little direct contact with the American Baptist Missionary Union until after 1914. Suffice it here, therefore, to note certain facts—that the first Baptist church in Lithuania was established in 1841 in Memel under the guidance of Oncken; the first baptisms on Latvian soil were held secretly on a night in September, 1861, when seventy-two believers were baptized as the result of the witness of Jakobsohn, a young ship's carpenter who had been influenced by German Baptists at Libau. Nine Esthonians were baptized on February 11, 1884, at Hapsal by the German pastor of a Baptist church in St. Petersburg, Russia. Although German Baptists carried on missionary work in Poland as early as the middle of the nineteenth century, the greater number of organized Baptist churches came into existence after the Edict of Toleration was issued in 1905 by the Russian Czar.[17]

Work in Russia proper was undertaken as early as 1851 by German Baptists on behalf of their fellow countrymen who had settled

---

[16] Peterson, *Missions in Europe,* pp. 19-20; *The Baptist Missionary Magazine,* Vol. 49, No. 1 (Jan., 1869), p. 26; No. 6 (June, 1869), pp. 176-79; Vol. 50, No. 7 (July, 1870), pp. 282-85; J. H. Rushbrooke, *Some Chapters of European Baptist History* (London, 1929), pp. 34-35; *Proceedings of the B.W.C.,* 1911, p. 42.

[17] That American Baptists took an interest in the work being conducted by European Baptists in these countries is evident from the frequent mention of them in *The Baptist Missionary Magazine.*

in the south of Russia. But the hostile policy of the Russian Government prevented the building of a Baptist meeting house until 1872. This effort was carried on in direct connection with the German Baptist Mission until 1884, when the Baptists in Russia withdrew from the German Baptist Conference and formed the Russian Baptist Union. Their action was prompted by regulations of the government that forbade religious work to be carried on in Russia in the name of foreign organizations. Since that time, appropriations made by the American Baptist Missionary Union for Russian work were separated from those made to the German Mission.

By 1910 the Russian Baptist Union was comprised of 159 churches of the five associations on the western border of the empire. Two of the associations were among the Lithuanians and Estonians of the Baltic Provinces. The three others were composed chiefly of German-speaking churches in west and south Russia. Its leading spirits were Basil Pavlov and Michael Ratushny. After 1905, when religious toleration was granted, the churches of native Russians, most of whom had come out from the Orthodox Church, formed themselves into the Union of Russian Baptist Churches. Its leader was Ivan Prokhanov, who differed with the larger Russian Baptist Union in interpreting Baptist principles. Moreover, his followers represented a different cultural stratum of society, being principally "the well-to-do peasants and Cossacks in the country and small shop-keepers and independent artisans in the towns." [18]

The prospects of Baptist advance in Russia, once the ban on religious toleration had been lifted, resulted in scores of new churches springing up in southern Russia, Russian Poland, Hungary, and Roumania. The deep dissatisfaction with the Orthodox Church felt by many in Russia and her satellites was evident in this trend, once the fear of persecution was removed. Impressed by these developments, the officials of the American Baptist Missionary Union voted in 1906 to give assistance to Baptist work in Russia.[19] The progress made in the years that followed justified their decision, for by 1914 there were 97,000 Baptists reported in the Russian Baptist Union and 8,472 in the Union of Russian Baptist Churches.

---

[18] Serge Bolshakoff, *Russian Nonconformity* (Philadelphia, 1950), p. 120. See also Peterson, *Missions in Europe,* pp. 20-21.

[19] Peterson, *op. cit.,* pp. 21-22; *Reports of A.B.M.U.* for 1906, pp. 418, 426.

Baptist Mission in Greece

The efforts of Baptist missionaries to conduct evangelistic work in Greece beginning in 1836 met with stern resistance throughout the entire history of the mission there. This was not surprising in a country where the Greek Orthodox Church prevailed. The chief means utilized in the evangelizing of the people were distribution of tracts, preaching, and the maintenance of schools for children. A revolution in 1843 won for the Greeks a new constitution which provided for religious toleration, but not the right of minorities to proselyte or interfere with the prevailing religion. This was the situation when the American Baptist Missionary Union faced financial embarrassment in 1845. A resolution to discontinue the mission as soon as possible was delayed in being put into operation only by the pleading of the workers on the field at Corfu and Piraeus.

The revolutions of 1848 on the continent did not precipitate an overthrow of political institutions within Greece, but they did serve as a check on the exercise of arbitrary power and they helped to spread more liberal views concerning political and religious rights. Hence Rufus Buell could write from Piraeus appreciatively of the favorable effect of the revolutions upon the government in Greece.[20]

In October, 1851, Albert N. Arnold moved the mission station at Corfu to Athens to be closer to Buell at Piraeus, the port-city of the Grecian capital, and also to establish a strategic contact in the cultural center of the nation. When Dr. Solomon Peck visited Greece on his famous deputation trip to the Missionary Union's fields in 1853, he was impressed favorably and urged a continuance of the mission there in spite of the discouragements. In the same year a chapel was opened in Athens. The work, however, did not prove enduring. By 1857 the mission in Greece was without workers, the Americans having returned home and Demetrius Z. Sakellarios, a native printer and Buel's assistant, having given up the work. Until 1871 the enterprise was suspended. Then the Board appointed Sakellarios, who just had completed his seminary course at Newton Theological Institution in Massachusetts, to be its missionary at Athens. This was a move that also was to end in failure, for by 1886 the Missionary Union finally discontinued its mission to Greece.[21]

---

[20] *The Baptist Missionary Magazine,* Vol. 29, No. 2 (Feb., 1849), pp. 58-59.

[21] *Ibid.,* Vol. 32, No. 7 (July, 1852), pp. 292-93; Vol. 33, No. 3 (March, 1853), pp. 65-72; Vol. 34, No. 3 (March, 1854), pp. 86, 89; Vol. 51, No. 5 (May, 1871), p. 142.

Mission in Spain

An equally difficult field was Spain where the Roman Catholic influence was strongly entrenched. Convinced that the religious life of the country was lacking in evangelical warmth and zeal, Dr. William J. Knapp, who had been for a time professor of Modern Languages in Vassar College, established in 1869 an independent missionary work in Madrid. The next year he requested and was granted appointment by the American Baptist Missionary Union. About the same time a second missionary was appointed, the Reverend John W. Terry, but he remained only a few months. In spite of the limitations of these beginnings, eighteen were baptized in 1870 and on August 10 of that year the first Baptist church in Madrid was organized with thirty-three members. The congregation employed two evangelists and two teachers for the schools it maintained respectively for boys and for girls. A second church was established at Valencia in 1871, and the nucleus of a third at Alicante. About the same time a number of converts were won in Portugal. By 1874 there were altogether four churches in Spain with four native pastors and an aggregate membership of 244. When Knapp returned to America in 1876 to become eventually a professor in Yale College, the work was continued entirely by Spanish leadership.

In 1885 the Missionary Union had but one representative in Spain, the Reverend Eric Lund, of Sweden, who began a work at Barcelona, in the northeastern part of the country. From that time Barcelona became the headquarters of the Baptist Mission in Spain. It served as the center for publication of tracts and the distribution of the Scriptures. In 1886 Lund was joined by the Reverend Manuel C. Marin, a native of Spain who had received training at Colby College and Newton Theological Institution in America. Together, they conducted evangelistic meetings in the villages, organizing small, independent churches under the leadership of one of the village people designated by the missionaries for the task. Although their efforts met with considerable success, opposition from the Roman Catholic priests was sufficiently strong to prompt the Missionary Union to consider discontinuing the Mission just before the outbreak of the Spanish-American War in 1898. Lund's urging dissuaded them. In the meantime, he and a young Filipino, Braulio Manikan, who had come to Spain to study civil engineering and had been converted, began to think in terms of a Baptist witness in the Philippine Islands.

Their vision took form when the Missionary Union appointed them for service in the new mission being opened there in 1900, following upon the accession of the Islands by the United States from Spain.[22]

From this cursory survey of the spread of the Baptist witness in Europe, it becomes evident that it was at times a most discouraging task. Yet, wherever a work was begun there were conversions and many who gladly paid a heavy price to hear the gospel that liberates from fear and oppression. The most successful areas were Germany, Sweden, and possibly Russia. Between 1832, when the first work in Europe was undertaken by the American Baptist Missionary Union in France, and 1914, the number of Baptists on the continent grew from virtually none to 138,291 who were organized in 1,173 churches.[23] It was a rewarding record for the Union after 80 years of guiding and encouraging a nationally directed work in many different countries and among people of varying cultures. While most of the Baptist churches in Europe asked only for sympathy and a slight degree of co-operation from the Missionary Union, it was that continuing and unfailing response that made the difference between success and failure, and sometimes even between survival and extinction of the Baptist witness in Europe.

---

[22] Peterson, *Missions in Europe,* pp. 28-30; *The Baptist Missionary Magazine,* Vol. 50, No. 10 (Oct., 1870), pp. 369-70, 383-85; No. 12 (Dec., 1870), pp. 448-49.

[23] *Missions,* Vol. 5, No. 1 (Jan., 1914), p. 73.

CHAPTER XXI

Appraisal of a Century

FACING a flag-festooned platform, a large company of American Baptists were gathered in Tremont Temple, Boston, to commemorate one hundred years of missionary service. The time was June 24-25, 1914. A large picture of Adoniram Judson was the focal point of attention as it hung above the platform in the center of a large banner on which were the words: The Judson Centennial. It was a memorable occasion, and the reports and addresses which were prepared for publication following those days of celebration provide an impressive testimonial to the significance of the event not only to Baptists, but to American Protestantism. For American Baptists had been among the pioneers of foreign missions just a century before. Their record had been in recent years impressive for co-operation with other Protestant groups. Moreover, Baptist successes in Burma, South India, and the Congo stood out as shining lights on the map of Protestant world missions. The centennial rightly called for commemoration, thanksgiving, and appraisal. A great century of missionary enterprise was past, and American Baptists stood on the threshold of an exciting new era, the nature of which few could even glimpse on those warm summer days just prior to the terrifying opening of the First World War.

Highlights of a Century

For twenty years after the organization of the Triennial Convention on May 21, 1814, foundations were laid slowly in Burma against intense government opposition. By 1833 there were three important centers—Rangoon, Moulmein, and Tavoy, with outposts at Mergui, Amherst, and in Arracan. There were in the country at the time twenty-two missionaries and 371 church members. From 1833 to

1838 was a period of marked enthusiasm at home. The Richmond Convention in 1835 voted, it will be recalled, "to establish new missions in every unoccupied place where there may be a reasonable prospect of success." [1] The results were seen before long in new work begun in Siam (1833) which spread eventually to China; in reinforcements of fifteen missionaries to Burma (1834); in a new mission to the Telugus in South India (1834); in an entrance into Assam by way of Sadiya (1836); in the opening of the Bengal-Orissa Mission by American Free Baptists (1838); in expansion in Europe to include Germany, Denmark, and Greece besides France; and in an unsuccessful effort in Haiti (1834–37).

Then came the time of testing that began with the schism of 1845. With problems of reorganization, the pressure of the American Civil War, and postwar adjustments, it was not until 1872 that another wave of advance carried the Baptist Mission forward. This new thrust included the opening of the Japan Mission in 1872, the taking over of the seven stations and twenty missionaries of the Livingstone Inland Mission in Belgian Congo in 1884, and the commencing of work on the Island of Panay in the Philippines in 1900. During this period, the problems at home were numerous, falling as we have seen into three distinct phases: a period of trial and error both on the field and at home (1846–1866), a period of progress (1866–1893), and an era of transition (1893–1913).

By 1914 the American Baptist Foreign Mission Society was able to report 700 missionaries "actively engaged in the work, either actually on the field or at home for needed furlough." [2] Annual contributions had increased from a little over $1,000 in 1813 to more than $1,000,000 in 1913, which included the receipts of the Woman's Foreign Missionary Societies. During the 100 years of mission service, American Baptists had contributed to the Union $31,000,000.[3]

The achievements over a century had been notable. The number of distinct mission fields was 11, on which 127 main stations had been established, which represented an average of 11 or 12 stations for each mission. These stations were central posts of leadership occupied by a permanent missionary staff of usually two or more per-

[1] Howard B. Grose and Fred P. Haggard, *The Judson Centennial, 1814–1914* (Philadelphia, 1914), p. 4. Statistical data in this section are drawn from pp. 3-10 of this volume.

[2] *Ibid.*, p. 5.

[3] *Ibid.*, p. 205.

sons. Burma and South India led with 23 and 29 stations respectively. In addition, there were 2,975 outstations which were permanently occupied by native preachers or teachers, or which were visited periodically by missionaries or their native associates.

For the work of evangelism, 6,106 nationals were engaged, of which 2,395 were preachers and Bible-women, while many were teacher-evangelists in village schools. A total of at least 308,000 converts had been baptized in 100 years of work, which represented the labors of missionaries and their associates. Membership of the churches on these mission fields in 1914 numbered over 166,000. With the 140,000 Baptists in Europe, the total membership was 306,000. The grand total of baptisms during the entire century for non-Christian lands and Europe amounted to 585,000.

Although the tension between evangelism and education was always present, most missionaries, to a greater or less degree, realized the value of educational work. We have noted how educational work as a part of missionary outreach was discouraged by the Deputation of 1853, and how many mission schools were thereafter discontinued in Burma and South India. We have seen also how some of the missionaries to the Karens actually withdrew from the Union for a time to maintain their schools. Baptists were not alone in facing this problem. The American Board of Commissioners (Congregational) passed through a similar conflict about the same time, but reacted in favor of educational work more quickly than the Baptists. The greatest strides in education among Baptists were taken in the latter years of the century in developing secondary schools and even college work (at Rangoon and Shanghai). Especially was this trend noticeable in Burma, China, and the Philippines. It was apparent to a lesser degree in South India, Japan, Assam, and Bengal-Orissa. Education received its greatest impetus and strengthening about 1912, following the adoption of the intensive policy.

Medical missions emerged even more slowly and received recognition almost begrudgingly. There again, the fear that evangelism might be supplanted from its primary place explains the reticence of the Missionary Union in this respect. Nevertheless, in the last third of the century it was possible to observe the development of dispensaries, hospitals, and nurses' training schools under the direction of able doctors, both men and women. Much credit is due the Woman's Foreign Missionary Societies for pioneering work in this field of medical missions. By the close of the century (1913) the Missionary Union was supporting 58 medical missionaries, 27 hospitals, 57 dispensaries, and treating over 6,000 in-patients and more than 94,000 out-patients within a single year. In China the Society was co-operating in union medical schools.[4]

Certainly another significant accomplishment of the century was the translation and circulation of the entire Bible in three languages of Burma, in Assamese, in Telugu, in Japanese, in two or three Chinese dialects, and in the Panayan language of the Philippines. Lesser portions of the Scriptures were distributed in varying dialects and languages of the hill tribes in Burma and Assam, and of the Bantus in the Belgian Congo.

A further achievement was the establishment of self-governing local churches. In 1914 there were in non-Christian lands 1,575 organized Baptist churches, of which 908 were self-supporting. In these Christian communities nationals received training in a democratic way of life which developed initiative and leadership among peoples, many of whom were the depressed and forgotten classes of society.

An Appraisal

As one seeks to appraise the work of a century, he becomes first of all aware of a gradual change in missionary methods. The early missionaries relied greatly upon distribution of printed tracts and portions of the Scriptures. In Burma, the *zayat,* a native gathering place for rest and conversation, was used widely by Judson and his successors. The ever-restless missionaries, eager to carry the gospel into untouched communities, placed increasing emphasis upon preaching in the villages which were scattered along the streams and rivers and on into the hills beyond the lowlands. This was the pattern that was favored in the early years by the Board in America and by many of the missionaries. It was deemed inadvisable for several missionaries to gather at a single station, even though it be a fairly large community like Moulmein. The scattering of the mission staff was regarded as the wisest use to which the limited leadership could be put. By many this might be viewed today as a mistaken strategy, since each missionary was left thereby with full responsibility for all phases of work to be done at each station. Specialization of duties

---

[4] Thomas S. Barbour, *A Contribution to Christian Missions* (New York, 1914), p. 18.

was almost impossible, although missionary wives and single women were relied upon for teaching in the schools. Yet, the result of this plan was frequently to leave a station in the complete charge of one or at best two women when the men were called away or removed by illness or furlough. On the other hand, much is to be said for the courageous zeal that impelled the missionaries ever on and out into new territories, cost what it might. Perhaps, however, a greater attention to the development of schools to train national leadership in the early years might have had rich results in strengthening the young churches and in exerting a greater impact upon the pagan culture of the country.

After the serious setback to education which resulted from the policies adopted by the Board in the middle of the nineteenth century, education came to have an ever greater place of importance in later years. Schools were developed on an enlarging scale partly as an evangelistic effort and partly to train Christian leadership. Then, as we have seen, medical missions and an emphasis upon agricultural and industrial training became an accepted part of the program. The latter emphases were justified at many stations, and particularly in South India and later in the Congo and the Philippines, as a means of partial self-support for pupils in school, but also as a means of lifting the level of livelihood for the struggling Christian communities just emerging from poverty and near-starvation.

Any fair appraisal of missionary methods must take into account also the acceptance in South India in particular of the principle of mass movements toward Christianity, when the Telugus were admitted in great numbers by Dr. John E. Clough. It should be admitted at once that Clough made every effort to screen carefully the candidates for admission to the Christian community by believer's baptism. However, there are some today who, looking back upon the period of great revivals, feel that many who came into the church under such circumstances had made only a superficial commitment to Christ. This criticism has been levelled especially against the great ingatherings among the hill tribes in Upper Burma in the early years of the twentieth century. Certainly, a reading of the journals of the missionaries responsible for these areas indicates that deep sincerity and soul-searching were exercised on their part. In many cases, particularly in the Philippines, there was the tendency to withhold baptism from converts out of fear of their making hasty or superficial decisions. Certainly something is to be said on both sides of the argument. On the whole, the Baptist emphasis upon a regenerate church and believer's (or adult) baptism served as a deterring force when masses began to move too quickly into the Christian church.

During the century of American Baptist missions under review, new forces became important factors in the work of the missionaries on the various fields. The rise of English military and political might in Burma and India played an important part in Baptist missionary work in those countries. It is very apparent that most of the missionaries developed an increasing reliance upon the protection and stability which British rule gave to the mission activities. Partly as a reaction against this close correlation between the Christian missions and imperial power in Far Eastern countries, antiforeign outbursts took place in China in the later years of the nineteenth century and during the early years of the twentieth century. They were expressive of a general resentment against Western exploitation rather than against Christianity as such, yet it was not always easy, in their thinking or in their emotional attitudes, for nationals to separate the two. This was a problem which was to become greatly accentuated in the years following the First World War.

At home new and virile movements within American Christianity were affecting favorably the missionary enterprise. One was the emergence of women into a leading role in the mission work of the church, with their special concern for educational and medical service to women and children in foreign lands. Another trend was the outpouring of student life into Christian missions after 1886 when the Student Volunteer Movement arose at Mount Hermon under Dwight L. Moody's leadership. With the able guidance of John R. Mott and Robert P. Wilder, and other youth leaders of the time, fresh energies were directed into every denomination which was engaged in a missionary outreach.

A third phenomenon to influence Baptist work in particular was the organization of the Northern Baptist Convention in 1907, which brought to the Mission Societies pressures from laymen to reorganize their structure for greater efficiency. At the same time, the new denominational pattern began to develop a sense of responsibility on the part of the churches for support of foreign missions which had been carried heretofore almost exclusively by individuals thoroughly committed to this task of the Christian community.

By the close of the nineteenth century there was developing a new concept of missions which was just beginning to express itself in the thinking of foreign society secretaries and thoughtful missionaries. Without rejecting the earlier impulse which stemmed from a conviction that people without Christ and his gospel were lost in their sins, there were many, as we have indicated in an earlier chapter, who began to justify missions on the more positive basis of the remedy which the gospel offered for people living in fear and hopelessness because of their spiritual darkness. Greater attention was given to studying the religious life and cultural patterns of the people to be served. There was less of an acceptance of the idea that Western culture was superior to Eastern cultures. Attempts were seriously made to avoid associating the gospel with Western civilization. Closely allied to this thinking, but not foreign to the philosophy of many earlier pioneer missionaries, like Clough and Abbott, was the determined objective of developing an indigenous church which would be self-governing, self-supporting, and self-propagating. Although the implementation of this basic philosophy of mission work came slowly on some fields, by 1914 it was the adopted policy of the Societies. Also closely related to the new thinking about the mission of the church was a growing tolerance toward interdenominational co-operation on the fields and even at home in certain areas. This was a trend which was to develop appreciably in the years after 1914.

The major change which the missionary enterprise underwent is perhaps most clearly and succinctly expressed in the descriptive words of a great church historian:

> Nineteenth century Christian missions were largely a paternalistic enterprise, a kind of spiritual imperialism. It was a benevolent imperialism, but it was imperialism. Not until the twentieth century did there come a decided change.[5]

The changes which began to manifest themselves in those early years and which were to develop in the period after 1914 may be summarized briefly here. First, there was a greater emphasis upon the intensive development of fields already in existence instead of expanding the mission to include new fields. Second, more stress was placed upon institutional work—schools, hospitals, agricultural and

[5] Kenneth Scott Latourette, *The Great Century in Europe and the United States of America, 1800–1914,* Vol. 4 of *A History of the Expansion of Christianity* (New York, 1941), p. 52.

industrial missions—all of which were intended to elevate the standard of life of the people. Third, there was a conscious effort to separate western civilization from the gospel. Fourth, greater specialization was encouraged among missionaries, which in turn necessitated more educational preparation. Fifth, a more efficient organizational structure was developed both at home and on the field. This was evident in the establishment of the Conference of Missionaries on each field with its Reference Committee and Mission Secretary. Sixth, wherever possible, increasing interdenominational co-operation was taking place in educational and medical work. Seventh, there began to emerge, with the organization of the Northern Baptist Convention, a more responsible church relationship and support of the denomination as a whole to the Baptist World Mission.

No appraisal of this great century of missionary advance would be complete without recording the channels of influence through which the Baptist minorities in country after country made their Christian impact upon pagan cultures. First, there was the reduction of many languages to writing. Second, there was the translation of the Scriptures into numerous languages and dialects. A third channel was comprised of schools, hospitals, and medical education which created abroad the nursing profession, promoted personal and public health, and helped to prevent famines and epidemics. A fourth avenue of influence was to be found in the churches which became the training ground for democratic expression and the development of leadership among peoples, many of whom hitherto had enjoyed no opportunity for taking a place of importance in society. Finally, national Christians arose to positions of leadership within their respective countries, making their Christian witness felt in various areas of life. Indeed, the manner in which the Christian message permeated the masses of plain people was truly remarkable. It motivated them to contribute to the propagation of their faith without thought of personal reward or gain for their country. There could be no more convincing evidence of the transforming power of the gospel.

PART 3 MATURING THROUGH TRIAL (1914–1954)

CHAPTER XXII

The New Era in Prospect

THE ASSASSINATION of the Archduke Francis Ferdinand in a relatively obscure town in Serbia on a June day in 1914 precipitated the war which was to break up old patterns and develop new and sometimes terrifying ones in a crucible of conflict. In a very real sense, therefore, the First World War ushered in a new era which made its impact upon all areas of life. The worldwide hostilities set in motion forces which eventually brought to an end the older imperialism which had raised Western Europe to a position of world ascendancy over a period of three exciting centuries of colonial expansion. The war also speeded up processes of industry and stimulated the development of new means of transportation which introduced a new way of living for millions. The democratic ideals which were presented as the reason for Allied participation in the great struggle evoked among subjugated and subservient peoples an unquenchable resolve to become free. At the same time, the devastation and displacements of war spread discontent and poverty. A disrupted postwar economy catapulted entire nations into severe depression and hysteria. The pall of insecurity and want gave rise in the twenties and thirties to new experiments in economic and political life, such as communism, fascism, nazism, and the social welfare state.

Because a new world was being fashioned by the forces of world revolution during the decades following 1914, it is the First World War rather than the organization of the Northern Baptist Convention (1907) which most plausibly may be made the point of division between Part Two and Part Three of our story. For the missionary enterprise of the churches was related so closely to world affairs that it was affected often more seriously by forces external to organized Christianity than by the factors inherent within itself. To understand, therefore, the impact of this tumultuous half century upon American Baptist missions in particular, we shall survey briefly the leading trends that were most significant in their effect upon church life at home and abroad.

Trends in the World at Large [1]

A most obvious feature of the period since 1914 is the prevalence of war on a global scale. The holocaust which broke upon the world during the course of the First World War terrified nations for a brief time into a crusade to end all wars through the League of Nations and through feeble efforts at disarmament. It was a noble attempt which ended in bitter disillusionment when it became evident in the thirties that the inequities of the peace settlements were leading to a renewal of conflict. The Second World War was far wider in scope than the first, deeper in its impact upon entire populations, and more ghastly in its destructive power. Once again, men began to plan for international responsibility which would eliminate war, this time through the United Nations. No sooner, however, had the organizational meeting at San Francisco closed in 1945 than the fearful fact became clear that the world had not truly moved beyond a war era, but was only caught in an uneasy truce. After 1947 the tension of universal fear was fed by a "cold war" between the United States and Soviet Russia, and by actual fighting in Indo-China and Korea for varying lengths of time.

The impoverishment of Western Europe as the result of two wars within fifty years plus colonial uprisings issued in a debilitating war-weariness and a decline in Europe's political and economic control. This shattered state of affairs became the signal for the revolts of peoples who had been dominated by European colonialism—first in British India, then in the Dutch East Indies, and later in French

---

[1] The author is indebted to Kenneth Scott Latourette's analysis in *The Christian World Mission in Our Day* (New York, 1954), chap. 3.

Indo-China. In such circumstances it is understandable that a wave of pessimism prevailed in Europe during these years, a mood which was in marked contrast to the easy optimism of the nineteenth century. This outlook reflected itself in the theological thought of the continent to the extent that the idealistic humanism of the liberal era gave way in the thirties and forties to a return to the traditional Christian view of man and sin under the judgment of God but capable of being redeemed by Jesus Christ.

Strangely enough, in recent years an air of hopefulness has been dominant in several other parts of the world. This has been especially true in those countries where Western rule has been thrown off. India, Pakistan, and Burma, for example, began to regard their future optimistically once independence from the Western powers had been achieved. Even Communist China, although under the influence of Soviet Russia, heralded the new order of the People's Republic with enthusiasm. On the other hand, deeply inherent within the social revolution through which Asia was passing was a fear that Western control might be renewed. It was for this reason that "foreign missionary *control*" and "the continued *dependence* of Asian Christians on foreign assistance" were resisted stoutly by Asiatic governments.[2]

Still another feature which has characterized the first half of the twentieth century has been the prevalence of revolutions which have swept away the ruling houses of the last century—the Romanovs in Russia, the Hapsburgs in Austria-Hungary, the Hohenzollerns in Germany, the Savoys in Italy, the Manchus in China, and independent princes in non-British India. In addition, there have been industrial and cultural revolutions in Russia, China, and Africa which exerted an influence upon other parts of the world as well. These have been accompanied by a hunger for bread on the part of the masses, and a restlessness for security and self-determinism. Communism has sought to capitalize on this restlessness to advance its world crusade to be accepted as the new way of life. Symbolizing the tension between the traditional outlook of the West and the new points of view has been the mounting struggle between the United States and Soviet Russia. This ideological conflict is between Anglo-Saxon democracy on the one hand and the communism of Marx and Lenin greatly modified by Stalin on the other.

---

[2] Paul D. Devanandan, "Asian Churches Look to Evanston," *The Christian Century*, Vol. 71, No. 29 (July 21, 1954), pp. 872-73.

Accompanying these revolutions and the break-up of old empires, and the intensifying of tensions, is the recession of white supremacy in the face of a rising demand by the peoples of color to gain prestige and favor in proportion to their numbers. Whether the power of the Christian gospel will be strong enough within the ranks of its adherents to resolve these tensions by helping to achieve justice and freedom for all remains to be seen.

Within the United States during this period, there has been a reflection of these forces, modified or complicated, as the case may be, by internal factors. For example, the severity of the impact of two world wars on the American people was cushioned in part by their vast resources of wealth and technical skills. These resources and skills made for a degree of prosperity which carried the United States through its deepest economic depression (1929–39). Even in the midst of the depression, except for a brief period, a spirit of optimism prevailed. This reflected itself in church life to an amazing degree. After both wars, major denominations entered upon ambitious crusades for reconstruction and missionary advance. While all religious faiths of mankind have been affected by the tumultuous changes since 1914, Christianity has displayed more vigor than the others, and has continued "the amazing geographic spread which marked the world of yesterday." [3] This has been particularly true of the churches in the United States where greater prosperity has combined with an optimistic mood to take the initiative in world missions.

Developments in the Christian Scene

One of the most significant developments within American Protestantism during the early years of the twentieth century was the Laymen's Missionary Movement. It came into existence on November 15, 1906, as an interdenominational effort to support missions. This was near the one-hundredth anniversary of the launching of the American foreign missionary enterprise under the auspices of the American Board of Commissioners for Foreign Missions. The Haystack Prayer Meeting, which gave the effective impulse to that enterprise, had occurred about 1806, although the date is debatable. The stimulus of this new Laymen's Missionary Movement resulted in a great increase in missionary giving. By 1924 the total contributions

[3] Latourette, *The Christian World Mission in Our Day*, p. 71.

received by mission boards in the United States and Canada amounted to $45,272,293 as compared with $8,980,488 received in 1906. During the same period, the number of North American Protestant missionaries increased from 5,708 to 16,754.[4] Undoubtedly the laymen's efforts had been inspired by the enthusiasm of the Student Volunteer Movement. Since its organization in 1886, it had provided the main source for the recruitment of mission staffs.

To be sure, the picture had its darker side as well. The Interchurch World Movement which was launched immediately after World War I proved to be only partially successful. Several reasons have been given for the limited results achieved. There appears to have been too little effort to select top leaders adequate for the task. The motivation in publicity was lacking in complete selflessness. Mission boards were quick to underwrite the effort on the basis of bank-loans. Thus, when the Movement failed, many boards were left in debt. Yet some good came from the effort, for it publicized a degree of unity among Protestants hitherto unheralded. Moreover, the surveys made in the campaign proved to be helpful resources for later fund-raising.[5]

In the late twenties missionary giving declined greatly, due to a number of factors: higher taxation, an increased standard of living at home even to the point of extravagance, weariness of financial drives during the war, inadequate methods of raising money, depression, and perhaps more important than was realized at the time, a diminishing sense of mission.[6] This declining enthusiasm for missions was due in part to a changing view of the task of the church and its relationship to non-Christian religions. During the first few decades of the century, the attitude of many thoughtful students had been influenced by scholarly studies which were being made of these other religions. They came to discover elements of value in them which they at once viewed as points of contact which Christianity should make. In other words, many came to view the task of Christian missions as providing the complement needed to complete the inadequacies of non-Christian religions, rather than as providing the

---

[4] John R. Mott, *Five Decades and a Forward View* (New York, 1939), p. 41.

[5] *Ibid.*, pp. 64-66.

[6] *Ibid.*, pp. 67-70, 83. During the Depression, the contraction of the work of mission boards ranged all the way from 30 to 60 per cent or more.

unique revelation of God to displace the erroneous religions of other peoples.

The Laymen's Missionary Inquiry, which was launched by an interdenominational group of American business men in 1930, dramatized this transition of thought concerning the missionary task of the church. The project was initiated by generous supporters of missions, many of whom had backed the Laymen's Movement. It was intended to discover the most effective approach of Christianity to non-Christian faiths. Accordingly, a survey was made of the work of American church mission boards in India, Burma, China, and Japan. The report which was published in 1932 in several volumes aroused a storm of protest from nearly all mission boards and missionaries. Although the Inquiry gave general endorsement to the mission program, it attacked the underlying presuppositions of the traditional missionary objective. Not only did it call attention to what were regarded as inefficiencies in missionary administration on the fields, but it criticized the strong evangelistic impulse which was the primary motivation for virtually all missions. The Report stressed the importance of co-operation with national cultures and religions rather than displacement of them. The task of the missionary was viewed as that of strengthening the older non-Christian religions by sharing the deepest insights of Christianity. The title of the popular summary volume, *Rethinking Missions,* pointed up the revolutionary character of the Report.

The most effective reply to the new point of view came not from America but from Europe. It was Professor Hendrik Kraemer's *The Christian Message in the Non-Christian World,* a volume prepared for the Madras Conference of the International Missionary Council in Madras, India, in 1938. Kraemer's view was that the Christian message is a unique revelation designed by God to displace other religions by an indigenous Christian church. He opposed the premise that Christianity has much in common with non-Christian faiths. His influence greatly weakened the more liberal concept of missions. By 1952 the Laymen's Inquiry had been virtually rejected as had been the theological suppositions upon which it was based. It called forth a severe appraisal from one historian:

> The Laymen's Inquiry was born out of a genuine Christian concern, but the majority of the appraisers were not sufficiently grounded in a personal knowledge of missions, the categories

employed were humanistic, and the missionaries themselves were ignored in the processes of the inquiry.[7]

Perhaps the most formative influence in this period was the rise of what has come to be called the ecumenical movement. This movement arose almost inevitably out of the missionary enterprise itself. The first World Missionary Conference was held at Edinburgh in 1910. It was the outgrowth and climax of a number of earlier gatherings held in England and America beginning as far back as 1854. A later expression of the same movement was the formation in 1893 of the Foreign Missions Conference of North America. Under the stimulus of the ecumenical interest, many other national missionary councils and national Christian councils came into being. In this connection it is interesting to note that the concept of interdenominational co-operation in world missions went back to a proposal of William Carey that a world missionary conference be held at Capetown, South Africa, in 1810. It was a full century before his proposal was acted on and the Edinburgh Conference of 1910 was convened. But once the movement got under way, it soon gathered momentum. The Edinburgh Conference, which was predominantly Anglo-American, set in motion a chain of events on mission fields which accomplished miracles in the strengthening of indigenous churches.

From October, 1912, to May, 1913, John R. Mott conducted a series of eighteen regional and three national conferences in Ceylon, India, Burma, Malaya, China, Korea, and Japan. As a consequence, the India National Conference recommended a plan for the formation of provincial representative councils of missions and of national missionary councils to be composed of delegates from the provincial bodies. The China Conference made specific proposals for greater co-operation in higher education, in theological instruction, in the production of Christian literature, and in reciprocal recognition of church discipline. In Japan the Conference did not go as far, although it favored the formation of a Christian university for the entire country and a first-class Christian college for women. In both countries, the Conferences helped to give new direction to denomina-

---

[7] R. Pierce Beaver, "North American Thought on the Fundamental Principles of Missions During the Twentieth Century," *Church History,* Vol. 21, No. 4 (Dec., 1952), p. 349. See also David G. Moses, "Christianity and the Non-Christian Religions," *The International Review of Missions,* Vol. 43, No. 170 (April, 1954).

tional mission policy for most of the major foreign mission agencies, including the two American Baptist Foreign Mission Societies.

The cause of interdenominational missionary effort was strengthened also in 1912 by the launching of *The International Review of Missions,* a quarterly dedicated to the discussion of major problems and issues involved in the spread of the gospel to non-Christian peoples. This quarterly almost from its beginning has been the journal of the International Missionary Council.

Although the First World War interrupted plans for another comprehensive missionary council, British and North American missionary agencies formed in 1918 the Emergency Committee of Co-operating Missions as a means of assisting the work of German Christians in particular. By October, 1921, co-operation had extended to the point that sixty-one representatives of mission boards from fourteen different countries chiefly from the West met at Lake Mohonk, New York, to organize the International Missionary Council. John R. Mott was chosen chairman and J. H. Oldham and A. L. Warnshuis, secretaries for London and New York offices respectively. The new Council was to meet every two years. Under its auspices a number of significant general missionary conferences were held, the first at Jerusalem in 1928, where the relations between the younger and older churches and the threat of secularism were recognized as major problems. The second was held at Tambaram, a small town near Madras, India, in 1938. There the leadership of the younger churches was clearly in evidence, and much emphasis was placed upon a study of the church in its relation to the task of world missions. In many respects the Madras Conference ushered in a new era of missionary co-operation.

During the Second World War, the International Missionary Council set up financial aid for "orphaned missions" of nations at war with Great Britain and the United States. In July, 1947, soon after the cessation of hostilities, the Council held an international meeting at Whitby in Ontario, Canada. There the delegates declared that all Christians of the older and younger churches are committed to be "partners in obedience to the Great Commission." Co-operation was stressed between the International Missionary Council and the World Council of Churches, which had been in existence under a provisional constitution since 1938 and which was to be formally and permanently constituted at Amsterdam in 1948. The next meeting of the Council was at Willingen, Germany, in 1952. "The church under the cross" provided the sobering theme as Christians from all parts of the world faced up to the hostile forces which were challenging the expansion of Christianity—a vigorous communism, an awakened nationalism in Asiatic countries, secularism, the ever-present problem of a fragmented Christianity, and the resurgence of life in the older religions of Buddhism, Hinduism, and Mohammedanism.

In the meantime there was increasing evidence of co-operation among Christians in the lands of the younger churches. In China, for example, interdenominational co-operation in educational institutions began before 1910, but it mounted steadily after the China Educational Commission, headed by Professor (later President) E. D. Burton of the University of Chicago (an American Baptist), made its survey in 1921–22. As a result most of the Christian colleges and several of the middle schools became union institutions in whose support two or more denominations joined. A National Christian Council included most of the denominations working in China, with the exception of the Lutherans and the Southern Baptists. In 1931 the Council created a National Commission on Religious Education, and in 1932 inaugurated a Five Year Movement to advance Christianity after the destructive anti-foreign, anti-Christian tide of the 1920s. In Japan a National Christian Council was organized in 1922, and early in 1941 the Church of Christ in Japan (or Kyodan) came into existence, partly in response to a desire for Christian unity and partly because of pressure from the state to have one responsible Protestant headquarters in the country. The National Missionary Council of India, Burma, and Ceylon, which was a product of plans issuing from the Edinburgh Conference (1910), was succeeded in 1922 by the National Christian Council of India, Burma, and Ceylon. Within it were regional councils for Burma and Ceylon. In 1949, with the independence of Burma, the Burma Christian Council received full autonomy. The South India United Church, which had been formed in 1908 as a result of the union of Presbyterian, Congregational, and Reformed bodies, became the pattern for similar planning for North India, although by 1954 the Union there had not yet been consummated. The National Christian Council of Thailand (formerly Siam) was organized in 1929.

In 1926 an international missionary conference was held at Le Zoute, Belgium, for interdenominational planning of Protestant work in Africa. Out of it came the International Committee on Christian Literature for Africa, which became a sub-committee of the International Missionary Council. Another result of this co-operative effort was the United Missions in the Copper Belt, in the southern part of the Belgian Congo and in Northern Rhodesia, through which Baptists, Congregationalists, Methodists, and Presbyterians sought to meet jointly the needs of the workers in the mines. All five denominations worked unitedly in the fields of education and social welfare in an attempt to fill the vacuum which the collapse of the African tribal culture had created. They felt that they must do something for those people who had been detached by Western industry and commerce from their traditional way of life.[8]

From this brief survey it is evident that Christianity is becoming rooted among peoples with whom it had no rootage a century and a half before. Protestants are especially active in transferring administration of church life and responsibility for the spread of the gospel to members of the national churches abroad. More and more the hymns, art forms, architecture, and organization of the Christian communions are manifesting the recession of western cultural patterns in favor of the Oriental. Indeed, the influence of Christianity upon mankind as a whole has deepened and widened in the course of the past few decades. This is particularly evident in the concessions which Ghandi made to the teachings of Jesus, although he never forsook his Hindu faith. It is revealed also in the spread of the Christian ideal of peace and brotherhood which motivated in part, at least, the creation of the League of Nations and later of the United Nations.[9]

The spectacular advances which Christianity has made against very great odds since 1914 have been achieved through methods which are a continuation of those of the nineteenth century. Yet the increasing costs and decline in mission staffs in the major denominations have made it more difficult to achieve the mobility to occupy new areas of need than once was possible. Indeed, mission boards

---

[8] There are several accounts of the Ecumenical Movement, the most recent and most complete being *A History of the Ecumenical Movement, 1517–1948,* edited by Ruth Rouse and Stephen Charles Neill (Philadelphia, 1954); see chapter 8 in particular. For an excellent analysis of the Whitby Conference in 1947, see Kenneth Scott Latourette and William Richey Hogg, *Tomorrow Is Here* (New York, 1948).

[9] Latourette, *The Christian World Mission in Our Day,* pp. 87-89.

have been hard-put in recent years to maintain established work, without entering new areas. As the process of transfer of mission responsibilities to nationals continues in non-Christian lands, the existence of large numbers of schools and hospitals presents a serious problem for churches that are not financially prepared to assume their care. In many instances, schools have become secularized because Christian communities have not had adequate leadership or funds necessary to maintain a distinctly Christian witness. Such problems call for the re-appraisal of older methods and policies in the face of new needs and situations.[10]

It is against this background that we turn now to a survey of the main developments of the American Baptist mission at home and abroad. The problems which have arisen since 1914 must be viewed, therefore, in the light of the larger world setting. The interaction of forces, religious and non-religious, often complicated issues to the point that a true perspective is all but lost. A retelling of the story may in some measure restore a sense of proportion against which the decisions of the future may be made.

---

[10] Latourette, *op. cit.*, pp. 133-35, 157-58

CHAPTER XXIII

Developments at Home: Progress Under Stress, 1914–1924

AGAINST THE BACKDROP of the trends just described, American Baptists entered upon one of the most trying periods of their history; for war, economic depression, internal conflicts over theology and organizational patterns, and international tensions abroad conspired at times to test their endurance and faith almost to the breaking point. For convenience we may divide the forty year span from 1914 to 1954 into three rather distinct periods: the first marked by a steady growth up to the postwar era of the twenties; the second by a time of financial stress and strain and retrenchment which continued roughly from 1924 to 1947 during a time of worldwide economic depression, internal theological dissension, and widening international tensions; the third by an advance in the face of most disheartening losses at home through controversy and losses abroad through the effects of the Second World War. This chapter will tell only the first part of the story, up to 1924; the next will report the main events from 1924 to 1954.

By way of reminder, it may be well to recall the leading developments in those few hopeful years at the opening of the century that preceded the First World War. The entrance of the United States into the orbit of world imperialism as the result of the Spanish-American War inspired missionary expansion into the Philippines in 1901. The organization of the Northern Baptist Convention in 1907 symbolized the assumption by Baptists in the North of greater denominational responsibility for missions. To a certain extent, this responsibility also involved a transfer of sovereignty formerly possessed solely by the Foreign Mission Societies. Pressures were exerted on the Boards to work for greater efficiency and economy. The budgets of foreign missions were subjected constantly to the expanding needs of a growing denomination whose interests were developing in many directions. By 1924 the appeal of the two foreign mission societies for funds, to some degree at least, had come under the control of the Board of Missionary Cooperation, the Convention's fund-raising agency. The promotional program for foreign missions was geared into that of the denomination as a whole.

The merger of the Free Baptists with the Northern Baptist Convention in 1911 brought another field, Bengal-Orissa, under the direction of the foreign societies. The unusual expansion on older mission fields—in the Kengtung area of northern Burma, in South India and Belgian Congo, and in China and Japan which had come to be known as the "New Orient" in the light of developments in those countries—these all prompted the Northern Baptist Convention in 1912 to recommend that the American Baptist Foreign Mission Society undertake an intensive work instead of entering upon new fields. This decision led to a series of major changes in policy from 1913 on; for the Board of Managers undertook an intensive development of stations which were then in existence and inadequately supported. The strategy was to develop strong Christian communities which would become permanent forces of evangelization. To implement this policy, a program of educational work was developed which was intended to produce a trained leadership adequate to guide an indigenous church. Because of the great cost of institutional work, Baptists undertook in some instances united projects with other denominations. This policy was destined, in the years to come, to produce some dissatisfaction on the field and at home.

Reflecting the enthusiasm of the times, the Convention authorized larger expenditures in those early years of the century than were warranted by the actual receipts collected; consequently a discouraging deficit was built up which necessitated some curtailment by 1914. Then came the war which threatened to envelope the entire globe, and the problems of missions were accentuated by the abnormal conditions which were produced by the events that followed.

The War Years (1914–1918)

Shortly after the outbreak of hostilities in Europe in August, 1914, the Board of Managers of the Foreign Society undertook to enlist Baptists throughout the country in a program of relief for the various missionary agencies in European countries then at war. At the same time a resolution was adopted by the Board in favor of an arbitrated peace and the support of a federation of nations with an international court and police force. The official publication of the society, *Missions,* hastened to repudiate war as a means of settling international disputes.[1]

The war itself was from the beginning somewhat disruptive to mission work. Although the spiritual morale of the American people arose to the point of sacrifice in meeting the emergency needs abroad, the transmission of funds and the transportation of missionaries became ever more difficult. European Baptists felt the debilitating effect of the draft of mission workers into the armed forces. In northern France and Belgium, church property was destroyed. In British India the Society found it necessary to assume responsibility for the care of missionaries of other missions, whose funds had been cut off. The increased cost of living presented a serious problem to missionaries already struggling with limited salaries and work appropriations. The accumulated deficits of the past few years added to the difficulties which the Societies faced in sending out missionary replacements. To counteract the effects of staff curtailment and to carry forward the intensive policy, greater attention was given to the development of schools to train nationals for leadership of the work abroad. To add to the problem, John D. Rockefeller, Baptist oil magnate who had given so generously to support Baptist missions, notified the Society that with his gift of $200,000 in 1915, he was inaugurating a policy of reducing the annual subsidies so that eventually they might be stopped altogether without detriment to the work.[2]

In 1916, however, the Society managed for the first time in six years to close the year without a deficit. Several legacies, an economy in home expenditures, and increased giving during a period of higher

---

[1] Records of the Board of Managers of A.B.F.M.S. for Sept. 16, 1914, pp. 340, 361; *Missions,* Vol. 5, No. 10 (Oct., 1914), p. 783.

[2] Northern Baptist Convention, *Annual,* 1915, pp. 339-40, 364-71. (This source will hereafter be referred to by its initials, N.B.C.) See also Records of Boards of Managers, 1915–16, p. 108.

incomes were largely responsible. Yet on the mission fields there were bitter complaints about budget curtailments and the application of the intensive policy. The war had produced conditions which reduced the giving of the churches on the field. In Burma and the Belgian Congo, a business depression and poor crops served further to reduce contributions. In Europe conditions grew steadily worse as churches in some countries were demolished and congregations scattered. Baptists contributed a large portion of America's relief money for Europe, and Baptist money was given without reference to the religious beliefs of those helped.[3]

During these years organizational changes were taking place at the headquarters of the Society. In March, 1915, the Board adopted new rules which provided for standing committees on the oversight of the missions, for educational work on the fields, for ways and means (a committee to raise funds), for finance (a committee to supervise the permanent funds and investments of the Society), for management of the Home Department, for candidates, for vacancies on the administrative staff of the board, and for representatives to serve on a Joint Council of the Foreign Society and the Woman's Society. For administration of the Society's affairs, an Officers Council was created, which consisted of the general secretary, who served as chairman, the home secretary, the foreign secretaries, the treasurer, the assistant secretaries, and the vice-treasurer, and *ex officio* the chairman and vice-chairman of the Board of Managers. In June, 1916, the Board adopted a revised plan of administration under which there were to be an Officers Council, a Foreign Department in charge of all field policy and administration, a Home Department in charge of collection of funds and promotion of the work within the United States, and a Treasury Department.[4] These changes reflected the growing complexity of the work of mission administration and also the increasing attention to more efficient methods of conducting the business of the Society.

The man who was possibly most instrumental in the initial stages of the reorganization of the Society was the home secretary, Dr. Fred P. Haggard, a skilled organizer. He had come to administrative work from service in Assam, becoming first assistant secretary and then

---

[3] *Ibid.*, 1916, pp. 441-49, 521, 595, 606-12; for 1917, pp. 822-28.

[4] Records of Board of Managers, A.B.F.M.S., 1915–16, pp. 85-89; for 1916–17, pp. 14-17.

home secretary in 1905 upon the retirement of Dr. Henry C. Mabie. During fifteen years of service, he reorganized and enlarged the literature department, improved methods of dealing with candidates, organized plans for using missionaries on furlough in deputation work, and improved the station plan of support. He also assisted in the development of lay support, and participated in the various interdenominational relationships of which the Society was a part. Against the background of his own missionary service, Haggard gave devoted service in administrative work. But certain personality traits and his aggressiveness aroused resentment among those who were slow to accept change in the organizational patterns of the Society. As a result he was obliged to resign in the fall of 1915.[5]

Administrative changes were developing on the field as well. For several years conferences of missionaries had been entrusted with an increasing amount of responsibility for the affairs of their respective fields. Some of the missions were urging an extension of their responsibility to include the power of final decision on the field. Faced with this request, the Board adopted a policy in 1915 of moving cautiously in taking any steps which would relinquish their own financial direction of the work. Even so, they did agree to encourage the growth of field administration in the various missions of the Society.[6]

As the war dragged on into its third and fourth years, its effects upon the mission fields became more marked and intense. Banking facilities were disorganized, mail was delayed in reaching the field, submarines endangered travel and imperilled the shipping of materials essential to the missions. When India, Assam, and Burma joined the Allies, American missionaries had the problem of maintaining their personal neutrality until their own country entered the war. Some missionaries volunteered for war service. The Reverend J. R. Bailey, M.D., and the Reverend W. C. Mason, both of Assam, served among the Nagas who were recruited as labor battalions in the British armed forces. Likewise, Reverend Robert Wellwood, Mr. H. J. Openshaw, and the Reverend I. B. Clark of West China went to France to labor among the Chinese coolies who were being used there. The Reverend Ernest Grigg of Burma spent his furlough in France among regiments of Burmese soldiers who were aiding the

---

[5] *Ibid.*, 1915–16, pp. 292-95, 419.

[6] *Missions,* Vol. 6, No. 7 (July–Aug., 1915), pp. 572-73; *Annual Report of A.B.F.M.S.* for 1916, p. 47.

British. Some fifteen other missionaries, many of them medical men, were engaged in various forms of humanitarian service. Members of the administrative staff at home and board representatives also were involved in the war.

During the course of the conflict, thirty-nine missionaries died and more than forty retired, creating a serious problem of replacement under wartime conditions. In Bengal-Orissa, one missionary was obliged to supervise the work of four stations in addition to his own. In South India six stations were cared for by two missionaries. A decline in evangelistic results occurred on many fields as non-Christians became cynical and disillusioned about so-called Christian nations engaged in war. In 1918 the total number of converts for all fields had dropped to 7,098 from more than 11,000 in 1915. It was the lowest number of baptisms in more than 20 years. To intensify the discouraging situation faced by the Societies, inflationary prices affected every mission field, and the unfavorable currency exchange added to the high cost of maintaining the barest essentials for carrying on the work.[7]

Meanwhile at home, the Board of the American Baptist Foreign Mission Society co-operated in every way with the Five Year Program launched by the Northern Baptist Convention in 1915 to raise funds and increase the missionary force on the fields. In 1917 the Foreign Society and the Woman's Society voted to unify their budgets, except in capital fund items, and make a joint appeal to the denomination, dividing the receipts on an apportionment plan. To offset in part at least the lack of an adequate missionary staff, the Board of the Foreign Society adopted a new policy for a larger use of women in general station work and in the performance of business matters, particularly in Burma. By joint planning between the two Societies, two missionaries were to be sent to stations where only one person had been at work. In spite of these emergency efforts, however, the missions were hard-hit. In the Orient, for example, the raising of armies deprived stations of the services of promising national leaders, thus adding to the burden of the missionaries.[8]

Through the leadership of Ambrose Swasey, of Cleveland, Ohio,

---

[7] William B. Lipphard, *The Second Century of Baptist Foreign Missions* (Philadelphia, 1926), chaps. 1-2.

[8] Annual Report of A.B.F.M.S. for 1916, pp. 19-20; Records of Board of Managers and Executive Committee of A.B.F.M.S., June 1914–May 1924, pp. 180-83; for 1917–18, p. 186; N.B.C., *Annual* for 1919, p. 406.

and F. W. Ayer, of Camden, New Jersey, a group of Baptist laymen met together in Chicago in January, 1918, to plan a campaign to raise $1,000,000 to cover the war-time needs of the various Baptist Societies. Dr. Fred P. Haggard, who, after his resignation as home secretary, had become secretary of the Laymen's Missionary Movement, an interdenominational venture, was selected as campaign director. A National Campaign Committee was formed, with Ayer as chairman and Swasey as treasurer. The American Baptist Foreign Mission Society was to receive $213,947 of the $1,000,000 to be raised. The effort, which was successful, developed great spiritual power and was the beginning of a vigorous laymen's work which took on added significance in later years.[9]

As the war progressed, Baptists reflected the world-consciousness and Wilsonian idealism which was gripping the imagination of the American people. They reaffirmed their Society's policy of co-operating with evangelicals of all denominations "whenever and wherever such co-operation can be undertaken without any sacrifice of principles." [10] This policy became apparent in many areas—on the fields in joint operations in medical and educational work; at home in the representation of the Society on committees of the Foreign Missions Conference, and on the Board of Managers of the Missionary Education Movement which outlined mission study themes and policies. Contacts were maintained also with the Laymen's Missionary Movement, the International Missionary Council, the Student Volunteer Movement, the Federal Council of Churches of Christ in America, and other interdenominational organizations.

The war years made Baptists conscious of several major needs. They became convinced of the necessity of making Christian principles basic to all international relationships. This in turn spurred interest in the missionary cause by which the gospel of love was to be spread around the world. As nationalism revived in the postwar era, particularly in countries where Baptists conducted missions, it became increasingly evident that the development of a strong national leadership in India, China, Japan, Burma, and elsewhere was imperative.

With such problems in mind, the two Societies held a significant missions conference at Newton Centre, Massachusetts, April 25—

---

[9] *Annual Report of A.B.F.M.S.* for 1918, pp. 14-15.
[10] N.B.C., *Annual,* 1918, p. 448.

May 8, 1917. The Board adopted the findings of this gathering of staff leaders and missionaries. They gave a broad interpretation to the fundamental objective of mission work, "to include within its scope all phases and relationships of individual and social life." They re-emphasized the proposition that no conflict should exist between evangelistic work and other forms of missionary endeavor, and that every form of mission work should be permeated with the evangelistic spirit. It was also decided that medical work should be stressed, in particular in China and the Belgian Congo, and especially for women in British India, and that larger attention should be given to Christian literature on all fields. The Conference was agreed that nationals should be encouraged to assume leadership, although they should not be given the right to say whether a missionary returns to his field of service from furlough or not, nor should they determine financial policies beyond participating in the Missionary Conference Plan then in operation.[11]

Expansion in Postwar Years (1919–1924)

The world of 1919 was in turmoil. Scarcely any part of the globe had escaped the devastating effects of the four-year struggle. Europe was in the throes of poverty and political confusion. From a reluctant Great Britain the millions of India were demanding self-determination. China was convulsed by civil war that threatened the existence of the young republic. Japan was in a financial crisis which was to be aggravated by the tragic earthquake of 1923. The Philippines were demanding independence from the United States on the score that Americans had much to say about the war to save democracy. To the white man Africa was becoming increasingly important for its vast natural resources.

The task of reconstruction on mission fields was made more difficult by the high cost of living which showed no appreciable decline. Yet Europe was in desperate need of material relief to stave off hunger and the suffering that accompanies disease and homelessness. There was the need also to re-establish friendly relations with Baptists in countries with which America had been at war. The spread of democracy to various countries on the continent opened new opportunities for evangelical Christianity. In countries where state churches still enjoyed political privilege, the rights of Baptist minor-

[11] Records of Board of Managers, A.B.F.M.S., 1917–18, pp. 478-83.

ities required protection. In non-Christian lands the Mission Societies faced the challenge to build new foundations which would meet the increasing demands for self-expression and self-control on the part of Christian nationals whose countries were struggling for independence from Western exploitation and political domination.[12]

As the Mission Societies prepared to meet the new needs, they manifested a broader view of missionary objectives than had been held in the preceding century. In addition to the threefold concern for evangelism, education, and medical missions, mission leaders became convinced that the problems resulting from the war were also their responsibility. They faced frankly "the industrial strife intensified by new economic rivalries, the intellectual unrest and the social turmoil accentuated by the war, the international jealousies left as a heritage of the great conflict, and the towering menace of race prejudice." [13] The task of Christian missions took on a fresh urgency as the ideal of brotherhood and world peace became clearly involved in the responsibility of the church.

The ministry of relief and reconstruction brought by the American Baptist Foreign Mission Society to Europe in the years immediately following the war will be described in a later chapter. Suffice it to say here that it did much to demonstrate the international quality of Christian brotherhood and in that respect was one of the most significant object lessons ever provided on the meaning of missions.

As the Societies engaged in the postwar tasks, important readjustments were being made at the home base. Budgets had to be raised in the face of continuing high costs. Increases authorized in missionary salaries as a war emergency were made permanent. The building program estimates had to be revised upward. Special gifts had to be sought to provide badly needed mission residences, school buildings, churches, and hospitals. The only bright spot in the financial situation was that the international rate of exchange returned to more normal figures, thus favoring the Societies' treasuries.

The work on the field also underwent study by means of a number of field visits. In the year 1920–21 Professor H. B. Robins, a member of the Board of the Foreign Society, visited the fields of the Far East. The year following, Secretaries J. C. Robbins and P. H. J.

---

[12] For a detailed account see Lipphard, *The Second Century of Baptist Foreign Missions,* chaps. 3-4.

[13] *Ibid.,* p. 54.

Lerrigo surveyed the British India missions and the Belgian Congo field respectively. In May, 1922, Secretary J. H. Franklin and Dr. C. W. Chamberlin, a member of the Board, studied the East China and South China Missions as well as the work in Japan. Thus for the first time in the Society's history, a simultaneous survey was made of the major fields of the Baptist world mission.

Both Societies took steps immediately following the war to overcome the serious shortage of missionary personnel resulting from wartime conditions. The first step was to create the office of candidate secretary. Dr. Lerrigo was appointed for the Foreign Society and Miss Helen Hunt for the Woman's Society. The two societies sent 66 new missionaries to the fields in the fall of 1919, 88 in 1920, and 90 in 1921, making a total of 244 replacements within three years after the war. Then came a decline in receipts and an accompanying increase in deficits for both Societies, forcing the Boards to reduce the number of new appointees to 27 in 1922, 35 in 1923, and 28 in 1924. Most of the 334 new missionaries sent out in those six years were women, increasing the staff of the Woman's Society by 40 per cent, while the staff of the Foreign Society showed only a 10 per cent gain.[14]

To face the financial problems that were mounting in these years, Northern Baptist Laymen called for the creation of a General Board of Promotion (now called Council on Missionary Co-operation) which should free the Societies from fund-raising burdens. The plan, which was adopted by the Northern Baptist Convention at Denver in 1919, called for an over-all effort to raise a single budget to be divided among the various agencies of the Convention. This new Board of Promotion was to be representative of all national, state, and city mission societies. The close connection of the Foreign Mission Society to the plan is indicated by the selection of Dr. J. Y. Aitchison, then home secretary, to become general director of the new Board. Under the Board's leadership, the Northern Baptist Convention entered upon a campaign to raise $100,000,000 for postwar advance. This great effort came to be known as the New World Movement.

At the same time, the Convention agreed to co-operate with the Interchurch World Movement, an interdenominational campaign in which participating denominations were asked to underwrite the fi-

[14] Lipphard, *The Second Century of Baptist Foreign Missions,* p. 104.

nancial goal by loans which would be repaid when the contributions from the churches were received. Northern Baptists contracted loans to the amount of $2,500,000 as their share. When the effort began to fail, the Northern Baptist Convention voted at its meeting in Buffalo in May, 1920, to withdraw.

Meanwhile, the date for completing the New World Movement drive was set for April 30, 1924. Fund-raising techniques reminiscent of the Liberty Loan Drives of the war years were used. "Minute men and women" brought the challenge to more than 3,000 Northern Baptist churches in 1920. In spite of an economic depression, through this co-operative effort more than $12,500,000 was received in the fiscal year 1920–1921. When the campaign reached the half-way mark in 1922, it was reported that 86 per cent of the churches had subscribed, yet only a little more than 50 per cent of the $100,000,000 goal had been reached.[15] The remainder was never raised.

During this same period the Foreign Mission Societies moved their headquarters in 1920 from Boston to New York. The first space occupied in New York was in the Holland Building at 276 Fifth Avenue. There they remained until November, 1929, when they agreed to join other agencies of the Northern Baptist Convention in leasing space in a new building at 152 Madison Avenue on the corner of East 32nd Street.

As the result of Dr. Aitchison's resignation as home secretary to become director of the Board of Promotion, Dr. Lerrigo was chosen as his successor in the Foreign Society. Dr. Lerrigo, formerly a medical missionary in the Philippines, had developed a Medical Service Department in addition to serving as candidate secretary. As home secretary he continued to perform these duties. His interest in the health of the missionaries had developed during his experience in recruiting missionary personnel. Under his direction arrangements were made for more thorough medical examinations of all candidates and for better care of the health of the missionary staff.

A number of circumstances combined in these years to inject into the already numerous problems of the Mission Societies charges of theological unsoundness. The greater emphasis placed by the Societies upon educational work on mission fields, the growing tendency to enter into union projects with other denominations, the participa-

---

[15] N.B.C., *Annual,* 1920, pp. 70-71; 1921, pp. 66, 148, 562-63; 1922, pp. 67, 73.

tion of the Northern Baptist Convention in the Interchurch World Movement, and the broadening concept of the missionary task of the church aroused suspicion and at times open criticism from some sections of the Convention. Indeed, the problem was not peculiar to Northern Baptists, for during the First World War and in the years immediately following, the forces of theological liberalism and fundamentalism had come to open conflict in several denominations across American Protestantism. Among Baptists the fundamentalists were divided. Some refused to have fellowship with the Northern Baptist Convention, while others, like J. C. Massee, William B. Riley, John Roach Straton, and Curtis Lee Laws, editor of the Baptist weekly, *The Watchman-Examiner,* led in 1920 in the organization of the Baptist Fundamentalist Fellowship of the Convention.

The Fundamentalist Fellowship denounced the Interchurch World Movement, and accused the Foreign Mission Society of having allowed trust funds to be used to pay the debt of the defunct Movement. It also initiated an investigation of Baptist schools by the Convention in 1920–21, many of which were suspected of harboring what had come to be called modernism. At the Indianapolis Convention in 1922, Dr. William B. Riley, of Minneapolis, sought to get the Convention committed to adoption of the New Hampshire Confession of Faith. Dr. Cornelius Woelfkin, a New York minister and a former president of the American Baptist Foreign Mission Society, was spokesman for those who opposed the use of creeds to attain doctrinal uniformity. On the convention floor, he offset Dr. Riley's proposal by a substitute motion to the effect that "the Northern Baptist Convention affirms that the New Testament is the all-sufficient ground of our faith and practice, and we need no other statement." By a vote of 1,264 to 637, Woelfkin's motion was carried.[16]

In the meantime, the general Home and general Foreign Mission Societies appointed a committee of fifteen to consider the acceptance of gifts subject to doctrinal conditions. The matter had been prompted by the fact that each of these two Societies had been offered a sizeable gift of money on the condition that they should maintain a specified orthodox creedal position. After due consideration, the Foreign Society voted in 1923 not to accept gifts with creedal conditions. In explanation, the officers made a distinction between "things which are believed" (in which sense all Baptists have a creed) and "things

[16] *Ibid.,* 1922, pp. 130, 133-34.

which must be believed" (in which sense Baptists refuse to have a creed). The Board members then reaffirmed their faith in the essentials of the redemptive gospel, and urged all donors "to trust the loyalty and integrity of our respective Societies and Boards, and to make their gifts to our denominational enterprises without doctrinal conditions."[17]

The problem was complicated further by charges made by Dr. John Roach Straton, pastor of the Cavalry Baptist Church, New York City, that reflected on the doctrinal views of missionaries of the Foreign Society. Dr. Straton claimed to have quotations from missionary correspondence. The officers of the Society insisted that these quotations had been taken out of their proper context and were being subjected to unfair interpretation. Dr. Straton, speaking for the Baptist Fundamentalist League of Greater New York and Vicinity for Ministers and Laymen, then requested access to the files of missionary correspondence in order to determine the theological views of certain missionaries suspected of "modernism." This the Officers Council refused to grant, while at the same time they offered to investigate the charges themselves. The Board approved the decision of its administrative leaders, and assured the constituency of its desire to follow through on any specific charges against any of its missionaries. Some few accusations were made against named missionaries. For example, a missionary of Bengal-Orissa had accused one of his associates of holding liberal theological views, and had sent a copy of his accusation to a fundamentalist leader in New York, as well as to Dr. Lerrigo, the home secretary.

In response to this situation, the Board of Managers of the Foreign Mission Society on October 23, 1923, issued a public statement answering the following charges made by Dr. Straton in his paper, *The Fundamentalist:* (1) That the Board neglected the work of personal evangelism in favor of education and social service. (2) That the Board permits teaching of liberal doctrines by its missionaries. (3) That the Board was not straightforward in its dealings with the denomination. The replies of the Board to these charges were not evasive. It was admitted that there was always the difficulty of maintaining a proper balance between evangelism, education, medical, and general humanitarian features of the work, but it was pointed out

---

[17] Records of Board of Managers, A.B.F.M.S., 1920–22, pp. 452-56; 1922–24, action of May 8, 1923.

that the majority of the conversions on the fields were traceable to the influence of schools and hospitals. The Board further explained that it made no secret of its policy of giving to its officers and missionaries considerable liberty of theological opinion so long as they held fast to "the vital message of the gospel of Christ." The Board also pointed to its statement issued in 1921 to the Convention that it "knew no missionaries who were teaching and preaching other than the evangelical gospel common to our Baptist faith." [18]

The Board did not allow the matter to rest there. A careful extract of confidential correspondence between missionaries involved in the charges and the secretaries of the Society was prepared by a committee of the Board for review at a four-hour session of the entire Board. The decision of the Board was that while some letters contained phrases which might be misunderstood or misinterpreted, the general spirit of them was evangelical in character. In January, 1924, the Board released an open letter to Northern Baptists answering in detail the charges made in *The Fundamentalist.* To the accusation that Shanghai Baptist College was teaching error, the Board pointed out that the charge had been based upon evidence presented by a young man who was not a missionary of the Society, but who had been engaged for a few months to teach English in a mission school remote from Shanghai. He had never had any connection with the College. Moreover, President F. J. White of Shanghai Baptist College, in a statement published in 1922, had answered the charges made by the youth. The second charge concerned the withdrawal of a missionary in West China who felt that his strong social views might embarrass the Society. The accusation was that the secretaries were indifferent to his views. Actually, they had agreed with the missionary that he should not continue in the work of the Society. A third accusation was, that of sixty missionaries in East China in 1922, only six were set apart for evangelistic work. This statement was pointed out as misleading because it did not include the wives of missionaries in the small figure, whereas they had been included in the large one. It was further explained that, with the exception of Kinhwa, which station was being turned over to the Chinese Christian leaders, there was a family in each station engaged in evangelistic work. A fourth charge was that the churches in France had been cut

[18] *Ibid.,* 1920–22, p. 413, 449-50; 1922–24, pp. 343-45, 350-52, 426-29, 450-53.

off from support by the Society because they were faithful to an orthodox Baptist position. It was answered that this statement was not true, and that the churches had withdrawn voluntarily from the Society's assistance, most of them entering upon a self-supporting basis.[19]

As a further step in its investigation, the Board of Managers sent to each missionary under attack a letter on March 11, 1924, requesting an expression of his doctrinal views for clarification. In April, the missionary from Bengal-Orissa, who had been accused of heresy, appeared before the Board to answer the charges made against him by his fellow worker. As a result, the Board voted to retain its confidence in him because of his essential faith in the gospel and because of the fruits of his work on the field.[20]

In spite of these efforts at clarification, the Fundamentalists were not satisfied. At the Milwaukee Convention in 1924, Dr. J. C. Massee, of Boston, presented a resolution calling for a commission of seven persons to be named by the president of the Convention to investigate and report as to the conduct, policies, and practices of the Board of Managers and Secretaries of the Foreign Society in the selection of new missionaries and in the doctrinal position of older appointees. The resolution was adopted with an allotment of $25,000 for expenses. The Society, in turn, presented to the Convention a statement prepared by the chairman of its Board of Managers, Professor Frederick L. Anderson of the Newton Theological Institution, describing its "evangelical policy," and defining the gospel as "the good news of the free forgiveness of sin and eternal life (beginning now and going on forever) through a vital union with the crucified and risen Christ, which brings men into union and fellowship with God. . . ." [21]

At the Convention meeting in 1925 in Seattle, Washington, the commission of seven presented its testimony and material in four volumes and offered a summary report as follows: (1) They did not find that the secretaries and the Board of Managers knowingly had appointed liberals because they were liberals; but they did find evidence that there had been a tendency to underestimate the value of

---

[19] *Ibid.*, 1922–24, pp. 513-15, 523-30.

[20] Records of Board of Managers, A.B.F.M.S., 1924–25, pp. 20-21, 64-70.

[21] N.B.C., *Annual*, 1924, pp. 51-52, 529-38; for full statement of Professor Anderson see Robert G. Torbet, *A History of the Baptists* (Philadelphia, 1950; revised, 1952), p. 415 ff.

thoroughly sound evangelical Christian views in a missionary. (2) They found that the Board followed what they termed an "inclusive" policy, i.e., "it would appoint and retain missionaries of varying theological beliefs provided they came within certain limits which the Board regarded as 'the limits of the gospel.' " (3) They found some evidence of wrong teaching among missionaries. (4) They noted that in the last ten years more emphasis had been placed upon education than evangelism, but that the reason was practical, not theological. These trends, so it appeared, had been due to the Board's eagerness to train an adequate number of capable national leaders for the indigenous churches.[22]

The Board received the report in good spirit and set up a committee to carry out the adoption of the constructive criticisms made. Not satisfied with this, the Reverend W. B. Hinson, of Oregon, presented a series of resolutions to the effect that men and women who were out of harmony with the evangelical faith, as he defined it in detail, be removed from their appointments. After much discussion, the Reverend R. V. Meigs of Illinois proposed amendments which eliminated the doctrinal statement, simply referring to the Indianapolis decision of 1922 to use the New Testament only, and leaving to the Board the action to be taken, in the light of facts discovered. The amendments were adopted by a vote of 742 to 574, indicating a wide divergence of opinion on this issue.[23]

The amount of attention devoted here to this particular trend in the affairs of the Foreign Mission Society is justified in view of the train of events which followed. The matter was by no means settled with the actions thus traced. It remained for many years to disturb the peace of the Convention and to weaken the confidence of many in its missionary work.

Nevertheless, the record of evangelistic work on the mission fields of Northern Baptists was encouraging. By 1921 the American Baptist Foreign Mission Society was reportedly the fourth largest foreign mission society in the world, with ten fields besides work in many countries in Europe. It was supporting 833 missionaries, 7,000 native workers, and there were 1,834 organized churches, 3,429 regular meeting places, 4 colleges, 2,737 schools of all grades with

[22] N.B.C., *Annual,* 1925, pp. 79-94. The committee members were A. W. Beaven, chairman, Mrs. H. F. Compton, Judson A. Crane, John F. Herget, J. C. Massee, Mrs. John Nuveen, H. F. Remington, secretary.

[23] *Ibid.,* pp. 94-96, 174-75.

89,752 under instruction, 24 hospitals, and 62 dispensaries. The number of baptisms in 1920 amounted to over 11,000. By 1924 the total was 18,415, the largest number of converts in any single year of the 110 years of the history of the Society.[24]

By 1924 the five-year New World Movement came to an end. Although only one half of the desired amount had been raised, the effort had been on the whole favorable. The general level of missionary giving had been lifted, and interest in missions had increased among both men and women. In addition, there had been created in the Board of Promotion an agency for the encouragement of stewardship as a denominational ideal. General giving had been raised, Baptist schools had been brought, for the first time, into the comprehensive missionary program of denominational support. There was developing among Baptists in the North, though under some stress, a denominational consciousness and sense of responsibility which was to strengthen the entire mission enterprise in years to come.

---

[24] *The Baptist,* Vol. 2, No. 22 (July 2, 1921), p. 289; Vol. 4, No. 50 (Jan. 12, 1924), p. 1580.

CHAPTER XXIV

Developments at Home: Forward Through Storm, 1924–1954

BY THE MID-TWENTIES a policy of retrenchment had become necessary in the conduct of the American Baptist world mission. This course continued into the thirties under the stress of a world-wide economic depression, internal theological conflict, and international political tensions. It is with these problems and their handling that this chapter deals. The story reveals both the strength and the weakness of the human vessels in whose hands the great missionary task of the church has been entrusted. It indicates also the interaction which takes place between the gospel and the forces that prevail in the environment in which it makes its impact. The fact that the Christian message not only maintained itself in many lands where disturbances were rife, but actually penetrated into new areas during this time of conflict reveals clearly the innate power of the gospel within a hostile world.

Retrenchment and Dissension (1924–1938)

With the culmination of the New World Movement, a decline in financial support again made retrenchment a necessity. The contributions to the unified budget of the Northern Baptist Convention's agencies dropped from $9,818,813.74 in 1920–1921 to $4,389,-612.68 in 1926–1927. The Foreign Society's share in these contributions declined from $1,371,636.84 to $832,955.14 in the same period.[1] In the face of such a shrinking income, the number of mis-

[1] N.B.C., *Annual,* 1927, p. 325.

sionary units (i.e. a family or single person) under appointment to the Foreign Society dropped from its peak of 313 in 1923 to 265 in 1929, to 240 in 1934, to 179 in 1939, a decline amounting to 43 per cent in 16 years. Between 1928 and 1938, the staff of the Woman's Society dropped from 204 to 153, a loss of 25 per cent.[2]

Such retrenchments represented a serious threat to the continuance of the successes which were taking place on most mission fields. In the South India Mission, for example, nearly 6,000 converts were baptized in 1925, the largest number for any one year in the Mission's history since the revival of 1878. In the Philippines, national leaders were coming forward to help the missionaries. Only in the Orient was there a serious obstacle; between 1925 and 1930, an anti-Christian feeling was aroused by those antiforeign propagandists among the Chinese intellectuals who saw in the missionary enterprise a "Western" movement. Nevertheless, the year 1927 witnessed a total of 20,482 baptisms in the ten fields of Northern Baptists—and that with a reduced staff of missionaries.[3] Such were the evidences of the ever-widening opportunities for missionary expansion at this critical juncture in the affairs of the Societies at home.

Several steps were undertaken during these years to deal with the pressing financial needs. In 1924 the fund-raising responsibility was transferred from the General Board of Promotion to a new Board of Missionary Co-operation. It was an effort to achieve further integration among the various agencies of the Convention. When the Northern Baptists met for their annual sessions in Seattle in June, 1925, Professor Frederick L. Anderson, chairman of the Board of Managers of the Foreign Society, startled the delegates into a full realization of the critical nature of the situation. Pointing out the serious reductions in appropriations to the various fields, he announced that a process of withdrawal from whole fields or from at least twenty or twenty-five mission stations would be imperative if a substantial increase in funds were not provided at once. As a result, the financial crisis was given main consideration, for no one desired missionary retrenchment. The solution which was approved by the Convention was an authorization of the two Foreign Societies to launch a "Lone Star Fund." Its name was reminiscent of the critical days more than

[2] P. H. J. Lerrigo and D. M. Amidon, eds., *All Kindreds and Tongues,* 4th issue (New York, 1940), p. 97.

[3] N.B.C., *Annual,* 1925, p. 415, 424, 430-33; 1927, p. 275-77; 1930, pp. 396-97.

sixty years before when the Lone Star Mission at Nellore in South India had been in the balance. The total amount to be raised by the two Societies was to be $263,622 over and above their respective budgets. Within a year $358,719 was raised—a creditable demonstration of the eagerness with which Baptists sought to maintain their missions at all costs.[4]

Late in the year 1925 a special conference of the Boards of Managers and delegates from the ten mission fields of the two Societies was held in New York to formulate policies in the face of the circumstances at home and abroad. The main recommendation was for the development of an indigenous Christianity on the fields, with the training of an adequate leadership, and the further development of women's work. Attention was given also to the strengthening of medical work so that skilled doctors going to the field might be able to carry on efficient medical practice along scientific lines. This was a far step forward from earlier times when medical missionaries were expected to be first of all evangelists and doctors only incidentally. Another significant decision made by the conference was to strengthen the existing joint organizations of nationals and missionaries on the respective fields. In Burma, for example, the committee of management of the Burma Baptist Convention had a majority membership of nationals. In Assam both the national convention and the Jorhat Christian Schools were managed jointly by missionaries and representatives of the associations of churches. In Bengal-Orissa the evangelistic board entrusted with supervision of the evangelistic work for the entire mission was representative of missionaries, ordained native pastors, and laymen of the churches. In South India, the Home Mission Society of the Telugu Baptist Convention, on which there was only one missionary elected by the Convention, had assumed charge of one entire mission field (Kandukuru). In South and East China, administration of the work was shifting rapidly to Chinese leadership. In West China the Szechuan Baptist Convention was comprised of both missionaries and Chinese. In Japan all matters of administration had been previously transferred to the Japan Joint Committee of twelve members equally divided between the Japan Baptist Convention and the Reference Committee of the Missionary Conference. In the Philippines certain mission schools had boards

[4] *Missions,* Vol. 16, No. 8 (Sept., 1925), pp. 452-74; *Annual Report of A.B.F.M.S.* for 1926, pp. 63-64.

of trustees composed exclusively of Filipinos, with the station missionary serving only as adviser. Large institutions, such as Central Philippine College and the Baptist Missionary Training School, were incorporated. A Home Mission Society, organized by the Jaro Baptist Church and participated in by other churches, was independent of missionary control. Such was the picture in 1925 on the 10 mission fields where 1,204 of the 2,003 churches were self-supporting. It was indicative of a marked effort to encourage self-support among the younger churches while at the same time responding to the growing desire of Christians abroad to assume a larger degree of supervision and control of their own church life.[5]

In 1927 the Board of the Foreign Society approved the organization of the Department of Budget and Research, with an administrative secretary, who was to serve as co-ordinating officer for the various departments of the organization. George B. Huntington was selected for this post. It was a further step forward to create greater efficiency in the management of an increasingly complex structure which was faced with the constant pressure of economies under mounting costs of operation. The Society was functioning on a reduced budget which represented only seventy per cent of the amount needed for basic essentials. Further retrenchment was avoided only by the fact of a greatly depleted missionary staff, an absolute minimum of new missionary appointees, elimination of practically all provision for new property needs on the fields, reduced appropriations for mission work, and timely acquisition of additional monies through legacies and the maturing of annuities and the success of the Lone Star Fund. Accordingly it became necessary to launch a second special drive for support in what was called the Judson Fund, which was to take the form of appeals to individuals for special gifts for a three-year period (1927–1930). Receipts were to be used to establish Judson College in Rangoon, Burma, on a new site where it would have greater opportunity for growth, to send out missionary reinforcements to the field, to enroll missionaries in the Pension Fund of the Ministers and Missionaries Benefit Board, and to provide for damages done by a cyclone in South India in 1927. To this Fund,

---

[5] For details see the 85-page booklet, *Foreign Mission Policies: A Report of the Special Conference of the Boards of Managers and Delegates from the Ten Missions of the American Baptist Foreign Mission Society and the W.A.B.F.M.S. held in New York, November 18–December 2, 1925.*

John D. Rockefeller contributed $290,000 to cover the entire cost of the new buildings for Judson College.[6]

In February, 1928, the Board of the Foreign Society lost the leadership of Professor Frederick L. Anderson, who had served for eight and a half years as its chairman. He resigned because of the pressure of his academic duties at the Newton Theological Institution, although he remained on the Board until his death in 1938. With two exceptions, Dr. Anderson had filled the longest term of service in 114 years of the Society's history. He had been the unfailing guide and promoter of the organization's work in one of the most trying periods of its history—at a time of the unification of denominational work, of theological controversy, of revolutionary changes in the Orient, and of falling financial receipts.[7] He was succeeded by Dr. Herbert J. White.

In 1929 a new basis of co-operation between the Foreign Society and the Woman's Society was adopted. Transition of the latter from an auxiliary to a co-ordinate status in mission work came about gradually, although it had been formally recognized in the reorganization of 1914. As a result, some of the old practices and attitudes had continued into the new relationship. The new plan sought "to modify some of these practices and to define more clearly the co-operative relationship of the two Societies." There continued to be consultation and sharing of information in regard to common work and interests on fields where missionaries of both Societies worked together. But in matters relating to the exclusive work of the Woman's Society, its sovereignty was recognized.[8]

The probable causes for this period of decline were numerous. They included the world-wide economic depression which reached its peak in 1933, the theological controversy which was responsible for some loss of contributions, and the tendency of the Societies to overexpand when funds were plentiful, without setting aside sufficient available reserves.

The effects of the depression accentuated the financial straits against which the Societies had been battling for several years. The actual appropriations to meet the budget for the American Baptist

---

[6] *Annual Report of A.B.F.M.S.* for 1928, pp. 49, 73; Records of Board of Managers, A.B.F.M.S., 1928–29, p. 193.

[7] *Annual Report of A.B.F.M.S.* for 1928, pp. 44-45.

[8] *Ibid.*, 1930, pp. 63-64; *Records of Board of Managers, A.B.F.M.S.*, pp. 29-32.

Foreign Mission Society for 1931–1932 were fifty thousand dollars less than the total appropriation for 1930–1931. This was but the beginning of more severe reductions to follow, which called for the most extreme measures. For example, in 1932, missionaries on the field were asked to join with Baptists at home in what was called "The Maintenance Movement." In some instances missionaries contributed as much as ten per cent of their annual salary. In order to cut expenses at home, the Board of Managers adopted a bimonthly schedule of meetings in place of the traditional monthly sessions. The same year the office of candidate secretary was temporarily discontinued. An arrangement was made with the secretaries of the Student Volunteer Movement, both of whom had been former missionaries of the Society (Jesse R. Wilson and R. P. Currier), to make contacts with students in behalf of the Candidate Department. Through lack of funds to return them to their stations, several missionaries on furlough were retained at home. A few were released from service. To cut travel costs, other missionaries on the field were being asked to defer their furloughs. In 1932 the Society sent out only nine new missionaries, the smallest group since 1885. In January, 1933, the Board was obliged to transfer the home for missionaries' children from Chicago and combine it with the Fannie Doane Home at Granville, Ohio, and to close the home at Newton Centre, Mass. The budget for 1933–1934 represented a decrease of almost one-third in three years' time. It provided for only one new missionary family. By 1934 the trend of benevolence giving had begun a very slow upturn. The depth of the depression had been reached, but the hills ahead were steep and treacherous to surmount. As late as November, 1935, the Board of the Foreign Society found it necessary to approve reductions in the budget for 1936–1937 totalling $100,000.[9]

Still another factor making it difficult to find adequate support for the missionary work was the theological dissension which had begun shortly after the First World War. It will be recalled that the mounting criticism of the doctrinal soundness of the Board's missionaries had resulted in the appointment of a Commission of Seven by the Milwaukee Convention in 1924. In its report, the Commission had

---

[9] *Annual Report of A.B.F.M.S.* for 1932, p. 18; 1932, pp. 42-43; 1933, pp 52-53, 55; N.B.C., *Annual,* 1932, p. 596; 1933, pp. 367, 400, 415; 1934, pp. 402, 447; Records of the Board of Managers, A.B.F.M.S., 1934–36, pp. 249-50,

counseled the Society to investigate the cases of eight missionaries, without implying that all of them were unsound. By 1927 it was possible for the Board to report that four of the eight had resigned and were no longer in the service of the Society. Theological charges against three others had been dismissed, and only one missionary remained to be examined. The officers of the Society, however, had made clear in a statement to the Northern Baptist Convention meeting at Washington, D.C., in 1926 that they refused to "harry our missionaries with any general inquisition into their opinion." At the same time, they pledged that any important charges presented in writing against any missionary or officer of the Society would be investigated. The Board intended to serve the whole denomination, but "within the limits of the Gospel." [10]

These efforts on the part of the American Baptist Foreign Mission Society to answer charges made against its policies did not prevent the creation, in 1928, of a new missionary agency known as "The Association of Baptists for World Evangelism, Inc." It was organized, with headquarters in Philadelphia, when three missionaries of the Foreign Society withdrew from its service over doctrinal differences and disagreement with what they regarded as liberal policies in the Northern Baptist Convention. They opened a new work in Manila early in that year on the basis of what might be termed a "faith mission." The Association required of its missionaries and board members the signing of a strongly fundamentalist creed, and discouraged fraternization with members of the Northern Baptist Convention. Baptist support came from about fifty churches which in 1933 withdrew from the Northern Baptist Convention to form the General Association of Regular Baptist Churches, North.[11]

Dissatisfaction continued within the Northern Baptist Convention. It stemmed from two major sources of friction. One was over what the critics of the Society called its "inclusive policy," by which they meant that the missionaries appointed might include those who were orthodox and those who were not. To offset this charge the Society in 1933 once again affirmed the statement of its "evangelical" policy

[10] For report concerning investigation of missionaries, see the Board's statement in *The Baptist,* Vol. 6, No. 44 (Dec. 5, 1925), p. 1347, and *Annual Report of A.B.F.M.S.* for 1927, p. 56. For policy statement made at Washington, D.C., see *Missions,* Vol. 17, No. 6 (June, 1926), pp. 388-400.

[11] See fuller account in Torbet, *A History of the Baptists* (Philadelphia, 1950; revised, 1952), pp. 411, 450-51.

issued in 1924. However, discontent remained, and it was claimed that missionary candidates were being appointed who denied the virgin birth of Jesus Christ, and that the Board's statement of policy did not require a specific affirmation of that doctrine.

The other source of friction was aroused by the degree of centralization in the denomination which the Board of Missionary Co-operation represented. Having arisen at a time of theological controversy between the advocates of liberalism and fundamentalism, it is not surprising that some saw in it a menace to their position because it seemed so far removed from the autonomy of the local churches who were asked to respond to its fund-raising efforts. In 1933 the Convention made an effort to remedy the situation by replacing the Board of Missionary Co-operation with a Council on Finance and Promotion, which should be representative of all Boards and Societies in the Convention. The Executive Committee of the abolished Board was replaced by a General Council designed to be an administrative agency for the Convention and one to which the various committees of the Convention should be responsible.[12] This attempted adjustment did not allay the fears of those who saw in the Convention a threat to democratic procedures in the local churches, nor did it mollify the persistent charges made against the Foreign Societies that they were not giving sufficient attention to orthodox teaching and direct evangelism in their work.

In the meantime, however, an interdenominational survey of the philosophy and methods of the Christian missions around the world aroused even more general discontent. It was the Laymen's Missionary Inquiry which has been described briefly in an earlier chapter. From its inception, Baptist laymen were prominent in the survey, five of them being members of the interdenominational committee of eight laymen who were to guide the undertaking. Indeed, the committee had been created by Baptists who had heard Dr. John R. Mott, chairman of the International Missionary Council, report in 1930 on his recent world tour of the mission fields. These laymen were intent upon determining how wisely and economically this enterprise had been administered during its more than one hundred years of existence. The survey, which required three years (1930–1933), was reported in six large volumes. A more popular summary of the findings and conclusions was published under the title, *Re-*

---

[12] For fuller treatment see *Ibid.*, pp. 456-57.

thinking Missions. The report pronounced the aim of Christian missions to be the presenting of the Christian way of living and thinking. Education, medicine, and similar allied pursuits of missionaries were commended as suitable ends in themselves quite apart from the direct motivation of evangelism. Missionaries were criticized for having a "limited outlook and capacity" and for seeking to establish Western-type churches in a sectarian manner. The committee advocated that missionaries refrain from attacking non-Christian systems of religion.

The basic point of view set forth by the Laymen's Inquiry was challenged by practically all mission board leaders across Protestantism, and certainly by most Baptists. The Board of the Foreign Society were of the decided conviction that the Laymen's Report did not do justice to the missionaries. Moreover, they took drastic exception to the philosophical interpretation of the basis and scope of the missionary enterprise. As they surveyed the character of their work, they were able to point to more than 4,000 schools, 30 hospitals, 61 dispensaries, leper asylums, orphanages, agricultural stations in China, Burma, and India, and to large indigenous churches among the Karens and Kachins in Burma, the Garos and Nagas of Assam, the Telugus of South India, the Bantus of the Congo, and the Chinese. They were able also to point to their social influence in the anti-opium efforts in the Orient, against foot-binding in China and child marriage in India, and in behalf of public health and literacy. In 1931, of the 3,000 Baptist churches in non-Christian lands 63 per cent had been reported as self-supporting.[13]

Further indication of the traditional point of view held by most Northern Baptist leaders with respect to the primary function of missions was made clear by the survey of mission education in India and Burma undertaken at the request of both Foreign Societies in 1932–1933. The study was made by Dr. Frank W. Padelford, executive secretary of the denomination's Board of Education, who traveled for 22 weeks in the company of Dr. Joseph C. Robbins, foreign secretary. The report revealed that Baptists far surpassed other missions in Burma, except in primary education. Because of generous support from Burmese Christians, it cost American Baptists only

---

[13] P. H. J. Lerrigo, compiler and ed., *Northern Baptists Rethink Missions: A Study of the Report of the Laymen's Foreign Missions Inquiry* (New York, 1933), pp. 24, 47-60, 69, 100. See also *Annual Report of A.B.F.M.S.* for 1933, pp. 27-29; Records of Board of Managers, A.B.F.M.S., 1933–34, pp. 24-30.

about $10,000 a year to conduct the two theological seminaries, two training schools, 22 high schools, 113 middle schools, and 675 primary schools involved in the over-all program. Missionaries and Burmese alike regarded the schools as the leading evangelistic agency in the Burma Baptist Mission. The report warned, however, that this large number of schools could be maintained only so long as pupils' fees and government grants-in-aid could be collected. The report also indicated that the girls' schools were distinctly superior to those for boys, due to the fact that the Woman's Board had followed a policy of concentration rather than of expansion. Under this policy, two women were placed at the head of each school, whereas the Board of the Foreign Society had followed the practice of placing each school for boys under the care of a man who also had large field responsibilities. It is significant, in view of the long tension between the rival emphases of education and evangelism on the field, that Dr. Padelford's opinion was "that the missionary has held too exclusively to the school as his avenue of approach." He also observed that in some countries the hospital and the dispensary had been substituted for the school, whereas in Burma the medical work was very limited. As an over-all strategy, Dr. Padelford recommended that two special missionaries of outstanding competence and training be sent to Burma and India respectively, solely to make contacts with the political and cultural leaders who were in a position to determine the future of their respective countries.[14] In this way, the most effective use could be made of education as a means of Christianizing the culture of the peoples involved.

The sixth year of financial depression and economic uncertainty (1935) brought the work of the Foreign Societies to a very critical situation. Donations from churches and individuals were still below normal, although the decrease was lower than in any previous year. From 1930 to 1935 receipts from this source had dropped from $807,822.51 to $438,936.47. To raise the missionary quotas of the churches, the Council on Finance and Promotion inaugurated in 1935 a denomination-wide movement to obtain from individuals "One More Dollar" as a gift over and above the regular pledges.[15]

---

[14] Frank W. Padelford, Report on Christian Education in India and Burma, 1932–33, (mimeographed, 40 pp.), pp. 4-11.

[15] N.B.C., *Annual,* 1935, pp. 405, 426. The decrease in donation receipts in 1931–32 was 15%; in 1932–33, 20% plus; in 1933–34, 12% plus; in 1934–35, 7% plus.

This effort was followed, during the next two years, by a Forward Movement Fund by which the Convention hoped to enable the mission societies to hold their own financially. Actually the contemplated budget provided for no new missionary appointees. In 1936 a slight increase in contributions was announced for the first time in seven years. By 1937 it was possible to send two new families to the foreign field. Although the industrial depression seemed to be receding, there was as yet no permanent increase in contributions in evidence.[16]

With the worst of the depression in the background, the Foreign Society and the Woman's Society engaged in several evaluation studies which were reported in June, 1936. In addition to detailed plans for the specific fields, they pointed to the accomplishment of several major aims: (1) To fill the gaps in the depleted missionary ranks. (2) To make more adequate provision for the needs of the missionaries. (3) To strengthen the work of evangelism on every field, and to give more guidance to the mass movements, while also following up openings among the more responsive peoples. (4) To develop further an indigenous leadership. (5) To cultivate self-support on all fields, making a distinction between subsidizing activities, which should be avoided, and supplying tools for effective work. (6) To place more emphasis upon the new rural community approach in Burma, China, and Japan. (7) To press forward in wise measures of co-operation with other Christian bodies. (8) To maintain close consultation between the two Boards so as to avoid overlapping in their work.[17] This ambitious program was not to be fulfilled at once, for ominous clouds of war were beginning to gather on the horizon.

An Era of War and Crisis (1939–1945)

The growing threat of world conflict during the nineteen-thirties intensified the problems of missionary administration. As the Fascist Axis in Europe laid claim, first, to Ethiopia, then to Austria, Czechoslovakia, and ultimately on September 1, 1939 to Poland, it became increasingly difficult to conduct affairs with any degree of normalcy. The entrance, that autumn, of the British and European democracies

---

[16] *Ibid.*, 1936, pp. 390-96; 1937, pp. 381, 424, 427; 1938, pp. 386-87, 409.

[17] *Ibid.*, 1937, pp. 422-24. For full report see Records of Board of Managers, A.B.F.M.S., 1934–36, pp. 415-36; 1936–37, pp. 37-41, 120-31, 347-55.

into open hostilities with the Axis Powers was the beginning of a terrifyingly prolonged agony of bloodshed, mass bombings, and desolation. The flames of burning villages and devastated cities spread swiftly over Europe, first to engulf the Lowlands and France, then to threaten Britain's very existence, and finally to destroy thousands of Russian towns as the Nazi armies moved relentlessly toward Stalingrad in 1942. In the meantime Japan's surprise attack upon Pearl Harbor on December 7, 1941, brought the United States into the war. This only increased the already serious hindrances to mission work in the Orient.

As early as 1931, China became the victim of an "undeclared" war by Japan, whose armies invaded Manchuria and eventually occupied large territories in East and South China. Fortunately for the Christian missions, many denominations, including the Baptists, had been gradually transferring leadership and responsibility to the Chinese Christians. Thus when the Japanese arrived and set up a puppet regime, the Chinese themselves in many cases determined the course of action to be taken. For example, from the outset of the Sino-Japanese struggle, the Chekiang-Shanghai Baptist Convention decided not to conduct its schools under the puppet regime. Accordingly, the primary schools were closed, and the middle schools were evacuated to Shanghai, where the East China Christian Co-operating Middle School was set up. This institution carried on the work formerly conducted by 16 Christian schools of various missions in the occupied territory near the city. Although housed in a crowded downtown office building, the school managed to care for 750 students until the Japanese attack on Pearl Harbor when it was disbanded.

Mission property was soon taken over by the Japanese who regarded it as their own. The Riverside Academy at Ningpo was put to use as a boys' school; the Riverbend campus in the same city was occupied by a cavalry unit of the Japanese army. Both Wayland Academy and the Hangchow Union Girls' School plants were used by the puppet regime. These examples were typical of what was occurring throughout occupied China.

Institutions of higher learning tended to follow the student trek to Free China in the West. In 1937 Ginling College and the University of Nanking evacuated to Chengtu in West China, where they continued to operate as guests of the West China Union University.

Nanking Theological Seminary was moved to Shanghai in 1938, to be manned by an entirely Chinese staff. By 1943 its work had been disrupted by the war, so that only one department continued and that in West China in co-operation with West China Union Theological College. When the Board of Directors of the University of Shanghai suspended work on January 27, 1942, the alumni opened the Shanghai Institute under the leadership of Dr. C. C. Chen, an outstanding biologist, to conduct a regular minimum of courses in the rooms of the China Baptist Publication Society. It was entirely self-supporting.

Medical work in East China was carried on after 1937 with unusual courage under increasingly difficult circumstances. By 1941 the Baptist hospitals at Shaohing and Ningpo were cut off from contacts with the Mission Headquarters at Shanghai when those cities were taken by the Japanese. Yet the staffs continued their work, the American missionaries not leaving until 1943.

By July, 1942, nearly all "enemy nationals" (Americans, British, etc.) in Japanese occupied areas were removed to larger cities near the coast—Peking, Tientsin, Chefoo, Tsingtao, Shanghai, Canton, and Hong Kong. The largest number were in Shanghai. For a time they could move about their business freely. But by the fall of 1942 they were required to wear armbands in public and were forbidden entrance to places of public entertainment. During this time they were obliged to support themselves by what personal savings they had, by the income obtained from the sale of personal effects, and in some cases by loans from the United States Government made through the Swiss Consulate-General. General internment came in February and March, 1943, in what were called "Civil Assembly Centers." Although the treatment was reportedly not "deliberately harsh," living conditions were difficult and there was much suffering and privation.

Mission property in East China, in at least one-third of the area, including the University of Shanghai, fell into Japanese hands. Hospitals were continued as public institutions under Japanese or local "puppet" supervision, or they were occupied as Japanese military institutions. Schools were allowed to continue under Japanese supervision, or operated as part of the public school system, or confiscated for other purposes. Churches fared better, many of them being permitted to function as heretofore, others being confiscated for non-religious purposes. For a time the Japanese talked in terms of turning mission properties over to the Chinese Christians. They also exerted great pressure on the churches to unify Christianity in China. In March, 1943, they succeeded in persuading the various churches in Shanghai to organize the Shanghai Christian Union Executive Committee which was to operate with Japanese oversight. This was to become the pattern for religious organization in other cities in China.

By 1943 Japanese soldiers occupied all cities in East China where Baptist work was being carried on—Huchow, Hangchow, Ningpo, Shaohing, and Kinhwa. Severe fighting took place in Shanghai, where the North Shanghai Baptist Church was destroyed. In Kinhwa and in Ningpo there was also some destruction to church property. Elsewhere some congregations had to relinquish their buildings. Yet church attendance, evangelistic zeal, and financial support maintained a surprisingly high level. The Chekiang-Shanghai Baptist Convention functioned well, and its executive secretary, Dr. T. C. Bau, gave admirable leadership during the trying times after the missionaries had been evacuated.

Baptist work in South China suffered from frequent air raids, and many of the things said concerning the East China Mission could be duplicated for the South China Mission. West China became the rallying point for the hopes of China's future. At Chengtu, Northern Baptists co-operated with other Protestant denominations in the West China Union University which served as host to the refugee schools of the invaded areas.[18]

Prior to the Japanese air attack on Pearl Harbor, the Protestant Church in Japan (Kyodan) had been organized in 1941, independent of foreign funds and official direction from missionaries. Through this means the educational and publication work as well as the evangelistic program of the various denominations at work in Japan was co-ordinated. Therefore, when hostilities broke out between Japan and the United States the Christian forces were already under general government oversight through the Department of Education.

---

[18] This survey of war conditions in China has been drawn from such sources as: *Toward the Mark: Baptist World Advance, 1940–1944,* p. 20; Lerrigo and Amidon, *All Kindreds and Tongues,* 1940, pp. 198, 205, 210-18; N.B.C., *Year Book,* 1942, p. 291; 1943, p. 206; reports provided by repatriated missionaries of East China in 1943, prepared in mimeographed form by the A.B.F.M.S.

This situation may have saved the Japanese Christians from persecution. The only hindrance which they experienced during the course of the war was the resentment which non-Christians felt toward Christianity because of its intimate association with American and British life.

Two days after Pearl Harbor, William Axling and his wife, veteran missionaries of the American Baptist Foreign Mission Society, were placed under "house-arrest." Then, on September 16, 1942, they were taken to separate concentration camps. In December, 1943, there were still thirty-nine Protestant missionaries in Japan, two of whom were on the staff of the Foreign Society, J. F. Gressitt and Mrs. H. W. Topping whose husband had died in Japan during the course of the war.

Church attendance among Christians in Japan declined during the war years. The lag was due in part to long working hours, to the fact that Protestant pastors and Roman Catholic priests, as well as Buddhist and Shinto priests, were required to spend some time in work essential to the war effort, and undoubtedly due also to the effects of the war itself. Much of the work in Japan was permitted to continue. The Mary L. Colby School, for example, underwent many changes after Pearl Harbor but remained open. By the end of April, 1942, all American teachers in the school were compelled to stop teaching, and a year later Bible study was discontinued by government order. The kindergartens and social centers carried on their usual service. Once again the transition to national leadership had been a wise move which paid rich dividends in such a time of crisis.[19]

When bombing began in the Philippines in December, 1941, most of the missionaries on Panay Island moved up country to towns and barrios between Calinoz and Dumalog. When the Japanese invaded the island, several of the missionaries were interned and placed eventually in the Santo Tomas Prison at Manila. The Central Philippine College was forced to close a few days after war was declared, mainly because so many students and faculty members left to join the army. The Iloilo Mission Hospital and Capiz Hospital were moved early in 1942 to Calinoz and Dumalog respectively, where they continued to function until the arrival of the Japanese army. The Jaro and

---

[19] *Toward the Mark,* pp. 23-24; N.B.C., *Year Book,* 1942, pp. 288-89; reports of repatriated missionaries of Japan in 1943 and a manuscript address delivered by Dr. Axling on his arrival in America that year.

Iloilo churches were closed with the outbreak of the war. All other churches continued, some up to the invasion, and others after the initial invasion. The Convention of Philippine Baptist Churches secured permission from the Japanese to carry on its work.

The invasion of the Philippines was costly for the Baptists, for it resulted not only in the almost total destruction of mission property at Iloilo, and elsewhere, but also in the loss of eleven missionaries and a thirteen-year-old boy who were arrested in their hide-out on Panay Island and executed by the Japanese military on December 20, 1943.[20] The other missionaries who had been held in various places of internment were liberated in 1945 by the American army.

Burma and Assam, being in the path of moving armies, first of the invading Japanese and then of the Allied Forces, suffered grievously in property damages and loss of lives, but not in Christian courage. In Burma and to a degree in Assam, as elsewhere in war-torn areas, the Baptist policy of having developed a strong national leadership proved its worth when in 1943 all of the missionaries were compelled to evacuate.

In the Belgian Congo the mission work was not disrupted by the war directly. In fact there was a continuance of the strong response to the gospel among the Bantus which had characterized them in earlier years of the mission's history. However, the acceleration of industrialization which accompanied the war period wrought a major change in the life of the Congolese people, for it removed them further from their uncomplicated tribal life and enticed them into a materialistic society for which they were unprepared. The problems which have ensued deserve the more detailed treatment which will be given in a later chapter.

The effects of the war on the mission fields have been dealt with in some detail because they give meaning to what was happening at home during the war years. The budget was raised in full during the year, 1942–1943, not only because of the rising income of a wartime economy, but because of a growing concern for the preservation of the mission enterprise at a time of great crisis. When the

---

[20] Report of repatriated missionaries of the Philippines in 1943 prepared by the A.B.F.M.S.; N.B.C., *Year Book,* 1943, p. 202; 1944, pp. 303, 310. For the story of the heroic martyrs, see Chapter XXX of this book; also *Through Shining Archway,* a pamphlet published by the American Baptist Foreign Mission Society and the Woman's American Baptist Foreign Mission Society (New York, 1945).

Northern Baptist Convention met at Wichita, Kansas, in 1941, approval was given to an undiminished budget. At the same time the decision to raise an additional $600,000 as a World Emergency Fund for wartime needs was made. The goal was reached. A new goal of $2,000,000 was set for the year 1944–1945. At the same time, missionaries were returning to their posts, many by circuitous and danger-infested routes. Others were already back. In spite of the hazards and complications of wartime travel, 157 new appointees and returning missionaries had sailed for foreign fields between the outbreak of war in 1939 and the spring of 1944.[21]

A move to integrate the two Foreign Mission Societies, which had been under consideration for some time, received an impetus from a temporary move made during this chaotic period. In 1942 a cabinet was established to be composed of nine members of the Board of the Foreign Society and six members of the Woman's Board. This joint body was to meet at least monthly, and to exercise all functions of the two Boards. Reports of its meetings were to be sent to the Boards, which were to hold two sessions annually. The reason for the move was that the problems of the two Societies had multiplied so greatly, owing to the war, that it was no longer practicable to depend upon quarterly meetings of the full boards. On the other hand, no step was taken to integrate the two Societies at that time. This was to be a later development.[22]

Because the war had curtailed the advance of mission work in China and in other areas involved in the war, the two Foreign Societies met with the two Home Societies of the denomination in April, 1942, to consider the possibility of opening a new field in South America. The Home Societies were involved because they traditionally had been responsible for mission work in Central America and would therefore be concerned about any extension of work in Latin America. It was the unanimous agreement of the conference that the proposal was not wise, for the prospect of sustained support after the war was uncertain. Moreover, Southern and Canadian Baptists, as well as other evangelical bodies, were already at work in South America. It was decided therefore to husband the resources which were accumulating for postwar developments.[23]

---

[21] N.B.C., *Year Book,* 1944, p. 313.
[22] Records of Board of Managers, A.B.F.M.S., 1940–42, pp. 450-52.
[23] *Ibid.,* 1942–43, pp. 7-8; *Missions,* Vol. 34, No. 6 (June, 1943), pp. 357-58.

Owing to wartime travel restrictions, the Northern Baptist Convention did not hold its annual meeting in 1943. Instead, representatives of the General Council, of the Council on Finance and Promotion, of the several national, state, and city agencies affiliated with it, and the Post-War Planning Commission met in Chicago in May, 1943, to consider the affairs of the denomination and to hold the annual meetings of the boards of the respective agencies. The Foreign Board was faced with demands from fundamentalist groups within the Convention to rescind their appointment of Dr. Elmer A. Fridell, of Berkeley, California, as foreign secretary for the Orient, because of dissatisfaction with his views on certain issues. After a full hearing, the Board reaffirmed the appointment which had been made in the previous February.

To add to the emerging dissatisfaction in the denomination, the General Council of the Convention, at its midyear meeting in December, 1943, authorized the purchase of a conference center for the denomination at Green Lake, Wisconsin, to be known as the Northern (now American) Baptist Assembly. The venture had been recommended by Dr. Luther Wesley Smith, the executive secretary of the Board of Education and Publication, with the unanimous support of representative secretaries of all the national agencies of the Convention. The property consisted of more than one thousand acres with two miles of lake-shore frontage, and although it was estimated to be worth $8,000,000, it was purchased for $300,000. Some objected to the decision because it had not come before the entire Convention for approval. Others objected that the money might be used more wisely in direct missionary work. Actually, its value as a national training and conference center for the denomination has been abundantly demonstrated in the years which have followed. The American Baptist Assembly's Board of Managers is representative of the various co-operating agencies of the Convention.[24]

The Fridell appointment had fanned the long smoldering dissatisfaction on the part of the Fundamentalists into a full flame. The instance at hand provided the occasion to press once again for an abandonment of what they called the "inclusive policy." Failing in accomplishing this at a joint conference with Board representatives in Chicago in September, 1943, they set out to organize a new for-

---

[24] *Missions,* Vol. 34, No. 6 (June, 1943), pp. 362-63; Vol. 35, No. 6 (Feb., 1944), pp. 104-06.

eign mission society which would appoint only those who subscribed to a creedal position which was to be embodied in its by-laws. Indicative of the point of view of its founders, the new agency was to be called The Conservative Baptist Foreign Mission Society. It came into being in Chicago on December 15, 1943, when a board of eighteen members was chosen, six each from the western, central, and eastern sections of the Northern Baptist territory. National headquarters were established in Chicago.

At least two missionaries of the American Baptist Foreign Mission Society resigned their posts to become affiliated with the new agency. In May, 1944, the Board of the Foreign Society adopted a statement repudiating the term "inclusive policy," as it had come to be used and misused by the Society's critics. It was voted:

> That because of the misunderstanding and unfortunate associations connected with the term 'inclusive policy' the American Baptist Foreign Mission Society is happy to go on record as disavowing the 'inclusive policy' in any sense that would imply an inclusion of appointees under the Board who are not in wholehearted agreement with our established evangelical policy . . . (the policy was then reiterated as stated in 1924).[25]

Meanwhile a Convention Committee on Conference and Co-operative Unity was at work, seeking to evolve some amicable solution to the tensions created by the existence of the competitive Society. In May, 1945, its majority report was adopted by the General Council of the Northern Baptist Convention, which met in Chicago to act for that body in the absence of a convention meeting which again was cancelled because of wartime restrictions. In substance, the report refused to recognize the new organization as "another society within the framework of the Northern Baptist Convention." Instead, it recommended that the name "conservative" be dropped and that the society become simply "a fellowship to encourage churches to contribute to the support of Convention missionaries whom it approves." A minority report presented by Dr. W. Theodore Taylor, president of the Conservative Baptist Foreign Mission Society, requesting recognition as "an independent foreign mission society, supported by Northern Baptist churches and members of Northern Baptist Convention churches" was rejected.[26] This action arose from

---

[25] Records of Board of Managers, A.B.F.M.S., 1942–43, p. 89.

[26] *Ibid.*, pp. 322-28; N.B.C., *Year Book,* 1945, pp. 51-52.

the view of many that the newly organized society constituted a rebellious element in the Convention, that it had been organized without consulting that body, and that it was unwilling to subject itself to the rules governing the activities of the co-operating agencies of the Convention.

The Conservative Baptist Foreign Mission Society accordingly continued its work without Convention recognition. It drew its support from non-Convention Baptist churches which previously had supported non-denominational "faith" missions and from individuals within the Convention who had become dissatisfied with the policies of the Foreign Society and of the Convention in general. It also sought funds from such churches within the Convention as would respond to its appeal.

Although the revival of theological controversy had thrown a pall over the Convention when it met at Atlantic City in 1944, there was plainly emerging a new spirit of consecration, unity, and sacrifice, which had been born of the era of conflict and discipline through which Northern Baptist had passed. Unified budget receipts for the year ending April 30, 1944, totalled $4,500,000, the highest in any single fiscal year since 1929–30. The Postwar Committee which had been appointed by the Board of the Foreign Society in 1943 to study plans for the reconstruction period reported in 1944 that they were engaged in studies concerning Japan, the Philippines, and the Congo as areas of special consideration for rebuilding when the war should end.

Postwar Planning and Progress (1945–1954)

By 1945 the Northern Baptist foreign mission enterprise was entering upon an era of advance in the face of great losses due to the war and the challenge of the tremendous needs for reconstruction. Indicative of the new trend was the report made in 1946 by the Postwar Committee which had been working for at least two years under the direction of Dr. C. L. Seasholes, of Dayton, Ohio. The findings revealed the changes which foreign missions were undergoing as the result of the war period. Personnel was regarded as the master key to the many problems facing the Societies. The missionary of the mid-century required a degree of specialization and competence unthought of in 1900. Suitable living quarters were considered important to his well-being, yet they should be of a type in keeping with the national level of living standards. The committee stressed the need to give support to the younger churches in rebuilding and rehabilitating workers. A distinction was made between assisting nationals by supplying necessary tools for their task and doing the job for them. Medical work, public health programs, the relief of hunger, and leadership training were all viewed as phases of the missionary task which should be continued and strengthened. It was very apparent that equipment needed modernization and new methods should be introduced as rapidly as possible. There was a determination to renew fellowship with the Christians in Japan, now that hostilities were at an end.[27]

The possibility of engaging in reconstruction work to any significant extent depended upon the willingness of the churches at home to increase their giving. To this end the General Council of the Northern Baptist Convention in 1945 approved plans for a World Mission Crusade to be conducted under the direction of the Council on Finance and Promotion for two fiscal years (1945–1947). The goal was $14,000,000, of which sum $10,000,000 was to be used to meet non-recurring needs of rehabilitation created by war, and $4,000,000 for recurring needs over and above those covered in the unified budget. This effort was coupled with a Christian Life Crusade designed to strengthen the local churches through emphasis on evangelism and stewardship. It was planned that nearly 63 per cent of the amount raised should be used for foreign and home mission projects.[28] When the Convention met in May, 1947, at Atlantic City, New Jersey, it was announced that the amount had been oversubscribed by more than $2,000,000. This great achievement was largely the result of the tireless leadership of Dr. Luther Wesley Smith, national director of the World Mission Crusade and executive secretary of the Board of Education and Publication, and of Dr. C. Oscar Johnson, general chairman of the Crusade and pastor of the Third Baptist Church in St. Louis, Missouri.

The optimism engendered by the success of the fund-raising effort was matched by activities on the mission fields. Missionaries who, because of war conditions, had been serving on fields other than their own were being transferred to their former posts. Families long sepa-

---

[27] Records of Board of Managers, A.B.F.M.S., 1946–47, pp. 97-100.

[28] N.B.C., *Year Book,* 1945, pp. 86-88, 114-18. See also *Crusader* (official denominational news magazine), No. 6 (May, 1946).

rated were reunited. Eighty-four adults and forty-six children secured passage in 1945–46 from America. In East China, Wayland Academy, in spite of a badly wrecked plant, was reopened with 1,400 boys in attendance. Evangelistic meetings held in many of the mission schools, including the University of Shanghai, brought a large number of conversions. In South China the two national conventions had maintained their identity during the period of semioccupation. A Chinese staff opened Bixby Memorial Hospital, and the Kwong Yit Girls' School continued without interruption throughout the war. As soon as missionaries arrived from their refuge in West China, the Mission was able to function once again. The West China Mission was the only Northern Baptist field in the Far East that had escaped invasion. Now that the war was over, refugee institutions in Chengtu began to return to their former locations.

The Burma Baptist Convention met in December, 1945, with over 600 present. In March, 1946, the Kachins of the Kutkai area held a local association meeting at which 1,500 were present. Later, the Pwo Karen associational gathering numbered 4,400 with over 400 women in attendance. All groups were planning for a vigorous future program, and churches were being restored before their homes were rebuilt.

The Filipino Christians in Iloilo set about at once to rebuild the completely destroyed Central Philippine College. Toward the rebuilding program, one hundred per cent of the faculty and staff made individual pledges, although ninety per cent of them had lost their homes and possessions during the course of the war. Japanese Baptists asked for sixteen missionaries to be sent to help them in their evangelistic and educational work. In the Belgian Congo steps were being taken to open a new station among the Bayaka tribe. Two new dispensaries and one new baby clinic in the Banza Manteke area brought the total to eight dispensaries and five clinics to serve the Bantus. The Ongole field in South India reported over a thousand baptisms in 1945–46, the largest number since 1929. Vellore Christian Medical College had won the right to teach the full M. B. and B. Sc. courses in medicine and surgery. Dr. John S. Carman and Dr. Carol E. Jameson of the Baptists were on its staff.[29]

Through the Foreign Society's special representative to Europe,

---

[29] *Gleanings Along Kingdom Highways,* a pamphlet of facts published by A.B.F.M.S. and W.A.B.F.M.S. in 1946.

Dr. Edwin A. Bell, relief and encouragement were being given to stricken Baptist congregations in many countries on the continent. Through World Service Relief, sponsored by the World Council of Churches, Baptists poured a steady stream of food and clothing into many parts of the world. Such was the response to the needs of the postwar period.

Both Societies were aware of the growing problem of maintaining permanent institutions abroad, such as schools, hospitals, and orphanages, in the face of increasing resentment of nationals against Western influence on the one hand, and of the inability of the younger churches to support them on the other hand. Yet the Boards determined to continue their support as long as possible. Thus, in November, 1947, they voted to reaffirm their responsibility for three distinctly Baptist institutions of higher learning: the University of Shanghai, Central Philippine College, and Judson College. At the same time they voted to continue to co-operate in eleven union institutions in China, Japan, India, and Belgian Congo. Keenly aware of the urgency of developing capable national leadership as rapidly as possible, the Boards decided in January, 1948, to give priority of financial support to theological training schools on their mission fields.[30]

A number of special gifts projects were authorized by the two Societies in March, 1948. They included plans for spending $200,000 for evangelistic work among the Hakkas in South China, the Japanese in Okinawa, the Santals in Bengal-Orissa, and the Nagas in Assam—all peoples whose responsiveness to the gospel was unusually encouraging. To provide for better equipment and to develop audio-visual materials and literature, especially for rural education, a sum of $100,000 was planned. For support of Bible training schools and seminaries in the Naga Hills in Upper Assam, at the Pwo Karen Bible Training School in Insein, Burma, and at the Nanking Theological Seminary in East China, $110,000 was to be raised. The Societies planned also to spend $260,000 to support medical work at the American Baptist Mission Hospital in Gauhati, Assam, to finance the South China Medical Program, to rebuild Iloilo Mission Hospital in the Philippines, and to strengthen the Briton Corlies Memorial Hospital in Yuan, West China. A sum of $100,000 was to be spent for bringing nationals to the United States

[30] Records of Board of Managers, A.B.F.M.S., 1947–48, pp. 230, 234.

for special training and for fellowship, and to make possible the visit of Americans to the mission fields, thereby developing better understanding between the older and the younger churches. A like amount was to be used to rebuild churches in Shanghai, East China, in Rangoon, Burma, and in Warsaw, Poland. Christian Training Centers for industrial and agricultural instruction in Bengal-Orissa, South India, and the Belgian Congo were to receive $130,000.[31] It was an ambitious program indicative of the progressive planning of missionary leaders aware of the changing needs that confronted them.

The successful achievement of such projects depended in large measure upon American support. Mission secretaries found themselves increasingly sensitive to the problems which confronted them on the home front as they sought to increase financial giving and to develop understanding of the grave changes that were taking place continuously on the fields. In November, 1949, Dr. Jesse R. Wilson, home secretary since 1940, outlined to the Board of the Foreign Society a number of the major problems which it faced in the performance of its work: (1) The seeds of suspicion that had been sown in the denomination through misunderstanding and hostile criticism. (2) The disposition of some state conventions and city societies to withhold for use in their areas an increasing proportion of the money raised for the unified budget. (3) The development of new agencies and causes that were laying claim to a share of the Unified Budget of the Convention. (4) Heavy taxation which absorbed an increasing proportion of income from which mission gifts must come. (5) The tendency of some to doubt the wisdom of supporting missions under circumstances of disturbed world conditions. (6) The inability of mission secretaries to find time or energy to concentrate on promotional efforts while under the pressure of accentuated administrative problems.[32]

Yet in spite of the complex problems to be faced, the missionary cause in the denomination gained favor. It had always supplied the main motivation for co-operative effort, and with the removal of many sources of tension, a chastened and more earnest Convention moved forward. In 1950, at its annual meeting in Boston, the Northern Baptist Convention changed its name to the American Baptist Convention. The Council on Finance and Promotion became

---

[31] *Ibid.*, pp. 301*a*-301*b*.

[32] *Ibid.*, 1949–50, pp. 161-62.

known as the Council on Missionary Co-operation, thereby restoring the missionary motive to fund-raising. In Buffalo in 1951, it was reported that receipts for the fiscal year, 1950–51, had amounted to nearly $6,000,000. There were increases each year thereafter, until by 1954 a budget of $7,800,000 was adopted.

The steady mounting of missionary support was due to a number of reasons. The Convention had regained a sense of urgency about its mission. The Council on Missionary Co-operation had developed new and effective techniques for training laymen and laywomen in the churches to assume their stewardship responsibilities. An increasing number of missionaries were being appointed each year for service on foreign fields, thirty-nine being dedicated in 1954 at the Convention meeting in Minneapolis, Minnesota. A third factor was the growing strength of the organized support of the women through the National Council of American Baptist Women which had been organized in 1951 to replace the older National Committee on Woman's Work. It paralleled the National Council of American Baptist Men, and sought to enlist an increasing proportion of the women of the churches in the Baptist world mission.

Commensurate with the growing support at home were the developments on the mission fields. In January, 1952, the Foreign Society extended its mission work to Thailand (Siam), nearly 117 years after William Dean had arrived in Bangkok to work among the Chinese and 83 years after missionary work for the Siamese had been abandoned in 1869. The resumption of service in this ancient land was to be among the Karens and the Swatow-dialect Chinese, many of whom were refugees from Baptist areas in Burma and China. The new field was staffed in part by missionaries evacuated from China in 1951 when work there became impossible after the triumph of the communist regime.

On the older fields there were encouraging results. In 1952 the number of baptisms totalled 24,620. To the growing churches was given increasing responsibilities as the administration of the fields was being transferred to them at a pace greatly accelerated over former years. The Burma Baptist Convention became an administrative body in 1954 with full approval of the Mission Societies. The Philippine Baptist Convention and the Shinseikai (the Baptist New Life Fellowship) of Japan were assuming larger administrative responsibilities. Even in the Belgian Congo, where general conditions had retarded the transfer of leadership, a Baptist fellowship body was formed and leading Congolese for the first time were admitted officially into the Mission Conference.

New approaches with the gospel were introduced on some fields. These included Christian Centers in crowded cities such as Hong Kong, Bangkok, Rangoon, and Leopoldville, into which great numbers of people had come in recent years, either to gain employment or to seek refuge from wartime conditions. Student Centers were built in or near government colleges in Burma, the Philippines, and Japan to provide a Christian ministry and message. This means of reaching the student populace proved to be less expensive than to found and support Christian colleges. Much attention was given to the development of rural programs in the Philippines, Japan, and Burma in particular. Public health programs also were emphasized. Christian leaders were being taught to utilize audio-visual aids, newspaper evangelism, and the preparation of Christian literature for the wider spread of the Christian message.[33]

According to reports for 1952 and 1953, the two Foreign Mission Societies were supporting 352 missionaries in Japan, the Philippines, Thailand, Burma, Assam, Bengal-Orissa, South India, and Belgian Congo. On these fields there were 4,298 organized churches (not counting 1,150 congregations in South India which had not been organized into churches). The total church membership numbered 501,070. Besides these areas of responsibility, the Foreign Society supported Dr. Edwin A. Bell as its representative to Europe, giving him an operating budget of approximately $35,000 with which to assist the churches. Additional sums in varying amounts were channeled through him for postwar relief, rehabilitation, and construction. In 1952–53 there were 750 Baptist churches and a total membership of 155,685 in Belgium, Finland, France, Germany, the Netherlands, Norway, and Sweden. In recent years, countries under the communist regime were closed to him.[34]

In 1950 a Committee on Integration of the two Foreign Mission Societies began to study the possibility of creating one Board to administer the work of the two agencies. By November, 1954, a plan of organization had been developed which seemed feasible, and it

---

[33] Jesse R. Wilson, *American Baptists Overseas: A Handbook of American Baptist Foreign Missions* (New York, 1954), chaps. 4 and 8.

[34] *Ibid.*, pp. 9-23.

was adopted at a joint Board meeting. At the meeting of the American Baptist Convention in Atlantic City in 1955, the integration was approved by both Societies.

From this survey of the developments at home, one is impressed with the high degree of consecration and eagerness on the part of mission leaders to meet the challenge of a changing world. The realism with which they faced the almost insurmountable problems was matched only by their boundless faith in the power of the gospel to transform human life and society regardless of circumstances. It has been a thrilling story, but even more exciting is the record of the accomplishments on the mission fields, often amidst tragic suffering and heartbreak.

CHAPTER XXV

Progress of Women's Work

A MAJOR FACTOR in the successful maintenance of the world mission of American Baptists through the four decades of war and world revolution was the vision, determination, and courage of Baptist women. They worked with marked effectiveness through the Woman's American Baptist Foreign Mission Society and numerous auxiliary state and local societies. Because their accomplishments were distinctive, although related closely to those of the American Baptist Foreign Mission Society, their work deserves separate treatment. For convenience, the highlights of the special developments and contributions for which they were responsible in the period following 1914 will be traced by decades.

New Ventures (1914–1921)

On June 16, 1914, it will be recalled, the Woman's American Baptist Foreign Mission Society, in Boston, completed its organization by formally adopting the new constitution and bylaws that merged the eastern and western societies of earlier days into one functioning unit. Mrs. Helen Barrett Montgomery became the first president, remaining in office until 1924 with the exception of the year 1921–1922, when she was released from her duties to serve as president of the Northern Baptist Convention. During that year Mrs. Andrew MacLeish took her place. The stability of the Society in these years was in no small measure due to the able leadership provided by Mrs. Montgomery, a woman of unusual stature in scholarship and Christian statesmanship.

Symbolic of the close relationship which was developing within the denomination between the several mission agencies was the merger in 1915 of the *Helping Hand,* the official periodical of the Woman's Society, with *Missions,* which had become the joint publication of home and foreign missions. In the same year, the Woman's Foreign Society united with the Woman's American Baptist Home Mission Society in organizing the World Wide Guild to enlist the interest of young girls in the missionary cause. By 1920 there were nearly 3,000 Guild Chapters across the Convention, with a combined membership of over 33,000 girls. This effort was followed by the initiating of a Children's World Crusade as a part of the general scheme to educate the very young to recognize and accept their missionary responsibility. The Guild and the Children's World Crusade were placed in that year under the direction of the Department of Missionary Education of the Convention's Board of Education. They still co-operated with the two Women's Boards and made regular contributions to their mission work.

In financial progress the most significant step taken by the Mission Societies in 1917 was the adoption of the Joint Apportionment Plan, whereby the two foreign boards presented a single appeal to the churches and divided the receipts on the basis of a previously agreed apportionment. This plan continued until still greater administrative co-operation between the Societies was achieved when the women moved their offices from Chicago and Boston to New York to join the Foreign Mission Society in establishing headquarters in the Holland Building on Fifth Avenue.

Achievements on the mission fields were keeping pace with the progress that was being made at home in this period. In 1918, for example, the Woman's Board had erected a new stucco school building at Sendai, Japan, to provide for 125 students. In East China, a women's building was opened at Huchow for the inauguration of a new type of work for married Chinese women; it was called a Homecraft School, where instruction was given in the development of a Christian home and in the care of children. In West China a hospital for women was begun on a small scale at Suifu.[1]

One of the most distinctive ventures of the Woman's Society was its participation in interdenominational institutions on the mission fields. As early as 1915 co-operation was given to the opening, at Madras, of the first Union College for women in India. This was

---

[1] *The Standard* (a Baptist weekly published in Chicago), Vol. 65, No. 39 (May 25, 1918), p. 1160.

followed by joining with four other Mission Boards in the establishment of the Woman's Christian College in Tokyo in 1918. It was the first attempt in Japan to provide high grade college education for women. Another project which attracted great interest among supporters of the Woman's Society was the hospital and Union Medical College for Women at Vellore, South India. These two institutions were the outcome of the notable work of Dr. Ida Scudder, a medical missionary in South India since 1900. Her work was widely supported by several Woman's Mission Boards in America, including the American Baptist. In 1920 Baptist women also co-operated with four other Boards in opening two institutions in East China, the Woman's Medical Training School at Shanghai and the Bible School for Chinese women at Nanking.[2]

Plans for the celebration of the fiftieth anniversary of the organized foreign mission work of Northern Baptist women were launched at the annual meeting of the Woman's Society at Atlantic City in 1918. These plans called for the raising of $365,000 to be secured by extra gifts and pledges before the Jubilee Celebration in 1921. By the time of the Northern Baptist Convention meeting in Des Moines, Iowa, in 1921, the Jubilee Fund was overpaid by more than $100,000. In addition to an anniversary celebration at the Convention and in 10 districts across the country, Jubilee meetings were held on the fields. Inspired by the occasion, the Telugu Baptist Woman's Home Mission Society was organized with 42 members, representing 23 villages. New work for women and children was begun in Poland and Czechoslovakia, where five Christian nurses and Bible teachers were supported by the Woman's Society.

Within 50 years, the number of missionaries sent out by Northern Baptist women had increased from 2 to 275. They were serving in 112 stations on the 10 Baptist mission fields. Their contribution to educational work had been most significant, as they determined the policy and supervised and supported more than 1,000 schools of all grades from kindergarten through high school. In addition, they were co-operating in three different countries in the founding and support of three liberal arts colleges and one medical college. In some respects they had become specialists in education, providing training of

---

[2] *Missionary Directory of Fields and Events: A Story of the Year, 1923–1924* (New York, 1924), see list of important events from 1871–1923 on pp. 83-99.

teachers, Bible women, and nurses. To the solution of social problems in many countries, Baptist women also had made a distinctive contribution by founding orphanages, homes for widows (many of them still children, as in India), schools for mothers, and Christian social work in the congested centers of large cities. The missionaries also directed the work of 300 Bible women who devoted full time to evangelistic teaching and preaching. They also became medical directors for 26 hospitals and dispensaries, training more than 100 native assistants since the beginning of medical missionary work. At home, Baptist women had become competent in the handling of funds. In 1920 the treasury department of the Society collected, invested, and disbursed more than $1,000,000.[3] In a half century of service, the women of the Northern Baptist Convention had made a notable contribution to Baptist missions, and the Jubilee year found them well qualified for the expanding tasks which lay ahead.

Expansion Under Trial (1921–1931)

The Jubilee Celebration was accompanied by an enthusiasm which was reflected in the large number of missionaries commissioned by the Woman's American Baptist Foreign Mission Society in 1921 and 1922, and in the expenditure of more than $1,000,000 for new buildings and an additional $200,000 for equipment and repairs on the field from 1921 to 1931. This was accomplished in spite of the fact that the budgeted amounts during the decade were reduced ultimately to 75 per cent of needs. Consequently special efforts to raise money became necessary. The Jubilee Fund, which was expended in its entirety during the period, made possible the erection of 10 new buildings, the establishing of scholarship funds for missionaries and foreign students to study in America, and the dispensing of relief for emergencies. The Lone Star Fund, which was authorized by the Northern Baptist Convention in 1925, proved a successful measure at a time of serious indebtedness and retrenchment. Then in 1929 the Judson Fund was launched by the two Societies to raise $1,000,000 from individuals, with no appeals to the churches. The women's share of the receipts raised by 1930 was $212,000, which facilitated the sending out of 10 new missionaries, the erecting of some new build-

[3] *Missions,* Vol. 12, No. 6 (June, 1921), pp. 324-33; *The Baptist,* Vol. 2, No. 19 (June 11, 1921), pp. 589-90; No. 20 (June 18, 1921), pp. 623-25; No. 49 (Jan. 7, 1922), p. 1555.

ings, the strengthening of educational and medical equipment in Assam, the investment for the first time of an adequate share in the development of the new Judson College which was being erected as a unit of Rangoon University, and provision for the pensioning of retired missionaries. Still another source of income in this period was the Laura Spelman Rockefeller Memorial Fund, a gift of $1,000,000 from the Rockefeller Foundation which was matched by an equal amount given to the Woman's American Baptist Home Mission Society. Only the interest on this capital, amounting to about $50,000 a year, was to be used, and that for new buildings, for the development of national leadership on the fields, and for support of interdenominational missionary work.[4]

During this decade a number of changes occurred in the leadership of the Society. In 1924, upon Mrs. Montgomery's retirement from the presidency, Mrs. Herbert E. Goodman, a widely traveled and capable woman, was elected. About the same time Mrs. Henry W. Peabody and Mrs. Andrew MacLeish withdrew for other interests. They were replaced by Mrs. Howard Wayne Smith, administrative vice-president, and Mrs. Nathan R. Wood, foreign vice-president. Following the death in 1925 of Mrs. T. E. Adams, veteran officer in the West and for twelve years recording secretary, her duties, which had multiplied with the years, were divided between Mrs. W. S. Abernethy of Washington, D.C., and Mrs. W. C. Coleman of Wichita, Kansas. The office of foreign secretary for the Society had been occupied by Miss Nellie G. Prescott from 1916 to 1921, followed successively by Miss Mabelle Rae McVeigh and Miss Minnie V. Sandberg. The post of administrative secretary was filled in turn by Miss Harriet E. Clark, Mrs. L. J. P. Bishop, and Miss Janet S. McKay. The treasurers of the Society in this decade were Miss Alice M. Hudson and Miss Frances K. Burr.

Several new departments were established within the administrative organization of the Society which were indicative of the expanding services which it was rendering. The Department of Designated Gifts and of Visualization of the Budget proved very helpful during the days of retrenchment. The Department of White Cross Supplies for Overseas caught up the enthusiasm that women had displayed for the Red Cross work during the First World War. Through this phase

[4] Isabel Warwick Wood, *What God Hath Wrought for the Woman's American Baptist Foreign Mission Society, 1921–1931* (New York, 1931), pp. 8-11.

of the work, materials for use in hospitals and dispensaries were prepared by women in the churches and shipped to the fields. The Administration Department and the Field Activities Committee of the Board of Missionary Co-operation directed deputation work of missionaries home on furlough. The Department of Mission Study, the World Wide Guild, the Children's World Crusade, and the Department of Missionary Education played important roles in developing a sense of stewardship responsibility in the churches for the support of foreign missions and the recruitment of new missionaries. In 1930 the Woman's Society, like the Foreign Society, transferred its headquarters from the Holland Building to 152 Madison Avenue in New York.

An important advance step in the Society's work from 1921 to 1931 was the development of national leadership among women on the fields. This was in keeping with the trend in the Foreign Society as well, and was in response to an evident desire of many of the younger churches for a larger participation in the administration of their work. The growing emancipation and prominence of women which had followed the First World War was evident in the rise of seven national missionary societies of women on the mission fields of Northern Baptists. In Burma there were two, the Karen Women's Missionary Society, founded in 1920, and the Burma Women's Missionary Society, established in 1923. The latter Society supported eight full-time evangelistic workers besides many part-time workers, and erected a home for Bible women and a rest-house for Christian Burman women. It looked forward to the time when it should be able to maintain the Burman Women's Training School. Similar societies were established in Bengal-Orissa, South India, Assam, and Japan. In South China the Women's Society was under the auspices of the Ling Tong Conference. On the three China fields, women were appointed to the national councils which were rapidly taking over responsibility for the administration of policies, expenditures, and personnel in East, South, and West China.[5]

At the beginning of this decade, the Woman's Foreign Society began to co-operate with five Christian colleges in Asia which had been organized interdenominationally during the World War period to develop the leadership of women. The Laura Spelman Rockefeller Memorial Fund made possible an appreciable increase in the yearly

[5] *Ibid.*, pp. 11-14.

appropriations to these institutions and an addition of four others to the list. The union institutions thus supported in 1931 included Woman's Christian College at Tokyo; Ginling College at Nanking, whose president, Dr. Wu Yi-Fang, was a Baptist; Shanghai Woman's Christian Medical College, connected with the Margaret Williamson Hospital which was the largest hospital for women in China; Madras Woman's Christian College; Vellore Union Medical College, founded by Dr. Ida Scudder; St. Christopher's Training College at Madras, which provided specialists in education; and West China Union University at Chengtu in Szechuan Province. In addition, the Woman's Society helped to support three strictly Baptist schools of higher learning: Judson College in Rangoon, Burma, to which Helen Hunt, the candidate secretary of the Woman's Society, was sent to be dean of women in 1919; Shanghai College, which began to admit women students in 1920; and Central Philippine College which had an enrollment of four hundred men and women.[6]

A brief summary of the achievements on the respective fields during the decade reveals something of the scope of the work and of its expansion. In the Belgian Congo, the Woman's Society had thirteen missionaries in 1931 as over against two in 1920. They had played an important role in training new converts won in the pentecost-like revivals at Sona Bata. They sought also to train the wives of young native pastors in Christian homemaking. Through the financial aid of the Jubilee Fund and the Laura Spelman Rockefeller Memorial Fund, new school buildings were provided at Sona Bata, Banza Manteke, Vanga, Kimpese, and Moanza. The Society also provided nurses to strengthen the medical work at Kimpese and other stations.

In Assam the Judson Fund enabled the Society to enlarge its educational work at Nowgong, where the first junior high school in the country was opened in 1929. At Jorhat, the Society built the Gale Memorial Building for the training of Bible women. The most outstanding women's achievement of the decade in Assam, however, was the opening of the Jubilee Hospital in 1924, which inaugurated medical work in that country. In Bengal-Orissa, where the women undertook work after the union with Free Baptists in 1911, the new Girls' High School at Balasore was the product of Jubilee Funds.

---

[6] *Ibid.*, pp. 14-17; on allocation of the Laura Spelman Rockefeller Memorial Fund, see Records of Board of Managers and Executive Committee of the W.A.B.F.M.S., June 1914–May 1924, pp. 7-8, 409-11.

The Sinclair Orphanage there was enlarged and newly equipped, while the Widows' Home was developed into an industrial school where the young girls left without support might learn to make a living. At Midnapore, the Society conducted the only medical unit in the province.

In Burma the Woman's Society maintained its greatest program in education, directing the work of 920 schools. Baptist women had four high schools for girls and co-operated in a number of others. Some of these institutions had as many as 500 girls, and did not call on the Society for any assistance other than the missionaries' salaries. Each of the three largest schools received a new building during the decade—Kemmendine and Mandalay from the Jubilee Fund, and Morton Lane in Moulmein from a special gift. The one piece of medical work conducted by the Society in Burma, the Ellen Mitchell Memorial Hospital, had grown to a large institution with three American doctors and a nurses' training school that sent out nearly 30 graduate nurses during the ten-year period.

In South India the Woman's Society made possible the erection of new buildings at Nellore—the Gurley Memorial Building for the Woman's Bible School (1922), the Emilie S. Coles Memorial Building, which houses the Elementary and Normal Training School and the Kindergarten Training School as well as school offices and a hostel (1926); and the Girls' High School (1929). The hospital at Nellore was enlarged and newly equipped, and renamed the New England Jubilee Building. It had four American doctors and a nurses' training school by 1931. The Woman's Society also maintained medical work at Ramapatnam and Nalgonda, and assisted the Foreign Society in medical work at several other stations. At Kavali, the women supported a work with children of criminal outcastes. In 1923 they built a Christian Community Center at Madras.

In East China the schools were strengthened by the addition of new buildings with Jubilee Funds at Riverside Academy at Ningpo and the School of Mothercraft at Huchow. The women also supported an industrial work at Shaohing in embroidery work, which employed hundreds of women who formerly were engaged in making paper money to be offered to idols. The Society provided nurses and conducted training schools for the two hospitals at Shaohsing and Ningpo. In South China the nationals took over administration of the schools in 1925. At Swatow two new buildings were provided for women's work during the decade. Rumors of war and the advance of communists into the Hakka area placed the women missionaries under severe strain for most of the period. The Woman's Bible Training School at Swatow continued to supply Chinese women evangelists for areas where the missionaries were unable to go. In West China, after the antiforeign riots of 1927, the work was resumed. The Woman's Society maintained boarding schools, day schools, and kindergartens, and participated in the West China Union University and its Union Normal School. At Suifu, the William Howard Doane Memorial Hospital was erected for the use of Dr. Emily Bretthauer, who had served for twenty-three years at that station.

In Japan the Woman's Society maintained three high schools for girls—the Mary L. Colby School in Kanagawa, a suburb of Yokohama, the Hinomoto Girls' School at Himeji, and the Ella O. Patrick Home School at Sendai which received a new building made possible by Lone Star Funds. In addition the women missionaries continued to conduct kindergartens and a Kindergarten Training School at Tokyo. To meet the pressing needs of congested city life, the Mead Christian Social Center was built at Osaka with Jubilee Funds; in Tokyo, the women had a part in building the new Misaki Tabernacle.

In the Philippines the women operated Doane Hall, established at Iloilo in 1921, and later called the Baptist Student Center. From this place, through a social and religious program, a Christian influence radiated out to the large student population of the city. A Bible and Kindergarten Training School was located there also and girls were sent out to teach the Bible and organize religious and social work. At Bacolod (on Negros Island) was a home for girls. For students studying at the University of Manila, dormitories were maintained to provide a Christian environment. At Capiz the women operated a "Home School" for orphans. The Woman's Society also co-operated with the General Society in the two Baptist medical institutions, Union Hospital at Iloilo and Emmanuel Hospital at Capiz.[7]

Yet this summary does not tell the entire story nor the record of discouragement that lay behind those achievements. From 1921 to 1931 the number of missionaries supported by the Woman's Foreign Society had dropped from 227 to 202. Only nine new appointments were made in the four years from 1923–1926; for lack of funds,

---

[7] The foregoing summary is based on Wood, *What God Hath Wrought*, pp. 17-34.

not a single new missionary was sent out in 1927–1928. It was the Judson Fund that turned the tide, making possible the appointment of ten young women in 1930.[8] It had been a trying period, but greater trials were yet to come.

Depression and Retrenchment (1931–1941)

The drop of nearly $1,500,000 in Convention income during the decade ending in 1931 brought a serious setback to the Woman's American Baptist Foreign Mission Society. That results were not more critical was due to a number of factors—the abnormally favorable rate of foreign exchange, the increase in financial support abroad, the heroic sacrifices of the missionary and native staff, and the income on the gift of $1,000,000 presented in memory of Laura Spelman Rockefeller. Yet, in spite of the valiant efforts to prevent further retrenchment, it was almost inevitable during the severe days of the great depression of 1929–39. Indeed, the effects of the economic depression were intensified by a decline in missionary interest among many as the validity of "foreign missions" came under question. At the same time, the churches abroad were taking root. By 1941 articles of agreement had been completed between the Baptist Boards in America and the Baptist Conventions in South, West, and East China, in Japan, and in the Philippines for the transfer of many administrative responsibilities from the missions to the nationals. In Burma and South India similar plans were in process, and within the later years of the decade, steps were being taken in Belgian Congo to transfer an increasing degree of responsibility to national leadership. Most rapid advance was made in the Philippines, where administrative control passed almost completely into the hands of the Convention there by the end of the ten-year period.

As a consequence of these developments—the increasing shortage of funds, the questioning of the missionary enterprise by some, and the rapid transfer of control to national leadership abroad—the mission staff shrank steadily during the years, 1931–1941. Although there were places where additional missionaries were needed badly and funds were lacking to send them out, in many cases the cut-back in mission staff from America had been caused by the transfer of responsibility to national leaders. At home this trend alarmed the Baptist constituency which was vitally concerned for the welfare of

---

[8] *Ibid.*, pp. 35-37

the foreign mission enterprise, and it resulted in a decrease in the number of missionaries available at home for deputation work. This meant that the Baptists in America were losing touch with the work of the younger churches in other lands at the time when these churches were developing most rapidly and undergoing the greatest change.

The problems which accompanied these trends were made the subject of careful study by the Boards. Like the General Society, the Woman's Society was concerned to adapt its program to meet the rapidly changing conditions. Stimulated by the findings of the Jerusalem Conference of the International Missionary Council (1928), the two Mission Boards saw that the sending churches needed to be aware of the relation which existed abroad between the social and economic backgrounds in the respective countries and the development of the younger churches. This led them to engage in a series of studies, in the middle of the decade, in consultation with the various Baptist conventions on the mission fields. The purpose was to evaluate the work which was being done with a view toward the concentration of mission forces in fewer areas, if world conditions seemed to warrant such a step. At the same time, the Boards were led to consider a fourth type of mission work to supplement evangelistic, educational, and medical missions. It was an attempt to improve the social and economic life of the people by agricultural and industrial guidance, and to increase the literacy of the masses by adult education.[9]

In the midst of these grave problems, the Woman's Society lost some of its ablest leaders. In 1933 Mrs. Herbert E. Goodman, who had served as president for nine years, resigned because of failing health. On July 31, 1934, she died. During her leadership of the Society, she had visited all of the fields except West China, and had been a delegate to the Jerusalem Conference. Three months later, Mrs. Helen Barrett Montgomery died, and with her passing an epoch seemed to have come to a close. In September, 1936, Mrs. John Edwin Scott died. She had been a pioneer in the women's missionary movement and president of the Woman's Society of the West (1899–1910) and honorary president of the Woman's American Baptist

---

[9] For a discussion of these trends, see Minnie Sandberg Sears, *The Seventh Decade of the Women's American Baptist Foreign Mission Society, 1931–1941* (Judson Press, 1941), pp. 9-16.

Foreign Mission Society (1914–36). By the close of the decade, Mrs. M. Grant Edmands had died at her home in Pasadena, California. She had been president of the Society of the East (1905–14) and honorary president of the Woman's Society from 1934 until her death.

In 1933 Mrs. Howard Wayne Smith, of Ardmore, Pennsylvania, was elevated from the post of administrative vice-president to president of the Society. In her new capacity, she visited all of the fields except West China and the Belgian Congo, and participated for many years in the work of the Foreign Missions Conference of North America. Mrs. Leslie E. Swain, of Cape Cod, Massachusetts, succeeded Mrs. Smith as administrative vice-president. In 1938 Mrs. Swain became a delegate to the Madras Conference of the International Missionary Council and visited the mission fields. Always a skillful promoter of missions in the churches, she became a recognized leader in the denomination and contributed much time and effort to the growing ecumenical movement. Mrs. Nathan R. Wood retired as foreign vice president in 1936, and was succeeded by Mrs. Charles H. Sears, the former Miss Minnie V. Sandberg, who had been a missionary in Japan and then had served as foreign secretary of the Board until her marriage in 1933. During her duties as secretary, Mrs. Sears had visited all of the missions except West China and the Congo. When she resigned as foreign secretary in 1933, she was succeeded first by Mrs. J. Charles Humphreys and three years later by Miss Hazel F. Shank, who had been a missionary in Burma. In 1936–37 Miss Frances K. Burr, formerly a missionary in Japan and now the treasurer of the Society, assumed the additional duties of budget secretary. The plan of having a budget secretary had been previously adopted by the General Society also.

In addition to new personnel, there were many organizational changes which reflected the growing needs of the Woman's Society. In 1937 the League of Interpreters was established. Members of the League were women who were able and willing on a volunteer basis to supplement the deputation work of the missionaries. In this effort nearly eight hundred women were enlisted to help interpret the missionary enterprise to the churches. To co-ordinate further the promotional aspects of the Society's work, the responsibility for the women's work was transferred from districts to the state women's missionary societies. From 1937 the president of each state society became the administrative officer in direct contact with the national agency. In 1936–37 the Committee of Conference which co-ordinated the women's work in the Northern Baptist Convention came to be known as the National Committee on Woman's Work. In May, 1937, the name of the Administrative Department of the Woman's American Baptist Foreign Mission Society was changed to Home Base Department, although the functions remained the same.

Since the organization of the White Cross work after the war, there had been no diminution of interest or of accomplishment in this endeavor. In 1940 there were fifty-two tons of supplies shipped abroad as compared with twenty-one tons in 1930—a remarkable record for an entirely voluntary project. The production of literature and publicity for the promotion of the Society's work was in charge of a committee composed of the treasurer and the foreign and home secretaries during most of the decade under consideration. Mrs. Leslie E. Swain and Mrs. Curtis Lee Laws of the Board made notable contributions to this task. After 1935 the preparation of such material was placed in the Home Base Department under the chairmanship of Miss Margaret T. Applegarth. The interdenominational World Day of Prayer was first observed in 1927. By 1934 this prayer fellowship of Christian women had spread to fifty countries. Contributions received on that day in the United States were designated for the Woman's Christian Colleges in the Orient and the migrant work in the United States.[10]

As early as 1934 there were those within the Northern Baptist Convention who believed that a merger of the two Foreign Mission Societies would effect economies and make for greater efficiency. The move was resisted by the Woman's Society in 1936 on the grounds that no economy would be effected, that the work of the women might be jeopardized by such a merger, and that the methods of women's work were unique and should not be sacrificed. The arguments were reminiscent of those which had been used in earlier years when the merger of the two women's societies had been under consideration. The matter was not dropped, however. In 1941 a joint committee of the two Foreign Mission Societies and the two Home Mission Societies proposed that the four agencies should maintain separate legal existence, but that the two Foreign Societies should elect a single United Foreign Mission Board, and the two Home Mis-

[10] The foregoing account is based on Sears, *op. cit.*, pp. 16-24.

sion Societies should elect a single United Home Mission Board. The critical conditions produced by the war overshadowed consideration of this problem during the next few years. However, as we have seen in the previous chapter, the two Foreign Mission Boards did create in 1942 a joint cabinet from among the members of the two Boards to deal with business during the war emergency, thus paving the way for a more favorable reaction to the plan of integration at a later time.[11]

In 1940 the World Wide Guild celebrated its 25th anniversary. During a quarter of a century approximately 700,000 girls had been members of this organization. Through the Guild's program of study, reading, book reviews, dramatic presentations, houseparties, and regular presentation of gift boxes for missions, the extent of missionary support was enlarged appreciably. For 24 years Miss Alma J. Noble, of Buffalo, New York, was the leader of the organization. Its pattern of work at times was adopted by the women, as in the case of the Guild House Party. This was begun in New York State and became popular across the country as it was adapted by the women's state organizations. In that 25-year period the Guild had contributed close to $750,000 to denominational missions.[12]

Any survey of women's work on the mission fields in this trying decade must be given against the backdrop of the exciting events described in previous chapters. Suffice it here but to touch highlights that illustrate the contributions which the women were making to the ongoing of the mission enterprise. In China, for example, times were difficult for the schools. The beautiful campus of Ginling College in Nanking became a refuge for ten thousand women and girls during the siege of the city in 1937. In time the work of the college was transferred to the campus of West China Union University in Chengtu. In Shanghai the Woman's Medical Christian College performed great service under most discouraging conditions. The Associated Boards for Christian Colleges in China, with headquarters in New York, did much to raise emergency funds so that the colleges might continue to operate in West China.

In 1937–38 the two Baptist Boards set out to raise a large sum known as the China Emergency Fund, to help meet the inflationary

---

[11] Records of Board of Managers and Executive Committee of W.A.B.F.M.S., June 1925–May 1936, pp. 724-26; May 1940–Nov. 1943, pp. 131-34, 217-20.

[12] *Missions,* Vol. 31, No. 8 (Oct., 1940), pp. 482-85.

situation and to give relief to human suffering. When the interdenominational Church Committee for China Relief was organized a little later, the Boards backed the new effort fully. In 1940 the Northern Baptist Convention set up the World Relief Committee, which endorsed the Church Committee for China Relief as the chief agency to aid the stricken land.

During the decade, 1931–41, the number of women in the Chekiang-Shanghai Baptist Convention increased from 36 per cent to 50 per cent of the total membership. They were able to take leadership responsibility, thanks to the training program of the Woman's Evangelistic Department of the Convention which had been carried on through lay leadership training conferences and short term Bible institutes.

In South China repeated bandit raids plagued the interior of the country, causing missionaries to flee and making travel virtually impossible. The Japanese invasion of the territory left many towns unprotected, thus encouraging bands of roving brigands to ravage the communities. At Swatow, it was difficult to keep the various educational institutions in operation during the flight of nearly eighty per cent of the population before the Japanese invaders. When the people began to return, however, Baptists opened a combined institution known as the Kakchieh American Baptist Religious Educational Institution, supported by both Societies. The Bible Training School for women passed its sixtieth anniversary during this decade of disruption. With remarkable courage the hospital staffs maintained the services of their respective institutions throughout the Baptist mission areas in China.

The first century of Baptist work in South India, Bengal-Orissa, and Assam came to a close in 1936 with elaborate pageants and exhibitions of the work done in the schools. Education for girls in South India progressed rapidly after the marriageable age for girls had been raised by the government. By vote of the Baptist Missionary Conference in 1934, coeducation was promoted wherever possible. A distinctive community service was rendered by women in South India during this decade as teams of three young women, an evangelist, a nurse, and a teacher, made a home together to serve a particular area. Meanwhile, the Christian women of India were enjoying increasing participation in church life. During these years, the Telugu Woman's Convention grew in strength, and from 1936 it carried responsibility for Sooriapett Hospital. In 1939 the Convention opened a home in Beswada for women in need of special protection.

When the American Baptist Foreign Mission Society decided in 1936 to curtail work among the Bengalis in Bengal-Orissa, the Woman's Board voted to continue support of the Girls' High School at Midnapore. New dormitories were erected there, as at Balasore. Young people's summer conferences were instituted with marked success.

In Assam the Sarah E. White Memorial Women's Hostel was built in 1938 to house students from Cotton College in Gauhati. The Girls' High School begun there in 1931 had an enrollment ten years later of two hundred, furnishing an important link in the Christian educational system of the country. The Woman's Hospital at Gauhati suffered during these years from a critical lack of leadership, although the Nursing School grew appreciably. The All-Assam Baptist Women's Union, which was completely in charge of the women themselves, indicated the progress made in women's leadership.

The work of the All-Burma Woman's Missionary Society and the Karen Woman's Missionary Society grew during this decade. Near the end of the period the Kachin women began to organize in a similar fashion. Because of the traditional freedom of women in Burma, many Christian women were occupying places of leadership in the church, in education, in medical work, and even in government service. The Woman's Society had done much to make this possible by its extensive program of educational work in nearly every corner of the country. During the decade, the three high schools for girls, at Kemmendine, Mandalay, and Moulmein, maintained their high standard. By 1939–40, approximately one-third of the more than five hundred students at Judson College were women. A new building at Insein to house the Burmese Bible Training School was erected in 1933, and the Moulmein Memorial Hospital's plant and equipment were enlarged. Yet, during this ten-year period, the staff of women missionaries in Burma had to be cut from fifty-two to thirty-three because of shrinking funds from America.

When the East Japan Baptist Convention was organized in the early nineteen-thirties to take over administration of all the work of Northern Baptists, a Woman's Department was created, under the chairmanship of Miss Chiyo Yamada, to be in charge of all work for women and girls. This Department spent much effort and money to organize Sunday schools all over Japan. The project gave new impetus to the women's work which had lagged for many years. The Bible Training School at Osaka was closed in 1936, and the Convention entered into a plan with the Methodist School in Tokyo for the religious training of young women. When the subsidies from America were shut off by government action in 1939, the Japanese found it difficult to maintain a high level of work in mission schools. Funds for additional equipment to allow for enlarged enrollment and increased income from fees were wholly insufficient.

The first All-Congo Women's Conference was held in June, 1933. By 1941, as evangelists, teachers, and medical assistants, forty-one Congolese Christian women were associated with the Baptist Mission in the Belgian Congo. In 1934 an interdenominational conference of missionary women was held at Leopoldville to plan ways of developing further the work for women and girls. As a result, handicraft and practical subjects for girls received more attention in later years in most of the schools in the Belgian Congo. Through the great work of Dr. Catherine L. Mabie at Kimpese, nurses were trained to provide much needed prenatal guidance in baby clinics, and to assist doctors in giving semiannual examinations for sleeping sickness required by the government of every person in the Lower Congo.

In 1937, two years after the Convention of Philippine Baptist Churches had been incorporated to administer all of the work of Northern Baptists in the Philippines, the Women's Committee of the Convention's Board of Trustees was formed. In October, 1937, the first conference of Baptist women from various parts of the field was held in Iloilo, bringing together representatives of local women's societies which had been in existence since about 1930. The influence of women in church life was greater in the Philippines than in most countries because they had an equal status with men. They received excellent training for leadership at the Baptist Missionary Training School at Iloilo, which was incorporated into the Central Philippine College in the nineteen-thirties as the Women's Department of the School of Theology. In 1939 a new building was erected for this work. The two nurses' training schools enabled women to make an important contribution to the medical work of the Islands.

The Woman's Society continued to give support to work begun in the previous decade for women and children in Czechoslovakia and Estonia.[13] The widespread influence of the work sponsored by Baptist women within the Northern Baptist Convention in spite of the depression and retrenchment was truly remarkable. Perhaps the most significant indication of progress was the manner in which the leadership of women had developed on every mission field. It was a fortunate trend in view of the events that were to take place after 1941.

War and Reconstruction (1941–1954)

During the year 1941, the Woman's American Baptist Foreign Mission Society celebrated its 70th anniversary by raising the sum of $70,000. The fund was apportioned to many projects in which the Society was engaged. A new department for women was developed in the Pyinmana Agricultural School in Burma. A part of the money was used to develop national leadership on the various fields, and to send out new doctors and nurses to replace retiring missionaries in the Society's medical program. An appropriation also was made to the retirement fund for aging missionaries.[14]

The effects of the war were felt more widely by 1942 as restrictions on shipping tightened and as the emergency needs of war-stricken areas increased. White Cross materials, which the Society furnished for hospitals on the mission fields, were sent abroad under the most trying difficulties owing to the scarcity of shipping facilities. Yet the need was becoming greater, as schools and churches as well as hospitals stood in dire need of material assistance. As soon as hostilities ended in 1945, the amount of goods sent abroad to devastated areas increased appreciably.

The Woman's Society underwent a change in leadership during this critical period. In 1943 Miss Janet S. McKay retired as Home Base Secretary after seventeen years of notable service. She was replaced by Dr. Irene A. Jones. Miss Annie E. Root became the treasurer of the Society, after two terms of service in East China as a missionary of the American Baptist Foreign Mission Society.

At the same time, in an effort to prepare for the post-war needs,

---

[13] The foregoing survey is based on Sears, *The Seventh Decade,* pp. 24-56.
[14] N.B.C., *Year Book* for 1941, p. 291.

the Board of Managers participated in joint planning conferences between 1942 and 1944 with the Board of the General Society. It was estimated that the minimum financial needs of the two Foreign Boards for the five-year period following the close of the war would be in excess of $5,000,000, and that the minimum staff reinforcements would be 80 new families and 40 single missionaries. The story of the World Emergency Forward Fund of 1944–45 and of the World Mission Crusade of 1945–47, as measures taken by American Baptists to meet the needs of reconstruction, has been told in a previous chapter. Suffice it here to say that the enthusiastic support of the women of the churches in these financial efforts was a large factor in their ultimate success. Equally important was the deeply spiritual quality which characterized their approach to postwar planning. In 1946, for example, the Woman's Society observed its 75th anniversary by an emphasis upon prayer, recruitment of new missionaries, and the development of greater stewardship responsibility in the churches.

Still another factor in the successful achievement of this period was the effective service rendered by the National Committee on Woman's Work, which was composed of representatives of the boards of the Woman's American Baptist Foreign Mission Society and the Woman's American Baptist Home Mission Society. Through its guidance, women in the local churches were mobilized for support of the Baptist World Mission. In the five-year period following the close of the war, the Baptist women of the Convention raised annual sums which at times exceeded $300,000 as their "Love Gift" over and above their regular support of the missionary budget of their churches. At the same time, the annual receipts of the Woman's American Baptist Foreign Mission Society totalled more than $500,000, which represented approximately one-third the amount received annually by the General Society.[15]

Between May, 1946, and the same month a year later, forty-four missionaries of the Woman's Society sailed to nine of the ten American Baptist fields, Japan being the exception. Of this number, seven were new appointees. During the next twelve-month period, twenty-seven sailed, of whom six were newly appointed. In 1947 Miss Hazel

[15] The foregoing account is based on reports in *Along Kingdom Highways*, 1943–53.

F. Shank, foreign secretary for India, Burma, Assam, Bengal-Orissa, and Belgian Congo, visited Burma and India to study the needs of women's work in those countries. The next year, Mrs. Charles H. Sears, secretary for Japan, China, and the Philippines, made a similar survey of the missions for which the Woman's Society was responsible in those lands.[16]

There were encouraging signs of evangelistic revival everywhere. In Burma more than 20,000 baptisms were reported for 1947. On the Vanga station alone in Belgian Congo, there were over 1,200 baptisms for the year. In the Philippines, a village-to-village mobile clinic and evangelistic mission reinforced the evangelistic work of the churches, schools, and hospitals, resulting in more than 3,000 baptisms since the close of the war. Reports of equal fervor were made by workers in China, Japan, and Assam.[17]

Although the process of devolution on the various fields was far advanced, whereby the church life came under the direction and, to some extent, the support of nationals, the need for missionary reinforcements continued. Between 1948 and 1953, the Woman's Society appointed on the average of six new missionaries each year, yet there was great need for more recruits. The loss of missionary personnel through withdrawals from the field on account of health and inability to adjust to the disturbed conditions abroad presented a serious problem. In an effort to make the impact of the mission enterprise felt in local areas of the Convention, the two Foreign Societies adopted the policy of holding meetings of the Boards of Managers in various cities across the country. This plan proved to be a pronounced success, for it brought the responsible task of the churches in their world outreach directly to the churches.

It will be obvious, from this summary of the work of the Woman's American Baptist Foreign Mission Society since 1914, that it had acquired a significant and permanent place in the life of the denomination. Whereas it once had occupied a subordinate relationship to the General Society, it now functioned on an equal basis. Indeed, the trend by the close of the period was in the direction of the integration of the two Boards for the greater efficiency of the work. Important areas of Baptist mission work, especially in the fields of edu-

---

[16] *Ibid.*, 1947, pp. 58-60; 1948, pp. 129-30.

[17] Records of Board of Managers and Executive Committee of W.A.B.F.M.S., Jan. 1947–Mar. 1949, pp. 178-79.

cation and medical care, had been strengthened immeasurably by the Woman's Society. At home, the Society had achieved an enviable record in the development of mission support by the rank and file of Baptists.

CHAPTER XXVI

Maturing Churches in Burma

FOLLOWING WORLD WAR ONE Burma, like other Asiatic countries, underwent revolutionary changes in political and social life which affected seriously the Christian missionary enterprise. The deep resentment against Western exploitation, and particularly British rule, came to the surface in more drastic form in this century than in any previous outbursts against white control. The spirit of nationalism was encouraged by the political idealism of Woodrow Wilson who sought to gain world acceptance of the principle of self-determinism for all peoples. It only remained for a world depression and a second world war so to weaken the Western powers that colonialism's hold upon Asia began to crumble. Little by little, the subject peoples of the British, French, and Dutch Empires won demands first for participation in government and then for full independence. During this period Burma achieved a high degree of autonomy after the passage of the Government of India Act in 1935. By 1937 it was separated from India, and by 1940 the country had made significant gains in economic and cultural life.

These changes were accompanied by many evidences of the influence of Western civilization. In 1920 a national university was established at Rangoon, the product of two schools formerly affiliated with Calcutta University—University College, which was the outgrowth of Rangoon College organized in 1885, and Judson College, the only Baptist institution of higher learning in the country. By 1930 there was added to Rangoon University, as the new institution was called, a Training College for Teachers and a Medical College. Judson College maintained its own existence as an affiliated unit of the University, and the strong Christian program continued without serious interruption until Burma gained full independence. From 1931 until 1937 Burma was the only province in British India to provide public education in the vernacular through high school. By 1940 there were 137 motion picture theaters in Burma, of which 16 were in Rangoon. The country enjoyed a program of socialized medicine, with 300 government hospitals and dispensaries making possible the treatment, usually free of charge, of more than three million patients a year.[1]

A significant phase of the developments in the new Burma was a resurgence of vitality in Buddhism, the predominant religion. In 1940 fewer than 10,000 Burmese were Christians. The other Burmese either remained loyal to Buddhism, as did the Shans, or they were animists. Among the Karens, only 17 per cent were Christians, yet they constituted two-thirds of the baptized Christians in Burma. The remainder were animists or Buddhists.[2] Thus it may be seen that Christian missions still faced a serious challenge in the land where Judson had planted the gospel in 1814.

The American Baptist Mission, from the time of Judson, continued to be the leading mission agency in Burma. In 1931 the Baptist membership represented 64 per cent of a total Christian community numbering 331,106. The remainder included Roman Catholics (27 per cent), Anglicans (7 per cent), and smaller groups of several societies (2 per cent). The total number of Christians grew to 350,000 by 1942. Baptist influence in Burma was felt particularly in education, through its numerous schools. It was felt also in medical work, through the Harper Memorial Hospital in Namkham, the Ellen Mitchell Hospital for Women in Moulmein, the Sir San C. Po Hospital in Bassein, and a smaller institution in Kengtung. The Mission exerted further influence through a program of rural reconstruction at the Pyinmina Agricultural School, and through the Baptist Mission Press at Rangoon.[3]

During these years the Mission made its impact upon public life through Baptist nationals who were prominent in the changing po-

---

[1] John Leroy Christian, *Modern Burma: A Survey of Political and Economic Development* (Berkeley and Los Angeles, 1942), chaps. 9 and 10.

[2] *Ibid.*, pp. 41, 203.

[3] *Ibid.*, pp. 205-06.

litical scene. Among the Christian members of the legislature in 1932–33 were U Tun Pe, professor of Burmese at Judson College, and Saw Pe Tha, a Karen graduate of Judson College, who presided as deputy president of the legislature during the heated sessions following the forced resignation of the president over the issue of the separation of Burma from British India. When a delegation from Burma, representing those who favored separation and those who opposed it, met with members of the Joint Select Committee of the British Parliament in December, 1933, to formulate a new constitution for Burma, the one woman delegate was Dr. Ma Saw Sa, a graduate of Judson College and the first woman physician of Burma. Another delegate was Sra Shwe Ba, a Pwo Karen and district evangelist in charge of the associational work of the Bassein Pwo Karens and a member of the Burma Legislative Assembly. When the new government was formed in 1936, four Baptist nationals were in the legislature and another, U Pe Tha, was a cabinet minister.[4]

This rise of national Christian leadership during the thirty years following 1914, particularly among the Karens, occasioned deep concern and resentment on the part of some Buddhist Burmese. They thought they saw in the Christian Karens a reason for the growing demands of the Karens generally for autonomy in the political life of Burma. When Burma finally gained full independence in 1948, civil strife developed between the Burmese government and the Karens who desired an autonomous state within the Union of Burma.

The dominant trend in the period since 1914 was the maturing of the churches in the Asiatic countries. In Burma, the oldest of the American Baptist mission fields, there was an early strengthening of national leadership and the transfer of administrative responsibility from the missionaries to the nationals. By the close of the Second World War it had become evident that an indigenous Christianity was capable of withstanding the stress and strain of war and revolution.

Self-Support and National Leadership in Burma

In 1915 Burma was being acclaimed among Baptists in the United States as a most impressive example of the development of self-governing and self-supporting churches on the mission fields. At the time 768 churches were self-supporting. The Burma Baptist Mis-

---

[4] *Annual Report of A.B.F.M.S.* for 1933, pp. 18-19; for 1938, p. 25.

sionary Convention was then 50 years old. Through it the nationals had achieved a marked degree of interest and efficiency in the work under their care, while the direct leadership of the missionaries had decreased. Burmese women were elected to membership for the first time in 1914. Here and there were notable laymen like Moung Shawloo, great great grandson of a Talaing king of Tennasserim Province, whose grandparents and parents had been baptized by Judson. Educated in the mission schools in Moulmein and trained for medicine in America, he rendered a great service in Moulmein as a physician and as a pillar in the Burmese church.[5]

At the same time a closer co-ordination was being affected between the Burma Baptist Mission Conference and the Board at home. In 1915, for example, the missionaries were granted authority to administer an enlarged emergency fund directly from the field. In response to the growing pressure for admitting nationals to leadership, the annual Mission Conference made room in 1917 for a half day or more of fellowship with delegates appointed by the Burmese and Karen Conventions. By 1921 the first national was elected president of the Burma Baptist Convention. He was Saya L. T. As Syoo, pastor of the Moulmein Burmese Church. In 1922 the president was a Karen, Saya Ba Te, a man who spoke Karen, Burmese, and English fluently and who was a master of parliamentary law.[6]

By 1922 the organized work of nationals was impressive. There were more than 1,000 Baptist churches comprising a total membership of 77,000, and nearly 800 schools with 30,000 pupils. Within the country there were 10 distinct divisions of the Burma Mission, serving the Burmese, the Sgaw Karens, the Pwo Karens, the Shans, the Kachins, the Chins, the Talaings, the Anglo-Indians, the Indians, and the Lahus respectively, each with its own language, customs, and particular problems. The Burmese churches were organized locally into five Burmese Baptist Associations which in turn were combined in the Burmese Baptist Conference. This Conference supported evangelistic and school work in Megwee, and was entirely responsible for all work in half of the large Myingyan field. Churches of the Burmese, Karens, and other groups were organized further in the

---

[5] *Missions,* Vol. 6, No. 7 (July-Aug., 1915), p. 573; No. 10 (Nov., 1915), pp. 816-17.

[6] *Annual Report of A.B.F.M.S.* for 1916, p. 46; for 1921, p. 30; for 1922, pp. 48, 86; *The News (Burma and Assam),* Vol. 30, No. 12 (Dec., 1917), p. 46.

Burma Baptist Convention, which was entirely independent and self-supporting. Its own program of service included support, in whole or in part, of evangelists in 15 fields, and maintenance of the All-Burma Baptist Orphanage at Moulmein.[7]

In 1924 the Board in the United States approved a request made by the Burma Mission Conference to enter into co-operation with the National Christian Council, thus evincing a desire to relate its work in Burma to the wider Christian fellowship. The annual contribution, to be sure, was meager, only $400, but it was a beginning. The growing strength of the Baptist churches in the country was indicated by the fact that contributions to their own work increased from over $130,000 in 1914 to more than $233,000 in 1924, a gain of 79 per cent. Over 81 per cent of the mission schools were financed on the field and received no aid from America. The Burma Mission Press in Rangoon, with its modern plant, was totally self-supporting even to paying the salaries of missionaries associated with it.[8]

When the Burma Baptist Convention met in October, 1928, at Tavoy to celebrate the Karen Centennial, an impressive baptismal service was conducted in the same pool in which Ko Tha Byu had been baptized 100 years before. Of the 951 Karen churches in Burma, 95 per cent were self-supporting. These humble people had come a long way within a single century. By contrast, the Burmese Christians numbered only 5,160 in 1927. Buddhism's hold on Burma was a major factor in deterring further progress among these people.[9]

A deputation to the Burma Mission in 1929, led by Foreign Secretary Joseph C. Robbins, was impressed by the need for a policy of more rapid "devolution," or transfer of administration to the national churches, in view of the strong nationalism in the country and of the depleted missionary staff. The process was encouraged by the organization in October of the Burma Baptist Missionary Committee, composed of nine nationals representing the Burma Baptist Missionary Society and three missionaries. The Joint Committee was to be responsible for the administration of all work and funds entrusted to it by the American Baptist Foreign Mission Society and the

---

[7] Joseph C. Robbins, *Following the Pioneers* (Philadelphia, 1922), pp. 31, 33.

[8] Records of Board of Managers of A.B.F.M.S., 1924–25, p. 13; *Missions*, Vol. 16, No. 6 (June, 1925), pp. 325-26.

[9] *Annual Report of A.B.F.M.S.* for 1929, pp. 33-35; *The News (Burma and Assam)*, Vol. 42, No. 12 (Dec. 1929), p. 85.

Burma Baptist Missionary Society. The plan had been devised on the field by the Reference Committee of the Mission Conference. A similar organization was established for the Karen work.[10]

The transfer of responsibility to the Christians of Burma was more gradual than in China and Japan, where sweeping changes were made between 1914 and 1930. The situation in the Burma Mission was complicated by the presence there of numerous tribes on the borders among whom missionary work was in its infancy, so that devolution could be considered seriously only for the advanced part of the Mission.

The decade of the 1930's was trying for the churches in Burma. In May, 1930, a series of earthquakes destroyed property and resulted in a heavy loss of life in Pegu and Rangoon. The damage to mission property, however, was relatively slight. Beginning later in the year, a series of bandit raids in several districts seriously disrupted Christian activity for a time; many Karen Christian villages were destroyed and numerous Burmese and Karens were killed. The disturbed area included districts in which the mission stations of Tharrawaddy and Thonze were located. Lesser outbreaks occurred in the vicinity of Pyapon, Pyinmana, Henzada, and Toungoo. The disturbances were partly due to an intense spirit of nationalism and the prevalent unrest with British rule, and partly also to the general lawlessness existing in that part of Burma. Furthermore economic depression was a contributing factor because it had produced a severe drop in the price of rice, Burma's staple crop. Interruption in the work of the Mission Society was only temporary, however, and normal conditions soon were restored.

When the British Government agreed to a Round Table Conference at the close of 1931 to discuss the political future of Burma, two of the fourteen national delegates were Sidney Loo Nee and Sra Shwe Ba, members of Karen Baptist churches. The conference pointed toward a plebescite to be held in the fall of 1932 to determine whether the people of Burma desired separation from India. During this difficult period, when the government temporarily withdrew financial support from Karen schools, the churches met the situation by increased donations. When Dr. C. A. Nichols, who had served in Bassein for fifty-two years, died in 1933, the Karen leader, Thra

---

[10] *Annual Report of A.B.F.M.S.* for 1930, pp. 46-47; Records of Board of Managers of A.B.F.M.S., 1928–29, pp. 480-84.

San Ba, took over direction of the educational work, while Sir San C. Po, M.D., long an honored figure among the Sgaw Karens, assumed charge of the evangelistic work.[11]

Under the new constitution, which gave to Burma in 1937 a large measure of self-government, nationalistic uprisings and internecine riots occurred. There were religious conflicts in 1939 between Burmese and Mohammedans and race riots between Burmese and Indians who had migrated to Burma, with the eventual forcing of thousands of Indians to return to their country. During this period of stress, it appeared for a time as though the University of Rangoon, with which Judson College was affiliated, would be brought under government control, but this was avoided by a cabinet change.

On October 24, 1940, the one hundredth anniversary of the completion of the Burmese Bible by Judson was celebrated in connection with the meeting of the Burma Baptist Convention in Rangoon. A year later several hundred Burmese and Karen women met to celebrate the seventieth anniversary of the organization of the Woman's American Baptist Foreign Mission Society. At the Convention which followed, the name of that body was changed to the "All-Burma Baptist Convention." To encourage stewardship for the support of its work, the Convention adopted what was known as "God's Acre Plan," whereby a proportion of farm produce would be sold for a "thank-offering" to God.[12] The church in Burma had taken root in the hearts of its people.

Advances in Evangelism and Education

In 1915 an independent movement of Baptist Burmese Christians undertook responsibility for evangelistic work at Magwe, a town in the extreme southern section of the area then under supervision of L. W. Hattersley, who was stationed at Myingyan. Through what was called the Burman Evangelistic Society, a church and school were organized at Magwe. Ten years later, this society volunteered to assume full responsibility for the Myingyan field, with the understanding that the missionary supervision of the school be continued. Through these moves the Burmese were taking initiative for the evangelizing of their own people as the Karens had done much earlier. In fact, Karen mis-

---

[11] *Annual Report of A.B.F.M.S.* for 1931, pp. 29-31; for 1932, pp. 27-28; for 1934, pp. 31-32; *The Baptist,* Vol. 5, No. 53 (Jan. 31, 1925), pp. 1260.

[12] *Along Kingdom Highways* for 1941, p. 20; for 1942, pp. 26-27.

sionaries at this time were conducting work among the Kachins, the Chins, the Shans, and the Taungthus of Upper Burma, and recently had undertaken a mission to the Lahu tribes of the Kengtung Province, where the converts were numbered by the tens of thousands.[13]

American Baptist missionaries included in their outreach numerous smaller groups of people, some of whom had come to Burma seeking employment. Among these were the Chinese immigrants, some of whom readily sought baptism in the cities. In Mandalay, where four Chinese evangelists were at work, Chinese Baptists erected a building for their work. There were also more than 1,000,000 Indian migrants. They were most numerous in Rangoon and Moulmein where Baptist schools ministered to their needs. Elsewhere, however, there were scattered groups of Indians from Mergui to Maymyo and from Moulmein to Bassein. Altogether there were more than 2,000 Baptists among the Indians of Burma in 18 churches. A third group were the Anglo-Indians and Anglo-Burmese who were chiefly the children of marriages between the women of the land and members of the British army. Many of them occupied high positions in governmental and educational circles. Converts among these people were to be found in the Immanuel Baptist Church at Rangoon and in English-speaking churches in Moulmein and Maymo. An English Girls' High School enrolled 150 Anglo-Indian students in Moulmein. Work among the Talaings chiefly centered in Moulmein. It had been reopened in 1902 by A. C. Darrow and his wife after an interruption of 40 years. By 1926 there were six churches, three of which were self-supporting and two others nearly so. More than 800 baptisms among these people had occurred during that period. Robert Halliday, who was a notable Talaing scholar, strengthened this mission by outstanding literary work in addition to his other duties.[14]

The schools and hospitals of the Burma Mission also engaged in evangelistic effort. Outstanding work was accomplished by teams of college and university students of Rangoon under the direction of the Reverend V. W. Dyer, the pastor of the Immanuel Baptist Church and the general evangelist for Burma. In a dozen campaigns

[13] *Annual Report of A.B.F.M.S.* for 1915, pp. 114-15; *The Standard,* Vol. 64, No. 4 (Sept. 23, 1916), pp. 77-78.

[14] Robbins, *Following the Pioneers,* p. 79; *Annual Report of A.B.F.M.S.* for 1926, p. 92; for 1935, pp. 73-74.

all over Burma, more than four hundred, mostly Buddhist Burmese, became Christians in 1925. In September, 1929, Dyer led a band of students to India in response to an invitation from the missionaries there. Gospel teams from Judson College also conducted successful meetings in mission high schools throughout Burma. During a seven-year period more than two hundred students from Judson College, from the theological seminaries, and from the Bible Schools for Women participated in this new approach to non-Christian youth.[15]

A virtual pentecost among the Pwo Karens began in 1933, when 353 were baptized on a single day in February at Inye-Kyun in Bassein district. By the close of 1934, nearly 2,000 baptisms had taken place among these people.[16] These are but illustrations of the evangelistic advance in Burma during these years. The remarkable successes experienced among the hill tribes of the country will be described in a later section of this chapter.

A significant advance in Christian education paralleled the evangelistic ministry. Most notable for its impact upon the political and cultural life of the country was Judson College (known until 1919 as Rangoon Baptist College). Beginning in 1914 this institution came increasingly under national leadership, and was affiliated with the theological seminaries for Karens and Burmese. When the University of Rangoon was established in December, 1920, Judson College and University College became constituent members of the new institution. This set in motion plans to transfer the Baptist school from its crowded downtown quarters to a new campus in the suburb of Kohine, four miles from the heart of Rangoon. A fifty-four acre site on Victoria Lake, a gift from the Government of Burma, furnished the new campus. Although the college was supported by the American Baptist Foreign Mission Society and the Woman's Society, along with annual grants from the government and gifts from interested citizens, it was administered by a widely representative Board of Governors. This included representatives of the Baptist Conferences of Burma (Burmese, Karen, European, and Indian), three representatives elected by the Burma Christian Council (an English Wesleyan, an American Methodist, and an Anglican), and repre-

---

15 *Annual Report of A.B.F.M.S.* for 1930, p. 109; Randolph L. Howard, *Baptists in Burma* (Philadelphia, 1931), pp. 94, 137-38.

16 *Annual Report of A.B.F.M.S.* for 1933, pp. 222-23; for 1934, p. 33.

sentatives from the missionary staff and alumni groups. Through the constituent relationship thus entered into with Rangoon University, Baptists gained a voice in the government of the new institution and were in a position to exercise a strong Christian influence upon the entire university.

Political unrest that reflected itself in a strike of students in 1920 proved a great strain on the health of President David C. Gilmore and later on the health of his successor, Dr. Elias W. Kelly, who served but three months. In the spring of 1921, therefore, Dr. Randolph L. Howard, a professor in the college since 1910, was elected president. Under his leadership, the institution returned to normal attendance within a few months following the student strike, and a period of steady growth began. Through his negotiations with the government, he obtained assurance that the school would retain full college status which it had gained in 1909. He also enlarged the campus and the number of buildings. In addition to his duties as president, Dr. Howard served as chairman of the executive committee of the Burma Mission and as a member of the Senate of the University of Rangoon. When his wife's health broke in 1924 he was forced to return to America, whereupon he was appointed to the administrative staff of the Society as associate secretary for India, Burma, China, Japan, and the Philippines. In his new capacity he helped to secure the $500,000 needed to supplement a like amount raised in Burma for the new buildings of Judson College.[17] By 1931 Judson College had 25 buildings in all on the campus, including a chapel which cost $100,000, the gift of John D. Rockefeller.

Dr. Howard's successor was Dr. Wallace St. John, who served for eight strenuous years during which time the college was transferred to its new campus. In 1933 he was succeeded by the Reverend Gordon S. Jury, who had served on the faculty for 15 years. By 1938 the enrollment was the highest in its history with 235 men and 102 women. Nine racial groups were represented in the student body: Burmese, Karens, Indians, Anglo-Burmese, Chinese, Chins, Kachins, Mons, and Shans. Nearly 56 per cent of the students were Christians, many of whom were assisting in evangelistic work and Christian instruction in nearby villages.

By educating young people in a Christian environment, Judson College did much to stabilize the mission work in Burma. It also

---

[17] Howard, *Baptists in Burma,* frontispiece.

furnished significant leadership for the new Burma which came into a separate national existence on April 1, 1937. Judson alumni were entering all phases of national life, political, medical, educational, and religious. Some were leaders in government like U Pe Tha, one of the six ministers of the Governor's Council, and Dr. Daw Saw Sa, the only woman senator and the leading woman physician of Rangoon. Others became leaders in church life, among whom were Thra San Ba, in charge of the Nichols Sgaw Karen High School at Bassein, Thra Chit Maung, who had taken over responsibility for the Karen work in Rangoon, Dr. Ma Ah Ma, staff doctor of the Ellen Mitchell Memorial Hospital in Moulmein, and Daw Eleanor San Tay, teacher at Judson and president of the Karen Baptist Women's Missionary Society.[18]

In 1940 the leadership of Judson College passed into national hands as Dr. G. S. Jury retired from the principalship in favor of Dr. U Hla Bu, a distinguished Burmese with a doctor's degree from the University of London. The choice was fortunate, for the institution was entering upon a period of increasingly difficult problems arising chiefly from the intensified nationalism within government circles. In the cabinet of the Burma Government were three Judson graduates, U Ba Yin, minister of education, Saw Pe Tha, judicial minister, and U Ba Than, minister of commerce and industry. It is easy to see how national leadership paved the way for greater public confidence in the institution. The enrollment in 1941 reached a total of 521, representing 16 racial groups, with Christians still predominant in influence and number.[19]

During the next few years, resistance to Western control in church life mounted. In 1942 all powers relating to the University of Rangoon were transferred to the government. In 1945 the University, including Judson College, was operated as a unitary teaching institution. When the Burma Government ruled in 1948 against a return to the constituent college plan, it negotiated with the Mission for the purchase of the buildings of Judson College. The Mission retained the chapel and the chaplain's residence to be used as a center for Christian work on the campus. Left without a Christian college in the country, a National Christian College Planning Committee began

[18] *Judson College, Rangoon, Burma,* a pamphlet published by A.B.F.M.S. and W.A.B.F.M.S., 1938, pp. 7-14.

[19] *Along Kingdom Highways* for 1941, p. 21.

laying plans at once for the establishment of a National Christian College in Moulmein, with a staff to be supplied by nationals. The project failed, however, to secure the approval of the government authorities. Thereupon the American Baptist Foreign Mission Society created out of the monies received for the sale of the buildings a Judson College Scholarship Fund to be used for higher education in Burma.[20]

Closely related in importance for the development of a Christian leadership were the theological seminaries. The oldest of these was the Karen Theological Seminary, at Insein, a suburb of Rangoon. The school had been in existence since 1845. During the last forty years of that period, Dr. D. A. W. Smith had been its president. Under his guidance a thousand young men had been trained for the ministry. Upon his retirement in 1916, Dr. W. F. Thomas, a missionary in Burma since 1880, became president. He occupied this position until 1921, when he was chosen by the Board to be general evangelist for all Burma, whereupon Dr. Harry I. Marshall was selected to succeed him. The Karens were devoted to their seminary and bore the greater part of its cost.

Also located at Insein was the Burman Theological Seminary. Upon the retirement of President J. C. Richardson in 1933 to take up work in the Burmese field at Henzada, the leadership passed into the hands of a national, Saya U Ba Han, who had been a member of the faculty for nearly eighteen years. An English Seminary offering courses in English to advanced students of all races was located likewise in Insein. In January, 1939, it was housed in a new building and renamed, in honor of the donor and his deceased wife, the Willis and Orlinda Pierce Divinity School.

By 1940 theological education had assumed primary consideration in the planning of the American Baptist Foreign Mission Society, as the process of devolution made urgent the increase in trained leadership. The task was made difficult by the multiplicity of races with their separate institutions for men and women in Burmese, Sgaw Karen, and Pwo Karen vernaculars at Insein and Rangoon. Plans were made to centralize the seminaries and Bible schools in Insein so that the missionaries designated to the vernacular institutions might also teach advanced courses in the Willis and Orlinda Pierce

---

[20] Records of Board of Managers, A.B.F.M.S. for 1948–49, pp. 21-22, 236; for 1952–53, pp. 9-10.

Divinity School. A policy of self-direction and self-support with missionary teaching and counsel was followed by the Board.[21]

Another type of specialized education encouraged by the Foreign Society was the Pyinmana Agricultural School, which had been established by Brayton C. Case in 1923 along the lines of the Allahabad Institute developed in 1912, in the United Provinces of India, by Sam Higginbottom, a Presbyterian missionary. Case, who had been born of missionary parents in Rangoon in 1887 and trained in agriculture as well as theology in America, was eminently suited for his appointment to missionary service in 1912. With keen understanding of the basic economic needs of the people of Burma, most of whom lived by the products of the soil, he established in 1917 at Pyinmana a Demonstration Farm as a center of instruction in improved agricultural methods. Six years later he founded the Pyinmana Agricultural School. The burning passion of his ministry may be described best in his own words concerning his call: ". . . to go back and preach the gospel to my friends in Burma and teach them how to do away with hunger and poverty and misery in their villages." [22]

For thirty-one years, Case pioneered in agricultural missions. His work was studied by mission boards around the world. His plan of combining evangelism with an intelligent and sympathetic attention to the economic needs of undeveloped peoples found sympathetic response in the meeting of the International Missionary Council at Jerusalem in 1928. That conference noted that the purpose of rural work in mission fields was "to lead in the effort to build a rural civilization that shall be Christian to the core," and one that should provide for farmers access to land, security, and low cost distribution of their products.[23] The Burma Government was sufficiently impressed by Case's work to make Pyinmana an experimental station of the agricultural college at Mandalay in 1917 and to contribute funds for Case's school in later years. While Case was home on furlough in 1928 he aroused the interest of several deans of agricultural colleges, who led in the development of two organizations, Agricultural Missions Incorporated and the Rural Missions Co-operating

[21] *Annual Report of A.B.F.M.S.* for 1940, pp. 36-37.

[22] Randolph L. Howard, *Lazy-Man-Rest-Not: the Burma Letters of Brayton C. Case* (Philadelphia, 1946), p. 8.

[23] Benjamin H. Hunnicutt and William W. Reid, *The Story of Agricultural Missions* (New York, 1931), p. 11.

Committee of the Foreign Missions Conference. Both organizations were administered by the same secretary, Dr. John Reisner.

By the 10th year of the existence of the Pyinmana Agricultural School, the enrollment had reached 104 as compared with 39 when it opened. The government contributed about one-half of the expenses involved in operating the institution, and shared equally with the Foreign Mission Society in providing buildings which cost $40,-000. In addition to a campus of 30 acres, the school maintained a farm of 150 acres well stocked with cattle, hogs, and fowl. Of the graduates 58 per cent returned to the farm and 88 per cent engaged in some work for the improvement of rural communities. In grateful recognition of Case's contribution to the life of Burma, the government at Mandalay on December 28, 1934, awarded him a medal.

In 1938 the Burma Government voted to underwrite full support of an additional missionary to establish and supervise Agricultural Demonstration Centers in the Kachin Hills. William Henry Cummings was designated to this work. In 1940 Case established an additional Demonstration Center in Kengtung State, at Pangwai. Following the death of Mrs. Case in 1939, the Board of the Woman's American Baptist Foreign Mission Society undertook to raise a memorial fund in 1940–41 for a Woman's Department at Pyinmana to provide training for girls in home building. The memorial became the Lena Tillman Case Home Crafts School.

In his work Brayton Case was careful to combine evangelism with instruction on agricultural problems. After a talk to Christians and non-Christians about farming, he would present an explanation of the Christian message. But always he avoided the practice of using help in terms of agriculture for bait to win non-Christians. Yet entire villages were transformed because the people were eager to hear the message of men whose counsel had brought them success in the cultivation of their rice-fields and farms.[24]

Space does not permit more than a summary of the vast system of Christian schools which the Baptists supported in Burma. The Mission operated a total of 708 schools in 1939 for all grades, in partial support of which the government appropriated grants that totaled more than $200,000. These schools served 35,000 pupils, of

[24] For the foregoing account, see Howard, *op. cit.*, pp. 8-87; see also Howard, *Baptists in Burma*, pp. 135-36.

which 2,022 boys and 1,108 girls were enrolled in high schools and college. In 1940 Judson College reported an enrollment in excess of 500 students. Among the outstanding schools for girls were Morton Lane High School in Moulmein, Kemmendine Girls' High School in Rangoon, and the American Baptist Mission Girls' High School in Mandalay.[25]

During the 20-year period from 1930 to 1950 the number of pupils enrolled in the schools associated with the Baptist churches of Burma remained fairly constant. Government grants dropped, however, from $354,155 in 1930 to $49,001 in 1950. Most of the latter amount was appropriated for hill schools in the Chin and Kachin areas. All of the plains schools were entirely self-supporting. While the appropriations of the Mission Societies in America remained substantially the same, a larger portion went in 1950 toward scholarship aid than toward direct support of the schools. This indicated that the national churches had assumed almost full support of the Christian school system of Baptists in Burma. Moreover, the schools were staffed chiefly by nationals. A heavy burden was thus placed upon the higher institutions of learning to find a sufficient number of adequately trained teachers.[26]

Medical Missions and Christian Publications

In 1920 there were four hospitals in Burma—the Ellen Mitchell Memorial Hospital at Moulmein, the Louise Hastings Memorial Hospital at Kengtung, the Emily Tyzzer Memorial Hospital at Haka, and the Mission Hospital at Mongnai. In addition there were two dispensaries, at Namkham and Taunggyi. Serving these institutions, most of which were extremely limited and inadequately staffed, were four doctors and three nurses from the United States. Medical work in Burma was not a sustained function of the Mission, largely because of inadequate funds and the availability in the country of government hospitals. The continuing medical centers of the Mission in those early years were the Ellen Mitchell Memorial Hospital at Moulmein, with its training school for nurses, and the Moulmein Leper Asylum which had been opened by Dr. Mitchell and Miss Susan Haswell before 1900. The Society also co-operated with the

---

[25] *Annual Report of A.B.F.M.S.* for 1940, p. 123.
[26] Records of the Board of Managers of A.B.F.M.S., 1952–53, pp. 238-39.

American Mission to the Lepers in the maintenance of a leper asylum at Kengtung in the Southern Shan States of Burma.[27]

Out of the dispensary at Namkham, on the northeastern border of Burma, there developed by 1938 a full-fledged hospital under the direction of Dr. Gordon S. Seagrave, who had begun his work there in 1922. He was the son of missionary parents and the great-grandson of the pioneer evangelist, the Reverend J. H. Vinton, who had entered Burma in 1832. With extremely limited resources, Dr. Seagrave developed a hospital and community health program which ministered to an increasing number of Shans, Palongs, and Kachins. A two-story stone hospital building of 100 beds was built in 1938 by Dr. Seagrave with the help of missionary associates at a cost of $40,000, one-half of which was provided by the Woodward Avenue Baptist Church of Detroit, Michigan. It was named the Harper Memorial Hospital in recognition of Dr. Robert Harper, a member of the Detroit church and Dr. Seagrave's predecessor at Namkham. A nurses' training school was developed in connection with the hospital for which Dr. Seagrave prepared a two-volume textbook in the Burmese language on nursing.[28]

Perhaps the most notable contribution to medical missions in Burma came from women who served as physicians and nurses, ministering especially to the physical needs of mothers and children. Among these were Americans sent out by the Woman's American Baptist Foreign Mission Society and nationals who had been encouraged by the missionaries to gain specialized training. A notable woman physician was Dr. Merlin Kingsley, member of an old Anglo-Indian family. She had been trained and inspired by Dr. Marie Coté, a medical missionary who had blazed the trail for women doctors in Rangoon. Dr. Kingsley not only practised as an obstetrician, but became the first woman alderman in Rangoon in order to fight for public health and against the white-slave trade. She was a leading member of the Immanuel Baptist Church until her death in 1927. A second example of nationals in medicine was Dr. Ma Saw Sa, a third generation Christian and daughter of a high government official. She

---

[27] See William B. Lipphard, *The Ministry of Healing* (Philadelphia, 1920); Randolph L. Howard, *Baptists in Burma,* pp. 128-29; *Annual Report of A.B.F.M.S.* for 1920, pp. 115-16; for 1932, p. 28; for 1935, p. 51.

[28] See Gordon S. Seagrave, *Waste-Basket Surgery* (Philadelphia, 1930) and *Tales of a Waste-Basket Surgeon* (Philadelphia, 1938).

had received her education at Judson College, Calcutta University Medical School, and the University of Dublin in Ireland. As the first Burmese woman to gain recognition as a physician, she inspired many young women to study medicine.[29]

The Baptist Mission Press at Rangoon was one of the most efficient publishing houses in the Orient. Its centennial was celebrated in Rangoon on October 15, 1916, with due recognition of the remarkable leadership of Frank D. Phinney, who had served as superintendent for thirty-five years since 1881. During its long history, the Press had issued the complete Bible in four languages of Burma—Burmese, Sgaw Karen, Pwo Karen, and Shan. At the time, a fifth, the Kachin Bible, was ready for publication. Portions of the Old and New Testaments had been published in Talaing. Since the coming of Phinney as superintendent, the Press had been self-supporting and was paying the salaries of its full staff.

On December 15, 1922, the distinguished career of Phinney came to an end with his death, forty years after he had taken up his work in Burma as successor to Cephas Bennett. His mechanical genius and religious zeal contributed to the outstanding success of the Mission Press in Burma. He was responsible for the erection of a fine building in Rangoon and for the design of several fonts of type, of the Burmese Remington typewriter, and of the Burmese and Karen linotype machines which were introduced in 1922. As a Christian layman, he served as a deacon and Sunday school superintendent of the Immanuel Baptist Church in Rangoon. He co-operated with the Burma branch of the Christian Literature Society and was prominent in the Burma Bible and Tract Society.[30] Phinney was succeeded as superintendent of the Mission Press by H. W. Smith.

In 1923 a revision of Judson's famed Burmese New Testament was completed by Dr. John McGuire, who had devoted nineteen years of work to the project while he carried on his regular missionary duties. This was typical of the untiring devotion which missionaries gave to the translation of the Bible and the production of Christian literature in the vernacular, a work most vital to the spread

[29] Howard, *Baptists in Burma,* pp. 97-99.

[30] *Annual Report of A.B.F.M.S.* for 1917, pp. 62-63; for 1919, p. 79; for 1922, p. 73; *The News (Burma and Assam),* Vol. 36, No. 1 (Jan. 1923), pp. 1-2.

of the gospel in Burma. The dissemination of Scriptures and the production of school textbooks and various forms of Christian literature continued unabated until the Japanese invasion of Burma during the Second World War brought widespread disruptions.

Awakening of Hill Tribes in Burma

Thus far we have traced the developments of the peoples on the plains of Burma, the Karens, Burmese, and smaller immigrant groups. Now we must turn to a brief summary of the remarkable awakening which was occurring among the tribes living in the hill country. In a previous chapter we noted the initial missionary appeal made to these people and their impressive response to the Christian message.

Notable among the tribes to receive the missionaries with enthusiasm were the Lahus and Was, among whom work had been begun in Kengtung State by the Reverend William M. Young in 1901. Within fourteen years, ten thousand converts were received. For sometime, questions of comity arose between the Presbyterian Board and the Baptists because the natural development of Presbyterian work from Siam and Baptist work on the eastern borders of Burma brought the two missions face to face. After a series of conferences, the Presbyterians waived claim to the greater part of Kengtung State, reserving only a five-mile strip along the eastern caravan route from Siam to China. Thus the field was left open to the Baptists.[31]

In 1919 a new station was opened at Mong Lem, on the northern border of Burma touching China. Across the border were at least seven thousand Christians who had been converted under Young's ministry at Kengtung Town, a hundred miles to the south. Seeing the advantage of this contact with China, Young moved to Mong Lem in 1920 where his first task was to win the friendship of the Chinese officials who had been persecuting the Christians in the area. Succeeding in this, Young with the assistance of several Karen preachers worked so effectively that within three years' time there were one hundred Lahu villages which had become entirely Christian. They had a total population of ten thousand believers. Later, Young's two sons, Harold and Vincent, came to work with him. Further reinforcements arrived in 1926 in the persons of Raymond B. Buker and his

---

[31] *Annual Report of A.B.F.M.S.* for 1915, pp. 54-55.

twin brother, Dr. Richard S. Buker, a medical missionary. Yet the staff was inadequate to care for the ever expanding Christian community which by that time numbered 170 villages with over 16,000 church members.

Meanwhile, from Kengtung, on the Burma side of this great harvest field, the Reverend James H. Telford was at work, expanding the services of the mission to at least six tribes in the area—the Lahus, Was, Kachins, and Kaws, all animists, and the Shans and Tailois, who were Buddhists. In 1927 the Lahu Mission was removed to Loimwe, a more healthful site, where the Central Lahu School was established. The Shan Mission remained at Kengtung under the direction of Dr. and Mrs. M. D. Miles, who supervised a hospital, school, and church.

In 1936 the Burma Government took under its care the unadministered Wa States lying between Burma and China. This move encouraged the Baptist Mission to expand its work into this area. By 1938 permission had been granted to establish a new station at Pang Yang on the Burma side of the border, to be under the direction of Harold Young and his wife. Vincent Young was in charge of the station to the east at Bana on the China side of the border. A neighboring station at Mong Mong was cared for by a Karen preacher. Within three years, Harold Young had built at Pang Yang a mission residence, a chapel, a dispensary, a small school building, and three houses for teachers—all hewn out of the local forest timber with primitive tools. In 1941 he and his brother at Bana received into the church four thousand members.[32]

The mission to the Kachins was well established by 1914. Since the opening of the century there had been great advance among these people through the work of evangelists and teachers who had carried the gospel and spelling book in the Kachin language as far as 250 miles north and 150 miles south of Bhamo. Through steady growth under the able leadership of Dr. and Mrs. Ola L. Hanson, Miss Eva C. Stark, and Miss Fannie D. Manning, three stations were developed—Bhamo, Myitkyina, and Namkham—with 70 outstations where regular work was done and many more where small groups came together for worship. The Christian community of Kachins in

---

[32] The foregoing account is based on reports in the *Annual Report of A.B.F.M.S.* for 1915, 1920–27, 1936, 1940–41.

1926 numbered nearly 3,000 members. There were 36 schools serving 1,400 pupils. For these people who were just emerging from illiteracy, the Bible was made available in their own language by Dr. Ola Hanson. Over a period of 30 years of unremitting toil, he also prepared a dictionary, a grammar, a hymn-book, textbooks for school use, and a monthly periodical, the *Kachin News*. For his remarkable achievements, he was honored when the Kachins celebrated their Jubilee at Bhamo in March, 1927.[33]

In the 1930's self-support was growing in the three areas of Kachin activity. Of the 21 preachers and evangelists of the Bhamo field, 17 were supported entirely by nationals, as were also two Bible women. Approximately 150 baptisms took place in 1932, and 1,800 rupees were contributed for evangelistic purposes. In the same year the ten preachers on the Myitkyina field baptized 208 converts; at Namkham 240 were received by the 18 preachers at work in that vicinity. Financial contributions almost matched those at Bhamo.[34]

By a process of co-operation between government officials and Baptist missionaries, a program was outlined during the next few years for the social uplift of the Kachins. The efforts included health care, rural advancement, curtailment of the sale of opium, and the promotion of an educational system. In 1939 a branch of the Pyinmana Agricultural School was opened with government support at Namkham under the direction of William H. Cummings, grandson of W. H. Roberts, the pioneer missionary to the Kachins. By 1941 mission work was extended into the "triangle area," a territory in Northern Burma hitherto unreached.[35]

By 1914, only 34 years after the first station had been opened among the Chins, there were 1,200 baptized believers. The real results began in 1919 and continued with gathering momentum. The work centered in two stations far up in the hills, Haka and Tiddim. Christianity wrought remarkable transformations in many Chin villages, eliminating fear of evil spirits, cattle stealing, and the sale of whiskey and opium. By 1926 there were 1,300 Chin Christians witnessing to their faith in all sections of the hills.

Dr. J. Herbert Cope was the leading missionary among these peo-

---

[33] *Ibid.*, for 1926, pp. 92-93; for 1927, pp. 41-42; for 1928, pp. 30-31.

[34] *The Burma News,* Vol. 46, Nos. 4 and 5 (Apr. and May, 1933), pp. 49-51.

[35] *Annual Report of A.B.F.M.S.* for 1938, pp. 24-25; for 1940, pp. 35-36; *Along Kingdom Highways,* 1942, p. 26.

ple, having opened his ministry to the Chins in 1908. He established and built churches among them, served as their pastor and teacher, encouraged better living conditions among them, and played a significant role in providing some thirty-five textbooks in the vernacular of three Chin dialects for village and station schools. In addition he gave the Tiddim Christians the New Testament and a hymnbook. In 1922, when the government took over all the schools, Dr. Cope was made Honorary Inspector of Schools. In 1927 he was awarded the Kaisar-i-Hind medal by the government in recognition of his unselfish service in behalf of the Chin people. On June 11, 1938, he died at Tiddim, and was succeeded in leadership by Chester U. Strait, who had been his associate since 1926.[36]

The close co-operation between the Christian community and the government in the operation of schools in the Chin Hills had several advantages. It assured the maintenance of some 30 schools with 1,500 pupils on a more adequate system than would have been possible for either the government, the Mission, or the churches to do alone. Moreover, it made a strong Christian impact upon general education.[37]

In addition to the work among the northern Chins so briefly described, the Burma Mission included stations for the southern Chins at Thayetmo and Sandoway, where an equally successful work was conducted through the years. In both areas Chin Christians achieved a remarkable degree of self-support by the midcentury in spite of their great poverty.

Developments in Burma Since World War II

Until 1942, Burma had been comparatively peaceful and prosperous for about a generation. The British rulers had granted self-government in the face of strong nationalistic feeling. Then suddenly came the Japanese invasion and conquest. In the disorder that followed, the Christian communities and the Burma Mission underwent a severe ordeal of testing. During the fighting in 1942 between the Japanese and United Nations' armies on a line from the Irrawaddy River on the west to the Sittang River on the east, Tavoy, Moulmein, Rangoon, Pegu, Shwegyin, and Tharrawaddy-Thonze fell into Japa-

---

[36] *Annual Report of A.B.F.M.S.* for 1926, pp. 93-94; *The Burma News,* Vol. 51, No. 7 (July, 1938), pp. 81-84.

[37] Howard, *Baptists in Burma,* p. 117.

nese hands. Mission work was disrupted in Lower Burma almost at once. Missionaries were forced to evacuate, some being transferred to other fields in Assam, Bengal-Orissa, and India. Only a handful of missionaries remained in Lower Burma until ordered out by the government. Headquarters for the Burma Mission were transferred to Mandalay. The treasurer, D. O. Smith, kept mission accounts and sought valiantly to supply the remaining missionaries with funds.

In Central Burma, Brayton Case remained at his post in Pyinmana, where he was endeavoring to collect food for the Chinese Army that was seeking to stem the Japanese invaders south of the city. Through work of fifth columnists, however, the city was fired, and Case, in the company of F. Dickason from Rangoon, turned the mission property and livestock over to the Christians of surrounding villages. They left by car, following a British convoy north toward Yamethin, where they met three trainloads of Chinese troops. Case urged Dickason to go on to Mandalay, while he returned to the fighting front with the soldiers. Thus he became a member of Lieutenant General Joseph W. Stilwell's staff and trekked with him across the mountains to India.

At Mandalay, the remaining missionaries helped in the huge refugee camps to the south of the city which were filled with thousands fleeing from Lower Burma where cholera and dysentery had broken out. When the Japanese bombed the city, the American Baptist Mission Girls' School was converted into a hospital under the care of Miss Lucy Wiatt. Finally, amidst demolition and incendiary bombs, the missionaries abandoned Mandalay. Miss Wiatt, one of the last to leave, followed the Burma Road into China. Others, like Dr. and Mrs. Gordon Jury, of Judson College, made their way on foot along the course of the Irrawaddy River and over the mountains to Assam. Chester Klein managed to get to Dibrugahr, Assam, only to die of sheer exhaustion. Miss Lucy P. Bonney and Miss Mary I. Laughlin fled from Myitkyina to the Kachin Hills, where they trekked through wild jungles for many weeks, arriving in India, ill and exhausted.

Dr. Gordon Seagrave, of Harper Memorial Hospital at Namkham, on the China border, aided Chinese soldiers under General Stilwell's command by his mobile hospital units. In this he was assisted by two Bible Church Mission Society doctors and twenty native nurses. During Stilwell's retreat they reached Assam by the Chindwin River.

Raymond Buker, Harold and Vincent Young, and James Telford,

on the border of Burma and Thailand, were nearly trapped. Vincent Young and Telford were cut off from the rest and obliged to make their way on foot to Kunming, China, through southern Yunnan Province. Gustaf Sword at Kutkai, a little town along the Burma Road, turned the mission over to the Kachin Christians. He and Buker made a hazardous escape across the border into China from whence they secured air-passage to India. After a month of waiting, they obtained sea accommodations to the United States by way of the Cape of Good Hope, Africa. In 1944 Dr. Sword accepted special service with the United States Office of War Information in Burma. Meanwhile the ordained pastors organized to serve as a board of missions to carry on the work.

A tragic casualty of the war was the death of Brayton Case on July 14, 1944. While engaged in a mission to supervise the planting of rice behind the fighting lines in Northern Burma, he was catapulted from a ferry boat as it listed heavily. His body, weighted down with a heavy pack, sank and was never recovered. His untimely death was a great loss, not only to the Burma Mission but also to the entire country that had come to depend upon his scientific efforts to help lift the level of agricultural production.[38]

By 1945, with the aid of the Allied Powers, the Japanese were expelled from the country. This was followed by serious disorders resulting from internal resistance to the restoration of British authority.

Much of the mission and church property had been destroyed or damaged seriously during the war, but emergency funds raised through the World Mission Crusade brought encouragement and help to the Baptists of Burma. By the middle of 1947 most of the necessary repairs had been made to the Ellen Mitchell Memorial Hospital at Moulmein. With new supplies to replace those which had been looted, the hospital resumed operations. Its nurses' training school was also revived.

Christian teachers all over Burma undertook to reopen the Christian schools without waiting for government aid or the return of the missionaries. Charging what fees they could, the nationals divided

---

[38] For a vivid account of war-time experiences of missionaries in Burma, see Gustaf A. Sword, *Come What May, or Triumphant Faith Along the Burma Road* (Chicago, 1943); also see *Along Kingdom Highways,* 1942, pp. 23-28; *Missions,* Vol. 34, No. 6 (June, 1943), pp. 346-49.

the income equally among the staff regardless of professional status. At a time when wages for servants and day laborers were rising sharply, the salaries of the teachers remained pitifully small. In Moulmein, where there had been four high schools under mission auspices before the war, only two could be placed in operation when hostilities ended. One was a coeducational school in the less damaged Morton Lane buildings; the other was the Karen coeducational school which resumed operations in its former location. Most of the buildings at Prome, one of the oldest cities in Burma, had been destroyed by the fighting. The Mission Girls' School and the Woman's Residence, although badly damaged, were the only brick structures left standing. The jungle had grown up about it and wild animals roamed freely through the area. At Henzada, the school was still operating, owing to the courage of Daw Thein, the Burmese headmistress who had refused to give possession of the property to the Japanese.

At Bassein, one of the largest mission stations in the world, the Karen Baptists were laying plans to raise funds to revitalize their evangelistic ministry, to open a hospital, to begin a medical service for the jungle villages, to establish a local Bible training school, and to inaugurate an agricultural project. Such determination to carry on the Christian mission was the more remarkable because many Karens as well as Burmese had suffered imprisonment or martyrdom in the Bassein-Myaungmya district during the war.

At Insein a gift from World Mission Crusade funds made possible the beginning of repairs on the Burman Women's Bible School. The Karen Women's Bible School reopened on Seminary Hill, using an unoccupied residence for a dormitory and sharing classrooms with the Karen Theological Seminary. Much financial support of the work of pastors, evangelists, and Bible women, and of the care of the poor came from the efforts of the Burmese Women's Missionary Society to co-ordinate the work of local groups. The women also assisted in the reconstruction of the schools.

At Rangoon the American Baptists and Methodists co-operated after the war in a flourishing coeducational Christian high school in the buildings of the former Cushing High School, a Baptist property. Most of the five buildings of the Kemmendine Girls' High School had been destroyed by bombing and fire. In the few remaining ones, former Kemmendine teachers maintained a Christian school. The buildings of Judson College were undamaged, although they had been stripped of equipment and library. During the first two years following the war, the College co-operated in the interim University of Rangoon, and in the second year it was possible to open the hostels for men and Benton Hall for women. At Toungoo, where much devastation had occurred, a coeducational Christian school was established in the buildings of the former Girls' High School.

Co-ordination of work was the pattern everywhere as valiant attempts were made to restore the services of the Mission in spite of the severe losses. Leading in this effort was the Burma Council of Baptist Churches, which sought in 1947 to co-ordinate and unify the Christian work of the different racial groups in the country in terms of higher education, agriculture, Christian publications, pensions, and home and foreign missions. The Council was an important adjunct to the Burma Baptist Convention.[39]

As a result of continued resistance to British rule, the United Kingdom entered into a treaty with Burma in January, 1948, granting complete independence. Burma, once free, refused to remain within the British Commonwealth of Nations. This severance of the British tie precipitated a civil strife between the Burma Government and the Karens, the largest of the minorities and a people who did not intend to return to a position of subjection to the Burmese. The spirit of self-determination spread to the hill tribes, some of whom also demanded guarantees of autonomy under the new government. Under such circumstances, the Burma Government, anxious to solidify its rule and to develop a national consciousness, looked with some suspicion upon the missionaries whose Western ideas were regarded as a divisive influence in the country, especially among the Karens and hill peoples.

Under the leadership of the dynamic Premier U Aung San, plans were formulated for a socialist democracy in which the natural resources and major industries would be nationalized and the large landed estates broken up and distributed among the peasantry. But it was not long before a series of crises stemming from internal dissension resulted in economic disorders and the assassination of the premier and several members of his cabinet. Communists who had promised co-operation with the socialist government went under-

---

[39] The foregoing account is based on the report of the visit of the foreign secretary of W.A.B.F.M.S. in 1947 to Burma: Hazel F. Shank, *The Planting of the Lord* (New York, 1948).

ground and began an armed campaign against it. Under the leadership of Thakin Nu, the new cabinet vacillated between brave words and indeterminate action. To aggravate the situation still further, the Karens began pressing for an independent state through their national union. Bitter feelings led to armed attacks which enabled the Karens to seize and hold a large sector of central Burma, where they established themselves as an independent state.

During the insurrection the mission stations at Pyinmana, Toungoo, Bassein, Maubin, and Insein were looted, burned, or totally destroyed. Many Christian villages were wiped out completely. Hundreds of people were made homeless and penniless, and became the victims of starvation and disease. Missionaries faced constant danger. One of them, Miss Selma Maxville, was kidnaped and murdered early in 1950.

Meanwhile, the harrassed government was unable to realize its program of social reform. Public education was set back because thousands of school buildings had been demolished in the war and the limited resources of the country made it impossible to rebuild them. Many boys of school age were gathered quickly into the numerous fighting units scattered over Burma. Immorality, cruelty, and poverty became the prevailing evils of the turbulent period. Much of Rangoon was not rebuilt, and large sections became mere "shack towns."

In the midst of such conditions, the problem of developing a trained Christian leadership became almost insuperable. The destruction of the schools in Bassein, the great damage to the theological seminaries at Insein, and the closing of Judson College by the government in 1949 made the need acute. At the same time, the government's unwillingness to admit missionaries in any large number left the churches without adequate resources to carry on a vigorous program of advance.

Yet, in spite of the civil war between Karens and the Burmese authorities, the number of Karen converts increased by several thousand. In 1948 alone, over 21,000 were added from all national groups to the Baptist churches of Burma. In the hill areas thousands were being won each year from among the Chins, the Kachins, the Was, and the Lahus. The ingatherings presented a serious problem of assimilating such large groups of new converts into the church and into Christian ways of living.

Under the difficulties, Christian literature became an increasingly powerful means of Christian evangelism in Burma. Owing to the complete destruction of the Baptist Mission Press during the war, the literature program was conducted jointly by the Burma Christian Literature Society and the Baptist Board of Publications. Specialized areas of mission service were relied upon more than ever as the government virtually restricted admission of new missionaries to specialists in education, agriculture, and medicine. We have noted already how many of the Christian schools were opened with limited staffs and crowded buildings. The famed center of agricultural missions at Pyinmana was reopened for a time following the war by Roger W. Getz and William N. Rice, only to be closed again when they were obliged to flee for their lives with the advance of communists and the outbreak of Karen revolts. All possessions as well as the Pyinmana stock and equipment were looted or destroyed. Medical work at Moulmein was reopened following the war. The Harper Memorial Hospital at Namkham was reopened by Dr. Gordon Seagrave, who had notified the Board of his intention of working independently. The work in Kentung was carried on by nationals alone until 1947 when Reverend Paul Lewis took charge of the station from his post at Pangwai. By November, 1950, Vincent Young was able to return to Kengtung to supervise the rebuilding program authorized by the Board at home. A number of dispensaries and clinics were maintained in other stations.[40]

By 1952 considerable progress had been made in the reconstruction of damaged property through the courageous efforts of the Baptists of Burma, with generous assistance from American Baptist World Mission Crusade funds. In addition to new buildings provided for schools at Bhamo, Myitkyina, Kutkai, Moulmein, and elsewhere, church edifices were replaced at Sumprabum, Mandalay, Prome, and Rangoon. Of special importance was the rebuilding of the Immanuel Baptist Church in the heart of Rangoon, on the broad plaza facing City Hall and the towering Sule Pagoda. The church had about one thousand members organized in four distinct congregations, each with

[40] The foregoing account is based upon reports from Burma by missionaries, nationals, and staff representatives of the A.B.F.M.S. See *Missions,* Vol. 147, No. 8 (Oct. 1949), pp. 462-67; Vol. 150, No. 6 (June 1952), pp. 340-44. See also Records of Board of W.A.B.F.M.S. for May 1949–June 1951, pp. 475-77.

its own pastor and schedule of services—the Telugu, Karen, Chinese, and Eurasian or English-speaking Christians. In addition to a ministry of preaching and teaching, the church maintained a clinic with the services of three doctors.

During this period the main leadership of the churches and schools within the area of the Burma Baptist Convention was in the hands of nationals. The Karen work was conducted almost entirely without the assistance of American missionaries. Indeed, Karen Christians, themselves, were engaged in an extensive program of evangelistic outreach in Burma and Thailand. While advance was slow among Burmese and Shans, there were 4,200 baptisms, reported by Baptists for 1951, among Chins and Kachins in the hill country. The major progress was clearly evident among the Karens whose numbers increased by nearly 16,000 in the same year. This was true in spite of the hardships of congregations separated from one another by civil strife and with many of their leaders imprisoned by the government for security reasons.

Political conditions in the country became more settled under the leadership of Prime Minister U Nu, who came to power in 1952. Many Karens were released from imprisonment, and a Karen state (Kawthulay) was established with government approval in 1953 within the Union of Burma. The new state included 2,000,000 Karens, smaller groups of Burmese, Mons, Taungthus, and other indigenous peoples. Its constitution guaranteed to all the basic freedoms of thought, speech, religion, vocation, and association, as well as equal participation in the cultural, economic, and educational life of Burma.

In spite of a revival of Buddhism which accompanied the emergence of the new regime in Burma, the people were more ready to hear the Christian message than before the war. An increasing number of Christian books and tracts were sold, local newspapers published Christian messages, and the Burma Broadcasting Station allotted time to a weekly program called "The Church Speaks." On Independence Day in 1952, the Burma Christian Council conducted a united service of worship in an open square in Rangoon. Although the Christians constituted not more than three per cent of the country's total population of 18,000,000, they continued to fill a significant role in the nation's life far out of proportion to their numbers. Christian leaders occupied key posts in several departments of government service.[41] In this and in many other ways the Christian churches of Burma were demonstrating their maturity and so fulfilling the purpose of the Baptist missionary enterprise which had been opened in that land nearly a century and a half before.

---

[41] *The International Review of Missions,* Vol. 42, No. 165 (Jan. 1953), pp. 25-26.

CHAPTER XXVII

Emergence of Indigenous Churches in India

INDIA, LIKE BURMA, underwent great changes after 1914. As an ally of Great Britain in the First World War, the country hoped for an early independence, which was not granted. Prodded by the stubborn resistance of Mahatma Ghandi, the British were forced little by little to make concessions in the years that followed. Through a series of intense nationalist movements, the country won its independence in 1947, when two governments were established, the Union of India and the Mohammedan state of Pakistan. Both, by their own choice, remained within the Commonwealth which has Great Britain as its nucleus.

Within the New India, revolutionary social and cultural changes were affected during this period. The disabilities of the depressed or outcaste classes were annulled, largely through the persistent efforts of Ghandi, who championed their cause although he himself was a caste Hindu. The introduction of new methods of agriculture and industry affected widespread economic improvements. The rising tide of nationalism was accompanied by a revitalization of Hinduism, which was regarded by India's leaders as an important factor in the struggle for cultural unity. At the same time, the new government was not unfriendly to Christianity so long as the movement was in the control of nationals. This attitude was motivated largely by a sense of gratitude for the contribution which Christian schools, medical centers, and rural co-operatives had made to the social uplift of India.

Since 1914 Christianity had made significant advance in the country, the proportion of communicants having arisen from a little more than one in a hundred to more than two in one hundred. Protestants had made the greater gains over Roman Catholics, the large majority of their converts coming from the depressed classes and the animistic hill tribes. Christian schools had opened a door to millions who hitherto had been despised and poverty-stricken. Through two medical schools, women physicians and surgeons were being prepared, especially at Vellore. Rural co-operatives did much to lift the economic level of life for the masses who depended upon the soil for their existence.

Within the area of greater India, American Baptists maintained during these years three distinct missions—in Assam, Bengal-Orissa, and South India. Only one of them, Bengal-Orissa, was of recent accession to American Baptists, having been turned over to the American Baptist Foreign Mission Society as the result of the merger of the Free Baptists with the Northern Baptist Convention in 1911. The other two were, next to Burma, the oldest fields operated by the American Baptist Foreign Mission Societies. Although each deserves extensive treatment, space will permit only a highlighting of major developments in each mission as an indigenous Christianity emerged.

Maturing of the Churches in Assam

Prior to 1914 a deterring factor in the progress of the Assam Mission was the lack of administrative unification. Its stations were so isolated that no effort had been made by missionaries to get together for conference until 1886, and it was not until 1914 that the first All-Assam Baptist Convention was held. The gathering brought together one thousand Christian leaders representing twenty different tribes and languages. To develop further co-ordination of the field as a whole and to establish educational work, in which Assam was sadly deficient, the missionaries elected one of their number, the Reverend A. J. Tuttle, to be conference secretary. The plan was endorsed by the Board and the Mission entered upon a new era of administration. A further advance was made the following year when the Convention formed the Woman's Council to encourage the leadership of nationals in women's work. Under the direction of these women, efforts were made to open a high school for the girls of Upper Assam in Jorhat and to establish a hospital for women and children at Gauhati.[1]

[1] *Annual Report of A.B.F.M.S.* for 1915, p. 137; *Annual of the Northern Baptist Convention* (hereafter referred to as N.B.C.) for 1915, pp. 953-54; for 1920, p. 702.

Although there were efforts to reach the upper classes among the Assamese people, Baptist missionaries experienced their greatest success among the animistic tribes in the hill areas. This was true both from the point of view of evangelistic results and the development of self-support. By 1920 there were among the Garos, who constituted the largest single hill tribe, 19 parent churches, each of which had several branch churches under its care. In 1921 there were 932 baptisms among these people. The Garo churches assumed an increasing responsibility for the Christianizing of their own tribe. Not only did they support their own village schools, but two of the stronger churches helped to maintain schools in weaker villages. More than one-third of the baptisms came through the 77 schools thus supported.[2]

When the veteran pioneer among the Garos, Dr. Marcus C. Mason, died in 1934 at his home in Albany, N. Y., there were 17,000 Baptist church members and 300 national workers listed among these people. Their language had been reduced to writing by Dr. Mason. To him and Dr. E. G. Phillips they owed their Bible in the vernacular. At the central station in Tura were a Girls' school, a Boys' School Hostel, a Mission Hospital, the Kalazar Asylum, and the Leper Asylum—a rewarding legacy of the patience and persistence of more than half a century of missionary endeavor.[3]

Similar success was experienced among the Nagas, with their many branches—the Aos, Angamis, Lothas, Semas, etc. They were found in Aizuto, Kangpokpi, Kohima (government center for the Naga Hills District), Impur, and Ukhrul. The variety of dialects placed a heavy burden upon the missionaries. In 1926, for example, the Reverend J. E. Tanquist completed the translation of the New Testament into the Angami language after four years of work. Yet, other Naga tribes were still without the Scriptures although whole villages were turning to Christianity. By 1928 it was possible to bring together for the first time in convention at Kangpokpi more than 1,100 Baptist Christians from nearly 10 tribes in Manipur State. Churches were assuming an increasing financial responsibility for their work, and were building more substantial and attractive meeting houses.[4]

---

[2] Joseph C. Robbins, *Following the Pioneers* (Philadelphia, 1922), p. 143.

[3] *Annual Report of A.B.F.M.S.* for 1935, pp. 56-57; *Missions,* Vol. 20, No. 5 (May, 1929), pp. 260-61.

[4] *The Baptist,* Vol. 7, No. 10 (Apr. 10, 1926), pp. 309-11; *Missions,* Vol. 19, No. 9 (Oct. 1928), pp. 551-53.

The centennial celebration of the Assam Mission was held early in 1936 at Jorhat, when 5,000 Christians crowded into a huge tabernacle erected for the occasion. There a moving pageant depicted the coming of the early missionaries by boats up the river to Sadiya in 1836, and many scenes of mission activity over a 100-year period. Long after nightfall, several hundred people, carrying lighted candles, formed a huge cross on the sloping bank of the river in a closing service of evangelistic appeal. It was symbolic of the emphasis which had marked the history of the Mission and had brought it from an almost futile beginning in Sadiya to a community of over 57,000 baptized believers in 908 churches. Under the leadership of 61 missionaries and 712 nationals, a vigorous program was maintained which included 407 schools, four hospitals, and five dispensaries.[5]

The centennial marked a significant step forward for the churches in Assam as nationals assumed an increasing measure of control of their work. For example, the North Lakimpur field was transferred to the Assamese General Convention in 1937, thus releasing a missionary for specialized service elsewhere. During the same year a separate Assam Christian Council was formed, in affiliation with the National Christian Council of India, Burma, and Ceylon.[6]

With the extension of the Second World War to the Far East in 1942, the Assam Mission felt its disruptive effects. The Woman's Hospital at Gauhati, reinforced by several missionaries evacuated from Burma, ministered to refugees and military personnel. Dr. Alice L. Randall, the physician in charge, was awarded the Kaisar-i-Hind Medal by the British Government for her fine public service. Other missionaries were diverted from their routine of work to unusual channels of service. A. F. Merrill, of Assam, and Harold M. Young and James H. Telford, of Burma, served as civilian officers in charge of Garo Porter Corps. John Selander, of Sadiya, carried on an adult literacy program in the camps of Garo troops. Several mission buildings near Cotton College at Gauhati, and still other buildings of the schools at Golaghat and Jorhat were requisitioned for military use. Missionaries took opportunity to work among the soldiers in these stations. Only the missions at Tura and Nowgong were able to carry on somewhat normal programs, and these had trenches dug on their compounds for protection against bombings.

---

[5] *Annual Report of A.B.F.M.S.* for 1936, pp. 21, 64.
[6] *Ibid.,* for 1938, p. 25.

In the spring of 1944 when the Japanese penetrated Manipur and the Naga Hills, extensive damage was done to churches and mission property in Kangpokpi, Manipur, and Kohima. Thousands were left homeless, hungry, and in need of medical aid. During this trying period, the Christians of Assam stood up bravely in the face of privation and danger. Many rendered courageous service to missionaries and allied soldiers at the cost of their own lives. The Mission continued to conduct evangelistic work among the nationals and the military personnel in the villages. The Woman's Hospital at Gauhati was obliged to extend its services and so came to be known as the American Baptist Mission Hospital. It accommodated a military medical unit and assisted the Reeder Memorial Home in caring for orphaned children. The Jorhat Hospital was likewise faced with overwhelming demands upon its facilities.

With the withdrawal of American troops in 1945, mission buildings requisitioned for their use, were returned to mission service. The schools became centers of a vigorous youth work in the years that followed. The remarkable evangelistic spirit of the Assam churches resulted, between 1945 and 1949, in an increase of Baptists, especially among the hill tribes, from 79,000 to 95,000.[7]

The war years underscored the importance of a closer co-ordination between the Assam Baptist Convention and the American Baptist Mission, with the Assam churches assuming a larger share of responsibility and with a pooling of resources which was destined finally to result in the merger of the two bodies into one organization. Accordingly, the Assam Baptist Missionary Conference and the Assam Baptist Convention met together in January, 1950, and established "The Council of Baptist Churches of Assam." In the new organization, the churches were given a larger share in the administration of the various aspects of Christian outreach and service than ever before. As further indication of its standing, the Council became a co-operating part of the interdenominational Assam Christian Council.[8]

With characteristic zeal, the Council of Baptist Churches of Assam planned to establish a chain of mission centers through the Naga

[7] For a report of the Assam Mission during the war years see *Along Kingdom Highways* for 1942–50; see also *Crusader,* Vol. 3, No. 8 (Jan. 1949), p. 17.

[8] Records of Board of Managers and Exec. Comm. of W.A.B.F.M.S., May 1949–June 1951, p. 671; *Along Kingdom Highways,* 1952, pp. 20-21.

Hills, in areas where missionaries were not allowed to go by the government. Each center was to have a church, a school, a medical clinic, and a conference center for training leaders and evangelists. By 1952 two were already established, and plans were being pushed for others along the border between Assam and Burma.[9]

There is no more spectacular example of maturing churches than those of the Garos, Nagas, and other peoples of the hills of Assam, who were little more than half a century out of the crudest and most barbaric forms of animism. Each "mother" church oversaw the work of a dozen or more "branch" churches, a pattern which was common in Assam. In the Garo Hills alone in 1952 were 29 such churches and 430 branch churches with an aggregate membership of more than 24,000. Church and associational evangelists and other trained workers carried much of the responsibility for this outreach of the mother church.[10]

Aiding measurably this advance among the hill tribes were the missionary-translators who in many cases reduced the tribal dialects to writing, then produced vernacular versions of the Scriptures besides hymnbooks, reading books, and school texts. To their labors is due much of the credit for the successful advance of the evangelists as they carried the gospel to their own people and neighboring tribes.

Educational and Medical Missions in Assam

The mission's educational program was important for two reasons: first, to develop a trained leadership for the churches and second, to provide laymen with a general preparation for making an adequate living. The Jorhat Christian Schools, which had been established in 1903, were dedicated to this dual function, and provided the center of Baptist educational work in Assam. They included a school of Bible instruction, a school of academic instruction, and a school of industrial crafts. For girls the Woman's American Baptist Foreign Mission Society maintained three well equipped institutions at Gauhati, Nowgong, and Golaghat. Although Baptists supported no college in Assam, they did maintain a hostel for students attending Cotton College, one of the two government colleges of the province. This evangelistic work was conducted by Dr. and Mrs. W. E. Witter in the early years of the period under consideration.

---

[9] *Along Kingdom Highways* for 1951, p. 7; for 1952, p. 20.
[10] *Missions,* Vol. 150, No. 9 (Nov., 1952), p. 545.

In 1932 the two Foreign Mission Societies requested Dr. Frank W. Padelford, executive secretary of the denomination's Board of Education, to conduct a survey of mission education in India and Burma. Concerning the program in Assam, he commended the achievements in the Garo Hills where the greatest concentration of effort had been placed, and recommended establishment of additional primary and secondary schools. His survey revealed that the large area covered by a thinly scattered line of stations was in special need of integration under a strong mission secretary.[11]

Soon after Cotton College opened its doors to women in 1932, Baptists established the Sarah E. White Memorial Hostel at Gauhati. There young women from the plains and the hill country received the Christian message and were encouraged to take leadership in the church life of Assam.

Following the disruptive influences of the Second World War, mission work among the hill tribes entered a new era. The Naga people expressed a growing desire for education. Private middle English and upper primary schools sprang up to meet the need. Nearly all of them included compulsory Bible training, which was supplied by teachers paid by the mission. At the same time the Jorhat Christian Schools were training over 200 boys a year from many tribes. By 1953 the Bible school had been developed into a theological seminary.[12]

In response to a demand from Assamese Christians for higher education under Christian auspices, the two Foreign Mission Boards allocated funds for partial support of the Assam Christian College, a union project of the Assam Christian Council. It opened at Barapani, near Shellong, on August 16, 1952, with eleven students, seven of whom were Baptists. Its campus of one thousand acres had been donated by the chief of a large hill tribe. Christian youth contributed voluntary labor for temporary buildings of mud-plastered bamboo with thatch roofs and dirt floors. It was a small, but hopeful, beginning of an institution dedicated to the training of young men and women who wish to serve the Christian cause.[13]

---

11 Frank W. Padelford, Report on Christian Education in India and Burma, 1932–33, pp. 1-13.

12 *Along Kingdom Highways* for 1947, pp. 39-40; for 1952, p. 22; for 1953, p. 6.

13 *Ibid.,* 1953, p. 6; Records of Board of Managers and Exec. Comm. of W.A.B.F.M.S. for Sept. 1951–Sept. 1953, p. 1187; Jesse R. Wilson, *American Baptists Overseas* (New York, 1954), p. 77.

Medical work likewise contributed to the uplift of the people of Assam. By 1936, American Baptists maintained four centers—three under the General Society at Tura, Kangpokpi, and Jorhat, and one under the Woman's Society at Gauhati. In each place there was a hospital and dispensary, although the work varied because of difference in location, staff, and equipment. Two colonies for lepers were maintained at Kangpokpi and Jorhat. The chief burden of medical leadership fell for many years on Dr. Henry W. Kirby and Dr. Jonas Ahlquist at Jorhat. In 1940 Dr. Kirby retired from active service, although he continued his interest in leper work. Dr. Ahlquist, famed for eye surgery, was obliged to give up his skilled practice in 1939 because of an eye defect. He was transferred to Kangpokpi for general work, but there he met with a fatal motor accident in 1941, cutting off prematurely his useful career.

Little by little, the medical program and staff were strengthened. By 1941 the hospital building at Jorhat was enlarged and supplied with X-ray equipment by the gift of a California donor, and named in his honor the Willis F. Pierce Memorial Hospital. By 1947 the staff consisted of five doctors, two laboratory technicians and an assistant, one compounder, and 11 nurses. A public health program was also administered which reached nearly 25,000 people in the area. Dr. Oliver Hasselblad, of the staff, contributed generously to support of the work by fees received in his private practice among the tea planters, making possible erection of a chapel and a modern tuberculosis sanitorium. Dr. Mary E. Kirby, daughter of Dr. Henry Kirby, took charge of the Women's Jubilee Hospital in Gauhati in 1945. Under her direction the facilities were greatly improved and enlarged. At Tura a new ward for women and children was completed by 1949. In 1952 the Mission agreed upon a plan for medical integration, whereby the staffs and special services of all medical units might be interchanged among the five hospitals.

Through the assistance of evangelists and Bible women attached to the hospital staffs, the medical work of the Baptist Mission in Assam continued to be a strong evangelizing agency. Thus there was integrated into the program of medical care and public health a spiritual service in keeping with the basic purpose of the Mission.[14]

[14] The foregoing summary is based on *Annual Report of A.B.F.M.S.* for 1936, p. 70; *Along Kingdom Highways* for 1941, pp. 24, 39-40; for 1947, p. 30; for 1949, p. 7; for 1950, p. 9; for 1952, p. 20; *Crusader,* Vol. 3, No. 6 (Nov., 1948), pp. 3-5.

Developments in Bengal-Orissa

In Bengal-Orissa, the field taken over by the American Baptists from the Free Baptists in 1911, the major development of the present century was the encouragement of national leadership. As a step in this direction, a home mission society was organized around 1911 to raise funds. Although it ceased to exist in time owing to staff bickerings, the nationals supported some of the workers in the Santal Field. The Santals were animists, a backward people for whom Dr. Jeremiah Phillips, of the Free Baptist Mission, had reduced their language to writing about 1871. Dr. Bacheler later opened the first school for them. By 1921 there were more than one hundred schools, including two middle boarding schools and a high school under construction. It was among the Santals that the greatest progress was made.

A more successful attempt at the transfer of leadership to nationals was undertaken in November, 1918, when the Foreign Mission Board approved a proposal of the yearly meeting of the mission to the effect that all funds used for preachers, colporteurs, Bible women, and zenana teachers be administered directly by the yearly meeting, which was composed of both nationals and missionaries. For this purpose an Evangelistic Board of six nationals and three missionaries was elected. In the years that followed, local committees appointed in the various stations were responsible for the conduct of evangelistic work on their respective fields. When the Santipore station was without a missionary in 1921, C. N. Mohapatra, a prominent lawyer in the Baptist church at Balasore, was appointed to take charge of the work at a salary which was one-third the amount he was receiving in his profession.[15]

In the Bengal-Orissa Mission, evangelistic and educational work advanced together. Most of the work was done among Bengalis, Oriyas, and Santals, with some work among the Telugu- and Hindi-speaking people at Khargpur and Jamshedpur. The multiplicity of languages complicated the task greatly. In one Indian church, four languages were used in every service, the Scriptures and hymns being read in Bengali, Oriya, Telugu, and Hindi, and the sermon being preached in Hindi, which was the common language of India.

---

[15] *Annual Report of A.B.F.M.S.* for 1919, pp. 94-95; for 1920, p. 137; for 1921, pp. 29, 103; for 1922, p. 40.

At Jamshedpur, a thriving industrial center, the Mission undertook a new work in 1919. Land was provided by the Tata Iron and Steel Company, and grants were obtained from both the English and the Indians for the establishment of the station. By 1924 there was in the city an English-speaking church with 60 members and an Indian church with 110 members. Through their ministry it was hoped to influence the increasing number of people being swept from poverty-stricken villages into this congested steel center of India.[16]

The prominent attention given to schools in the Bengal-Orissa Mission was largely responsible for the capable and well-trained laity in the churches. The center of educational work was at Bhimpore and Balasore. The Balasore Industrial School, established in 1906, rendered a significant contribution to the life of the country by training Christian youth to enter into a trade with skill and confidence. By 1925 there was an enrollment of 75, half of whom were Christians who spent part of their free time in evangelistic efforts at the bazaars. The Boys' High School at Balasore had an enrollment of 212 in 1932, of whom 65 were Christians. At Bhimpore, the main work was carried on among the Santals. Until 1916 the numerous village schools operated from that station were supported entirely by the Mission, but in 1917 the Santal Education Board was constituted to assume responsibility for them, with the missionary at Bhimpore acting as Supervisor of Schools for the community.[17]

The acceptance of government assistance in support of the schools became an issue with the Foreign Mission Board around 1921. Dr. Frederick L. Anderson, chairman of the Board at the time, regarded the practice as a violation of the Baptist principle of the separation of church and state. To deal with the issue, a conference was held at Kurnool in the Telugu field, to which the four Indian missions sent representatives. The Bengal-Orissa and Assam Missions voted to give up the grants and aid. The Burma Mission did not do so on the grounds that the masses of people, particularly in Bassein, where the schools were most numerous, were citizens and therefore entitled to the use of government funds for the support of their schools. The missionaries were quite willing to give up the government grants

---

[16] *Ibid.*, for 1920, pp. 141-42; for 1925, p. 143; for 1928, p. 121; for 1930, p. 49.

[17] *Ibid.*, for 1920, p. 25; for 1925, p. 327; Frank W. Padelford, Report on Christian Education in India and Burma, 1932–33, pp. 1-3.

if the Board would make up the difference. When the Board, however, failed to supply the funds, the Burma missionaries continued to accept the grants.

For the training of preachers, the Bengal-Orissa Mission was dependent for many years upon the English Baptists' Christian Training College in Cuttack. In 1935 the Reverend H. I. Frost, of the American Baptist Mission, served as principal of the school. At the time there were nineteen students enrolled, thirteen of whom were from the Bengal-Orissa Mission.[18]

The centennial celebration of the Mission was held in 1936, with the main observance in Balasore and local recognitions given in three of the large towns and five of the outlying stations. At the time there were 40 churches with 2,848 members; 120 schools with 4,161 pupils; and 3 dispensaries serving over 9,000 patients annually. The staff consisted of 24 missionaries from the American Baptist Foreign Mission Society, 7 from the Woman's Society, and 270 nationals. Although there had been no mass movements on this field, there were notable evidences of effective Christian growth. The barriers of caste were beginning to yield to Christian influence to the degree that high-caste Hindus were willing to allow their children to live together with Christians in hostels. Women, formerly under strict regulations, were emerging to occupy positions of prominence. Moreover, there was a stirring among the Santals and Koras, lower class peoples of the country. The growing leadership of nationals was evident in the formation in 1935 of an enlarged Home Mission Board of 12 members, only four of whom were missionaries. This Board took over full administrative responsibility for the mission's primary schools.[19]

From 1936 on, the Bengal-Orissa Mission seems to have experienced a steady, although unspectacular progress. The Mission Conference in 1936 voted to join the newly formed All-India Baptist Union, a step in the direction of closer co-ordination of Baptist work in greater India. When the Congress Party came into power in India in 1937, the leaders in Orissa were friendly to Christians. In fact the Christian community was represented in the legislature by one elected member, the principal of an important college in South Orissa, and by three members nominated to represent the Santals and other

---

[18] *Annual Report of A.B.F.M.S.* for 1935, pp. 29-30.
[19] *Ibid.,* for 1936, pp. 21, 84-85, 89

Christian groups of the lower classes. With the growing response of the Santals to the Christian message, the need for adequate leadership became pressing. The Bengal Christian Council urged the increase of missionaries, especially of women, to work among these people, and the extension of lay witnessing among them. Bible women were particularly needed to help overcome illiteracy, which was a major problem among these people. Through the introduction of new charts for teaching Santali by the Laubach method, great progress was made from 1940 on, with the co-operation of the Bengal Christian Council.[20]

During the Second World War, the expansion in the industrial life of Bengal-Orissa confronted the missionaries with unprecedented opportunities for evangelism as village people moved into the towns and troops came in contact with the mission stations. During those years the mission staff was strengthened by the assistance of missionaries evacuated from Burma. At the same time, the spiraling cost of food presented a serious problem as the limited diet affected the health of missionaries and nationals alike. Grants from the World Emergency Fund at home enabled many workers to maintain themselves, even if only a little above the subsistence level. In 1943 devastation from cyclone and famine intensified the suffering. The two Mission Boards sent more than $30,000 for relief and rehabilitation. The mission orphanages made a valiant effort to care for children left homeless during this time of stress. When they were old enough, they were taken into the schools, where they were fed, clothed, and educated.

In the midst of these years of famine and war, the work of evangelism went on steadily, the most spectacular results being among the Santals and Koras in the vicinity of Jhargram, a station which had been opened in 1939. These animistic people were the most responsive of any race in the mission. Indeed, the Santal Christian Council, made up of representatives of eight missions of different denominations, was indicative of the Protestant impact being made upon these people in Bengal, Assam, Bihar, and Orissa.

The postwar period presented new problems. With the increasing disposition of Asians to demand independence of Western influence and leadership, the Societies undertook to merge the Mission and the churches into one body. This effort was begun in 1946 with the

---

[20] *Ibid.*, pp. 40-41; *Annual of N.B.C.* for 1940, p. 585.

appointment of a Joint Integration Committee. In 1950 the Santal Education Board took over from the Mission the supervision of the village schools. This transfer, which was initiated by the government, was met with some reluctance on the part of the Mission because of a fear that the schools would no longer remain Christian. To strengthen the Christian teachers, the Mission in 1952 inaugurated annual conferences of Christian teachers from both mission and government schools with gratifying response. At the same time the Mission undertook to reorganize its high schools and technical schools in the interest of providing better technical training and Christian opportunities for young people.

In 1952 the retirement of the Reverend H. I. Frost and his wife, after forty years of missionary service on the field, signalized the departure of the last family to have been appointed by the Free Mission Society before it merged with the American Baptist Mission in 1911. Among his many services was his contribution to the revision of the Oriya Bible, which came from the press just before he left the field.[21]

The progress made in Bengal-Orissa after 116 years of missionary endeavor had been distressingly slow. By the close of 1952, there were no more than 4,000 church members in the entire field. There had been none of the mass-movement response to the gospel which had occurred in South India, in the hills of Assam, or in the Belgian Congo. With the possible exception of Japan and West China, Bengal-Orissa was the most difficult American Baptist mission field. There were several reasons for this fact: the missionaries had to cope with five major language groups; villages were separated by unbridged rivers and connected only with unmanageable roads; a resurgence of Hinduism had taken place in recent years; and the missionary staff was woefully inadequate, with only five married couples and eight single missionaries for the entire area.

Yet there were obvious signs of hope and encouragement. For in 1953 the schools enjoyed a record enrollment, with 218 at the Boys' High School at Bhimpore, 75 at the Girls' High School, and 180 in the Primary School there. At Midnapore there were 525 in the Girls' High School. At Balasore the Girls' High School had 400 students, the Boys' High School 325, and the Boys' Technical School 90. At

---

[21] The foregoing account is drawn from issues of *Along Kingdom Highways* for 1943 through 1953.

Hatigarh 190 were enrolled in the co-educational Middle School. In addition, there were large enrollments in the primary schools in many villages. The number of college-trained people in the churches was increasing. Upon such leadership depended the future influence of the Christian community in an area in which the new industrialized India was being born.[22]

Medical work in Bengal-Orissa had never been large. It had been confined to clinics at Hatigarh and Bhimpore and the supervision of a leprosy colony at Hatigarh. But with the postwar period of industrial expansion and widening opportunities, a woman doctor and nurse were appointed and plans were well under way to do more medical work on this field.[23]

Growth Toward Maturity in South India

In the years immediately following 1914, the American Baptist Mission in South India underwent a transition period as the older missionaries retired and as the administrative responsibilities for the work began to be transferred gradually to the nationals. Indicative of the trend was the resignation in 1914 of Dr. David Downie at Nellore as treasurer of the mission, after forty-one years of service in that capacity. Out of consideration for his advancing years, he was transferred the next year to Coonoor, a beautiful town in the hill-country, where he worked under easier circumstances until his final return to America in 1927. Further indication of the transition taking place was the transfer in 1918 to the Telugu Baptist Convention of responsibility for the management of the entire mission station at Kandukuru. This was the first step in a plan for ultimate national control of the American Baptist Telugu Mission.[24]

At Ongole, where Dr. John E. Clough had developed a great work, changes likewise were occurring. In 1918 erection of the Clough Memorial Hospital was begun in honor of the pioneer missionary. The funds had been raised jointly by the Ongole Christians and Baptists in America through the efforts of Clough's successor, Dr. James M. Baker. Ongole College, which had been fathered by Dr. Clough, was absorbed into Madras Christian College, a union institution. In 1925 the Central Boys School was turned over to the

---

[22] *Missions,* Vol. 150, No. 10 (Dec. 1952), pp. 588-91.
[23] Jesse R. Wilson, *American Baptists Overseas,* p. 29.
[24] *Missions,* Vol. 10, No. 5 (May, 1919), p. 330.

management of Anaparti Abraham, son of the Baptist Bible woman at Addanki. He had been a deputy inspector of schools for the government, and in this transfer he took a personal loss in income to accept the new position.[25]

A record year of evangelistic results were reported in 1925 for South India, with nearly 6,000 baptisms within the year and a total of 14,000 over a three-year period. Indeed, the South India Mission was one of the most successful at work in the country. It had 218 churches with 80,521 members; 1,265 schools serving 33,470 pupils; seven hospitals, eight dispensaries; and 2,157 national workers and 127 missionaries from America on the field. Commensurate with this remarkable growth was a notable achievement in self-support, particularly in Ongole and Kurnool, where the cost of the actual work done on the field, exclusive of the salaries of the missionaries, was borne by the Indian churches.[26] At Kurnool, within a period of but 50 years (1877–1927), 12 organized churches with over 4,000 members were conducting work in 133 different villages in the environs of the city. In Kurnool itself there were five schools for boys and girls including a high school with 200 boys. Under the guidance of Dr. William A. Stanton, who spent 40 years on this field (1895–1935), a policy of complete support and direction of the village work was carried out through a home mission society known as the Kurnool Field Association.[27]

A significant indication of the broadening influence of the Telugu Christian community between 1925 and 1935 was the response of the Sudras to the gospel. They were a village people of caste status who comprised the major portion of the population in the Telugu country. Within the 10-year period 30,000 had been baptized by preachers who were themselves recruited from the outcastes. Never before in the history of Protestant missions in India had there been such a widespread movement of village people of the middle and higher castes to unite with Christians who had been won by an earlier movement among the outcastes. In a very real measure, it was a

---

[25] For the record of the remarkable leadership given to the Ongole field by Dr. Baker until his retirement in 1929, see his book *Contending the Grade in India* (Ashville, N. C., 1947), pp. 150 ff.

[26] *Missions,* Vol. 16, No. 6 (June, 1925), pp. 327-28.

[27] *Missions,* Vol. 19, No. 1 (Jan. 1928), pp. 8-9; *Annual Report of A.B.F.M.S.* for 1928, p. 34; William A. Stanton, *The Awakening of India: Forty Years Among the Telugus* (Portland, Me., 1950).

tribute to the growing impact of the Telugu Christians upon the life of the country. Indeed, among the Sudras, Christianity had become identified with "social justice and opportunity for the oppressed," and therefore made an appeal to those who favored those ideals.[28]

When the South India Mission celebrated its centennial anniversary in 1936 at Ongole, 7,000 Christians were in attendance. The Baptist community had grown to more than 114,000 church members gathered into 380 churches. A total of 2,704 national leaders carried the day-to-day responsibility for 30 stations in more than 3,000 villages, chiefly among the outcastes. There were 1,332 schools attended by 39,306 pupils. The number of hospitals had increased to 6, and the number of dispensaries to 12. The missionary staff included 60 representatives of the Foreign Society and 27 of the Woman's Society.[29] In few missions was so much being accomplished in proportion to the funds and staff available.

Changing political developments in India within the next few years intensified the desire of many in the country to revive Hinduism and to free themselves of western influence and control. The Congress Party, which came into power in 1937, worked for economic and social reforms, including passage of a law prohibiting the sale of intoxicants in the Madras Presidency. The rising social consciousness of the leaders of India was an encouraging sign. Likewise, the movement to promote adult literacy under the guidance of Dr. Frank C. Laubach was given hearty co-operation by Christians and non-Christians alike. At the same time the outcastes of the Bombay Presidency were being weaned away from Hinduism by their leader, Dr. B. R. Ambedkar, who saw in India's national religion a hindrance to the freedom of his people. There were some who looked for even greater mass movements on the part of the outcaste peoples to Christianity, as some 200,000 converts a year were coming into the churches of all denominations in India.[30]

A major step in the direction of consolidating the Baptist fellowship in India was the organization of the Baptist Union of India, Burma, and Ceylon in 1939. Its first assembly was held at Cocanada, India, January 3 to 7. There were representatives present from the

---

[28] *Annual Report of A.B.F.M.S.* for 1935, pp. 26-27; J. Waskom Pickett, *Christian Mass Movements in India* (New York, 1933), p. 298.

[29] *Annual Report of A.B.F.M.S.* for 1936, pp. 73, 83.

[30] *Ibid.*, for 1938, pp. 20-21; for 1939, pp. 16-17, 26.

American Baptist, British Baptist, Canadian Baptist, Australian Baptist, and New Zealand Baptist Missions. But the gathering was especially notable for the contribution made by Karens and Burmans, Telugus, Punjabis and Bengalis, Assamese, and the representatives of the hill tribes from the northern forests. It was a fortunate development in the life of the churches, fortifying them for the strain and stress of the war years that followed.

When Great Britain declared war on Germany in September, 1939, the Viceroy of India immediately placed India and its army on the side of the Allies. Reaction in the country was varied. Ghandi indicated sympathy with the British cause. An extremist section of the Congress Party declared for complete independence and no compromise. A Moslem group at the other extreme offered complete loyalty to Britain. The Indian State with remarkable unanimity gave their support to the war effort.

In spite of war, political rioting within India, and rising prices, the Telugu Christians maintained their support of the churches and carried forward their evangelistic work. The Telugu Baptist Women's Convention sponsored in 1943 a School of Methods at Ramapatnam to strengthen the leadership of women in the churches. A vigorous adult literacy program constituted a major concern of the Telugu leaders generally. Financial problems multiplied as the price level climbed 300 per cent above the prewar level. It became virtually impossible to maintain the boarding departments of mission schools. The declining number of missionaries, as replacements became increasingly difficult, was offset in part by the services of Burma missionaries who had been obliged to evacuate that country. But the major burden was undertaken by nationals, themselves, who arose valiantly to the occasion.[31]

Educational and Medical Work in South India

Although the Telugu Mission had always been known for its ardent evangelism, education was not neglected. In the whole mission, more than 25,000 boys and girls and young men and women were receiving training in 936 institutions. Of these, 912 were elementary schools and 14 were secondary schools other than high schools. There were four high schools, three for boys at Nellore, Ongole, and Kurnool,

[31] *Annual Report of A.B.F.M.S.* for 1940, p. 17; *Along Kingdom Highways* for 1943, pp. 25-30; for 1944, pp. 24-27.

and one for girls at Nellore. The normal training schools for women teachers were located at Ongole and Nellore, while a similar institution for men was situated at Bapatla. The mission also supported vocational schools for boys at Nellore and Kurnool. The interest of the mission extended beyond its own border to include joint support with other denominations of Madras Christian College. The Woman's Society helped to support the Woman's Christian College, which was opened in 1915, and the Vellore Medical School. To reach college students with the gospel, the Day Memorial Church in Madras, composed of English-speaking Indians, contributed $15,000 for the erection of a student hostel in that city.[32]

The theological seminary at Ramapatnam made a significant contribution to the training of leadership for the churches. For a brief time, between 1920 and 1924, the seminary was strengthened by the participation of Canadian Baptists. By the celebration of its 50th anniversary in 1925, the school had trained close to 1,500 students. In that year 114 students were enrolled, and 489 alumni were active in Baptist missions, while 84 were engaged in the work of other missions.

The mission accomplished much in the development of a trained laity among the Telugu Christians. Much of the training provided was of a vocational nature which enabled converts to achieve skills that would provide them with an adequate living. The Telugu mission was among the first of the Baptist fields to recognize the importance of industrial work and to make provision for it. The lifting of the standards of life of the laity, which resulted from this policy, was a source of strength to the churches. In 1923 a Telugu Baptist Laymen's Movement was organized at Markapur, to promote self-support in the churches.[33]

It will be recalled that the issue of the separation of church and state was raised by the Board in 1921–22 over the policy followed by the missionaries on the Asian fields of accepting grants-in-aid from the British government for the support of mission schools. A special conference brought together representatives from Burma, Assam, South India, and Bengal-Orissa at Kurnool in January, 1922,

[32] Robbins, *Following the Pioneers,* p. 100.

[33] *Annual Report of A.B.F.M.S.* for 1921, pp. 44-45; for 1925, p. 132; Henry C. Vedder, *A Short History of Baptist Missions* (Philadelphia, 1927), pp. 74-77.

for a consideration of the matter. In November of the same year, the Board at home recommended that the custom of accepting grants-in-aid be discontinued as soon as possible by the missionaries, although no attempt was made to interfere with the practice of the indigenous churches. Because the Board was not able to enlarge its appropriations to the mission, the application of the new policy was placed in operation only gradually on the Telugu field.[34]

Although obvious progress had been made in the educational work of the Telugu Mission, the achievements in this respect came under severe criticism in 1932–33, when a survey was made of Christian education in India and Burma under the auspices of the Boards at home. The report warned that there was a very real danger that the Mission in South India might lose out in evangelistic work if it did not adopt a more vigorous program of developing national leadership. It claimed that some of the older missionaries did not see the importance of encouraging the converts to acquire a full high school education. In a sense they reflected the tension which had always existed among the missionaries between the advocates of an exclusive emphasis upon evangelism and those who would supplement the work of evangelism with a strong educational program. The pressure to transfer leadership of the work to nationals gave the warning added significance.[35]

Medical work in the South India Mission had developed from humble beginnings in small dispensaries established at Ramapatnam and other places by the Woman's American Baptist Foreign Mission Society. By 1921 there were hospitals at Nellore, Udayagiri, Hanamakonda, Mahbubnagar, Nalgonda, Sooriapett, and Ongole. By 1922, the new Clough Memorial Hospital, consisting of 25 stone buildings, was completed at Ongole. It was one of the finest in Indian missions, caring for 500 in-patients a year and serving 16,000 annually through its clinics which were held in villages within a radius of 35 miles of Ongole. At Nellore a training school for nurses was in operation. There were also dispensaries at Ramapatnam and Sattenapalle. At Vellore, Baptists participated in the Union Medical School for the training of Indian women for medical service.

---

[34] *Annual Report of A.B.F.M.S.* for 1923, pp. 56-57.

[35] Frank W. Padelford, Report on Christian Education in India and Burma, 1932–33, pp. 1, 10-11.

In 1931 the Clough Memorial Hospital at Ongole expanded its services by accepting responsibility for a new dispensary just erected at Podili by the Reverend T. W. Witter. Five years later Dr. Ernest Holsted, a member of the Ongole Hospital staff, became the full-time director of the dispensary. During the Second World War, the Clough Memorial Hospital escaped from serious damage owing to the presence of the Royal Air Force south of the city. In 1946 expansion of its facilities was made possible by gifts from the youngest daughter of Dr. Clough (Gratia Upjohn). In that year the hospital served more than 4,000 in-patients, of whom one-half were women and children. In addition there were over 13,000 out-patients who received treatment.[36]

Postwar Developments in South India

Although the South India field escaped the devastation of war, spiraling prices and scarcity of supplies affected seriously the work in schools and hospitals. Because the mission was understaffed during the course of the war, Telugu leaders took over an increasing number of positions. At Hanumakonda, for example, Indian physicians took full charge of the Victoria Memorial Hospital, thus releasing Dr. John S. Carman to become Acting Professor of Surgery at the All-India Christian Medical College at Vellore. The war also affected the life of India's women, transforming them into confident and aggressive participants in the growing industrial life of the country. An increasing number of caste people were open to the gospel.

Greater co-operation between Christians of various denominations also characterized the postwar period. By 1947 Baptists, Lutherans, and Anglicans were co-operating in Andhra Christian College, an institution of the United Lutheran Mission at Guntur. At the same time negotiations were in process for the eventual union of the American Baptist Theological Seminary at Ramapatnam and the Canadian Baptist Seminary at Cocanada. The policy of co-operation did not extend, however, to the United Church of South India, which was inaugurated in September, 1947, bringing together Congregationalists, Presbyterians, British Methodists, and Anglicans. Telugu Bap-

[36] *Missions,* Vol. 12, No. 6 (June, 1921), pp. 360-61; *Annual Report of A.B.F.M.S.* for 1923, p. 139; for 1937, pp. 90-91; Baker, *Contending the Grade in India,* pp. 289, 293.

tists did not join because of basic creedal differences relative to baptism and the nature of the ministry.[37]

The political developments, following the war, which brought to India independence from British rule in 1948, had a mixed effect upon the Baptist work in the country. Uprisings which took place in Hyderabad State in South India in protest to the Union of India disrupted the lives of the missionaries but did not drive them from their stations. Legislation against the age-long practice of "untouchability" broke the waning grip of caste upon the life of India and made easier the lot of Christians, so many of whom came from the outcaste groups. The new status of India made changes necessary in the conduct of missionary work. Since the government was administered by Hindus, many of whom were eager to advance Hinduism, the official attitude towards missionaries underwent change. By the end of 1951, the government gave recognition to fifty missionary societies from outside of the British Commonwealth, and were giving consideration to admitting sixteen others. It was plain that only those who had specialized training to supplement the work of nationals were to be admitted for mission work in the country.

To meet the new situation, the Mission and the Telugu Baptist Convention agreed to transfer further responsibility to national leaders. A joint council of missionaries and nationals directed the work, the majority of members being nationals. At the same time, new methods of evangelism were being developed to increase the Christian impact upon society. Among these was newspaper evangelism conducted through two leading daily newspapers. This effort was sponsored jointly by the American Baptist and United Lutheran Missions. Another plan was known as the Home and Family Emphasis to encourage witnessing to the Christian faith in family life.[38]

Medical and educational work in South India was being transferred rapidly to national management in the postwar period. In 1948, a board of Indian leaders was set up to share in the management of the Clough Memorial Hospital. Other steps were to follow

---

[37] The foregoing account is based on *Along Kingdom Highways* for 1945, pp. 26-28; for 1946, pp 23-25; for 1947, pp. 68-69; for 1948, pp. 60-62.

[38] *Ibid.,* for 1948, pp. 59, 69; for 1950, pp. 7-8; *Crusader,* Vol. 6, No. 7 (Dec. 1951), p. 4; Records of Board of Managers and Exec. Comm. of W.A.B.F.M.S., May 1949–June 1951, p. 475; *The International Review of Missions,* Vol. 42, No. 165 (Jan. 1953), p. 18; Wilson, *American Baptists Overseas,* pp. 69, 74-79.

until the entire control of the institution should be in the hands of nationals. This was the same pattern which had been followed even more rapidly in the schools. With the growing demands being made upon Indian leadership, the Union Medical College at Vellore and the Theological Seminary at Ramapatnam became of primary importance. As an economy move the Women's Bible Training School at Nellore was closed and its training responsibility transferred to Ramapatnam Seminary. A further step in the co-ordination of theological education was taken when plans were developed in 1949 for the co-operation with Canadian Baptists and the Church of South India in a program of ministerial training at Ramapatnam.[39]

In a certain sense a new era in the missionary enterprise was entered upon in the years immediately following the close of the war. What character it was ultimately to take in the new India, only time could tell. But this much was certain. The Telugu churches had achieved a remarkable degree of maturity and were prepared and eager to fulfill their responsibilities of leadership. The future of the Christian witness in India was in their hands.

---

[39] *Along Kingdom Highways* for 1948, pp. 68-71; Records of Board of Managers and Exec. Comm. of W.A.B.F.M.S., May 1949–June 1951, p. 560; for Sept. 1951–Sept. 1953, p. 1029.

CHAPTER XXVIII

Ordeal in China

FOR CHINA the period since 1914 was an almost constant struggle against internal political dissension, the threat of exploitation and invasion from without, and the perennial problem of floods and famine. When the ancient Confucian dynasty disappeared in the Revolution of 1911–12, the country was quite unprepared. Although rival war-lords were somewhat suppressed in the 1920's by the Kuomintang under the leadership of Chiang Kai-shek, communism was interjected into the picture under Russian direction to complicate the situation still further. Then in the 1930's the Japanese encroached on China, first seizing Manchuria in 1931, then launching a full-scale invasion in 1937, followed by an occupation of much of the country in the 1940's. When in 1945 the Japanese were expelled by Allied help, the Nationalist Government of Chiang Kai-shek was too exhausted to assert itself, to check inflation, or to rehabilitate the transportation system. Meanwhile the old Confucian cultural patterns were disintegrating. The stabilizing family system was breaking down, and Buddhism and Taoism were being discarded.

The situation into which communism was fully prepared to move was marked not only by a cultural disintegration, but by an utter lack of political and military strength. Communists were able therefore to win control of China in the first instance by political trickery and military power. Even if Christianity had been stronger and more widespread, it could not alone have prevented the advancing tide of communism. Thus by 1949 the Communists replaced the Kuomintang and the rule of Chiang Kai-shek, who had lost the confidence of the country. On October 1, 1949, they set up "the People's Republic of China," working in close co-operation with Russia and denouncing the United States as an imperialistic threat to the peace of the world. A complete re-education of the nation was initiated by the Communists which threatened the very existence of the Christian witness in China.

It is indicative of the remarkable persistence of Chinese Christianity that Christian conversions continued throughout the entire period from 1914 through the dark days of the Japanese invasion. The increase for all denominations mounted from 257,431 in 1914 to 402,539 in 1924, to 567,390 in 1936, then to 623,506 in 1946. The total number of converts in 1948 was 750,000. There was evidence also that Christianity was taking root in China. In 1922 the National Christian Council was constituted. In 1927 the Church of Christ in China brought most of the Protestants together, including the Presbyterians, the United Brethren, many of the Congregationalists, and some of the Baptists and former Methodists. By a process of devolution, mission boards were transferring administrative responsibility for the extension of the gospel in China to national leadership. The Chinese Christians had taken their place in the ecumenical movement and were filling places of responsible leadership within the life of their own country.

But with the advent of the communist regime, the picture began to change. Theological education dwindled under the numerous restrictions placed upon the church schools and ministerial leadership. The churches were obliged to endorse the "People's Republic" and its program. Many Christian pastors submitted to government pressure, some undoubtedly with secret reservations. The connection of Christianity in China with Western civilization and mission support was a distinct liability, for the Communists were determined to uproot any movement that was associated with the capitalistic West. Moreover, the very nature of the gospel precluded Christians from bringing to its support the weapons employed against it by the Communists.[1]

The Christians during the four decades of history in China, now to be surveyed in this chapter, experienced an ordeal more severe than any other group of Christians were called upon to bear in this troubled era. It will be our purpose to trace briefly the main developments of American Baptist work in China, against which it may

---

[1] For the foregoing analysis, the author is indebted to Kenneth Scott Latourette, *The Christian World Mission in Our Day* (New York, 1954), pp. 116-27.

be possible to project summaries of the work on the three mission fields in that country. At the end of the chapter, we shall tell briefly the story of the transfer of mission effort to the Chinese-speaking peoples of Thailand in 1952, when the doors to China were closed to further assistance from the West.

Main Trends in the China Missions

In the years following the First World War, China experienced considerable confusion and unrest. Emboldened by her new position in world affairs, Japan made demands upon China which would have subjected that nation to her economic control had they been granted. At the same time, the Chinese people resented the transfer of Shantung to Japan by the Peace Treaty of Versailles in 1919. This feeling deepened during the years which followed into a wide-spread agitation against foreign interference in Chinese life. Accordingly, China demanded control of her own tariffs, the abolition of extraterritorial privileges given to citizens of Western powers living in the cities along the coast, the return of certain ports which had been conceded to European governments for commercial purposes, and the complete exercise of the normal rights of a sovereign nation.

A series of antiforeign uprisings gave dramatic expression to the underlying tensions which existed over these issues. In 1925, for example, the shooting of Chinese students by British police in Shanghai aroused bitter hostilities against all Westerners. A similarly deplorable tragedy occurred at Canton a few months later, and another antiforeign outburst took place in 1927 which resulted in the bombardment of Nanking by foreign gunboats. In each instance, angry mobs endangered the lives of missionaries and commercialists alike. Irate college students boycotted the Western schools and sought to turn the minds of Christian youth against the Christian missions. Missionaries were evacuated from some centers, and Chinese Christians were obliged to carry on the work until their return, often at some peril to their own safety. These events occurred simultaneously with civil disorders in various areas between rival war lords, and with outbreaks of banditry and communist-inspired violence.

To complicate the situation still further, a decline in the number of American Baptist missionaries set in after 1922. This trend was due to several factors: (1) reduced financial resources and higher costs involved in administering the fields, (2) the disturbed conditions in China, (3) the increase in the Chinese staff which diminished the need for outside assistance in some instances, and (4) a decline in missionary spirit in American Christianity.[2] The trend affected not only Baptists but other denominational missions as well.

In view of the changing situation, five hundred representatives from all of the larger evangelical denominations at work in China met with an equal number of Chinese leaders in an epoch-making National Christian Conference at Shanghai in May, 1922. The American Baptist Foreign Mission Society was represented by two board members, the Reverend Carey W. Chamberlin and Professor Kenneth Scott Latourette, and by the foreign secretary, Dr. James H. Franklin. A major outcome of the meeting was the formation of a National Christian Council for China, which was to be a strictly advisory body to assist in co-ordinating Protestant work in China and to encourage integration of the missions with the national churches. American Baptists, on advice of the missionaries, gave limited support to the new Council, after having received assurances that its own work would not be hindered in any way.

Following this conference, representatives of the three American Baptist missions in China met at Shanghai to lay plans for the unification of their work. As a result, two significant organizations came into being. One was the Chinese Baptist Council, which was composed of representatives of the missionary staff of the three missions and representatives of the three Chinese conventions within the territory of the missions. The other was the Chinese Inter-Mission Committee, composed of missionary representatives of the three missions. This was a far-reaching step, for hitherto there had been only slight relationship between the several missions of China. Through the new agencies thus established it was hoped to overcome barriers created by language differences and the great distances which separated the three missions.[3]

The trend toward the co-ordination of Christian work in China did not go unnoticed by the sensitive nationalists. The meeting of the World's Christian Student Federation in Peking in 1922 aroused a widespread agitation against foreign connections with Christianity. In the summer of 1924 anti-Christian sentiment was renewed, which

---

[2] William B. Lipphard, *Out of the Storm in China* (Philadelphia, 1932), p. 131.

[3] *Annual Report of A.B.F.M.S.* for 1923, pp. 48-49, 144.

prompted Chinese provincial educational associations to demand that education should be separated entirely from religion, and that foreigners no longer should be allowed to control educational institutions. During the uprising against foreigners that followed in 1925, armed forces, organized by Russian Communists, moved northward. By the end of March, 1927, all of China south of the Yangtze was controlled by invaders. Special objects of attack were mission schools and hospitals and foreign-operated commercial businesses. When the nationalist army invaded Nanking, a violent attack was begun on the missions. Actually, it was an effort to discredit Chiang Kai-shek rather than to injure the foreigners. The crisis convinced Chiang that Soviet power in the ranks of the Kuomintang was too strong. Accordingly, he broke with the communist element and purged the party. In June, 1928, Peking fell into his hands and soon the whole country was under the control of the Nationalist Government. Even then there was not complete unity, for jealousy of Chiang's power prompted a rival government to arise in Canton, while the Communists kept up an agitation against his government. Yet the friendly disposition of Chiang Kai-shek towards Christianity gave the missions a brighter outlook for the immediate future.[4]

The turmoil of these trying years had far-reaching effects upon the course of Baptist work in China. By 1927 a large-scale evacuation of missionaries had taken place. All missionaries in South China withdrew to Swatow; all but one in East China came to Shanghai, and all but five in West China left their stations and proceeded in constant peril of their lives to Shanghai. It was part of a mass exodus of Christian missionaries of all denominations. By July, only five hundred remained at their stations in interior China, and five thousand of approximately eight thousand Protestant missionaries had left the country. No doubt this year was the darkest in the history of Protestant missions in China up to that time.[5]

Yet no note of defeat crept into the consultations of Baptist missionaries who gathered in Shanghai. Instead, they had urged the Board, as early as 1925, to allow them to return to their stations as soon as conditions permitted, assuring the Board that they would take personal responsibility for any risks involved. The Board ac-

[4] Kenneth G. Hobart, A Comparative History of the East China and South China Missions (unpublished typescript), pp. 584-91.

[5] Lipphard, *Out of the Storm in China,* pp. 32-33; Kenneth Scott Latourette, *A History of Christian Missions in China* (New York, 1929), p. 821.

quiesced, while at the same time making clear that they would ask no special privilege for their missions or staff in China. This was to allay the suspicion harbored by many Chinese that mission boards were seeking the military protection of their governments to sustain their enterprises abroad. The Board took an even stronger position in 1927, when it went on record as approving the United States' policy of non-intervention in China, and again directed its missionaries to take no part in Chinese political movements.[6]

A second outcome of the antiforeign uprisings was the rapid increase in the process of devolution from 1925 onward. In the absence of the missionaries from West China, the Szechuan Baptist Convention carried on with a Chinese executive committee. The Chekiang-Shanghai Baptist Convention in East China assumed new areas of responsibility. In 1925, amidst the strain of antiforeignism, the South China Baptists issued a declaration of independence from Western control, which resulted in the organization of the Ling Tong Baptist Council, with full approval of both missionaries and the Boards at home. In 1927 the Council found itself under pressure to demonstrate to Chinese officials that the churches were not under Western imperialistic control, but under Chinese leadership. Fortunately, for the future of the Baptist witness in China, the China Baptist Council, organized at Shanghai in 1922, was able to co-ordinate the three autonomous bodies which had come into being during the transition period. The Council, composed of five Chinese and three missionaries from each of the three fields, met in 1927 and again in 1930 for prayer and planning. Out of these gatherings came a decision to co-operate with the National Christian Council's Five Year Movement for evangelism. Further indication of the growing strength of the Chinese churches was evident in the organization in 1930 of the China Baptist Alliance, which brought together the Chinese churches regardless of the foreign society under which they had arisen.[7]

A third outcome of the situation in China in these years was the obligation placed upon mission schools to be registered with the government, thus bringing them under government standards and requiring that religious exercises for students be voluntary rather than

[6] *Ibid.*, p. 35; *Annual Report of A.B.F.M.S.* for 1926, pp. 22-23; Records of Board of Managers of A.B.F.M.S., 1927–28, pp. 145-46.

[7] Lipphard, *op. cit.*, pp. 62-69; *Annual Report of the A.B.F.M.S.* for 1931, pp. 18-23.

compulsory as before. It was also required that the heads of such schools be nationals. While the new policy had much in its favor in that it accelerated the transfer of leadership to the Chinese Christians, it presented a problem of maintaining distinctly Christian institutions under circumstances where the majority of students, in some cases, were non-Christians and could not be obliged, under the government restriction, to take courses in religion or to participate in worship services.

By 1931 the Baptist missions in China had undergone basic changes and adjustments to problems which had been little understood by Baptists prior to 1914. It now had become obvious that missionaries were associated with Western imperialism simply because of their citizenship status. The establishing of mission schools, which once had been welcomed by the Chinese, was now being questioned. The subsidizing of Chinese churches with American funds was coming under criticism. Church unity had become a matter of major importance to the Chinese Christians. Missionaries, once regarded as superior to the nationals, were now given only equal status. Mission property presented problems in the transfer of responsibility and administration of the work to nationals.[8] At home, Baptists had to become accustomed to regarding their Chinese brethren as equals with like pattern of church life, yet with differences of cultural expression in worship and theological formulation.

The degree to which church life in China had become institutionalized may be seen from the status of the missions in 1931. A staff of 151 missionaries, including wives and unmarried women, plus 1,065 nationals, served as pastors, teachers, and physicians in the three areas of China where American Baptists conducted work. The three fields reported a total of 145 Baptist churches, with more than 11,000 members. To serve nearly 14,000 students, 188 schools were maintained. These ranged from primary grade to union women's schools and women's medical colleges, the University of Shanghai (Baptist), Ginling College for Women, Nanking University, and the West China Union University. The three last-mentioned institutions were union schools in which Baptists co-operated with other denominations. Medical work supported by American Baptists included 12 hospitals and an equal number of dispensaries. This was a form of service greatly appreciated by the Chinese, and they paid in fees

[8] Lipphard, *op. cit.*, pp. 152-55.

approximately three-fourths of the total cost, exclusive of the salaries of missionary doctors. The total investment from the United States in the Baptist work in China for the fiscal year 1931–32 amounted to $251,853.09, of which $130,403.02 paid the salaries of missionaries. The remainder was used to maintain the properties, to support Chinese workers, and to defray transportation costs and other miscellaneous expenses.[9]

The Japanese occupation of Manchuria in 1931–32 brought a greater degree of unity to the Nationalist Government of Chiang Kai-shek than it had been able to achieve up to that time. At the same time there was, during the next few years, a Christian advance in China. The churches co-operated with the government's "New Life Movement," which concerned itself with the education of illiterates, with village sanitation, and the improvement of the ethical conduct of petty officials. Christian leaders took occasion to tell of the new life through Christ, thus giving spiritual content to the program. More settled conditions throughout the country encouraged the extension of evangelistic efforts, most of which were carried on by the Chinese themselves. Increased attention was given also to rural needs of the people, the vast number of whom earned their living in country villages. The University of Nanking, with which Baptists co-operated, was the center for this emphasis.[10]

When the Japanese aggression spread into a full-scale invasion of China proper in 1937, the picture darkened again. In the areas of penetration along the seacoast, industry and trade became stagnant and banditry broke out. Food prices spiraled as war, floods, and famine combined to increase the misery of the Chinese people. Five stations of American Baptist missions were in the "occupied" area of China. Only two of the stations in Free China escaped bombing raids. Schools in occupied areas were closed down. The middle schools and many of the primary schools in Free China were removed from the cities to improvised quarters in country districts out of danger of air attack. The mission hospitals, all in Free China, kept their doors open day and night. Missionaries found themselves absorbed with relief work in behalf of refugees fleeing from the invader.

---

[9] *Ibid.*, pp. 7-8.

[10] *Annual Report of A.B.F.M.S.* for 1935, pp. 22-23; for 1937, pp. 31-32, 471-72.

During these difficult times, twelve Christian colleges in China, including Shanghai University and the three union schools in which American Baptists participated—Nanking, Ginling, and West China Union University—received financial assistance from the Associated Boards for Christian Colleges in China, which had headquarters in the United States. Entire student bodies were transferred to West China so that higher education might not be wiped out completely by war. At the same time, the churches remained open, even in occupied towns and villages. Lay leadership was developed through church training programs, especially in East China. In every way the Chinese Christians were showing a determination to maintain their church life at all costs.[11]

As the situation worsened, the Board of the American Baptist Foreign Mission Society adopted a policy in October, 1940, which gave wide discretion to the Officers Council of the Society and to the mission staffs on the fields to evacuate missionaries from occupied China to Free China, and from Japan, where necessary, to other missions, especially in Burma and India. To meet the growing problem of inflation, emergency appropriations of more than $26,000 were voted for the China Missions.[12]

With the bombing of Pearl Harbor on December 7, 1941, the war in Asia widened to include the United States. Of the two Baptist Societies, twenty-four missionaries were in occupied China; only four were in Kinhwa, the one remaining free station. In South China, six were in Japanese hands at Swatow, while twelve were in the free stations at Kityang, Ungkung, Meihsien, and Hopo. In West China thirty-seven missionaries were at their posts. Thus in the three China missions, thirty of the mission staff were in Japanese-held territory, and fifty-three in Chinese-controlled areas, completely free to carry on their work. By March, 1942, it was possible for the Societies at home to make contacts with its missionaries in occupied China through the International Red Cross and the Swiss Diplomatic authorities.[13]

With China's capital and the Nationalist Government in West China, the mission work there became of most strategic importance.

---

[11] *Ibid.*, for 1940, pp. 18-20; *Along Kingdom Highways,* 1941, pp. 13-16; *Missions,* Vol. 31, No. 4 (April, 1940), pp. 206-10.

[12] Records of Board of Managers of A.B.F.M.S., 1940–42, pp. 127, 147.

[13] *Along Kingdom Highways,* 1942, pp. 9-11, 15-18, 77-78.

Chengtu became the major center of Christian education for all China. Gingling College and Nanking University were located on the campus of West China Union University. Union Theological College, a comparatively young institution which had arisen out of the war crisis, was training approximately sixty men and women for Christian leadership. The National Christian Council had established its new headquarters at Chungking, from whence it was directing a program of evangelism, with special attention to students. In this it had the support of most major mission boards, including the American Baptist. In East China, on the other hand, the work of the University of Shanghai came to a standstill after Pearl Harbor. The Union Middle School in Shanghai likewise had closed. In South China the schools faced a difficult time under the puppet government of the Japanese.[14]

The defeat of Japan by the Allied forces in 1945 did not lessen the internal problems of China. For, by 1948, the country was again engulfed in civil war between the Communists and the troops of the Nationalist Government. At first the fighting did not interfere seriously with American Baptist missions because none were located in North China, the scene of the initial conflicts. But as the Communists moved southward, eventually taking control of the entire country, the plight of the missions became grave indeed. During the years which followed the formation of the People's Republic of China on October 1, 1949, Christian churches were closed, less than five per cent of the buildings being reserved for purposes of religious service. Church buildings were appropriated for troop barracks, government and Party offices, storehouses, and halls for public propaganda schools. Pastors were ordered to earn their living by manual labor. All responsible laymen and laywomen in the churches were investigated in an effort to discredit their witness in their respective communities. Schools and social institutions were either closed or taken over by the government; every effort was made to destroy the very memory of their former association with the missionary enterprise. All contacts between Chinese Christians and the outside world were cut off in a determined policy to isolate the church and weaken its position.[15]

---

[14] *Ibid.*, pp. 19, 29; N.B.C., *Annual* for 1942, pp. 290-91; for 1944, pp. 296, 299.

[15] Based on reports of American Baptist missionaries who were among the last Americans to leave China in 1952–53. See also *Missions*, Vol. 149, No. 4

Many Christian leaders refused to sign the Christian Manifesto, a directive to the churches to purge their ranks of "pro-Western and anti-Communist" members. Some Chinese ministers continued to preach the gospel in spite of the personal danger involved. Many theological students refused to accept subsidies from the government for their education.[16] With such courage and determination to maintain a Christian witness against all odds, the survival of the church in China was not improbable.

The South China Mission

For the first ten years after 1914, the South China Mission, like the other fields in the country, was involved in the development of the intensive policy adopted by the Boards in 1912. This called for a concentration upon present stations, the improvement of facilities, and the strengthening of national leadership. In the area of evangelism, the policy was not as well developed as in education, partly because of the impatience of some of the South China missionaries with any curtailment of establishing new stations and partly because of a reluctance to consolidate the scattered congregations on this field. In fact the multiplication of churches went on unchecked, so that by the close of 1925 there were 143 organized churches with a total of 5,721 members. To serve these churches there were only 13 missionaries, nine ordained and 77 unordained ministers, most of whom acted also as teachers for schools connected with the chapels. While the results in the number of baptisms were noteworthy, progress towards self-support was very slow.

Contrary to the policy of not undertaking new stations, the Board was persuaded to support a new station at Changning, upon the urging of the Reverend C. E. Bousefield. Early in 1916 the churches of the Basel Mission were taken into it, so that the number of churches was increased to three with 166 communicants. The work was especially notable for reaching people of all classes in society.

Contacts with the city populace of Swatow were strengthened during this same period when an institutional church was developed

---

(April 1951) for a report on the Christian Manifesto, the communist-inspired directive to the Christian churches of China (pp. 215-18). Note in addition *The International Review of Missions,* Vol. 42, No. 165 (Jan. 1953), pp. 285-96; Vol. 43, No. 169 (Jan. 1954), p. 10.

[16] Wallace C. Merwin, "Can the Church Survive in China?" *The Christian Century,* Vol. 70, No. 44 (Nov. 4, 1953), pp. 1257-1259.

under the leadership of the Reverend Jacob Speicher. A new structure was completed in 1920 which provided facilities for health programs, educational classes for children, supervision of the leper colony which had been founded by the municipal government, and nightly evangelistic meetings. Through this means an impact was made upon the life of the community which fortified the evangelistic appeal of the mission.[17]

In educational work, the intensive policy was more marked. In 1913 a study had been made of the schools under the mission's direction, with the result that plans were developed to have primary schools in every chapel, to maintain eleven boarding schools of grammar grade and two academies, one at Swatow and the other at Kaying, and to support Bible training schools for women at Swatow and Kaying. For higher education, the mission undertook to co-operate with Canton Christian College and other schools in the area. The academy at Swatow proved to be a success. By 1924 it had nearly 500 pupils, and was serving as a feeder for Shanghai College. By 1925 all eight stations of the South China Mission had boarding schools for boys and five had them for girls. Buildings had been erected between 1918 and 1920 at Hopo, Kaying, Ungkung, Kityang, and Swatow.

By 1918, the Mission became acutely conscious of the need for trained ministers, and began to send students to America for training. The service rendered by the Ashmore Theological Seminary at Swatow was sporadic, depending on whether Ashmore was on furlough or not. In the 1920's there were efforts to get the academies to offer pre-theological training, and about 1922 or 1923 annual summer institutes were inaugurated at Swatow for preachers.[18]

Reinforcements for medical work of the Mission came in 1913 with the arrival of Dr. H. W. Newman, Dr. Mildred Scott, and Mrs. Fannie Northcott, R.N. In 1916 the Mission adopted a five-year program, which included the establishing of a strong central hospital at Swatow, with dispensaries at the central stations conducted by Chinese doctors under American supervision. Dr. Newman was placed in charge of the program. The work was delayed for three years while the Mission and the Board debated the proper location

[17] Hobart, A Comparative History of the East China and South China Missions, pp. 456-69; *Annual Report of A.B.F.M.S.* for 1915, pp. 157-58; for 1921, pp. 31-32.

[18] Hobart, *op. cit.*, pp. 471-97.

of the hospital. Finally, Dr. Newman resigned in 1921, on the grounds that the Mission did not intend to develop hospital work on a high scientific level. Dr. and Mrs. C. B. Lesher, who returned to China late in the year, were designated to the Bixby Memorial Hospital at Kityang, which was to be developed into the general hospital for the entire field in view of the situation precipitated by Dr. Newman's stand. But some unfortunate clashes with local Chinese undermined Dr. Lesher's usefulness, and he severed his connection with the Mission in 1927. For several years thereafter, no real progress was made toward making Kityang the general hospital. Meanwhile, a new hospital was constructed after 1922 at Hopo, with civic assistance, under the direction of Dr. Newman, whose continuance with the Mission had been assured by this new responsibility. Thus there were four hospitals in operation in the South China Mission: the Josephine Bixby Memorial Hospital at Kityang, the Edward Payson Scott and Martha Thresher Memorial Hospital for women at Swatow, the True Word Hospital at Ungking, and the most recent hospital at Hopo.[19]

During this period from 1914 to 1925, not so much progress in the transfer of leadership to Chinese was forthcoming as might have been expected under the intensive policy. In 1913 the Board introduced the system of appropriating funds in gross to be administered on the field, but this was done by the Missionary conference which did not include Chinese. The convention of Chinese Baptist churches virtually ceased to exist after 1924 or 1925, simply because it had no responsibility beyond providing fellowship. Meanwhile, the various associations grew stronger because they had their own home mission societies, and so had a reason for existing. More responsibility was placed on Chinese for the internal administration of the mission schools. After 1921 there were co-principals (a missionary and a Chinese) at Swatow Academy and the Ashmore Theological Seminary.[20] The slowness in the process of devolution in the South China Mission was traceable, in part at least, to a generation of older missionaries who were reluctant to relinquish control of the work which they had developed. In part also, it may have been due to the more decentralized character of the church life in South China, where

---

[19] *Ibid.*, pp. 500-09; William B. Lipphard, *The Ministry of Healing* (Philadelphia, 1920), appendix.

[20] Hobart, *op. cit.*, pp. 511-17.

the associations rather than the wider convention assumed what functions were assigned to the Chinese leaders.

It is not surprising, therefore, that during the tense political situation in China in 1925, a group of young men of the Tie Chiu Baptist churches issued "a declaration of independence" from all foreign control. They urged that the administration and responsibility for the work should be given to the Chinese in order to develop an indigenous church and to make clear the absence of all connection between Christianity in China and foreign control. As we have noted previously, this action was received favorably by the Board, whereupon the Ling Tong Baptist Convention was organized and administrative machinery was set up to take over the work from the missionaries. At first, the missionaries were only advisers in the new organization, with no power to vote; but with the passing of antiforeign feeling, the Council of the Convention was reduced in size and missionaries were given a vote. In keeping with the new trend, many of the schools abandoned the policy of having co-principals in favor of full Chinese administration.[21]

The course of the new Convention was not smooth during the next several years. Jealousies among Chinese leaders brought internal dissension, while the reluctance of the associations to recognize its authority brought difficulties from without. The failure of the churches to give adequate financial support necessitated a cutback in the Convention's program. Conditions were so unsettled that no general secretary would serve longer than two years. Yet, in spite of the obstacles, some achievements were registered. The Convention authorized the reopening of the Ashmore Theological Seminary in 1928, after six years of inactivity. Because of economic strain, the brave attempt to undertake theological training failed once again, and it was decided to discontinue the school and send students to the Methodist Seminary at Foochow and to the Southern Baptist school at Canton.

More favorable progress was made in the development of the women's work of the Convention. Bible women were often able to continue their preaching schedule during the unsettled period after 1925 when male evangelists could not. Women's work was well organized in the local churches and the associations. A strong central organization co-ordinated their activities with marked success.

---

[21] Hobart, *op. cit.*, pp. 597-602.

From 1929 to 1934 abnormal conditions prevailed in the Hakka country, with banditry, pillaging, kidnaping, and murder rampant. Church buildings were destroyed, services were disrupted, and missionaries and Chinese co-laborers were forced to withdraw. Those who withdrew turned their attention to the Hakkas who lived in Swatow. There an interdenominational work was undertaken by missionaries of various denominations, and ultimately a Hakka church was established.

By 1936 the full force of the world economic depression was being felt in South China. Appropriations from the United States had decreased almost fifty per cent within four years. In the interest of economy, the Ling Tong Convention undertook some reorganization of its work. The Hakka Convention organized a Home Mission Society to secure funds for the relief of the work in Kaying and Hopo, where the reduced appropriations were threatening the continuance of the stations. Yet the picture was not all dark, for when the centennial of Baptist work in China was observed in 1936 by Swedish, English, Southern and Northern Baptist Missions, it was pointed out that there were more than 70,000 Baptists in China. Under their auspices there were many hospitals, dispensaries, and clinics. There were schools for the blind and homes for orphans and the aged. A complete system of Christian education from the nursery through secondary and higher schools ministered to more than 20,000 children and youths. Of the 83 missionaries on all three of the China fields, 29 were in South China. Of the 156 churches with 14,478 members, 116 churches were in South China, but with only 7,627 members, which indicated a certain lack of consolidation of church life in that field. Five of the 11 Baptist hospitals in the country were in South China, and 9 of the 16 dispensaries.[22]

During the early years of the Sino-Japanese War which opened in 1937, South China was spared most of the dislocation suffered by East China. It was not until June 21, 1939, that the Japanese occupied Swatow and a small adjoining area. From that time on, the struggle began against hunger, disease, and aerial attacks. The inland mission centers at Kityang, Hopo, and Meihsien became increasingly important as work along the coast was disrupted. But by 1944

[22] The foregoing account is based on Hobart, *op. cit.*, pp. 607-29; N.B.C., *Annual*, 1933, p. 441; *Annual Report of A.B.F.M.S.* for 1936, p. 96; for 1937, pp. 32-33, 98, 107-08.

it became necessary for the missionaries to evacuate those areas as the Japanese advanced inland. Some returned to the United States; others relocated in West China at Chengtu. In those trying times, the Ling Tong and Hakka Conventions maintained their identity under the able leadership of the Reverend S. K. Lo and others. In spite of the difficulties of travel, evangelistic work was continued, Bible women often serving as pastors of churches.

When the war with Japan ended in 1945, every effort was made to resume the work of the Mission. The staff at Bixby Memorial Hospital began a limited ministry without waiting for the missionaries to return. They used supplies which they had hidden away before the arrival of the Japanese in 1944. As missionaries returned to their posts, a keen loss was felt in the resignation of Dr. Kenneth G. Hobart, who had served as Mission Secretary during the dark days of the war. He remained in the United States as a professor in the Berkeley Baptist Divinity School in California.[23]

The postwar reconstruction included the reopening of seminary classes at the Ashmore Theological Seminary in co-operation with the Woman's Bible Training School, a program of relief work for needy people, and a strengthening of the medical program with the Bixby Memorial Hospital at Kityang as the center. The prospects which seemed so bright in 1946 were clouded as the Nationalists engaged in a bitter struggle with the Communists for control of the war-torn country. By 1949, as we have seen, all of China was under the communist regime, and the South China Mission, like the other fields, was faced with a new ordeal of suffering and testing.

By the close of 1952 the last American Baptist missionaries in the country were evacuated from South China. The Mission's only remaining contacts with the Chinese people were in Hong Kong, a part of the British Crown Colony off the southeast coast of China, and in Thailand. From the summer of 1951 until her furlough in 1953, Miss Edna Smith, a South China missionary under the Woman's American Baptist Foreign Mission Society, worked among some 150,000 Swatow-dialect-speaking Baptists who had come to Hong Kong to escape the communist regime and to make a new life for themselves. In the fall of 1954 the Reverend and Mrs. L. E. Noren, also formerly of the South China Mission, were placed in

---

[23] *Annual Report of A.B.F.M.S.* for 1940, pp. 42 43; *Along Kingdom Highways,* 1944, pp. 32-37; for 1945, pp. 33-35; for 1946, pp. 25-27.

charge of the work, and Miss Smith was designated for return to the United States. Thus Hong Kong, which had been a steppingstone to China for American Baptists more than a century before, was now an interim-station for the China Mission while the doors of China proper remained closed.[24]

The East China Mission

As we have noted in an earlier chapter, the East China Mission was far in advance of the other American Baptist fields in the country with respect to the consolidation of its work and the development of the intensive policy of the Foreign Mission Societies. It will be recalled, also, that this Mission looked favorably upon the discontinuance of the Central China Mission at the outset of this period, although the decision was frowned upon by the South China Mission as a serious retreat.

Perhaps no other field was so highly institutionalized as the East China Mission. This had come through the strong emphasis upon educational and medical missions. In view of this fact it is the more remarkable that the missionaries so early encouraged a transition of responsibility to Chinese leaders. By 1914, for example, exclusively foreign educational and evangelistic committees had given way to joint bodies consisting of Chinese and missionaries. In 1918 the Chekiang Baptist Convention was reorganized under the leadership of Dr. J. T. Proctor, the Mission Secretary since 1913, and Dr. T. C. Bau, pastor of the Hangchow Baptist Church. The purpose was to enable the Chinese to assume a large degree of control in the Mission. To its executive committee, composed of seven Chinese and two missionaries, the Mission turned over full administrative control of the entire evangelistic program and of the day-schools that were conducted in the chapels. In 1919, the sum of $18,000 was placed at its disposal for this work. Because there had been no local associations, as in the South China Mission, there were organized in 1919–20 four district associations in Ningpo, Shaohing, Kinhwa, and Huchow, with a joint executive committee for each. The mission secretary was made the Convention's adviser, and other missionaries were selected to serve as advisers for the evangelistic work and the

---

[24] For details concerning the closing years of the Mission's work in China, see *Along Kingdom Highways,* 1948–1954; *Crusader,* Vol. 7, No. 10 (March 1953), pp. 8-9; Wilson, *American Baptists Overseas,* pp. 12-14.

women's work. The missionaries had no vote on the executive committee of the Convention. In 1922 Dr. T. C. Bau was chosen to be the first executive secretary of the Chekiang-Shanghai Convention, as the new body was then called. He and Dr. Proctor worked closely together until the missionary's death in 1927. In 1928 the Mission transferred all of its work to the Convention, thus completing the process of devolution.[25]

The successful operation of the Chekiang-Shanghai Convention was due in part to a half century of experience in home mission work conducted by the Chinese themselves, and also to the leadership of Dr. Proctor. Upon Dr. Proctor's death, one of his fellow missionaries observed that it was to his election as secretary of the mission more than to any other one factor that Baptists in China owed "the orderly growth of the mission and the convention as organizations, their gradual preparation for the change in relationship which was bound soon to come, and the perfect harmony which marked the actual transfer of administrative authority which took place in 1927–28." [26]

The evangelistic ministry of the churches in the period after 1914 was complemented by the development of two institutional church projects, one at Hangchow, under Dr. T. C. Bau until his election as Convention secretary in 1922; the other at Ningpo under the direction of the Reverend C. L. Bromley and his wife. This social service approach had been stimulated by the success of the Yangtzepoo Social Center operated by the students at Shanghai College. The projects continued for several years, but failed to root themselves in the Chinese community life so as to gain full support. Within the area of the East China Mission, at the close of 1925 there were 41 organized churches, of which only four were self-supporting. Altogether there were 61 places of regular meeting for religious services. The total number of church members was 3,174.[27]

The educational work of the East China Mission was far advanced over many other fields. American Baptists worked jointly with Southern Baptists in the Shanghai Baptist College and Theo-

---

[25] Hobart, A Comparative History of the East China and South China Missions, pp. 561-69.

[26] Frank W. Goddard, *Century of Baptist Missions to the Chinese* (1933), cited in A. Frank Ufford, The East China Baptist Mission: 1843–1943 (a typecript), pp. 28-29.

[27] Hobart, *op. cit.*, pp. 524-27.

logical Seminary. They co-operated in several union institutions, including Nanking University and Medical School, the Hangchow Union Girls' School, the Huchow Union Hospital, and the Ginling College. There was also a working agreement in boy's educational work with the China Inland Mission at Kinhwa and with the Church Missionary Society of England in Shaohing. The Mission began to send selected students to the United States for advanced training by 1919. By the end of 1924 the Mission had 13 middle schools with nearly 1900 students, and 13 secondary or grammar schools with approximately 600 pupils. In 1926 Shanghai Baptist College celebrated its 20th anniversary with a student body of about 700, of whom 66 were women. Its buildings and equipment were valued at over $1,000,000. One of the most significant projects for the home training of women was the Memorial School of Mothercraft at Huchow, which had been established in 1918 by Miss Mary I. Jones. It was the only institution of its kind in China and drew students from Peking to Canton.

The East China Mission also gave leadership in this period to interdenominational enterprises that were of an educational nature. The Reverend E. H. Cressey served as secretary of the East China Education Association in addition to being principal of the Wayland Academy at Hangchow. The Mission co-operated for many years in the Council of Health Education by making an annual grant. Dr. T. C. Bau represented the Mission and the Chekiang-Shanghai Baptist Convention in the Daily Vacation Bible School Movement.[28]

Medical work also went forward during these years. Four hospitals were established at Huchow, Kinhwa, Ningpo, and Shaohing; certain efforts were made for co-operative medical service with other denominations; and work actually was begun in a union medical college at Nanking.

Although the South China Mission actively supported the China Baptist Publication Society, in which Southern and Northern Baptists co-operated, the East China Mission lost interest in it, largely because Dr. Proctor and others feared that it was engaged in a narrowly denominational propaganda.[29]

In the period from 1925 to 1935, the Mission experienced the

---

[28] The foregoing survey is based upon Hobart, *op. cit.*, pp. 530-45; Ufford, *op. cit.*, p. 15.

[29] Hobart, *op. cit.*, pp. 547-552.

disruptive influence of the antiforeign uprisings. Dr. J. S. Grant and his wife at Ningpo escaped harm only when someone in the mob attacking his home recognized it as the home of the mission doctor. Early in 1927 all of the Mission's schools were closed temporarily. Some church buildings and schools were occupied by soldiers and abused. In the absence of the missionaries from their posts during the hostilities, the Chinese Christians displayed great loyalty and courage. The testing had the effect of purging the ranks, for the number of churches dropped from 41 in 1925 to 38 and the membership from 3,174 to 2,704.

In response to the demands of the government for control of the schools, the Boards at home gave formal approval in September, 1927, for the registration of mission schools, and transferred the internal management of them to the nationals. Shanghai Baptist College obtained its first Chinese president on February 25, 1928, in the election of Dr. Herman C. E. Liu. The institution made excellent progress under his leadership. In 1931 it became the "University of Shanghai"; a Downtown School of Commerce was established the next year. The internal administration of hospitals likewise was transferred to nationals. At Huchow, the union with the Southern Methodist Mission was dissolved, and the plant was turned over to the Methodists to operate.

The China Baptist Publication Society sold its plant in Canton and moved to Shanghai in 1926. From this time, the East China Mission took more interest in it, and it came under Chinese management.

The transition of administrative responsibility to the Chinese in these years freed the missionaries to devote more time to the training of lay members of the churches. Under Chinese leadership, more youth and women's work was developed. Women enjoyed an equal share with the men in the Chekiang-Shanghai Baptist Convention. When the Church of Christ in China was formed in 1927, the Convention did not unite with it for much the same reasons as Telugu Baptists had not joined the Church of South India.[30]

The outbreak of the Sino-Japanese War in 1937 brought devastating results to the East China field. With the attack upon Shanghai in August, the University of Shanghai had to be evacuated. At the end of November, Huchow fell into Japanese hands. Many sur-

---

[30] *Ibid.*, pp. 635-66

rounding towns in which Baptists conducted work were almost wholly evacuated by Chinese and foreigners alike. Nanking and Hangchow fell in December. Only Kinhwa, Shaohing, and Ningpo were spared actual invasion, although they were at one time or another subjected to aerial attack. Although property losses to the Baptists were serious, they were not so great as those suffered by other missions.

Most of the missionaries remained at their posts for as long as possible, their wives and children having been evacuated. The University of Shanghai continued its work for a time in a crowded downtown office building. Other school work came to a standstill. The hospitals were kept open. Under the guidance of the National Christian Council, the churches were active in welfare and relief work. At Hangchow, the Reverend E. H. Clayton gave noble service in providing a refuge for thousands of women and children at Wayland Academy. For such courageous assistance, the missionaries gained in the affection of the Chinese people. Indeed, the demonstration of Christian vitality in the churches made a deep impression upon the nation during those dark days. By his fearless leadership, Dr. T. C. Bau contributed much to the stability of the Baptist witness.

One of the deepest tragedies of the war was the assassination, on April 7, 1938, of President Liu, of Shanghai University. His death was the direct result of his bold stand against the invaders of his country.

We already have alluded to the tense situation created for American missionaries in China by the opening of hostilities between Japan and the United States on December 7, 1941. When the Japanese made their drive on Kinhwa in the summer of 1942, the four missionaries who had stayed until it was evident that the city was doomed, barely escaped with their lives. Making their way into Free China, they found places of useful service in hospital and relief work.

By 1944 the Japanese had occupied all of the cities in East China. Where church buildings were taken over by the invader, congregations divided into small groups to worship in homes. At great personal sacrifice, many pastors stayed by their charges. Local churches became distributing centers for food, clothing, and medicines to the victims of the war. The hospitals in Ningpo and Shaohing continued to operate after occupation. Special care had been taken previously to select a board of directors who could manage them as independent Chinese organizations sponsored by local and district Baptist churches. Nurses continued their training at Ningpo. At Shanghai, the Margaret Williamson Hospital continued its work under Chinese management and staff, although the Woman's Christian Medical College suspended its activities. The Pickford Memorial Hospital at Kinhwa, being forced to evacuate one place after another before the invaders, with losses each time, finally made its way into Free China. During the war years, the Chekiang-Shanghai Baptist Convention continued to maintain its program against the greatest odds.[31]

Following the cessation of hostilities in 1945, the return of missionaries to East China was more rapid than to South China because of its greater accessibility and also because of the immediate need of strengthening its institutions. Some missionaries came from West China or India, others from America. Two new families were under appointment. The loss of personnel for the schools and the destruction of property created major problems for the reconstruction period. Immediately upon the re-opening of institutional work, the usual plans for evangelistic work in the schools were resumed. Under the leadership of Principal B. Y. Hsu, Wayland Academy, faced with a badly wrecked plant and the loss of every particle of equipment, planned at once a series of evangelistic services for the 500 boys and girls, nearly all of whom were non-Christians. In the fall of 1946, when the University of Shanghai reopened, 1,000 students were enrolled.

At the time of the celebration of the centennial of the East China Mission at Ningpo in April, 1948, five years after the actual date, there were more than 5,000 Christians in 34 Baptist churches. The Chekiang-Shanghai Convention also had three hospitals, eight primary schools, an equal number of middle schools, a Bible Training School for women, and the University of Shanghai. Dr. T. C. Bau was honored for twenty-five years of service as executive secretary of the Convention, whose headquarters were now in Hangchow.

Within less than ten months, the advance of the communist forces from the north made the evacuation of missionaries necessary for the protection of the Chinese Christians whose relationship with Western people imperilled their safety. By December, approximately nine missionaries were transferred to the Philippines, seven to Japan,

---

[31] The foregoing account is based on the *Annual Report of A.B.F.M.S.* for 1938, pp. 15-16, 88; *Missions,* Vol. 29, No. 6 (June 1938), pp. 358-59; *Along Kingdom Highways,* 1943, pp. 30-32; 1944, pp. 29-30; 1945, pp. 32-33.

and twelve to the United States. In October, 1949, communist efforts to destroy the power plant of Ningpo brought serious damage to the Baptist hospital there. In the same month, the People's Republic of China replaced the Nationalist Government of Chiang Kai-shek. By 1952 the last missionaries had left the country. The future was in the hands of the Chekiang-Shanghai Baptist Convention.[32]

The West China Mission

The decision of the American Baptist Foreign Mission Society to close the Central China field greatly strengthened the work in West China after 1914. It was thereby possible to add several missionaries to the staff, including Dr. Emily Bretthauer and Miss L. Jennie Crawford, who opened in 1916 a medical service for women and children at Suifu under the support of the Woman's Board. They began their work in a rented house which was used as a dispensary and headquarters until land could be purchased and regular hospital buildings erected. A year later the Woman's Society established the first high school for girls in West China at Suifu.

The progress of educational work was aided greatly by the influence of West China Union University, with which Chengtu Baptist College was affiliated. A steady stream of leaders for the churches, for schools, and for other professions came out of this Christian institution.[33]

In 1923, at the meeting of the West China Baptist Convention, the first Chinese pastor was ordained. In the same year a Home Mission Society was organized to conduct evangelistic work among the aborigines in West China. When the missionaries were obliged to leave their posts during the uprisings of 1925 and 1927, the Convention gave stability to the churches. Its leadership was recognized by the Mission in 1928, when the Convention was entrusted with the administration of funds from America for all pastoral, educational, and medical work except the union medical and educational projects at Chengtu. To handle the new responsibility, the Convention appointed an Executive Committee of five members and a Finance

---

32 *Along Kingdom Highways,* 1946, pp. 27-30; for 1947, p. 44; for 1948, pp. 81-82; *East China News Letter,* May 1, 1948 and Dec. 1948; *Crusader,* Vol. 4, No. 10 (March, 1950), pp. 8-9.

33 Salquist, Anna M., West China Baptist Mission Records, 1889–1944 (a typescript), pp. 24-25; N.B.C., *Annual* for 1917, p. 671; for 1919, p. 466; *Missions,* Vol. 16, No. 6 (June, 1925), pp. 329-330.

Committee with strong missionary representation. The Reverend Harry J. Openshaw was made secretary of the Convention. The process of devolution thus proceeded with a marked spirit of harmony.[34]

The years, 1933–1935, were marked by a series of disturbances which might have proved disruptive to the churches had they not already made real progress in the development of national leadership. An earthquake in 1933 was followed in 1934 by the threat of communist invasion into Szechuan Province. Late in 1935 the Red Army was swept by the Nationalist forces toward Yachow, forcing the missionaries and many of the Chinese church leaders to evacuate to Kiating for safety. By 1937, Szechuan Province had become a refuge for thousands of persons fleeing before the Japanese invasion of the coastal cities. The situation presented to the West China Mission its greatest opportunity for evangelism as the area became the focal point for refugee schools, government officials, and for the greatest migration of Chinese in the history of the country.

Between 1937 and the Japanese defeat in 1945, the Mission was engaged in a variety of work. It co-operated with the West China Union University, the Union Middle School for Boys, and the West China Theological College at Chengtu. The Woman's Society gave support to the program of the Union Normal School for Women. The Mission supported evangelistic and social service projects, hospital and dispensary work, and its own schools. In addition it joined in various enterprises conducted by the National Christian Council.[35]

The problems were legion, as inflation caused operation costs to spiral and as the demands of the war emergency placed hospitals and the churches under unusual pressure for personnel and material aid for the relief of human misery. The burden upon an overworked staff was lightened temporarily by the transfer of a few missionaries from Burma, when war conditions drove them out of that country. With five refugee universities from East China on the campus of West China Union University at Chengtu, the demands for student work upon the mission staff and the Chinese leaders were great.

A notable Baptist contribution was made to higher education by the Reverend E. H. Cressey, who was executive secretary of the

---

[34] *Annual Report of A.B.F.M.S.* for 1928, p. 23; Salquist, West China Baptist Mission Records, p. 12.

[35] Salquist, West China Baptist Mission Records, pp. 9-10.

interdenominational Council of Higher Education of China. During the six years of war, the burden of this work necessarily was centered in West China. Dr. Cressey maintained throughout the period offices in Chengtu and Chungking. Under his direction, the Council gave guidance for the spiritual program not only of the Christian colleges, but also of 117 Christian middle schools and 53 Christian nursing schools operating in Free China.

Early in 1945 Chungking as the wartime capital of the Nationalist Government was in great jeopardy. It had been subjected to merciless bombardment, and many looked for the city to fall into enemy hands momentarily. The missions at work in western China were strongly urged by the government to evacuate all but a skeleton staff of missionary personnel. The sense of impending disaster brought virtual panic to the populace. At this critical juncture, the West China Baptist Mission's firm stand against any withdrawal stiffened morale appreciably. With heroic devotion, the depleted staff carried on in the face of constant danger. By the close of the year there were only fifteen missionaries on the field, ten from the General Society and five from the Woman's Society. There had been no replacements since 1940 to meet the losses due to death, retirement, and enforced furloughs of those unable to secure permission to return to their posts. The Chinese Convention, like the Mission, faced its share of the work with depleted personnel. Its general secretary, Dr. G. B. Fuh, rendered a most needed service at great personal sacrifice. He served not only the Baptist churches, but the larger Christian enterprise through his membership on the Szechuan Christian Council.

During these years great progress was made in the development of lay leadership in the churches. Women achieved a place of equality with men in the community as well as in church responsibility. Stress was placed on Christianizing Chinese family life. Every effort was made to counteract the demoralizing influences of war conditions. There is little doubt that the Christian witness during this trying period was of inestimable value to the people of China.[36]

The postwar era was nearly as fraught with danger for returning missionaries as in the previous years. The Reverend Robert A. Vick and his wife were killed along with their three year old son in a

---

[36] The foregoing account is based upon *Annual Reports of the A.B.F.M.S.* 1937–40, and *Along Kingdom Highways,* 1941–46.

plane crash while enroute to their station; a second son recovered from injuries and was returned to the United States. When the first postwar conference of missionaries was held in West China at Loshan (the new name for Kiating) in July, 1947, it required six days for missionaries from Ipin (formerly Suifu), to make the journey through bandit-infested country. The threat of communist aggression added further danger to the lot of the missionaries.[37] The story of the eventual overthrow of the Nationalist Government by the Communists has been told. The course of events in West China was similar to that on other Baptist fields in the country, as missionaries were obliged to withdraw, leaving to the Chinese Christians full responsibility for the future of the churches.

Reopening of Thailand (Siam) Mission

Because of the close relationship between the early work begun in Siam in 1833 and the Baptist Mission in China, a brief survey is included here of developments in that ancient land which came to be known after 1932 as Thailand. From 1845, the American Baptist Missionary Union centered its main attention upon China, giving only peripheral support to Siam which had been regarded from the inception of the mission as a steppingstone to China. Within this limitation, missionaries were assigned periodically by the American Baptist Foreign Mission Society to the work at Bangkok, and the South China Baptist Mission gave what assistance it could to the Chinese-speaking work. For many years the Bangkok church included both Siamese and Chinese converts. Only four of the missionaries sent out by the American Baptist Missionary Union spent more than four years on the field, owing to the enervating climate and the discouraging difficulties in penetrating the Buddhist culture with the Christian message. They were Dr. William Dean, who spent a total of ten years in the country, dividing his time between Thailand and China; the Reverend R. Telford, who remained nine years until ill health forced him to transfer to Hong Kong in 1863; the Reverend Josiah Goddard, who devoted seven and a half years to the country prior to his work in China; and William Ashmore, whose long missionary career in South China was preceded by seven years of service in Thailand.

During those years the number of converts among the Siamese

---

[37] *Ibid.*, 1948, pp. 90-95.

was relatively few. The main accomplishment of the mission was to translate the Bible into the language of the country, a task to which Dr. John Taylor Jones devoted his missionary career, although he died in 1851 before completing the work. The press in the Siam Department of the Mission was kept going by funds from the American Bible Union, The American Bible Society, and earnings from job work.

On April 8, 1861, the church at Bangkok was divided, eleven Chinese members withdrawing under the leadership of the Telfords to organize a strictly Chinese congregation. This seems to have been the beginning of an upturn in the work among the Chinese immigrants. In 1868 an awakening occurred, when forty persons were baptized, most of the converts having been won from the outstations. The church obtained that year its first ordained pastor, Ban Pla Soi.[38]

With the work in China well under way, the Executive Committee of the American Baptist Missionary Union proposed suspension of the Siam Department of the Mission in 1869 as an economy measure. The Chinese Department, which by this time had 149 Chinese, was to be continued. But only two years later, the Committee questioned the wisdom of maintaining the Chinese work at Bangkok since it served only a transient group of people who might be reached by the South China Baptist Mission. Dr. William Dean pled for the continuance of the enterprise on the grounds that the Chinese constituted the commercial class of Thailand.[39]

In 1872 the Reverend C. H. Carpenter, of Bassein, Burma, led a group of Karen Christians to Thailand, for the purpose of beginning a mission to the Karens living in the mountains along the Burma-Thailand border. He looked for support of his venture from the Canadian Baptists, who showed interest in establishing an independent mission to the Karens in that area. It was not until 1884 that the work actually was undertaken by the Karen Baptist Home Mission Society and the Bassein Karen Home Mission Society.

In the meantime, little was heard of the Siam Mission in the records of the Missionary Union until 1905, when it was called "a lone star," with only a single station at Bangkok. The missionary in

---

[38] The foregoing summary is based upon reports in scattered issues of *The Baptist Missionary Magazine* from 1847 to 1869.

[39] *Ibid.*, Vol. 50, No. 7 (July 1870), pp. 259-60; Vol. 52, No. 7 (July 1852), pp. 273-75.

charge was Dr. Hans Adamsen, a physician who was honored by the government for his success in making vaccine. Out of a full schedule, he gave what time he could to all three language groups, the Siamese, the Peguans, and the Chinese. There had been no missionary since 1890 who could speak the Chinese language, hence the Chinese church was obliged to continue its work unaided.[40]

In 1929 circumstances once again turned attention to the Bangkok mission. The sale of a property in the business district of the city which had belonged to the Foreign Mission Society netted a sum of $50,000. The Board therefore sent the Reverend A. H. Page, Mission Secretary of the South China Mission, to Bangkok to consult with the Chinese Baptist Church and the Presbyterian missionaries, who were at work in the city, for a more active ministry to Chinese immigrants from Swatow. As a result, the Foreign Society sent, in 1931, the Reverend and Mrs. A. F. Groesbeck, of Chaoyang, China, to assist in a building project which would get the Chinese Baptist Church into a more strategic location. In September, 1935, the new building was completed. It was located on a main thoroughfare, with an auditorium which seated five hundred persons and with rooms for a community program.[41]

Until 1932 Thailand was an absolute monarchy. In that year, by a bloodless revolution, the king was persuaded to grant a constitution and the country moved in the direction of democracy. Universal suffrage was granted to all persons over eighteen years of age. Efforts of the government to develop a single educational system were disrupted by a strong minority of nearly five million Chinese, the traders and bankers of Thailand, who insisted upon education for their children in their own language. During the Second World War and since, the United States maintained friendly relations with the government, and gave extensive technical and military aid. In 1949 Dr. Frank Laubach conducted a ten-week literacy campaign in the country, but the work begun was not carried forward after his departure.

Economically, Thailand prospered during these years. Private as well as government schools were filled to capacity. The Presbyterian Mission, which was alone among Protestants in sponsoring ele-

---

[40] *Ibid.,* Vol. 85, No. 7 (July 1905), p. 272; Vol. 86, No. 6 (June 1906), p. 225.

[41] *Annual Report of A.B.F.M.S.* for 1929, p. 27; for 1933, p. 98; for 1936, pp 38-39, 97.

mentary and secondary education, sought, after the war, to establish a national Christian university, but failed to secure government permission. Whereupon, they and the Church of Christ (British) established a student hostel in Bangkok, where students attending the two state universities might have Christian instruction and influence. The two denominations also developed a co-operative farm in Chiengrai, and inaugurated a program of work camps for young people which accomplished much in teaching the dignity of work and in strengthening the spiritual witness of youth.

Upon the urging of the Church of Christ in Thailand and faced with a forced withdrawal of missionaries from China, the Board of managers of the American Baptist Foreign Mission Society formally voted in January, 1952, to open new work in that country among the Karens of the Burma-Thailand border, and among the Swatow-speaking Chinese in the metropolitan area of Bangkok. The decision was welcomed by Karen Baptist congregations in the mountains of northwestern Thailand and by the Chinese Baptists in Bangkok. Accordingly, the Reverend and Mrs. Alfred Q. Van Benschoten were appointed to work among the Karens at Chiengmai, while the Reverend and Mrs. Carl M. Capen were designated for work among the Chinese in Bangkok. Capen is the son of the late Reverend and Mrs. Randall T. Capen, who had served for approximately thirty-five years in South China. Thus once again the two mission fields were associated in the ministry to the Swatow-speaking Chinese. Still another American Baptist missionary, Dr. Richard Buker, was lent by the Foreign Society to the Presbyterians, to be in charge of the leper colony at Chiengmai and twenty-two segregation villages in outlying areas through which he sought to prevent the spread of leprosy which affects nearly 100,000 victims in Thailand.[42]

With only 75,000 Christians in a population of 18,000,000, the reopening of work in Thailand proved to be a challenging opportunity. Moreover, it made possible the relocation of missionaries no longer able to serve in the Swatow-speaking area of South China.

---

[42] This brief survey is based on Horace W. Ryburn, "The Challenge to the Church in Thailand Today," *The International Review of Missions,* Vol. 41, No. 163 (July, 1952), pp. 288-300; Records of Board of Managers of A.B.F.M.S., 1952–53, pp. 352-55; *Missions,* Vol. 150, No. 4 (April, 1952), p. 204; Vol. 151, No. 9 (Nov. 1953), pp. 25-29; Dorothy A. Stevens, ed., *Baptists Under the Cross* (Philadelphia, 1953), pp. 53-54; *A Book of Remembrance,* 1954, p. 62.

In addition it brought reinforcements to the Karen Baptists who have been at work in the mountains of Thailand since 1884. Thus, in a remarkable way there was a reuniting of forces which once again might prove to be the means of a fresh entrance into China.

CHAPTER XXIX

Maturing Witness in Japan

THE STORY of Baptist work in Japan since 1914 is in some respects distinct from that of missionary efforts in other countries. Its appeal was mainly to the middle class of society, and it displayed a stronger interdenominational character than elsewhere, except possibly in East China. There was no mass-movement response; instead, the winning of converts was gradual, and usually one by one. In a very real sense, the Baptist witness in Japan matured through patience and persistence.

Main Developments to 1937

In 1914 evangelism received major attention among Japanese Baptists. They participated in a three-year interdenominational evangelistic campaign opened in the spring of the year under Japanese leadership. In the Inland Sea, the Gospel Ship, *Fukuin Maru,* continued its ministry among the island peoples until December, when the government forbade neutral ships to pass through the area unless engaged in foreign trade.

At the same time, the educational phase of the work continued to grow. Sixteen missionaries of the Woman's American Baptist Foreign Mission Society were conducting kindergartens and schools for girls in seven mission stations throughout the country. The Duncan Academy for boys at Tokyo passed its twentieth anniversary in 1916 with the largest entering class in its history. Some college work was being offered through a plan of co-operation with the Presbyterians. At the Misaki Tabernacle in Tokyo, Dr. Axling was providing a variety of educational opportunities in an institutional church program. Sunday schools, not encouraged in the earlier years of the Baptist Mission in Japan, were increasing in number.

In October, 1916, a Joint Conference of missionaries and representatives of the Board of the Foreign Society was held in Tokyo to study the Baptist educational situation in Japan. As a result, it was decided to discontinue Duncan Academy in Tokyo and to establish a new middle school in Yokohama, where there was no Christian school for boys. Plans were made to erect additional hostels at Waseda University to provide a Christian homelife for students. The theological seminary was to be located permanently in the vacated buildings of Duncan Academy. Japanese leaders were to have a larger share in the administration of schools.

Under a new plan of field administration, the Japanese pastors were given greater responsibility, and a program of self-support was encouraged. This was an important step, for only five of the thirty-three Baptist churches in the area of the American Baptist Mission were assuming their full support and contributing their share toward evangelistic work. Because many of the congregations were hindered in their effectiveness by inadequate meeting houses, the Board set up a church edifice fund to help finance the construction of new buildings.[1]

In 1918 another major step was taken when the mission staff set up a joint committee of six missionaries and six Japanese leaders to prepare all budgets and apportionments and to supervise the placement of missionaries on the field. The decision was supported by the General Society, the Woman's Society delaying action on the new policy until a later date. The women did vote, however, to have Japanese boards of directors appointed for the girls' schools, the Kindergarten Training School, and the Women's Bible Training School. At the same time the office of mission secretary was created to co-ordinate the work of the mission staff itself. Dr. C. B. Tenny was the first to hold that office.[2]

The effects of the First World War were widely felt in Japan. Hardly a phase of life remained unchanged. Many demands were made for universal suffrage, and some attention was being given by political leaders to the formation of a labor party. As education received a fresh impetus from the new forces at work, a Woman's Christian College was established jointly by several denominational

[1] The foregoing account is based on *Annual Reports of the A.B.F.M.S.*, 1915–17, and the Records of the Board of Managers of A.B.F.M.S., 1916–17, pp. 207-09

[2] *The Standard*, Vol. 65, No. 48 (Aug. 2, 1918), p. 1426.

missions. By 1920 the Mabie Memorial School, the new middle school for boys, was opened by the Baptists at Yokohama, with an entering class of three hundred students. Dr. Yugoro Chiba, an outstanding Japanese Christian, became the president of the theological seminary at Tokyo. At Waseda University, Dr. Harry B. Benninghoff supervised the Christian activities on a campus of ten thousand students. Although he was supported by the American Baptist Foreign Mission Society, his work was interdenominational. Early in 1922, Scott Hall, the second hostel to be erected since 1908, was completed. It became an important center of Christian influence for university students throughout the city.

The Woman's American Baptist Foreign Mission Society supported four high schools for girls at Sendai, Tokyo, Kanagawa, and Himeji, through which nearly seven hundred young women were brought under Christian influence each year. Between thirty-five and forty Sunday schools were conducted in the surrounding territory by students of these schools. The Society encouraged higher education by its support of the Woman's Christian College in Tokyo. Leadership for women's work was being prepared by the Bible Women's Training School in Osaka and the Kindergarten Training School in Tokyo. The Bible women and kindergarten teachers provided an important link between the church and the home.[3]

In the midst of these years of unprecedented progress in the Baptist work in Japan came the devastating earthquake of 1923. Nearly three-fourths of the property erected by the Mission in the preceding ten years was damaged or destroyed. Three Japanese teachers at Mabie Memorial School lost their lives in the destruction of the building in which they were at work. The Tokyo Baptist Tabernacle lay in ruins. Scott Hall at Waseda University and the new Yotsuya Baptist Church in Tokyo were damaged. The two Mission Boards sent a commission to Japan at once to make plans for reconstruction. By April, 1924, American Baptists had contributed $146,628 for this purpose. The distribution of emergency supplies was made under the direction of Dr. Axling through a relief headquarters established in the gutted Tokyo Baptist Tabernacle.[4]

Almost before reconstruction could get under way, a second event

---

[3] *Missions,* Vol. 12, No. 6 (June, 1921), p. 359.

[4] *The Baptist,* Vol. 4, No. 35 (Sept. 29, 1923), p. 1106; No. 42 (Nov. 17, 1923), pp. 1321-22; *Annual Report of A.B.F.M.S.* for 1924, pp. 20-26.

struck the churches a severe blow. It was the passage of a new immigration law by the United States Congress in 1924 which excluded Japanese from the country. The good will gained by the generous relief efforts following the earthquake was virtually dissipated in the resentment which the new legislation aroused. Missionaries found it difficult to enlist new students in the work. The people of the Inland Sea, where the Gospel Ship had resumed its work after the war, became hostile. Although the political disturbances occasioned by the Act had subsided by 1926, the Baptist Mission was weakened seriously. Not quite $200,000 had been received to replace the destruction of property which had amounted to more than $500,000. The only major rebuilding accomplished by this time was the remodeling of the Baptist Tabernacle at Tokyo, which had resumed its varied activities in full force.[5]

Between 1926 and 1937 the development of an indigenous church life among Japanese Baptists was accelerated. Although Japanese leaders shared in the administration of the Mission through a Joint Committee, they openly asked for full control. With the example before them of the Congregationalists, who had earlier made this transition with success, the Baptist Boards effected further changes in organization of the Mission. The Woman's Society agreed for the first time to place its work in Japan under the supervision of a joint woman's committee composed of its own appointees and of representatives of the Japanese Baptists, the latter constituting a majority status. The Joint Committee, which had been directing the work of the General Society for several years, was reconstituted to give the Japanese a majority rather than a fifty-fifty representation with the missionaries as before.[6]

Other changes were also made in the operation of the Mission. The Gospel Ship was sold in 1927 and a plan was developed to concentrate the work in the Inland Sea in a few strategic centers. The great cost of operating the ship plus the fact that travel facilities had improved among the islands had dictated the change. For the future it was felt that the development of a stronger church life would be more effective than an itinerant evangelistic program. Within the next few years, the Reverend and Mrs. M. D. Farnum were designated to

[5] *Annual Report of A.B.F.M.S.* for 1925, pp. 27-33; for 1926, pp. 18, 146; *Missions,* Vol. 16, No. 6 (June, 1925), p. 330.

[6] *Annual Report of A.B.F.M.S.* for 1927, pp. 151-52.

this field, with headquarters at Sheigei. At the northern end of the island group, the Reverend W. F. Topping was endeavoring to develop a co-operative farming plan to improve the economic status of the people.[7]

A further change in the plan of the mission work was effected in 1927, when the Japan Baptist Theological School and its preparatory department (Tokyo Gakuin) were removed to Yokohama, to be coordinated with the Mabie Memorial School for Boys. The new institution was composed thereby of three schools: a middle school for boys, a college which included a social service department and a department of commerce, and a theological school. In the fall of 1928 the Yokohama Memorial Church dedicated its reconstructed building, five years after having been damaged by earthquake and fire.

During the next several years, Baptists were influenced by the Kingdom of God Movement, introduced to Japan in 1929 by Toyohiko Kagawa. It was an evangelistic effort to reach every class in Japanese society, especially the farmers, the industrial workers, the fishermen, and the miners, who had been virtually unreached by the gospel. All of the major denominations at work in the country cooperated through the National Christian Council of Japan. It proved to be an effective corrective to the middle-class trend in Japanese church life.

In 1932 new Baptist headquarters were established in Tokyo in a modest office building erected on land at the rear of the Tokyo Baptist Tabernacle. In connection with the great institutional church, the headquarters became a center for Baptist life and a symbol of Baptist unity. In 1933 the Tabernacle completed a quarter of a century of service. Its work extended into the industrial areas of the city through the Fukagawa Christian Center established after the earthquake. By a diversified program of evening classes for employed people, of medical dispensaries and children's clinics, recreation clubs, and children's educational work, the masses of the city were being reached with considerable success. The Central Baptist Church, which made the Tabernacle its home, was a self-supporting and self-governing center around which the various social welfare and educational features of the Tabernacle were conducted.

---

[7] *Ibid.*, for 1926, pp. 34-35; for 1928, pp. 27-28, 147; for 1931, pp. 26-27; for 1933, pp. 105-06.

In 1934 the transfer of control of the Baptist Mission in Japan was completed, when the East Japan Baptist Convention (the churches of the American Baptist Mission as over against the West Japan Baptist Convention of churches affiliated with the Southern Baptist Mission) was merged with the Japan Baptist Mission. By this reorganization, the Mission disappeared as a legislating body outside of the Convention. Responsibility for administration was placed in the hands of an executive committee of the Convention, composed of nine men and three women. The women's work was placed under the control of a subcommittee composed of Japanese Baptist women and missionaries of the Woman's Foreign Society.[8]

As international tensions began to mount in the 1930's, church leaders in Japan sought to bring about church union. In 1935 a plan was formulated by a Commission on Church Union, but it was rejected as premature by the Baptists, the Lutherans, the Episcopalians, and a few other groups. Representatives of the East Baptist Convention argued that unity with the churches under the Southern Baptist Convention should be effected before they entered a larger body.[9]

Theological education was a constant problem to the Baptists of Japan, for they were not numerous enough to have a strong seminary. As a solution, the theological department conducted at Mabie Memorial School in Yokohama was transferred in 1936 to Aoyama Gakuin, the Methodist College and Seminary in Tokyo. Aoyama Gakuin was a coeducational institution in which the United Church of Canada, the Evangelicals, and the Disciples also co-operated. Under the new arrangement, the Baptists were to supply a Japanese and an American teacher.[10]

The War Years (1937–1945)

When Japan entered upon a course of war, first with China, then with the Western powers, the churches underwent severe testing. The military invasion of China was unpopular with the greater number of Christians in the country. Yet, once engaged in the conflict, the churches sought ways and means of serving Japanese troops on the battlefronts. Some pastors, like Saburo Yasamura, director of

---

[8] N.B.C., *Annual* for 1932, p. 722; for 1933, p. 462; for 1934, pp. 532-33.

[9] *The International Review of Missions,* Vol. 41, No. 162 (April 1952) p. 198

[10] *Annual Report of A.B.F.M.S.* for 1937, pp. 36-37, 114.

Mead Christian Center in Osaka, enlisted as chaplains. The international outlook of Christianity caused missionaries and Japanese Christians alike to be viewed with suspicion by intense nationalists. There was no strong church group in Japan to withstand the war party in the government. Many Christians found it difficult to distinguish between the bounds of loyalty to the emperor and devotion to God.

Yet in spite of these countertides, Baptist work, in common with the entire Christian movement, showed some evidence of progress during the early years of war. Regardless of a slump in church attendance, contributions remained on the upgrade and self-support made real gains. The Christian schools continued to operate without serious setback. But as the war deepened, Japanese finances became perilous, and uncontrollable inflation threatened the nation. Acute shortages in food, coal, electric power, and manpower caused suffering and restlessness among the people.

In 1940 the Religious Organizations Bill became a law, giving full legal standing and formal recognition to Christianity as one of the religions of the Japanese Empire. The Bill was designed to bring all religious organizations under supervision of the government. Passage of the new law hastened a process already in operation among Baptists of Japan to unite their two Conventions into one organization. The new body was known as the "Nippon Baputesto Kirisuto Kyodan" (the Japan Baptist Christian Denomination). Dr. Yugoro Chiba was elected its first president. In 1941, to forestall compulsory action by the government, the Christian churches drew together into the Church of Christ in Japan (Nippon Kirisuto Kyodan). It was to be free from foreign funds and official direction from missionaries. The Japan Baptist Kyodan approved the union in principle and joined with forty other denominations. The change caused a minimum of dislocation in the life of Baptist churches and institutions because the Japanese Christians had long been in complete control of Baptist work in Japan, with the missionaries serving under the Japan Baptist Convention. Moreover, by mutual agreement, financial subsidies from the United States had ceased on April 20, 1941. The first secretary of the Church of Christ in Japan was a Baptist, the Reverend Isamu Chiba, son of the great Baptist leader.

As the political situation between Japan and the West worsened in 1941, missionaries' wives and children were urged to evacuate. By

December 7, when Japanese planes attacked Pearl Harbor, the entire missionary force had been reduced to about one-fourth the usual staff. Only six missionaries, three from each Society, were in Japan proper. They were restricted in their movements, but were allowed for a time to continue their work. Ultimately, all of them were interned except Mrs. H. W. Topping, who was eighty years of age and retired, her husband having died in 1942, and the Reverend James F. Gressitt, who was allowed to remain in active service. He served until his death in 1945 as treasurer of the Japan Baptist Mission and treasurer of the Kagawa Co-operators, the organization which supported Kagawa in his program of social work and evangelization. In December, 1943 Dr. and Mrs. William Axling, Miss Winifred M. Acock, and Miss Thomasine Allen were repatriated.

Japanese Christians did not suffer severe persecution during the war years. There was a decline in church attendance throughout the country as war-work distracted many from their normal pursuits. The Christian schools carried on with undiminished zeal, their greatest problem being that of securing competent Christian teachers. The Mabie Memorial College at Yokohama had an enrollment of two thousand students in 1943. The Hinomoto Girls' School at Himeji, through the generous gifts of parents, graduates, and friends, was able to raise its full endowment and form a property-holding body. The Kindergarten Training School in Tokyo had eighty girls in training and seventy-five children in school. The former Baptist Theological Seminary building at Tokyo was chosen to house the new Woman's Union Theological Seminary, a merger of nineteen schools brought together in 1943. The Baptist Tabernacle in Tokyo maintained its full program of service to the working classes of the city.[11]

Postwar Developments (1946–1954)

The death of Dr. Yugoro Chiba, secretary of the Japan Baptist Convention, on Easter Sunday, April 21, 1946, was a severe loss to the churches. He had served as a representative of the Christians of his country in ecumenical gatherings. His stand against militarism had been unwavering during the entire course of the war. His leadership

[11] This brief survey is based on *Annual Reports of A.B.F.M.S.,* 1938–40; *Along Kingdom Highways,* 1941–45; Kenneth Scott Latourette, *The Christian World Mission in Our Day* (New York, 1954), pp. 128-30; Henry P. Van Dusen, *For the Healing of the Nations* (New York, 1940), pp. 73-77.

in the Convention had given stability to the Baptist churches at a critical time in their history.[12]

War damage to churches in Japan was extensive. Out of about 1800 Protestant churches, 540 were bombed by American planes and 200 more were dismantled or dynamited by Japanese authorities to prevent fires from spreading. As a result, about one-half of the Christions in the country were left without church buildings. In Tokyo, the Fukagawa Christian Center was a mass of rubble. The Immanuel Baptist Church was utterly destroyed. Of the Baptist Kindergarten Training School, three buildings were demolished, and only one remained for use after the war. Scott Hall at Waseda University, which had housed Baptist student work, had been sold during the war. The Baptist Women's Dormitory was demolished. At Yokohama, Mabie Memorial College was wiped out except for one building, and the ten buildings of the Mary L. Colby Girls' School were destroyed completely. Both institutions operated after the war in temporary quarters. Behind the ruins of the Kanagawa Baptist Church a plyboard chapel was erected to provide for worship services. At Himeji almost the entire city was destroyed. The Baptist church and parsonage were burned. Saburo Namioka, principal of the Hinomoto Girls' School, served a period in prison because of his Christian attitude during the war. Upon his release, he reorganized the school once again on a sound Christian basis. At Osaka, the four buildings of the Mead Christian Center were demolished entirely. Miss Margaret E. Cuddeback returned after the war to resume her work in the home of a friendly Japanese family.[13]

With World Mission Crusade funds collected in the United States, the two Mission Societies helped the Japanese Baptists to rebuild the most needed churches among the twenty-three edifices destroyed during the war. The Woman's Society sent, through Church World Service, two prefabricated dwellings for residences to house their missionaries. American Baptists participated in an interdenominational agency known as "Heifers for Relief," to supply a source of milk for the undernourished.

In 1948 the Board of Managers of the American Baptist Foreign

[12] Records of Board of Managers and Executive Committee of W.A.B.F.M.S., Jan. 1944–Nov. 1946, pp. 412-14.

[13] *Missions,* Vol. 38, No. 1 (Jan. 1947), pp. 12-16; No. 10 (Dec. 1947), pp. 597-600; *Crusader,* Vol. 3, No. 4 (Sept. 1948), pp. 3-7; *Along Kingdom Highways,* 1947, p. 51; 1948, p. 99.

Mission Society voted to participate in the organization of an interdenominational Christian university for Japan. On April 13, 1953, the new institutions, known as the International Christian University in Japan, was officially opened on a 365-acre campus seventeen miles northwest of the heart of Tokyo. It is a union venture of fourteen Mission Boards and one in which American Baptists have a share, thus bringing to fulfillment a fifty-year-old dream.[14]

By 1949 communism had infiltrated into student centers, industrial areas, and rural sections of Japan. The severe shortages in food, clothing, medical needs, and leadership provided fertile soil for its propaganda. Legislation, however, which barred party members from public office and banned communist literature, offset its influence to a large degree, and materially contributed to the acceptability of Christian teaching and the general mission program.[15]

Following the war, the relations of Baptists to united Protestantism in Japan underwent change. Baptist churches, formerly related to American Baptists, organized within the framework of the Kyodan their own fellowship, known as the Shinseikai. It was instrumental in determining Baptist policy and plans. The trend away from church union, hinted at in this effort of Baptists to protect their own principles and work, prevailed among other groups as well. Many strong denominations that once co-operated under the pressure of the war years went their own way in the postwar period. These included the Lutherans, Southern Presbyterians, and Southern Baptists. The Shinseikai, although nominally a member of the Kyodan, was moving away from it, largely because the Baptist ministry was not recognized by some other communions and because there were differences over the concept of the church and believer's baptism. The Baptist Convention maintained its own departments of women's work and young people's work, and began to train its own workers in the Institute of Christian Studies, opened after the war as a part of the Mabie Memorial School (Kanto Gakuin). Baptists continued to look to the Union Theological Seminary in Tokyo for the training of its pastors.[16]

---

14 Records of Board of Managers, A.B.F.M.S., 1948–49, p. 86; *Year Book of the American Baptist Convention, 1954,* p. 213.

15 *Missions,* Vol. 147, No. 1 (Jan. 1949), p. 39; *Along Kingdom Highways,* 1951, p. 10.

16 *Along Kingdom Highways* for 1951, p. 11; for 1952, p. 5; *Missions,* Vol. 150, No. 4 (April 1952), p. 210.

By 1950 American Baptist missionaries were working under the direction of the Japanese Baptist Convention in seven stations. The major educational institutions included the Mabie Memorial School for men and women in Yokohama, with the college opened temporarily at Oppama, a former Japanese Naval Training Center; schools for girls in Himeji, Yokohama, and Sendai; and the great student center at Waseda University in Tokyo. In addition, the Baptists participated in a rural training school for pastors, located twenty-six miles from Tokyo; they shared in the work of the Tokyo Woman's Christian College; and were actively engaged in helping to establish the International Christian University for work on the graduate level. Large Christian centers were maintained in Tokyo, Osaka, and Kuji to minister to the factory workers of heavily industrialized areas. A summer conference ground developed a camping program for youth at Inagawa, near Osaka. There were strong churches in Himeji, Kobe, Osaka, Yokohama, Tokyo, and Sendai, and smaller ones elsewhere. The two Societies supported twenty-six missionaries in the country, five of whom had been evacuated from their fields in China.[17]

New types of work undertaken after the war included medical clinics at the Christian Centers in Kuji and Osaka; a Rural Reconstruction Center dedicated in 1950 at Rifu, which was intended to demonstate improved farming methods and to orient students for the ministry to the needs of rural people; and the launching of a new Gospel Ship in 1951 to sail again the Inland Sea of Japan. A new Christian Center Building was opened in Fukagawa in 1952, erected through World Mission Crusade funds. A new campus for the Mabie Memorial School, now known as Kanto Gakuin University, was purchased in 1952.[18] These accomplishments were materially aided by substantial sums of money raised in the United States in 1950 by a special effort which the Foreign Societies called the Japan Opportunity Fund.

Since the war the number of Christians in Japan has increased, but not so rapidly as some had hoped. At the close of 1949 there were about 186,000, which was considerably less than before the war. In spite of the withdrawal of some denominations, the Kyodan

---

[17] *Ibid.*, for 1950, pp. 14-15.

[18] Wilson, *American Baptists Overseas*, pp. 29, 72-73; *Along Kingdom Highways*, 1952, p. 5.

still had about two-thirds of the Protestants. In 1952 there were 55 Baptist churches in the country related to the American Baptist Foreign Mission Societies. The aggregate membership totaled about 4,000, recruited largely from the 600 converts a year since the war. This figure represented a drop of 2,000 from the total membership of Baptist churches before the war.[19]

It is clear that the response to the Christian message excited no mass movement in Japan, and that the growth of the Christian community was the result of an uphill pull. The reasons were not far to see—a highly developed culture, an association of Christianity with Western imperialism, and a shortsighted policy on the part of the American Baptist Mission in earlier years of not placing sufficient stress on higher education for the more adequate training of a national leadership. Yet, it also may be observed that the quality of church life among Japanese Baptists remained high in spite of the limitations, and the churches matured with remarkable success.

---

[19] Latourette, *The Christian World Mission in Our Day,* pp. 128-30; *Missions,* Vol. 150, No. 4 (April 1952), pp. 207-08.

CHAPTER XXX

Advance Through Trial in the Philippines

THE AMERICAN Baptist Mission in the Philippines was the youngest of the ten fields developed by 1914, yet it was one of the fastest growing in numbers and in responsible leadership. The notable advances which were made took place within a forty-year period that opened with the First World War and closed in an era of reconstruction that followed the Second World War. When the story of the Filipino churches is understood against this background, it becomes one of the most challenging in the annals of missionary history.

Developments to 1941

The theological dissension which troubled the American Baptist Foreign Mission Society during the period after 1914 was discussed in a previous chapter. It was within that context that the Baptist Mission in the Philippines suffered from divisiveness. The factors were as much due to personalities as to doctrinal differences. As early as 1917 Dr. Raphael C. Thomas, medical missionary at Iloilo, where the Presbyterians and Baptists supported a Union Hospital, separated himself from the Mission on the grounds that his work was distinct from that of other missionaries who were engaged in evangelistic and educational services. His implied criticism was shared by a minority group of missionaries who were dissatisfied with the policies of the Mission, particularly at the point of comity agreements and inter-denominational projects. When pressure was placed on the Society not to return to the field certain missionaries at home on furlough, the Board took decisive action on December 11, 1917, notifying the Reference Committee that the missionaries were no longer to involve themselves in a judgment about the return of staff members on furlough. The Board also indicated that it would take more direct control of the administration of the field, limiting the Reference Committee to an advisory capacity, except in matters specifically referred to it with power. Any missionaries not satisfied with the policy of the Board were invited to return home.

The unrest remained, however, to plague the Mission for several years. It centered chiefly in the variant viewpoints of missionaries concerning such matters as comity agreements and the proper emphasis upon education and evangelism. In many respects the dissension reflected the dissatisfaction at the time within the Northern Baptist Convention concerning the policies of the Foreign Mission Boards on the various fields. In 1926 attention once again focussed upon Dr. Thomas, when he requested the Board to assign him to an evangelistic field. About the same time, the Board received criticism of his management of the Union Hospital at Iloilo of which he was then superintendent. When they notified him that a Commission was on its way to the Islands to investigate the situation before they made their decision on his reassignment, he refused to await its arrival, and returned home at once. Upon his arrival in New York, he engaged in a nine-hour conference with the Board, at the close of which he resigned as a missionary of the Society "because of inability loyally to support the administration in the Philippines." His resignation was accepted.

Within a short time, two other missionaries resigned from the Philippine Mission staff because of doctrinal differences and disagreement with what they regarded as liberal policies in the Northern Baptist Convention. The withdrawal of this minority group gave rise to the creation of a new missionary agency in 1928, known as "The Association of Baptists for World Evangelism, Inc." Under its auspices, a new work was opened at once in Manila. *The Sunday School Times,* a strongly fundamentalist organ in sympathy with the new mission agency, interpreted Dr. Thomas' resignation as an indication that he had been ousted because of his orthodoxy and evangelistic loyalty. Faced with such a charge, the Board of the Foreign Mission Society published the facts surrounding the long history of Dr. Thomas' dissatisfaction with the Mission.[1]

[1] Records of Board of Managers of A.B.F.M.S., 1917–18, pp. 92-94; 1928–29, pp. 318-20. The issue of *The Sunday School Times* referred to is for Feb. 9, 1929.

In spite of these difficulties in the Philippines, a number of important developments were in process during these years. In 1922 the Jaro Industrial School was raised to junior college status, to be known as Central Philippine College. In 1924 the Presbyterians, who had worked together with the Baptists in Iloilo on Panay Island for several years, withdrew to consolidate their work. Their action left full responsibility to the Baptists for the Union Hospital at Iloilo and the Dunwoody Dormitory at La Paz, seat of a large government school. Friends of Dr. Thomas, who was then still associated with the Mission, provided the funds for the Board to purchase the Presbyterian buildings.[2]

In 1925, the 25th anniversary of Baptist work in the Philippines was observed. At the time, the Mission was maintaining three stations: Iloilo and Capiz on Panay Island, and Bacolod on Negros Island, with a staff composed of 34 missionaries and 232 Filipino workers. Associated with the Mission were 86 churches with 5,581 church members, 23 schools with 1,875 pupils, 2 hospitals, and 4 dormitories for students attending government schools. More than 400 students were enrolled in Central Philippine College. On the Bacolod field, there had been over 1,200 baptisms in a single year.[3] It was a notable record for only a quarter of a century of work.

During the next few years, however, there was a decline in the number of baptisms, reflecting the growing opposition of the Roman Catholic Church to Protestant evangelism. The loss of many new converts, who had been too easily won, made evident the need for a better-trained ministry which would appeal successfully to the influential student and professional classes. A notable contribution in this direction had been made by Dr. Eric Lund, the pioneer missionary to the Philippines, who died in retirement in California in 1933. Until the close of his life he had engaged in prolific literary labors, publishing the amazing total of 171 books, pamphlets, and tracts in six different languages. His greatest achievement was the translation of the entire Bible into Panayan, the New Testament into Cebuan, and the Four Gospels and Acts into Samarenyo, these being the three dialects of the Visayan people.[4]

In 1934 the Filipinos gained the promise of independence from

---

[2] *Annual Report of A.B.F.M.S.* for 1925, p. 40.
[3] *Missions,* Vol. 16, No. 6 (June, 1925), pp. 330-31.
[4] *Annual Report of A.B.F.M.S.* for 1928, p. 149; for 1933, p. 49.

the United States within a ten-year period. Passage of the Philippine Independence Bill by the American Congress had a marked effect upon the course of mission policy in the Islands. The feeling of nationalism which it engendered prompted the Filipino Christians to desire greater responsibility in the conduct of their church life. As a consequence, the Western Visayan Convention was reorganized in 1935 into the Convention of Philippine Baptist Churches, Inc. Instead of the mission work being directed and carried on by the Joint Committee which was composed of the Executive Committee of the old Filipino Convention and the Reference Committee of the Mission, the work henceforth was to be conducted by the new Convention's Board of Trustees. This administrative group was composed of nine Filipinos and six missionaries, all elected by the Convention itself. In accordance with the new plan, the old Mission Conference was reorganized under the less pretentious name of Missionary Group. The Reference Committee of the missionaries became a smaller Mission Business Committee. The former responsibilities of the Mission were transferred to the Convention, only the personal matters of the missionaries being reserved to the Missionary Group.[5]

The institutional work of the new Convention was strengthened perceptibly. In 1935, when many of the schools in the Islands experienced a drop in enrollment, Central Philippine College maintained its usual level in spite of opposition from Roman Catholic leaders. In 1938 the Baptist Missionary Training School, located at the Student Center at La Paz, was merged with the School of Theology of the College. At the same time, the college curriculum was adjusted to a full four-year course. A program of nurses' training was conducted at Emmanuel Hospital in Capiz and at Iloilo Hospital. In 1940 the latter institution had for the first time a Filipino director, Dr. Porras, and a Filipino woman physician. Both hospitals were operating under their own Boards, subject to the oversight of the Convention.[6]

The War Years and Reconstruction (1941–1954)

The quiet progress which prevailed in all of the work in the Philippines during the months prior to December, 1941, was shattered by the declaration of war which followed the Japanese attack on Pearl

[5] *Ibid.*, for 1936, pp. 42, 107.
[6] *Ibid.*, 1934–40.

Harbor. At that time, the combined mission staff of the two Foreign Mission Societies totalled twenty-two, of whom nineteen were on the field and three at home on furlough. Central Philippine College was closed two days after war broke out, most of the students taking up arms. Both mission hospitals carried on their full program, including nurses' training. In April, 1942, the Japanese took over the Iloilo Hospital and operated it for their own troops until March, 1945. During the period of American advance, the property was badly damaged by bombing. It was finally occupied by the 37th United States Field Hospital, after necessary repairs had been made. With the evacuation of American forces in 1946, the property was returned to the Baptists. The Emmanuel Hospital at Capiz, which was smaller, maintained an effective traveling dispensary service during the earlier war years. The Convention of Philippine Baptist Churches was recognized by the invading authorities and continued to carry on as best it could under the confused circumstances of wartime. Many of the people deserted the larger centers and retreated to the interior. Under the strained conditions, some fell away from Christianity, but the majority remained faithful.[7]

The fate of the twenty-one American Baptist missionaries in the Philippines varied with the circumstances in which they found themselves after Pearl Harbor Day. Two who were engaged in Chinese language study at Baguio on the Island of Luzon were interned there by the rapidly advancing Japanese. Later, they were transferred to Bilibid Prison. Two others, on the Island of Negros, were first interned at Bacalod, and then in Santo Tomas, and later at Los Baños. The majority, seventeen in number, were on the Island of Panay. Six of these, who had been connected with the mission hospital at Iloilo, were put in prison there. Eleven months later, they were transferred to the Santo Tomas internment camp on Luzon. All ten of the missionaries who had been interned on Luzon and Panay were liberated in February, 1945, by the American forces.

The remaining eleven, which included the entire staff at Capiz, and the thirteen-year-old son of two of the missionaries, escaped internment by retreating to the hills. There, at a small mountain retreat which they called "Hopevale," they sought to elude capture and to carry on their ministry to the Filipinos. They were discovered by

[7] For details, see *Along Kingdom Highways,* 1941–43; *Missions,* Vol. 147, No. 5 (May 1949), p. 273; *Crusader,* Vol. 4, No. 1 (May 1949), p. 12.

Japanese soldiers, apparently on December 19, 1943, and put to death the next day. Their remains were later buried in a common grave beneath the communion table of the Katipunan Baptist Church, near Hopevale, in grateful recognition of their supreme sacrifice for the Christians of the Philippine Islands.[8] The tragic loss left Capiz without a single missionary and wiped out more than half of the entire staff of the Philippine Mission.

In the fall of 1945 Dr. Elmer A. Fridell, foreign secretary for the Orient, visited the Philippines to calculate the damage done and to plan relief for the suffering people and the reconstruction of the property. He reported that eighty per cent of the churches on Panay Island and sixty per cent of those on Negros Island had been destroyed. The Iloilo Mission Hospital, having been repaired by American troops, was in usable condition. With a complete medical unit purchased from the United States Navy, it was possible to reopen the hospital in 1948 under a Filipino director, Dr. Cesar G. Jayme. Although Emmanuel Hospital at Capiz had not been destroyed, it had been thoroughly looted. All twenty buildings of Central Philippine College were completely destroyed. A further loss to the churches was the disappearance of the manuscript of the revision of the Visayan translation of the Bible.

The task of reconstruction was enormous. The Board of Managers of the Foreign Mission Society appropriated funds in 1946 for the erection of temporary quarters for Central Philippine College. In 1949, $10,000 was appropriated towards the rebuilding of Franklin Hall and the last of the then available war damage claims were released for the use of the College. By 1947 the institutions were operating once again with more than 1,000 students in attendance. In the next two years its student body increased to 1,500, and the Theological College and Woman's Department doubled their enrollment and had eight teams of students going out into the villages conducting the evangelistic and educational ministry.

In 1949 Jose Yap, the executive secretary of the Convention of

---

[8] The story is told in *Along Kingdom Highways,* 1945, pp. 40, 60-61; *Missions,* Vol. 37, No. 4 (April 1946), pp. 206-11; and in *Through Shining Archway* (New York, 1945). The twelve who died were: Miss Jennie C. Adams, Miss Dorothy A. Dowell, Miss Signe A. Erickson, Mr. and Mrs. James H. Covell, Rev. and Mrs. Erle F. Rounds, Rev. and Mrs. Francis H. Rose, Dr. and Mrs. Frederick W. Meyer, and Erle Douglas Rounds, thirteen-year-old son of the Rounds.

Baptist Churches of the Philippines, pleaded for an agricultural missionary who would help his people to improve the output of the soil and so overcome the great poverty which they suffered. By the spring of that year, Mr. and Mrs. Burl A. Slocum arrived from East China to develop a department of agriculture at Central Philippine College. Under Dr. Slocum's guidance, rural institutes were held and the churches became centers for community work in guiding the people to better farming methods. It was a practical program which greatly strengthened the impact of the evangelistic emphasis of the churches.

By 1950 the medical work at Capiz was reinforced by the arrival of Dr. and Mrs. Robert Ainslie and a missionary nurse, Miss Elizabeth Swanson, from West China. They were a welcome addition to the Emmanuel Hospital, which had been reopened after the war by Filipino doctors and a single missionary nurse, Miss Ethel Boggs. At Iloilo a new nurses' home was dedicated in the same year.

When the 50th anniversary of Baptist work in the Philippines was observed at Central Philippine College in 1950, there were 150 Baptist churches with a total membership that exceeded 8,000. A mission staff of 29 missionaries was being supported by the two Foreign Mission Societies to supplement the leadership of the Convention.[9]

During the next few years there were encouraging signs of progress. The Convention churches were assuming responsibility for self-support, encouraged by the stewardship institutes conducted in 1951 by the Reverend Dean R. Kirkwood, who had come from West China. The Women's Federation of the Convention gave further expression to the developing self-reliance of the Filipino Christians. The youth work of the Convention assumed new importance under the guidance of the Reverend and Mrs. J. L. Sprigg, who had been transferred from West China to supervise the Student Center at La Paz and to direct the Youth Department of the Convention. In 1953 the Central Philippine College attained the status of a university, with an enrollment which exceeded 2,500. The institution had eight new permanent buildings which had been erected with the help of World Mission Crusade funds from the United States. Dr. Almus O. Larsen came in 1952 to be the new president. The agricultural program con-

---

[9] This brief survey is drawn from *Along Kingdom Highways,* 1948–50; *Crusader,* Vol. 4, No. 1 (May 1949), p. 13; Vol. 5, No. 5 (Oct., 1950), pp. 6-7; *Missions,* Vol. 148, No. 10 (Dec., 1950), pp. 600-02.

ducted by Mr. Slocum through the University was attracting national attention. Nearly 600 farmers were enrolled in farm study classes. A Bible Institute was set up to teach pastors and lay-workers in rural communities who had not had the advantage of formal education.

By 1953 the Convention was composed of 173 churches with almost 12,000 members. They co-operated with the Philippine Federation of Christian Churches in projects of evangelism, Christian education, church extension, and Christian family life. When, however, the United Church of Christ in the Philippines was formed in 1948, the Baptists did not join, but promised to give the matter further study.[10]

The witness of the Baptist churches in the Philippines was of strategic importance, for it provided an evangelical message in a land where Roman Catholicism had grown decadent. Moreover the importance of the Filipinos in the spread of the Christian message was increased by the fact that their Islands constituted a bridge between the Occident and the Orient. The Christian schools and hospitals, subsidized by outside funds, did much to offset the problems created by the great poverty of the people. As the membership of the churches increased ten per cent each year, the enthusiasm of Filipino Baptists mounted and their hope for the future brightened.

---

[10] See *Along Kingdom Highways,* 1951–53; *Missions,* Vol. 150, No. 5 May 1952), pp. 271-74; *Crusader,* Vol. 4, No. 1 (May 1949), p. 12; Vol. 8, No. 4 Sept., 1953), pp. 3-5.

CHAPTER XXXI

Growth in the Changing Congo

THE REMARKABLE STORY of the American Baptist Mission in the Belgian Congo needs to be viewed against the backdrop of the rapidly changing scene in which that work took place after 1914. As the potentialities of the African continent became more fully recognized, industry developed to the point where the slow-moving life of the African people was accelerated at a confusing pace. In Central Africa, in particular, the development of copper mines exerted a marked effect upon Christian mission work. It provided in some instances an opportunity to evangelize village peoples who had left home to live in new industrial centers, uprooted from their moorings and searching for a new set of values. As Africans learned the use of money, some became less generous in their giving to the support of the church. Bright and energetic young men found in the mines a freedom from the tutelage of the Christian mission, and many of them launched out as organizers of independent native denominations. In some cases entire districts became partially depopulated. Artisans, laborers, house-boys, and even teachers and evangelists deserted the mission stations for the Copper Belt.[1]

With industrialization came secularism that presented to many a false sense of values—that things are the good in life. New means of transportation brought a new life to thousands of Africans. At Kano, in the heart of the Congo, where once there were inaccessible villages

[1] J. Merle Davis, *Modern Industry and the African* (London, 1933), p. 9; ——————, *The Economic and Social Environment of the Younger Churches* (London, 1939), pp. 23-24.

far removed from the bustle of modern civilization, a large airport was built after the Second World War. Leopoldville became a thriving city with stock piles of a variety of goods, the latest motor cars, and heavy machinery for modern construction of roads and buildings—all brought from the coast by a single track narrow gauge railroad from Matadi. Overnight, villagers recruited for day-labor found themselves transferred from a simple village life to an urban culture in which they were made familiar with Western customs and modern machinery of all kinds.[2]

The vigor of the Christian churches in the Congo during this transition period was astonishing. Congregations were large. Church discipline was exercised faithfully for such offenses as polygamy, witchcraft, heathen practices, drunkenness, and unlawful pagan dances. But the more observant noted that although the church had vitality, it was deficient in solidity through a lack of trained African leadership.[3] Owing to the illiteracy and poverty of the people, the process of developing an indigenous church life was slow. But the trend was accelerated in the years following the Second World War.

It is the purpose of this chapter to trace this gradual growth toward Christian maturity among the Congolese peoples who had come under the ministry of the American Baptist Mission. For convenience the record will follow rather distinct periods of activity during the four decades under consideration. Because the educational and medical work was interwoven so intimately with the evangelistic ministry of the mission, no effort will be made to treat these phases of the enterprise separately.

The First World War and Its Effects

Although the Africans in the Congo escaped immediate contact with the destructiveness of war, its effects were felt among them nonetheless. Many were overwhelmed and mystified by the reported savagery of white men with whom they associated the Christian gospel. Shipping restrictions hindered regular mail service and the securing of adequate supplies for the mission needs. Most of the Congo missionaries were subjected to unusual dangers from submarine warfare in

---

[2] G. J. M., Pearce, *Congo Background* (London, 1954), pp. 62-77; articles by Leonard Gittings, American Baptist missionary to the Belgian-Congo, in the Battle Creek (Mich.) *Enquirer and News,* Aug. 29, 1948 and May 22, 1949.

[3] Pearce, *op. cit.,* p. 108.

their travel to the field or in their return to the United States for furlough during the period of hostilities. Over the five-year period after 1914, only one new family received appointment to the Congo. Meanwhile the morale of the mission staff was tested severely in the face of the shortage of personnel and materials. The influenza epidemic of 1918 took a heavy toll of life among the undernourished people. Mission schools remained closed from November of that year until the following January. The Congo Evangelical Training Institution, for the education of church leaders, was closed for an entire year because of the illness of the missionaries in charge.[4]

In the summer of 1921 the mission was disturbed by a spontaneous movement of a politico-religious nature which arose in the Lower Congo. It was led by a self-styled prophet, Kibangu, who claimed to be a Messiah and a miracle-worker. He aroused strong hostility against white men and called for a return of the country to the Africans. Fearing that the movement was part of the current Pan-African movements which had been aroused by the peace propaganda for self-determinism at Versailles, the Belgian government suppressed the movement by sentencing Kibangu to death and consigning many of his followers to prison or to exile. Later, King Albert reprieved Kibangu from the death sentence. Meantime, his followers became disillusioned when he failed to work the expected miracles.

The Prophet Movement, as it was called, left its mark on the Christian missions. Roman Catholic missions suffered most because a large number of their adherents went over to the "prophets." Most of the Protestant Christians remained in association with their churches, although there was a strong insistence in many districts upon shifting missionary control and oversight to nationals. In 1924 there was a recrudescence of the movement in the Sona Bata area, when 3,000 members of the Baptist community were led to separate themselves from the mission. The movement accentuated the need for providing a national leadership that would be stable and thoroughly trained.[5]

During the latter half of 1921, Dr. P. H. J. Lerrigo, home secretary of the American Baptist Foreign Mission Society and secretary for Africa, visited the Belgian Congo Mission. This was the first

---

[4] *Annual Report of the A.B.F.M.S.*, for 1915, pp. 182-83; for 1918, pp. 39-40; for 1919, p. 124; for 1920, p. 44.

[5] *Ibid.*, for 1922, pp. 47-48, 144-45; for 1923, p. 177, 182; for 1925, p. 43.

time a representative of the Board had come to the field since a visit by Dr. James H. Franklin in 1910. It was the beginning of a deepening interest in the Congo stations which had been overshadowed for some time by developments in India, Japan, and China. Dr. Lerrigo's visit enabled him to participate in a General Conference of Protestant Missionaries in the Congo, which was held at Bolenge in the fall of 1921. On that occasion, consideration was given to the findings of a Commission, which had come to Africa under the joint auspices of the Foreign Missions Conference of North America and the Phelps-Stokes Foundation in 1920–21. Under the direction of Dr. Thomas Jesse Jones, the Commission had visited the various stations of Central Africa and the Belgian Congo to study the educational situation. Dr. Catherine L. Mabie, medical missionary and teacher at Kimpese, represented the American Baptist Mission in the Congo. Out of the Commission's work, Protestant missionaries were made aware of the importance of raising the standards of education and broadening its scope in the interest of an adequately trained ministry and teaching staff with which to conserve the results of evangelism. Because the findings revealed the fact that mass education in the Congo was being provided entirely by Roman Catholic and Protestant Missions, it became plain that the government either should help to finance these schools, or establish a public school system.

In consequence of the Commission's report, the American Baptist Missionary Conference adopted plans for better supervision of village schools, for establishing boarding schools for boys and girls at all central stations, and for development of union higher schools in the larger language areas. About the same time the Belgian Government's Colonial Service established a policy of subsidizing mission schools which measured up to their standards. At first, the Roman Catholic institutions received the greater benefit from this policy, but in later years a more equitable treatment of Protestant schools was worked out.[6]

Beginning in 1921 and continuing almost unabated for several years, a great mass movement toward Christianity took place in the Lower Congo, at Sona Bata. Previous to 1921 there had been a

---

[6] *Ibid.*, for 1922, pp. 45-47, 143-44; Catherine L. Mabie, *Congo Cameos* (Philadelphia, 1952), pp. 110-12. For an excellent discussion of this topic, see Orval J. Davis, "Educational Development in the Belgian Congo," *The International Review of Missions*, Vol. 43, No. 172 (Oct. 1954), pp. 421-28.

church membership on that field of about 1,500, and baptisms had averaged nearly 150 each year. From 1921 to 1924, however, more than 10,000 baptisms were reported. Under the impetus of the new interest aroused among Baptists in the United States by these stirring events in the Belgian Congo, new reinforcements were sent out in 1924, making it possible to open a new field of operation at Moanza, which for a number of years had been only an outpost of the Vanga station. The Reverend and Mrs. Thomas Hill undertook this pioneer work with a background growing out of more than three decades of service in the Congo.

Between 1914 and 1924 the increase in church membership in the entire Belgian Congo Mission totaled 230 per cent, a growth of 4,506 to 14,871. The number of organized churches had arisen from 20 to 36, representing an increase of 80 per cent. Of these 20 were self-supporting as over against 8 in 1914. While the number of missionaries had dropped from 47 to 44 over the 10-year period, the Congolese staff had increased from 294 to 778.

The cultural and social contributions of the Mission were equally impressive. The Congo Evangelical Training Institute at Kimpese had provided in the 15 years since its establishment 137 graduates, 73 men and 64 women, of whom more than 70 per cent were actively engaged in Christian service. Six small mission hospitals provided greatly needed medical care at Banza Manteke, Ntondo-Ikoko (now called Tondo), Kimpese, Mukimvika, Matadi, and Vanga, with the assistance of the Colonial Medical Service which furnished free medicines. Medical missionaries co-operated with the Belgian Government in a vigorous campaign against sleeping sickness, a disease that prevailed in the area. At Sona Bata, Dr. J. C. King introduced a new drug for the treatment of the disease. Dr. W. H. Leslie, veteran medical missionary at Vanga for more than thirty years, was honored by the Belgian king in 1924 for his contribution to the health of the Congolese people. At Tondo, a valuable industrial work was conducted in an effort to train Christian converts in practical skills whereby they might make an adequate living and become valuable citizens in their communities. Through such means, the Mission contributed to the social well-being of the Belgian Congo while it won converts to the Christian faith.[7]

[7] The foregoing account is based on the *Annual Report of A.B.F.M.S.* for 1922–25; *Missions,* Vol. 16, No. 6 (June, 1925), p. 331; and William B. Lipphard, *The Ministry of Healing* (Philadelphia, 1920), the appendix.

A Period of Marked Progress (1925–1939)

From 1925 until the Second World War, the American Baptist Mission in the Congo made significant progress. Because the Roman Catholic influence was growing in strength, Protestant missions found it advantageous to co-operate with one another wherever possible in the conduct of their work. This trend had been encouraged by the Continuation Committee for Africa that had resulted from the World Missionary Conference of 1910 at Edinburgh. From this, there emerged in 1925 the Congo Protestant Council, under the secretaryship of Dr. Emory Ross. The new organization became increasingly important as a means of cementing the co-operating missions into a strong union. It also provided a clearing institution for problems of comity and the settlement of other issues. Through its services, general planning conferences were arranged, a Union Mission Hostel was established to accommodate missionaries on tour, and a quarterly, *The Congo Mission News,* was published. The Council also did much to assist the medical program of the co-operating missions. Through its services, pre-medical training for nurses, midwives, and doctors' assistants eventually was made possible.[8]

Further evidence of interdenominational co-operation in the African mission enterprise was the International Conference which was held at Le Zoute, Belgium, in September, 1926, to study the strategy for the Christian mission in Africa. The 221 delegates from 14 countries included six American Baptists; Dr. Catherine L. Mabie, the Reverend Joseph Clark, the Reverend Henry Erickson, Dr. John Hope, the Reverend Leslie B. Moss, and Dr. P. H. J. Lerrigo. The Conference underscored the social character of African life, with its tribal units and customs. The principle of the Christian society built upon Christian family life was commended. It was urged that African customs which were not incompatible with the Christian life should not be condemned. The problem of illiteracy was faced realistically by the Conference, and the need for a Christian literature was stressed. Dr. Mabie returned to Kimpese deeply impressed by what she had heard, and determined to do her share in the production of a vernacular literature. From that time she began to prepare textbooks in the language of the people, with the assistance of Vingadio, a de-

---

[8] Mabie, *Congo Cameos,* p. 146-50.

voted Congolese woman. The earliest ones were mimeographed; others were printed on a small printing press.[9]

The years 1928–29 were particularly important for the American Baptist Mission in the Congo. The Annual Conference met in 1928 at the time of the Jubilee celebration for the completion of fifty years of Protestant work in the Congo. A special deputation from the American Baptist Foreign Mission Society and the Woman's Society were present for the dual occasion. It included Dr. E. C. Kunkle of New York, Dr. A. C. Baldwin of Philadelphia, Dr. and Mrs. P. H. J. Lerrigo of New York, Mrs. H. E. Goodman, Miss Grace Goodman, and Mrs. M. E. Shirk, all of Chicago. Out of a total of thirty-four recommendations made to the Boards at home by the missionaries and the deputation, the most important, which were adopted early in 1929, were as follows: (1) The mission work at Matadi, which had been operated jointly by the American Baptist Mission, the Swedish Missions Forbundet (Covenant), and the British Baptist Mission, was transferred to the sole responsibility of the Swedish Mission. (2) The office of the treasurer of the Congo Baptist Mission was transferred from Matadi to Leopoldville, which recently had become the new headquarters of the Belgian government. It was natural, therefore, that work at Leopoldville should be reopened and that it should be made the new headquarters for the Baptist Mission. (3) The Reverend E. A. MacDiarmid was elected the first mission secretary in the history of the Congo work. (4) Approval was given to a plan to increase support of the Congo Protestant Council so that the secretary, Dr. Ross, might serve on a full-time basis. A tract of land was given by the Mission to the Council for the erection of a headquarters building at Leopoldville. (5) Specific recommendations pertaining to the development of several stations, the enlargement of the Congo Evangelical Institute at Kimpese, and the possible transfer of Tshumbiri to the Baptist Mission Society of England were assigned to a special committee for study and later adopted. The trend in mission administration thus begun was continued when the next biennial Mission Conference met in 1930. The functioning of the hitherto separate and isolated stations of the Congo Mission was unified. An equally important accomplishment was the election of a woman as vice-chairman of the Conference and the appointment of a Woman's

---

[9] *Ibid.*, pp. 121-22; Edwin W. Smith, *The Christian Mission in Africa* (London, 1926), pp. 25-28, 47-48, 50-51, 70, 105.

Committee, indicating the acceptance of women as fully-accredited missionaries. The 1930 Conference was also significant for the reason that it was held simultaneously with the first Baptist conference of African Christians associated with the Mission.[10]

In 1929 a new station was opened at Kikongo, in a relatively untouched area to the north of Vanga and Moanza in the Kwangu district. The Reverend and Mrs. Charles E. Smith were the pioneers in this new field. Within a year they had a congregation of five hundred baptized believers and over forty young men enrolled in the training school at Kimpese to take leadership in the churches. At the same time the Moanza station was growing under the direction of the Hills and a new missionary family, the Reverend and Mrs. Theodore E. Bubeck.[11]

The growing concern of Protestant missions to provide an adequate Christian literature for new converts, which had been aroused by the Le Zoute Conference of 1926, found expression in the organization three years later of the International Committee on Christian Literature for Africa (known as I. C. C. L. A.) It was an interdenominational project to provide books for the churches in Africa and to help the growth of good literature which would keep pace with the many-sided developments of African life. It was sponsored by the International Missionary Council; its first secretary was Miss Margaret Wrong, a Canadian of outstanding ability. The new undertaking was timely, for a number of factors affected positively the literary needs of the Africans. Among these were the constant mobility of the populace and the creation of urban centers which created changes in language groups. An illustration of the problem which this presented to the missionaries was evident at Leopoldville, where the American Baptist Mission found in a Ki-Kongo language center that fifty-one per cent of the people spoke Lingala. Another factor was the rising income of the African laborer, which made it possible for him to purchase books. A third factor was the coming of new missionary societies which placed exclusive stress on preaching. While their position favored the translating of portions of the Bible into several languages, it did not encourage the production of a general literature for Christians. The need was great for the

[10] *Annual Report of A.B.F.M.S.* for 1929, pp. 37-42; Records of the Board of Managers of A.B.F.M.S., 1928–29, pp. 203-06, 254; *Congo News Letter,* Vol. 21, No. 4 (Oct. 1930), pp. 3-12; N.B.C., *Annual* for 1931, p. 410.

[11] *Annual Report of A.B.F.M.S.* for 1930, p. 53.

development of African authors who could relate the Christian message to the growing urban population as well as to the village peoples.[12]

In 1932 Protestants in Belgian Congo became aware of a plan of the Roman Catholic Church to consolidate the Belgian Congo as a Roman Catholic mission field to the exclusion of Protestant missions. To offset this trend, the American Congo Committee, which represented the Protestant missions concerned, engaged Dr. J. H. Oldham, secretary of the International Missionary Council, to visit Brussels in order to enter a plea with the Belgian government to place Protestant missions on an equal basis with Roman Catholic missions with respect to government standards for the inspection of schools and hospitals and the admission of these institutions to examination for government subsidies.[13]

At the same time the various missions sought to adjust their programs to meet government standards and to avoid complaints that might prejudice the government against them. The American Baptists had in 1932 a total of 1,260 schools with over 55,000 pupils. Most of these were in villages where many of the teachers had but a rudimentary education. At Banza Manteke and Sona Bata, the government standards were followed closely. At Kimpese the Congo Evangelical Institute introduced a dual curriculum, a two-year course for slow students and a three-year course for advanced students. In the advanced grades of elementary schools and in all of the secondary schools, more attention was given to the teaching of French, the official government language.

In August, 1933, an education conference was held at Kimpese of representatives of the co-operating missions to discuss the establishment of a Normal Training School to serve the evangelical missions of the Lower Congo. With the full approval and co-operation of the trustees of the Baptists' Evangelical Training Institution at Kimpese, plans were laid for the necessary modification of its curriculum. The new name of the school became *École de Pasteurs et d'Instituteurs* (School for Pastors and Teachers). Thus from September, 1933, the school offered a three-year theological course, a two-year Bible training course, and a two-year normal course. In addition there was

---

[12] Claude De Mestral, "Christian Literature for Africa," *The International Review of Missions,* Vol. 43, No. 172 (Oct. 1954), pp. 436-42.

[13] *Annual Report of A.B.F.M.S.* for 1933, pp. 19-20.

a school for women. The children of the students attended the practice school for the fledgling teachers.

Following this conference, plans were made at once by the medical missionaries of the Baptist Mission to open a medical training school at Sona Bata, to be known as the *École Protestante des Auxiliaires Medicaux au Congo*. The new institution was to be administered by the Mission, with the door open to other denominational missions which might desire to co-operate. The Conference also decided to continue hospital service at Banza Manteke, Tondo, and Vanga, with a doctor and nurse at each; and a minimum dispensary service at Moanza and Kikongo.[14]

The effects of the world economic depression of the 1930's were felt in the Belgian Congo mission field as elsewhere. In response to a request from the Board to study economies in their work, the Congo Mission recommended in 1935 the possible transfer of one of the stations to a neighboring mission. At the time, the Mission had approximately three thousand schools with a wide influence upon village life. The growing work among women was releasing many from the thraldom of age-old beliefs and customs. The general attitude towards Protestant work in the Congo was increasingly favorable in spite of the enlarging sphere of Roman Catholic influence. The number of church members in the Baptist community was over thirty thousand as compared with three thousand in 1901.[15]

As a step in the direction of the ultimate transfer of mission responsibility to the Congolese, a "Native Council" was created in 1936 as an auxiliary to the Reference Committee of the Congo Mission. The same year the Native Council received an urgent appeal from the Bayaka tribe for teachers. These people, who lived in deep superstition and paganism, occupied an area within the triangle formed by the Sona Bata, Kikongo, and Moanza fields in the Kwangu region. Unable to secure reinforcements from the Board, the missionaries pledged five per cent of their meagre salaries in addition to their tithe over a period of five years to make a beginning of work in the new area.[16]

---

[14] The foregoing survey is based on the *Congo News Letter,* Vol. 25, No. 3 (July, 1933), pp. 21-22; No. 4 (Oct. 1933), pp. 12-14; *Annual Report of A.B.F.M.S.* for 1934, pp. 38, 114-16.

[15] *Annual Report of A.B.F.M.S.* for 1936, p. 112; *Developing Africa's Riches in Christ* (a pamphlet), pp. 12-16.

[16] *Annual Report of A.B.F.M.S.* for 1937, pp. 122-24.

In spite of the financial handicaps of these years, the Mission continued to expand its services. In 1936 Dr. George W. Carpenter, who had served for ten years on the faculty of the training school at Kimpese, was appointed by the Congo Protestant Council as educational advisor for all Protestant missions in the Congo. In 1937 the Swedish Missions Forbundet entered into agreement with the American Baptist Foreign Mission Society and the English Baptists to help support the training school at Kimpese (*École de Pasteurs et d'Instituteurs*), thus were united three out of four Protestant missions working in this Kikongo dialect area.[17]

In the same year, the Board of the American Baptist Foreign Mission Society voted to assume all responsibility for the administration of the Tondo Mission in the Upper Congo. This station, located eight hundred miles inland and four hundred miles from the nearest American Baptist station, was in the Lontumba language area. Its beautiful compound of brick buildings and its hospital built by funds from Tremont Temple Baptist Church in Boston and dedicated in 1928 as the Tremont Temple Hospital, was a monument to the devoted labors of Joseph Clark and his wife. The Clarks had been pioneer missionaries of the Congo Mission until his death in 1930. The work had been supported for many years by contributions from the First Baptist Church of Pontiac, Michigan, and other churches not previously co-operating with the unified budget of the Northern Baptist Convention. During the fundamentalist controversy in the denomination over the policies of the Foreign Mission Society, the Pontiac Church came into disagreement with the Board over the basis of continuing support. The outcome of the issue was for the Board to take full responsibility for the station until such time as it could effect a transfer of the Tondo field to the Baptist Missionary Society of England or the United Christian Missionary Society, then at work in the Upper Congo. The services of Dr. and Mrs. Westcott at the station were discontinued.[18]

With funds provided by the American Leprosy Mission, American Baptists were enabled in 1937 to construct a leprosy camp near Sona Bata. Within the next few years a group of brick buildings

---

[17] *Ibid.*, for 1936, p. 44; for 1937, p. 125; for 1938, pp. 26-27, 105.

[18] Records of Board of Managers and Executive Committee of W.A.B.F.M.S., September 1936–Febuary 1940, pp. 88, 172, 239-40.

housed the patients of the area who came for medical treatment. At the same time, they were given an opportunity to hear the gospel.

In June, 1938, the American and English Baptists in Leopoldville were hosts to the gathering of representatives of twenty mission societies working in the Congo who came together to celebrate the sixtieth anniversary of Protestant work in the Congo. The event signalized the growing unity among the Protestant missions. It also paved the way for the American Baptists to transfer to the Swedish Missions Forbundet within the next two years, fifty-one villages on the north side of the Congo River in the vicinity of Banza Manteke in exchange for thirty villages on the south side of the river. This re-establishment of mission boundary lines was indicative of the spirit of unity and co-operation between missionaries and nationals on the Congo field.[19]

The War Years and Since

Although the Second World War which involved Belgium was at first far removed from the Congo, its effects were felt in rising prices, delayed mail deliveries, increased cost of transportation, and difficulties encountered in passage to and from the field. The deeper effects became evident as the Congolese people's respect for the white man lowered as they witnessed his destructiveness. Twice in 1940 the developments in the European war occasioned tense hours for the missionaries in the Congo. The first time was when Belgian troops surrendered to the Germans, raising the question as to the future status of the Belgian Congo. Word soon went out, however, that the Belgians outside of Belgium proper would continue at war with Germany. The second instance was when France concluded an armistice with the Germans, thereby opening the question of the destiny of French Equatorial Africa. When that Colony announced its stand with the Free French forces, the missionaries in Belgian Congo were relieved.

The war occasioned a revival of the Prophet Movement, which had followed closely upon the First World War. It reflected the Africans' disillusionment with the white men who were at war among themselves in various parts of the world. The first prophets came from among the Bayaka people. Their leader was Kiala, a former

[19] *Annual Report of A.B.F.M.S.* for 1938, p. 37; for 1930, pp. 31-32; for 1940, p. 49; for 1942, p. 40.

Christian who had returned to polygamy and fetishism. Professing to receive his instructions from heaven, he urged the people to throw away all papers that linked them to the white man—their medical passports, their tax books, and their gun permits. Dozens of other prophets arose in rapid succession, calling the people to leave their daily occupations and form an exclusive group within their respective villages. The prophetic utterances of some fanatical leaders, purporting to give new interpretations of certain biblical prophecies, actually encouraged immorality, leading hundreds of Christians astray and giving Jesuit missionaries occasion to discredit the Protestant faith, although some Roman Catholic converts also were involved.

The government, fearing that the movement would lead to antigovernment demonstrations, took strict measures to suppress it. As many had been led by the prophets to destroy their fetishes, the government decided to consider as suspect any who did not possess fetishes. Christians, who had destroyed their fetishes for a very different reason, were therefore alarmed and many of them, out of their fear, secured new fetishes from the witch doctors. This created a serious problem for the missionaries. The Kikongo station was the most seriously affected of the American Baptist missions, but even there the loss of converts was relatively small and whole sections of the church which temporarily had aligned themselves with the movement were won back.[20]

The most serious problem for the missionaries during the war period was the lack of an adequate staff. In 1941 the renowned medical missionary and teacher, Dr. Catherine L. Mabie, retired after a lifetime of service. Although she continued to prepare textbooks in the Kikongo dialect for the Mission, her leadership was missed greatly. Missionaries home on furlough found it impossible to secure passage back to the field. In 1942, after seven years without any new missionary families, during which time there had been many losses, the Reverend Roland G. Metzger, son of missionaries to the Congo, sailed for the field with his wife.

In 1943 a joint conference of missionaries and national leaders was held to plan for the eventual transfer of responsibility for the

---

[20] The foregoing is based on accounts in the *Annual Report of A.B.F.M.S.* for 1940, p. 49-50; *Along Kingdom Highways* for 1941, pp. 28-29; for 1942, pp. 37-38; *Congo News Letter,* Vol. 41, No. 3 (July, 1949), pp. 26-29.

established work to the Congolese, thus leaving the missionaries free to launch out into unreached areas. The problem of holding able leaders in the churches was becoming acute as Christian teachers and preachers found themselves able to secure an income from three to twenty times what they received on the basis of the Mission's salary scale. As the Congo women became increasingly conscious of their importance and were eager for training, it was evident that the educational program for girls needed to be raised to a higher standard and broadened. This development among women pointed also to a need for more women missionaries to itinerate in the villages.[21]

The perennial problem of providing an adequate literature for Christians in the Congo required co-operative effort for its solution. In 1945, therefore, there was formed a union publishing enterprise known as *La Librairie Évangélique au Congo* (LECO) at Leopoldville for the purpose of providing Christian literature for the several Protestant missions in the Congo. It was developed out of the Bible depository and book depot which had been opened in July, 1935, under the joint sponsorship of the British and Foreign Bible Society and the Congo Protestant Council, and in charge of Dr. George W. Carpenter, of the American Baptist Mission. During the war years, when it was difficult to secure books and supplies from Belgium, this organization was particularly valuable. Dr. Carpenter was the manager of LECO from its inception until December, 1952. Under his direction, a two-story building was erected on ground provided by the Baptist Missionary Society of England. It was equipped with presses and type-casting equipment which was very important in a country where many languages were used. Few projects have made a greater contribution to the churches of the Congo.[22]

Space permits only a brief survey of the developments on American Baptist Mission stations in the years immediately following the war. In 1945 the Tondo station was transferred to the Baptist Missionary Society of England. During the same year the first conference of Congolese Christian women from all eight of the Amer-

---

[21] *Along Kingdom Highways* for 1942, p. 41; for 1943, pp. 16-17; for 1944, pp. 14-15; for 1945, pp. 41-43; *Missions,* Vol. 36, No. 1 (Jan. 1945), pp. 34-40.

[22] George W. Carpenter, "Co-operation in Christian Literature Production in Belgian Congo," *The International Review of Missions,* Vol. 43, No. 172 (Oct. 1954), pp. 414-20; *Along Kingdom Highways,* for 1947, pp. 48-49; for 1948, p. 111.

ican Baptist stations met at Banza Manteke to discuss their place in the church and in the home. At Vanga one of the greatest mass movements in the history of the Mission resulted from a carefully planned program of church extension. Across 15,000 square miles of jungle and bush country that was inhabited by 175,000 members of the Bayanzi, Bahungana, and Bambala tribes, 26 church centers, each with a staff of pastor, evangelist, and teachers, had been planted. Between 1946 and 1950, more than 10,000 converts were baptized. When the missionary in charge, the Reverend Leonard Gittings, left the field in 1950 to return to America, an additional 12,000 probationers were under instruction preparatory to baptism. Between December, 1951, and October, 1953, the Reverend Chester Jump baptized, after careful examination, nearly 10,000 converts. In the Sona Bata field all of the 49 churches were self-governing and self-supporting, and were organized into the Sona Bata Association. The Leper Colony three miles from the mission station and the hospital at Sona Bata were under the care of Dr. Glen W. Tuttle. In 1949 a new station was opened at Boko, on a vast plain east of Moanza and south of Kikongo. This was an extension of the work which had been begun among the Bayakas at Kikongo in 1929. The station, which included a school and a dispensary, was under the care of the Reverend and Mrs. W. F. Robbins and Miss Eva Shepard.[23]

The educational work of the entire American Baptist Mission was given a forward impetus when the Congo Protestant Council won approval from the Belgian government for granting subsidies to those Protestant schools which could meet official requirements. The decision represented a victory for Protestants, who had been urging for many years equal status with Roman Catholic institutions. The government action resulted in the lifting of standards and the accomplishment of more intensive work in Protestant schools. This, in turn, increased the need for new equipment and higher trained teachers. It also necessitated that new missionaries spend a longer period of study in Belgium in preparation for work in the Congo. Although some Baptists regarded the subsidies as a violation of the principle of separation of church and state, the majority of missionaries felt

---

[23] *Along Kingdom Highways* for 1946, pp. 38-39; for 1948, p. 115; *Congo News Letter,* Vol. 42, No. 2 (April 1951), pp. 12-15; No. 3 (July 1951), pp. 3-6; *Crusader,* Vol. 6, No. 3 (Summer, 1951), pp. 14-15; Vol. 8, No. 7 (December, 1953), p. 4.

that they could not refuse the financial aid and be fair to African Christians who were dependent upon mission schools for their education.[24]

The new status of mission schools gave encouragement also to the medical training program. In 1952 a new Protestant medical school, known as the *Institut Médical Évangélique,* was opened at Kimpese as the joint enterprise of five missions: the American Baptist Foreign Mission Societies, the Baptist Missionary Society of England, the Christian and Missionary Alliance, the Disciples of Christ Congo Mission, and the Swedish Missions Forbundet. Dr. Glen W. Tuttle, Baptist missionary in charge of the Sona Bata Hospital, was among the medical missionaries on the teaching staff. With a five-year course it was prepared to train African personnel for medical work. The Baptist-initiated medical training program for nurses and midwives at Sona Bata (known as the *École Protestante des Auxiliaires Medicaux au Congo*) was transferred to the new union institution at Kimpese in 1953. The station, however, continued its medical program of hospital, clinic, and outlying dispensaries.[25]

By 1951 the American Baptist Mission was able to report 113 Baptist churches with an aggregate membership of over 40,000. Of the 113 churches, 96 were entirely self-supporting. Baptisms for the year totaled 1,726. The eight stations of the Mission were scattered widely over a territory covering 40,000 square miles. For this vast area the Society supported only 40 missionaries on the field. With the main goal of the Mission being to develop a capable Congolese leadership to carry on the work of evangelism among their own people, the educational program was of great importance. Foremost in this effort was the School for Pastors and Teachers at Kimpese. The chief lack in the training program, however, was the scarcity of trained women leaders. Out of nearly 4,000 pupils in grammar schools, for example, only 209 were girls. The Baptists maintained only two high schools in the Congo with a combined enrollment of 87 boys and only 16 girls. The neglect in training women and girls was unfortunately not solely a Baptist deficiency;

---

[24] *Along Kingdom Highways* for 1948, p. 111; for 1949, p. 15; for 1951, p. 13; Records of Board of Managers and Executive Committee of W.A.B. F.M.S., May 1949–June 1951, p. 475; *Congo News Letter,* Vol. 43, No. 3 (July, 1952), p. 9.

[25] *Along Kingdom Highways* for 1952, p. 24; for 1953, p. 17.

it prevailed in other missions as well, a fact which was given much attention by interdenominational conferences on Africa missions held in the United States in 1952.

Of the 52 Protestant mission hospitals in the Belgian Congo in 1952, American Baptists maintained six, besides 24 dispensaries. The entire missionary medical staff, however, consisted of only four doctors and six nurses. There were 60 Congolese nurses and another hundred in training. At the same time, the *Institut Médical Évangélique* at Kimpese gave promise of the development of African doctors to meet the grave need for medical care.[26]

In summary, it may be said that the Congo Mission had enjoyed unusual growth in number of converts and in the development of mission stations which have become centers of evangelistic outreach carried on by Congolese Christians under the direction of the missionaries. The very extensiveness of the areas covered by each of the eight stations, with a limited mission staff, has of necessity left much to be desired in meeting the need for an intensive cultivation of evangelism, education, and health measures. While the Congolese ministry has been poorly trained, the lay members of the church have been in worse condition, for they have received little instruction beyond the preparation for a year prior to their baptism. American Baptists have sought to overcome this problem by offering a "certificate of growth in Christian knowledge" to those who will take additional instruction. In the Congo, where the transfer of leadship has been retarded by general conditions such as have been described, a Baptist fellowship has nevertheless been developed, and in recent years leading nationals have become officially active in the Mission Conference for the first time.

In the changing Congo, perhaps the most encouraging factor has been the united witness of Protestant missions in the Protestant Council of the Congo. Through its united efforts, Protestants have been able to provide schools of secondary and higher grade which have begun to bear fruit in an able and prepared leadership for the churches. In a very real sense, the Christian community has presented a stabilizing influence to the people of the Congo at a time

---

[26] *Missions,* Vol. 150, No. 8 (Oct. 1952), pp. 460-65; *Along Kingdom Highways* for 1953, pp. 17-18; *The International Review of Missions,* Vol. 43, No. 169 (Jan. 1954), p. 43.

when they have been lifted out of their ancient tribal life into a confused and complex world of strange and distorted values.[27]

---

[27] For further reading see Kenneth Scott Latourette, *The Christian World Mission in Our Day* (New York, 1954), pp. 102-08; and H. D. Brown, "The Church and Its Missionary Task in Congo," *The International Review of Missions,* Vol. 41, No. 163 (July, 1952), pp. 301-09.

CHAPTER XXXII

Continuing Witness in Europe

EUROPE HAS BEEN a unique field among those in which the American Baptist Foreign Mission Societies have conducted missions. With few exceptions, it has received from these Societies no missionaries from the United States, only financial assistance and friendly counsel. In each country where European Baptists have received funds from abroad, the principle of acknowledging the autonomy of national organizations has been observed. Aid has been channeled through a special representative of the Societies to responsible Baptist Unions, churches, or institutions which handle and disburse the monies received with complete freedom from outside control. Therefore, within the limits of this chapter, the major attention will be placed upon the manner in which the Societies have enabled small Baptist groups on the Continent to maintain a witness during the tumultuous years since 1914.[1]

The First World War and Rehabilitation (1914–1939)

At the time of the outbreak of the war in Europe in 1914, the American Baptist Foreign Mission Society was planning to send a commission to the Continent to study possible adjustments in the work there. Instead, the Board of Managers found itself faced with the pressing needs of Baptist minorities who were experiencing the devastation of war. In France church buildings were destroyed, congregations were scattered, and pastors were called into the service. The work in Southern Belgium, ever small, was almost entirely disrupted. In Germany as many as twenty-five per cent of the mem-

[1] For a summary of developments in Baptist church life in Europe, see Robert G. Torbet, *A History of the Baptists* (Philadelphia, 1950; revised, 1952), Ch. 7.

bers of individual congregations were called into military service. Many of the church buildings in areas overrun by opposing armies were damaged or destroyed, and economic suffering among the people was great in the latter years of the war. Although the Scandinavian countries escaped the ravages of actual fighting, wartime restrictions on trade made it difficult for many churches to pay the salaries of their ministers. Baptist church life in Russia was brought almost to a standstill because most able-bodied men were called to the armed services. Many Russian Baptists, however, refused for conscience sake to go to fight, although they expressed willingness to perform noncombatant service for the Army. In 1915 twelve preachers who were regarded as dangerous to the government were reported exiled along with many other Protestant church leaders.[2]

To administer relief and to plan for the rehabilitation of Baptist work in Europe, the American Baptist Foreign Mission Society took a number of steps almost immediately upon the cessation of hostilities. In March, 1919, Foreign Secretary Dr. James H. Franklin made a six-week visit to the Continent. Six relief centers were established by the Society in Northern France and Southern Belgium under the direction of the Reverend Oliva Brouillette. In 1920 Dr. Charles A. Brooks, secretary for the foreign-speaking work of the American Baptist Home Mission Society, was lent to the Foreign Society for several months to study conditions in Europe. In July, 1920, a Baptist Conference of representatives of nearly all Baptist bodies in the United States, Canada, Great Britain, and Europe met in London under the auspices of the Executive Committee of the Baptist World Alliance. The American Baptist Foreign Mission Society, through Dr. Emory W. Hunt and Dr. Franklin, united with the Foreign Board of the Southern Baptist Convention and the Canadian Baptists in adopting a co-ordinated and unified policy for relief and reconstruction work in Europe. In the division of territory, the American Baptist Foreign Mission Society agreed to care for the needs of Baptist groups in Germany, France, Belgium, and French-speaking Switzerland; in Czechoslovakia (in co-operation with British Baptists); in Poland (in co-operation with German-speaking Baptists in America); in Norway and Denmark; in Latvia, Lithuania, Estonia, and Northern Russia (in co-operation with British

---

[2] Based upon scattered reports in *Annual Reports of A.B.F.M.S.*, 1915–1918.

and Canadian Baptists). Dr. J. H. Rushbrooke, of London, was elected Baptist Commissioner to Europe for the co-operating Societies.

At home more than four thousand Baptist churches in the Northern Baptist Convention contributed three thousand heavy bales of clothing and barrels of much needed relief supplies. These were sent to Europe during the winter of 1921–22 for distribution under the direction of Dr. William B. Lipphard, an associate secretary of the Foreign Society. This relief effort was in co-operation with Herbert Hoover's American Relief Administration. The next year Dr. W. O. Lewis, the newly appointed special representative of the Foreign Society, sailed for Europe to devote close attention to problems in France and to Russia, where a famine was taking its toll of human life. A second large shipment of clothing was sent from America in the winter of 1922–23. Several members of the Board conducted evangelistic tours on the Continent during the summers of 1922 and 1923.[3]

The great interest in Europe which had been aroused by its sad plight following the war had made it possible for the Society to raise special funds for relief work and also larger sums than usual for the support of churches, evangelists, and schools in European countries. By 1930, however, declining receipts made it necessary to discontinue the relief work almost entirely, while appropriations for other purposes were steadily reduced. In view of the limited resources, the chief emphasis was placed on support of several schools in strategic centers which were essential to the training of Baptist leaders. Among these was the theological seminary in Hamburg, the endowment of which had vanished during the war. The Society helped to put the buildings in order and made regular contributions toward the support of the professors. In co-operation with the Baptists of England, assistance also was given to Baptist schools in Poland, Estonia, Latvia, and Czechoslovakia. A substantial amount was appropriated for the theological school in Norway. By 1930 the small appropriation to the Bethel Seminary in Stockholm was discontinued, as Swedish Baptist work became entirely self-supporting.[4]

The administration of financial aid to autonomous Baptist groups

---

[3] *Ibid.*, 1920–23; *The Baptist*, Vol. 5, No. 22 (June 28, 1924), pp. 522-23.

[4] *Annual Report of A.B.F.M.S.* for 1929, pp. 43-44; for 1930, p. 186; for 1934, p. 55.

on the Continent was not without its problems. In France, for example, the situation was complicated by the existence of two groups of Baptists, the Franco-Belgian Association led by M. Philemon Vincent, a teacher and scholar of broad evangelical views, and the Franco-Swiss Association led by M. R. Saillens, an evangelist and pulpit orator who held ultra-conservative views on doctrine. Both groups, which did not number together more than two thousand members, were persuaded by Dr. Franklin in 1920 to unite in what was called the Federation of Evangelical Baptist Churches of France. But the union was not permanent, for differences developed between the two groups over the theological character of a proposed training school for pastors. Within a short time seven churches withdrew from the Federation. Those of this number who were receiving financial assistance from the American Baptist Foreign Mission Society felt that their connection with the Society must end. They therefore organized the Evangelical Baptist Association. The Tabernacle Church of Paris, of which Saillens was pastor, did not join this group, but it remained independent of both organizations. The issues which had caused the break were three: (1) theological criticism of some of the pastors being supported by the Foreign Mission Society, (2) objection to allegedly unscriptural methods of mission work, such as vacation Bible schools and preaching on social themes, (3) resentment that the Baptist Federation belonged to the Protestant Federation of France, which included in its membership churches with theological positions called in question by the dissenting groups.[5]

A second instance in which the Board of the Foreign Mission Society was called upon to exercise great patience was in Poland, where a rivalry existed between Slavic Baptists and German-speaking Baptists. In 1923 a union of Baptists and Evangelical Christians was effected under the leadership of K. W. Strzelec. Personality conflicts prevented the union from becoming a success. In 1925 the Slav Baptist Union was organized and grew in numbers and influence. The American Baptist Foreign Mission Society chose to co-operate with this body because of its stability. The government, on the other hand, refused to grant the Union legal standing, preferring to recog-

[5] W. O. Lewis, "The Situation in France," a mimeographed paper of 14 pages prepared in March, 1924, and revised in August, 1931, for distribution to Board members of A.B.F.M.S.

nize the all but defunct Slav Union Baptists and Evangelical Christians.

After the war the Woman's American Baptist Foreign Mission Society purchased a well equipped hospital in Lodz which came to be known as the Peabody-Montgomery Hospital. It opened in 1922 with sixty beds, and a program of nurses' training. The Baptists of the area purchased a Deaconess' home which was to be associated with the hospital.

In 1926 the Foreign Society, which had been supporting the Compass Publishing House, was obliged to withdraw its support because of failure of the business to remain solvent, and to cause the building to be sold. The Compass Fund, from the sale of the property, was to be transferred to the Home Office in New York. In 1931 the Society was once again involved in negotiations with the Polish Baptists, through Dr. Lewis, concerning funds for the purchase of a church property in Warsaw. With an exaggerated impression of the financial reserves of the Society, the Polish Baptists had contracted for a property much beyond their financial means. The situation illustrates the difficulties faced by the Society and its representative abroad in handling mission aid in a mutually satisfactory manner.[6]

After the Russian Revolution of 1917, the relations of the Mission Societies to Baptists in Russia were complex and difficult. The disorders which followed that event, including the famine of 1920–21, provided a climate of opinion in which the growth of the sects was encouraged. Baptists and Evangelicals, in particular, attracted many new converts because many Russians associated the Russian Orthodox Church with the regime which had oppressed them under the Czars. Indeed, between 1914 and 1923 the number of Baptists increased from well over 100,000 to 1,000,000. Some even estimated the figure at 2,000,000, while one government official expressed his belief that there were 3,000,000 Baptists in the country. The Communists welcomed the sects as a potential means of weakening the Orthodox Church.

Although the Soviet Government did not view the Baptists as a

---

[6] William O. Lewis, "After Ten Years in Poland," a mimeographed paper of 13 pages prepared for the Board of A.B.F.M.S. on Sept. 15, 1931, in connection with correspondence over the purchase of church property in Warsaw. See also correspondence between Dr. J. H. Franklin and Dr. W. O. Lewis on the same subject, July 16–Oct. 28, 1931. These documents are in possession of the American Baptist Historical Society Library, Rochester, N. Y.

political menace, it did set obstacles in the way of their work, particularly with children and young people, by forbidding organized religious education of children under eighteen years of age, and by demanding the service of all able-bodied young citizens in the Army. After 1929 the government became as severe with the sects as with the Orthodox Church. Because of their evangelistic zeal, hundreds of Baptists and other evangelical Christians were arrested. Pastors were disfranchised, deprived of food tickets, subjected to special taxation, forbidden to teach their children except at home, forbidden to circulate Bibles, and forbidden to hold services in their churches. In spite of persecution, however, Baptists continued to make converts to an extent alarming to the official press. By 1940 it was estimated that there were 5,000,000 Baptist sympathizers in Russia. But direct contact with them by their fellow Christians abroad was an impossibility.[7]

The rise of Hitler to power in 1933 and the consequent spread of Nazism in Europe became a threat to a free Baptist witness in countries where it prevailed. In Germany the Baptists followed a policy of cautious expediency. They voted to suspend the constitution of the Baptist Union temporarily and authorized Dr. F. W. Simoleit with three other men to represent them in denominational affairs and to be responsible to the government for the Baptist denomination in Germany. Their strong antipathy to involvement of the church in politics in any way, plus their recognition that the new regime did not hinder their work since they were not a state-church, caused them for a time to be somewhat blinded to the real issues involved in the emergence of totalitarianism. In 1934 they entertained in Berlin, without interference from the state, the fifth Baptist World Congress. During the same year, however, pressure from the government to align the German Baptist Young People's Union with the Hitler Youth organization prompted the Baptists to dissolve their national organization for youth rather than to yield to the demands made upon them. Before the end of the year it was becoming increasingly clear that the Hitler regime was hostile to Christianity.[8]

Repercussions of the Hitler movement were being felt in the Baltic

[7] For details see *Annual Reports of A.B.F.M.S.*, 1922–1938; William B. Lipphard, *Communing with Communism* (Philadelphia, 1931); Kenneth Scott Latourette, *Advance Through Storm*, Vol. VII of *A History of the Expansion of Christianity* (New York, 1945), pp. 86-87.

[8] *Annual Report of A.B.F.M.S.* for 1934, p. 118; for 1935, pp. 137-38.

States. By 1935, Estonia, Latvia, and Lithuania had come under a sort of dictatorship, with laws guaranteeing freedom of the press and freedom of assembly for political and religious purposes either modified or suspended altogether. The dismemberment of Czechoslovakia in October, 1938, and the disappearance of the country as an independent nation in March, 1939, raised serious problems for the people. The school in Prague was still open as was the Peabody-Montgomery Children's Home which had been founded by the Woman's American Baptist Foreign Mission Society in 1922. But the Baptists were carrying on against fearful odds.[9]

The Second World War and Since (1939–1954)

With the outbreak of war in Europe in 1939, contacts between the Foreign Mission Boards in the United States and Baptists in most of the countries on the Continent became increasingly difficult. It was known, however, that many European Baptists had lost their homes, some had been killed, others were in concentration camps, and still others had been called to military service. Where it was feasible, the Board continued a minimum of financial aid, but the currency control in certain countries and the ever-widening area of war made it impossible to do constructive building. Plans were laid, nevertheless, to renew aid and help at the earliest possible moment. In the meantime, the Foreign Societies endeavored to do what they could through their special representative, Dr. Walter O. Lewis. In 1939, when Dr. Lewis was elected general secretary of the Baptist World Alliance, he continued to devote part of his time to the affairs of the American Baptist Foreign Mission Society until 1944, when he was succeeded in that phase of his work by Dr. Edwin A. Bell.

After the United States entered the conflict in 1941, American Baptists were obliged to channel their relief funds through interdenominational agencies such as the World's Committee of the Y.M.C.A. (for prisoners of war), the American Friends' Service Committee (for civilians), and the International Missionary Council (for aid to orphaned missions of German Baptists). Ultimately, the overseas program of relief and reconstruction was co-ordinated by a special committee consisting of twenty-four representatives of the Foreign Missions Conference of North America and the Federal Council of Churches of Christ in America. Early in 1943 Northern

---

[9] *Ibid.*, for 1935, pp. 138-39; for 1939, p. 34.

and Southern Baptists entered into joint conversations concerning postwar relief and reconstruction. In December of that year, European Baptist leaders who were marooned in the United States met with representatives of the American Baptist Mission Societies in Chicago for a conference on the rehabilitation of Baptist work in Europe after the war. As a consequence, the two Boards adopted a policy of co-operating with European Baptists for a ten-year period after the cessation of hostilities. It also was agreed to raise $500,000 over a period of five years for relief work, for the re-establishment of Baptist institutions, and for the reconstruction of churches and chapels damaged or destroyed by bombing.

When peace came in 1945, Dr. Bell lost no time in visiting Baptist groups in European countries. As a result of consultations which he conducted with Baptist leaders on the continent, programs were developed for France, Belgium, and Czechoslovakia, by which American assistance might be made available to the national Baptist bodies for evangelism, youth work, ministerial training, the preparation of literature, and for direct relief. By maintaining constant contact with officials of the World Council of Churches at Geneva and of the Baptist World Alliance in London, Dr. Bell helped to advance many co-operative plans for general relief work and the care of displaced persons. The Foreign Society entered into conversations with the North American Baptist General Conference (German) with respect to the reopening of work in Germany, and with the British Baptists relative to Finland and Czechoslovakia. Communications with Baptists in Poland remained very difficult, while no entrance could be effected into the Russian-occupied states of Latvia, Estonia, and Lithuania.

Before it was possible to get bulk shipments of relief materials to Europe, the Foreign Society began to send small food and clothing packages to Baptist leaders in Europe. These supplies went in time to France, Belgium, Norway, Poland, and Czechoslovakia. Almost $15,000 worth of equipment for home use was purchased from the United States Army in Europe for distribution to Baptist families. Food was purchased in Denmark and sent to Baptists in Holland, Poland, Finland, and Czechoslovakia. Money was sent to Sweden to be used for immediate relief among Baltic refugees, many of whom were Baptists. The White Cross Department of the Woman's Society undertook several relief projects in addition to its regular work. By

1948 American Baptists were entering upon a program of bringing displaced Baptists from Eastern Europe to the United States under provision of an Act of Congress which opened the doors of the nation to unfortunates of all faiths who were fleeing from persecution and oppression in their homelands. These efforts were part of a larger relief program co-ordinated by the World Relief Committee organized by the Northern Baptist Convention in 1940.

By 1951 it was possible for Dr. Bell to report that more than $500,000 of World Mission Crusade funds had gone to Europe. The reconstruction and relief work had covered a wide variety of services. Two theological schools were reopened in Poland and Czechoslovakia which had been closed by the war. Assistance was given in the establishing of a new training school for ministers in Finland. Funds were provided for new buildings for the theological school in Oslo, Norway, and for the reconstruction of the seminary in Hamburg. Several European students were aided in their education, some in American and British schools, and others in European institutions. Many war-damaged church buildings had been repaired and some new chapels erected for refugees and displaced persons. Many thousands of individuals had been supplied, through local churches, with food, clothing, medicines, and other vital necessities of life. Evangelism and youth programs were encouraged by substantial gifts of money and equipment.

The meeting of the seventh congress of the Baptist World Alliance in Copenhagen, Denmark, provided a tremendous stimulus to morale for the Baptists of Europe. Initial steps were taken at that time to form a European Baptist Federation which would draw together the 700,000 Baptists of Europe (exclusive of those in Russia) for fellowship and more effective service. Organization of the Federation was completed in 1952. Included within the administrative council of the new body were representatives of each Baptist Union in Europe, the European members of the Executive Committee of the Baptist World Alliance, and representatives of each of the co-operating mission boards.[10]

Space permits only a brief survey of the developments since the war in the various European countries where the American Baptist

---

[10] The foregoing account is based on the *Annual Report of A.B.F.M.S.* for 1940, pp. 52-53; scattered references to the work in Europe in *Along Kingdom Highways,* 1941–53; *Crusader,* Vol. 3, No. 9 (Feb. 1949), pp. 3-5; Vol. 4, No. 5 (Oct. 1949), pp. 8-9; Vol. 7, No. 10 (March, 1953), p. 2.

Foreign Mission Societies have given assistance. In France there were not more than 2,500 Baptists gathered in 30 churches served by 20 pastors. They were sadly divided, only the churches of the Federation maintaining relations with the Foreign Societies. With American funds, a new orphanage was equipped, summer camps for children and youth were developed, and tents for evangelistic campaigns were provided. In Belgium, along the French border, there were but five Baptist churches related to the Foreign Societies, one Polish and four French-speaking, with a total constituency of not over three hundred. Buildings were repaired and pastors' salaries were subsidized by mission funds.[11]

German Baptists, who had been completely self-supporting prior to the Second World War, suffered greatly from the bombing raids and the complete disorganization of German life. The three seminary buildings at Hamburg were restored with American Baptist help. Groups of American Baptist young people spent the summers of 1949 and 1951 in Hamburg donating their labor to this project. The American Baptist Foreign Mission Society made available to the Baptist Union of Germany the sum of $80,000 to rebuild some of the 74 churches which were destroyed and the 190 which were damaged by air raids, and to provide chapels for new Baptist congregations of refugees from Eastern Germany and other parts of Eastern Europe. Assistance also was given to the enlarging of the Publishing House at Kassel, and to the development of a strong youth program which was intended to offset the influences of the Hitler regime and the war years.[12]

Baptists in Sweden were the most vigorous Baptist group on the Continent after the war. They gave generously to relief work among the Baptists of Norway, Finland, Poland, and Germany, in addition to supporting a theological seminary at Stockholm, a Publication Society, a flourishing youth program, and foreign mission work in China and the Congo. Norwegian Baptists were self-supporting except for their school program. They received some financial assistance for a building to house their growing theological seminary at Oslo

---

[11] *Along Kingdom Highways,* 1948, pp. 119, 122; 1951, p. 15; *Crusader,* Vol. 6, No. 5 (Oct. 1951), p. 4; Vol. 7, No. 10 (March 1953), p. 5.

[12] *Along Kingdom Highways,* 1948, pp. 122-23; 1952, pp. 26-27; 1953, pp. 19-20; *Crusader,* Vol. 4, No. 5 (Oct. 1949), p. 10; Vol. 6, No. 5 (Oct. 1951), pp. 3-6; Vol. 7, No. 2 (June, 1952), pp. 4-5; Vol. 7, No. 10 (March 1953), p. 4; Vol. 8, No. 6 (Nov., 1953), p. 9.

and for the restoration of the Fisherman's Hostel at Honigsvog, in the northern part of the country, which had been utterly destroyed in 1945 when the Germans retreated from Finland and Norway. Norwegian Baptists also supported twenty-two missionaries in the Belgian Congo. The Baptists of Denmark had made a distinctive contribution to the relief work in Germany and Holland. They conducted a vigorous mission work in the Congo and maintained a flourishing theological school in Töllöse, near Copenhagen. The institution included a Folk High School and an Academy.[13]

From Russia came word in 1944 that the Baptists had entered into a union with the Evangelical Christians. In August, 1945, the Pentecostals were invited to join. The federation was known as the Council of the United Baptists, Evangelical Christians, and Pentecostal Churches and groups in the U.S.S.R. The new organization functioned like the British National Council of Free Churches. The officially reported membership of Baptists was 350,000, with an unofficial following of sympathizers who were estimated to be as many as three million. The rigid government requirements for gaining recognition as an organized church prevented many groups from being registered in the actual membership of the Baptists. There also seem to have been many who remained aloof from the government-sponsored organization. Within recent years some of the Baptist leaders in Russia have been permitted to visit Baptists in Finland and Sweden, where they also met representatives of American and British Baptists. In 1954 several British, American, and European leaders were permitted to visit Baptist churches in Russia. This renewal of contacts, although limited, was encouraging to Baptists around the world.[14]

The American Baptist Foreign Mission Society extended aid to small Baptist groups in Finland and to the refugees from the Baltic States who had fled to Sweden and Germany to escape communist rule in their countries. Through the gift of two tents, the Swedish-speaking Baptists and the Finnish-speaking Baptists in Finland were assisted in conducting evangelistic meetings during the summer months. The Foreign Society also contributed to the preparation of

---

[13] *Along Kingdom Highways,* 1948, pp. 120-24; 1951, p. 14; 1952, p. 26; *Crusader,* Vol. 7, No. 2 (June, 1952), pp. 5-6.

[14] *Along Kingdom Highways,* 1948, pp. 123-24; Serge Bolshakoff, *Russian Nonconformity* (Philadelphia, 1950), p. 122.

new quarters for the Finnish-speaking Baptist Theological School. With American help the Baptist Unions of Estonia, Latvia, and Lithuania continued their work among those of their numbers who had fled to Sweden and Germany. The Latvian Baptist Union moved bodily to Germany during the break-up of the front in the East, and all of its officers were housed in camps for displaced persons. Their intention was to move as congregations to other parts of the world to begin life anew. Approximately twenty thousand Estonians fled to Sweden, of whom many were Baptists. They were given help by the American Baptist Foreign Mission Society and Estonian Baptists in the United States.[15]

By 1947 three homes for children in Poland were being maintained in co-operation with Baptist Relief in Poland, an organization through which Scandinavian, English, and American Baptists were working. A theological seminary was opened in Warsaw. Owing to the removal of the entire German-speaking Baptists from the country and the loss of large numbers of Slavic-speaking Baptists along the eastern frontier in the territory taken over by Russia, there were only about four thousand Baptists left in Poland as compared with sixteen thousand prior to the war.[16]

In spite of the advent of a communist regime in Czechoslovakia following the close of the war, the Baptists of that country, with help from the United States, were courageously restoring damaged buildings; re-establishing the theological seminary at Prague, which had been closed since 1939; renovating the orphange at Ceklis; and founding new churches among the Slovaks being repatriated from Hungary. By 1951, however, the country was closed to any help from the West; all pastors and theological schools were brought under the support of the government. In June, 1953, Baptists in Austria, whose ranks had been increased by the immigration of many German-speaking refugees from the Balkan states and Eastern Europe, organized the Baptist Union of Austria. The American Baptist Foreign Mission Society made contributions toward the purchase of land and the erection of buildings for Austrian Baptists.[17]

---

[15] *Along Kingdom Highways,* 1945, p. 46; 1948, pp. 121-22; 1950, p. 22; *Crusader,* Vol. 7, No. 2 (June, 1952), p. 6.

[16] *Along Kingdom Highways,* 1947, p. 33; 1948, p. 123; 1951, p. 15.

[17] *Ibid.,* 1948, p. 120; 1951, p. 15; *Crusader,* Vol. 8, No. 8 (Jan. 1954), p. 13.

This brief story of the continuing Baptist witness in Europe gives us a basis of hope for the future. On a continent where the Protestant state churches have lost their former power and influence, except perhaps in a very limited degree and in small groups within their own fellowship, the hope of evangelical Christianity seems to rest largely with the minority groups—the small denominations like the Baptists, the Methodists, the Presbyterians, and a few others. In the evangelistic zeal and the steadfast devotion to the cause of religious liberty, characteristic of these groups, one sees the kind of power which can revitalize the church life of Europe.

CHAPTER XXXIII

In Retrospect

IN ONE HUNDRED AND FORTY YEARS American Baptists have crowded an amazingly broad program of missionary effort. It has taken them into three continents and many countries. The investment of lives and material resources alone provides a thrilling record in the annals of missionary history. The development of churches in Asia, Africa, and Europe remains as a worthy legacy for future generations. The story of this impressive enterprise has been told, certainly not fully, but in sufficient detail to highlight the main developments in the work of the two agencies responsible for the undertaking, namely, the American Baptist Foreign Mission Society and the Woman's American Baptist Foreign Mission Society. An effort has been made to bring alive the exciting events at home and on the mission fields, and to show wherever possible the interaction of factors, both religious and non-religious, which influenced the ongoing missionary movement.

Many names have been mentioned, some have been described at length, others but briefly; but many others have been omitted entirely because of the brevity of this survey. Yet the achievements of nearly a century and a half have been the product of the sacrifices and contributions of hundreds of missionaries, of numerous staff secretaries, and of thousands of Baptist people in the churches at home and abroad. Not every event has been signalized on these pages. Undoubtedly, there is room for debate concerning the justification for the inclusion of some and only the passing reference to, or even the exclusion of, others. The vessels chosen to fulfill the purpose of God in this great enterprise were in many cases ordinary men and women who were subject to the limitations and imperfections of human kind. Among them were stalwarts, yet even these were not without flaws. Nevertheless, all were used of God in a venture of faith.

Highlights and Contrasts

The record which we have traced in this volume has fallen into three major periods, each demarcated by its own watersheds. The thirty years from 1814 to 1845 opened with the dramatic call to American Baptists to organize a national agency for the support of a daring young couple who had landed in Rangoon, Burma, with no assets but their faith in God. These initial years witnessed the laying of foundations both at home and abroad, as a denomination was being organized to extend its message of hope and salvation to the peoples of Asia, Africa, and Europe. It will be recalled that by 1845 stations had been established in Burma, Assam, South India, and Liberia, while Free Baptists had made a beginning of the Bengal-Orissa Mission. In addition small groups of European Baptists were being encouraged and financially aided in their witness in Germany, Denmark, Greece, and France.

The eighty years between 1845 and 1914 were influenced strongly by forces at work within the Baptist ranks and by others from without. The period opened with a schism which for a time drew the Mission Society into a period of severe testing, the effects of which were felt also on the fields. By 1872, however, a sufficient measure of stability had been achieved at home to overcome the trend of uncertainty. As a result the American Baptist Missionary Union entered upon an era of progress, strengthened by the organization in 1871 of women's Baptist foreign mission societies. In addition to steady gains in evangelism, in education, and in the translation and circulation of the Bible into many languages and dialects, the Societies experienced in some respects their most spectacular achievements in the years that followed. These were high-lighted by great ingatherings in South India and the Belgian Congo and by steady growth of self-supporting churches among the Karens in Burma and the Swedish and German Baptists in Europe.

In the closing years of the nineteenth century and the years prior to the First World War, a gradual change took place in missionary strategy in response to the emergence of new forces. We have noted the increasing emphasis placed upon education in these later years of the period as the missionaries sought to develop a trained national leadership to assume eventual responsibility for the new churches being established on the respective fields. We have observed also the growing place given to medical work and agricultural and industrial missions in an effort to lift the level of life for the people to whom the gospel was being preached. At the same time a more efficient organizational structure was being developed both at home and on the fields. We have seen also evidence of an increasing trend toward interdenominational co-operation particularly in institutional work. Outbursts of antiforeign feeling in China indicated a rising nationalism which was to emerge as a major problem after 1914. With the organization of the Northern Baptist Convention in 1907, it was possible to develop a more responsible church relationship and denominational support of the Baptist world mission.

Simultaneously with these developments, we have witnessed the transforming influence of the gospel as it permeated the masses of plain people on mission fields, motivating them to contribute to the propagation of their faith without thought of personal reward or gain for their country. We saw, too, the rise of outstanding Christian leaders in the political and cultural life of various countries. We have noted also the by-products of the missionaries' labors in the rising literacy rate, the developing health programs, and the cultural impact of the schools.

The last forty years (1914–1954) have been characterized by a sharp demarcation from the century which closed on the eve of the First World War. During this brief period, as we have seen, new forces were set in motion and older ones were accelerated, resulting in a virtually different world from that of the nineteenth century. In an era of prolonged world wars, the imperialism that had given to the Western nations ascendancy and power came to an end. The acceleration of industrial processes and the means of transportation introduced a new way of living even to peoples hitherto untouched by the machine age. Numerous groups of Asian and African peoples sought to free themselves of Western domination, many of them achieving success. The spread of discontent and poverty, as the result of war and economic disruption, gave rise to new experiments in economic life. Among these the most virile and dangerous to Christianity was communism, with its materialistic philosophy and its unabashed hostility to the spiritual values of the Christian gospel.

The effects which these forces exerted upon the missionary situation around the world have been so startling as to all but revolutionize the conduct of the mission task. The sending-churches have found themselves faced with several disturbing factors: (1) the loss of initiative in Western Europe, particularly on the part of Great Britain, whose military strength in Asia had given protection to Western missions for more than a century; (2) the widespread and rapid growth of nationalism in Asia and Africa; (3) a growing enlightenment among the peasant people of underprivileged countries, as they became aware of the technical resources which can bring them a materially more abundant life; (4) a rapid increase in the world's population which threatens disastrous famine if the problems of adequate agricultural methods and distribution are not solved in time; and (5) the determined and vigorous hostility of communism which boasts in 1954 of having taken over a large part of Asia and of holding the solution to the basic economic needs of mankind.[1]

In response, the sending-churches have been forced to develop a new approach to missions, which takes into account the cultural and economic environment of the people to whom the Christian gospel can become a transforming power. In the consummation of this task the churches of the West are hindered by certain limitations. In their eagerness to win converts, they tend sometimes to proceed too hastily. When they fail to understand the social and cultural aspects of the society in which they conduct mission work, their evangelism at times causes a social disintegration which presents serious problems, as in Africa. The sending-churches face also the necessity of adapting the church to rural needs. The missions are often embarrassed by other agents of Western countries who were present on the fields, but who did not represent the Christian gospel. A further source of limitation stems from an assumption of cultural superiority on the part of some of the sending-churches, which reflects itself in a paternalistic attitude.[2]

After the Second World War, the ground was laid for new lines of missionary thinking. It was what Charles W. Ranson, executive secretary of the International Missionary Council, called "a period of

---

[1] M. A. C. Warren, "The Missionary Obligation of the Church in the Present Historical Situation," *The International Review of Missions,* Vol. 39, No. 156 (Oct. 1950), pp. 393-98.

[2] J. Merle Davis, *New Buildings on Old Foundations: A Handbook on Stabilizing the Younger Churches in Their Environment* (New York, 1945), pp. 23-43, 62.

questioning and reconstruction." The way was paved by a new theological climate in the United States which had been stimulated by postwar problems, the rise of neo-orthodoxy, the ecumenical movement, and a rediscovery of the doctrine of the church. The challenge of communism also impelled Christians to think seriously about the fundamental principles of the Christian faith and the precise relation of the church to its mission.[3]

The Baptist Response to the New Era

The response of American Baptists to these new forces indicated a sensitivity to the growing tensions and accumulated problems of the "revolutionary" century. Since 1914 there has been a concerted effort on the part of mission leaders to carry out a policy of devolution whereby full responsibility is transferred as rapidly as possible to nationals. This trend was accelerated greatly by the developments of the Second World War. On the fields there also has been a growing co-operation with other Christian bodies in national church councils, union schools and hospitals, and projects to relieve the sufferings of war-stricken peoples. New methods have been introduced on mission fields with rewarding success. Among these have been the development of specialized leadership by which guidance is given to entire areas in better farming techniques, in the conduct of literacy campaigns to teach entire communities to read, in the use of visual aids in presenting the gospel message, in the development of organized women's work, and in the introduction of camping programs for youth.

Extensive studies were made of all the fields after the Second World War with a view to developing an effective strategy which would enable the missionaries to be more effective in helping the national churches. At home, steps were being taken toward the integration of the work of the American Baptist Foreign Mission Society and the Woman's Society. This integration was consummated in May, 1955. At the same time, a more responsible support was being developed among the churches through the Council on Missionary Cooperation of the American Baptist Convention.

---

[3] R. Pierce Beaver, "North American Thought on the Fundamental Principles of Missions During the Twentieth Century," *Church History,* Vol. 21, No. 4 (Dec. 1952), pp. 345-64; Charles W. Ranson, "The Christian World Mission in the Perspective of History," *The International Review of Missions,* Vol. 43, No. 172 (Oct. 1954), pp. 381-89.

As American Baptists face the future, mission leaders are intent upon building their enterprises more on the basis of the church universal than has been true in the past.[4] They seek to encourage a greater two-way traffic in the movement of church leaders between the sending- and the receiving-churches. They endeavor to maintain a better balance between the message and the ministry, and to develop a Christian theology which will enable the evangelist to become more effectively articulate and intelligent about the content of the Christian faith. Plans are envisaged whereby the Mission Societies can keep their work more mobile and flexible, so as to make possible an easier concentration of resources at points of special need. A greater concern is being expressed for community solidarity as the Christian witness takes root in the culture of the people to whom it is proclaimed. That which had begun as a venture of faith is continuing in a changing world with no diminution of dependence upon the Holy Spirit through whose power ordinary men and women have across the decades sustained hope in the face of despair and courage in the midst of defeat, and have at times accomplished miracles of grace in the name of Jesus Christ.

---

[4] See a forecast by Jesse R. Wilson in *American Baptists Overseas* (New York, 1954), pp. 86-89.

Bibliography

NOTE: The titles in this bibliography, selected from among the many examined by the author, are those which proved to be of most value in the preparation of this history.

Albaugh, Dana M., *Between Two Centuries: A Study of Four Mission Fields, Assam, South India, Bengal-Orissa, and South China.* Philadelphia: The Judson Press, 1935. 245 pp.

American Baptist Foreign Mission Society, *Annual Reports, 1826–1954.* 67 volumes. These may be found in the offices of the Society in New York. The Society was known as the General Missionary Convention of the Baptist Denomination in the United States from 1814 to 1845. Then the name was changed to the American Baptist Missionary Union. In 1910 a second change was made to the present name. From 1941 to 1954 the reports of this Society and of the Woman's Society are included in a volume called, *Along Kingdom Highways.*

———, Records of the Board of Managers and the Executive Committee, 1814–1954. Typed copies of the original hand-written records of the Board Proceedings of the General Missionary Convention for May 18, 1814–May 3, 1847 (6 volumes) are in possession of the Society in New York. The originals are stored for safekeeping. The Records of the Executive Committee of the American Baptist Missionary Union for 1846–1902 are in handwritten ledger books in possession of the Society. An index to them for the years 1846 to 1882 was prepared by Dr. Edmund F. Merriam and continued to 1904 by Miss Mansfield. The records of the Board of Managers and the Executive Committee for later years are also in ledgers, but in typed form for recent years.

Azariah, V. S., *India and the Christian Movement.* New York: The National Council of the Protestant Episcopal Church, 1938. 106 pp.

Baker, James M., *Contending the Grade in India.* Ashville, N. C.: The Biltmore Press, 1947. 297 pp. The autobiography of Clough's successor at Ongole, India.

Baker, Oren Huling, ed., *Albert William Beaven: Pastor, Educator, World Christian*. Philadelphia: The Judson Press, 1944. 97 pp.

The Baptist. Chicago, 1920–26. File in the library of The Eastern Baptist Theological Seminary, Philadelphia, Pa.

Baptist Missionary Magazine. Boston and New York. 93 volumes under various titles: *Massachusetts Baptist Missionary Magazine* (1803–1816), *The American Baptist Magazine and Missionary Intelligencer* (1817–1824), *The American Baptist Magazine* (published by the Baptist Missionary Society of Massachusetts from 1825–1826 and by the Board of Managers of the Baptist General Convention from 1827–1845), *The Baptist Missionary Magazine* (published by the Executive Committee of the American Baptist Missionary Union from 1846–1909). A complete file is in the library of the American Baptist Foreign Mission Society in New York, N. Y.

Baptist Missionary Review, The. Madras and Cuttack, 1895–1905, 1917–1919. A monthly publication of the South India Mission, valuable for the missionary point of view on the field.

Baptist World Congress, *Proceedings,* 1905–1950. 7 volumes.

Barbour, Thomas, *A Contribution to Christian Missions—One Hundred Years in the Work of the American Baptist Foreign Mission Society,* 1914. A pamphlet in the Backus Historical Collection, Newton Centre, Mass.

Beaver, R. Pierce, Pioneer Single Women Missionaries. New York: Missionary Research Library. Mimeographed Bulletin No. 12 of Vol. IV (Sept. 30, 1953). 7 pp.

Bennett, Mela Isabel, *A Sketch of the Life and Character of Albert Arnold Bennett, D.D*. Providence, R. I., published by the author, 1913. 107 pp. Very sketchy.

Binney, J. P., *Twenty-Six Years in Burmah.* 384 pp.

Bixby, Olive Jennie, *My Child-Life in Burmah*. Boston, 1880. 172 pp.

Bowers, A. C., *Under Head-Hunters' Eyes*. Philadelphia: The Judson Press, 1929. 248 pp. Provides an interesting picture of pioneer work in the region of Sibsagar, Assam.

Brief View of the Baptist Missions and Translations compiled from the Printed Account of the Baptist Missionary Society. Boston: Wells and Lilly, 1815. 40 pp. An interesting account preserved in the Massachusetts Historical Society, Boston.

Briggs, Charles W., *The Progressing Philippines*. Philadelphia: The Griffith & Rowland Press, 1913. 174 pp. Helpful.

Brockett, L. P., *The Story of the Karen Mission in Bassein, 1838–1890*. Philadelphia: American Baptist Publication Society, 1891. 160 pp. A valuable account.

Brown, E. B., *The Whole World Kin: A Pioneer Experience Among Remote Tribes, and Other Labors of Nathan Brown*. Philadelphia: Hubbard Brothers, 1890. 607 pp. Valuable.

Burma News, The. Rangoon, 1888–1940. 53 volumes. Valuable insights from the field.

Butterfield, Kenyon L., *The Christian Mission in Rural India: Report and Recommendations.* New York: International Missionary Council, 1930. vi, 162 pp. A helpful analysis.

———, *The Rural Mission of the Church in Eastern Asia: Report and Recommendations.* New York: International Missionary Council, 1931. 222 pp. Helpful.

Carpenter, C. H., *Self-Support, Illustrated in the History of the Bassein Karen Mission from 1840 to 1880.* Boston: Rand, Avery & Co., 1883. xxi, 426 pp.

A Century of Service by Baptist Women. New York: The Woman's American Baptist Foreign Mission Society, 1933. A pamphlet containing an excellent summary of early history and organization.

Chambers, R. Fred, Central Philippine College: An Historical Study in the Light of Philippine Historical and Cultural Background. Doctoral dissertation, the University of Colorado, 1949. Part Two, 103 pp. Ably written.

Chaplin, Ada C., *Our Gold-Mines, the Story of the American Baptist Missions in India.* Boston, W. G. Corthell, 1882. 416 pp.

China Baptist Publication Society, The, Canton, China (1899–1909): Our Tenth Year. Canton, 1909. 34 pp.

Christian, John Leroy, *Modern Burma: A Survey of Political and Economic Development.* Berkeley and Los Angeles: University of California Press, 1942. 381 pp. Helpful.

Christian College in India, The: The Report of the Commission on Christian Higher Education in India. London: Humphrey Milford, 1931. xiii, 388 pp. Valuable.

Christian Movement in Japan Including Korea and Formosa, The, 1903–1927. After 1927, this series was continued as *The Japan Christian Year Book.* Partial file in library of The Woman's American Baptist Foreign Mission Society, New York.

Church, Pharcellus, *Theodosia Dean, Wife of Rev. William Dean, Missionary to China.* Philadelphia: American Baptist Publication Society, 1850. 288 pp. Fair.

Churchill, Elizabeth R., *History of the Karen Missionary Association of the Baptist Church of Gloversville, N. Y., 1845–1907.* A pamphlet.

Clayton, E. H., *Heaven Below.* New York: Prentice-Hall, Inc., 1944. 282 pp.

Clough, John Everett, *From Darkness to Light: A Story of the Telugu Awakening.* Philadelphia: American Baptist Publication Society, 1882. 288 pp. Valuable.

———, *Social Christianity in the Orient.* New York: The Macmillan Co., 1914. xiii, 409 pp. Valuable.

Congo Missionary Conference, *Reports,* 1906–08, 1911, 1918, 1921, 1924. Annual reports of the Congo General Conference of Protestant Missionaries.

Congo News Letter. Banza Manteke, 1924–1953. A quarterly published by missionaries of the American Baptist Foreign Mission Society. The first volume appeared in 1910.

Cooke, John Hunt, *Johann Gerhard Oncken: His Life and Work*. London: S. W. Partidge & Co., 1908. 187 pp. Fair.

Davis, J. Merle, *The Economic and Social Environment of the Younger Churches*. London: Edinburgh House Press, 1939. xiii, 231 pp.

———, *Modern Industry and the African*. London: Macmillan Co., 1933. xviii, 425 pp.

———, *New Buildings on Old Foundations*. New York: International Missionary Council, 1945. 320 pp. Excellent.

Dean, William, *The China Mission*. New York: Sheldon & Co., 1859. 396 pp. A valuable account by the pioneer Baptist missionary to China.

Deming, John Howard, *Centennial Survey—A Study of Baptist Missionary Achievement*. A pamphlet in the Backus Historical Collection, Newton Centre, Mass.

Dennis, James S., *Christian Missions and Social Progress*. 3 volumes. New York: Fleming H. Revell Co., 1897, 1899, 1906. 1625 pp.

Developing Africa's Riches in Christ. A pamphlet published by the American Baptist Foreign Mission Society in 1935. Good summary.

Downie, David, *The History of the Telugu Mission of the American Baptist Missionary Union*. Philadelphia: American Baptist Publication Society, 1893. 232 pp. Draws on primary sources and the author's own experiences as a missionary.

———, *From the Mill to the Mission Field: An Autobiography*. Philadelphia: The Judson Press, 1928. 194 pp. Valuable.

East China Projects of the Chekiang-Shanghai Baptist Convention, the American Baptist Foreign Mission Society, and the Woman's American Baptist Foreign Mission Society. 1936. 57 pp.

Eaton, W. H., *Historical Sketch of the Massachusetts Baptist Missionary Society and Convention, 1802–1902*. Boston: Massachusetts Baptist Convention, 1903. 240 pp.

Eddy, Sherwood, *India Awakening*. Philadelphia: American Baptist Publication Society, 1911. xii, 257 pp.

Edmond, A. M., *Memoir of Mrs. Sarah D. Comstock*. Philadelphia, 1854. 228 pp.

Endymion, *Tribute to the Memory of Mrs. Maria M. Dean*. Bangkok: S. J. Smith's Publishing House, 1883. 149 pp. Chiefly letters and extracts from Mrs. Dean's Journal.

Enquirer and News. Battle Creek, Mich., 1946–50. Contained a series of articles on the Belgian Congo written by the Reverend Leonard Gettings, an American Baptist missionary.

European Baptist Congress, *Proceedings,* 1908. London: Baptist Union Publication Department, 1908.

Felton, Ralph A., *The Rural Church in the Far East: Studies Prepared for the Tambaram Meeting of the International Missionary Council.* Calcutta: Baptist Mission Press, 1938. x, 258, xxxii pp. Helpful.

Fishman, Alvin T., *Culture Change and the Underprivileged: A Study of Madigas in South India Under Christian Guidance.* Madras: The Christian Literature Society for India, 1941. 207 pp. A doctoral dissertation for Yale University.

Fleming, Daniel J., *Contacts with Non-Christian Cultures: A Case Book in the Christian Movement Abroad.* New York: George H. Doran Co., 1923. xiv, 189 pp. Very helpful.

Foreign Mission Policies: A Report of the Special Conference of the Boards of Managers and Delegates from the Ten Missions of the American Baptist Foreign Mission Society and the Woman's American Baptist Foreign Mission Society held in New York City, Nov. 18–Dec. 2, 1925. 85 pp.

Forrester, Fanny, *Memoir of Sarah Judson.* New York, 1848. 250 pp.

Franklin, James H., *The Christian Crisis in China.* New York: American Baptist Foreign Mission Society, 1931. 149 pp. Important.

———, *In the Track of the Storm.* Philadelphia: American Baptist Publication Society, 1919. 140 pp.

The Freewill Baptist Mission in India. A pamphlet issued by the Free Will Baptist Female Mission Society. No date.

Fridell, Elmer A., Mimeographed Materials on American Baptist Work in the Philippines. Loaned by the author. Valuable.

Frost, Harold I., Achievements and Possibilities of the Orissa Section of the Bengal-Orissa Mission and Steps Needed to Make the Work More Effective. A manuscript loaned by the author. Helpful.

Gammell, William, *A History of American Baptist Missions in Asia, Africa, Europe and North America.* Boston: Gould, Kendall and Lincoln, 1849. 359 pp.

Goddard, Francis Wayland, *Called to Cathay.* New York: Baptist Literature Bureau, privately printed, 1948. 160 pp. Excellent biographies of William Dean, Josiah Goddard, Josiah Ripley Goddard, Francis Wayland Goddard, and Stephen Josiah Goddard.

Goddard, Josiah R., *The East China Baptist Mission, Historical Notes.* Ningpo, 1911. 65 pp. Valuable.

Grose, Howard B. and Fred P. Haggard, editors, *The Judson Centennial, 1814–1914.* Philadelphia: American Baptist Publication Society, 1914. 305 pp.

Gunn, Harriette Bronson, *In a Far Country.* Philadelphia: American Baptist Publication Society, 1911. 244 pp.

Hamlen, George H., *The Balasore High School.* 1904. A pamphlet.

———, *A Free Baptist Foreign Mission Catechism.* 1904. A pamphlet.

Harrington, Charles Kendall, *Captain Bickel of the Inland Sea.* New York: Fleming H. Revell Co., 1919. 301 pp.

Harris, E. A. and B. E. H. Harris, editors, *American Baptist Missions in Burma, 1920.* Rangoon: American Baptist Mission Press, 1921. 173 pp.

Harris, Edward Norman, *A Star in the East; an Account of American*

Baptist Missions to the Karens of Burma. New York: Fleming H. Revell Co., 1920. 223 pp.

Harris, Mrs. J. E., *History of the Shwegyin Karen Mission.* Revised by her son, the Reverend E. N. Harris. Chicago: The Englewood Press, 1907. 53 pp. Valuable for a missionary's view of the field.

Harvey, H., *Memoir of Alfred Bennett.* New York, 1852. 231 pp.

Herman, Stewart W., *Report from Christian Europe.* New York: Friendship Press, 1953. xii, 212 pp. Good analysis of trends since the Second World War.

Hervey, G. Winfred, *The Story of Baptist Missions in Foreign Lands from the Time of Carey to the Present Date.* St. Louis: Chaney R. Barnes, 1886. 820 pp. Limited in value.

Hill, Viola C. and C. H. Barlow, M.D., *Glimpses into East China.* Shanghai: Printed at American Presbyterian Mission Press, 1920. 42 pp. Loaned by the author. Helpful.

Hill, Viola C., A History of the East China Mission. A typescript written in 1927. Loaned by the author.

Hines, Herbert Waldo, *Clough: Kingdom-Builder in South India.* Philadelphia: The Judson Press, 1929. 168 pp. Good.

Hobart, Kenneth Gray, A Comparative History of the East China and South China Missions of the American Baptist Foreign Mission Society, 1833–1935: A Study of the Intensive versus the Extensive Policy in Mission Work. A doctoral dissertation for Yale University, 1937. xiii, 772 pp. Excellent.

Holmes, Ella Marie, *Sowing Seed in Assam.* New York: Fleming H. Revell Co., 1925. 195 pp.

Howard, Randolph L., *Baptists in Burma.* Philadelphia: The Judson Press, 1931. 168 pp. Very good.

———, *It Began in Burma.* Philadelphia: The Judson Press, 1942. 124 pp. Useful.

———, *Lazy-Man-Rest-Not: The Burma Letters of Brayton C. Case.* Philadelphia: The Judson Press, 1946. 128 pp.

Hubbard, Ethel Daniels, *Ann of Ava.* New York: Missionary Education Movement of the U. S. and Canada, 1913. 245 pp.

Hughes, Lizbeth B., ed., *The Evangel in Burma, being a Review for a Quarter Century, 1900–1925, of the Work of the American Baptist Foreign Mission Society in Burma.* Rangoon: American Baptist Mission Press, 1926. 225 pp.

Hunnicutt, Benjamin H. and William W. Reid, *The Story of Agricultural Missions.* New York: Missionary Education Movement of the U. S. and Canada, 1931. 180 pp.

International Review of Missions, The. London, 1912 ff. The standard Protestant journal on foreign missions.

Jeffery, Mary Pauline, *Dr. Ida: India—The Life Story of Ida S. Scudder.* New York: Fleming H. Revell Co., 1938. 212 pp.

Johnson, Jennie Bixby, *The Life and Work of Moses Homan Bixby.* New York: Burdett and Co., 1904. xviii, 157 pp.

Jones, Eliza G., *Memoir of Mrs. Eliza G. Jones, Missionary to Burmah and Siam*. Philadelphia: American Baptist Publication and Sunday School Society. New and enlarged edition, 1853. iv, 212 pp.

Judd, Mrs. Bertha Grimmell, *Fifty Golden Years: the First Half Century of the Woman's American Baptist Foreign Mission Society, 1877–1927*. Rochester: The Du Bois Press, 1927. 281 pp.

Judson, Adoniram, Miscellaneous Letters. Massachusetts Historical Society and the Backus Historical Collection.

Judson, Ann Hasseltine, *Relation of the American Baptist Mission to the Burman Empire*. Washington, D. C.: John S. Meehan, 1823. 315 pp.

Judson, Emily C., *Biographical Sketch with Portrait*. No date. Included with letters to Mrs. Judson (1851–53) in the Backus Historical Collection.

Judson, Edward, *The Life of Adoniram Judson*. New York: Anson D. F. Randolph & Co., 1883. 601 pp. Valuable.

Kelley, Jennie B., *A Consecrated Life: Portraiture of Rev. Edwin Delmont Kelley, Missionary in Burmah*. Boston: D. Lothrop & Co., 1879. 277 pp.

Kendrick, A. C., *Life and Letters of Mrs. Emily C. Judson*. New York: Sheldon & Co., 1860. 426 pp.

King, Alonzo, *Memoir of George Dana Boardman, Late Missionary to Burmah*. Boston: Gould, Kendall & Lincoln, 1839. xxxv, 319 pp.

Knowles, James D., *Memoir of Mrs. Ann H. Judson*. Boston: Lincoln & Edmands, 1829. 324 pp.

Kraemer, Hendrik, *The Christian Message in a Non-Christian World*. New York: International Missionary Council, 1947. xviii, 455 pp.

Latourette, Kenneth Scott, *The American Record in the Far East, 1945–1951*. New York: The Macmillan Co., 1952. 208 pp.

———, *The Christian Outlook*. New York: Harper & Brothers, 1948. 229 pp.

———, *The Christian World Mission in Our Day*. New York: Harper & Brothers, 1954. 192 pp. Excellent analysis of current trends.

———, *The Emergence of a World Christian Community*. New Haven: Yale University Press, 1949. 91 pp.

———, *A History of the Expansion of Christianity*. 7 volumes. New York: Harper & Brothers, 1937–1944. Volumes 3-7 were of particular value for background material.

———, *The United States Moves Across the Pacific*. New York: Harper & Brothers, 1946. ix, 174 pp.

Latourette, Kenneth Scott and William Richey Hogg, *World Christian Community in Action*. New York: International Missionary Council, 1949. 42 pp.

———, *Tomorrow Is Here*. New York: Friendship Press. 1948. xiv, 145 pp.

Laymen's Foreign Missions Inquiry. 7 volumes. New York: Harper & Brothers, 1933.

Leber, Charles Tudor, *World Faith in Action*. Indianapolis and New York: The Bobbs-Merrill Co., Inc., 1951. 345 pp.

Lennox, William G., *The Health and Turnover of Missionaries*. Published by the Advisory Committee of the Foreign Missions Conference, New York, 1933. 217 pp.

Lerrigo, P. H. J., *God's Dynamite*. Philadelphia: The Judson Press, 1925. 184 pp. A popular study book on American Baptist mission fields.

———, compiler and editor, *Northern Baptists Rethink Missions: A Study of the Layman's Foreign Missions Inquiry*. New York: Baptist Board of Education, Dept. of Missionary Education, 1933. 128 pp. Valuable.

Lerrigo, P. H. J. and Doris M. Amidon, editors, *All Kindred and Tongues: An Illustrated Survey of the Foreign Mission Enterprise of Northern Baptists*. (Fourth Issue) New York: American Baptist Foreign Mission Society and the Woman's American Baptist Foreign Mission Society, 1940. 298 pp.

Levy, George E., *The Baptists of the Maritime Provinces, 1753–1946*. St. John, New Brunswick: Barnes-Hopkins, Ltd., 1946. xii, 336 pp.

Lewis, W. O., After Ten Years in Poland. A mimeographed paper of thirteen pages prepared for the Board of the American Baptist Foreign Mission Society, September 15, 1931. In possession of the library of the American Baptist Historical Society, Rochester, N. Y.

———, The Situation in France. A mimeographed paper of fourteen pages prepared for the Society in March, 1924, and revised in August, 1931. In possession of the American Baptist Historical Society.

Lewis, W. O., Correspondence to Dr. James H. Franklin Concerning Polish Baptists. 1931. In possession of A.B.F.M.S. and the American Baptist Historical Society.

Lipphard, William B., *Communing with Communism: A Narrative of Impressions of Soviet Russia*. Philadelphia: The Judson Press, 1931. 153 pp.

———, *The Ministry of Healing: A Study of Medical Missionary Endeavor on Baptist Foreign Mission Fields*. Philadelphia: American Baptist Publication Society, 1920. 126 pp. Valuable survey and interpretation.

———, *Out of the Storm in China: A Review of Recent Developments in Baptist Mission Fields*. Philadelphia: The Judson Press, 1932. 201 pp. Excellent survey.

———, *The Second Century of Baptist Foreign Missions*. Philadelphia: The Judson Press, 1926. 253 pp. Valuable interpretation.

The Lone Star Jubilee. Madras: Addison and Co., 1886. iv, 264 pp.

Longley, William J., The First Thirty-Five Years: A Short Account of Foreign Mission Beginnings in the United States. An unpublished manuscript of 66 pages in possession of the author.

Lord, Fred Townley, *Achievement; a Short History of the Baptist Missionary Society, 1792–1942*. London: The Carey Press, 1941. vii, 150 pp.

Luther, Calista V., *The Vintons and the Karens: Memorials of Rev. Justus H. Vinton and Calista H. Vinton.* Boston: W. G. Corthell, 1880. xi, 252 pp.

Lynd, S. W., ed., *Memoir of the Rev. William Staughton, D.D.* Boston, 1834.

McKenzie, W. S., *The Lone Star, a Sketch of the Teloogoo Mission.* Boston: G. J. Stiles. 24 pp.

Mabie, Catherine L., *Congo Cameos.* Philadelphia: The Judson Press, 1952. 191 pp. Delightfully informative.

Mabie, Henry Clay, *From Romance to Reality: The Merging of a Life in a World Movement.* Boston: 1917. 396 pp. Valuable autobiography.

Mackay, John A., *Christianity on the Frontier.* New York: The Macmillan Co., 1950. 206 pp.

Malcom, Howard, *Travels in Southeastern Asia, Embracing Hindustan, Malaya, Siam, and China; with Notices of Numerous Mission Stations, and a Full Account of the Burman Empire; with Dissertations, Tables, etc.* 2 volumes. Boston: Gould, Kendall, and Lincoln, 1839. 273 and 321 pp. Valuable.

Marshall, Harry I., *Naw Su: A Story of Burma.* Portland, Me., Falmouth Publishing House, 1947. 351 pp. A novel that reflects customs, etc.

Mason, Mrs. Ellen H. B., *Civilizing Mountain Men, or Sketches of Mission Work Among the Karens.* Third edition. London: James Nisbet & Co., 1864. x, 372 pp.

Mason, Francis, *The Karen Apostle: or Memoir of Ko Thah-Byu, the First Karen Convert, with Notices Concerning His Nation.* First American edition revised by H. J. Ripley. Boston: Gould, Kendall & Lincoln, 1843. 153 pp.

Massachusetts Baptist Convention, *Records for 1824–1835* and *Letter Book for 1835–1839.* 2 volumes.

Maulmain (sic.) Missionary Society, *Annual Reports,* 1841–1859. Maulmain: American Baptist Mission Press.

Merriam, Edmund Franklin, *The American Baptist Missionary Union and Its Missions.* Boston, 1897. 233 pp. Valuable.

———, *A History of American Baptist Missions.* Philadelphia: American Baptist Publication Society, 1913. 278 pp.

Missionary Directory of Fields and Events: A Story of the Year, 1923–1924. New York: Woman's American Baptist Foreign Mission Society, 1924. 109 pp. Provides a list of important events from 1871 to 1923.

The Missionary Jubilee . . . of the American Baptist Missionary Union, 1864. New York, 1869. 500 pp.

Missions. New York, 1910–1954. This periodical was formed by the union of various Baptist missionary journals. It was successor to the *Baptist Missionary Magazine* (Boston). Complete file in library of American Baptist Historical Society, Rochester, N. Y.

Montgomery, Helen Barrett, *Following the Sunrise: A Century of Baptist*

Missions, 1813–1913. Philadelphia: American Baptist Publication Society, 1913. 291 pp. Helpful.

———, ed., *Our Work in the Orient; an Account of the Progress of the Women's Baptist Foreign Missionary Societies, 1909–10*. Boston, 1910. 202 pp.

———, *Western Women in Eastern Lands: an Outline Study of Fifty Years of Woman's Work in Foreign Missions*. New York: The Macmillan Co., 1911. 286 pp.

Moore, Mrs. Pitt H., ed., *Twenty Years in Assam, or Leaves from My Journal*. Nowgong, Assam, 1901. xiv, 222 pp. Covers 1879–99.

———, ed., *Further Leaves from Assam*. Nowgong, Assam, 1907. xi, 191 pp. Covers 1900–1907.

———, ed., *Autumn Leaves from Assam*. Nowgong, Assam, 1910. x, 96 pp. Covers 1908–10.

———, ed., *Stray Leaves from Assam*. Rochester, 1916. xi, 128 pp. Covers 1911–16.

Morrow, Honore Willsie, *Splendor of God*. New York: William Morrow & Co., 1929. 376 pp.

Mott, John R., *Five Decades and a Forward View*. New York: Harper & Brothers, 1939. 133 pp.

Munger, H. W., History of the Philippine Baptist Mission. An unpublished manuscript prepared between 1925 and 1929. It covers the early beginnings of the Mission to 1908. 117 pp. Useful.

Murphy, Howard R., From Lone Prairies to Teeming Jungles. An unpublished manuscript by a missionary of the Free Baptist Foreign Mission Society to Bengal, India. 197 pp. Interesting.

Myers, J. B., ed., *Baptist Missionary Society Centenary Volume, 1792–1892*. London, 1892 (Second edition). viii, 344 pp.

Neill, Stephen, *The Christian Society*. London: Nisbet & Co., 1952. xv, 334 pp. Excellent interpretation of the missionary movement of the past two centuries in particular.

Neill, Stephen and Ruth Rouse, *A History of the Ecumenical Movement, 1517–1948*. Philadelphia: The Westminster Press, 1954. xxiv, 822 pp.

Osgood, William C. *et al.*, History of the Free Will Baptist Work in Bengal-Orissa. An unpublished manuscript prepared by several missionaries and loaned to the writer.

Patton, A. S., *The Hero Missionary: Eugenio Kincaid*. New York, 1858. 312 pp.

Pearce, G. J. M., *Congo Background*. London: The Carey Kingsgate Press, Ltd., 1954. 119 pp. Very useful.

Pease, Charles S., Luther Rice, Missionary and Educational Pioneer. An unpublished manuscript prepared in 1909 in Northborough, Mass. 123 pp. In the library of Andover-Newton Theological Institution, Newton Centre, Mass.

Peterson, Frank, *Missions in Europe*. Boston: American Baptist Foreign Mission Society, 1911. A pamphlet that provides a valuable survey.

Phillips, Mrs. J. L., *Dr. J. L. Phillips; Missionary to the Children of India.* London: The Sunday School Union, 1898. 264 pp.

Pickett, J. Waskom, *Christian Mass Movements in India: A Study with Recommendations.* New York: The Abingdon Press, 1933. 382 pp. Informative.

Pollard, Edward B., *Luther Rice, Pioneer in Missions and Education.* Edited and completed by Daniel G. Stevens. Philadelphia: The Judson Press, 1928. vii, 125 pp. Good.

Poteat, Gordon, *Stand By for China.* New York: Friendship Press, 1940. x, 181 pp. Interpretation of effects which new movements in China had on missions.

Ranney, Ruth W., *A Sketch of the Lives and Missionary Work of Rev. Cephas Bennett and His Wife.* New York, 1892. 142 pp.

Ranson, Charles W., *The Christian Minister in India: His Vocation and Training.* London: Lutterworth Press, 1945. 317 pp. Good.

———, *Renewal and Advance.* London: Edinburgh House Press, 1948. 228 pp.

Reischauer, Edwin O., *Japan Past and Present.* New York: Alfred A. Knopf, 1947. 192 pp. Useful.

Report of Inter-Mission Conference of Delegates from Associations and Missions In China Connected with the American Baptist Foreign Mission Society, 1922. 35 pp.

Rivenburg, Narola, ed., *The Star of the Naga Hills: Letters from Rev. Sidney and Hattie Rivenburg, Pioneer Missionaries in Assam, 1883–1923.* Philadelphia: The Judson Press, 1941. 147 pp.

Robbins, Joseph C., *Following the Pioneers; a Story of American Baptist Mission Work in India and Burma.* Philadelphia: The Judson Press, 1922. 162 pp. Good.

Ross, Emory, *African Heritage.* New York: Friendship Press, 1952. 145 pp. Careful analysis of problems faced by missions.

Rushbrooke, J. H., *The Baptist Movement in the Continent of Europe.* London: The Kingsgate Press, 1915. viii, 207 pp. A revised edition appeared in 1923.

———, *Some Chapters of European Baptist History.* London: The Kingsgate Press, 1929. 131 pp.

Safford, Mrs. Henry G., *The Golden Jubilee.* New York: Woman's American Baptist Foreign Mission Society, 1921. 263 pp. Valuable.

Salquist, West China Baptist Mission Records, 1889–1944. A typed manuscript of 60 pages in possession of the American Baptist Foreign Mission Society.

Seagrave, Gordon S., *Burma Surgeon.* New York: W. W. Norton & Co., 1943. 295 pp.

———, *Burma Surgeon Returns.* New York: W. W. Norton & Co., 1946. 268 pp.

———, *Tales of a Waste-Basket Surgeon.* Philadelphia: The Judson Press, 1938. 265 pp.

———, *Waste-Basket Surgery*. Philadelphia: The Judson Press, 1930. 174 pp.

Sears, Minnie Sandberg, *The Seventh Decade of the Woman's American Baptist Foreign Mission Society, 1931–1941*. New York: The Council on Finance and Promotion of the Northern Baptist Convention, n. d. 57 pp. Excellent survey.

Skoglund, John E., *The Spirit Tree: The Story of Baptist Work Among Primitive Peoples*. Philadelphia: The Judson Press, 1951. 95 pp.

Smith, D. A. W., *A Sketch of the Life of Edward Abiel Stevens, D.D.* Rangoon: American Baptist Mission Press, 1886. 27 pp.

Smith, Edwin W., *The Christian Mission in Africa*. London: The International Missionary Council, 1926. viii, 192 pp. A study based on the Le Zoute Conference.

Smith, S. F., *Missionary Sketches*. Boston: W. G. Corthell, 1879. 400 pp.

Stacy, Thomas H., *Life of Otis Robinson Bacheler, Missionary to India*. Boston: The Morning Star Publishing House, 1904. xv, 512 pp. Not well organized.

The Standard. Chicago, 1915–1920. A Baptist weekly.

Stanton, William Arthur, *The Awakening of India: Forty Years Among the Telugus*. Portland, Me.: Falmouth Publishing House, 1950. 213 pp.

Stevens, Edward Abiel, *Inexcusableness of the Heathen; a Discourse*. Rangoon, 1862. 23 pp.

Stevens, Summer Wynne, *A Half-Century in Burma: A Memorial Sketch of Edward Abiel Stevens, D.D.* Philadelphia: American Baptist Publication Society, 1897. 32 pp. Helpful.

Stiansen, Peder, *History of the Baptists in Norway*. Chicago: The Blessing Press, 1933. xi, 176 pp. Very useful.

Swanson, O. L., *In Village and Tea Gardens; Forty-Three Years of Missionary Work in Assam*. Second edition. Chicago: Conference Press, 1944. 208 pp. Helpful.

Sword, Gustaf A., *Come What May, or Triumphant Faith Along the Burma Road*. Chicago: Conference Press, 1943. 159 pp. Very good.

———, *Light in the Jungle: Life Story of Ola Hanson of Burma*. Chicago: Baptist Conference Press, 1954. 189 pp. Very useful.

Sword, Victor Hugo, *Baptists in Assam: A Century of Missionary Service, 1836–1936*. Chicago: Missionary Press, 1935. 160 pp. Very good.

Taylor, Joseph, West of the Yangtze Gorges. A mimeographed manuscript issued by the American Baptist Foreign Mission Society in 1944, but written in 1936. 153 pp.

Through Shining Archway. New York, 1945. A pamphlet published jointly by the American Baptist Foreign Mission Society and the Woman's American Baptist Foreign Mission Society to memoralize the martyrdom of Baptist missionaries in the Philippines during the Second World War.

Titterington, Sophie Bronson, *A Century of Baptist Foreign Missions: An*

Outline Sketch. Philadelphia: American Baptist Publication Society, 1891. 297 pp. Limited in usefulness.

Torbet, Robert G., *A History of the Baptists*. Philadelphia: The Judson Press, 1950, revised edition 1952. 540 pp.

———, *A Social History of the Philadelphia Baptist Association, 1907–1940*. Philadelphia: Westbrook Publishing Co., 1944. 247 pp.

Trueblood, Elwyn J., *The Dawn of the Post-Modern Era*. New York: The Philosophical Library, 1954. xii, 198 pp. An analysis of trends since 1914.

Ufford, A. Frank, The East China Baptist Mission, 1843–1943. An unpublished paper presented at the Centennial Observance, Ningpo, China, April 18, 1948.

Van Dusen, Henry P., *For the Healing of the Nations*. New York: Charles Scribner's Sons, 1940. 227 pp.

Vail, Albert L., *The Morning Hour of American Baptist Missions*. Philadelphia: American Baptist Publication Society, 1907. 477 pp. Valuable.

Vedder, Henry C., *A Short History of Baptist Missions*. Philadelphia: The Judson Press, 1927. 559 pp. Useful.

Vickland, E. Elizabeth, *Women of Assam*. Philadelphia: The Judson Press, 1928. 179 pp.

Warburton, Stacy R., *Eastward, the Story of Adoniram Judson*. New York: Round Table Press, 1937. 240 pp. Excellent.

Wayland, Francis, *A Memoir of the Life and Labors of the Rev. Adoniram Judson, D.D.* 2 volumes. Boston: Phillips, Sampson, and Co., 1853. 544 and 522 pp. Very useful.

Wha Mai Hospital, Ningpo, China, with Report for 1922 in Connection with the American Baptist Foreign Mission Society. Shanghai: Printed at the Presbyterian Mission Press, 1923. A pamphlet.

Wilson, Jesse R., *American Baptists Overseas: A Handbook of American Baptist Foreign Missions*. New York: American Baptist Foreign Mission Society and the Woman's American Baptist Foreign Mission Society, 1954. 96 pp. Very useful.

Woman's Baptist Foreign Missionary Society of the East, *Annual Reports*, 1871–1914. 8 volumes. These include reports of the Executive Board Meetings as well as of annual meetings.

———, Records of Board of Directors, 1871–1914. 13 volumes. These are handwritten journals of minutes, which are fuller than the printed records.

Woman's Baptist Foreign Missionary Society of the West, *Annual Reports*, 1871–1914. 7 volumes. These include reports of Executive Board Meetings as well as of annual meetings.

———, Records of the Meetings of the Society and of the Executive Board, 1875–1914. 12 volumes. These are handwritten journals of minutes which are fuller than the printed records.

Woman's American Baptist Foreign Mission Society, Records of Board of Managers and Executive Committee, 1914–1954. 12 volumes. These are handwritten in ledgers; later volumes are typed.

Wood, Isabel Warwick, *What God Hath Wrought for the Woman's American Baptist Foreign Mission Society, 1921–1931*. n. d. A pamphlet telling the story of the sixth decade of women's organized work.

Wyeth, M. N., *A Galaxy in the Burman Sky*. Philadelphia, 1892. 196 pp.

———, *Emily C. Judson*. Philadelphia, 1890. 179 pp.

———, *Sarah B. Judson*. Philadelphia, 1889. 179 pp.

———, *The Wades: Jonathan Wade and Deborah B. L. Wade*. Philadelphia, 1891. 196 pp.

Wynd, William, *Seventy Years in Japan: A Saga of Northern Baptists.* Privately printed, n. d. vi, 284 pp. Valuable.

Index